READING AND WRITING IN ELEMENTARY CLASSROOMS
Strategies and Observations

Third Edition

Patricia M. Cunningham
Wake Forest University

Sharon Arthur Moore
Arizona State University West

James W. Cunningham
University of North Carolina, Chapel Hill

David W. Moore
Arizona State University West

Longman *Publishers USA*

Reading and Writing in Elementary Classrooms: Strategies and Observations, Third Edition

Longman, 10 Bank Street, White Plains, N.Y. 10606

Associated companies:
Longman Group Ltd., London
Longman Cheshire Pty., Melbourne
Longman Paul Pty., Auckland
Copp Clark Longman Ltd., Toronto

Senior acquisitions editor: Laura McKenna
Production editor: Linda W. Witzling
Text design adaptation: David Levy
Cover design: Joseph DePinho
Production supervisor: Richard Bretan

Library of Congress Cataloging-in-Publication Data
Reading and writing in elementary classrooms : strategies and
    observations / Patricia Cunningham . . . [et al.].—3rd ed.
        p.   cm.
    Rev. ed. of: Reading in elementary classrooms. c1989.
    Includes bibliographical references and index.
    ISBN 0-8013-1264-7
    1. Reading (Elementary)   2. English language—Composition and
exercises—Study and teaching (Elementary)   3. Language arts
(Elementary)   I. Cunningham, Patricia Marr.   II. Reading in
elementary classrooms.
LB1573.R279   1995
372.4—dc20   —dc20
[372.4]
                                                    94-29678
                                                      CIP

6 7 8 9 10-MA-98

For Lane, who took a chance and gave us a start

Contents Overview

PART II: . . . IN ELEMENTARY CLASSROOMS   283

Contents

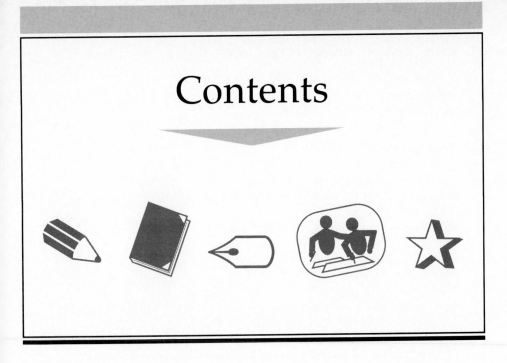

Preface

Teaching children to read and write at high levels of literacy is a complex, long-term commitment that our society and our schools must make if we are going to remain competitive in the twenty-first century. In this third edition of *Reading and Writing in Elementary Classrooms*, we have taken into consideration the latest research and best thinking from literacy and language studies, curriculum and instructional practices, and psychology. Culling through the best of what we have traditionally done and pulling together the best current practices, we present a balanced long-term view of literacy development and approaches.

SHARED FEATURES OF THE SECOND AND THIRD EDITIONS

The third edition of Reading and Writing in Elementary Classrooms retains those features of the second edition that our students and colleagues found especially noteworthy. These include:

Focus on Thinking Processes

Chapter 1 describes nine thinking processes that are critical to reading and writing. These thinking processes—*call up, connect, organize, predict, image, monitor, generalize, evaluate,* and *apply*—underlie the activities and strategies presented in later chapters and help to provide a coherent framework for the development of high-level literacy.

Focus on Reading and Writing as Language

One of the key ideas in Chapter 1 is that *reading and writing are language*. Reading and writing build on the oral/aural language foundation the child brings to school and reading and writing support each other and the overall linguistic ability of the child. Throughout the chapters, activities and strategies that promote the total development of all the language abilities of children are suggested.

Focus on Affective Domain

Children are both thinking and feeling people. Their likes and dislikes, attitudes and interests must be developed and given attention. Applications for the key idea that *reading and writing are feeling* established in Chapter 1 are found in all the other chapters in the book.

Focus on Balanced Literacy Instruction

The field of reading appears to be continually under siege by various factions arguing for one approach over another. The fact that children learn in different ways and that acquiring high levels of literacy is a complex long-term process mitigates against any single, narrow approach. This edition, like the earlier editions, promotes a balanced diet of authentic reading and writing activities along with instruction in appropriate strategies as indicated by careful observation of the learners. The best literacy instruction blends features from a variety of approaches to reading and writing.

Narrative Chapters

Teachers often bemoan the fact that children have many more skills and strategies than they actually use. The same can be said of teachers. To use knowledge, one must know not only what to do but when and why, for how long, and with which children and in connection to what! The narrative chapters in Part II were created to give teachers concrete examples of how the various ideas and activities presented in Part I might be implemented in different classrooms at different grade levels with a variety of different children by teachers with a range of different teaching styles.

In Part II, we transport our readers to an imaginary school, Merritt Elementary School, where we follow an imaginary class of children from kindergarten to fifth grade. With help and support from the principal, Mr. Topps, and the central office facilitator, Sue Port, the various teachers use a variety of approaches to make literacy a reality for all their children. The children emerge into literacy under the enthusiastic tutelage of their kindergarten teacher, Miss Launch. Mrs. Wright provides a balanced approach in her first-grade classroom. She emphasizes shared and guided reading, words, writing, and self-selected reading, and demonstrates how the instruction changes as the children's literacy develops. Miss Nouveau, a first-year teacher, takes the class through second grade. She gets off to a somewhat rocky start, but with help from Mr. Topps, Sue Port, and other teachers, she makes great strides by the end of the year. Mrs. Wise is the third-grade teacher. Mrs. Wise has through all her years of teaching acquired huge stores of knowledge and books and she carries out an integrated language arts program with literature as the centerpiece. The fourth-grade teacher, Ms. Maverick, also integrates, but her focus is on integrating across the curriculum. Mr. Dunn, the fifth-grade teacher, carries out a balanced program that emphasizes studying, independence, and technology. The teachers in this edition are familiar to users of the earlier editions, but they, too, have been updated and have some new "tricks up their sleeves."

Organizing Features

To increase the comprehensibility of our text, we have included Looking Ahead and Looking Back sections, which preview and then summarize each chapter's major concepts. We have also identified four to six key ideas for each chapter and organized the information under these key ideas. The narrative chapters all have locators in the margin that connect the instruction in the narratives with the key ideas in the first nine chapters.

Application Activities

Believing that we learn best when we evaluate and apply what we are learning, we have included activities in each chapter that promote application. Many of these activities can be incorporated easily into a field experience, which is often part of the reading methods course. Listen, Look, and Learn boxes contain suggestions for visiting classrooms, viewing videotapes of classrooms, and interviewing teachers and students to check out the ideas presented and learn more about actual classroom practice. Try It Out boxes suggest lessons and activities students might plan and often suggest trying out some of these with a child or small group of children. Do It Together boxes suggest cooperative activities in which readers pool their knowledge and experiences with particular concepts and compare their collective experiences with what they are learning in the text. Add to Your Journal boxes end each chapter and suggest ways in which the reader might use writing to reflect upon the ideas in the chapter.

NEW FEATURES OF THE THIRD EDITION

Two New Chapters—"Developing Prior Knowledge and Meaning Vocabulary" and "Writing"

There were always many suggestions for developing prior knowledge/vocabulary and writing in the earlier editions, but the recognition of the critical role played by prior knowledge in comprehension and the surge in classroom writing and knowledge about how to teach writing prompted us to add these two chapters. Both chapters give an overall theory of the development of prior knowledge/vocabulary and writing and many practical suggestions for developing them. Because we believe that both prior knowledge/vocabulary and writing are critical to instruction in all content areas, we have devoted a major section of each chapter to cross-curricular activities.

Major Revisions of the Original Chapters

All chapters have been updated to reflect the latest research and best practice. Chapter 2 on emergent literacy has a new section on *phonological awareness* because the relationship between phonological awareness and success in beginning reading is now clearly established. In addition, Chapter 2 has more practical information on the use of *Big Books* and *shared reading* as major ways to help children take the first steps to literacy. Chapter 3 has been completely rewritten and reflects the current understandings about the importance of *analogy in decoding, the important connections between spelling and decoding knowledge, and the need to connect word fluency instruction with real reading and writing.* Chapter 8 has new sections on *portfolio assessment* and *anecdotal records,* which are more authentic assessment devices. Chapter 9 has a new section on *planning* and another new section on *making special provisions for children with special needs.* Because we believe that reading and writing are best developed across the entire school day and throughout the curriculum, each chapter contains a major section on *content-area reading and writing strategies.*

For Children with Special Needs

All the practical chapters contain special activities that have been found to be successful when teaching children with particular needs and talents.

Theory and Research behind Strategies

Each instructional chapter ends with a section that succinctly summarizes the major research and theoretical base for the ideas and strategies presented in the chapter.

Additional Readings

Each chapter ends with an expanded and updated annotated bibliography of additional readings.

Instructor's Edition

The instructor's edition contains many of the extras we use when teaching courses with this text. For each chapter in Part I, it contains such features as student projects, essay questions, and transparency masters.

ACKNOWLEDGMENTS

We would like to thank the students and colleagues who have read and commented on earlier editions of this book. They have helped us improve it. We would also like to thank the following reviewers for their helpful suggestions:

Janice F. Almasi, University of Nebraska at Omaha

June Brown, Southwest Missouri State University

Joyce Choate, Northeast Louisiana University

Nancy B. Cothern, Indiana University, Fort Wayne

Luisa Duran, University of New Mexico

Sandra Fradd, University of Miami

Paul Gathercoal, Gustavus Adolphus College

Cynthia M. Getty, University of Tennessee

Marjorie R. Hancock, Kansas State University

Nancy S. Haugen, Ottawa University

Ila Dean Horn, University of Nebraska at Omaha

Dennis J. Kear, Wichita State University

Pat Koskinen, University of Maryland, College Park

Carol V. Lloyd, University of Nebraska at Omaha

Sam Miller, University of North Carolina, Greensboro

Sue R. Mohrmann, Texas A & I University

Gary A. Negin, California State University, San Bernardino

Elinor P. Ross, Tennessee Technological University

John A. Smith, Utah State University

Lynn C. Smith, Southern Illinois University

Marilou R. Sorensen, University of Utah

We also want to thank Tracy Seiler and Leigh Wayne Miller, two Wake Forest University undergraduates. Tracy took most of the photos and drew most of the illustrations. Leigh Wayne typed, proofed, tracked down elusive references, and learned to use Powerpoint to do some nice graphics. We are grateful for their time, talents, and enthusiasm!

READING AND WRITING . . .

CHAPTER 1

About Reading and Writing

LOOKING AHEAD

The next eight chapters of *Reading and Writing in Elementary Classrooms* will describe the major components of effective reading and writing instruction, the theoretical framework for each, and specific teaching activities that you can use to foster the development of high-level literacy for all children. Each chapter has key ideas that summarize the most important information in that chapter. The key ideas in this chapter relate to the nature of reading and writing and to the individual nature of the children we are teaching. The key ideas in this chapter are the foundation for the key ideas in all the other chapters.

As you read this book, you will find a variety of effective ways to teach children to read and write. But you already have a lifetime of experiences with reading and writing yourself. To begin, then, we suggest that you recall what you have experienced over the years so that you can relate, or connect, your own experiences with learning to read and write to teaching others to read and write. Here is an anecdote of one child's reading and writing history.

A tiny baby, David, sits on his grandmother's lap. He can't yet talk, but Grandma holds up objects and makes sounds. "Hey diddle diddle, the cat and the fiddle," she says with a smile. She points to blobs of black and color on a page. "See the funny cat?" she asks. "See the fiddle?" The baby doesn't know what's going on, but he feels good sitting with Grandma, who rocks him and makes nice sounds. A year or so later, David looks forward each evening to being put to bed by Daddy, who stays with him and shows him pictures in books. Frequently, Daddy reads the same book over and over, and David begins to recognize the rhythms and patterns of the words—even, perhaps, the way they look on the page.

One day David, now three, surprises his parents by pointing to an ad in the evening paper and shouting, "Pizza Hut!" Mommy and Daddy are amazed, but Daddy points out that, after all, it *is* David's favorite restaurant, and he sees the Pizza Hut sign an average of once every 10 days. When he's four or five, David enjoys going with Mommy to the grocery store. He writes his own "list," a page of scribbles, and delights Mommy by telling her what each "word" means—fruit, cookies, cereal—and crossing each one off as Mommy picks it off the shelf. At about the same age, David begins to write "real" words—*David, Mommy, Daddy, love*—when a grown-up spells them out for him. He pretends to read favorite books to his stuffed bear and insists indignantly that he is not pretending at all.

When David starts kindergarten, he learns about libraries; he even has his own library card. Mommy takes him to storytime at the public library on Saturdays, and he can now read signs along the road as they drive: *Stop, Exit, No Parking.* Often he listens to tapes of stories and enjoys the activity because he can back up and listen to his favorite parts again and again. But he also likes to have Mommy and Daddy read to him because he can ask questions. In kindergarten, the children make "chart stories"—a series of sentences that describe a field trip or special event. In first grade, David is put into the "foxes" reading group; his group, to his surprise, finishes four books before the "bunnies" group is even through with their second. He spends time at the reading center, picking out books that interest him and listening to tapes; he enjoys that much more than the worksheets. Sometimes he forgets what a picture is supposed to be and puts *p* for *puppy* next to a picture that is supposed to be a *dog.* He can write words and sometimes sentences of his own, but his teacher is concerned about his occasional inability to do his phonics worksheets correctly.

David does a lot of acting and art activities with his reading in the third grade. "Close your eyes," his teacher says. "Can you hear the waves? Can you smell the salt air?" His third-grade teacher has each child keep a journal and has her students write in it every day. Fourth grade, however, is a disaster. The teacher has everyone read in turn, and David frequently stops paying attention once he has figured out when his turn will come. In science and social studies, David and his classmates do nothing but read the text and answer the questions at the end of each chapter. He can't wait to move on. Fortunately, fifth grade is better. When the children read, the teacher asks them to look at headings and illustrations first and to predict what might happen in the story. The teacher is supportive even when the predictions are wrong: "Your way might have made a better story!" he says. What David dislikes most in fifth grade is The Kit. Each student is assigned a set of colored cards with a paragraph to be read and questions to be answered on each card. The topics are often boring, and the questions are similar from one color to the next; sometimes David answers the questions without doing the reading.

In the eighth grade, David's teacher presents Preview, Question, Read, Recite, Review (PQ3R). To David, it seems only common sense, but the process seems to remind some of the other students of what they should be doing when they read, and many are especially helped by the reminder to review what they've read. In ninth-grade science, David learns about outlining and "webbing"—ways to organize information. His tenth-grade English teacher actually reads aloud to the class—a technique that brings snickers from the class the first few times but one that students eventually look forward to. The books the teacher chooses are exciting and intriguing, and some students who have never liked reading are excited about it for the first time.

Did the preceding story bring back some memories of your own years of learning to read and write? Do you remember having some of the same experiences? Did you respond to them as David did, or were your responses different? We shared this imaginary reading history with you for two reasons: First, it may help you to recall and evaluate your own experiences in learning to read and write, to recognize how many varied approaches are used in learning to read and write, and to connect what you are about to read with your own experiences. Second, we wanted to set the stage for the key ideas in this chapter:

1. Reading and writing are learned in a variety of ways.
2. Reading and writing are thinking.
3. Reading and writing are feeling.
4. Reading and writing are language.
5. There are individual, cultural, and language differences among the children we teach.
6. Children need a balanced literacy program.

READING AND WRITING ARE LEARNED IN A VARIETY OF WAYS

Children learn a great many things about reading and writing before coming to school. The foundation for reading and writing is being built when they are too young even to know what reading and writing are and what books are for. When children are read to, they begin to get a sense of how written language sounds. They learn many concepts from someone reading and talking about the pictures in the books. They also come to realize that it is the "funny little black marks" that people are looking at as they read. Young children who are read to regularly go through a "pretend reading" stage. Although they don't yet recognize most of the words in the book, they can pretend to read a favorite book because they have heard it read many times and they know which things to say for which pictures. Books that children can pretend read after several hearings are called predictable books because the pictures, rhyme, and sentence patterns let you predict what the words will say. Perhaps you remember some predictable books such as *Are You My Mother?* (Eastman, 1960), *One Fish, Two Fish, Red Fish, Blue Fish* (Seuss, 1960) and *Brown Bear, Brown Bear* (Martin, 1970).

In addition to learning to read by being read to, many children have books that are recorded on tape. As they relisten to favorite books, they learn meanings for words, increase their oral language facility, and often learn to read some of the books.

Young children learn to read the signs and labels that are such a big part of their world. Through their excursions to stores and restaurants, they learn to read words such as *Pizza Hut, McDonald's,* and *Stop.* At first, they can recognize these words only when they see them on the sign. But later, they begin to iden- tify the words regardless of whether the pictures, shapes, or other cues are there.

At the same time that these young children are engaging in all these reading activities, most children are also trying to write. Their first writing attempts are usually scribbles and then become collections of circles and lines that resemble letters. The first "real" words most children write are their own names, along with the names of pets and family members. They often copy words to make signs (*Keep Out* is commonly found on young children's bedroom doors). Most children write before they can spell. They ask others to spell words for them, copy favorite words from books, signs, and greeting cards, and invent the spelling of words by putting down some letters they hear.

For many children these fledgling reading and writing attempts happen in the preschool years. Print-rich kindergartens promote continued literacy devel- opment by providing lots of reading to children, shared reading of predictable Big Books, and many opportunities for children to write. Children who have not had these literacy experiences at home need to be placed in these print-rich kindergarten environments.

As children move into the primary grades, the reading to children, shared reading, and opportunities for writing should continue to be a large part of their literacy experience. In addition, children need to begin reading books on their own. Whole language classrooms are classrooms in which children spend most of their time reading real books for their own purposes and writing authentic texts. Whole language classrooms place a high priority on good literature, on self-selected reading and writing, and on children sharing their reading and writing with one another.

In many classrooms, some of the reading instruction is carried out with an adopted basal reading series. These series have books for each grade level (some- times called literature anthologies) that contain a variety of literature, including contemporary fiction, historical fiction, science fiction, fantasy, biography, and nonfiction informational selections. Often, in addition to the basal reader or literature anthology, children do some work in an accompanying workbook or respond to literature in an accompanying journal. Most basal series contain periodic tests and other instruments teachers use to assess how children are progressing in their reading. In some classrooms, basal reading instruction is carried out in ability groups. In other classrooms, the teacher uses a variety of whole class instruction, flexible groups, and pairing arrangements instead of fixed reading groups.

Writing is also learned through a variety of activities. In most primary classrooms, teachers record children's ideas and display these on a chart. These activities, sometimes called language experience activities (LEA) or shared writing, are opportunities for children to watch the teacher write. Through participation in language experience or shared writing activities, children learn that what you say can be written down and then read back. They also learn how we write and begin to understand the left-right conventions of writing as well as develop some beginning sense of punctuation and sentence/paragraph formation.

In addition to participating in activities where the teacher writes down the ideas, children learn to write by writing. Writers' Workshop is the popular term for a process approach to writing in which children write, share, edit, revise, and publish. Teachers teach minilessons in which they demonstrate how to write in various forms, the mechanics of writing and editing, and revision strategies. In many classrooms, children write in a journal, which may include personal writing as well as responses to literature and to what is being learned in the content areas of science and social studies. In many classrooms, children use computers to write, edit, and publish their pieces.

Phonics and spelling instruction have a role to play in moving all children toward literacy. Children need to learn to read and spell high-frequency words such as *was*, *have*, and *they*, which are sometimes referred to as sight words. Children also need to develop strategies for figuring out the probable pronunciation of a word they have never seen before. This figuring out of unfamiliar words is what is usually referred to as phonics or decoding. Children also need to learn the most common English spelling patterns so that they can move through the stages of invented spelling toward conventional spelling.

Most of the reading and writing activities just described would take place during the language arts/reading part of the day. In many classrooms, teachers integrate the reading, writing, and other language activities and carry out an integrated language arts program. But children are reading and writing throughout the school day, and these literacy experiences they have while learning in the content areas of science, social studies, math, and health also contribute to their achievement of high literacy levels. These content-area subjects are the place where much new vocabulary is encountered, and teachers use this opportunity to help children build new concepts and learn new words. Children need to learn how to read textbooks as well as other informational sources. Many teachers include study strategies such as PQ3R, organizing strategies such as webbing and data charts, and research strategies such as locating information and note taking in their content-area instruction. In these classrooms, integration occurs not just within the integrated language arts block but across the various content subjects as well.

Learning to read and write with fluency and confidence are long-term, multi-faceted goals. Effective classrooms do not have one approach to reading and writing. Rather, they use numerous approaches to provide a wide variety of reading and writing experiences throughout the day and across the curriculum.

LISTEN, LOOK, AND LEARN

Interview a teacher you respect at a grade level you would like to teach. Find out how that teacher teaches reading and writing. Create some questions and ask the teacher to describe a typical daily/weekly schedule. Try to determine if the teacher reads to the students daily and provides time for the children to read materials of their own choosing. What part does writing play in the curriculum? Is a basal reader used, and if so, what part does it play in the total language arts program? How much time is devoted to phonics and spelling activities, and are these integrated with the reading and writing that occur? How much is language integrated into the content areas of science, social studies, and math? Summarize what you found in your interview by relating it to the information in the *reading and writing are learned in a variety of ways* key idea.

READING AND WRITING ARE THINKING

Imagine that you come upon someone who is sitting, pen in hand or fingertips poised over the keyboard, and staring at the blank page or the blank screen and you ask, "What are you doing?" The person will often respond, "I'm thinking!" Continue to observe and you will see the person eventually move into the writing phase, but the writing is not nonstop. There are constant pauses, and if you are rude enough to interrupt during one of these pauses and ask, "What are you doing?" the writer will again probably respond, "I'm thinking!!!"

Eventually, the writer finishes the writing, or, more accurately, finishes the first draft of the writing. The writer may put the writing away for a while or may ask someone, "Take a look at this and tell me what you think." Later the writer will return to the writing to revise and edit it. Words will be changed, paragraphs added, moved, or deleted. Again, the writer will pause from time to time during this after-writing phase, and if you ask what the writer is doing, you will get the familiar response, "I'M THINKING!"

We offer this common scenario as proof that writing is at its essence thinking and that even the most naive writer knows this basic truth. Because writing is thinking and because learning requires thinking, students who write as they are learning think more and thus learn more.

When asked what *reading* is, most people would reply, "It's saying words written down." According to that definition, you would be reading if you read the following sentence:

Serny wugs dree biffles.

FIGURE 1.1 When reading and writing, we use some or all of the nine thinking processes.

Although most people can say these made-up words, doing so is not really reading because reading implies not only the ability to say the words but also the ability to know what you have said. Either saying the words aloud or thinking them in your mind is the word-identification part of reading. Knowing what you have read is the comprehension part. You could not comprehend the meaning of the sentence above because the made-up words had no meaning. But how do you comprehend the meanings of the many and varied sentences you read every day? Comprehension—figuring out the meaning of what you read—is accomplished in your brain as your brain processes the meanings of the words. In simplest terms, your brain thinks about what you read. But what is *thinking*, and how does it occur? What do you mean when you say, "I'm thinking"?

For more than a century, psychologists have tried to determine the exact nature of thinking, and there are many lists of the possible components of thinking. But because thinking is a complex process, it is difficult to describe. Nevertheless, because thinking is how your brain allows you to comprehend what you are reading, it is important for people who teach reading and writing to have some understanding of what some of those components might be. Although there is disagreement about which thinking processes are used in reading comprehension, nine processes seem to play a large part in reading comprehension and writing (Moore, Moore, Cunningham, & Cunningham, 1994). These processes are not clearly distinguished from one another, and reading and writing often involve several of them. The nine thinking processes are as follows:

1. *Call Up.* Imagine that you are planning a trip to Hawaii and buy a Hawaii travel guide to help you plan your trip. As soon as you begin to read the book, you will recall some of the things you already know about Hawaii. As you continue to read, what you read will help you to recall other pieces of information you didn't remember at first. The more experiences you are able to recall, the more you will have available to relate to what you read.

   Perhaps our reading history that began this chapter helped you to recall your own reading memories, although you might have remembered some of these experiences anyway. Memories you can call up without prompting are said to be at your "recall" level. Our scene may also have described some experiences that you didn't recall on your own but that when you read about them, you thought, "Oh, I remember that!" These memories were also part of your knowledge and experience, but they happened so long ago or were so insignificant that you had trouble recalling them. You did, however, recognize them when our scene jogged your memory. Therefore, you had these experiences not at the recall level but at the "recognition" level. As we read, we recall and recognize experiences and knowledge already stored in our brain. We will refer to this recall and recognition as *call up.*

2. *Connect.* Not only do we call up our own experiences, but we also usually try to relate them to whatever we are reading about. Imagine a list in your brain titled "Everything I Know about Hawaii." When you have finished reading, that list will be a lot longer. It is sometimes difficult for people to understand the difference between the processes of "calling up" and "connecting" because in reality, they almost always happen together. The reason we call up our experiences is so that we can relate, or connect, new information to what we know.

3. *Organize.* Organizing the information you gain from reading is a way of making connections. As you are reading about Hawaii, you will read about its history, beaches, climate, hotels, and so on. You will indeed connect this information to what you already knew before reading. But if we could look inside your brain when you finished, the new and old information would probably not look like a list. What we would probably see might look more like an outline with major headings and information under each. We might also see a part that looks like a time line with a listing of dates and important events in Hawaiian history. One part might look like a chart with the various beaches listed across

the top and different features listed under each one. Organizing information helps us to remember what we've read and to sequence what we write.

4. *Image.* As you are reading about Hawaii, you will probably be imagining what it would be like to be there. You might close your eyes and picture the beaches. You might feel the heat of the tropical sun on your back. You might hear the waves crashing when the surf is up. You might smell the pig roasting for the luau, and your mouth might water as you think about eating it. As we read, we use our senses to imagine what is happening. Based on our past experiences, we create sights, sounds, smells, tastes, and feelings that make the book come alive. We call this thinking process of using some or all of our senses to relate to what we are reading *imaging.*

5. *Predict.* Another way we use our brain to think as we are reading is to predict. A *prediction* is a guess about what is coming next. As you are reading about the Japanese bombing of Pearl Harbor, you realize that this probably bodes ill for the many people of Japanese descent living on the islands. Your further reading confirms this prediction that the Japanese-Hawaiians are in for a hard time. Sometimes your predictions are not confirmed. As you are reading about how to get to Kauai, you discover that you can fly directly to the small island without changing planes in Honolulu. Your surprise indicates that you had made a prediction. Predictions are important to reading comprehension because they are one of our brain's ways of actively involving us with our reading.

6. *Monitor.* You will know that your brain is constantly monitoring the incoming information when you recall those times in your reading when you have stopped and thought, "That can't be right!" Imagine that you were reading about hotels in Hawaii and saw that one that sounded just right charged $1,000 for a double room. "That can't be right!" you would think. "It must be a misprint of an extra zero." You would check further and might conclude that (1) it was indeed a misprint, (2) the $1,000 was a weekly rate, or (3) you have very expensive taste in hotels! Monitoring is our brain's way of double-checking information. When we read, we monitor constantly. We are usually aware of the monitoring only when we realize that something has gone wrong.

7. *Generalize.* Generalizing is another thinking process that is closely linked to reading and writing. It is the process by which the brain takes several small pieces of information and from these small pieces comes to some larger conclusion. As you study the charts giving the average rainfall and average high and low temperatures for each month, you might realize that there is not much variation. It's a little warmer in the summer months and a little cooler in the winter months, but the climate is pretty moderate and they have lots of sunny days year-round. Drawing conclusions and forming generalizations based on facts is of

critical importance because these "big ideas" are more easily remembered than the facts on which they were based. Months after reading about Hawaii, you probably cannot remember the average rainfall and temperatures for each month but you probably do remember your generalization that the weather is pretty moderate with lots of sunny days year-round.

8. *Apply.* To apply something is to use it. When you call your travel agent and make your Hawaii trip plans, you are probably basing some of your decisions about when to go, which islands to go to, and where to stay on what you read in the travel guide.

9. *Evaluate.* To evaluate is to make judgments about things. You evaluate when you decide that the treatment of the Japanese-Hawaiians was "not right." You evaluate when you decide you probably won't like poi, a native Hawaiian dish. Applying often includes evaluation. You probably decided which islands to go to based on your judgments about which islands had more things you would like. You evaluated and then applied that knowledge to planning your trip. Had you been reading the Hawaii travel book with no prospects of ever going to Hawaii, you still would have made evaluations, but you would, unfortunately, not have used these judgments to plan your trip.

Thinking is something we do all the time. We daydream, plan, worry, scheme, and ponder. As we think, we use a variety of thinking processes. To comprehend what we read, we think as we are reading. The nine processes we have described here are some of the components of thinking that seem to be the most useful while reading. To help you think about "thinking," we have described each one separately, but in reality, several processes are going on simultaneously. In the remaining chapters of this book, you will find many activities designed to help students become better readers and writers. Because reading and writing are so intimately bound up with thinking, you will find that these activities help students become better at using the nine thinking processes as they read and write.

TRY IT OUT

 Find a short magazine article on a topic of interest to you. Read the magazine article and try to be aware of where you use the thinking process. What do you call up from your own experiences as you read? What connections do you make between the magazine information and your own background knowledge, and what connections do you make between various pieces of information in the magazine article? Do you organize any of the information by mentally categorizing it or seeing time or other relationships? At what point do you image? Predict? Is there a point at which you become aware of the omnipresent monitoring function of your brain because something seems not to click? Could you use or apply anything you have learned in your own life? What generalizations and judgments did you make about what you read?

For each of the thinking processes, explain how you used it to comprehend this article or why you think you did not use it.

READING AND WRITING ARE FEELING

People are both thinking and feeling creatures. When we talk about thinking, we are referring to the cognitive part of us. The feeling part of us is referred to as the affective domain. We have feelings or emotional responses to all of the important parts of our lives. We like certain foods and hate others; we fear certain social situations and eagerly anticipate others. These feelings are important because, to a large extent, they determine how we will respond in various situations.

The imaginary reader in the scene that opened this chapter had mostly positive feelings about reading. Even before he knew what the words meant, he liked the feeling of being rocked and read to. He enjoyed being read to and writing messages on his chalkboard. When he went to school, he continued to have good feelings about reading and about himself as a reader. With the exception of some seatwork activities—workbooks and The Kit—our reader liked most reading-related things.

Unfortunately, not all children's interactions with reading are that positive. Many children are not read to and given opportunities and encouragement to write before coming to school. These children start out behind. They don't really understand what reading is. They lack meanings for many words and language patterns commonly used in picture books. They can't read their own name and may not even realize that their name can be written. Kindergarten and first-grade teachers must immerse these children in a variety of language activities so that they can learn those concepts that are learned by many others before coming to school.

Even with good instruction, some children find that learning to read and write is difficult. When something is difficult, we tend to feel negative toward it. Children in the lowest reading group usually have negative and defeatist attitudes toward reading. Also, children who find reading difficult seldom become good readers because they don't read much (Allington, 1984). Reading, like any other skill, requires both instruction and practice. Children who don't succeed well in reading don't like to read. Children who don't like to read don't choose to read books. They read only what is assigned and never develop the fluency and ease that comes from lots of easy reading.

How a teacher teaches reading and writing has a great impact on how successful children are and on their attitudes toward reading. Teachers who teach reading not just in reading groups but also through language experience and writing activities give children more than just one way to learn to read. Teachers who provide students with strategies for organizing and remembering information read in science and social studies increase the success of students in those subjects and improve their attitudes toward those subjects and toward reading. Perhaps the most important thing teachers can do to promote good reading and writing attitudes is to read to children and provide time, books, and opportunities for them to read books of their own choosing and to write on topics they care about.

How children feel about reading and writing is directly related to how successful they are, how much they read and write, and how their teachers teach reading and writing. Throughout this book, you will find teaching strategies that help children become better readers and writers. These same strategies will create children who like to read and write.

READING AND WRITING ARE LANGUAGE

We would like to take another imaginary trip now. This time we will go to the island of Norite.

The island of Norite is a tropical paradise of white sandy beaches and constant sun. The people who live there are intelligent people who have a variety of occupations. People work in restaurants, hotels, schools, and factories. Here, as in all places, each person is different from the others. Some are short and others are tall; some are fat and others are skinny; some are smart and others are not so smart. They even have television and telephones. The people of Norite have a rich and wonderful language, with even 19 words for types of waves.

Imagine that you somehow get stranded on this island. The people are gracious and treat you like an honored guest, and you are given everything you need to survive. However, you don't speak their language and they don't speak English; you communicate with gestures and motions and by pointing to objects. Quickly, you begin to learn some basic words in their language, and after several weeks there, you want to write down some notes about this strange island. You look around for pens and paper but don't see any. You approach your host and make "writing gestures" to show you want writing implements, but your host shows no understanding at all. You look around your hotel and then walk through the shops, and as you do this, you suddenly realize that you have not seen a single written thing or anything to write with. "It can't be" is your first response, but even as you think this, you realize that you have become stranded on an island with no written language.

You walk to the school and talk to the principal—the smartest person on the island. You make writing gestures, and when you see by the blank expression on her face that even she has no conception of reading and writing, you grab her hand and take her to the beach. You say "sand" and use a stick to write the English word *sand* in the sand. She must think you want to know her word for sand because she picks some up and says something that sounds like "jid." Unsure about how to spell it but desperately wanting to communicate what writing is, you use your stick to write *jid* in the sand. You say her name, "Raheeta," and write it, too, and then say your name and write it. You repeat these three words several times and trace the word written in the sand each time. Just when you think you will not be able to make her understand, her eyes get wide and she points to the word *Raheeta* and to herself and asks, "Raheeta?" "Yes, yes!" you shout. The two of you stay on the beach scratching words in the sand until it is too dark to see.

Working with Raheeta, you write down the language of the island. It is easy to write the words that stand for concrete things such as sand, water, swim, and Raheeta. It is harder to write the words used to connect these concrete words. These words are never said by themselves, and even Raheeta does not know them as separate words. When she says "Jidabhuss" as she touches the sand, you know that *jid* means *sand* and *huss* means *hot,* and you figure out that the sound "ab" between them must be a linking word like *is.* These abstract connecting words are the hardest for you to hear and for Raheeta to learn.

As you teach Raheeta to read and write, you realize how many things all readers take for granted that must be taught to someone who is ignorant of reading and writing. When Raheeta begins writing words, she just puts the words where they fit rather than going from left to right. She has to learn that you leave a space after words and what punctuation marks like periods, commas, and question marks signal. Written language has all of these conventions or arbitrary rules that you don't need to know to carry on a conversation but that are essential to written language. She also doesn't understand the meanings of words we commonly use to talk about reading and writing. Terms such as *letter, word,* and *sentence* all have to be explained and are quite confusing in the beginning.

After many months of constant writing in the sand, however, Raheeta knows the written words for most of the common spoken words in her language. By then, everyone on Norite has learned about this strange new way to communicate, and Raheeta and you take on the job of making the whole island—young and old alike—literate. You are very old by the time you are rescued, but you have accomplished what few have ever done. You have helped people with a rich spoken language learn to read and write that language.

We can learn something from this imaginary adventure on Norite that we all take for granted. Reading and writing are language. Language is primarily oral. People first learn to talk and to listen and then learn that what they say can be written down and read back. Because reading and writing are integrally bound to listening and speaking abilities, reading instruction must build on students' oral language. Simultaneously, we must increase their facility with oral language so that we have more to build on. Reading and writing abilities develop together for most children. Children who write become better readers and children who read become better writers.

Throughout this book, you will find suggestions for involving children in discussion, dramatic, and other oral language activities that increase the number of words in their speaking vocabularies and the ways in which they can combine these words to express themselves clearly and cleverly. You will find listening-comprehension strategies that increase children's ability to listen to a story or piece of informational text that is read to them as well as increase their ability to understand and respond to what they have listened to. You will find writing activities that help children learn to express their ideas using written language. As children write their own ideas, they become more aware of how authors communicate ideas, and they use this knowledge to understand better what they read. Reading is language. Children become better readers and writers when teachers develop all of the language arts—speaking, listening, reading, and writing—and use each one to support the others.

In thinking about the next key idea it is important for you to keep in mind the critical dependence of reading and writing on oral language because many children come to school speaking a language other than English. These children must learn to speak and listen in the language they are also learning to read and write.

THERE ARE INDIVIDUAL, CULTURAL, AND LANGUAGE DIFFERENCES AMONG THE CHILDREN WE TEACH

Think about your own family, or a family you know well, with two or more children. Have you noticed and heard others remark on "how different the children are"? One child must have a clearly defined routine and set of rules while the other child does better if allowed more flexibility and self-determination. One child is neat; the other a slob. (Let's hope they don't have to share the same bedroom!) One child has a restless, creative, problem-solving mind and personality. The other child is as smart (perhaps smarter on standardized tests) but unimaginative.

Anyone who has ever observed how children from the same family differ knows that all children do not learn/respond/think in the same manner. Successful parents recognize the differences in their children and adjust their rules, routines, interactions, and so forth to maximize the possibilities for each of their different children.

In addition to these individual differences among children, there are some important cultural and linguistic differences we must think about. Our nation has always had a diverse population coming from many different countries and bringing a variety of languages and customs. Demographic data suggest that we are becoming a more multicultural society. In 1990, 40 percent of the school-age population of New York State belonged to ethnic minority groups. In California, the "minority" has become the majority with over 50 percent of the school-age population identifying themselves as nonwhite or Hispanic. In addition to cultural differences, many school-age children speak a language other than

English. Estimates are that nationwide we now have 10 million children in our schools living in homes where English is not spoken. Many teachers currectly teach in classrooms in which more than half of their students are non-native-English speakers, and most teachers will teach in classrooms in which at least one student speaks a language other than English. The classrooms in which we help children become literate will increasingly contain larger numbers of children whose cultural and linguistic heritage is quite different from the heritage of the teacher.

Describing all the cultural and linguistic differences that exist among children is impossible and beyond the scope of this book, but since we believe that learning is best accomplished through real, concrete experiences, here are a few examples. Children from some ethnic groups live in large cooperative family groups in which hugs and other displays of affection, social interaction, and sharing are an integral part of their daily lives. Children take responsibility for each other and cooperation is highly valued. Other children are used to more formal interactions and are taught "not to speak unless spoken to" and always to wait for and follow adult directions. These children would expect some social distance to be kept between children and adults—particularly adult authority figures such as teachers. Some Native American children live in a culture in which cooperation rather than competition is valued and often don't understand why they can't help each other on a test. Many Native American children are taught in their homes to be keen observers, and a greater priority is placed on doing than on talking. There are also a variety of cultural differences relating to eye contact and the amount of physical distance normally kept between two people who are conversing with one another.

Many children who have recently immigrated from Russia cannot speak, read, or write English but they can speak, read, and write two other languages—Russian and Hebrew. Hmong children from the mountains of Laos often come speaking a little English but are unable to read or write in any language. Some Korean children have difficulty learning to use articles and verbs in speaking and writing English because the Korean language contains no articles and verbs are not inflected for tense or number.

These few examples of cultural and linguistic differences are not intended to be inclusive and certainly aren't meant to stereotype any group. They are included only to try to make real for you the idea that children bring with them expectations, behavior patterns, and varying knowledge based on what they have experienced in their homes and communities. In order to achieve the goal of high levels of literacy for all the diverse children we teach, teachers must know that differences exist and that these differences affect how children learn. The most successful teachers are keen observers. When they have a child in their classroom who comes from a cultural or linguistic environment different from theirs, they watch and think about the child's reaction to the classroom routines and seek information about parents, other members of that cultural/linguistic group, and other sources and make whatever accommodations they can in the classroom routine.

DO IT TOGETHER

 Form groups of four or five and pool your knowledge of individual differences among children. Think back to your own experiences in school and in any classrooms you have observed or taught in. Think about yourself as a learner. How were you different from the crowd? Then think of other children you know well—family members, friends, neighbors. What differences do you have personal experience with and how did teachers respond to those differences? Try to think of instances in which the teacher adapted to the learner and instances in which the learner had to do the adapting. Summarize your findings and make a list of ways you think teachers can adapt to the differences children bring with them.

CHILDREN NEED A BALANCED LITERACY PROGRAM

Not only do children bring to school huge differences in the amount of reading/writing experiences they have had, they also come with their own "personalities." Some children need and like the structure of basal readers. They know exactly what they are going to read and what to do after they read. Skills are introduced and reviewed in a predictable, logical order. Some children even take pleasure in completing each story and noting the visible signs that they are progressing.

This same order and predictability that allow some children to thrive in basal approaches can be a total turnoff to children with other personalities. "Reading is always the same," they say. "You talk about what you are going to read, learn some new words, read the story, and do two pages in your workbook! Boring!" These adventuresome types like variety—in what they read, when they read it, and what they do before and after reading. Put these children in a literature approach based on self-selection and a variety of ways of sharing and they are more apt to become readers.

To some children, their own ideas and imaginations are much more interesting than anything some "faraway" author might have written. These children love to "express themselves." They love to talk and tell stories and be the center of attention. These expressive children also love to write, and as they write, they use and learn words that they then read. The writing personalities will read—but for them reading is a means, not an end. Reading is one of their sources for ideas about which they can write!

Likewise, some children are better at learning and using letter-sound relationships. They have "an ear" for sounds—much like the ear of some who become musicians. Other children labor over the letters and sounds and aren't able to blend the sounds they know into words they know.

One of the major reasons for providing a balanced literacy program is that children bring differences with them into our schools. While it is not possible to clearly determine which children will learn best with which approach, it is clear that when a teacher provides more routes to the goal of literacy, more children will find a route that will take them there.

Another reason balance and variety are called for relates to the cultural differences among children. Classrooms with children from many different cultural backgrounds will want to have some activities that are more formal or more guided or require individual participation, along with other activities that are less formal or more self-selected or that promote cooperative learning. The cooperative groupings will include not only small groups but working partnerships and some tutoring arrangements. Balanced classrooms offer children opportunities to respond orally and in writing along with opportunities to make things and respond artistically.

Language differences also suggest a balance of classroom activities. In some schools, non-native-English speakers are taught English while the rest of their instruction is carried on in their first language. They learn content and learn to read and write in their native language while simultaneously learning to speak English. Programs in which children are taught for the first several years in their native language are most common in schools in which most non-native-English speakers speak one other language. In other schools, children come from a variety of different language backgrounds. In these schools, children are usually given some special instruction in English and for the rest of the day, they are "immersed" in an English-speaking classroom. When children for whom English is not their first language are in an English-speaking classroom, they benefit from a wide variety of language opportunities.

LOOKING BACK

In this chapter, we have begun to think about reading and writing by introducing six key ideas. These ideas are key to an understanding of not only this chapter, but the entire book.

1. To enable you to begin with a broad rather than a narrow understanding, we have stressed that *reading and writing are learned in a variety of ways.* Because of this, teachers need to have in their repertoires a wide variety of different teaching strategies and approaches.

2. Since *reading and writing are thinking,* as you teach them, you both call upon and develop children's thinking processes.

3. Because *reading and writing are feeling,* you must constantly consider student attitudes and interests as you plan reading and writing activities.

4. Since *reading and writing are language,* they are supported by and connected to the other language functions, speaking and listening. Reading and writing are best developed in integrated language arts classrooms in which reading and writing are connected to each other and to speaking and listening.

5. The fact that *there are individual, cultural, and language differences among the children we teach* leads us directly to the final and biggest key idea.
6. *Children need a balanced literacy program.*

ADD TO YOUR JOURNAL

 One of the big ideas in this chapter was that both reading and writing are primarily thinking. That idea is the major reason you find this journal-writing prompt at the end of each chapter. This journal is a place for you to think about what you are reading. As you write in this journal, try to use the nine thinking processes described in this chapter. *Call up* your past experiences with learning to read and write and with teaching. *Connect* these experiences to what you are reading. *Organize* the new information in a way that will help you to remember it. Try to *image* your classroom and *predict* how the different students in your class might respond to various approaches. *Monitor* your reading for what makes sense and what is confusing. Think about what big *generalizations* or conclusions you can make based on your experience and your reading. *Apply* as much as you can to whatever experiences you currently have working with children. *Evaluate* the big ideas and decide what is most important to you. Use your journal to think about each of the key ideas and to record your own personal responses to what you are learning.

REFERENCES

Allington, R. L. (1984). Content coverage and contextual reading in reading groups. *Journal of Reading Behavior, 16,* 85–96.
Moore, D. W., Moore, S. A., Cunningham, P. M., & Cunningham, J. W. (1994). *Developing readers and writers in the content areas, K–12* (2nd ed.). White Plains, NY: Longman.

Children's Books/Materials Cited

Are You My Mother? by P. D. Eastman, Random House, 1960.
Brown Bear, Brown Bear, What Do You See? by Bill Martin, Holt, Rinehart, & Winston, 1970.
One Fish, Two Fish, Red Fish, Blue Fish, by Dr. Seuss, Random House, 1960.

ADDITIONAL READINGS

Since reading and writing are language, classrooms that integrate the language arts provide children with a variety of ways to learn to read and write. These books and articles explore the interconnections between listening, speaking, reading, and writing and suggest a variety of ways classrooms can provide integrated language and content-area instructional programs.

Britton, J. (1994). *Language and learning.* Portsmouth, NH: Heinemann.

Goodman, K. (1986). *What's whole in whole language?* Portsmouth, NH: Heinemann.

Hart-Hewins, L., & Wells, J. (1990). *Real books for reading: Learning to read with children's literature.* Portsmouth, NH: Heinemann.

Heller, M. F. (1991). *Reading-writing connections: From theory to practice.* New York: Longman.

Irwin, J. W., & Doyle, M. A. (Eds.). (1992). *Reading/writing connections: Learning from research.* Newark, DE: International Reading Association.

McCracken, R., & McCracken, M. (1988). *Songs, stories and poetry to teach reading and writing.* Manitoba, Canada: Peguis.

Noyce, R. M., & Christie, J. F. (1989). *Integrating reading and writing instruction in grades K–8.* Boston: Allyn & Bacon.

Pappas, C. C., Kiefer, B. Z., & Levstik, L. S. (1990). *An integrated language perspective in the elementary school* (2nd ed.). White Plains, NY: Longman.

Pigdon, K., & Wooley, M. (Eds.). (1993). *The big picture: Integrating children's learning.* Portsmouth, NH: Heinemann.

Routman, R. (1988). *Transitions.* Portsmouth, NH: Heinemann.

Routman, R. (1991). *Invitations.* Portsmouth, NH: Heinemann.

Stevenson, C., & Carr, J. F. (Eds.). (1993). *Integrated studies in the middle grades.* New York: Teachers College Press.

Tierney, R. J., & Shanahan, T. (1991). Research on the reading-writing relationship: Interactions, transactions, and outcomes. In R. Barr, M. D. Kamil, P. B. Mosenthal, & P. D. Pearson (Eds.). *Handbook of reading research* (Vol. 2, pp. 246–280). White Plains, NY: Longman.

Walmsley, S. A., & Walp, T. (1990). Integrating literature and composing into the language arts curriculum. *Elementary School Journal, 90,* 251–274.

Weaver, C., Stephens, D., & Vance, J. (1990). *Understanding whole language: From principles to practice.* Portsmouth, NH: Heinemann.

Young, K. (1994). *Constructing buildings, bridges and minds: Building an integrated curriculum through social studies.* Portsmouth, NH: Heinemann.

How the brain functions and how thinking occurs are explored in terms that are relatively easy to understand in these two books.

Caine, R. N., & Caine, G. (1991). *Teaching and the human brain.* Alexandria, VA: Association for Supervision and Curriculum Development.

Vygotsky, L. S. (1978). *Mind in society.* Cambridge, MA: Harvard University Press.

Because reading and writing are feeling, motivating students to enjoy reading and writing is essential. The research on motivation and 33 research-based motivational strategies are summarized in this excellent article.

Brophy, J. (1987). Synthesis of research on strategies for motivating students to learn. *Educational Leadership, 45,* 40–48.

These books and articles reflect the latest research and best practice about teaching multicultural, multilingual children.

Au, K. H. (1993). *Literacy instruction in multicultural settings.* San Diego, CA: Harcourt Brace College Publishers.

Early, M. (1990). Enabling first and second language learners in the classroom. *Language Arts, 67*, 567–581.

Faltis, C. J. (1993). *Joinfostering: Adapting teaching strategies for the multilingual classroom.* New York: Merrill.

Fitzgerald, J. (1993). Literacy and students who are learning English as a second language. *The Reading Teacher, 46*, 638–647.

Freeman, Y. S., & Freeman, D. E. (1992). *Whole language for second language learners.* Portsmouth, NH: Heinemann.

Gibbons, P. (1993). *Learning to learn in a second language.* Portsmouth, NH: Heinemann.

Language arts in multilingual/multicultural education. (1989, September). *Language Arts, 66*.

Nurss, J. R., & Hough, R. A. (1992). Reading and the ESL student. In S. J. Samuels & A. E. Farstrup (Eds.), *What research has to say about reading instruction* (2nd ed., pp. 277–313). Newark, DE: International Reading Association.

Weber, R. (1991). Linguistic diversity and reading in American society. In R. Barr, M. L. Kamil, P. B. Mosenthal, & P. D. Pearson (Eds.), *Handbook of reading research* (Vol. 2, pp. 97–119). White Plains, NY: Longman.

A summary of important research that supports the development of balanced literacy programs can be found in the following two books.

Anderson, R. C., Hiebert, E., Scott, J. A., & Wilkinson, I. A. G. (1985). *Becoming a nation of readers.* Washington, DC: National Institute of Education.

Samuels, S. J., & Farstrup, A. E. (Eds.). (1992). *What research has to say about reading instruction.* Newark, DE: International Reading Association.

Emergent Literacy

LOOKING AHEAD

Like most other complex behaviors, literacy develops gradually and through a variety of experiences with reading and writing. The stage of development during which children are making their fledgling attempts at reading and writing is called emergent literacy. When children enter school, they have very different levels of literacy development. Some precocious children are already reading and writing fluently. Children who have had many informal reading and writing encounters move easily into independent reading and writing. Children who have had few experiences with print need a print-saturated environment in which to begin their explorations of reading and writing.

In the past decade, we have had a tremendous amount of research, usually included under the term *emergent literacy*, that has shown us what happens in the homes of children where literacy is a priority. We now know that children born into homes where someone spends time with them in reading and writing activities walk into our schools with an incredible foundation upon which our instruction can easily build. These children experience an average of over 1,000 hours of quality one-on-one reading and writing activities (Adams, 1990).

Parents (or parent substitutes including grandmothers, cousins, uncles, and big sisters) read to children and talk with them about what they are reading. This reading is usually done in the "lap position," where the child can see the pictures as well as the words used to tell about the pictures. Favorite books are read again and again, and eventually most children have a book that they "pretend read"—usually to a younger friend or a stuffed animal.

In addition to reading, these children are exposed to writing at an early age. They scribble and make up ways to spell words. They ask (and are told) how to spell favorite words. They make words from the magnetic letters and copy favorite words from books. From all of these over 1,000 hours of reading and writing experiences, these children learn some incredibly important concepts and attitudes. This chapter will describe these concepts and attitudes and four activities that foster them. The key ideas are:

1. Emerging readers and writers develop crucial understandings.
2. Reading to children supports emergent literacy.
3. Shared reading with predictable Big Books supports emergent literacy.
4. Shared writing and language experience activities support emergent literacy.
5. Helping children write supports emergent literacy.

EMERGING READERS AND WRITERS DEVELOP CRUCIAL UNDERSTANDINGS

A great many important concepts and attitudes are developed as children encounter print in various forms. Seven of these stand out and differentiate children who have had many print experiences from those who have not. Children who have had many print experiences know why we read and write, have greater knowledge stores, understand the conventions and jargon of print, have higher levels of phonological awareness, can read some important-to-them words, know some letter names and sounds, and are eager and confident in their fledgling reading and writing attempts.

What Reading and Writing Are For

This is one of those "so obvious it is overlooked" variables. Ask five-year-olds from strong literacy backgrounds why people need to read and write and they reel off a string of answers:

> *Well, you have to able to read. You read books and signs and cereal boxes and birthday cards that come in the mail and recipes and. . . . You write notes and stories and signs and lists and you write on the computer and you send postcards when you are on a trip and you write to your aunt and . . .*

You can tell from their answers that these children who come to school with clear ideas about the functions of reading and writing have had lots of real-world experiences with reading and writing. Reading and writing are things all the bigger people they know do and they intend to do them, too!

Background Knowledge and Concepts

A lot of what we know about the world we learn from reading. This is also true of young children. Imagine a child who has just had read as bedtime stories *The Ocean Alphabet Book* by Jerry Pallotta and *The Bear Scouts* by Stan and Jan Berenstain and pores over Richard Scarry's *Best Word Book Ever* before turning out the light. Think about all the concepts and words about the ocean developed from the informational alphabet book. Even though *The Bear Scouts* is fiction, the information about scouting, camping, and the outdoors is true. The Richard Scarry book, of course, builds concepts with clear pictures arranged around different categories.

As you will learn in Chapter 6, comprehension is directly tied to prior knowledge. The more you know about any topic, the greater will be your understanding of what you read related to that topic. Word identification is also closely related to topic knowledge. Children who know a lot about oceans can figure out a word like *jellyfish* from the context, pictures, and beginning sounds, but children who don't have the word and concept for jellyfish stored in their brain's ocean knowledge folder can't. Your store of background knowledge and concepts directly affects how well you read, and children who have had many books read to them know more than children who haven't.

Concepts about Print

Print is what you read and write. Print includes all the funny little marks—letters, punctuation, space between words and paragraphs—that translate into familiar spoken language. In English, we read across the page in a left-to-right fashion. Because our eyes can see only a few words during each stop (called a fixation), we must actually move our eyes several times to read one line of print. When we finish that line, we make a return sweep and start all over again. If there are sentences at the top of a page and a picture in the middle and more sentences at the bottom, we read the top first and then the bottom. We start at the front of a book and go toward the back. These arbitrary rules about how we proceed through the print are called conventions.

Jargon refers to all the words we use to talk about reading and writing. Jargon includes such terms as *word, letter, sentence,* and *sound.* We use this jargon constantly as we try to teach children how to read: "Look at the first word in the second sentence. How does that word begin? What letter makes that sound?"

Using some jargon is essential to talking with children about reading and writing, but children who don't come from rich literacy backgrounds are often hopelessly confused by this jargon. Although all children speak in words, they don't know words exist as separate entities until they are put in the presence of reading and writing. To many children, letters are what you get in the mailbox, sounds are horns and bells and doors slamming, and sentences are what you have to serve if you get caught committing a crime! These children are unable to follow our "simple" instructions because we are using words for which they have no meaning or an entirely different meaning.

Many children come to school knowing these print concepts. From being read to in the lap position, they have noticed how the eyes "jump" across the lines of print as someone is reading. They have watched people write grocery lists and thank-you letters to Grandma and have observed the top-bottom, left-right movement. Often, they have typed on the computer and observed these print conventions. Because they have had someone to talk with them about reading and writing, they have learned much of the jargon.

While writing down a dictated thank-you note to Grandma, Dad may say, "Say your sentence one word at a time if you want me to write it. I can't write as fast as you can talk."

When the child asks how to spell *birthday*, he may be told, "It starts with the letter *b*, just like your dog Buddy's name. *Birthday* and *Buddy* start with the same sound and the same letter."

These children know how to look at print and what teachers are talking about as they give them information about print. All children need to develop these critical understandings in order to learn to read and write.

Phonological Awareness

Have you listened to kindergartners on the playgound when they want to tease one another? What do they say? Often you hear chants such as Billy is Silly; Saggy, Baggy Maggie; Fat Pat—she's a rat! Making rhymes and playing with words is one of the most reliable indicators that children are getting control of language. They are becoming aware of words and sounds and can manipulate these to express themselves—and to impress others!

This ability to manipulate sounds is called phonological awareness, and children's level of phonological awareness is very highly correlated with their success in beginning reading. Phonological awareness develops through a series of stages during which children first become aware that language is made up of individual words, that words are made up of syllables, and that syllables are made up of phonemes. It is important to note here that it is not the "jargon" children learn. Five-year-olds cannot tell you there are three syllables in *dinosaur* and one syllable in *Rex*. What they can do is clap out the beats in *dinosaur* and the one beat in *Rex*. Likewise, they cannot tell you that the first phoneme in *mice* is *m*, but they can tell you what you would have if you took the first sound off *mice—ice*.

Children develop this phonological awareness as a result of the oral and written language they are exposed to during the preschool years. Nursery rhymes, chants, and Dr. Seuss books usually play a large role in this development. Lap reading in which children can see the print being read to them also seems to play an important role. Most children who have the luxury of being read to on demand will select a favorite book that they insist on having read again and again. They will ask questions about the words: "Where does it say, 'snort'?" "Is that *zizzerzazzerzuzz*?"

Children also develop a sense of sounds and words as they try to write. In the beginning, many children let a single letter stand for an entire word. Later, they put more letters and often say the word they want to write, dragging out its sounds to hear what letters they might use. Children who are allowed and encouraged to "invent spell" develop an early and strong sense of phonological awareness.

Some Concrete Words

If you sit down with first graders on the first day of school and try to determine if they can read by giving them a simple book to read or testing them on some common words such as *the, and, of,* or *with,* you would probably conclude that most first graders can't read yet. But many first graders can read and write some words. Here are some words a boy named David knew when he began first grade:

David
Mama
Daddy
Bear Bear (his favorite stuffed animal)
Carolina (his favorite basketball team)
Pizza Hut
I love you (Written on notes on good days)
I hate you (Written on notes on bad days!)

Most children who have had reading and writing experiences have learned some words. The words they learn are usually "important-to-them" concrete words. Knowing 10 to 15 words is important not because you can read much with these few words, but because in learning these first words, you have accomplished a critical task. Children who come to school already able to read or write some concrete words have accomplished an important and difficult task. They have learned how to learn words.

Some Letter Names and Sounds

Many children have learned some letter names and sounds. They can't usually recognize all 26 letters in both upper- and lowercase and they often don't know the sound of *w* or *c,* but they have learned the names and sounds for the most common letters. Usually, the letter names and sounds children know are based on those concrete words they can read and write.

The Desire to Learn to Read and Write

The final distinguishing characteristic of children who have had lots of early literacy encounters is that they can't wait to do it! All the big people can do it and they can't and they want to. They pretend read books and scribble write and then "read" their scribbling because they want to be able to do it! We all know of children who come home disappointed after the first day of first grade because "We were there all day and we didn't learn to read!" This "can't wait" attitude is a legacy of their literate environments, and the motivation sustains them through some of the work and effort required to become an independent reader and writer.

As you can tell, a lot is happening in the minds and hearts of young children during their early literacy encounters. Many children have these experiences at home. School just helps them continue their process toward literacy. Other children, unfortunately, have few reading and writing experiences before coming to school. For them, we must simulate as closely as possible the experiences

FIGURE 2.1   All children can develop these crucial understandings when immersed in appropriate reading and writing activities.

they missed. In the remainder of this chapter, we will describe four activities that form the cornerstone of an emergent literacy program through which all children can develop the critical understandings. None of these activities by itself is broad enough to develop all seven understandings but each activity develops several. With all four activities occurring regularly, children have multiple opportunities to realize why people read and write, expand their knowledge stores, learn print conventions and jargon, develop phonological awareness, learn to read and write some words, learn some letter names and sounds, and develop an "I can't wait" attitude!

READING TO CHILDREN
SUPPORTS EMERGENT LITERACY

Children are question machines. They come to school asking lots of questions, although the numbers of questions children ask seem to decrease with each year of schooling. One reason these lucky children do so well in school is that they have had their questions answered as they asked them, and they continue to ask questions and expect responses. As teachers read to young children, they ought to be modeling how they think as they encounter print, just as some parents do when they read aloud to their children (Roser & Martinez, 1985; Heath, 1982; Taylor, 1983).

Teachers need to model for children how they as readers call up, connect, organize, predict, monitor, image, evaluate, generalize, and apply by making statements throughout a read-aloud session. One way of modeling is a Think Link. A Think Link demonstrates what the teacher is thinking about at various times, linking the thinking to the essential thinking skills given in Chapter 1. For example, while reading *Jumanji* (Van Allsburg, 1981), the teacher might say, "I wonder what will happen next! I'll bet those rhinoceroses make a real mess in the house" (predict). "This is sort of like some games I have played" (connect). "I can just see that snake slithering down off the mantle" (image).

Through reading to and talking with children, the children learn at least three of the critical "knowings." They learn that being a reader is important and fun and that they want to become readers and writers themselves. They gain a broader understanding of the world as they encounter concepts and vocabulary that are unfamiliar. Children learn the different reasons that people write as things are read to them that inform or entertain.

The world of literature for young children is incredibly rich and varied. Chapter 5 describes some of the wonderful categories of books available. Because there are so many different kinds of books and because different understandings are increased by different kinds of books, teachers should read a great variety of books to children. In addition to storybooks and informational books, teachers should read poetry and nursery rhymes.

One of the best indicators of how well children will learn to read is their ability to recite nursery rhymes when they walk into the kindergarten. Children should learn to recite these rhymes, should sing the rhymes, should clap to the rhymes, act out the rhymes, and pantomime the rhymes. In some kindergarten class-rooms, they develop "raps" for the rhymes.

Once the children can recite lots of rhymes, nursery rhymes can be used to teach the concept of rhyme. The class can be divided into two halves—one half say the nursery rhyme but stop when they get to the rhyming word. The other half chime in with the rhyming word at the appropriate moment:

FIRST HALF: There was an old woman who lived in a shoe. She had so many children, she didn't know what to

SECOND HALF: do.

FIRST HALF: She gave them some broth without any bread and spanked them all soundly and put them to

SECOND HALF: bed.

Nursery and other rhymes have been a part of our oral heritage for generations. Now we know that the rhythm and rhyme inherent in nursery rhymes are important vehicles for the beginning development of phonological awareness. They should play a large role in any kindergarten curriculum.

While on the subject of things that have stood the test of time, do you remember being read *Hop on Pop? One Fish, Two Fish, Red Fish, Blue Fish? There's a Wocket in My Pocket?* These books hold universal appeal for young children and from them children develop important understandings. You can nudge those under-standings on a bit, if you help the children notice that many of the words that rhyme are also spelled alike. As you reread one of these favorite books, let the children point out the rhyming words and make lists of these on the board. Read the words together. Add other words that are spelled like that and rhyme, and make rhymes with those. Make up "silly words" and make them rhyme too, and decide what they might be and illustrate them! If you can have a wocket in your pocket, you can have a hocket in your pocket. What would a hocket be? What could you do with it?

The most important reasons for reading to young children relate to the power-ful role of read-alouds in concept development, the understanding of what reading is for, and the development of the desire to learn to read. Including lots of rhyming books in the read-aloud program has the added benefit of promoting phonological awareness and helping children develop some early understand-ings of letter-sound relationships.

SHARED READING WITH PREDICTABLE BIG BOOKS SUPPORTS EMERGENT LITERACY

Kindergarten and first-grade teachers have always recognized the importance of reading a variety of books to children. There is one particular kind of book and one particular kind of reading, however, that has special benefits for building reading and writing foundations—shared reading with predictable Big Books.

Shared reading is a term used to describe the process in which the teacher and the children read a book together. The book is read and reread many times. On the first several readings, the teacher does most of the reading. As the children become more familiar with the book, they join in and "share" the reading.

The best kind of books to use with shared reading is predictable books. Predictable books are books in which repeated patterns, refrains, pictures, and rhyme allow children to "pretend read" a book that has been read to them several times. Pretend reading is a stage most children go through with a favorite book that some patient adult has read and reread to them. Perhaps you remember pretend reading with such popular predictable books as *Goodnight Moon, Are You My Mother?* or *Brown Bear, Brown Bear.* Shared reading of predictable books allows all children to experience this pretend reading. From this pretend reading, they learn what reading is and they develop the confidence that they will be able to do it.

When children are read to "lap style" they have the opportunity to observe the print and the eyes of the person reading. They notice that the reader always reads the top print first, then the bottom print. They notice the eyes moving from left to right and then making the return sweep at the end of the line. Children who can see the words of a favorite book as that book is being read notice that some words occur again and again and eventually come to recognize some of these words. As they learn words, they notice recurring letter-sound relationships.

To simulate lap reading, many teachers use Big Books, in which the pictures and the print are enlarged. Not all Big Books are predictable, however. Not all Big Books have good story lines and wonderful artwork. If you want to get the maximum benefits from shared reading with Big Books, you should select carefully.

In choosing a book for shared readings in a kindergarten or first-grade class, consider three criteria. First, the book must be very predictable. The most important goal for shared reading is that even children with little experience with books and stories will be able to pretend read the book after several readings and develop the confidence that goes along with that accomplishment. Thus, you want a book without too much print and one in which the sentence patterns are very repetitive and the pictures support those sentence patterns. Second, you want a book that will be very appealing to the children. Since the whole class of children will work with the same Big Book and since the book will be read and reread, you should try to choose a book that many children will fall in love with. Finally, the book should take you someplace conceptually. Many teachers choose Big Books to fit their units or build units around the books.

In doing shared reading with big, predictable books, we try to simulate what would happen in the home as a child insists upon having a favorite book read again and again. First, we focus on the book itself, on enjoying it, rereading it, and acting it out. As we do this, we develop concepts and oral language. When most of the children can pretend read the book, we focus their attention on the print. We do writing activities related to the book and help children learn print conventions, jargon, and concrete words. When children know some concrete words, we use these words to begin to build phonological awareness and letter-sound knowledge.

A Sample Shared Reading Experience

To illustrate the many activities you might do with a predictable Big Book, we will use the Big Book *Ten Little Bears* (Ruwe, 1988). The opening page of the *Ten Little Bears* Big Book shows 10 bears of various colors and sizes sitting around a living room looking extremely bored. The text on these two pages reads:

> *Ten little bears were sitting at home.*
> *They wanted something to do.*

On the following page, you see a bear looking very unbored, joyously riding a sailboat on a pond. The text reads:

> *One little bear went for a ride in a sailboat.*

The picture on page 4 shows 9 of the original 10 bears in their same bored positions. The text reads:

> *Then nine little bears were left at home.*

Pages 5 and 6 continue the pattern established:

> *One little bear went for a ride in a car.*
> *Then eight little bears were left at home.*

The teacher and children are reading *Ten Little Bears.*

In the following pages the pattern continues as one by one, the bears ride off in a truck, in a helicopter, on a tractor, in a moving van, on a train, in a jet, and in a fire truck. Finally,

Then one little bear was left at home.
He was fast asleep.
Soon nine little bears came home.
Then one little bear woke up.
He said, "Let's go to the park to play."
Nine little bears said, "No. Let's eat."

Ten Little Bears offers many opportunities for concept development. It can be part of a unit on vehicles or a unit on travel. Number concepts can be developed as each bear leaves, leaving one fewer bored bear. Here are some activities teachers have used, as described in Cunningham and Allington (1991).

READ AND TALK ABOUT THE BOOK   Observational research of children being read to shows that parents not only read to children but engage the children in conversation about the book and reread favorite books. We try to promote this kind of conversation and interaction as each book is read. After reading the first two pages ("Ten little bears were sitting at home. They wanted something to do"), the teacher would encourage predictions by asking, "What do you think they might do?" Children would be encouraged to infer character feelings by responding to questions such as "How are these bears feeling?"

They relate their own experience to the book by responding to "Have you ever been bored? What do you do when you are bored?"

As the book continues and it becomes apparent that each bear is going to go for a ride in some kind of vehicle, children are asked which bear they think is going next and what kind of a vehicle that bear will ride in. Finally, only one bear is left—the sleeping bear. The teacher encourages thinking, language, and book engagement by asking such questions as "What will this bear want to do when he wakes up? Why do you think the sleeping bear wants to go to the park to play and all the other bears want to eat?"

The first reading of any book should engage the children by talking and thinking about what is happening in the book. All the thinking processes can be engaged. Children can call up their own experiences with being bored, with bears, with vehicles. They can connect their experiences and emotions with those portrayed in the book. They can make predictions, form images, and make generalizations. As they predict what will happen next, evaluate the story and the characters, and apply what they learn to their own lives, they are interacting with the book in a very child-centered way.

ACT OUT THE BOOK   Prepare for this activity by making cards that designate which bear is which. The simplest procedure is to make a simple line drawing of each of the vehicles on construction paper, writing the word (*sailboat, car,* etc.) on the back of the paper. For the last bear who doesn't ride in a vehicle, draw a sleeping bear. Punch two holes and put yarn through so that children can wear the cards around their necks. Laminate these so you can use them again and again.

Distribute the cards to 10 children and let them come up and sit around on the floor looking very bored. Reread the book, letting the appropriate children go off to ride in their vehicles. Letting the children make vehicle noises as they ride adds to the fun of this activity. Before you turn each page, ask the children who are watching which little bear is going next. Count after each bear leaves to see how many are left, then let the children help you read the refrains: "Then seven little bears were left at home."

Act out the book enough times so that each child has a chance to be one of the little bears. You may want to leave the book and the laminated cards in a center so that children can act out and read the book again and again.

RECORD THE BOOK WITH CHILDREN "READING" DIFFERENT PARTS   Let the children help you make an audiotape of the book. You may want to read some pages and designate certain children to read the pages that tell what each bear rides off in. Let the whole group read the refrain pages that tell how many bears were left at home. Put this tape in a listening center so that children can listen to themselves reading!

DEVELOP PRINT CONCEPTS BY POINTING OUT FEATURES OF THE BOOK Make sure children can find the front and back of the book as well as the title and author's name. Have individual children come and point to words as everyone reads to make sure that they know that the words are what you read and that you move in a left-right fashion across each line of print. Have children use their hands to show you just one word, the first word in a sentence, the last word, the longest word, and so forth.

IF AVAILABLE, PUT REGULAR-SIZED COPIES OF THE BIG BOOK OUT FOR CHILDREN TO ENJOY   Many Big Books come in sets with several regular-sized copies of the same book. Once children have read and enjoyed the Big Book, they love reading—or pretending to read—the little books.

LEARN MORE ABOUT VEHICLES   Let the children help you reread the book and list all the vehicles on the board. You may want to make a web that shows certain categories (land, sea, and air, perhaps). Lead children to name other vehicles and add these to the web. Have children describe the vehicles and tell what they are used for. Read them some informational books about vehicles. Have them find pictures of vehicles and make a collage bulletin board. You may want to have a "Bring Your Vehicles Day" on which children bring their favorite little cars, trucks, and airplanes. Be sure to compare and contrast the vehicles brought and use them in a writing activity. Describe the vehicles brought.

STUDY BEARS AND COMPARE REAL BEARS AND FICTIONAL BEARS   Re-read the book and ask the children questions that will help them understand the differences between real bears and storybook bears: "Do real bears live in

These children are acting out *Ten Little Bears*. The children in the top photo are the bored bears at the beginning of the book before they go off in the various vehicles. The little girl is the last bear, who is fast asleep.

houses? Where do real bears live?" Read them some informational books about real bears and help them understand the difference between fantasy and informational text. You may want to have a "Bring Your Bear Day."

LET THE CHILDREN BE THE WORDS   In this activity, children are given the words and they come up and make the sentences. They do this by matching their word to the words in the book. Two pages of the book are matched at a time. To prepare for this activity, write all the words on sentence strips and cut them to match the size of the word. Do not make duplicate words unless they are needed to make the sentences on the two pages of the book that will be displayed simultaneously. Do make separate cards for any words that are sometimes shown with a capital letter and sometimes used with a small letter. Make separate cards for each punctuation mark needed. Laminate these cards so that you can use them over and over.

Begin the activity by passing out all the cards containing the words and punctuation marks. Let the children look at their words and point out the distinction between words and punctuation marks. Tell the children that these are going to be their words and that they will come up and make the sentences in the book.

Open the book to display the first two pages. Ask the children to help you read the sentences.

Ten little bears were sitting at home.
They wanted something to do.

Point to each word as you reread the sentences and have the children look to see if their word matches any of the words they see in the book. Explain that you don't say anything when you get to the period but that it lets you know the sentence is over. Have all the children who have a word or punctuation mark in this sentence come up and get in the right order to make the sentence. Help the children to arrange themselves in the appropriate left-to-right order, to get the periods at the end of the sentences, and to hold the words right side up. When everyone is in order, have the children not in the sentence read the sentence as you move behind each child who is a word.

Have all the words sit down, display the next two pages, and have the children read from the book.

One little bear went for a ride in a sailboat.
Then nine little bears were left at home.

Again, have the children come up and arrange themselves. Let the children sitting down read the sentences from the word cards as you walk behind each word. Continue until children have made all the sentences in the book.

Being the Words is one of the very favorite activities of most children and they ask to do it again and again. Through this activity, children learn what words are, that words make up sentences, and that a period signals the end of the sentence but is not read. They also practice the left-to-right order of print and realize that the order the words are in makes a difference in what you read.

These children are "being the words" for one page in *Ten Little Bears*.

Many children also learn many of the words during this activity. You will observe this as you give out the words to do the activity a second or third time and hear children say things like, "Oh, boy, I'm the helicopter!" Many teachers put the book and the laminated words in a center. Children delight in turning the pages of the book and laying out the words on the floor to make the sentences.

SORT THE WORDS ACCORDING TO LENGTH This is another activity that uses the laminated words from Being the Words. Again distribute all the words to the children (excluding duplicates and punctuation marks). Tell the children that they are going to help you sort the words according to how many letters they have. Write the numeral 1 on a piece of paper and ask all children who have a word with just one letter in it to come up. The child with the word *a* should come up. Place this word along the chalk ledge behind the numeral 1. Continue with words that have two letters—*at, to, do, in, on, he, up, go, no*—and three letters, and so on until you get the ten-letter word *helicopter*. Put all the words on the chalk ledge behind the appropriate numeral. When all the words are in the right place, have the children guess which number has the most words. Let them help you count each group and write the number found above the numeral. After doing this activity with the whole class, many teachers put the numeral cards and word cards in a center and have children work with a partner to sort them.

Sorting the words according to length is a good activity to integrate reading and math. It also helps children become clear about the distinction between words and letters and helps them learn to focus on the individual letters in words. In addition, you can compare the words and help the children learn such jargon as long, short, longer, shorter, longest, shortest.

SORT ALL THE WORDS ACCORDING TO LETTERS   Pass out to the children all the laminated words used in Being the Words. Tape a long strip of butcher paper across the chalkboard. Draw lines and divide it into 26 bars, labeled *A* to *Z* (both capital and small). Beginning with *a*, let all the children whose word contains that letter come up. Once all the children are up in front, have each child make a tally mark in the appropriate letter bar. (If a word has two of the designated letter, that child should make two tally marks.) Count the tally marks and write the total number. Have the children with the words containing the letter *a* sit down and go on with the *b*s, *c*s, and so on. Children are generally amazed to see that there are 27 *t*s and 33 *e*s! They are disappointed to discover that there is not a single *z* in the entire book!

Sorting the letters takes some time, but the children love to do it and become much more aware of the individual letters in words. (One child in a kindergarten excitedly announced that *Zak*, his name, had a *z*! Another child brought to school the next day a Pizza Hut advertisement to show there were *z*s in words!) Sorting the letters is a good math activity also. Some teachers, instead of using simple tally marks, have the children color in bars to indicate the designated letter. The *e* bar is colored in almost to the top. The *z* bar has no coloring at all. Graphs allow the children to ''graphically'' see the number relationships.

SORT THE WORDS FOR JUST ONE LETTER   In this activity you help the children to focus their attention on just one letter. The *t*, for example, occurs in 24 of the words. To do this activity, you would pass out only those words that contain the letter *t*. Have children come up and display their word in response to questions such as which words have:

T as the first letter (*ten, two, three, they, to, then, truck, tractor, train, the*)

T as the last letter (*eight, at, went, left, fast, sailboat, jet, eat*)

T somewhere in the word but not first or last (*little, sitting, wanted, something, helicopter, tractor, let's*)

Two *t*s in the word (*sitting, tractor*)

T with an *h* after it (*three, they, something, then, the*)

T with an *r* after it (*truck, tractor, train*)

In addition to sorting words according to where the letters appear, the words can be sorted according to the sound children hear. Tell the children that *t* usually has the sound you hear at the beginning of *ten*, the end of *jet*, and in the middle of *tractor*. Have the children with the words *ten*, *jet*, and *tractor* come and stand on one side of you. Tell the children that sometimes *t* has other sounds, as in the word *three*. Have the child with the word *three* come and stand on the other side of you. Then have all the children bring their words and decide by listening whether the *t* has the sound in *ten, jet,* and *tractor* or another sound, and stand on the appropriate side. Conclude the lesson by having the children count the words on the *ten, jet, tractor* side and on the *three* side. Help them to generalize that *t* usually has the sound you hear in *ten, jet,* and *tractor* but that it can have other sounds.

USE WORDS WITH PURE INITIAL SOUNDS AS KEY WORDS   Letter sounds, like other learnings, can be learned by rote or by association. Learning the common sound for *b* by trying to remember it or by trying to remember that it begins the word *bears* when you can't read the word *bears* requires rote learning. Once you can read the word *bears* and realize that the common sound for *b* is heard at the beginning of *bears,* you no longer have to just remember the sound. You can now associate the sound of *b* with something already known, the word *bears.* Associative learning is the easiest, quickest, and longest lasting.

Children from print-rich environments know some concrete words when they come to school. As they are taught letter-sounds, they probably associate these with the words they know, thus making the learning of these sounds easier and longer lasting. We can provide this opportunity for associative learning for children who did not know words when they came to school by capitalizing on the words they have learned from *Ten Little Bears.*

The number of letter-sounds you wish to focus on from one book will depend on what your children already know. If their knowledge of beginning sounds is minimal, you may want to teach only five or six sounds that have clear, concrete key words most of the children have learned. The words *bear, car, five, go, helicopter, jet, little, no, park, ride, sailboat, ten,* and *van* have clear initial sounds and are apt to be learned easily by most children because they are repeated often or because they are "exciting" words.

Regardless of how many letter-sounds you teach using the *Ten Little Bears* key words, the procedure should be the same. Begin with two letters that are very different in look and sound and that are made in different places in the mouth—*b* and *l,* for example. Show the children the two words—*bear* and *little*—that will serve as key words for these letters. Tell the children to pronounce the two key words and to notice the position of their tongues and teeth as they do. Have one child stand in the front of the room and hold the word *bear.* Have another child hold the word *little.* Say several concrete words (*bike, lemon, box, book, ladder, lady, boy*) that begin like *bear* or *little,* and have the children say them after you. Have them notice where their tongue and teeth are as they say the words. Let the children point to the child holding *bear* or *little* to indicate how the word begins.

Begin a key word bulletin board on which you put the letters *b* and *l* and the key words *bear* and *little.* Repeat the activity just described using other *b* and *l* words until most of the children begin to understand the difference in the letter-sound. Then add a third letter and key word—perhaps *n* and *no.* Have them listen for and repeat words beginning with all three letters—*b, l, n.* Be sure to point out that the words they already know will help them remember the sound.

DEVELOP PHONOLOGICAL AWARENESS BY BLENDING RHYMING
WORDS   One component of phonological awareness is the ability to take words
apart and blend words together. The easiest words with which to teach this
blending principle are words to which you can add letters to make new words.
In *Ten Little Bears*, there are four such words—*at, in, up,* and *eat.* To teach this
lesson, put a word such as *at* on the board. Tell children that by blending some
of the beginning sounds they know with *at*, they can make lots of new words.
Use only those initial letters for which you have taught a sound and, if you have
a bulletin board of key words for the initial sound, remind children to look at
it to help them remember the sound for the first letters. Under the word *at*,
write *at* again and then add a letter to "magically" change *at* to a new word.
Let children read each new word and talk about what it means.

TRY IT OUT

 Find or make a predictable Big Book and use it with a group of children.
(When choosing your book, consider the three criteria—the book
should be very predictable and appealing and should help children
develop important concepts.) Try some of the activities suggested for *Ten Little
Bears* as well as others that fit your book better. As you read and reread the
book with the children, be sure that you encourage their participation in the
talking as well as the reading. Help them make connections and predictions and
express their feelings. Encourage the whole range of thinking children can do
with books. If possible, find a way for them to act out the book. Once the
children have read and enjoyed the book several different times in different
ways, do some activities that help them to focus on words and letters. As you
plan and carry out your Big Book activities, decide which of the seven critical
understandings are developed in each activity. (Of course, several understandings can and probably will be a part of each activity.) Summarize what you did
and how the various activities developed each of the critical understandings.

Shared Reading with Poems, Songs, and Chants

In addition to books, many teachers write favorite poems, chants, songs, and
finger plays on long sheets of paper and these become some of the first things
children can actually read (for an example, see Figure 2.2). Most teachers teach
the poem, chant, song, or finger play to the children first. Once the children
have learned to say, chant, or sing it, they then are shown what the words look
like. The progression to reading is a natural one and children soon develop the
critical "Of course I can read" self-confidence. Once children can read the piece,
many teachers duplicate it and send it home for the child to read to parents and
other family members.

   We hope you can see that shared reading can be used to develop all seven
critical understandings. Even though *Ten Little Bears* is a fictional book, there
are concepts to be learned when you expand the book to study bears or vehicles.

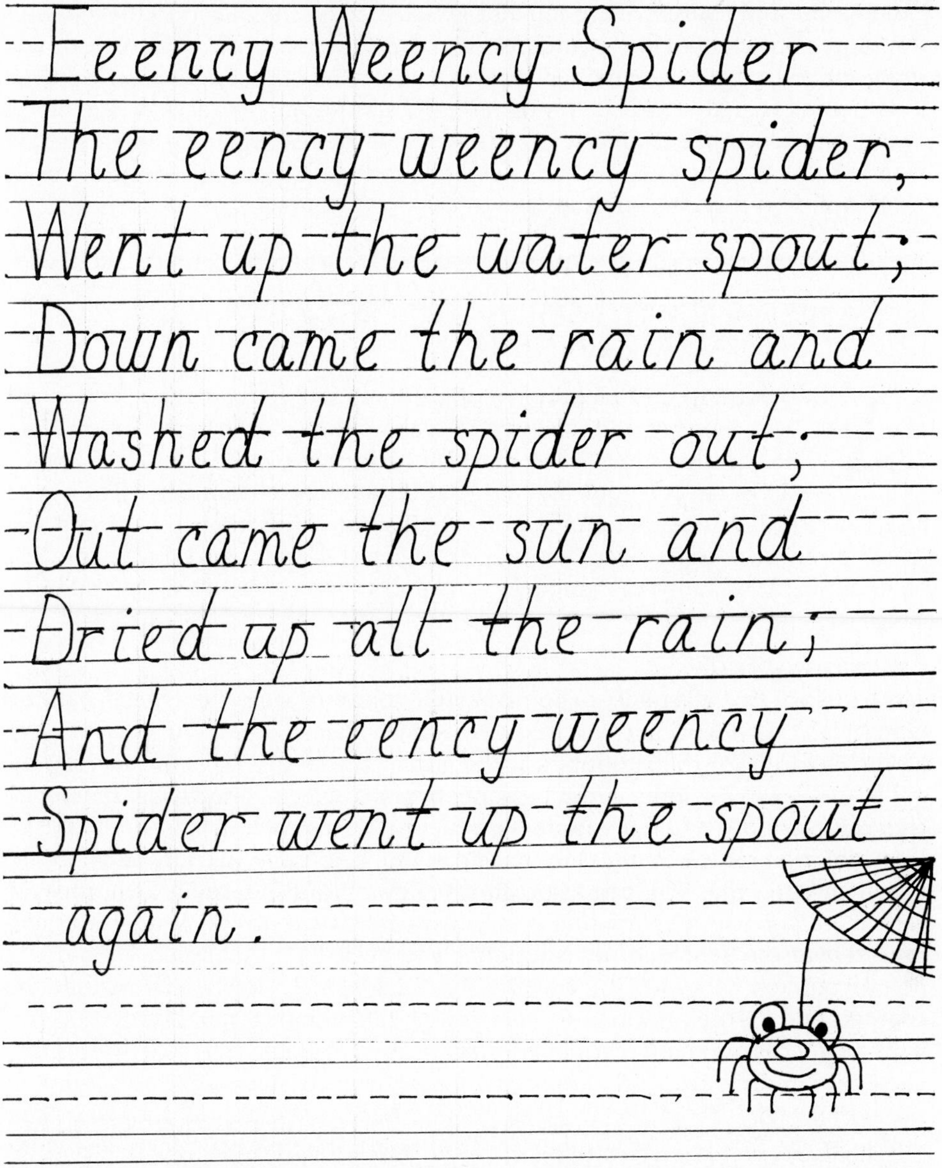

Eency Weency Spider

The eency weency spider,
Went up the water spout;
Down came the rain and
Washed the spider out;
Out came the sun and
Dried up all the rain;
And the eency weency
Spider went up the spout
again.

FIGURE 2.2   Once children have learned to say or sing rhymes, songs, and poems, they enjoy reading them together and taking them home to show that they are indeed learning to read.

Children develop left-right, top-bottom print conventions as they read with you and when they "become the words" to make the sentences. They also understand that words make up sentences. When they sort the words for specific letters or letter length, they realize that words are composed of letters. When they compare the sounds of different parts of different words, they begin to understand that letters represent sounds. Through all these activities, they firm up their under-standing of critical jargon—words, sentences, letters, sounds. When reading a predictable Big Book is extended by word and letter-sound activities, children learn some concrete words, letter names, and sounds and increase phonological awareness. Of course, children learn that one of the reasons we read is to enjoy wonderful books such as *Ten Little Bears.* Shared reading also promotes "I can't wait" and "I can do it" attitudes!

FOR CHILDREN WITH SPECIAL NEEDS— PHONOLOGIAL AWARENESS

Rhyming and blending activities help children see how words are put together and taken apart. Taking the syllable apart and putting it back together is the most difficult phonological awareness task. Most children quickly understand how speech is made up of words and how words are made up of syllables, but some children need extra practice to grasp those concepts. Here are two strategies you might try if some children have difficulty dividing the language stream into words or the words into syl-lables.

Counting Words
To do this activity, all children should have 10 counters in a paper cup. (Anything manipulable is fine. Some teachers use edibles such as cereal or Ritz Bits and let the children eat their counters at the end of the lesson. This makes cleanup quick and easy!) Begin by counting some familiar objects in the room having all children place one of their counters on their desks as each object is pointed to. Have children return counters to the cup before beginning to count each object.

Tell children that you can also count words by putting down a counter for each word you say. Explain that you will say a sentence in the normal way and then repeat the sentence, pausing after each word. The children should put down counters as you say the words in the sentence slowly, then count the counters and decide how many words you said. Children generally attend better if the sentences are about them. (*Carlos has a new lunch box. Miguel is a good listener.*) Once the children catch on to the activity, let them say some sentences—first in the normal way, then one word at a time. Listen carefully as they say their sentences the first time because they will often need help saying them one word at a time. Not only do children enjoy this activity and learn to separate out words in speech, but they are also practicing critical counting skills!

Clapping Syllables
Once children get fairly automatic at separating the speech stream into words, they are ready to begin thinking about separating words into some components. The first division most children make is syllables. Clapping seems to be the easiest way to get every child involved, and the children's names are the naturally appealing words to clap. Say the first name of one child. Say the name again and this time, clap the syllables. Continue saying first names and then clapping

the syllables as you say them the second time and invite the children to join in clapping with you. As children catch on, say some middle or last names. The term *syllables* is a little jargony and foreign to most young children, so you may want to refer to the syllables as beats. Children should realize by clapping that *Fay* is a one-beat word, *Wendy* a two-beat word, and *Robinson* a three-beat word.

Once children can clap syllables and decide how many beats a given word has, help them to see that one-beat words are usually shorter than three-beat words—that is, they take fewer letters to write. To do this, write some words children cannot read on sentence strips and cut the strips into words so that short words have short strips and long words have long strips. Have some of the words begin with the same letters but be different lengths so that children will need to think about word length to decide which word is which.

For the category "foods," you might write ham and hamburgers, milk and muffins, and soup, sausage, and strawberries. Tell the children that you are going to say the names of foods and they should clap to show how many beats the word has. (Do not show them the words yet!) Say the first pair, one at a time (*ham/hamburgers*). Help children to decide that *ham* is a one-beat word and *hamburgers* takes a lot more claps and is a three-beat word. Now, show them the two words and say, "One of these words is *ham* and the other is *hamburgers*. Who thinks they can figure out which one is *ham* and which one is *hamburgers*?" Help the children to explain that because *hamburgers* takes so many beats to say, it probably takes more letters to write.

SHARED WRITING AND LANGUAGE EXPERIENCE ACTIVITIES SUPPORT EMERGENT LITERACY

Shared writing is a process in which the teacher and children write together. Generally, the teacher leads the children to share ideas and then records the ideas as the children watch. Shared writing, like individual writing, can be used to write a wide variety of things. Regie Routman (1991), in her wonderfully practical, readable book *Invitations*, includes this list of some of the possibilities (p. 60):

Wall stories and Big Books

Stories, essays, and poems

Original story endings

Retellings of stories

Class journal entries

Class observations of pets, plants, and science experiments

Shared experiences such as field trips and special visitors

Class rules and charts

Weekly newsletter to parents

News of the day

Curriculum-related writing
Reports
Informational books
Evaluations of books and activities

Shared writing is similar to language experience in that the teacher writes as the children watch but is different in one important feature. One of the cardinal principles of language experience has always been that the teacher should write down exactly what the child said. Allen and Allen (1966), Stauffer (1980), and others who promoted language experience as an approach to beginning reading and writing argued that children must learn that what they say can be written down and then read back. This important learning can occur only if the child's exact words are recorded. The problem, for teachers, arises when a child's spoken dialect differs from standard written English. Teachers find it difficult to record sentences such as:

She ain't got no money.
I done hit my head.

Most teachers, when working with individual children, however, will write down the sentences just as they are spoken because they realize that the child will read the sentence the way it was spoken. If the sentence

She ain't got no money

is changed to the standard

She doesn't have any money

the child, remembering what was said, will read the word *don't* as "ain't," *have* as "got," and *any* as "no."
Likewise, if the child's spoken

I done hit my head

is changed to the standard

I hit my head

the child, remembering what was said, will say "done" while looking at *hit,* "hit" while looking at *my,* "my" while looking at *head,* and run out of written words before finishing the spoken sentence.

If language experience is being used with an individual child to help the child understand what reading and writing are and that you can write and read what you can say, then the child's exact words must be written down. To do anything else will hopelessly confuse the child about the very things you are using individual language experience to try to clarify.

The situation changes, however, when you are working with a class or small group of children. The group invariably includes children who use a variety of different language structures. Recording sentences such as the above when you are working with children whose language usage varies will lead to confusion, and sometimes ridicule, on the part of children whose spoken language is closer to standard written English. In addition, the charts, letters, books, and so on that you create during shared writing are apt to be displayed in the classroom and/or sent home to parents. It is difficult to explain to parents why nonstandard usage should be written down, and there are even examples of teachers being accused of not knowing how to "write good English."

Shared writing differs from language experience in that the teacher and the children all "share" the construction of the writing. In creating a daily entry in the class journal, the teacher asks the children what important things they think should be included. She listens to all suggestions, accepting whatever kind of spoken dialect children use. After listening to the suggestions, she records them, using standard written English and imposing some kind of order and cohesion on them. She then reads aloud the sentences she has written. Because the teacher listens to the suggestions of many children and then records the "gist" but not the "exact words" of any child, the problem of recording and reading nonstandard usage does not occur.

Both shared writing and individual language experience are valuable tools to use with children whose reading and writing experiences at home and at school have been limited. In individually dictated language experience situations, children's exact words should be written down. In working with a group to create something for public consumption, however, shared writing in which all the children share the ideas and the teacher writes a composite seems to be the best alternative.

Both shared writing and language experience are usually about something the children are learning. Often, they summarize important concept-building experiences such as field trips or science experiments. Thus shared writing is an extension of the concept-building experience. As children watch the teacher record their ideas, they notice the left-right, top-bottom, and other conventions used in writing.

As with shared reading, children begin to note patterns of repeated letters and sounds in their dictated texts. Teachers can facilitate the process by having children dictate rhyming words in simple poems they create. For example, you might begin the poem by saying, "Let's make up a poem today. I'll write one line, and you tell me another one to write. For today I have this poem started. Can you help me finish it?" On chart paper, an overhead transparency, or the chalkboard, you might write:

I like to play

The children might add a line such as

with the clay

or

every day

or

with my friend Ray.

Creating simple two-line poems can be the beginning step for creating longer ones later. After children can hear the rhymes and see how the ending letters are alike, they can start to note the association of letter sounds and names with spelling patterns.

The teacher can explicitly point out words that begin with the same letter and have children identify them. For example, the teacher might ask children to come to the dictated text and underline all words that begin with *m*. Saying the *m* words one after another with a slight emphasis on the beginning sound helps to build connections among the letters and sounds of our language. Many teachers create a typed copy of dictated text and make multiple copies to use with children. Making multiple copies allows teachers to do some word- and sentence-matching activities. It also encourages the development of sight words through repeated exposures to the words. Children learn words by seeing and using them many times in many ways.

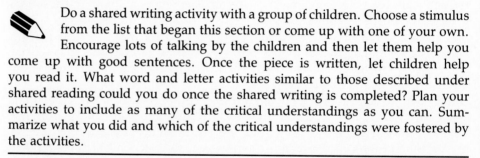

TRY IT OUT

Do a shared writing activity with a group of children. Choose a stimulus from the list that began this section or come up with one of your own. Encourage lots of talking by the children and then let them help you come up with good sentences. Once the piece is written, let children help you read it. What word and letter activities similar to those described under shared reading could you do once the shared writing is completed? Plan your activities to include as many of the critical understandings as you can. Summarize what you did and which of the critical understandings were fostered by the activities.

FOR CHILDREN WITH SPECIAL NEEDS—TRACKING PRINT/CONCRETE WORDS

Some children have a great deal of difficulty learning to track print. In spite of the group-shared reading and writing activities they participate in, they don't learn how you must move from left to right and so forth. Often, these are the same children who don't learn any of the concrete words included in the shared reading and shared writing stories. These children can learn to track print and learn some concrete words with some focused individual language experience activities. Here is what one teacher does with the one or two children each year who don't learn to track print and/or don't learn any words from the group activities.

DAY ONE

1. Sit down with the individual child and begin a simple book. (This book can be constructed with half sheets of ditto paper stapled between half-sheet construction paper covers.) Explain to the child that she is going to make a book about herself. Talk with the child and decide on one sentence

to go on the first page. Try to have a sentence long enough that it takes two lines to write. Write that sentence as the child watches.

> Ebony is in the first grade at
> Clemmons School.

2. Help the child read the sentence by moving her hand under each word. Read it together, pointing to each word until the child can read it and point to the words by herself.

3. As the child watches and says the individual words, write the sentence again on a sentence strip. Have the child read the sentence, pointing to each word, from the sentence strip.

4. As the child watches, cut the sentence from the strip into words. Mix these words up and have the child put the words in order to make the sentence, using the sentence in the book to match to.

5. Put all the cut-up words in an envelope and label the envelope and the page of the book with a 1.

6. Let the child draw a picture to illustrate page 1 of the book.

DAY TWO

1. Reread the sentence on page 1. Take the words from the envelope and put them in order by matching to the book sentence.

2. Together, compose another sentence about the child for page 2. Write that sentence as the child watches.

> Ebony comes to school on
> Bus 19.

3. Have the child read the sentence with you several times, helping the child to point to words while reading them.

4. Write this sentence on a strip, cut it apart, have it matched to the book sentence, and put it in an envelope labeled 2. Let the child illustrate page 2 of her book.

DAY THREE

1. Reread the sentences on pages 1 and 2. Take the words from the envelopes and put them in order by matching to both sentences.

2. Have the child find any duplicate words and decide that they are the same word and what that word is. In our example, the words *Ebony* and *school* are repeated.

3. Come up with a third sentence for page 3. Use the same procedures of writing this sentence on the sentence strip, cutting, matching, and illustrating.

> Ebony likes to eat pizza and
> apple pie.

DAY FOUR THROUGH BOOK COMPLETION
Continue adding a page each day, matching the words and looking for repeated words. Read the whole book each day, but when you have five or more pages, match just the two or three most recent preceding ones. Look for duplicate words and observe which ones the child is learning. When the book is finished, have the child read the whole book and ask the child to find words from the envelopes that she can read. Most children learn to track print and accumulate 8 to 10 words through doing one 12- to 15-page book. A few children need to do a second book, using the same procedure. Help the child construct the second book in the same way on a topic the child is particularly interested in.

HAVING CHILDREN WRITE SUPPORTS EMERGENT LITERACY

Until recently, the theory was that if children were allowed to write before they could spell and make the letters correctly, they would get into "bad habits" that would be hard to break later. There is a certain logic in this argument, but this logic does not hold up to scrutiny when you actually look at children before they come to school.

Just as children from literacy-oriented homes read before they can read by pretend reading a memorized book, they write before they can write. Their writing is usually not decipherable by anyone besides themselves, and sometimes they read the same scribbling different ways. They write with pens, markers, crayons, paint, chalk, and with normal-sized pencils with erasers on the ends. They write on chalkboards, magic slates, paper, and—alas—walls!

They write in scribbles, which first go anywhere and then show a definite left-to-right orientation. They make letterlike forms. They let single letters stand for entire words. They draw pictures and intersperse letters with the pictures. They make shopping lists by copying words off packages. They copy favorite words from books. They write love letters (I love Joshua) and hate mail (I hate Joshua).

Experience and research in the last decade have shown us that children are not ruined by being allowed to write before they can write. Rather, they learn many important concepts and develop the confidence that they can write. Here are some activities that promote writing for all.

Model Writing for the Children

As children watch you write, they observe that you always start in a certain place, go in certain directions, and leave space between words. In addition to these print conventions, they observe that writing is "talk written down." There are numerous opportunities in every classroom for the teacher to write as the children watch—and sometimes help—with what to write.

In many classrooms, the teacher begins the day by writing a morning message on the board. The teacher writes this short message as the children watch. The teacher then reads the message, pointing to each word and inviting the children to join in on any words they know. Sometimes, teachers take a few minutes to point out some things students might notice from the morning message.

How many sentences did I write today?

How can we tell how many there are?

What do we call this mark I put at the end of this sentence?

Which words begin with the same letters?

Which is the shortest word?

These and similar questions help children learn conventions and jargon of print and focus their attention on words and letters.

Class books are another opportunity for children to watch teachers write. During a unit on animals, children told what their favorite animals were. The teacher recorded each child's favorites on one page, which that child illustrated. The pages were bound together into a class book on *Animals We Like*.

Provide a Variety of Things to Write With and On

Children view writing as a "creation" and are often motivated to write by various media. Many teachers grab all free postcards, scratch pads, counter checks, pens, and pencils, and haunt yard sales—always on the lookout for an extra chalkboard or an old but still working typewriter. A letter home to parents at the beginning of the year asking them to clean out desks and drawers and donate writing utensils and various kinds of paper often brings unexpected treasures. In addition to the usual writing media, young children like to write with sticks in sand, with sponges on chalkboards, and with chocolate pudding and shaving cream.

Help Children Find Writing Purposes through Center Activities

For most young children, the purpose of writing is to get something told or done. Children will find some real purposes for writing if you incorporate writing in all your centers. Encourage children to make grocery lists while they are playing in the housekeeping center. Menus, ordering pads, and receipts are a natural part of a restaurant center. An office center would include various writing implements, a typewriter, or computer, along with index cards, phone books, and appointment books. Children can make birthday cards for friends or relatives or write notes to you or one of their classmates and then mail them in the post office center. They can make signs (Keep Out! Girls Only!) and post them as part of their dramatic play. When children put a lot of time into building a particularly wonderful creation from the blocks or Legos, they often don't want to have it taken apart so that something else can be built. Many teachers keep a large pad of tablet paper in the construction center. Children can draw and label records of their constructions before disassembling them. Once you start looking for them, there are numerous opportunities for children to write for real purposes as they carry out their creative and dramatic play in various centers.

Provide a Print-Rich Classroom

Classrooms in which children write have lots of print in them. In addition to books, there are magazines and newspapers. There are charts of recipes made and directions for building things. Children's names are on their desks and on many different objects. There are class books, bulletin boards with labeled pictures of animals under study, and labels on almost everything. Children's drawings and all kinds of writing are displayed. In these classrooms, children see that all kinds of writing are valued. Equally important, children who want to write "the grown-up way" can find lots of words to make their own.

Accept Whatever Writing They Do

Accepting a variety of writing—from scribbling to one-letter representations to invented spellings to copied words—is the key to having young children write before they can write. Sometimes it is the children and not the teacher who reject beginning attempts. If more advanced children give less advanced children a hard time about their "scribbling," the teacher must intervene and firmly state a policy such as this:

> There are many different ways to communicate through writing. We use pictures and letters and words. Sometimes we just scribble but the scribbling helps us remember what we were thinking. We use all these different ways in this classroom!

Without this attitude of acceptance, the very children who most need to explore language through writing will be afraid to write.

LISTEN, LOOK, AND LEARN

 Visit a classroom for young children. Spend the whole day if possible. Look for evidence of the four emergent literacy–promoting activities. What evidence is there that reading and talking with the children about books is an everyday—more than once a day—occurrence? Are shared reading and shared writing important parts of the daily routine? What evidence is there that children write? Are there lots of writing utensils? Is writing incorporated in center activities? Would you describe the classroom atmosphere as print-rich? Consider all the activities you observe in light of your knowledge about the seven critical understandings. Which of these understandings is most and least promoted by the classroom instruction and environment you observe? What would you change if you were suddenly the teacher in this classroom?

THE THEORY AND RESEARCH BASE
FOR EMERGENT LITERACY

In the first edition of this book, there was no chapter on emergent literacy. There was, instead, a chapter on reading readiness. Readiness—or lack of readiness—for reading and writing instruction was the dominant view until the mid-1980s. The change characterized by the shift from readiness to emergent literacy is much more than just a change in terminology. It represents a fundamental change in how we view literacy and the years leading up to literacy. To help you understand what an important and drastic change has occurred in our thinking, we will briefly summarize the readiness and emergent literacy theories.

For most of this century, educators believed that reading instruction should be delayed until children reached a certain level of mental readiness. They believed that for most children, this level of readiness would be achieved when they were about six years old. The most influential study (Morphett & Washburne, 1931) actually specified a mental age of six and one-half years as the right age to begin reading instruction. Many educators believed that writing should be delayed until reading abilities were firmly in place and recommended that children begin writing when they were eight or nine years old.

To determine which children were ready to read, most first graders were given readiness tests after six weeks of first grade. These readiness tests tested the skills believed to be critical for success in beginning reading instruction. Most tests included the skills of visual discrimination (Find the shape that is just like the first shape), auditory discrimination (Find the two pictures whose names begin with the same sound), letter naming, matching pictures with their beginning sounds, high-frequency word knowledge, and measures of oral language and meaning vocabulary.

First graders who scored high on these readiness tests were put into groups, and reading instruction—usually with a basal reader—was begun. There were two schools of thought about how to proceed with children who scored poorly on the readiness tests. Some schools and teachers felt it was best to "wait" for the readiness to develop. Other schools and teachers taught the skills—visual discrimination of shapes, auditory discrimination of sounds, letter names, and so forth—in an attempt to develop readiness.

Emergent literacy research began in the homes of young children. The research traces the literacy development of young children from birth until the time that they read and write in conventional ways (Heath, 1982; Harste, Woodward, & Burke, 1984; Teale & Sulzby, 1986; Sulzby & Teale, 1991). From this observational research, it became apparent that chidren in literate home environments engage in reading and writing long before they begin formal reading instruction. They use reading and writing in a variety of ways and pass through a series of predictable stages on their voyage from pretend and scribbling to conventional reading and writing. When parents read to children, interact with them about print they see in the world (signs, cereal boxes, advertisements), and encourage and support early writing efforts, reading and writing develop and grow along with listening and speaking—concurrently rather than sequentially.

In short, the observational research on young children debunked the readiness/mental age theories on which we had operated for half a century. Rather than needing to learn skills (auditory discrimination, letter names and sounds, etc.) before they began reading and writing, children exposed to lots of print experiences learned skills as they began reading and writing. Readiness to read has more to do with experiences with books than with any subset of skills or mental age.

This chapter is based on the emergent literacy research that shows the kinds of literacy behaviors young children engage in that result in their developing understandings essential to successful independent reading and writing. There has long been a debate over whether kindergartens should be primarily for play and socialization or for more academic work. Emergent literacy research supports neither kindergartens in which children play and socialize while we wait for literacy development nor kindergartens in which children work on isolated readiness skills. Rather than wait or teach separate skills for children who have not had these early literacy experiences before coming to school, kindergartens and other early school experiences should simulate as closely as possible the "at-home" experiences observed in the research. We call these kindergartens "literate home simulation" kindergartens.

LOOKING BACK

For most teachers, learning to read and write were relatively easy, pleasant activities. The ease with which most teachers learned to read probably reflects the fact that most teachers grew up in literate home environments in which reading and writing were modeled, encouraged, and supported. Emergent literacy observational research has shown us the tremendous impact of these early literacy experiences. In this chapter we have presented the practical implications of the emergent literacy research. The key ideas are:

1. Emerging readers and writers develop critical understandings.
2. Reading to children supports emergent literacy.
3. Shared reading with predictable Big Books supports emergent literacy.
4. Shared writing and language experience activities support emergent literacy.
5. Having children write supports emergent literacy.

ADD TO YOUR JOURNAL

 What do you remember about your early literacy experiences at home and at school? Did you come to school with many of the seven crucial understandings already established? Did you know why people read and wrote? Did you have a big vocabulary that represented lots of background knowledge and concepts? Could you track print as you pretended to read a book, and did you know common jargon—word, letter, sound, sentence? Could you read some important-to-you words like your own name, the names of other family members, pets, favorite restaurants? Could you name lots of the alphabet letters, and did you know the sounds for some of these? Did you know that words were made up of sounds, and could you mentally take words apart and put them back together again? Were you one of those children who just couldn't wait to learn to read?

Think about how critical these understandings are and then consider the four activities presented in the chapter—reading to and talking with children, shared reading with predictable Big Books, shared writing and lanuage experience, and writing. Which of these were part of your early school experience? Which do you believe are most important for developing the seven critical understandings if children come without them? If you teach young children, what role will these four activities play in your classroom? If you teach older children, do these four activities have any usefulness for older remedial readers?

REFERENCES

Adams, M. J. (1990). *Beginning to read: Thinking and learning about print*. Cambridge, MA: MIT Press.

Allen, R. V., & Allen, C. (1966). *Language experiences in reading: Teachers' resource book*. Chicago: Encyclopaedia Britannica Press.

Cunningham, P. M., & Allington, R. L. (1991). Words, letters, sounds and big books. *Learning, 20,* 91–95.

Harste, J. E., Woodward, V. A., & Burke, C. L. (1984). *Language stories and literacy lessons*. Portsmouth, NH: Heinemann.

Heath, S. B. (1982). What no bedtime story means: Narrative skills at home and school. *Language and Society, 11*(2), 49–76.

McCracken, R., & McCracken, M. (1988). *Songs, stories and poetry to teach reading and writing*. Manitoba, Canada: Peguis.

Morphett, V., & Washburne, C. (1931). When should children begin to read? *Elementary School Journal, 31,* 495–503.

Roser, N., & Martinez, M. (1985). Roles adults play in preschoolers' response to literature. *Language Arts, 62,* 485–490.

Routman, R. (1991). *Invitations*. Portsmouth, NH: Heinemann.

Stauffer, R. G. (1980). *The language-experience approach to the teaching of reading* (2nd ed.). New York: Harper & Row.

Sulzby, E., & Teale, W. (1991). Emergent literacy. In R. Barr, M. Kamil, P. Mosenthal, & P. D. Pearson (Eds.), *Handbook of reading research* (Vol. 2, pp. 727–757). White Plains, NY: Longman.

Taylor, D. (1983). *Family literacy*. Portsmouth, NH: Heinemann.

Teale, W. H., & Sulzby, E. (Eds.). (1986). *Emergent literacy: Writing and reading*. Norwood, NJ: Ablex.

Children's Books/Materials Cited

Are You My Mother? by P. D. Eastman, Random House, 1960.

The Bear Scouts, by Stan and Jan Berenstain, Random House, 1967.

Best Word Book Ever, by Richard Scarry, Golden Press, 1980.

Brown Bear, Brown Bear, What Do You See? by Bill Martin, Holt, Rinehart & Winston, 1970.
Goodnight Moon, by Marcia Brown, Holt, Rinehart & Winston, 1969.
Hop on Pop, by Dr. Seuss, Random House, 1987.
Jumanji, by Chris Van Allsburg, Harcourt Brace Jovanovich, 1981.
The Ocean Alphabet Book, by Jerry Pallotta, Charlesbridge Publishers, 1991.
One Fish, Two Fish, Red Fish, Blue Fish, by Dr. Seuss, Random House, 1960.
Ten Little Bears, by Mike Ruwe, Scott Foresman, 1988.
There's a Wocket in My Pocket, by Dr. Seuss, Random House, 1974.

ADDITIONAL READINGS

These books and chapters give an overview of emergent literacy research findings as well as some appropriate strategies and activities.

Strickland, D. S., & Morrow, L. M. (Eds.). (1989). *Emergent literacy: Young children learn to read and write.* Newark, DE: International Reading Association.
Sulzby, E., & Teale, W. (1991). Emergent literacy. In R. Barr, M. Kamil, P. Mosenthal, & P. D. Pearson (Eds.), *Handbook of reading research* (Vol. 2, pp. 727–757). White Plains, NY: Longman.

This article explains the theoretical basis for the importance of phonological awareness to reading development and suggests appropriate instructional activities.

Lundberg, I., Frost, J., & Petersen, O. P. (1988). Effects of an extensive program for stimulating phonological awareness in preschool children. *Reading Research Quarterly, 23,* 264–284.

Kindergartens that foster emergent literacy are the focus of these two practical books.

Fisher, B. (1991). *Joyful learning: A whole language kindergarten.* Portsmouth, NH: Heinemann.
Walmsley, B. B., Camp, A. M., & Walmsley, S. A. (1992). *Teaching kindergarten: A developmentally appropriate approach.* Portsmouth, NH: Heinemann.

Reading Recovery is a highly successful tutoring program for young children who experience difficulty in beginning reading and writing. These books describe the reading recovery instruction and assessment as well as a holistic theory of emergent literacy.

Clay, M. M. (1991). *Becoming literate: The construction of inner control.* Portsmouth, NH: Heinemann.
Clay, M. M. (1993). *An observation survey: Of early literacy achievement.* Portsmouth, NH: Heinemann.
Clay, M. M. (1993). *Reading recovery: A guidebook for teachers in training.* Portsmouth, NH: Heinemann.
DeFord, D. E., Lyons, C. A., & Pinnell, G. S. (1991). *Bridges to literacy: Learning from reading recovery.* Portsmouth, NH: Heinemann.

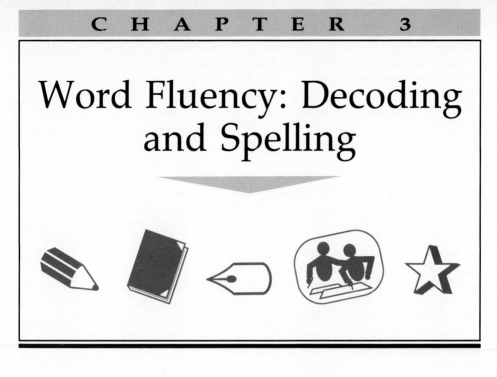

Word Fluency: Decoding and Spelling

LOOKING AHEAD

Reading and writing are the construction and communication of meaning. This meaning can be constructed and communicated only if readers can quickly and effortlessly recognize thousands of words. Writers express their ideas using words. Comprehension, communication, and construction of meaning are the big goals of reading and writing. Meaning is more than the sum of the individual words, but the individual words are the building blocks for constructing that meaning. This chapter will describe the complex relationship between decoding/spelling abilities and fluent reading and writing. Practical activities for helping children develop effective decoding and spelling strategies will be described.

Right now, as you are reading these words, your brain is simultaneously performing two complex functions. Your eyes focus on each word and your brain identifies each word. Your working memory remembers each word until you have identified enough words—a phrase or short sentence—from which your brain can construct meaning. This meaning is then shifted into long-term memory and your working memory space is once again freed up to hold the words identified by your brain, from which you will construct a little more meaning that can then shift to long-term memory, freeing up more working memory space and on and on until you finish reading. These two complex functions of identifying words and then using these words to construct meaning happen simultaneously and in parallel. In fact, this work that your brain is now doing is called "parallel distributed processing" (Rumelhart & McClelland, 1986).

Imagine that, while reading, you encounter the word *desufnoc*. When your eyes see the letters of a word you have never seen before, your brain cannot immediately identify that word. You must stop and figure out the word. This figuring out may include figuring out the pronunciation for the word and the meaning for the word. In this case, you can probably pronounce *desufnoc*, but since no meaning is triggered by your pronunciation, this word can't just join the others in working memory and help them construct some meaning to shift to long-term memory. Your reading is "stalled" by the intrusion of this unknown word. You have to either figure out what it is and what it means or decide one word is probably not very important and ignore it and continue reading, hoping the other words—the context—will allow you to continue constructing meaning even though you don't know the word *desufnoc*. A bit confused (which is *desufnoc* backward), you press forward!

We hope this little simulation in which you participated gives you some appreciation for the complex parallel processes that your brain carries out every time you read or write. When you are reading or writing, your brain is busy constructing meaning and is simultaneously identifying or spelling words. Most of the time, you don't even know that you are identifying or spelling words because you have read or written these words so many times that their identification and spelling has become "automatic." Automatic means without any conscious effort or thought. The concept of automaticity is critical to your understanding of the words/meaning construction relationship because your brain can carry out many automatic functions simultaneously (perhaps you have some background music on right now and are listening automatically as you identify words automatically too), but the brain can do only one nonautomatic function. Meaning construction is the nonautomatic function. When your brain is stopped by a word you can't immediately and automatically identify or spell, the brain's attention is diverted from meaning to words. In order to read and write fluently, readers and writers must be able to immediately recognize and spell the vast majority of the words. They must also have some strategies for identifying and spelling the occasional word that is not automatic for them. The key ideas in this chapter are:

1. Lots of reading and writing are crucial for the development of decoding and spelling.
2. Fluent reading and writing require immediate, automatic recognition and spelling of high-frequency words.
3. Fluent reading and writing require that students have strategies for pronouncing and spelling unfamiliar words.
4. Fluent reading requires cross-checking meaning with probable pronunciations.
5. Word fluency is developed in the content areas across the curriculum.

LOTS OF READING AND WRITING ARE CRUCIAL FOR THE DEVELOPMENT OF DECODING AND SPELLING

Imagine that in the next century, when all kinds of technological wonders are being invented and mass-marketed, someone invents a readowritometer. This marvelous device, when implanted in a child's brain, would tally up the number of words that child read or wrote across all the home and school hours—school days and weekends. Imagine that various children had their readowritometers constantly running for their first three years of school. At the end of these three years, the children would all be given a test that would determine how many words they could immediately recognize and how fast and accurate they were at figuring out how to pronounce and spell unfamiliar words. The number of words read and written would be an incredibly good predictor of each child's word fluency. Children who read and wrote a lot would instantly recognize huge numbers of words and be much faster and more accurate at decoding and spelling than children who read little. The first and most important component of good word instruction is large doses of successful reading and writing.

SQUIRT

SQUIRT stands for Sustained QUIet Reading Time. There are many other names for this important idea. Hunt (1970), who popularized the idea, called it USSR—Uninterrupted Sustained Silent Reading. DEAR—Drop Everything and Read—is another common name. In many classrooms, it is just called self-selected reading. Regardless of what you call it, some significant amount of time every day in every classroom should be devoted to children choosing for themselves something to read and then settling down to read it. Self-selected reading is often promoted in terms of the motivation and interest children develop as they have time to pursue their own personal interests through books. Remembering from Chapter 1 the big idea that *reading and writing are feeling* should convince you that self-selected reading is a critical component of how children develop positive attitudes toward reading. In the context of this chapter, whose purpose is to describe ways to help children become fluent decoders and spellers, we want to begin by emphasizing that the amount of reading children do is the biggest variable in their word fluency and that children who engage in regular self-selected reading do a lot more reading than children who don't.

Daily Writing with Invented Spelling

In addition to quantity reading, quantity writing helps children become better decoders and spellers. This is especially true when young children are encouraged to invent spell the words they need but haven't yet learned to spell. Clarke (1988) compared the decoding ability of end-of-the-year first graders and found that first graders who had been encouraged to invent spell in first grade were better at decoding words than first graders from classrooms that emphasized correct spelling. One of the biggest concerns teachers express as they teach young children about sound and letter patterns is that the children don't apply what they know to actually figuring out words while reading. To invent spell a word, however, you have to apply what you know because using your letter-sound knowledge is the way you get some letters to represent the word.

Children who are given time to write each day write more than children who aren't. Children who are encouraged to invent spell words they need as they write have daily opportunities to put to use what they are learning about letters and sounds. Writing is important for many reasons, and these reasons, the writing process, and ways to support children's writing are described in Chapter 7. In this chapter, we want to point out that in addition to all its other benefits, daily writing with invented spelling helps children become better decoders and spellers.

Oral Reading

Most of the reading children do should be silent reading where the focus is on understanding and enjoying what they read. It is also helpful and fun for children to have times when they read aloud. Young children like to read aloud, and as they are reading aloud, teachers have a chance to see how they are using their strategies and to coach them in the appropriate use.

When children read aloud, they always produce a few misreadings. It is these misreadings that allow teachers a "window on the mind" of the reader. It is in responding to these misreadings that teachers have a chance to coach children into strategic reading. Here are some suggestions for making oral reading an enjoyable and profitable endeavor (Cunningham, 1995).

HAVE CHILDREN READ SILENTLY BEFORE READING ORALLY Making sure that silent reading for comprehension precedes oral reading will ensure that students do not lose track of the fact that reading is first and foremost to understand and react to the meaning of the printed words. Young children who are just beginning to read should also read material to themselves or with a partner before reading it orally to a group or the teacher. When beginning readers read, however, it is seldom silent. They don't yet know how to think the words in their minds, and their reading to themselves can be described as "mumble" or "whisper" reading.

ORAL READING SHOULD BE IN EASY MATERIAL Material that students read orally should be easy enough that they will make no more than five errors per hundred words read. If the average sentence length is seven words, this would be no more than one error every three sentences. It is very important that children not make too many errors, because their ability to cross-check drops dramatically when they are making so many errors that they can't make sense of it.

CHILDREN SHOULD NEVER CORRECT EACH OTHER Allowing students to interrupt and correct the misreadings inhibits the reader's ability to self-correct and forces the reader to try for "word-perfect reading." The same is true when the teacher interrupts and corrects the reader. While it might seem that striving for word-perfect reading would be a worthy goal, it is not, because of the way our eyes move when we read.

When you read, your eyes move across the line of print in little jumps. The eyes then stop and look at the words. The average reader can see about 12 letters at a time–one large word, two medium words, or three small words. When your eyes stop, they can see only the letters they have stopped on. The following letters are not visible until the eyes move forward and stop once again. Once your eyes have moved forward, you can't see the words you saw during the last stop. As you read orally, your eyes move out ahead of your voice. This is how you can read with expression, because the intonation and emphasis you give to a particular word can be determined only when you have seen the words that follow it. The space between where your eyes are and where your voice is we call your eye-voice span. Fluent readers reading easy material have an eye-voice span of five to six words.

Good readers read with expression because their voice is trailing their eyes. When they say a particular word, their eyes are no longer on that word but rather several words down the line. This explains something that all good readers do. They make little non-meaning-changing errors when they read orally. They read "can't" when the actual printed words were *can not*. They read "car" when the actual printed word was *automobile*. Non-meaning-changing errors are a sign of good reading! They indicate that the eyes are out there ahead of the voice, using the later words in the sentence to confirm the meaning, pronunciation, and expression given to previous words. The reader who says "car" for *automobile* must have correctly recognized or decoded *automobile* or that reader could not have substituted the synonym *car*. When the reader says "car," the word *automobile* can no longer be seen because the eyes have moved on.

Good readers make small non-meaning-changing errors because their eyes are not right on the words they are saying. If other children are allowed to follow along while the oral reader reads, they will interrupt the reader to point out these errors. If children are allowed to correct non-meaning-changing errors, children learn that when reading orally, you should keep your eyes right on the very word you are saying! This fosters word-by-word reading. Too much oral reading with each error corrected by the children or the teacher will result in children not developing the eye-voice span all good fluent readers have. Constant interruptions by the teacher or other children also work against developing appropriate cross-checking strategies and spontaneous self-corrections.

Eliminating interruptions by other children is not easy but can be accomplished by having all the children not reading put their finger in their books and close them! When one child is reading the others should not be "following along" with the words. Rather, they should be listening to the reader read and "following along with the meaning."

IGNORE ERRORS THAT DON'T CHANGE MEANING   Small, non-meaning-changing errors—*can't* for *can not*—are a sign of good eye-voice span and should not be corrected.

WHEN THE READER MAKES A MEANING-CHANGING ERROR—WAIT! Control the urge to stop and correct the reader immediately. Rather, wait until the reader finishes the sentence or paragraph. What follows the error is often the information the reader needs in order to self-correct. Students who self-correct errors based on subsequent words read should be praised because they are demonstrating their use of cross-checking while reading. Students who are interrupted immediately never learn to self-correct. Instead, they wait for some-one else to correct them. Without self-correcting and self-monitoring, children will never become good readers.

IF WAITING DOESN'T WORK, GIVE HELPFUL FEEDBACK If the reader continues on beyond the end of the sentence in which he or she made a meaning-changing error, the teacher should stop the reader by saying something like:

> Wait a minute. You read, "Then the magician stubbled and fell." Does that make sense?

The teacher has now reinforced a major understanding all readers must use if they are to decode words well. The word must have the right letters and make sense. The letters in *stubbled* are very close to the letters in *stumbled*, but *stubbled* does not make sense. The teacher should pause and see if the reader can find a way to fix it. If so, the teacher should say,

> Yes, *stumbled* makes sense. Good. Continue reading.

If not, the teacher should say something like,

> Look at the word you called *stubbled*. What word do you know that looks like that and is something people often do before they fall?

If that does not help, the teacher might just pronounce the word. Later, it may be useful to return to that page, review the misreading, and point out the *m* before the *b*, or suggest a known rhyming word such as *crumbled* or *tumbled*.

Oral reading provides the "teachable moment"—a time for teachers to help students use the sense of what they are reading and the letter-sound relationships they know. When teachers respond to an error by waiting until a meaningful juncture is reached and responding first with a "Did that make sense?" question, children focus more on meaning and begin to correct their own errors. The rest of the group hear how the teacher responds to the error. As they listen, they learn how they should use "sense" and decoding skills as they are actually reading. Feedback that encourages readers to self-correct and monitor their reading sends a "You can do it" message.

FOR CHILDREN WITH SPECIAL NEEDS—FLUENCY

All children need lots of successful reading and writing in order to develop fluency. Children experiencing difficulty in learning to read or older remedial readers need these successful experiences even more, but their resistance to reading often means they do very little successful reading. Here are three strategies that have demonstrated effectiveness in providing successful reading for readers of all ages:

CHORAL READING

Pick a piece of poetry or a chant the children are familiar with. Decide what parts everyone—the chorus—should read and what parts will make good solos. Duplicate the material or use a chart or overhead to make the print visible to everyone. Assign the solos and practice the piece several times. Emphasize how to speak dramatically and include some sound effects if the piece allows that. Once you have practiced several times, perform the choral reading for a group or make a video- or audiotape of your performance.

IMITATIVE READING

In Chapter 2 you learned how to use predictable books to help children become readers. When the children listened to the book again and again until they had it memorized, they were doing a type of imitative reading. Imitative reading can also be done with older readers with a variety of books, stories, or magazine articles. Find a selection that would interest the student and that is not too long or too difficult. Record the selection in an appealing and dramatic manner. Then instruct the student to listen to the tape and follow along in the book until he or she can read the selection fluently (without meaning-changing errors, at a satisfactory rate, with expression). If the student is an extremely poor and laborious reader, use a very easy and very short selection at first. Be patient and allow the student to listen to or read the selection during any free time or at home. When the student is able to read the selection fluently without the aid of the tape, he or she should receive praise and ample opportunities to read the selection to parents, other teachers, fellow students, and young children in kindergarten or first grade. Although the student has not really memorized the selection (the student could not read the selection without having the book to follow), a combination of memorization and reading enables the student to have the real experience of successful, effective, and fluent reading. Several students can receive such instruction simultaneously, each one with a different book. The limit is defined by how many tape recorders are available. Or a group of students can learn the same book simultaneously if you have multiple copies of an appropriate book.

PERFECTION AND REPEATED READING

For repeated reading, a passage of probable interest to the student that is also at the student's instructional level is used. The passage should be short, no more than 150 words. Give the student the passage and tell him or her to read it silently and to get ready to read it orally with few errors and at a comfortable rate. After silent reading, have the student read the passage to you, count the oral reading errors, and time the reading. If the student makes more than five errors per hundred words, the passage is too difficult to use, and an easier one should be chosen. If no more than five errors per hundred words are made by the student, tell the reader the time it took and suggest that the student practice the material silently again. Repeat this process until the student has read the passage three or four times. While some students are practicing, another can be reading to you, which makes it possible to use repeated readings with a small group of readers. Perfection reading is just like repeated reading but without timing. In other words, the student rereads a passage but only to make fewer errors, not to increase rate. Students can be paired for perfection or repeated reading. They like listening to each other read to count errors or record time. Teachers should make sure, however, that students do not interrupt each other during reading but wait until the selection is finished before making corrections.

FLUENT READING AND WRITING REQUIRE IMMEDIATE, AUTOMATIC RECOGNITION AND SPELLING OF HIGH-FREQUENCY WORDS

In order to read and write, children must learn to quickly and automatically recognize and spell the most commonly occurring words. The most frequently occurring words are meaningless, abstract, connecting words (*of, and, the, is,* etc.). Children use these words in their speech but they are not aware of them as separate entities. Read these sentences in a natural speech pattern and notice how you pronounce the italicized words.

What do you see?

I want that piece *of* cake.

What are *they?*

In natural speech, the *what* and the *do* are slurred together and sound like "wudoo." The *of* is pronounced like "uh." The *they* is tacked on to the end of *are* and sounds like "ah-thay." All children use the highly frequent words such as *what, of,* and *they* in their speech, but they are not aware of these words as they are of the more concrete, tangible words such as *want* and *pie.* To make life more difficult, many of these high-frequency words are not spelled in a regular, predictable way. *What* should rhyme with *at, bat,* and *cat. Of* should be spelled *u-v. They,* which clearly rhymes with *day, may,* and *way,* should be spelled the way many children do spell it—*t-h-a-y.*

When you consider that most frequent words are usually meaningless, abstract words that children use but don't realize are separate words and that many of these words are irregular in spelling/pronunciation, it is a wonder that any children learn to recognize and spell them! In order to read and write fluently, however, children must learn to instantly recognize and automatically spell these words. The good news about these high-frequency words is that their number is limited. Ten words—*the, of, and, a, to, in, is, you, that,* and *it*—account for almost one-quarter of all the words children read and write. Half the words can be accounted for by just 100 words!

Since these words occur so often, children who read and write will encounter them in their reading and need to spell them as they write. In addition to daily reading and writing, many teachers have found it effective to display the high-frequency words in a highly visible spot in their classroom and provide daily practice with these words. Teachers often refer to the place where the words are displayed as their word wall.

Words on the Wall

Select five words each week and add them to a wall or bulletin board in the room. The selection of the words varies from classroom to classroom but the selection principle is the same. Include words that students will need often in their reading and writing and that are easily confused with other words. First-grade teachers who are using a basal often select some high-frequency words taught in that basal. Others select high-frequency words from Big Books or other trade books that they are reading to children or that children are reading. After reading and enjoying *Brown Bear, Brown Bear, What Do You See?* (Martin, 1970), a first-grade teacher added the high-frequency words *what, do, you, see,* and *at* to the classroom word wall. Children knew these words from the *Brown Bear* book and used them frequently in their own writing, Some children wrote sentences in the pattern of *Brown Bear* and used names of children in the classroom.

Manny, Manny, what do you see?
I see Lakesia looking at me.

Another way to know which words to put on the wall is to look in the first-draft writing of the children for commonly misspelled words. A look at the writing of some typical third graders will often find these common misspellings: *thay, peeple, waznt,* and *freind,* along with confusions about homophones such as *their/there, to/too/two,* and *wood/would.*

The word wall grows as the year goes on. The words on the word wall are written on different colored construction paper scraps with a thick black permanent marker. Words are placed on the wall alphabetically by first letter, and the first words added are very different from one another. When confusable words are added, put them on papers colored differently from the other words they are usually confused with.

Word Wall Activities

Most teachers add five new words each week and do at least one daily activity in which the children find, write, and chant the spelling of the words. The activity takes longer on the day you add words because you will want to take time to make sure students associate meanings with the words and you point out how the words are different from words they may be confused with. Many teachers also do a handwriting lesson with the five words on the day these words are added.

To do the daily practice, have students number a sheet of paper from one to five. Call out the five words, putting each word in a sentence. As you call out each word, have a child find and point to that word and have all the children clap and chant its spelling before writing it. When all five words have been written, point to the words and have volunteers spell each word as students check and fix their own papers.

On the day you add words, call out the five new words. During the rest of the week, however, any five words from the wall can be called out. Words with which children need much practice should be called out almost every day. In addition to calling out five words and having the children chant, write, and check them, many teachers do an additional "two-minute" on-the-back activity with the words. Children who have written the wall words *go, want, skate, phone,* and *talk* on the front may be asked to write the words *going, wanted, skating, phoned,* and *talking* on the back. This provides practice with endings and spelling changes that are needed when certain endings are needed. Children who have written the wall words *big, coat, drink, nice,* and *name* on the front may be asked to write the rhyming words *twig, float, think, twice,* and *shame* on the back. This activity helps the children to see that words you know can help you spell rhyming words, which often have the same spelling pattern.

Word Walls Support Fluent Reading and Writing

In the first section of this chapter, the importance of quantity writing with invented spelling to decoding and spelling fluency was described. Children who write *motorcycle* as *motrsikl* are not in danger of spelling *motorcycle* that way forever because they don't need to write the word *motorcycle* too often. Unlike *motorcycle,* words like *they,* which children spell *thay,* are written so often that many children become automatic at spelling *they* as *thay.* The way things become automatic is by doing them over and over until they require none of your conscious attention. Words on the wall are words we don't want children to invent spell, and in most classrooms the rule is, "If it's up on our word wall, we have to spell it correctly!"

Once you have a word wall growing in your room, there will be no doubt that your students use it as they are reading and writing. You will see their eyes quickly glance to the exact spot where a word they want to write is displayed. Even when children are reading, they will sometimes glance over to the word wall to help them remember a particularly troublesome word.

A word wall provides children with an immediately accessible dictionary for the most troublesome words. Because the words are added gradually, stay in the same spot forever, are alphabetical by first letter, are visually distinctive by different colors of paper, and because of the daily practice in finding, writing, and chanting these words, most children learn to read and spell almost all the words. Because the words you selected are words needed constantly in reading and writing, children's recognition of these words becomes automatic and attention can be devoted to less frequent words and to constructing meaning as they read and write. For a list of high-utility wall words and how they were selected, see Figure 3.1, on p. 66.

FOR CHILDREN WITH SPECIAL NEEDS—
HIGH-FREQUENCY WORDS

 Some children have a great deal of difficulty learning the function words, particularly the confusable ones such as *that, they, them, then, with, will, of, for, from.* The Drastic Strategy (Cunningham, 1980) summarized here was developed for teaching these hardest-to-learn words.

Step 1: Select a function word, and write it on a vocabulary card for each child. Locate a story for storytelling, or spontaneously create a story, in which you use the word many times. Before you begin your story, instruct the children to hold up their card every time they hear the word printed on their card As you tell the story, pause briefly each time you come to the word in the text.

Step 2: Ask children to volunteer to make up a story using the word on their card. Listeners should hold up their card each time they hear their classmate use the function word.

Step 3: Ask the children to study the word on their card. Next, go around to each child and cut the word into letters (or have them do it for themselves). Have the children try to arrange the letters to make the word. Check each child's attempt for accuracy. They should mix up the letters and try to make the word again several times. Each child should be able to do this before moving on to the next step. Put the letters into an envelope and write the word outside. Children should be encouraged to practice making the word during free times.

Step 4: Write the word on the chalkboard and ask children to pretend their eyes are like a camera and to take a picture of the word and put it in their mind. Have them close their eyes and try to see it in their mind. Next, they should open their eyes and check the board to see if they correctly imagined the word. They should do this three times. The last activity is for them to write the word from memory after the chalkboard has been erased, then check their spelling when it is rewritten on the chalkboard. This should be repeated three times.

Step 5: Write several sentences on the board containing a blank in the place of the word under study. As you come to the missing word in the sentences, invite a child to come to the board and write the word in the blank space provided.

Step 6: Give children real books or text in which the function word appears. Ask them to read through the story, and whenever they find the word being studied, they should lightly underline (in pencil) the new word. When they have done this, read the text to them and pause each time you come to the word so the students may read it chorally.

Teachers make their own decisions about which words to add to their word walls by observing which words children use frequently in their writing. This list is intended to be an example of the kinds of words that might be included if the word wall is to have the highest utility for the children. This list has high utility in multiple ways:

1. It includes words that account for 50 percent of the words children read and write.
2. It has an example word for each initial consonant, *b, c, d, f, g, h, j, k, l, m, n, p, r, s, t, v, w, y,* and *z* (including both common sounds for *c* and *g*).
3. It includes an example for the common blends *bl, br, cl, cr, dr, fl, fr, gr, pl, pr, sk, sl, sm, sn, sp, st, str,* and *tr.*
4. It includes an example for the common digraphs *ch, sh, th,* and *wh* and for the two-letter combinations *ph, wr, kn,* and *qu.*
5. It includes an example for the most common vowel spelling patterns:
   at, make, rain, day, car, saw, caught
   went, eat, see, her, new
   in, like, night, girl, thing
   not, those, coat, go, for, how, slow, out, boy, look, school, us, use, hurt
   my, very
6. It includes an example for the highest-utility phonograms (Wylie & Durrell, 1970):
   ack, ail, ain, ake, ale, ame, an, ank, ap, ash, at, ate, aw, ay, eat, ell, est, ice, ick, ide, ight, ill, in, ine, ing, ink, ip, it, ock, oke, op, ore, ot, uck, ug, ump, unk.
7. It includes the most common contractions: *can't, didn't, don't, it's, won't.*
8. It includes common homophones: *to, too, two; their, there; right, write; no, know; one, won.*
9. It includes words such as *favorite, teacher, school, family, sister,* and so on that don't occur on any high-frequency list but that young children use frequently in their writing.

a	clock	gym	made
about	coat	had	mail
after	come	has	make
all	could	have	many
am	crash	he	me
an	day	her	more
and	did	here	mother
animal	didn't	him	my
are	do	his	name
as	don't	house	new
at	down	how	nice
be	drink	hurt	night
because	each	I	no
been	eat	if	not
best	family	in	now
big	father	into	of
black	favorite	is	old
boy	first	it	on
brother	fly	it's	one
bug	for	joke	or
but	friend	jump	other
by	from	junk	out
call	fun	kick	over
can	get	know	people
can't	girl	like	phone
car	give	line	play
caught	go	little	presents
children	good	long	question
city	green	look	rain

FIGURE 3.1   High-Utility Wall Words (Cunningham, 1995)

ride	stop	time	what
right	street	to	when
run	talk	too	where
said	teacher	trip	which
sale	tell	truck	who
saw	than	two	why
school	thank	up	will
see	that	us	with
she	the	use	won
sister	their	very	won't
skate	them	want	would
slow	then	was	write
small	these	water	you
snap	they	way	your
so	thing	we	zoo
some	this	went	
sports	those	were	

FLUENT READING AND WRITING REQUIRE THAT STUDENTS HAVE STRATEGIES FOR PRONOUNCING AND SPELLING UNFAMILIAR WORDS

In addition to learning to instantly recognize and spell the most frequent words, children must learn how to figure out the pronunciation/spelling of words they do not know. All proficient readers have the ability to look at regular words they have never seen before and assign probable pronunciations. Witness your ability to pronounce these made-up words:

cate   frow   perdap   midulition

Now of course you weren't "reading" because, having pronounced these words, you wouldn't construct any meaning. But if you were in the position of most young readers who have many more words in their listening/meaning vocabularies than in their sight reading vocabularies, you would often meet words familiar in speech but unfamiliar in print. The ability you demonstrated to rapidly figure out the pronunciation of unfamiliar-in-print words would enable you to make use of your huge store of familiar-in-speech words and thus create meaning.

Before we go on, how did you pronounce the made-up word *frow?* Did it rhyme with *cow* or with *snow?* Because English is not a one-sound, one-letter language, there are different ways to pronounce certain letter patterns, but the number of different ways is limited and with real words, unlike made-up words, your speaking vocabulary lets you know which pronunciation to assign.

Not only do readers use their phonics knowledge to read words they have not seen before, this same knowledge enables them to write. If the four made-up words had been dictated to you and you had to write them, you would have spelled them reasonably close to the way we spelled them.

All good readers and writers develop this ability to come up with pronunciations and spelling for words they have never read or written before. Many poor readers do not. When good readers see a word they have never before seen in print, they stop momentarily and study the word—attending to print detail, looking at every letter in a left-to-right sequence. As they look at all the letters, they are not thinking a sound for each letter, because good readers know that sounds are determined not by individual letters but by letter patterns. Good readers look for patterns of letters they have seen together before and then search their mental word banks looking for words with similar letter patterns. If the new word is a big word, they "chunk" it—that is, they put letters together to make familiar chunks.

Based on their careful inspection of the letters and their search through their mental bank for words with the same letter patterns, good readers try out a pronunciation. If the first try doesn't result in a word they have heard and stored in their mental word bank, they will usually try another pronunciation. Finally, they produce a pronunciation that they "recognize" as sounding like a real word that they know. They then go back and reread the sentence that contained the unfamiliar-in-print word and see if their pronunciation makes sense given the meaning they are getting from the context of surrounding words. If the pronunciation they came up with makes sense, they continue reading. If not, they look again at all the letters of the unfamiliar word and see what else would "look like this and make sense."

Imagine a young boy reading this sentence:

The dancer came out and took a bow.

Imagine that he pauses at the last word and then pronounces *bow* so that it rhymes with *low*. Since that is a real word that he remembers hearing, his eyes then glance back and he quickly rereads the sentence. He then realizes, "That doesn't make sense." He studies all the letters of *bow* again and searches for similar letter patterns in his mental word store. Perhaps he now accesses words such as *how* and *now*. This gives him another possible pronunciation for this letter pattern, one that is also recognized as a previously heard word. He tries this pronunciation, quickly rereads, realizes his sentence now "sounds right," and continues reading.

From this scenario, we can infer the strategies this good reader used to successfully decode an unfamiliar-in-print word:

1. Recognize that this is an unfamiliar word and look at all the letters in a left-to-right sequence.
2. Search your mental store for similar letter patterns and the sounds associated with them.
3. Produce a pronunciation that matches that of a real word that you know.
4. Reread the sentence to cross-check your possible pronunciation with meaning. If meaning confirms pronunciation, continue reading. If not, try again!

Had this unfamiliar-in-print word been a big word, the reader would have had to use a fifth strategy:

5. Chunk the word by putting letters together that usually go together in the words you know.

There are many activities that help children learn common spelling patterns. Six versatile activities described in this section are Rhyming Word Charts, Word Sorting, Making Words, Chunking Big Words, Prefix/Suffix Activities, and What Looks Right?

Rhyming Word Charts

Children love rhyme and they love to make up silly rhymes and jingles. There are also wonderful books that have catchy, memorable rhymes in them. When you read favorite books to your children, be on the lookout for some rhyming words. Begin a chart with the rhyming words from books and then help children to come up with other words that are spelled the same and rhyme (for an example, see Figure 3.2). Some artistic teachers draw little pictures from the books to help the children remember that these words and rhymes are found in real books. Other teachers simply place books from which the rhymes came next to the chart.

Many teachers add one chart each week and read the words on the old charts as they add the new one. While writing, children will look up at the charts when they realize they need words that are on the rhyming charts. Children also enjoy writing silly rhymes. In classrooms where rhyming books are read and charts of rhyming words from these books are made with the children and left on display, children soon learn that words with the same spelling patterns usually rhyme. Once they have this critical understanding, they can begin to use words they know as keys to pronouncing and spelling unfamiliar words.

Word Sorting

Word sorts can be done with the words on the wall or any group of words the teacher wants students to concentrate on. The purpose of word sorts is to focus student attention on the various features of the words. To do a word sort, have students write 10 to 15 words on separate slips of paper. Then have the students sort the words into different piles depending on some features certain words share. Students may sort all words with a certain number of letters, all words that begin with a certain letter, or all words that have a certain letter anywhere in them. Sometimes the teacher tells the students the criterion on which to sort, for example, all words with an *a* in them. Other times, the teacher tells students which words to select—*boy, try, my, day*—and the students must guess how these words are all alike. In this case, they are all of the words that end in the letter *y*. Sorting words based on the number of letters and on the different letters and sounds represented by the letters helps students attend to those letters.

Words can also be sorted according to semantic features. Students might

The Cat in the Hat

at   rat   scat

bat   sat

cat   chat

fat   that

hat   brat

mat   flat

pat   spat

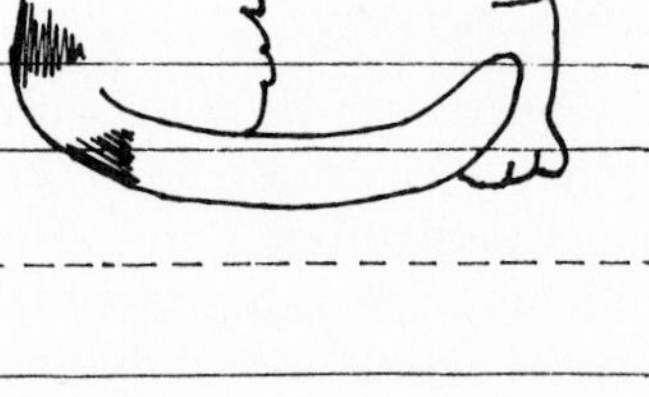

FIGURE 3.2   Here is a chart of rhyming words based on the old favorite *The Cat in the Hat* by Dr. Seuss.

choose all of the things or all of the words that name people. Words that describe things, words that tell what you can do, and words that name things found outside are some of the many possibilities for sorting based on semantic features. Once students understand the various ways the words can be sorted, they can play teacher and tell which words to choose or a criterion for sorting the words.

Making Words

Making Words (Cunningham & Cunningham, 1992) is an activity in which children are given some letters and use these letters to make words. They make little words and then bigger words until the final word is made. The final word always includes all the letters they have and children are always eager to figure out what word can be made from all the letters. Making Words is an active, hands-on, manipulative activity in which children learn how to look for patterns in words and how changing one letter or where you put letters changes the whole word. Here is an example of a Making Words lesson done in one first-grade classroom after children read an informational book about spiders.

For this lesson, each child had four consonants, *d, p, r,* and *s,* and two vowels, *e* and *i.* In the pocket chart at the front of the room, the teacher had large cards with the same six letters. Her cards, like the small letter cards used by the children, had the uppercase letter on one side and lowercase letter on the other side. The consonant letters were written in black and the two vowels were in red.

The teacher began by making sure that each child had all the letters needed. "What two vowels will we use to make words today?" she asked. The children held up their red *i* and *e* and responded appropriately.

The teacher than wrote the numeral 2 on the board and said, "We will make some easy two-letter words first to get warmed up. Take two letters and make *Ed.*" She watched as the children quickly put the letters *Ed* in their holders and she then sent someone who had correctly spelled *Ed* to the pocket chart to make *Ed* with the big letters. She got that child to explain that you needed to start *Ed* with a capital *E* because it was a name. She then put an index card with the word *Ed* in the pocket chart.

Next, she erased the 2 and wrote a 3 on the board. "Turn your *e* to its lowercase side and add just one letter to *ed* to make the three-letter word *red,*" she instructed. The lesson continued with children making words with their individual letter cards, a child going to the pocket chart to make the word, and the teacher putting a card with that word in the pocket chart.

The children changed *red* to *rid.* Next they made *sip* and *pie.* The teacher erased the 3 and wrote a 4 on the board and asked them to add just one letter to *pie* to make the word *pies.* Next they changed one letter to change *pies* to *dies.* At this point, the teacher said, "Don't take any letters out and don't add any. Just change where the letters are and you can change *dies* into *side.*"

They then changed *side* to *ride,* then to *ripe* and *rise.* The teacher erased the 4 and wrote a 5, and they used five of their letters to make the words *pride* and *drips.*

The teacher and children are ready to begin the Making Words activity. The letters *e, i, d, p, r,* and *s* are in the pocket chart and each child has these letters and a holder in which to make words.

As a child was making *drips* at the pocket chart, many of the other children were manipulating all their letters trying to come up with a word. They knew that each lesson ended with a word that used all their letters and they always liked to figure it out. Today, several children were waving their hands, eager to tell the word—*spider!* The teacher praised their sophisticated word-sleuthing skills and then told them to take all six letters and make a bug that they were going to read about in science—*spider.*

To conlude the lesson and draw children's attention to letter patterns, the teacher drew their attention to the words in the pocket chart.

Ed red rid sip pie pies dies side ride ripe rise pride drips spider

She picked up *Ed*, placed it at the bottom of the pocket chart, and asked, "Who can come and hand me a word that rhymes with *Ed?*" A child handed her the word *red*. She then had children find the two words that rhymed with *ride—side* and *pride*. The children spelled the rhyming pairs and decided that these words all had the same letters from the vowel onward. The teacher reminded the children that words that have the same spelling pattern usually rhyme and that this is one way many good readers and writers read and spell words. "What if

In the first photo are all the words the children made. The second photo shows how the children sorted the words for rhyming patterns.

I wanted to spell *fed?* What words that you made does *fed* rhyme with?'' The children decided that *fed* rhymed with *Ed* and *red* and would probably be spelled *f-e-d.* They also decided that *slide* rhymed with *ride, side,* and *pride* and would probably be spelled *s-l-i-d-e.*

As you can see from this sample lesson, Making Words is an activity that keeps the children involved and helps them learn to look for patterns. To plan a Making Words lesson, you begin with the word you want to end with. Many teachers choose this word from a book or story the children have been reading. You write this word on an index card and then consider what other words you could have the children make. There are always more words than you can make in a 15-minute lesson, so you select the words and the order in which you have children make them so that they begin to see that when you change or add a letter, the word changes in a predictable way.

TRY IT OUT

 Plan a Making Words lesson you could teach to a first- or second-grade class. Follow these steps:

1. Decide what ''big word'' can be made with all the letters. In choosing this word, consider books the children are reading, and what letter-sound patterns you can draw children's attention to through the sorting at the end.
2. Make a list of other words you can make from these letters.
3. From all the words you could make, pick 12 to 15 words using these criteria:
   a. Words that you can sort for the pattern you want to emphasize.
   b. Little words and big words, so that the lesson is a multilevel lesson. (Making the little words helps your slowest students; making the big words challenges your most accelerated students.)
   c. Words that can be made with the same letters in different places (barn/ bran) so that children are reminded that when spelling words, the ordering of the letters is crucial.
   d. A proper name or two to remind students that we use capital letters.
   e. Words that most students have in their listening vocabularies.
4. Write all the words on index cards and order them from smallest to biggest.
5. Once you have the two-letter and three-letter words together and so on, order them so that you can emphasize letter patterns and how changing the position of the letters or changing/adding just one letter results in a different word.
6. Store the cards in an envelope. Write on the envelope the words in order and the patterns you will sort for.

Once a Making Words lesson has been planned, it is easy to teach. For the steps to follow in teaching a Making Words lesson, see Figure 3.3.

Steps in Teaching a Making Words Lesson

1. Place the large letter cards needed in a pocket chart or along the chalk ledge.
2. Have designated children each give one letter to each child. Let the designated children keep the Ziploc bags or paper cups containing those letters and have each child collect the proper letter when the lesson is over.
3. Hold up and name the letters on the large letter cards and have the children hold up their matching small letter cards.
4. Write the numeral 2 on the board (or 3 if there are no two-letter words in this lesson) and have the children hold up two fingers. Tell them to take two letters and make the first word. Put the word in a sentence after you say the word.
5. Ask a child who has made the first word correctly to make the same word with the large letter cards on the chalk ledge or pocket chart. Encourage those who didn't make the word correctly at first to fix the word when they see it made correctly.
6. Continue to make the remaining two-letter words, giving students clues such as "Change just the first letter" or "Move the same letters around and you can make a different word" or "Take all you letters out and make another word." Send children who made the word correctly to make that word with the large letter cards.
7. Erase the 2 and write a 3 on the board. Have the children hold up three fingers and tell them that these words will take three of their letters.
8. Continue having them make words, erasing and changing the number on the board to indicate the number of letters needed. Use the words in simple sentences to make sure they access meaning. Remember to cue them about whether they are just changing one letter, changing letters around, or taking all their letters out to make a word from scratch. When you have them make a name, cue them that it is a name and send a child who has started that name with a capital letter to make the word with the big letters.
9. Before telling them the last word, ask, "Has anyone figured out what word we can make with all our letters?" Congratulate a child who did so and have him or her make it. If not, say something like, "I love it when I can stump you. Use all your letters and make. . . . "
10. (Some teachers make the words on one day and then do this sorting for pattern activity on the following day.) Once all the words have been made, take the index cards on which you have written the words and place them one at a time (in the same order that children made them) along the chalk ledge or in the pocket chart. Have children say and spell the words with you as you do this. Use these words for sorting and pointing out patterns. Pick a word and point out a particular spelling pattern. Ask children to find other words with that same pattern. Line these words up so the pattern is visible.
11. To get maximum transfer to reading and writing, have children use patterns they have sorted to read and spell a few new words.

FIGURE 3.3   Here is a lesson one teacher planned for the word *turtles* after the children read a book about turtles. The words to be made are written on index cards and placed in the envelope. On the outside of the envelope, the teacher writes the words children will make and the patterns they will sort for.

Here are three Making Big Words lessons. After cutting the letters from the top, the children manipulated the letters to make words and wrote the words in the boxes. The big word is connected to a theme or topic they are studying.

Making Big Words

Making Words lessons can also be done with big words and older children. When doing a Making Big Words lesson, print the letters needed at the top of a piece of paper (vowels first, then consonants in alphabetical order so as not to give away the big word). Make boxes for children to write and sort words on the rest of the paper. The children cut apart letters from the top of the sheet and manipulate them to make words. Finally, children write the words they make in the boxes.

When the children have had five to six minutes to make words and write them on their paper, let them each tell one word they made. Children spell the word, and if it is spelled correctly and can be made from the letters they have, words are written on index cards and put in the pocket chart. Once the children have contributed all the words they made, the words in the pocket chart are sorted for patterns, with the teacher and students suggesting various ways to sort them.

DO IT TOGETHER

Here are the letters of a big word.

a a i o u d g n r t

Write these letters on torn scraps of paper and manipulate them to form words. Keep a list of the words you can make in five minutes. When the time is up, compile a list of all the words made by everyone in the group. Write these words on index cards and sort them into patterns. Did anyone figure out the big word that can be made with all these letters? Summarize how Making Words helps you focus on spelling patterns and how it is a multilevel activity from which children could gain a variety of understandings about spelling patterns in big and little words.

Chunking Big Words

Many long words such as *entertainment* have chunks that students know from other words. The word *entertainment* begins with a familiar chunk, *enter,* and then has two other chunks that students should recognize from other words such as main*tain* and argu*ment.* As you introduce polysyllabic words to students, point out to them the familiar chunks. You might introduce *entertainment* by writing *entertainment* on the board and saying something like this:

> This is a long word, but it is not very hard to figure out if you use some other words you know. [Cover all but *enter.*] The first chunk is a word you know. The second chunk you know from words like *maintain* and *contain.* [Write *maintain* and *contain* on the board, underlining the *tain.*] Finally, you know the last chunk if you know *argument* or *moment.* [Write *argument* and *moment* on the board, underling the *ment.*]

Since English is not a language in which letters or chunks have only one sound, you might also write the word *mountain* on the board, underlining the *tain* and pointing out to students that the letters *tain* also commonly have the sound you hear at the end of *mountain.* Have students try pronouncing *entertainment* with the different sounds for the *tain* chunk. Point out that it sounds right and makes a word you know when you use the sound of *tain* that you know from *maintain* and *contain.* Remind students that if they use the probable sound of letters and the sense of what they are reading, they can figure out many more words than if they just pay attention to the letter sounds, ignoring what makes sense, or just guess something that makes sense, ignoring the letter sounds.

You may have been taught to decode polysyllabic words by learning a set of syllabication and accent rules. Do you remember learning to divide between two consonants unless the consonants are a digraph or a blend? Did you learn that the next-to-the-last syllable is often accented? Syllabication and accent rules have been the traditional strategies taught to help students figure out polysyllabic words. Unfortunately, research (Canney & Schreiner, 1977) reports that although students can learn the rules, knowing the rules is not related to the ability to decode polysyllabic words. The syllabication and accent rules were well intended. Good readers see polysyllabic words in chunks, and they know enough to accent the *tain* in *entertainment,* thus making it sound like the accented *tain* in *contain* rather than the unaccented *tain* in *mountain.* But good readers do not seem to do this by using rules. Rather, they look for chunks based on words they already know. Often as in *entertainment,* the chunk (*enter*) may be larger than a syllable. Accent is usually determined not by applying accent rules but by pronouncing a word different ways until one way sounds correct.

Polysyllabic words present serious decoding problems for many readers because when they see a word with more than seven letters, they don't even attempt to figure it out. Introducing words on a regular basis as suggested for the sample word *entertainment* will help students learn that big words can be decoded if they look across the words for familiar chunks and then are sure that the word they end up with "sounds right" and makes sense.

Prefix/Suffix Activities

Many big words are only small words with lots of added prefixes and suffixes. Often morphemic instruction focuses solely on prefixes or suffixes as they provide clues to the meanings of words. Students are taught that *inter* means between or among and use this to figure out that *international* means between nations. Unfortunately, prefixes such as *inter* also begin many words such as *interfere, interruption,* and *internal* in which there is a "between/among" meaning to the *inter* chunk but the rest of the word is not a known root word. Most students could not figure out the meaning of *interfere* by combining their knowledge of the Latin root *fere* with the meaning of between or among associated with *inter.*

Most readers know what an *autograph* is and can use the two chunks *auto* and *graph* to decode the word *autograph* if it is unfamiliar to them in printed form. Most readers do not need to (and are indeed not able to) use the morphemes in *autograph* to derive a meaning for the word. If children are taught that *mis* means "bad" or "wrong" and the next two words they see are *Mississippi* and *miscellaneous,* they tend to disbelieve our instruction and ignore morphemic clues. Even when the meaning link is there, as it is for the *uni* in *university, uniform,* or *unicorn,* most children could not use the *uni* to figure out the meanings of these words. Fortunately, most children know what the words *university, uniform,* and *unicorn* mean and can use the prefix *uni* as a pronunciation chunk. Children need to learn to look for morphemic units and to use them as pronunciation patterns as well as clues to meaning. Here is an example of a prefix activity (Cunningham, 1995) that focuses on meaning and chunks:

Write nine words that begin with *re* on index cards. Include three words in which *re* means back, three words in which *re* means again, and three words in which the *re* is just the first syllable and has no apparent meaning. Use words for which your students are apt to have meanings. Here are some possible words:

rebound	redo	record
return	replay	refuse
replace	rework	reveal

Place these words randomly along the chalk ledge, have them pronounced, and ask students what "chunk" the words all have. Once students notice that they all begin with *re*, arrange the words in three columns and tell the students to think about why you have put *rebound*, *return*, and *replace* together, *redo*, *replay*, and *rework* together, and *record*, *refuse*, and *reveal* together. If students need help, tell them that for one column of *re* words, you can put the word *again* in place of the *re* and have the meaning of the word. Explain that for another column, you can put the word *back* in place of *re*. Once students have figured out in which column the *re* means back and in which *re* means again, label these columns *back* and *again*. Help students to see that when you refuse something, you don't fuse it back or fuse it again. Do the same with *record* and *reveal*.

Have students set up their own papers in three columns, the first two headed by *back* and *again* and the last not headed, and write the words written on the board. Then say some *re* words and have students write them in the column they think they belong in. As each word is written, ask students where they wrote it and how they spelled it. Write it in the appropriate column on the board. Conclude the activity by having all the *re* words read and replacing the *re* with *back* or *again* when appropriate. Help students summarize that sometimes *re* mean back, sometimes *re* means again, and sometimes *re* is just the first chunk of the word. Here are some words you might use:

reusable	retire	retreat	rewind
recall	respond	remote	responsible
recoil	rewrite	refund	relief

A similar activity could be done for words that begin with *un*. Include words in which *un* means not or the opposite of, in which *uni* means one, and in which the *un* is just the first chunk. Use words your students are apt to know to start the lists, such as:

unfair	unicorn	under
unpack	united	uncle
unarmed	uniform	undertaker

The prefixes *un*, *re*, and *in* are the most common. Other common prefixes include *inter*, *dis*, *non*, *pre*, *post*, *mis*, *sub*, *super*, *trans*, and *semi*. Regardless of which prefixes you are teaching, your message to students should be the same. Prefixes are chunks at the front of words that have predictable pronunciations. Look for them and depend on them to help you chunk and pronounce new words. Sometimes, they also give you meaning clues. If you are unsure about the meaning of a word, see is a common meaning for the prefix can help.

Suffixes, like prefixes, are predictable indicators of pronunciation and sometimes signal a meaning relationship. The meaning signaled by suffixes, however, is not usually a meaning change, but rather a change in how and in what position the word can be used in the sentence. *Compose* is what you do. The *composer* is the person doing it. A *composition* is what you have once you have composed. Students need to become aware of how words change when they are signaling different relationships. They also need to realize that there are slight pronunciation changes to root words when suffixes are added. Common suffixes include *ly, er, or, ist, ful, less, al, ous, ness, ment, ize, ance/ence, ant/ent, tion/sion,* and *able/ible*.

What Looks Right?

What Looks Right? is an activity through which children learn that good spelling requires visual memory and how to use their visual memory for words along with a dictionary to determine the correct spelling of a word. In English, words that have the same spelling pattern usually rhyme. If you are reading and you come to the unknown words *plight* and *trite,* you can easily figure out their pronunciation by accessing the pronunciation associated with other *ight* or *ite* words you can read and spell. The fact that there are two common spelling patterns with the same pronunciation is not a problem when you are trying to read an unfamiliar-in-print word, but it is a problem when you are trying to spell it. If you were writing and trying to spell *trite* or *plight,* they could easily be spelled *t-r-i-g-h-t* and *p-l-i-t-e.* The only way to know which is the correct spelling is to write it one way and see if it "looks right" or check your probable spelling in a dictionary. What Looks Right? is an activity to help children learn how to use these two important self-monitoring spelling strategies.

Here is a sample lesson for the *ight/ite* pattern. Using an overhead or the board, create two columns and head each with an *ite/ight* word most of your children can both read and spell. Have the children set up two columns on their paper to match your model:

bite   fight

Have the children pronounce and spell the words and lead them to realize that the words rhyme but have a different spelling pattern. Tell them that there are many words that rhyme with *bite* and *fight* and that you can't tell by just saying the words which spelling patterns they will have. Next, say a word that rhymes with *bite* and *fight* and write it both ways, saying, "If the word is spelled like *bite,* it will be *t-i-t-e,* if it is spelled like *right,* it will be *t-i-g-h-t.*" Write these two possible spellings under the appropriate word.

Tell the children to decide which one "looks right to them" and to write only the one they think is correct. As soon as each child decides which one looks right and writes it in the correct column, have each child use the dictionary to see if that spelling can be found. If the child cannot find the one that looked right, then the other possible spelling should be looked up. Cross out the one you wrote that is not the correct spelling and continue with some more examples. For each word, say something like, "If it is spelled like *bite*, it will be *k-i-t-e*, but if it is spelled like *fight*, it will be *k-i-g-h-t*. Write the word both ways and have each child write it the way it looks right and then look in the dictionary to see if the word is spelled the way the child thought.

Here is what your columns of words would look like after several examples:

bite   fight
~~tite~~   tight
kite   ~~kight~~
quite   ~~quight~~
~~fite~~   fright
spite   ~~spight~~
~~slite~~   slight

Once you have given several examples in which there is only one correct spelling, give an example such as *site/sight* where both spellings are correct because there are two different words with different meanings and different spellings. Don't tell the children they are both correct. Use the regular procedure of having them decide which one looks right, write it in the correct column, and then find it in the dictionary. When children realize that both are there, take this opportunity to talk with them about the fact that some words are homophones—they are pronounced the same but have different spellings and meanings—and use the dictionary definitions to talk about the different meanings for *site* and *sight*. Use a few more homophone examples and help children to realize that they can use the dictionary both to check a probable spelling and to determine the meaning and spelling of a homophone. Here is what your board might look like at the end of the lesson:

bite   fight
~~tite~~   tight
kite   ~~kight~~
quite   ~~quight~~
~~fite~~   fright
spite   ~~spight~~
~~slite~~   slight
site   sight
mite   might
write   right

What Looks Right? is an activity format that can be used to draw children's attention to any spelling patterns, such as *ale/ali*, *ane/ain*, *oat/ote*, and *eat/eet*, that share a common pronunciation. In addition to one-syllable patterns, What Looks Right? can be used to help children determine whether the last part of a big word is spelled *t-i-o-n* like *vacation* or *s-i-o-n* like *television*, *a-b-l-e* like *movable* or *i-b-l-e* like *incredible, a-n-c-e* like *resistance* or *e-n-c-e* like *difference*. Children learn that you can use the words you know to generate probable spellings for other words but that some pronunciations have two common spelling patterns. When you write an unfamiliar word, you can increase the probability of spelling it correctly if you stop and consider whether or not it "looks right" and/or use a dictionary to see if your probable spelling is correct.

FLUENT READING REQUIRES CROSS-CHECKING MEANING WITH PROBABLE PRONUNCIATIONS

The ability to use some letters in a word along with the sentence or story context is an important decoding strategy. You must do two things simultaneously—think about what would make sense and think about letters and sounds. For sophisticated readers, this simultaneous use of meaning and letter-sound clues appears to be automatic, but many beginning readers have difficulty performing these two complex actions simultaneously. The most important thing teachers can do to foster the development of cross-checking is to respond to oral reading in the meaning-oriented "Does that make sense?" manner described in the first section of this chapter. Two gamelike activities, Guess the Covered Word and The Wheel, provide some additional practice with cross-checking.

Guess the Covered Word

Prepare for this activity by writing several sentences on the board. Cover one word in each sentence with two Post-it notes, one of which covers only the first letter or letters. Cut the Post-it notes so that the word length is obvious. Have students read the first sentence and guess what the covered word is. Next to the sentence, write each guess that makes sense. (If a guess does not make sense, explain why, but do not write this guess.) Once you have written several guesses, remove the paper that covers the first letter or letters. Cross out any guesses that are no longer possible and ask if there are any more guesses that "make sense and start with a *p*." If there are more guesses, write these. Be sure all guesses both make sense and start correctly. Some children will begin guessing anything that begins with *p*. Respond with something like, "*Peach* does begin with a *p*, but I can't write *peach* because people can't go to a peach." When you have written all guesses that make sense and begin correctly, uncover the word and have the whole sentence read.

After several Guess the Covered Word activities, you will be able to tell that your students are getting the point that guesses made based on meaning, beginning letters, and word length are much better than "wild guesses." They will not want to make guesses until the first letters are revealed and will beg you to "just go ahead and show us the first letters!" You will also notice them rejecting guesses with statements like, "No, it can't be *watermelon;* the word's not long enough." (For an example of a Guess the Covered Word lesson, see Chapter 11).

The Wheel

The popular game show *Wheel of Fortune* is premised on the idea that meaning and some letters allow you to figure out many words. In *Wheel of Fortune*, meaning is provided by the category to which the word belongs. A variation of this game can be used to introduce big words and teach students to use meaning and all the letters they know. Here is how to play The Wheel (Cunningham & Allington, 1994).

Remind students that many words can be figured out even if we can't decode all the parts if we think about what makes sense and has the parts we do know in the right places. Ask students who have watched *Wheel of Fortune* to explain how it is played. Then explain how your version of The Wheel will be different:

1. Contestants guess all letters without considering if they are consonants or vowels.
2. They must have all letters filled in before they can say the word.
3. The word must fit in a sentence rather than in a category.
4. They will win paper clips instead of great prizes.
5. Vanna will not be there to turn letters.

Write a sentence on the board and draw blanks for each letter of an important word. Here is an example.

If you were to travel to Antarctica, you would be struck by its almost unbelievable __ __ __ __ __ __ __ __ __ __ __.

Have a student begin by asking, "Is there a . . . ?" If the student guesses a correct letter, fill that letter in. Give that student one paper clip for each time that letter occurs. Let the student continue to guess letters until he or she gets a "No!" When a student asks for a letter that is not there, write the letter above the puzzle and go on to the next student.

Make sure that all letters are filled in before anyone is allowed to guess. (This really shows them the importance of spelling and attending to common spelling patterns!) Give the person who correctly guesses the word five bonus paper clips. Just as in other games, if someone says the answer out of turn, immediately award the bonus paper clips to the person whose turn it was. The student having the most paper clips at the end is the winner.

For our example, a student might ask if there is an *r*. ("Sorry, no *r*!")

The next student asks for an *s*. One *s* is filled in.

If you were to travel to Antarctica, you would be struck by its almost unbelievable __ __ s __ __ __ __ __ __ __.

The student is given one paper clip and continues to ask. "Is there a *t*?" "Yes, one *t*!"

If you were to travel to Antarctica, you would be struck by its almost unbelievable __ __ s __ __ __ t __ __ __.

The student asks for an *o*. Two *o*s are filled in and the student receives two more paper clips.

> If you were to travel to Antarctica, you would be struck by its almost unbelievable __ __ s o __ __ t __ o __.

Next the student asks for an *i* and then for an *n*.

> If you were to travel to Antarctica, you would be struck by its almost unbelievable __ __ s o __ __ t i o n.

After much thought, the student asks for an *m*. Unfortunately, there is no *m*, so play passes to the next student, who asks for an *e*, an *a*, a *d*, and an *l* and correctly spells out *d e s o l a t i o n!* (The teacher points out that desolation is also the emotion felt by the previous student who came so close to winning!) Play continues with another big word introduced in a sentence context.

Students who are introduced to vocabulary by playing The Wheel pay close attention to letter patterns in big words and get in the habit of making sure words they figure out based on some letters fit the meaning of sentences in which they occur.

WORD FLUENCY IS DEVELOPED IN THE CONTENT AREAS ACROSS THE CURRICULUM

In most elementary classrooms, two hours of the instructional day are devoted to reading and the other language arts. During the rest of the day, children are learning in a variety of curriculum areas including math, science, and social studies. Although we often don't think of it, these content-area subjects are perfect places to help children build their word fluency skills. In order to read and write in content areas, they must learn fairly specialized vocabulary. Often, the words to be learned are big words that the children need help learning to recognize and spell. This section will describe two activities for improving word fluency and learning important content-area vocabulary simultaneously.

Content Word Boards

Reserve one of the bulletin boards in your room for use as a content word board. As you teach science and social studies units, identify 15 to 25 big words that are key to understanding. Write these on large index cards with a black, thick permanent marker. Do not overwhelm your students by presenting all the words at once. Rather, add three or four each day as you introduce these words. As you put the words on the board, have the students chant the spelling (cheerleader style) with you. Then, have them close their eyes and chant the spelling again. Next, have them write a sentence that uses as many of the words as they can and still makes a sensible sentence.

Once the words are displayed on the board, draw students' attention to these words as they occur in lectures, films, experiments, or discussions. As students write about what they are learning, encourage them to use the big words and to refer to the board for correct spellings. Help students to develop positive attitudes toward learning big words by pointing out that every discipline has some critical big words, the use of which separates the pros from the amateurs.

Look at the big words on the Antarctica Big Word Board in Figure 3.4. Notice how many of the common polysyllabic patterns are illustrated by just this one set of words. Students who can read and write *exploration, exploitation, regulation, conservation,* and *confrontation* now have several big known words that end in that reliable but totally unexplainable letter pattern *t-i-o-n,* which we pronounce "shun"! The words *geologists, conservationists,* and *environmentalists* contain the suffix *ists,* which usually transforms a word from "the thing" to "the people who work on or worry about the thing." Including two important forms of the same base word *(conservation, conservationists; environment, environmentalists; geologic, geologists)* allows students to see how endings of words determine what part of the sentence they can be used in. If your students are not very sophisticated word users, you can greatly extend the control they have over language by pointing out how words change and the similarities and differences in pronunciation, use, and spelling.

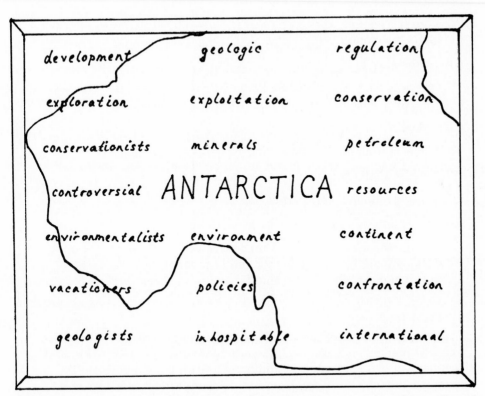

FIGURE 3.4 Here is a content word board containing numerous words students will need as they read and write about Antarctica.

Content Vocabulary Introduction

Many elementary teachers bemoan the fact that there are so many big, unknown words for students to learn in the content areas of science and social studies. This problem can be turned to your advantage if you seize the opportunity when introducing vocabulary in the content areas to model for students how you figure out the pronunciation of a word. Modeling is more than just telling them pronunciation, it is sharing the thinking that goes on when you come across big words.

Words should be shown in sentences so that students are reminded that words must have the right letters in the right places and make sense. Here is an example of how you might model for students one way to decode *international* (Cunningham, 1995).

Write on the board or overhead:

The thinning of the ozone layer is an *international* problem.

Then say to the class:

Today, we are going to look at a big word that is really just a little word with a prefix added to the beginning and a suffix at the end.

(Underline *nation.*)

Who can tell me this word? Yes, that is the word *nation.* Now, let's look at the prefix that comes before *nation.*

(Underline *inter.*)

This prefix is *inter.* You probably know *inter* from words like *interrupt* and *internal.* Now, let's look at what follows *inter* and *nation.*

(Underline *al.*)

You know *al* from many words such as *unusual* and *critical.*

(Write *unusual* and *critical* and underline the *al.*)

Listen as I pronounce this part of the word.

(Underline and pronounce *national.*)

Notice how the pronunciation of *nation* changes when we put *a-l* on it. Now let's put all the parts together and pronounce the word—*inter nation al.* Let's read the sentence and make sure *international* makes sense.

(Have the sentence read and confirm that ozone thinning is indeed a problem for many nations to solve.)

You can figure out the pronunciation of many big words if you look for common prefixes such as *inter,* common root words such as *nation,* and common suffixes such as *al.* In addition to helping you figure out the pronunciation of a word, prefixes and suffixes sometimes help you know what the word means or where in a sentence we can use the word. The word *nation* names a thing. When we describe a nation, we add the suffix *al* and have *national.* The prefix *inter* often means "between or among."

Something that is *international* is between many nations. The Olympics are the best example of an *international* sports event.

This sample lesson for introducing the word *international* demonstrates how a teacher can help students see and use morphemes to decode words needed for content-area learning. Notice that the teacher points out words students might know that have the same parts. In addition, meaning clues provided by the morphemes are provided whenever appropriate.

A similar procedure could be used to model how you would decode a word that didn't contain suffixes or prefixes. For the word *resources,* for example, the teacher would draw students' attention to the familiar first syllable *re* and then point out the known word *sources*. For *geologic,* the teacher might write and underline the *geo* in the known word *geography* and then point out the known word *logic. Policies* might be compared to *politics* and *agencies*.

Modeling is simply thinking aloud how you might go about figuring out an unfamiliar word. It takes just a few extra minutes to point out the morphemes in *international* and to show how *policies* is like *politics* and *agencies,* but these extra few minutes are quickly paid back as students begin to develop some independence in figuring out big words that carry so much content.

TRY IT OUT

 Look through some science or social studies books and identify some polysyllabic key words. Make a list of about a dozen and think about how you could model for students how you figure out how to pronounce and spell big words. Use the modeling example in the previous section and write out a script for how you would "think aloud" about the patterns—prefixes, suffixes, morphemes, and so on—as you introduce these important content-specific words.

THE THEORY AND RESEARCH BASE FOR WORD FLUENCY INSTRUCTION

Within the last decade, advances in technology have allowed researchers, mainly in the areas of psychology and artificial intelligence, to investigate brain functions, eye movements, and other basic reading processes. The focus of this research was not on how to teach reading or on comparisons of various approaches but rather on what happens internally when we read and how this changes as readers move from beginning stages to more sophisticated reading. We know a great deal more today than we did two decades ago about basic reading processes. Here are some major findings that provide the research base for the ideas and activities in this chapter:

Readers Look at Virtually All of the Words and Almost All the Letters in Those Words (Rayner & Pollatsek, 1989)   For many years, it was generally believed that sophisticated readers sampled text. Because of predictions about what words and letters they would see, readers were thought to look at words and letters just enough to see if their predictions were confirmed. Eye-movement research carried out with computerized tracking has proven that, in reality, readers look at every word and almost every letter of each word. The amount of time spent processing each letter is incredibly small, only a few hundredths of a second. The astonishingly fast letter recognition for letters within familiar words and patterns is explained by the fact that our brains expect certain letters to occur in sequence with other letters.

Readers Usually Recode Printed Words into Sound (McCutchen, Bell, France, & Perfetti, 1991)   Although it is possible to read without any internal speech, we rarely do. Most of the time as we read, we think the words in our mind. This phonological information is then checked with the information we received visually by analyzing the word for familiar spelling patterns. Saying the words aloud or thinking the words also seems to perform an important function in holding words in auditory memory until enough words are read to create meaning.

Readers Recognize Most Words Immediately and Automatically without Using Context (Stanovich, 1991; Nicholson, 1991)   Good readers use context to see if what they are reading makes sense. Context is also important for disambiguating the meaning of some words (I had a *ball* throwing the *ball* at the *ball*). Occasionally, readers use context to figure out words. Most of the time, however, words are identified based on their familiar spelling and the association of that spelling with a pronunciation. Context comes into play after, not before, the word is identified based on the brain's processing of the letter-by-letter information it receives. Several studies have found that poor readers rely more on context than do good readers.

Readers Accurately and Quickly Pronounce Infrequent, Phonetically Regular Words (Daneman, 1991)   When presented with unfamiliar but phonetically regular words—*kirn, miracidium*—good readers immediately and seemingly effortlessly assign them a pronunciation. This happens so quickly that readers are often unaware that they have not seen the word before and that they had to "figure it out."

Readers Use Spelling Patterns and Analogy to Decode Words (Adams, 1990; Goswami & Bryant, 1990)   For a long time, the phonics debate centered on whether to teach using a synthetic or analytic approach. Synthetic approaches generally teach children to go letter by letter, assigning a pronunciation to each letter and then blending individual letters together. Analytic approaches teach rules (the *e* on the end makes the vowel long). Brain research, however, suggests that the brain is a pattern detector, not a rule applier, and that, while we look at single letters, we are looking at them considering all the letter patterns we know. Successfully decoding a word occurs when the brain recognizes a familiar spelling pattern or, if the pattern itself is not familiar, searches through its store of words with similar patterns.

To decode the unfamiliar word *knob*, for example, a child who knew many words that began with *kn* would immediately assign to the *kn* the "n" sound. The initial *kn* would be stored in the brain as a spelling pattern. If the child knew only a few other words with *kn* and hadn't read these words very often, that child would probably not have *kn* as a known spelling pattern and thus would have to do a quick search for known words that began with *kn*. If the child found the words *know* and *knew* and then tried this same sound on the unknown word *knob*, that child would have used the analogy strategy. Likewise, a child might know the pronunciation for *ob* because of having correctly read so many words containing the *ob* spelling pattern, or might have had to access some words with *ob* to use them to come up with the pronunciation. The child who had no stored spelling patterns for *kn* or *ob* and no known words to access and compare to would be unlikely to successfully pronounce the unknown word *knob*.

To summarize what the brain does to identify words is to run the risk of oversimplification, but it seems necessary if we want our instructional practices to be compatible with what we know about brain processes. As we read, we look very quickly at almost all letters of each word. For most words, this visual information is recognized as familiar patterns with which spoken words are identified and pronounced (aloud or through internal speech). Words we have read before are instantly recognized as we see them. Words we have not read before are almost instantly pronounced based on spelling patterns the brain has seen in other words. Meanings are accessed through visual word recognition, but the sounds of words support the visual information and help to hold words in memory.

LOOKING BACK

Reading and writing are meaning-constructing activities that are both dependent on words. All good readers and writers have stores of high-frequency words that they read and spell instantly and automatically. Good readers and writers can also decode and spell most regular words. In this chapter, we have presented a theoretical framework for word fluency instruction as well as some practical activities consistent with current theory. The five key ideas are:

1. Lots of reading and writing are crucial for the development of decoding and spelling.
2. Fluent reading and writing require immediate, automatic recognition and spelling of high-frequency words.
3. Fluent reading and writing require that students have strategies for pronouncing and spelling unfamiliar words.
4. Fluent reading requires cross-checking meaning with probable pronunciations.
5. Word fluency is developed in the content areas across the curriculum.

ADD TO YOUR JOURNAL

This chapter has presented a lot of information, some of which is probably new to you and some of which probably contradicts what you remember about learning to read. Do you remember teachers spelling words for you as you wrote or requiring that you spell every word correctly? This requirement probably helped you produce more perfect papers but it probably didn't move you very far forward in your understanding of our English spelling system. Do you remember learning a series of vowel rules—the *e* on the end makes the vowel long? This rule describes how some vowel patterns work, but brain research suggests that the brain is a pattern detector rather than a rule applier. Perhaps this explains why many teachers decry the fact that "they know the rules—they just don't use them!" Call up what you remember about learning sight words, phonics, and spelling and compare it to what is presented in this chapter. Evaluate your own experience and the ideas presented here and apply this to your own personal teaching framework.

REFERENCES

Adams, M. J. (1990). *Beginning to read: Thinking and learning about print*. Cambridge, MA: MIT Press.

Canney, G., & Schreiner, R. (1977). A study of the effectiveness of selected syllabication rules and phonogram patterns for word attack. *Reading Research Quarterly, 12,* 102–124.

Clarke, L. K. (1988). Invented versus traditional spelling in first graders' writings: Effects on learning to spell and read. *Research in the Teaching of English, 22,* 281–309.

Cunningham, P. M. (1980). Teaching were, with, what and other "four-letter words." *The Reading Teacher, 34,* 160–163.

Cunningham, P. M. (1995). *Phonics they use: Words for reading and writing* (2nd ed.). New York: HarperCollins.

Cunningham, P. M., & Allington, R. L. (1994). *Classrooms that work: They can all read and write*. New York: HarperCollins.

Cunningham, P. M., & Cunningham, J. W. (1992). Making words: Enhancing the invented spelling-decoding connection. *The Reading Teacher, 46,* 106–107.

Daneman, M. (1991). Individual differences in reading skills. In R. Barr, M. L. Kamil, P. B. Mosenthal, & P. D. Pearson (Eds.), *Handbook of Reading Research* (Vol. 2, pp. 512–538). White Plains, NY: Longman.

Goswami, U., & Bryant, P. (1990). *Phonological skills and learning to read*. East Sussex, U.K.: Erlbaum Associates.

Hunt, L. C., Jr. (1970). The effects of self-selection, interest, and motivation upon independent, instructional, and frustration levels. *Reading Teacher, 24*(2), 146–151, 158.

McCutchen, D., Bell, L. C., France, I. M., & Perfetti, C. A. (1991). Phoneme-specific interference in reading: The tongue-twister effect revisited. *Reading Research Quarterly, 26,* 87–103.

Nicholson, T. (1991). Do children read words better in context or in lists? A classic study revisited. *Journal of Educational Psychology, 83,* 444–450.

Rayner, K., & Pollatsek, A. (1989). *The psychology of reading.* Englewood Cliffs, NJ: Prentice-Hall.

Rumelhart, D. E., & McClelland, J. L. (Eds.). (1986). *Parallel distributed processing: Vol. 1. Psychological and biological models.* Cambridge, MA: MIT Press.

Stanovich, K. E. (1991). Word recognition: Changing perspectives. In R. Barr, M. L. Kamil, P. B. Mosenthal, & P. D. Pearson (Eds.), *Handbook of Reading Research* (Vol. 2, pp. 418–452). White Plains, NY: Longman.

Wylie, R. E., & Durrell, D. D. (1970). Teaching vowels through phonograms. *Elementary English, 47,* 787–791.

Children's Books/Materials Cited

Brown Bear, Brown Bear, What Do You See? by Bill Martin, Holt, Rinehart, & Winston, 1970.

The Cat in the Hat, by Dr. Seuss, Random House, 1957.

In a People House, by Theo. Le Sieg, Random House, 1972.

ADDITIONAL READINGS

These books and chapters review the research on how we learn to read words.

Adams, M. J. (1990). *Beginning to read: Thinking and learning about print.* Cambridge, MA: MIT Press.

Ehri, L. C. (1991). Development of the ability to read words. In R. Barr, M. L. Kamil, P. B. Mosenthal, & P. D. Pearson (Eds.), *Handbook of Reading Research* (Vol. 2, pp. 383–417). White Plains, NY: Longman.

These articles present a balanced view of reading and writing and the role of phonics in that instruction.

Spiegel, D. L. (1993). Balance. *The Reading Teacher, 46,* 38–48.

Stahl, S. A. (1992). Saying the "p" word: Nine guidelines for exemplary phonics instruction. *The Reading Teacher, 45,* 618–625.

These three books have a variety of practical strategies for helping children of all ages develop spelling strategies.

Bolton, F., & Snowball, D. (1994). *Teaching spelling: A practical resource.* Portsmouth, NH: Heinemann.

Bolton, F., & Snowball, D. (1994). *Ideas for spelling.* Portsmouth, NH: Heinemann.

Gentry, J. R., & Gillet, J. W. (1993). *Teaching kids to spell.* Portsmouth, NH: Heinemann.

This article explains how invented spelling plays an important role in writing and how to avoid having children come to think that "anything goes."

Routman, R. (May/June, 1993). The uses and abuses of invented spelling. *Instructor, 102*(9), 36–39.

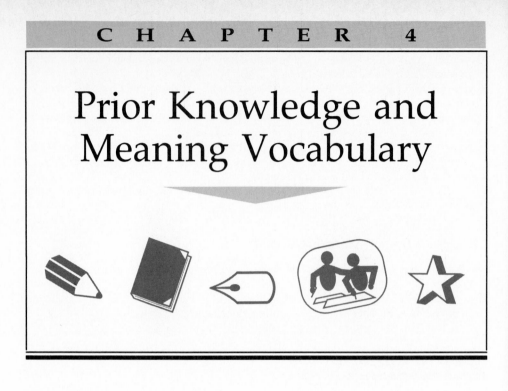

CHAPTER 4

Prior Knowledge and Meaning Vocabulary

LOOKING AHEAD

Reading and writing performance increases and decreases according to students' knowledge of what they are reading or writing about. Students who activate prior knowledge in preparation for literacy tasks have advantages over those who do not. Along with activating prior knowledge, readers and writers access the meanings of countless words. Teachers and students use several techniques to activate prior knowledge and access word meanings.

Imagine trying to read or write a passage when you know practically nothing about its topic. For example, reading a technical manual on subatomic particles such as quarks, baryons, kaons, and leptons would frustrate many people. Writing an essay about these units of physics also would be torturous. Many readers and writers simply don't know enough about subatomic particles to make sense of them. They lack the necessary prior knowledge and meaning vocabulary.

Like all readers and writers, elementary school students require appropriate prior knowledge and meaning vocabulary to make sense during their reading and writing. For instance, a child who chooses a book about the atom might find it too complex. Perhaps the author uses terms like *charm* and *quantum* to explain current atomic theory, although the child might not even know about molecules or electrons. The child's failure to comprehend would be due to a lack of background information rather than a lack of interest or intelligence. Moreover, if the child wanted to write or talk about atoms, he or she probably would need to consult several simplified books and other print and nonprint materials for basic information.

This chapter on prior knowledge and meaning vocabulary first explains their role in literacy. Then it describes how teachers and students put them to work. This chapter contains six key ideas:

1. Prior knowledge activation plays an essential role in reading and writing.
2. Prior knowledge can be activated many ways.
3. Meaningful encounters with words promote vocabulary development.
4. Teachers can use many strategies when presenting and reviewing vocabulary.
5. Students can develop independence in vocabulary learning.
6. Prior knowledge and meaning vocabulary are developed in the content areas across the curriculum.

PRIOR KNOWLEDGE ACTIVATION PLAYS AN ESSENTIAL ROLE IN READING AND WRITING

The first term in the heading of this section, *prior*, is very important. *Prior* adds the nuance of earlier or previous to the meaning of *knowledge*. This modification indicates that learners already have certain knowledge before they encounter something new. Prior knowledge is the intellectual substance someone has when beginning to explore unfamiliar topics. This knowledge is prerequisite to—or at least facilitative of—learners' accomplishments. Thus, prior knowledge is a means to an end; it allows readers and writers to accomplish literacy tasks. Prior knowledge is indispensable for at least three reasons.

Those who view literacy as a constructive process place prior knowledge as a prerequisite for reading and writing. Accoring to this view, authors do not code meanings into texts. Instead, authors produce texts that suggest and constrain messages readers may construct (Goodman, 1984).

One analogy for this constructivist view of literacy compares reading and writing to constructing a new building. Writers are said to be like architects. Writers, like architects, envision structures and produce plans for others to follow. Architects conceptualize and lay out designs for buildings, yet they go only so far. It is builders, not architects or blueprints, who actually perform the construction. Readers, like builders, bring in materials and put them together in response to plans. What underlies the plans writers produce and what makes up the materials readers use when following writers' plans is prior knowledge. Prior knowledge, then, is an indispensable part of literacy.

A second case for the value of prior knowledge involves students' misconceptions about the world (Chinn & Brewer, 1993; Guzzetti, Snyder, Glass, & Gamas, 1993). Especially when they read science content, students' prior knowledge sometimes interferes with learning because their incorrect preconceived ideas override verifiable content. For instance, many young students believe that prehistoric people lived during the time of the dinosaurs, that wild animals are always ferocious, that heavier objects fall faster than lighter ones, that a ball released from a curved track will continue to curve, and that summer is warmer than winter because the earth moves closer to the sun. Students might become confused by or simply discount passages containing alternative concepts. To counteract this situation, students should call up their prior knowledge. Once students are clear about what they believe, they can compare it with conflicting information and form reasoned judgments.

A final reason why activating prior knowledge is important is that it motivates learners. Children naturally want to know about their worlds; they want to make sense of what often seem to be chaotic situations. When exploring something new in a nonthreatening situation and realizing an opportunity to extend their previous understandings, children become motivated. This goes far in promoting literacy.

PRIOR KNOWLEDGE CAN BE ACTIVATED MANY WAYS

Successful teachers and students know that learning occurs best when prior knowledge is activated, so they devote attention to this when preparing to read and write. They call up what they know about a topic before reading a single passage, a section of a book, a whole book, or several books. They activate their prior knowledge before writing a letter, a journal entry, an essay, or a research report. Practically every classroom lesson begins with attention to prior knowledge.

In order to clarify what is already known, teachers often encourage their classes to call up what they can associate with a topic before beginning a unit on it. In other situations small groups of students discuss an author's books before beginning his or her newest one. Pleasure readers stop for a minute before beginning Chapter 10 of their nighttime novel to remind themselves what has happened so far. Distant relatives think about what they want to say before writing friendly letters. At least six general ways to activate prior knowledge before reading or writing are appropriate: brainstorming, graphically representing information, questioning, predicting, writing, and discussing.

Brainstorming

Brainstorming is perhaps the most basic way to call up what is already known about a topic. Learners spontaneously associate concepts, producing connected ideas in a freewheeling manner. Ideas can be jotted down on paper at students' desks, on a chalkboard, or on an overhead transparency. If students were preparing for the topic of Africa, they might call out concepts related to the land, the people, and the plants and animals. Items associated with the land might include jungle, the Sahara, dry grasslands, Congo River, Nile River, and rain forest.

Brainstorming frequently is a first step toward the exploration of a topic or a novel. Once numerous items are listed, teachers and students work to organize them and put them into a productive form. The following strategies accomplish this.

Constructing Graphic Organizers

Graphic organizers show the relations among facts and concepts. In effect, they are maps of a passage or unit of study. Just as maps help travelers navigate unfamiliar territory, graphic organizers help learners move through their reading and writing. Graphic representations of ideas provide stable, clear depictions of what is being studied.

Depicting categories of information about Africa would be useful because the topic is so large that students could get lost easily. As Figure 4.1 shows, one way to graphically represent information about Africa would be with a web. The main topic would be written in the center, and subtopics and facts would radiate outward.

Data charts also are good ways to organize information. As with Figure 4.2, students can fill known cells with information and leave other cells blank. Recording brainstormed facts this way crystallizes what is already known and focuses on what is still needed. Data charts also allow learners to make comparisons.

Figure 4.3 displays a way to categorize knowledge about Africa according to students' levels of understanding. Having columns for what is known and what is not known indicates the state of an individual's or group's prior knowledge.

Questioning

Asking and answering questions before reading and writing probably is the most common prereading and prewriting strategy. Students who produce questions about a topic before exploring it have an advantage over those who simply begin reading and writing. The topic, Africa, could be posted and presented briefly, and students then would have free rein to pose questions about it. Searching their minds and available resources for questions to answer activates students' prior knowledge. After an introduction to the topic of Africa, students might pose questions such as the following:

Who are the Bedouins, the Boers, and the Bantu?

How does Africa's climate compare with North America's?

What animals are found only in Africa?

Why were European countries able to colonize Africa?

What are some common features of traditional African folktales?

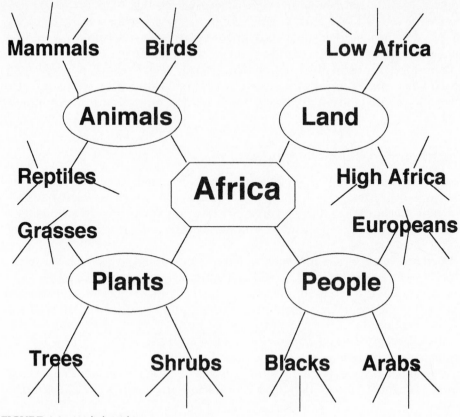

FIGURE 4.1   Web for Africa

Using what they already knew, students first would answer one or more of these questions as completely as possible. Then they would explore whatever resources were avilable to build on what they had.

Predicting

Making predictions about what will happen in a story is a time-honored, student-centered knowledge activation strategy. Teachers might inform students that a story about to be shared is an African folktale and ask what to expect from it. Later in the tale students can predict the characters' next logical moves. Teachers frequently record the predictions while moving through a passage and then have students confirm or disconfirm them.

Predictions about informative passages also are appropriate. When studying African land forms, students might access what they know about Niagara Falls and Mount Whitney to predict what they will learn about Victoria Falls and Mount Kilimanjaro. Using what they know about the Rocky Mountains' effect

Regions	People	Plants	Animals	Land
Desert				
Semiarid				
Tropical				

FIGURE 4.2   Data Chart for Africa

African People

What We Know	What We Don't Know
-- Many types of people live in Africa.	-- Exactly what is an ethnic group?
-- Family ties are very strong.	-- Why is the life expectancy in so many countries so low?
-- Most Africans live in rural villages.	-- What were the ancient African civilizations that were highly developed?

FIGURE 4.3   Graphic Organizer for What We Know and Don't Know about African People

on the U.S. climate, students might predict how the Atlas Mountains affect Africa.

Writing

The prior knowledge activation strategies listed above could include writing, but they do not emphasize it. Brainstorming, graphically representing information, questioning, and predicting use writing mainly to list concepts for future reference. This section emphasizes writing to compose complete coherent thoughts and for learners to engage themselves more fully in their learning.

Students who write from the perspective of a story character before reading about the character go far in activating prior knowledge. Students might assume the role of a young Masai hunter in Kenya and describe his impressions of his first hunt. Then they would read a passage describing such a hunt. Students might write to convince outsiders that they should live in the tropical rain forests of central Africa. Writing brief entries on this topic before investigating it further would access what is already known and prepare students for new learnings.

Discussing

Discussions are especially useful for exploring problematic or controversial issues. Discussions consist of free-flowing exchanges of ideas. Unlike recitations, discussions do not involve the teacher in holding the single correct answer in mind; there is a give-and-take dialogue. Discussions related to Africa might center about the following assertions:

Preserving the environment is Africa's biggest problem.

The colonization of Africa was disastrous.

African stories are more enlightening than American ones.

Nigeria is the most desirable African country to live in.

One way for all students to participate in a discussion is to use an adaptation of the Discussion Web procedure (Alvermann, 1991). As Figure 4.4 shows, a Discussion Web contains a statement or question in the middle, room for pro and con statements on the sides, and space for a conclusion at the bottom. Students fill in the web as much as possible before exploring resources.

Students first should work on the web in pairs, trying to list equal numbers of pro and con statements. After the pairs have had sufficient time brainstorming, exploring resources, and reaching conclusions, combine the pairs to form groups of four. After the groups reach a conclusion, they note the most convincing reason for it. A spokesperson for each group then takes about three minutes to present to the class their conclusion and strongest reason for it. As a follow-up activity, individuals might write their own conclusions to the issue.

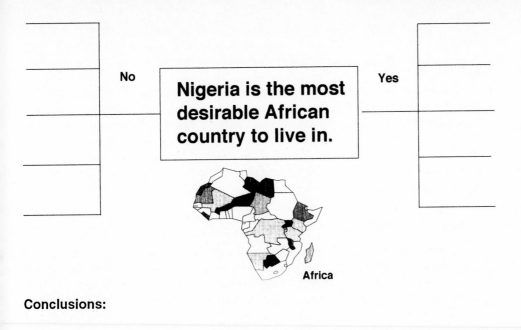

No

Nigeria is the most desirable African country to live in.

Yes

Africa

Conclusions:

FIGURE 4.4   Discussion Web for African Countries

LISTEN, LOOK, AND LEARN

Observe at least one class session where students are encountering new concepts, such as the introduction to a new unit of study or to a new topic within an ongoing unit. Note how students' prior knowledge is activated. What did they do to call up and connect what they already knew with what they were preparing to learn? Ask the teacher how he or she prefers activating prior knowledge. What techniques does the teacher prefer? How do they compare with the ones suggested in this section?

MEANINGFUL ENCOUNTERS WITH WORDS PROMOTE VOCABULARY DEVELOPMENT

Along with activating prior knowledge before reading and writing, literate students understand and use an extensive vocabulary. Many of the difficulties students have with reading and writing can be traced to difficulties they have with particular words. For example, it is difficult to paraphrase the sentence

"His hirple was becoming steadily worse" if you don't know that a hirple is a lame walk, or hobble. It is difficult to describe a story character in any depth when the only descriptive words you know are *nice, mean, good,* and *bad.*

This section on vocabulary instruction presents three teaching principles that underlie the instructional strategies presented in the next section. Use these principles to guide your decisions about students' vocabulary development. The principles are (a) whenever possible provide direct or indirect experience to support word meanings encountered in print, (b) provide many and varied experiences with the vocabulary being studied, and (c) teach vocabulary in conceptually related sets.

Direct or Indirect Experience

Children come to school with thousands of well-developed concepts built through experience. If you have ever been around young children, you know that their first words relate directly to objects and realities they have experienced. *Daddy, mama, milk, cookies, hot, up, bye-bye, fall down,* and *no* are among the first words of many children. The children learned the words by hearing them used while they simultaneously experienced them. Furthermore, young children cannot define the words they know. Rather, they show us that they know *cookies* by pointing to the cookie jar and saying "cookies"; pointing to the television when a commerical for Oreos comes on and saying "cookies"; and pointing to the crumbly mess on the floor, which has obviously been stepped on and rolled in, and saying "cookies"! Later, these same young children will add hundreds and thousands of words to their vocabulary by being in the presence of an object or reality and hearing the words used to describe the object or reality. We refer to the fact of actually being there to experience an object or reality as *direct experience.*

Not all vocabulary terms that young children bring to school with them, however, were learned through direct experience. Many young children have a concept for mountain even if they have never been in the presence of a mountain. Most young children can recognize zebras, elephants, and monkeys even though they may never have been to a zoo, circus, or other place with these animals. Some children who have never sailed or been in a canoe have the concepts represented by these words. How did they learn them? Did someone explain to them what a mountain was? Was the dictionary definition of monkeys read to them? Did some adult attempt to explain or define a canoe?

In most cases, when children have concepts for objects and realities they have never directly experienced, they have seen these objects or realities portrayed on television, in movies, or in picture books. We refer to this experience in which the learner sees the object or reality represented and hears the appropriate words used to describe the object or reality as *indirect experience.* All children in our culture come to school with many terms learned through indirect visual experience via television, movies, and pictures.

Learning by Connection

There is another way in which vocabulary is learned. Sometimes, we tell the meaning of or define a word. If, for example, a young child overheard you use the word *cancel* and asked, "What does cancel mean?" you might respond by telling or explaining: "Cancel means to have something but then decide not to have it anymore. Sometimes, school is canceled because of bad weather." In this case, the child might not have experienced *canceled* directly or indirectly but has only heard it defined and described. We refer to this way of learning words as *learning by connection*. Learners use the connect thinking process to associate known information with the new. Learning word meanings by connection is strengthened when some direct or indirect experiences are added. If, for example, the same child on the following day arrived at a music lesson only to discover that it has been canceled because the music teacher was sick, that child would have had direct experience with the concept of canceled and would be apt to remember what *canceled* means the next time he or she encountered the word.

Concepts that we have never experienced directly or indirectly but have only heard about or read about typically are the least well developed concepts, and the words used to represent them are often forgotten. Thus, our first principle for vocabulary development is as follows: *Whenever possible, provide direct or indirect experience to support word meanings encountered in print.*

FOR CHILDREN WITH SPECIAL NEEDS—DIRECT AND INDIRECT EXPERIENCES

 Children with limited prior knowledge or who speak a language other than the language of instruction often develop their vocabularies best when there is special attention to direct and indirect experiences. These students build a strong base for understanding and producing language when they manipulate and talk about concrete and visual products.

Begin with students' reading materials as the basis for deciding which direct and indirect experiences students might encounter. A sports topic could lead to you or your students bringing in the equipment noted in the passage; Native American folktales might elicit feathers, jewelry, animal figures, or weapons. If actual objects or models of the objects are not possible, bring in representative pictures.

Another technique is for students to produce pictures or displays of concepts presented in their readings. Having students show and describe what they produced allows them to use the new vocabulary in meaningful social situations.

As you and your students move through passages, seize opportunities to develop concepts. If the word *ledge* appears, point out any window or table ledges within sight. If *alley* comes up, ask for students to describe one or compare one with a street outside the school building. *Pierce* can be connected with students' pierced ears, or you might punch a little hole in a piece of paper to demonstrate piercing.

Many and Varied Experiences

We have been explaining vocabulary development as if it were a one-shot affair. This is seldom the case. Most words for which we have well-developed concepts have been encountered on a number of occasions. Some of these encounters have involved direct experience, some visual experience, and some only other words. Think of the concept represented by the word *hot*, for example. Maybe you first experienced the reality of *hot* when you burned your finger touching food that came right from the stove. As you cried out, your mother repeated, "Hot! I've told you never to touch anything hot from the stove. Even when the food is out, it stays hot for a long time. You see how hot things burn. Never, never touch hot things again." This experience and the word *hot* are not likely to be forgotten. But at this point, you have only a limited concept of hot. This concept will be broadened as you hear that word in relationship to many direct experiences—a hot summer day; the soup's too hot, blow on it; Dad got hot when his team fumbled the ball. You may also see a hot desert on television. Your concept of hot will be broadened by hearing the word in relationship to these indirect experiences. You may also broaden your concept of hot by reading that a suspect was arrested with hot goods and by hearing someone comment that their team's center was hot under the basket last night. These encounters with hot further broaden and delineate your concept for this simple word.

You might think of concepts as developing like an onion—one layer at a time. Each experience, whether direct, indirect, or verbal, gives shape and adds layers to developing concepts. This leads us to the second principle that teachers should keep in mind when helping children develop concepts: *Provide many and varied experiences with the vocabulary being studied.*

Conceptually Related Sets of Words

Let us return for a moment to the experience of burning your finger on hot food. Our focus when discussing that encounter was on the experience with the concept of hot. This word *hot*, however, was not the only word being learned. The experience and ensuing conversation were also helping to build concepts for stove ("never touch anything hot from the stove") and burn ("see how hot things burn"). Thus the terms, *hot, stove,* and *burn* were all being developed simultaneously through this one direct experience.

We seldom if ever know a word without knowing other words that relate to the same topic. Take the word *clock*, for example. People who know the word *clock* don't just know it as a piece of machinery for keeping time. People who know the word *clock* also have the concept of where different clocks are generally found (alarm clocks in bedrooms, grandfather clocks in living rooms, clocks in classrooms, clocks in cars, clocks in airports, etc.). Most people know uses for clocks and words associated with time keeping. Some people know the names for different parts of different kinds of clocks.

Because word meanings never exist in isolation but always in relationship to other words that make up the topic, we develop meanings for words while studying topics. Thus, our final principle for vocabulary development is this: *Teach vocabulary in conceptually related sets.*

FOR CHILDREN WITH SPECIAL NEEDS—ENGLISH VOCABULARY

Many children have small English vocabularies because English is their second language. Perhaps the main guideline regarding vocabulary instruction with these students is to honor both languages. Let students know that you respect their first language and that you expect them to learn English too. Display words written both in children's dominant languages and in English. Have students interact with specific terms in their first and second languages. Have students name concepts in their primary language and connect the names with their English counterparts. Accept children's accents, focusing on word meanings more than word pronunciations. Focus on the meaning of what children are communicating more than the form. Correct language miscues gently and quickly or after first attending to the content of children's messages.

When exploring subject matter with second-language children, provide literacy-rich environments. Use visual aids, demonstrations, and experiments that emphasize print. After guest speakers have presented information about a topic under examination, list the ideas they shared.

TEACHERS CAN USE MANY STRATEGIES WHEN PRESENTING AND REVIEWING VOCABULARY

This section presents numerous ways to plan lessons so that children build concepts for particular topics and words. The following lessons can be teacher- or student-directed. They are divided here between presenting and reviewing vocabulary. Presenting vocabulary stresses introducing terms; reviewing vocabulary emphasizes practicing terms already introduced.

Presenting Vocabulary

Presenting vocabulary consists of attempts to teach specific words and their meanings. Teachers and students identify particular words and attach meanings to them through direct, indirect, and verbal means. Presenting vocabulary according to the following strategies provides deep understandings of relatively few words.

COMPARING   Learners constantly compare new objects and realities with old ones in order to make sense of the new. To compare information for students, think of something they already know that is like the unknown thing you wish to teach. Tell students how the two concepts are alike and how they are different.

For instance, if you were comparing the term *magma* for students, you might say something like this:

> Magma is like tar. Do you remember the tar that was put on the roof last year? Magma is like tar because they both are a sticky and slow-moving liquid when they are hot. When they cool, they both become extremely hard. Magma differs from tar because magma consists of melted rocks and is found beneath the earth's crust; tar comes from plants and usually is made by people.

An important point about comparing is that your students must know the concept being used to teach the unfamiliar concept. If students don't know what tar is, the connection presented above will not be effective. Explaining that the British game of rounders is like cricket is not helpful if you don't know the game of cricket.

Once students have initial understandings of concepts, they can form their own comparisons. Children do this all the time on their own; encourage this natural tendency in your classroom. If a passage is about insects, encourage children to compare ones they have experienced. Open the class to allow spontaneous comments about how what is being studied compares with what is already known. Use the graphic organizers presented earlier in this chapter as a way to activate prior knowledge and develop meaning vocabulary. Webs and data charts are especially useful for comparing terms.

WORD DRAMA   Another favorite method for use with elementary students is word drama. When used with a set of related words, the different word dramas, or skits, for the different words promote deep understanding.

The method proceeds in either of two ways, depending in part on the age and sophistication of the students: Either the teacher or small groups of students make up skits. To make up a skit, take a word from a unit and develop a scenario in which students can extemporaneously act and speak to certain specifications so that the meaning of the word being taught becomes clear. The skit is acted out in front of the class and then both the skit and the word being taught are discussed by the class. For instance, imagine that you wish to teach a class of first graders the word *curious*. Consider how acting out the following skit might serve as a good introduction to the word *curious*:

> A girl and a boy pretend to be a boy and his mother walking down a street. Two children pretend to be playing hopscotch at one place along the street. Two more children pretend to be brothers and/or sisters arguing over whose turn it is to help clean up after dinner. As the "mother and son" walk down the street, the boy keeps listening to each conversation, or watching the game, asking questions to try to find out who's winning or what someone said. All this time, the mother keeps trying to get him to come along, for she is in a hurry. The mother and everyone else keep remarking how curious the boy is.

When the actors finish the skit, the teacher asks the audience what *curious* means. Most children have had direct experience being curious even if they did not attach the word *curious* to the experience. The teacher can help children remember the direct experience they have had by asking, "What have you been curious about? Have you ever been in a situation where someone got into trouble for being too curious? Do you know someone who is an exceptionally curious person?" While not providing children with the direct experience of *curious*, these questions help children call up from their experience a situation in which they were curious and connect the term *curious* to that experience.

WORD POSTERS   In this method, students select one word from a unit and illustrate it on a poster. You can have students sign up for words so that no two posters are about the same word, or you can let repetition occur where it will. Both approaches have their advantages and disadvantages. In either case, the students may use whatever textual or human sources are available to determine an understanding of the word chosen and then look for or draw pictures that illustrate the word. In addition, a student may use a short caption for each picture to add to the poster's clarity in representing the word. Word posters are a meaningful homework assignment.

DO IT TOGETHER

In small groups decide how you would present about five terms from this chapter using the suggestions above. Are the terms conducive to comparisons, dramas, or posters? Brainstorm ways to present the terms to students who do not know them already.

Reviewing Vocabulary

The strategies for vocabulary instruction presented so far are good ways to introduce words. But a good introduction to a word is only a beginning. Students typically need frequent encounters with new terms to understand them deeply and remember them.

Wide reading and writing is perhaps the best way to review vocabulary. Students who regularly utilize new terms in the context of interesting and important materials gain control over those terms. Along with providing regular opportunities to read and write, teachers often plan direct review of specific words. The following are some ways to accomplish this.

WORD WALL   Words on the Wall is an appropriate way to structure practice sessions attaching meanings to words. Words are displayed on a wall so that all students can see them. Methods such as forming connections, discussing images, and noting context are used to introduce the words. Once the words are up, review them using the following techniques that emphasize their meanings.

BE A MIND READER   Be a Mind Reader is a good review activity that gives students meaning-oriented clues. For instance, the following clues might be given for one of the key words from a passage on volcanoes.

1. It's one of the words on the wall.
2. Sometimes it is extremely hot.
3. It has two syllables.
4. It is called one name when it is inside the ground and another name when it is on top of the ground.

After giving all of the clues, see how many students guess *magma* when each clue is given. Students who guess the word after the first clue are the mind readers.

CAN THESE TWO GO TOGETHER?   Can These Two Go Together? is another technique useful for reviewing vocabulary. Put two words together in a question that students can answer only with yes or no. You or your students can be the ones to make up the sentences. The responses can be written or stated orally, or hands can be raised for yes and then for no. For instance, the following questions might be asked about words associated with volcanoes:

1. Do igneous rocks come from magma?
2. Are volcanoes made from lava?
3. Would you find igneous rocks around volcanoes?
4. Is magma the same thing as lava?

GROUP AND LABEL   Another way to review the words displayed on the wall is to Group and Label them. The students study the words listed on the wall and categorize them. Category names can be provided before or after the groupings are made. If you provide category names before students group the words, correct answers would be expected. If students are allowed to invent their own categories, correctness is based on the students' explanations for the categories.

WORD BOOKS   Many students make Word Books—vocabulary notebooks in which to record the words they are learning. Students may use a notebook or sheets of paper stapled together and decorated with an interesting cover. Words are then usually entered according to their first letter, but in the sequence in which they are introduced, alphabetical by first letter only. Depending on the age of the children and the type of word being studied, different information can be included with each word. Many teachers like children to write a personal example for each word ("*Frigid* is a February day when the thermometer hits 20°F") as well as a definitional sentence ("*Frigid* means very, very cold"). Although children may consult the dictionary for help, it is best not to let them copy dictionary definitions, since this requires little thought or understanding. In addition to the example and definitional sentence, other information may be included when it is helpful. A phonetic respelling may help students remember the spelling of irregular words. Sometimes, a common opposite is helpful in remembering the word. If the word has a common prefix, root, or suffix that will jog students' memory of its meaning, this can be noted. For some words, pictures, diagrams, or cartoons are helpful reminders.

TWENTY QUESTIONS

1. Establish the subject area and select one word.
2. Have students ask questions that can be answered only by yes or no. (The questions should progress from general to specific, e.g., "Is it an animal?" "Is it four-legged?" "Is it domestic?" "Is it a cat?")
3. If the word is discovered within 20 or fewer questions, points might be given based on how many questions were asked.

CHARADES

1. Divide the class into small groups of four or five.
2. Choose a vocabulary word from a word wall or content-area vocabulary list.
3. Present a word to the first person in the first group.
4. Have the first person act out the word using such devices as "sounds like," "rhymes with," or "first syllable."
5. Keep track of time until the correct response is given, with a maximum time of about 120 seconds to guess the word.
6. A round consists of one person from each group acting out a word. Terminate the game at the end of any complete round.
7. The winner is the team with the lowest cumulative time.

OPTIONAL PROCEDURE: Have one student go to the front and act out a word for the whole class. The student who guesses the word gets to be the next one to act out a word.

REVIEW SENTENCES

1. List key vocabulary on the chalkboard or on chart paper, or use wall words.
2. The teacher calls for sentences containing at least two words from the list to be dictated about the passages.
3. Information may be contributed in any order; the sequence of dictated sentences need not be in the same order as the original presentation of information.
4. Example words:

evaporate	fog
condense	moisture
water vapor	rises
invisible	clouds

Possible dictated senstences:

As water *condenses*, it turns into *fog*.

Clouds are formed by *evaporating* water.

Heat causes water to change from a liquid into an *invisible* gas called *water vapor*.

5. After the dictation of the sentences, the students turn to their texts or notes to check the accuracy of the statements.
6. Inconsistencies and errors are corrected, and important missing information is added.
7. This information may be organized and stored in students' notebooks for future use, if desired.

STUDENTS CAN DEVELOP INDEPENDENCE IN VOCABULARY LEARNING

Children's vocabulary increases at a rate of about 3,000 words per year (Nagy & Herman, 1987). This huge number of words learned during students' elementary school years indicates that presenting individual terms directly and intensively goes only so far. Students clearly learn vocabulary on their own.

Perhaps the best way to promote independent growth in vocabulary is to immerse students in rich natural language. Students who engage meaningful ideas while reading, writing, listening, and speaking aquire new terms. Students who interact regularly with books, guest speakers, field trips, informative media, and each other gain vocabulary that is not available to students in antiseptic environments filled with worksheets and rote work.

Along with immersing students in language-rich environments, teachers can promote students' independence in vocabulary learning by refining their strategies. Unlike the procedures for presenting and reviewing words described above, procedures for teaching independent vocabulary strategies emphasize ways for students to aquire word meanings on their own.

Using Context

Using context refers to determining the meaning of an unfamiliar word by noting the way it is presented in a passage. Passages frequently provide clear, direct explanations of unfamiliar words, so students should learn to pay attention to those explanations. For instance, a passage might contain these sentences: "All rocks that were formed from fiery-hot magma, whether they cooled above or below the earth's surface, are called igneous rocks. Igneous means 'fire-formed.'" Focusing students' attention on these sentences during a comprehension lesson would go far in teaching the meaning of *igneous*.

One caution about relying on context is that is does not always reveal the meanings of unfamiliar words. For example, the sentence presented earlier, "His hirple was becoming steadily worse," does not provide enough information about *hirple* to enable you to form an adequate meaning. You know that hirple is something a male can have, but that is all. You need to inform students during comprehension lessons that some word meanings can be inferred from context and some cannot. The strategy of using context to determine word meanings is best summarized as follows: "When there's a hard word in the sentence, look for other words that tell you more about that word" (Carnine, Kameenui, & Coyle, 1984, p. 198).

Using Morphemes

As described in Chapter 3, morphemes consist of prefixes, roots, and suffixes, which are meaningful parts of words. *Morphemic analysis* consists of identifying prefixes, roots, and suffixes found in derived words; it also consists of identifying meaningful parts found in compound words and contractions. Morphemes differ from syllables because morphemes are portions of meaning, and syllables are portions of sound. For instance, *disagreeable* contains three morphemes (*dis/agree/able*) and five syllables (*dis/a/gree/a/ble*). Analyzing the three morphemes in *disagreeable* helps readers determine its meaning.

Teaching students to note morphemes is a valuable way to remember words and to determine independently the meanings of unfamiliar words. To do this teaching, analyze the parts of derived words as presented in Chapter 3. That is, if *international* is a key word, point out how *inter* and *al* are attached to *nation*, and describe the effect the affixes have on the root.

Another way to teach students to use morphemes to improve their vocabulary knowledge as well as vocabulary learning strategies is to present morphemic word families. A morphemic word family consists of words derived from the same root, or base. For instance, *volcano, volcanoes,* and *volcanic* make up a morphemic word family. *Igneous, ignite,* and *ignition; grass, grassy,* and *grassland;* and *history, historical,* and *historian* represent three morphemic word families. To teach students morphemic word families, take a key word from a passage and write its derived forms in a column. Underline the common word part and tell students its meaning. Present each word in a sentence or short paragraph so that students learn how the meaning of the common element remains constant even though the derived words are different.

Using Spanish-English Cognates

An assumption of many bilingual educators is that learners transfer some of the knowledge and skills of their first language to their second language. In the case of Spanish-speaking students, cognates seem to be one aspect of their language that has much potential for help with English; similarly, English-speaking students can use cognates for help with Spanish. Cognates are words derived from the same earlier form. These are some Spanish-English cognates:

naturalmente	naturally
clima	climate
curioso	curious

novelas   novels
decidir   decide

Instruction in Spanish-English cognates should follow the guidelines for instruction in using morphemes described above. Indeed, a shared morpheme is what makes up a cognate pair. Students who are sensitive to meaningful parts of words can decide whether or not the parts are related across languages. Systematic relationships (e.g., reality–realidad, exactly–exactamente) are especially good candidates for special attention.

Using the Dictionary

Look at the following word and notice how incredibly fast a meaning pops into your mind:

purple

Now think of the definition of *purple*. Are you finding that instead of having a definition of purple memorized, you are having to use your understanding of purple to make one up? In other words, your understanding of words can be used to construct definitions, but your understanding of words is not a set of definitions. In fact, your understanding of words is really a set of nonverbal sensations (images, etc.) and related words. Generally, the only words for which you have memorized definitions stored in your memory are those words that you do not understand. For years, one of us kept trying to understand *existentialism* as a philosophy or school of thought. He never understood it, but then, and to this day, he always remembered the definition: "The philosophy that existence precedes essence." Perhaps had he ever come to understand *existentialism*, he would have forgotten that definition. Having students memorize definitions of words as a means of building their meaning vocabularies cannot succeed because understanding a word means that you do *not* have a definition stored in memory for it. Reading dictionary definitions can *remind* us of meanings we already understand or can refine or add precision to meanings we already have. Expecting a definition to provide the package of related words necessary to understanding a word meaning to the point of usefulness is like expecting a photograph to be an adequate substitute for getting to know someone.

Think back to your elementary school days. Do you remember looking up words and copying their definitions? If the word had several definitions (as most words do), which one did you copy? The first one? The shortest one? What did you do if the dictionary definition contained a word for which you didn't know the meaning? Most of us have had the experience of looking up words, copying the definition (first or shortest), and then memorizing it for a test regardless of whether we understood it. As soon as the test was over, however, most of the really unfamiliar words were forgotten. Those words for which you already had some associations were remembered, however, and their meanings were probably broadened by the experience of checking the dictionary definition. That brings us to our dictionary principle: *Have students use the dictionary to check or add to a word's meaning. Do not allow students to copy definitions.*

There are a variety of ways to promote *active* use of the dictionary that help students broaden their concepts and also teach students what a valuable resource the dictionary is. Students should learn to turn to the dictionary to find out what an unfamiliar word on the scavenger hunt list is. Often, they will find a picture of the unfamiliar object that can be traced or drawn. In Chapter 14, Ms. Maverick leads her students through a lesson in which they try to guess the meaning of an unfamiliar word based on the context surrounding that word. The final step in this lesson is for the students to check the appropriate dictionary definition to see how close their definition based on context matches that in the dictionary.

Students Selecting Key Words

Have students preview materials to be read with the purpose of listing two words they consider important and relatively unknown. Help students to define *important* as occurring many times in the material to be read. Help them also to consider whether the word is unknown not by their ability or inability to pronounce it but by their "I wonder what that word means" reaction.

Students Teaching Key Words

After the teacher has directed the students' lessons, students should know that we can build meanings for words by providing direct experience, indirect experience, or comparison. Students can work individually or in pairs to prepare their own lessons, which might include bringing in a model; finding a picture, including films, filmstrips, and slides; creating a skit for a word; and creating an analogy. Students will need some initial help with this work, but as time goes on, they become more independent. As students teach their lessons, the teacher should remind them that they can perform some of these activities whenever they meet a word for which they do not have meaning. "Where could I find a picture? I wonder if there is one in my text" and "Is this like anything I already know?" are models for how students should think when faced with an unknown, important word.

Moving toward Independence

In order to maximize student involvement in their vocabulary learning, have them take stock of their strategy use at various intervals. Prompt them to suggest ways to learn terms being encountered. You might ask, "What are some things you might do to understand and remember the new words we will meet today?" At other times, simply remind them of vocabulary learning strategies: "Remember what you know about using word parts when you come across new words in this unit." When making comparisons, be sure to get your class in on the act: "Today, we will continue reading about circuits and how electrons move only through a complete circuit. As you read, try to think of how open and closed circuits are a lot like something you already know. When you have finished, we will share all our ideas for what circuits are like." When students finish reading, accept all reasonable analogies, helping students to state how their comparisons are similar to and different from the new concept. As the teacher, you can of course share your own analogy with students, but be sure not to give them the idea that there is only one right comparison.

LISTEN, LOOK, AND LEARN

 As you observe a class, note how vocabulary is treated. Record how terms are presented, how they are reviewed, and how student independence with vocabulary is fostered. Compare your notes with others in class and produce generalizations about daily classroom vocabulary instruction. Evaluate the common practices that you have observed.

PRIOR KNOWLEDGE AND MEANING VOCABULARY ARE DEVELOPED IN THE CONTENT AREAS ACROSS THE CURRICULUM

Vocabulary instruction should be going on all day, every day in the elementary classroom. Field trips that take children out of the classroom and guests and objects brought into the classroom provide direct experiences for concept development. Teachers make maximum use of these opportunities by preparing the children ahead of time for what they will experience and by leading them through discussions and other language-oriented activities after the experience. This helps children sort through the information learned and store it away with other information for later use.

Reading to children and involving children in literature response activities following reading are vocabulary development activities. Picture books help children learn rich concepts for unfamiliar words and information about various topics. The content of reading across the curriculum is not just textbooks; the content includes informational books and periodicals also. Reading across the curriculum helps children understand and better organize the world in which they live; informational books provide a wonderful way to do that. They are often more interesting than textbooks because the authors of children's informational books know that their products will be purchased and read by children only if the children enjoy them.

Having students learn what a passage says about terms such as *magma, lava, igneous rocks,* and *volcanoes* is valuable. But learning word meanings from books and other printed materials is a verbal experience, so teaching these terms through direct and indirect means also is appropriate. For instance, you could bring in examples of igneous rocks, watch a movie about volcanoes, and demonstrate volcanic action.

Films and filmstrips are another source that many teachers use to help children develop concepts for things that they have not directly experienced. Even the pervasive "show and tell" period presents concept development opportunities. Questions related to the objects brought to share such as "What is this object made of?" "Is this object more than one foot long?" "Where would we find these objects?'' and "Can anyone think of other objects that are usually this color?'' help focus the children's attention on vocabulary development as it relates to the objects the children are directly experiencing. Group discussions and writing foster vocabulary development as children clarify concepts by talking and writing about them. Science and social studies should have as their primary goal helping children develop rich concepts for events, places, people, and phenomena.

All the instructional strategies presented so far in this chapter apply to the prior knowledge and vocabulary emphasized across the curriculum. Students graphically represent information, predict, write, experience concepts directly, produce word posters, play charades, and use morphemes with terms from the content areas. What follows are two additional teaching suggestions for prior knowledge and meaning vocabulary development in the content areas across the curriculum.

Scavenger Hunts

Scavenger hunts are a way of gathering objects and pictures to represent concepts that need developing (Vaughn, Crawley, & Mountain, 1979). Imagine that you are about to begin a science unit on weather. You look through the passages your students are going to read; preview films, filmstrips, and other teaching aids; and make a list of the unfamiliar vocabulary you will teach as you increase their store of information on the topic of weather. Your list includes *evaporation, condensation, cirrus clouds, cumulus clouds, stratus clouds, precipitation, temperature, humidity, barometer, thermometer, cyclone, tornado, hurricane, meterorologist, wind vane, rain gauge,* and a variety of other words. Of these words, some can be represented by pictures (indirect experience) and objects (direct experience). Other words such as *evaporation, condensation, precipitation, temperature,* and *humidity* cannot be represented directly or indirectly. Take all of the words on your list that can be represented by pictures or objects—*cirrus clouds, cumulus clouds, stratus clouds, barometer, thermometer, cyclone, tornado, hurricane, meteorologist, wind vane,* and *rain gauge*—and add to these terms some familiar, picturable words related to the topic of weather such as *snow, rain, ice, lightning, fog, frost,* and *rainbow* until you have a list of 20 to 25 picturable words that relate to the topic of weather. You now have your list of things for which your students will scavenge.

Assign your students to teams of four or five and provide each team with the list. Explain that on _____ (a date a week or two from when the list is provided) the teams are to bring a picture and/or object representing as many of the items on the list as they can find. To the students' inevitable question, "How can I bring a hurricane?'' your response will be, "You can bring a *picture* of a hurricane.'' Two points are given for each object and one point for each picture. Pictures can be illustrations, photographs, tracings, or drawings, as long as they actually represent the word. Allow the team time to discuss what the different words mean and who might be able to find an object and/or picture representing each. If some of the words are truly unfamiliar to your students, a question such as "What's a rain gauge?'' may arise. Depending on the maturity of your students and on whether this is their first or their tenth scavenger hunt, you may choose to respond by explaining what each word means or by saying, "I guess you will have to look it up somewhere. It's hard to find a picture or object that represents something if you don't know what that something is." This response should send your teams to their dictionaries or other reference sources.

Allow the teams to meet several times during the time they are scavenging. They should check things off the list as pictures and objects are found. Do not, however, allow any pictures or objects to come to school before the appointed date. Teams should be cautioned to keep secret what they find and where they found it. On the appointed day, each team will assemble and show their pictures and objects. The teacher will total the points for each team (two for each object, one for each picture—only one picture and object per word per team). The team with the most points is the winner. Since winners like to get a prize, what better prize than being allowed to create the bulletin board? What bulletin board? The *weather* bulletin board! You would not want to let all of those pictures go to waste. The winning team, therefore, should design the bulletin board so that each word is printed in large letters and the different pictures that represent it are displayed with the word. (A word without any pictures might be displayed by itself—a challenge to someone to find a picture.) What about the objects? Any objects that are valuable, dangerous, or live must be taken back home. But the rest can be displayed on the table you place underneath the bulletin board. Also, you will need to say in big bold letters somewhere: WEATHER BULLETIN BOARD CREATED BY WINNERS OF WEATHER SCAVENGER HUNT, and include a list of the winner's names.

You are now ready to begin your unit on weather. More important, your students are now ready. Having spent the previous week or two collecting objects and pictures related to the topic of weather has increased their general knowledge of that topic (perhaps they talked to the local meteorologist, or watched the weather report, or even read an intriguing section of the reference book from which they traced their picture of cirrus clouds) and has greatly increased their interest in the topic of weather. You also have a marvelous bulletin board with representations of the portion of your meaning vocabulary words that can be represented by objects and pictures. Some of your meaning vocabulary that could not be directly or indirectly represented can be easily understood with reference to the pictures and objects: *precipitation* is a form of moisture such as *rain* or *snow; temperature* is measured with *thermometers*.

Now that the children have enjoyed their first scavenger hunt and have begun their actual study of weather, what next? Perhaps you plan to study Mexico soon, and your Mexico topic includes words such as *Copper Canyon, pyramids,* and *desert;* maybe you are developing a unit on animals, and words such as *polar bears, cobras,* and *gerbils* are part of it. The children will certainly be ready for another scavenger hunt. This time, having learned how to hunt for objects and pictures, how to find out what unfamiliar words mean, and how to create a bulletin board, they will be much more ready to get right to work on locating these representations.

Vocabulary scavenger hunts are a highly recommended concept development strategy for a variety of reasons:

1. The principle of providing direct and indirect experience with unfamiliar words is adhered to as the students collect objects and pictures.

2. The principle of providing for a variety of different experiences is adhered to, since there will be many different pictures and/or objects representing each word and since the students will be talking about them with other team members and resource people as they look for them.

3. The principle of developing word meanings as they relate to topics is adhered to, since the objects and pictures being sought all relate to the same topic.

4. Students become involved and interested in the topic to be studied.

5. Students sharpen their reference skills.

6. Once the teacher makes the list, the students are collecting the representations and making the bulletin board. Thus the students, not the teacher, are doing most of the work.

List, Group, and Label

List, Group, and Label lessons (Taba, 1967) help children see how words can belong in a variety of groups. A teacher begins a List, Group, and Label lesson by asking students to list all of the words they think of when they think of a certain topic (weather, Mexico, or animals, for example). The teacher records on a chart or on the board the words the children list. When a substantial list has been generated, the children are asked to think of some words that "seem to go together in some way." Children thus form groups of words (younger children tell words in their groups—older children write words in their groups). As different children volunteer what is included in their group, they are asked, "Why did you put those words together?" and "What would you call or label that group?" List, Group, and Label lessons can be done as "unit openers" to diagnose how much children know about a topic and to activate prior knowledge. They can also be used as a culminating activity to evaluate how much children have learned.

FOR CHILDREN WITH SPECIAL NEEDS—KWL

 KWL is a flexible and popular way to guide students' thinking toward textual information (Ogle, 1986; Carr & Ogle, 1987). It focuses attention on the meanings of words as well as passages, working especially well with informational text. The letters of KWL stand for what we *K*now, what we *W*ant to find out, and what we have *L*earned.

Imagine that your class is about to study our nation's capital, Washington, D.C. You might begin the lesson by pointing out Washington, D.C., on a map and asking if any students have been there. Share some pictures and picture books of this city. To begin KWL, present a chart such as the following:

Washington, D.C.

What we know	What we want to find out	What we have learned

The students brainstorm what they know about Washington, D.C., and the teacher writes the responses in the first column. When the children have brainstormed their prior knowledge, the chart might look like this:

Washington, D.C.

What we know	What we want to find out	What we have learned
capital		
White House		
president lives there		
lots of drugs		
cherry blossoms in spring		
cold in winter		
near Virginia		
near Maryland		

Next, the teacher would direct the students' attention to the second column and ask them what they would like to find out about Washington, D.C. Their questions would be listed in the second column:

Washington, D.C.

What we know	What we want to find out	What we have learned
capital	How old is it?	
White House	How big is the White House?	
president lives there	What else is in D.C.?	
lots of drugs	Where is the CIA?	
cherry blossoms in spring	What kind of government does D.C. have?	
cold in winter	Why is it not a state?	
near Virginia	How many people live there?	
near Maryland	What do the people do who aren't in the government?	

Once the questions are listed, students read in order to see which of their questions can be answered and to find other information they think is important. After reading, the teacher begins by determining which of the questions were answered and then leads the students to add other interesting facts. This information is recorded in the third column. All members of the class are encouraged to contribute to this group task; no one looks back at the book until all initial responses are shared. Disputed or unclear information is marked with question marks.

After recording this first draft of what the class has learned, the children go back to the text to clarify, prove, or fill in gaps. Have the children read the relevant parts aloud and help them explain their thinking. When the information on the chart is complete and accurate, note the list of vocabulary terms that students now have access to. Point out how much was learned and how efficiently the chart helped record it. Inevitably, there are questions that were not answered in the reading, and a natural follow-up to this lesson is to help the children use additional resources to locate the answers to these questions.

THE THEORY AND RESEARCH BASE FOR PRIOR KNOWLEDGE ACTIVATION AND MEANING VOCABULARY INSTRUCTION

For quite some time educational researchers have appreciated the fact that readers and writers rely on prior knowledge (Herbart, 1898) and meaning vocabulary (Thorndike, 1921). The 1980s and early 1990s research on these topics worked to specify how students use prior knowledge and meaning vocabulary and how to promote this practice. Some research focused on writing (DeGroff, 1987), but most was devoted to reading comprehension.

Research into prior knowledge continues to date (e.g., Pressley, Wood, & Woloshyn, 1992), but the best general explanation of how it facilitates reading comprehension still is the 1984 review of schema theory by Anderson and Pearson. In this review prior knowledge is said to provide a schema, which is a framework or knowledge structure that facilitates thinking. For instance, readers familiar with sports can predict that a passage about a baseball game will have nine players on each side, the players will field different positions, some will be better than others, one team will win and another will lose, and so on.

Prior knowledge also allows readers to assimilate information readily. Readers map ideas from a text onto preexisting ideas. Sports-minded readers can readily understand and remember the progress of a baseball game because they have a general idea of what should happen.

In addition, prior knowledge helps readers perform inferential elaboration; it helps readers "fill in the blanks" left by authors. Authors assume their readers share common understandings, so they do not thoroughly explain everything in a passage. For instance, baseball fans have an advantage understanding snide comments about designated hitters' fielding abilities because they know that these players are expected only to bat and not to field.

The role of prior knowledge explained through schema theory does not account for the entire reading comprehension process (Carver, 1992; Sadoski, Paivio, & Goetz, 1991). For instance, schema theory does not explain readers' images nor readers' seemingly effortless apprehension of ideas contained in easy-to-read materials. But it explains enough to warrant educators' attention to prior knowledge.

Stahl and his colleagues (Stahl, Jacobson, Davis, & Davis, 1989; Stahl, Hare, Sinatra, & Gregory, 1991) investigated the roles prior knowledge and meaning vocabulary play in passage comprehension. These studies showed that students' knowledge of a passage's topic affected comprehension differently than did their knowledge of a passage's vocabulary. Prior knowledge influenced understanding the gist of a passage, whereas vocabulary knowledge affected comprehending details. These studies showed that teachers should attend to both prior knowledge and meaning vocabulary because they play independent roles in reading comprehension.

Three excellent research reviews covering a range of vocabulary acquisition issues are by Baumann and Kameenui (1991), Beck and McKeown (1991), and Graves (1986). These reviews clarify distinctions between teaching specific words and teaching students how to learn words independently. Another point to remember from these reviews is that vocabulary instruction should emphasize motivational aspects. Teachers should help students develop a sense of curiosity about words, an appreciation for their nuances of meaning, and an enjoyment and satisfaction in their wise use.

LOOKING BACK

Reading and writing performance is strongly affected by students' knowledge of what they are reading and writing about. Thus, prior knowledge activation is a crucial part of preparing to read and write, and it can be accomplished many ways. Along with activating prior knowledge, students require access to word meanings when reading and writing. This access also can be accomplished many ways. Six key ideas were developed in this chapter:

1. Prior knowledge activation plays an essential role in reading and writing.
2. Prior knowledge can be activated many ways.
3. Meaningful encounters with words promote vocabulary development.
4. Teachers can use many strategies when presenting and reviewing vocabulary.
5. Students can develop independence in vocabulary learning.
6. Prior knowledge and meaning vocabulary are developed in the content areas across the curriculum.

ADD TO YOUR JOURNAL

State the role prior knowledge activation plays in reading and writing. Can you give specific personal examples of how activating your prior knowledge helped you in the past to understand and remember particular materials? Describe the techniques you remember your best teachers using to activate your prior knowledge in preparation for new learning. What did they do that was similar to or different from the techniques presented here?

List about three words that you have learned in the past few months. Distinguish between words that you were taught and ones that you learned entirely on your own. Describe the situations where you encountered the words, how you came to understand them, and why you remembered their meaning.

REFERENCES

Alvermann, D. E. (1991). The discussion web: A graphic aid for learning across the curriculum. *The Reading Teacher, 45,* 92–99.

Anderson, R. C., & Pearson, P. D. (1984). A schema-theoretic view of basic processes in reading comprehension. In P. D. Pearson (Ed.), *Handbook of reading research* (pp. 255–291). New York: Longman.

Baumann, J. F., & Kameenui, E. J. (1991). Research on vocabulary instruction: Ode to Voltaire. In J. Flood, J. M. Jensen, D. Lapp, & J. R. Squire (Eds.), *Handbook of research on teaching the English language arts* (pp. 604–632). New York: Macmillan.

Beck, I., & McKeown, M. (1991). Conditions of vocabulary acquisition. In R. Barr, M. L. Kamil, P. B. Mosenthal, & P. D. Pearson (Eds.), *Handbook of reading research* (Vol. 2, pp. 789–814). White Plains, NY: Longman.

Carnine, D., Kameenui, E., & Coyle, G. (1984). Utilization of contextual information in determining the meanings of unfamiliar words in context. *Reading Research Quarterly, 19,* 188–204.

Carr, E., & Ogle, D. (1987). K-W-L plus: A strategy for comprehension and summarization. *Journal of Reading, 30,* 626–631.

Carver, R. P. (1992). Commentary: Effect of prediction activities, prior knowledge, and text type upon amount comprehended: Using rauding theory to critique schema theory research. *Reading Research Quarterly, 27,* 164–174.

Chinn, C. A., & Brewer, W. F. (1993). The role of anomalous data in knowledge acquisition: A theoretical framework and implications for science instruction. *Review of Educational Research, 63,* 1–50.

DeGroff, L. (1987). The influence of prior knowledge on writing, conferencing, and revising. *Elementary School Journal, 88,* 105–118.

Goodman, K. S. (1984). Unity in reading. In A. C. Purves & O. Niles (Eds.), *Becoming readers in a complex society* (Eighty-third Yearbook of the National Society for the Study of Education) (pp. 79–114). Chicago: National Society for the Study of Education.

Graves, M. (1986). Vocabulary learning and instruction. In E. Z. Rothkoph (Ed.), *Review of research in education* (Vol. 13, pp. 49–90). Washington, DC: American Educational Research Association.

Guzzetti, B. J., Snyder, T. E., Glass, G. V., & Gamas, W. S. (1993). Promoting conceptual change in science: A comparative meta-analysis of instructional interventions from reading education and science education. *Reading Research Quarterly, 28,* 116–161.

Herbart, J. (B. C. Mulliner, Ed. and Trans.). (1898). *The application of psychology to the science of education.* London: Swan Sonnenschein.

Moore, D. W., Moore, S. A., Cunningham, P. M., & Cunningham, J. W. (1994). *Developing readers and writers in the content areas, K–12* (2nd ed.). White Plains, NY: Longman.

Nagy, W. E., & Herman, P. A. (1987). Depth and breadth of vocabulary knowledge: Implications for acquisition and instruction. In M. G. McKeown & M. E. Curtis (Eds.), *The nature of vocabulary acquisition* (pp. 19–35). Hillsdale, NJ: Erlbaum.

Ogle, D. (1986). K-W-L: A teaching model that develops active reading of expository text. *The Reading Teacher, 39,* 564–570.

Pressley, M., Wood, E., & Woloshyn, V. E. (1992). Encouraging mindful use of prior knowledge: Attempting to construct explanatory answers facilitates learning. *Educational Psychologist, 27,* 91–109.

Sadoski, M., Paivio, A., & Goetz, E. T. (1991). Commentary: A critique of schema theory in reading and a dual encoding alternative. *Reading Research Quarterly, 26,* 463–484.

Stahl, S. A., Hare, V. C., Sinatra, R., & Gregory, J. F. (1991). Defining the role of prior knowledge and vocabulary in reading comprehension: The retiring of number 41. *Journal of Reading Behavior, 23,* 487–508.

Stahl, S. A., Jacobson, M. G., Davis, C. E., & Davis, R. L. (1989). Prior knowledge and difficult vocabulary in the comprehension of unfamiliar text. *Reading Research Quarterly, 24,* 27–43.

Taba, H. (1967). *Teachers' handbook for elementary social studies.* Palo Alto, CA: Addison-Wesley.

Thorndike, E. L. (1921). *The teacher's word book.* New York: Columbia University, Teachers College.

Vaughn, S., Crawley, S., & Mountain, L. A. (1979). A multiple-modality approach to word study: Vocabulary scavenger hunts. *The Reading Teacher, 32,* 434–437.

ADDITIONAL READINGS

The following is a straightforward explanation of how teachers can capitalize on the effects of prior knowledge.

Wood, K. D. (1988). The influence of prior knowledge on understanding. *Middle School Journal, 19,* 11–13.

Attention to unfamiliar words before reading helps activate prior knowledge, which this article details.

Wood, K. D., & Robinson, N. (1983). Vocabulary, language, and prediction: A prereading strategy. *The Reading Teacher, 36,* 392–395.

This report offers a strong case for wide reading as one of the best ways to promote vocabulary.

Anderson, R. C., & Nagy, W. E. (1993). *The vocabulary conundrum* (Tech. Rep. No. 570). Urbana-Champaign, IL: University of Illinois, Center for the Study of Reading.

These two articles describe how to concentrate on words within a holistic instructional approach.

Blachowicz, C. L. Z., & Lee, J. J. (1991). Vocabulary development in the whole literacy classroom. *The Reading Teacher, 45,* 188–195.

Iwicki, A. L. (1992). Vocabulary connections. *The Reading Teacher, 45,* 736.

The following articles offer perspective and strategies for teaching students how to learn words independently.

Hillerich, R. L. (1989). Developing independence in word meaning. *Teaching PreK–8, 20,* 26–28.

White, T., Sowell, J., & Yanagihara, A. (1989). Teaching elementary students to use word-part clues. *The Reading Teacher, 43,* 302–308.

Buikema, J. L., & Graves, M. F. (1993). Teaching students to use context cues to infer word meanings. *Journal of Reading, 36,* 450–457.

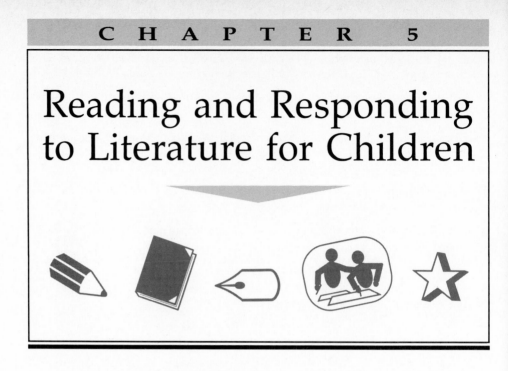

CHAPTER 5

Reading and Responding to Literature for Children

LOOKING AHEAD

Countless reading materials are available for children in libraries and bookstores and through the mail. These materials play a crucial role in promoting reading development. Children who have access to books and magazines have an advantage over children who are deprived of these materials. When children read literature, they discover and apply reading strategies. Children also become accustomed to whole stories; they encounter books that are divided into chapters. Teachers can do much to help students enjoy and benefit from literature for children. Teachers can provide students time and motivation to read interesting materials and develop students' responses to the materials.

In the galaxy of literature, a world of books exists for children. These books contain some of the very best writing currently being produced. Children may read a variety of materials, including the books and magazines of adults, but the field labeled "children's literature" consists of books that are expressly written for children and that achieve literary and artistic excellence. Various awards are presented to the authors and illustrators of children's literature, encouraging them to strive for this excellence. These awards include the John Newbery Medal, the Randolph Caldecott Medal, the National Book Award, and the Boston Globe–Horn Book Award. However, not all literature for children consists of books that have been in contention for any of these awards. Most of you probably grew up reading the Nancy Drew or Hardy Boys series books. Although they are not "quality" books as defined by the award givers and book reviewers, they are nonetheless books that children read and enjoy and search out. Because of the existence and popularity of these types of books, we have purposely used the terms *literature for children* and *children's books* in this chapter. We are discussing classroom uses of books that children can and will read, as well as books judged by adults to be quality pieces. We subscribe to the idea that children need a balanced literary diet. After all, what was the last piece of literature you read? Was it a classic or was it the latest best-seller?

Children's tastes in literature are varied, and fortunately, the world of literature for children is broad and encompassing. Not everyone realizes how broad and encompassing this world is; in fact, there are entire books written about literature for children that detail the varied genres, describe the books within those genres, describe the authors and illustrators of those books, and provide ways to involve children with literature. In this chapter we introduce the world of children's literature and ways to use this literature. You will encounter six key ideas:

1. A diverse world of literature exists for children.
2. Engaging children with literature promotes many outcomes.
3. Teachers can vary in their classroom use of literature.
4. Immersing children in literature is accomplished in many ways.
5. Children can respond to literature in a variety of ways.
6. Literature enriches the content areas across the curriculum.

A DIVERSE WORLD OF LITERATURE EXISTS FOR CHILDREN

The world of children's literature reflects the world in which we live. There are books about all kinds of people, places, and topics. Gone are the days when children's books were filled with white, middle-class characters living carefree existences. Today's books for children reflect the multicultural, diverse society in which we live. Through books, children learn more about their own daily world and they develop sensitivity to the different cultures of all the children in their classrooms. All teachers should provide rich and varied literature experiences for children. The additional readings at the end of this chapter include some excellent resources for children's books that reflect the diverse, multicultural society in which we live.

There are children's books for all ages and interests. The genres of books include poetry, folk literature, fantasy, modern and historical fiction, alphabet and counting books, wordless books, mystery, biography, and informational books. Three of these literature types, folk literature, fantasy, and informational books, might not be familiar to everyone by the title we have used. Because of this, we describe these three very carefully. At the same time, by seeing how broad these three genres are, you can see that all genres might be broader than some would suspect.

Folk literature encompasses fairy tales, folktales, epics, myths, and fables. Although modern fairy tales such as *Dove Isabeau* and *The Rainbabies** may be written, we normally think of fairy tales as part of folk literature. Folk literature consists of tales for which there is no identifiable single author or for whom authorship is in doubt because the stories have been in existence for so long. Cinderella stories are common tales in all culture groups, and many of us grew up with tales of the "Threes": pigs, goats, and bears. These stories were first part of the oral tradition and written down only much later. For this reason, the so-called modern fairy tales are included in the genre known as fantasy.

Fantasy is also a broad genre. It includes both classic fantasies (such as *Alice's Adventures in Wonderland* and *Charlotte's Web*) and modern ones (such as *Jumanji, Polar Express,* and *Tuesday*) as well as science fiction and science fantasy. The distinction between the last two may be somewhat blurry. But essentially, science fiction books contain scientific facts that have the possibility of being extrapolated from reality; science fantasy books involve the supernatural or are so futuristic that currently known scientific facts do not allow the extrapolation that occurs. A good example of science fiction is *This Time of Darkness*, whereas *A Wrinkle in Time* embodies the essence of science fantasies.

Another type of book is the *informational book.* This category contains factual materials for science, social studies, cooking, and other content areas, as well as "concept books" for the very young dealing with the alphabet or relationships of time, space, and amount (such as *The Handmade Alphabet, Exactly the Opposite,* and *Of Colors and Things*). When we think of informational books, often an image of dull, pedantic, sterile writing comes to mind. If that ever were characteristic of informational books, it certainly is no longer. The illustrations and photographs of many current informational books enrich the text and are high quality; the writing is lively and entertaining.

Informational books explain something to children or teach them how to do something. For example, there are many children's cookbooks, such as *Kitchen Fun for Kids: Healthy Recipes and Nutrition Facts for 7- to 12-year-old Cooks.* Other books explain science concepts to children in a clear yet interesting way, with books such as *Robots: Your High-Tech World; Coral Reef; The Magic School Bus on the Ocean Floor; Ouch! A Book about Cuts, Scratches, and Scrapes;* and *Why Do Volcanoes Erupt: Questions about Our Unique Planet.* . . . Children learn about life in prehistoric times with *Dinosaur Valley* and learn how to make many fun and interesting objects in *Nature Crafts* and *Papier-Mache Project Book.* There are also books such as *Bears* that describe the life cycle of a particular species of animal.

Rather than describe other genres of literature for children, the remainder of this chapter focuses on the uses of books in classrooms. Additional information about the contents of literature for children and guidelines for book selection are contained in the Additional Readings references at the end of this chapter.

---

* References for these children's books and others in this chapter are located at the end of the chapter.

ENGAGING CHILDREN WITH LITERATURE PROMOTES MANY OUTCOMES

Involving children with literature from the genres just described as well as other genres is essential to your reading program because it promotes many outcomes. In this section we will describe how literature promotes three outcomes: knowledge of the world, positive feelings, and strategies.

Reading to Develop Knowledge of the World

Literature for children expands and deepens their knowledge of the world. It allows children to learn about people, events, and locations that are beyond the possibility of face-to-face contact. Literature expands children's horizons by presenting to them people such as Marco Polo and Geronimo, events such as the Crusades and the first landing on the moon, and locations such as the Amazon and the North Pole. Young readers can be transported to other times and other places and learn about new things. They can learn about life on the American prairie during the late 1800s in *Sarah, Plain and Tall*, and they can travel to America with a Japanese immigrant in *Grandfather's Journey*. Additionally, children can learn that they are not alone in their wishes, successes, and rejections. The insights gained about characters' dilemmas and solutions to dilemmas give children perspectives that allow them to broaden their understanding of human relationships.

Literature not only expands children's knowledge of the world, but it also deepens that knowledge. When children emotionally identify with story characters, they can experience the events more deeply than if they only read about the events in a textbook. Children who read *Roll of Thunder, Hear My Cry* learn well what life was like for rural blacks in the South during the Depression. This learning takes hold and becomes meaningful because readers share Cassie's anger at her and her family's persecution; readers do not simply read a catalog of problems that black people in those circumstances had to face. As readers enter into the world suggested by an author, they strip away objective detachment and participate emotionally in that world. Such participation deepens understandings of what they read.

Reading literature to develop knowledge of the world is important because such knowledge is a vital component of the reading comprehension process. In addition, teaching students knowledge of the world is a primary goal during subject-matter instruction.

Reading to Develop Positive Feelings

One of the key ideas presented in Chapter 1 was that *reading is feeling*. This means that students respond emotionally to reading materials. This idea is important to remember because the intellectual side of reading frequently is emphasized far beyond the feeling side; yet both sides deserve attention. Literature develops positive feelings by eliciting aesthetic experiences and by promoting attitudes.

When readers become deeply absorbed in books' ideas as well as in the manner by which those ideas are presented, reading becomes an aesthetic experience. The ideas expressed in a book and the method of expression are equally important during aesthetic reading. This type of reading has a liberating effect because readers transcend their perceptions of individual aspects of a literary work and perceive all aspects in a synthesis of senses, understandings, and feelings. For instance, countless children have read or listened to *The Elephant's Child* primarily at the aesthetic level. They become absorbed by the language cadence and rhythm, the imagery, and their identification with the young elephant who runs away to "the great grey-green, greasy Limpopo River." Young children generally appreciate this story for its exquisite writing as much as for its message about curiosity.

Another way to explain the nature of reading as an aesthetic experience is to point out that aesthetic reading requires an encounter with the literary work itself (Rosenblatt, 1983). In practical reading, an exact paraphrase of a passage can be as useful and have as much impact as the original. Reading an exact paraphrase of a biology textbook has the same effect as reading the original. However, in aesthetic reading the actual literary work needs to be encountered. For example, consider the following poem by Langston Hughes (1932):

APRIL RAIN SONG

Let the rain kiss you.
Let the rain beat upon your head with silver liquid drops.
Let the rain sing you a lullaby.

The rain makes still pools on the sidewalk.
The rain makes running pools in the gutter.
The rain plays a little sleep-song on our roof at night—

And I love the rain.

Any attempt to paraphrase this poem would destroy its essence because the delicacy of the language would be lost. Aesthetic reading involves qualities of language beyond the direct, specific meanings denoted by words.

Reading literature also promotes attitudes toward reading. The Dr. Seuss books, *Winnie-the-Pooh,* and *Frog and Toad Together* are examples of books that exist mainly for the joy of reading. Escaping into a good mystery or fantasy can provide the release many children need to cope with the pressures of the outside world. Children can identify with Max, in *Where the Wild Things Are,* who is sent to his room but who escapes through his imagination to the land of the Wild Things. After holding a wild rumpus, Max leaves the land of the Wild Things and returns to his real-life home and finds dinner still hot and waiting for him. Like Max, children often need to escape to other worlds and let their imaginations run free.

Some reading programs devote exclusive attention toward teaching students *how* to read. That is, young students work daily on developing their word identification and comprehension skills by reading short instructional passages and by completing worksheets that are related to the passages. The problem with these programs is that they fail to show students *why* they should read.

The skills work frequently is done at the expense of developing attitudes toward reading, and the result is students who can read but who have no desire to do so. Including literature for children as a regular part of a classroom reading program helps ensure that this does not happen.

Reading to Apply Strategies

Using literature in your classroom provides an excellent opportunity for applying strategies.

One way that literature helps readers apply strategies is by leading readers to use them naturally. Good readers organize information, connect familiar ideas with unfamiliar ideas, form images, monitor their progress, and so on. When these readers encounter difficult text, they consciously and deliberately apply their strategies. A good reader who faces a difficult passage might think to himself or herself, "Uh oh, this is getting tricky. I'd better slow down and make sure I get things organized." This reader would have monitored and would have begun deliberately to organize his or her thinking. On the other hand, well-written text allows readers to organize information effortlessly because it is presented in a well-organized fashion. Good writers make strategies such as organizing, imaging, connecting, and predicting seem effortless for readers.

Another way that literature is useful for teaching students to apply comprehension strategies is when it is the basis for Think Links. Think Links call for teachers to take a passage, read a portion of it orally, and then describe the strategies they would use to comprehend the portion. Teachers read a passage, thinking through the process aloud. Think Links make public the private strategies individuals use when reading. Teachers should demonstrate Think Links with students to demonstrate how comprehension strategies are applied.

The following exemplifies a scripted Think Link that is appropriate for a second-grade class that has had the story *Frederick* read to it several times. This Think Link covers only the first few lines of the story. As can be seen, Think Links call for teachers to read a little and then interject how they are making sense of the passage. After you perform Think Links for your class, you might have students volunteer to present their own Think Links.

Frederick, by Leo Lionni. By looking at the cover I see that this story is about a mouse named Frederick. I bet he's friendly because he looks nice [connect]. I wonder what he does in the story? [predict]

"All along the meadow where the cows grazed and the horses ran, there was an old stone wall." When I lived in Connecticut I saw a lot of stone walls instead of wire fences [connect].

"In that wall, not far from the barn and the granary, a chatty family of field mice had their home." Now I know the story is not going to be true because mice aren't chatty [monitor, connect].

"But the farmers had moved away, the barn was abandoned, and the granary stood empty. And since winter was not far off, the little mice began to gather corn and nuts and wheat and straw." I see that they need food because it is not going to be readily available [connect]. This family of mice seems to be responsible [evaluate].

"They all worked day and night. All—except Frederick." Now I see a problem beginning [monitor]. I wonder what the mice do about Frederick not working [predict].

FOR CHILDREN WITH SPECIAL NEEDS—JUST THE RIGHT BOOK

 Books do so many things for all children that children with special needs are sure to find a variety of books they will enjoy and relate to. There are, however, some particular books you should know about. There are books written about all kinds of special situations children face. There are books about children who face physical challenges, children whose families are having problems, gifted children, and children who feel different from everyone else. The books are too numerous to list here but you should know that a large variety of these books exist. To track these books down, you can look under books for bibliotherapy and also use special bibliographies such as these:

Accept Me As I Am: Best Books of Juvenile Nonfiction on Impairments and Disabilities, by Joan Brest Friedberg. New York: Bowker, 1985.

Books for the Gifted Child, Vol. 2, by Paula Hauser and Gail A. Nelson. New York: Bowker, 1988.

Books to Help Children Cope with Separation and Loss, Vol. 3, by Joanne E. Bernstein and Masha K. Rudman. New York: Bowker, 1988.

The Single-Parent Family in Children's Books: An Annotated Bibliography (2nd ed.), by Catherine Townsend Horner. Metuchen, NJ: Scarecrow, 1988.

TEACHERS CAN VARY IN THEIR CLASSROOM USES OF LITERATURE

You can view the use of literature in your classroom reading program along a continuum. To make an analogy, let's say that you are on the Reading Railroad and are traveling on the literature tracks. You get on at New Teacher Station and settle into your seat for the trip. As the train clicks down the tracks, you begin to talk with some of your fellow travelers about their destinations. You had no idea that there were several stops on these tracks! The people you are with are getting off at three literature stations: SomeLit, LottaLit, and AllLit.

NoLit Station

The train doesn't even slow down as you pass NoLit Station. "What station is that?" you ask. Some experienced teachers explain, "Oh, that! That station closed down in the eighties. It was a popular stop in the seventies when skills were the 'be all and end all' of reading instruction. Many teachers were so overwhelmed by all the skills they thought they had to teach that they didn't find any regular time for literature in their curriculum. Fortunately, the train doesn't stop there anymore!"

SomeLit Station

The teachers getting off at SomeLit Station like literature and wish that they had more time to use books in their classrooms, but they believe they can justify only some time for children to become involved with it.

The SomeLit teachers like to draw on literature for some of their strategy development as when, for instance, teaching children to interpret figurative language. They teach that strategy to children and then ask them to locate examples of figurative language in the books they have checked out of the library.

Their students, too, follow the school's schedule of weekly or biweekly visits to the school library, but SomeLit teachers permit some time, about 15 minutes, for children to examine their new books after the library trip. The SomeLit teachers encourage their students to take the books home from school and remind them the day before library day that they need to return their books if they intend to get more. They don't turn their classroom libraries over to the school; the books gathered by previous teachers in that room are lined up on shelves on the side of the classroom. Although the books are a little tattered and many are woefully out of date, the SomeLit teachers ask if you have any idea how expensive it is to buy books. However, they occasionally receive some new books whenever their class places a large enough book club order so that the class is entitled to a free book.

SomeLit teachers like to read to children, they tell you, but with all there is to be accomplished, they can afford only one or two sessions a week for this reading. Occasionally, they will choose chapter books to read to the children, but generally, they select books, short stories, or poems that can be completed in a single reading. The SomeLit teachers feel good that they are able to allow children time to read every week; children are permitted to choose free reading Friday afternoons for 20 minutes.

Basically, SomeLit teachers believe that if they are going to allow children time for reading, they should check on how much the children learned from it. Consequently, oral and written book reports are the general practice, although children occasionally put on a skit or display other creative responses to books read.

LottaLit Station

"But you don't have to stop there!" interrupt the teachers who are bound for LottaLit Station. "There are lots of worthwhile ways to use children's books in the classroom reading program." LottaLit teachers often use the basal stories as jumping-off points to get children into whole books. If, for instance, a story in their basal is an excerpted chapter from a novel, they will plan ahead and locate enough copies of that book for the children to read. They will then take a break from the basal and allow children to read the novel. These teachers feel compelled to ensure that their students are taught the strategies their basal lays out, but they don't feel that they must have the children read all of the stories in a particular reader. They know that the strategies can be taught in a variety of ways and with a variety of materials.

The LottaLit teachers have talked with their librarians and have an arrangement whereby children can check out new books whenever they return the ones they borrowed last visit. This allows some children to go to the library daily because they go through a lot of books. These teachers also have an arrangement that allows children to check out one more book than they would normally be allowed to have. The children keep that book at school for their free-reading period, which is held daily. The children from LottaLit classrooms are often seen in the library before school and during recesses. LottaLit teachers believe that it is important to have a classroom library that will encourage independent reading by children. They don't change the materials much, but they are constantly looking for ways to increase their libraries, such as having children bring some of their own books to school to lend to the room library for a few weeks. Their libraries include a variety of books at many different reading and interest levels, and they try to make the area attractive to children by having rugs and floor pillows for the children to use while reading. These teachers try to attract children to the area with displays of books on different topics or by featuring an author or illustrator of the month.

Children are encouraged to read materials from the classroom library after they finish their assigned work, but LottaLit teachers ensure that all students have daily free reading by planning the free-reading period as a regularly scheduled event. LottaLit teachers have made and purchased many tapes of books. Children who can't read very well but would like to "read" a good story follow along in the book as the taped voice reads the story.

The teachers at LottaLit Station frequently read aloud chapter books so that children have the opportunity to see characters develop through a long work and because the teachers know that children enjoy a long piece and look forward to coming to school to find out what will happen in the next chapter. These teachers always read at least once a day to their students, and most weeks they find that they have read more than once a day.

Children have the opportunity to select, within a certain range, the type of response activities they will do after reading. Sharing these responses is always encouraged. The teachers may give them three activities to choose from unless the students can come up with one of their own that they would prefer. The types of responses that are offered generally include one written, one oral, and one artistic response.

AllLit Station

"How interesting," the AllLit group of teachers chimes in. They tell you that literature *is* their reading program. They use basal readers and all other adopted texts as supplements to the overall literature program. They consider adopted materials simply another type of reading material of which they have multiple copies. AllLit teachers occasionally require multiple copies of some reading matter so that they can work with small groups of children. The emphasis in their reading program is on reading entire works rather than the one-chapter excerpts that tend to be found in basal readers. Groups of children get together for reading because of a common interest rather than being grouped by the teacher. The AllLit teachers provide reading instruction and monitor children's reading progress through individual conferences and by keeping individual checklists of skills that good readers should possess.

An important aspect of the reading program at AllLit Station is that children continually share what they are reading through discussion with the teacher and with other children. Children may choose to write or give oral book reports, but they are not required. The teachers encourage ways of sharing books that involve an integration of the language arts of reading, writing, listening, and speaking. Children may turn a story into a play and perform it for a small group, since it is unlikely that the whole class would be interested in the same topic. AllLit classrooms include many types of response activities to literature, since that is a major component in their evaluation of children's reading progress.

AllLit teachers have made some sort of arrangement with the school librarian so that children can go to the library whenever they need to or want to during the school day. Children check out as many books as they wish because they use the library for obtaining both reference and pleasure-reading sources. The AllLit teachers encourage children to go to the library before school starts and during recesses as alternative activities to occupy their time. Far from having given their classroom libraries back to the school library, the AllLit teachers have built up their classroom collections to include borrowings from the county and school libraries, donations, books borrowed from students within the class, and books from the teachers' own personal collections of children's books. They change these books periodically so that there are always some appealing new additions. The classroom library is attractive and inviting with plants, a bathtub filled with pillows, and a seat from an old car. These teachers believe that displaying the books attractively is part of the lure, and so they have bookstands and shelves to display the front covers of many of the books in their libraries.

These teachers take every opportunity to read to children during the school day. There is scheduled reading time built into their lesson-plan books, but in addition, they take advantage of all of the transition times that occur. They keep a book of poems handy so that while the children wait in line to go to the lunchroom, they can read the poems to them.

AllLit teachers find that beginning the day by reading to children helps to set the tone and that ending the day by reading to children helps them to go home feeling good about school. By the same token, the children they teach read frequently. There is no planned free-reading time because AllLit teachers see to it that reading is what the day mainly consists of.

But now it is up to you. You look around the group and study the various teachers getting off at SomeLit, LottaLit, and AllLit Stations. They have given you much to think about. "Well," they ask as they all turn to you, "what's your destination?"

DO IT TOGETHER

 Think back to classrooms you have been in and try to recall a teacher who was at each of the stations. Have you experienced classrooms at the NoLit, SomeLit, LottaLit, and AllLit stations? For each station, write down any classrooms you remember. Share your memories with those of three or four peers. Summarize what your group has jointly experienced. Finally, decide which station you think is reasonable for your own teaching style.

IMMERSING CHILDREN IN LITERATURE IS ACCOMPLISHED IN MANY WAYS

Learning from books, vividly experiencing the sensations stimulated by books, improving reading abilities, and bettering attitudes toward reading are outcomes that do not occur automatically. They need to be cultivated. One of the best ways to cultivate these outcomes in children is to immerse them in books. Designing your classroom to approximate the LottaLit Station goes far in meeting this end. Surrounding children with literature and allowing them to plunge into the materials they choose develops effective, well-rounded readers. This section describes specific ways to immerse children in reading materials.

Sustained Silent Reading

Sustained Silent Reading (SSR) involves students in reading self-selected materials for a certain period (Hunt, 1971). SSR requires extensive, varied reading materials because all students and adults read during this time. Thus a wide selection of books, magazines, newspapers, and pamphlets is needed.

SSR is characterized by free-reading time, a quiet place, abundant materials, and an adult role model (Moore, Jones, & Miller, 1980). The goal is to induce students to read large quantities of material.

To begin an SSR program in your classrooms, collect a large assortment of reading materials. (We describe how to build a classroom library in the section entitled "Acquiring Literature for Children.") Once reading materials are obtained, set aside a certain time of the school day for SSR. Some teachers set it aside immediately after breaks in the day such as lunch or recess because SSR typically settles children down. Specify an exact amount of time for this activity, and keep your class to that time. It can be gradually increased as your students become better able to stay with a sustained reading task. Some teachers start off primary-grade children with 5 minutes a session and then try to increase gradually to 15 minutes by the end of the year.

Before beginning an SSR session, have your students select the material they will read. Then inform your class that everybody is to read silently for the specified time. It is important that you read too. Teachers who grade tests, file papers, or do other administrative tasks during reading time communicate to students that SSR really isn't very important. After the reading time is up, return the reading materials and proceed to the next activity of the day.

No formal response activities should be assigned during or following SSR. After all, continued attention to a specific passage is a response by itself. Furthermore, at some time, most of us have experienced a powerful, compelling book or movie and then immediately afterward have been asked, "Well, what did you think of it?" Do you recall how frustrating and maddening that question can be? Often we need time to sift through our thoughts. Even after we've figured them out, we'd like to let them simmer inside a while for our own gratification and not share them with others. Children work the same way. They share experiences with one another all of the time—including experiences with books. Children should be offered the opportunity to share what they have been reading during SSR time, but requiring reports of each book read violates the spirit of this activity.

A practice that is related to SSR, but that is not the same, is to encourage students to read on their own after they have completed their assigned schoolwork. Students take out a book and read at their desks or go to a designated area. This practice is helpful for those students who finish quickly but discriminates against those who seldom finish early. All students deserve an opportunity to read freely.

Reading Aloud to Children

Children of all ages benefit from listening to passages read aloud by an accomplished reader. Teachers, aides, and parents can be the ones to read to children; tape recordings also are appropriate. No matter who reads aloud, it is important that the person present a model of good reading behavior for children to imitate.

When reading aloud, your voice and gestures should convey enthusiasm and positive feelings for the book. Since familiarity with the passage is essential for effective oral reading, first read to yourself what you will later read orally to your students. Teachers generally introduce a book to a class by connecting its author, illustrator, or contents with materials the children already know. If the book contains pictures, share them with the children when appropriate. Follow-up discussion, writing, or art projects are appropriate when used in moderation. Also, reading comprehension techniques are appropriate for listening comprehension. Finally, you might encourage students to borrow a book just shared with a group in order for them to read it individually.

Selecting the books you intend to read aloud and the order in which you will present them is an important aspect of immersing children in literature. Many teachers present clusters of books by the same author, illustrator, or topic. For instance, the topic might be tied into the subject matter being presented in social studies or science; *Doomsday Book* could be read when students study the Middle Ages. Primary-grade teachers reread favorite stories several times so that students can respond to them at different levels. This practice is similar to bedtime story–reading practices wherein children experience the identical book many times. Selecting books that stretch students' imaginations and concepts is an important part of a read-aloud program. You can share materials with children that they would have difficulty reading on their own. School librarians will suggest books appropriate for oral reading, and they might be able to tell you which books teachers in other grades read aloud to their children so that you can avoid overlap. In addition, two references about reading aloud are included in the Additional Readings at the end of this chapter, and Huck, Hepler, and Hickman (1987) presented in the endpaper of their text an excellent graded list of 100 books to read aloud to children.

Book Talks

Teachers and librarians frequently introduce materials to students through book talks, which are designed to entice children to read the books that are presented. Book talks consist of brief summaries of parts of books, readings of excerpts, and comments about the contents. Those who present book talks share the contents of the materials in intriguing ways so that students want to read the entire work. Evaluative comments such as "this is one I'm sure you'll like" are kept to a minimum because the contents that are shared are meant to serve as motivation. After talking about books and showing them to the audience, make the books available so that students can borrow the ones they want as soon as possible.

Book Displays

Like book talks, book displays serve to entice children to read selected materials. Book displays are advertisements for a particular cluster of reading materials. Bulletin boards, pictures, decorations, and concrete objects are used to draw readers to the books just as department stores set up displays to attract consumers to their products. Teachers and librarians frequently choose an author or illustrator, learn the month when that person was born, and then set up displays promoting the person's work during that month. As is done with book talks, the materials to be promoted in book displays might be grouped because they are new, relate to a certain topic, have general wide appeal, or were produced by the same person.

Young Readers' Book Awards

Many classes, schools, school districts, and states participate in young readers' book awards. Primary- and intermediate-age groups typically are designated, and awards go to the authors or illustrators of books voted to be the favorites of the age groups.

Representatives of the group sponsoring the young readers' award produce a master list of about 20 book titles for a certain year. The lists are then distributed to teachers, librarians, and school administrators. Displays featuring the nominated books, school assemblies, posters, and other devices are used to promote the nominated books. To vote, children need to read or listen to about half of the books on the list. Children rank order their favorite books by a certain date, send their votes to a central location, and the winner is determined. An assembly typically is held wherein the winning author or illustrator receives appropriate recognition. These assemblies can be elaborate; in many cases, book fairs are held, small groups of students meet to discuss their favorite books, the winning author or other adult authors share their craft with children, and parents attend informational sessions.

Acquiring Literature for Children

Most classroom teachers endorse the idea of having a large quantity of literature for children in their classrooms. However, the problem is how to acquire a sufficient quantity of such materials. Stocking a classroom with bright, new books purchased with school district money frequently can become a distant dream. Nevertheless, we encourage you to search for book monies among the labyrinth of school budgets and outside grants. School administrators generally don't advertise that they have extra funds available, but if you present a specific, already prepared book order that requires only a signature and a school purchase order, you might be pleasantly surprised. However, if that doesn't work, or if it does work but you need still more books to fill a classroom library, consider the following options.

BORROWING FROM LIBRARIES   Sharing books among classrooms and borrowing a quantity of books at one time from the school library are ways to bring literature into your classroom. Rotating books this way allows you to get the most mileage out of what currently is available at your school. Furthermore, a close working relationship with your school librarian can do wonders toward acquiring and promoting children's literature. Most schools have scheduled times for classes to visit the library and check books out, but inviting the librarian to come into your classroom to promote books that have just arrived can be done also. Another important service that the school librarian can perform is to compile books that relate to a certain unit or theme that you are exploring with your class. Literature can be collected at your city or county library and brought into your class for a certain period too. Up to 20 books at a time usually may be acquired this way.

INVOLVING PARENTS   The PTA and other groups of concerned parents can be mobilized. Parents often want to help out, but they don't know what to do. Asking them to gather, borrow, and buy literature for children directs them toward a worthwhile goal. When Christmas arrives and you prepare to receive presents from your class, you might suggest books. Perfume, handkerchiefs, and neckties are nice, but you probably would do better with a good, new piece of children's literature to share with your class. Another way to stock your classroom library is to have children bring in books from their personal collections to share with the class. Children enjoy reading their favorite books to their peers and then placing that book in the library.

BUILDING CHILDREN'S COLLECTIONS Helping students acquire books for their personal collections at home also deserves attention. Book fairs can be held wherein representatives from one or more book companies come to your school and display their books for sale. Although book fairs are designed ostensibly to sell books, they also seem to sell enthusiasm and interest in reading. Watching young students move among all of the new books as they prepare to purchase a book confirms this second outcome. In addition, the money earned from book fairs can go toward purchasing materials for your classroom library.

Another way to help students build a personal collection is to participate in book clubs such as Lucky, See Saw, and Troll. Such clubs typically mail teachers invitations to participate. In book clubs, students' orders are sent to a specific company. The bonus books that come with a minimum order are good additions to the classroom library.

Subscriptions to children's periodicals such as *Your Big Backyard, Ranger Rick, Kids Discover, Zoobooks,* and *Boys' Life* are good ways to build children's collections of reading materials. Few techniques seem better at encouraging children to read than receiving magazines through the mail.

CHILDREN CAN RESPOND TO LITERATURE IN A VARIETY OF WAYS

In this section we describe response activities that are designed to help students refine their interpretations and value judgments of literature. The sophistication of children's literary understanding begins at a rudimentary level and develops into advanced levels with time and instruction (Applebee, 1978; Cullinan, Harwood, & Galda, 1983). Mature readers focus more on story themes than on plots. They recall the gist of stories more than memorable events. Mature readers relate the events of a story to the plan the author apparently followed in order to produce an overall effect. They note the metaphors and symbols authors use to represent real-world situations. To illustrate, sophisticated readers of *The Three Little Pigs* would focus on the message that being industrious leads to protection from danger. These readers would produce a general summary of the story rather than expand on the wolf's huffing and puffing to blow down houses. The encounters between the wolf and pigs numbers one and two would be seen as a necessary contrast to the confrontation between the wolf and pig number three. Mature readers would note that the pigs represent people, and the wolf symbolizes the dangers of an uncaring and hostile world.

Perhaps the greatest contribution of response activities is that they enable students to determine for themselves how thoroughly and imaginatively they comprehended a piece of literature. To produce an overt response to what has been read, students need to "step back" and sort out their thinking. If they find their comprehension to be inadequate, they can rethink and reread the passage to obtain a deeper insight. Without response activities, students often become stranded at superficial levels of comprehension.

Response activities also get students into the habit of processing literature thoughtfully. That is, as you regularly help students interpret and evaluate literature, they can learn to interpret and evaluate it on their own. Students then become used to expecting insight from what they read, and they are not satisfied until such insight is obtained. In essence, response activities lead students to a mature understanding of literature.

There are numerous ways to elicit responses from students about what they have read. The following are some that we have found to be effective.

Literature Response Journals

Many teachers find that an easy and natural way to connect reading and writing is to have students keep literature response journals (Routman, 1991). Children are encouraged to take some time after reading each day and record their thoughts, feelings, and predictions (see Figure 5.1 for examples). Teachers model this by recording some of their personal responses. From time to time, children and their teachers can share the responses they have written. This is often a good basis for promoting discussion of divergent responses to the same story.

Sudduth (1989) reported that many of her third graders didn't really know what to record in their literature journals. This was especially true of those children who were finding learning to read difficult. She outlined the step-by-step instruction she took them through:

At first, have the students read the same book. They can read this silently or with a partner or listen to a tape recording or to a teacher reading aloud. Have specific stopping points in the reading and help the children to verbalize what they are thinking and feeling.

On chart paper or the overhead, record some of the students' responses and have children copy the ones they agree with into their logs. Use "frames," such as:

I was surprised when _____.

Since _____ and _____ happened, I predict that _____ will happen next.

The story reminds me of the time I _____.

As students understand the various open-ended ways in which they can respond to literature, move them toward independence. Continue the discussions but don't write down what they say. Rather, have them write their own personal entries following the discussions. Have the class brainstorm a list of log topics and frames and display these so students can refer to them when they need "starters."

Have students choose books they want to read and do their own response journals. Divide the time available for self-selected reading into reading time and journal-writing time, perhaps 20 minutes to read and 10 minutes to write. Once children are reading individual books, provide time each week for sharing what they have written in small groups.

book Meanwhile back at the ranch.

I like meanwhile back at the ranch a lot it makes me laugh cuse rancher hicks goes out to sleepy gulch and elnas gettin evry thing!

Book: *Meanwhile Back at the Ranch.* I like *Meanwhile Back at the Ranch* a lot. It makes me laugh 'cause Rancher Hicks goes out to Sleepy Gulch and Elna's getting everything!

The War of the Worlds

The War of the Worlds is my favorite book that I've read. It was an exciting story. Although the end was predictable the rest of the story was nearly perfect.

I was somewhat disapointed by the ending. I am also confused at how the story caused so much panic when it aired as a radio play in 1939. Still it was a near perfect book.

FIGURE 5.1 These two examples were taken from the literature response journals of a first grader and a fifth grader.

Literature Discussion Groups

In many classrooms, literature discussion groups go hand in hand with literature response journals. They are an opportunity for small groups of children to come together as they are reading particular books to share reactions about their reading. Teachers meet with the groups from time to time, but the teacher's goal should be to have a lot of student talk and to gradually turn over the direction of the discussions to the students.

To begin a book discussion, use an open-ended question or directive. Questions such as "What should we know about the story?" and "What will you remember most about the story?" get students talking about what they have read. To maintain the discussion, comments can be made, such as "Tell me more about that" and "Why did that happen?" If the students' comments are unclear or fragmentary, ask for restatements or clarifications with questions such as "What do you mean?" Questions that fit only the story being discussed also are appropriate. For instance, the Junior Great Books Program suggests that its discussion leaders begin a second-grade discussion of *Jack and the Beanstalk* by asking whether Jack succeeds mainly by luck or by his own abilities (Kuenzer, 1978). An important rule for teachers to follow throughout these discussions is to ask only those questions that have more than one correct answer. When teachers are sure of the answer to a question, the discussion becomes a closed search for what is in the teacher's mind rather than an open exploration of ideas. Book discussions provide children with the opportunity to talk about what they have read, sharing what they know and investigating what is vague or unknown. Book discussions offer children a chance to explore their ideas about books. Young people work together to uncover new meanings in literature and support their interpretations with ideas and facts from the materials. The teacher's role is to initiate and encourage responses; the goal is to keep students talking. Indeed, ideal discussions consist of conversations between students as opposed to question-and-answer recitations between a teacher and the class.

When children are allowed to discuss books around a single central idea, the discussion web (Alvermann, 1991) that results has many features that contribute to children's understanding. Children learn to work with pairs and then larger groups in order to discuss one topic. Models of reasoning and articulated thoughts show other children how books can be examined. Children engage in higher-order thinking rather than mere rote recall, using the details and sequence to support perspectives. In a discussion web, children try to come to a conclusion about how they feel about a central yes/no question in the book. They work through pros and cons of the question in small groups and then, having the benefit of all the thinking in the classroom, arrive at their own conclusion.

We have conducted numerous discussion webs with all ages of elementary school children. The two discussion webs shown here (Figures 5.2 and 5.3) were done with picture books. *Two Bad Ants,* a book used with bilingual first graders, tells of two ants who decide to stay in a house that has a sugar bowl the ants have been pirating to feed their queen. The book details the adventures of the two ants during their one day on their own. The central question the children

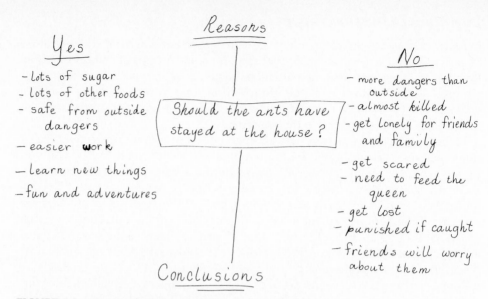

FIGURE 5.2 First-Grade Discussion Web for *Two Bad Ants*

were to discuss was whether or not the ants should have stayed at the house. An equally valid question for discussion relates to the title: Are they really two *bad* ants? The second discussion web shown was done with bilingual fifth graders for the book *Stellaluna*. Children and teacher learn a lot about fruit bats with this book about a small fruit bat separated from her mother and reared by birds.

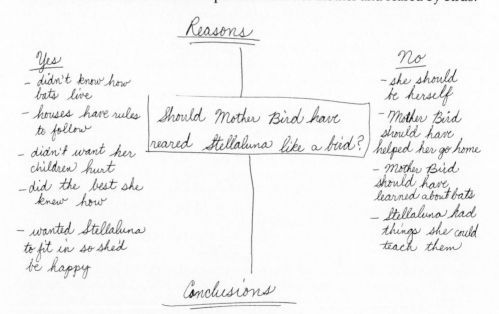

FIGURE 5.3 Fifth-Grade Discussion Web for *Stellaluna*

She has to learn how to behave like a bird and eliminate her bat ways. Eventually she is reunited with her fruit bat colony and must adjust to yet another lifestyle change. The central question for children was whether or not Mother Bird was justified in forcing Stellaluna to live like a bird. Another possible question that could be raised was whether or not Stellaluna could be happy living with only one culture.

Readers' Theater

Most intermediate-grade students like to read plays. However, locating and affording quantities of plays appropriate for classrooms are difficult, so many teachers turn to readers' theater as an alternative. Many variations of readers' theater are available (Sloyer, 1982); the following is a basic explanation of how to produce a readers' theater in a busy classroom.

Readers' theater consists of designating readers as particular story characters or the narrator and having them orally read the appropriate dialogue and narrative of a story. When introducing this technique for whole-class participation, have the students follow along in a story as a small group demonstrates the technique. Another way to introduce readers' theater is to reproduce part of a story on an overhead transparency or the chalkboard and demonstrate how a group would orally read the selection.

To have whole-class participation in readers' theater, first select a story with much dialogue. A short story, perhaps one from the adopted basal reader or an excerpt from a longer passage, can be used. When first using readers' theater, young students do best when the narrator orally reads the *he said* and *she said* parts; experienced students can omit these portions of the text. Divide the characters' and the narrator's parts among pages so that all students have a speaking role (for example, have one student narrate the story for the first two pages, have another student narrate the second two pages, and so on). Display the divisions, such as the one presented in Figure 5.4, so that students' names can be listed according to their assigned roles. Then help the students prepare for their parts by directing silent reading of the entire story and study of selected speaking parts. Ensure that students know when they are to speak and how to convey their role. If a whole class is presenting the story, students remain at their seats and read their parts as they arise, but if a small group is presenting a story, the students come to the front of the class.

To refine readers' theater presentations, sound effects and simple props might be used. Some teachers tape-record the presentations to allow later critiques of the performance. Older students who become enthused about readers' theater might form groups, select a passage, prepare it, and then present it before the class as a special project.

Young and Vardell (1993) not only describe the process and benefits of readers' theater, they tell how to adapt scripts. The major focus, however, is on moving readers' theater out of "reading" time and into the rest of the curriculum.

Pages

Role	23	24	25	26	27	28	29
Narrator							
Jill	X				X		
Gwen	X		X				
Coach	X	X		X	X	X	X
Marshall	X	X	X				
Erica	X	X	X		X	X	X
Ben	X	X	X		X	X	X

Place students' names in blank spaces.
X = no speaking part on this page.

FIGURE 5.4   Readers' Theater Setup for "Something Strange at the Ballpark"

Story Retellings and Re-creations

Retelling and re-creating stories help children respond to literature by sharing what they have read or listened to. Retellings and re-creations consist of activities such as puppetry, story acting, lap stories, flannel boards, acetate stories, and written retellings.

Some general guidelines are appropriate for conducting story retellings and re-creations. The following steps are the framework for retelling or re-creating a story:

1. Have students read the story knowing that it will be performed or written about later.
2. Describe the key characters, summarize the key events, and block scenes.
3. List props for the performance or written retelling; prepare props, if needed.
4. Narrate the story and have children supply the dialogue while manipulating the props, or have children write it in play or story form.

When the teacher performs the narrator's role, control over the presentation is maintained. The children who are performing certain roles can be readily directed to speak when their turn arises. If a child does not know what to say, the teacher may help out as long as the designated child actually speaks for the character. Memorizing dialogue or reading directly from a script while manipulating story characters might be appropriate in certain situations, but having students produce dialogue as needed seems to promote better understanding of passages.

Numerous variations of folk and fairy tales exist in children's literature. Western (1980) and Worthy and Bloodgood (1993) describe numerous activities to engage children in comparisons of folk literature variants. The variants that children read act as models for their own creations. Additionally, higher-order thinking is required of children as they compare variants. You might select, for example, to engage children in variants of *The Three Little Pigs*. You would bring into your classroom titles such as *The Three Little Pigs* (Galdone and Zemach versions), *The Three Little Javelinas, Three Little Pigs and the Big Bad Wolf, The True Story of the Three Little Pigs,* and *The Three Little Wolves and the Big Bad Pig.* Western details the steps in comparing story structure elements across variants. Worthy and Bloodgood list several comparison tasks for children to engage in. Having children write variations once they have read and analyzed numerous examples is a logical next step. Of course, children could also create a production for their variation instead.

Children would also enjoy hunting for variants if you start them with a single title such as *How Many Spots Does a Leopard Have? and Other Tales* or *The Stinky Cheese Man and Other Fairly Stupid Tales.* Many children also enjoy creating variants of friends' original stories in the classroom.

PUPPETRY   Children can and will make puppets out of any material. We found that having some books on how to make puppets (e.g., Currel, 1980) and having boxes that contain raw materials such as socks, papier-mâché, colored paper, and other colorful materials provide enough for children to produce puppets for story retellings. Large and small stages are needed for children to crouch behind to present their stories. Many teachers simply turn a table over on its side to create a puppet stage.

STORY ACTING   With very few props, children can act out stories that have been read. Teachers often allow groups of children who particularly enjoyed a story to dramatize it, and others have children in a reading group act out a story. It is best to begin story acting with small segments that children mime as the story is read aloud. A simple passage with only a few events should be used at first. Later, you can move to more complex passages containing several characters and much action. Dialogue can be added when the children seem ready.

LAP STORIES   The lap story requires a small painted or covered board that will fit in your lap and sheets of unlined paper to tear into the shapes of story characters. If you desire, clay can be used for molding. Ask, "Who is in this story?'' and as a child names a character, give the child a sheet of paper or a lump of clay. Direct the child to create the character by tearing the paper or molding the clay into a representative form. No drawing or cutting is allowed. However, if children are tearing paper, they can be given colored markers to add details after the tearing is done. Although clay can be used to make the characters, we believe it is best to have children tear paper into shapes because it seems to reduce anxiety about art. We've had children say "I can't draw a bear," but practically everyone can *tear* a bear, and the children know it. For this activity, we want to decrease the emphasis on art and increase the emphasis on storytelling.

After various children have been given paper or clay for the creation of characters, ask them, "What else do we need for this story?" Children should identify needed major props such as the bridge for *The Three Billy Goats Gruff* or three porridge bowls, three chairs, and three beds for *Goldilocks and the Three Bears.* Children may also want to include nonessential props such as the forest or other items of furniture. The only limitation you have is based on how much your lap can hold and how much your hands can manipulate. We have gotten ourselves into a pretty pickle on occasion by allowing all the children to create items for the lap story, only to find a lap insufficient to hold it all.

With younger children, prepare the paper in advance for certain stories. For *The Three Billy Goats Gruff,* for instance, three sizes of paper are provided so that the goats don't end up being the same size. When the lap story is finished, the characters and props can be placed in a large envelope, labeled with the story name, and placed in a learning center or story box. Then children can get the envelope and retell the story whenever they wish. Even when the paper shapes become tattered, we have found that it is no great problem. For one thing, they represent very little time or money investment, and children can easily replace the tattered forms with new ones. Finally, we take the salvageable shapes from several envelopes (tossing out the ruined ones) and put them together in a "Make a New Story" envelope to derive even more use.

Lap stories are more easily done with small groups of children, but they also work well with entire classes. The only caution is to seat the children close enough to you so that all can see and enjoy the story.

FLANNEL-BOARD STORIES   Another type of story retelling that is common in the elementary school classroom is done with the use of the flannel board. Story retellings can be done with a surface covered with a material with a nap (such as felt or flannel) and objects representing characters and props that will stick to the surface of the flannel board. The size of the surface used for flannel boards ranges from very large, heavy easels that are virtually untransportable to small stationery boxes with hinged lids that children can use individually at their seats.

Some people make their characters and props all from colorful felt pieces and glue on contrasting felt or draw with colored markers for details. Others cut out paper characters from books or draw paper characters that they seal with clear adhesive paper to protect the figure and give it more substance. A small piece of felt or sandpaper is glued onto the back of these paper figures so that they will adhere to the surface of the flannel board. Again, these characters are manipulated by the teacher as narrator with children providing the dialogue, or children use the flannel boards by themselves to retell familiar stories.

ACETATE STORIES   Acetate stories call for the creation of miniature transparencies of story characters and props. Place a sheet of acetate, such as that used to make overhead transparencies, over the illustrations in the book you want to use for story retelling. It is important that the pictures are not too large; an overhead projector enlarges what it projects, and you may have a wall full of dragon without room for any other characters or props on the screen.

When the acetate has been carefully placed over the desired picture, trace around the shape of the illustration with a thin-line, permanent-ink marker. It is important to use the permanent-ink markers because watercolor ink will not adhere to the acetate. After the shapes and internal details are outlined, fill them in with thin-line, permanent-ink markers in various colors. After the acetate pictures have dried (it takes only a few moments), peel back part of the backing from a sheet of clear adhesive plastic. Place the side of the acetate you just colored on the sticky side of the clear adhesive plastic. Cut around the edges of your characters and props so that you have the tiny acetate figures to go with a story the children know. What remains is a little transparency that can be projected on a screen for you and your children to use in story retellings.

Visuals

Creating visuals such as collages, posters, and book jackets helps students learn to form mental images of what they read. Furthermore, students manipulate and develop ideas through visual, artistic forms of expression just as they do through oral and written forms. Creating visuals is the mainstay of many response activities in primary-grade classrooms because young students often can put into a picture what they cannot put into writing. The following visuals provide a nonverbal outlet that often is the most effective way for students to represent their ideas on paper.

ILLUSTRATIONS   Students often draw pictures of characters, scenes, or locations they encounter in literature. The criteria for deciding what to illustrate can depend on what your students consider to be their favorite, most important, or most exciting topic. In addition, posters and bulletin boards frequently are designed by students in response to what they read.

COLLAGES   Assembling a group of pictures, cloth or wood pieces, and other materials in response to what has been read is a favorite activity of older students. They especially seem to enjoy hunting through magazines, catalogs, and newspapers for just the right pictures or printed phrases that symbolize a character or the general theme of a novel.

MAPS Showing where a character went in a story requires careful reading. After deciding what locations to represent, students map them out on paper, label them, and often illustrate them for greater detail. Maps can depict story characters' travels in any area. For example, the locations within a single house as well as the locations within a community, state, nation, or world can be mapped.

TIME LINES Time lines comprise a set of illustrations that portray the key events of a passage. Different groups of students can be responsible for individual illustrations, or one student can complete the entire project. The illustrations may be separated on different pieces of paper for others to arrange in correct sequence, they can be placed in different segments of a single sheet, or they can be drawn on poster paper to make a mural.

COMIC STRIPS This activity combines aspects of several other activities described here. Students depict a series of story events into a time line and produce dialogue for the story characters within that time line. Retelling a story through this comic strip format is a somewhat advanced task.

BOOK JACKETS Designing a book jacket that differs from the original directs students' thinking toward the central focus of the book. To choose a character or scene to portray on the cover, students need to judge what deserves emphasis. This is a high-level reading task.

DISPLAY ADS Creating a display ad is similar to creating book jackets; however, display ads openly attempt to convince readers to buy a certain book. They generally include more information about a book than its jacket does, and they include brief pieces of persuasive writing along with examples of what to expect.

Choosing Appropriate Activities

When deciding upon appropriate literature response activities such as the ones described, consider several points. First, matching the right activity with the right book and the right student is an uncertain undertaking. The best method we know for making proper matches might be termed "enlightened trial and error." You simply try certain activities that seem right for certain students and then pay attention to the results. If your students work comfortably with the project and if they gain insight into the material they have read, you have evidence that a worthwhile match was made. If the results you obtain are not so positive, try another activity.

Second, response activities can be viewed as products for instruction or as products for testing. For example, questions can be instructional when they are used to expand students' thinking about certain aspects of a story. In the children's novel *Number the Stars*, children can explore the horrors of the Nazi occupation of Denmark, the bravery of the resisters, and the terror felt by the Jewish children hiding from their occupiers. Children can discuss issues related to whether or not they might risk their lives and the lives of their families in order to protest atrocities against others. Questions comparing the treatment of African Americans and Native Americans in this country to the Nazis' treatment of Jews, gypsies, and the physically and mentally challenged can stimulate thinking and discussion. At the other extreme, students' answers to that question can be written down and then graded with no constructive feedback. When response activities such as questioning are used as a product only to be graded and not discussed, commented upon, or elaborated in some way, they are being misused.

Third, overt responses are important because they elicit active thinking and allow students to receive feedback, but time spent reading is important too. Discussing ideas, writing down ideas, and creating artistic responses can be counterproductive. We caution against "killing the butterfly." The beauty of books and the beauty of butterflies come from viewing their intricacies, their form, and their color in their entirety. Consequently, it is important to preserve children's feelings for the wholeness and overall impact of pieces of literature. Well-written and well-illustrated books, like butterflies, fall apart when their parts are dissected and overanalyzed. Literature can be presented with no teacher intervention, and children will enjoy and respond to it on their own. Anyone who has seen a child cry when reading or listening to *Stone Fox* knows what we are talking about. Because of this, knowing when *not* to require overt responses to literature is as important as knowing which response activities are most appropriate when they are required.

LISTEN, LOOK, AND LEARN

Visit a classroom and interview the teacher about the various ways children in that classroom respond to literature. Do the children keep any kind of response log? How are discussions conducted? Are there any readers' theater activities? What kind of story retellings and re-creations are used? Do the children create visual responses to books? How is the decision made about what kind of response activities will be used for particular books? Do the students have some choice about how they will respond? Is there variety in the response options? Summarize what you learned and decide how you can relate this to your own classroom.

LITERATURE ENRICHES THE CONTENT AREAS ACROSS THE CURRICULUM

In many elementary classrooms today, the curriculum is not fragmented into little time blocks for the different subjects. Rather, teachers integrate instruction around various themes or topics. (For an example of an integrated curriculum classroom, read about Ms. Maverick, the fourth-grade teacher in Chapter 14 of this book, who integrates her whole curriculum around varius content-area topics). Once a teacher has chosen a topic and outlined the major learning goals for that topic, a wide variety of resources and activities are used. These resources and activities include various media, real things and people, simulations, dramatizations, interviews, experiments, and a myriad of possibilities too numerous to list here. For any topic or theme under study, a wide variety of children's books can enrich the study of that topic. Many media centers have collections of books and other media arranged according to topic or theme. There are also commercially marketed collections of books that provide a wide diversity of information about a particular topic.

TRY IT OUT

 Come up with a science or social studies topic for a unit. Find five books that you and the students could read that would enrich learning and increase motivation. List these five books and how each will contribute to the unit.

Curriculum Webbing

A good way to organize a unit of study based on a book or on a topic such as animals, families, or weather is through curriculum webbing. To construct a curriculum web, write the title of the unit in the center of a large sheet of paper. Then brainstorm activities and materials appropriate for the unit and list them in categories branching out from the center. The categories could be labeled reading, writing, listening, and speaking, or they could come from information associated with the unit. For example, if families were the title, categories such as family members and reasons for families might be generated.

Curriculum webs provide a graphic organizer of the contents of a unit that helps initiate planning and maintains balance among activities. Figure 5.5 presents a model curriculum web for plants.

The curriculum web is an example of one way to take a specific topic and find various books and other activities that help you integrate the curriculum. Another way to use books to enrich all areas of the curriculum is to look at some of the wonderful books you share with children and ask yourself, "Where does this book lead us?"

Thematic Connections with Children's Books

Many of the best-loved children's books provide wonderful lead-ins to learning about particular topics. Children who read the Laura Ingalls Wilder books are usually eager to learn more about the settlement of our country. Children who read stories about children who live in other countries are intrigued to learn more about the countries in which those children live. Many teachers use maps to chart geographic locales in stories and textbooks. As stories are read to or by the children, the settings are located on the maps. While reading *Turn Homeward,*

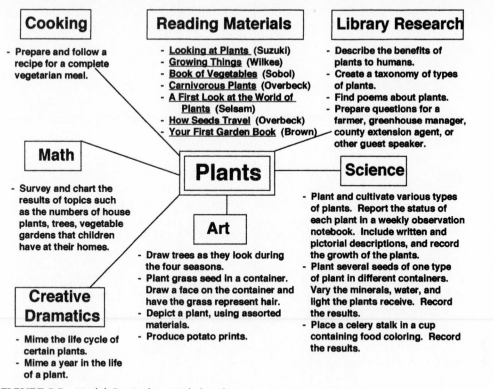

Cooking

- Prepare and follow a recipe for a complete vegetarian meal.

Reading Materials

- <u>Looking at Plants</u> (Suzuki)
- <u>Growing Things</u> (Wilkes)
- <u>Book of Vegetables</u> (Sobol)
- <u>Carnivorous Plants</u> (Overbeck)
- <u>A First Look at the World of Plants</u> (Selsam)
- <u>How Seeds Travel</u> (Overbeck)
- <u>Your First Garden Book</u> (Brown)

Library Research

- Describe the benefits of plants to humans.
- Create a taxonomy of types of plants.
- Find poems about plants.
- Prepare questions for a farmer, greenhouse manager, county extension agent, or other guest speaker.

Math

- Survey and chart the results of topics such as the numbers of house plants, trees, vegetable gardens that children have at their homes.

Plants

Art

- Draw trees as they look during the four seasons.
- Plant grass seed in a container. Draw a face on the container and have the grass represent hair.
- Depict a plant, using assorted materials.
- Produce potato prints.

Science

- Plant and cultivate various types of plants. Report the status of each plant in a weekly observation notebook. Include written and pictorial descriptions, and record the growth of the plants.
- Plant several seeds of one type of plant in different containers. Vary the minerals, water, and light the plants receive. Record the results.
- Place a celery stalk in a cup containing food coloring. Record the results.

Creative Dramatics

- Mime the life cycle of certain plants.
- Mime a year in the life of a plant.

FIGURE 5.5   Model Curriculum Web for Plants

Hannalee aloud to children, a teacher helped the children plot Hannalee's journey on the prison train from Athens, Georgia, to Indiana and then her return to her mother and her home through the war-torn South.

Books can take us to all kinds of places and both forward and backward in time. Books can help make math, science, and social studies concepts relate to the real world. As students read and enjoy *The Very Hungry Caterpillar* by Eric Carle, they can count and add all the things this caterpillar eats on his way to becoming a butterfly. Other math concepts included in this wonderful book are the measurement concept of the days of the week and some fraction concepts related to the parts of foods he eats. Many teachers connect this book with a science unit on animals and changes.

In *Ten, Nine, Eight* by Molly Bang, a father helps his daughter get ready for bed and they count down from "10 small toes all washed and warm" to "1 big girl all ready for bed." This book emphasizes counting and has African-American characters. It fits nicely into a social studies unit on families. Another book with a father as a major character is *Dad's Diet* by Barbara Comber. This book is a hilarious description of Dad's attempts to lose weight. Dad ends up weighing only six-sevenths of his previous weight. Since the book *Dad's Diet* takes place in Australia, Dad's weight is given in kilos. Work with fractions and with measurements can easily stem from this book. Children will enjoy figuring their own weights and the weights of their family and friends in kilos and determining how much each would weigh if they lost six-sevenths of their mass.

Informational books such as those listed at the beginning of this chapter can and should be part of your curriculum planning. Learning content through children's literature enlivens and enhances comprehension.

TRY IT OUT

 Find five children's books you think would appeal to children you teach or will teach. Read them and consider how they might enrich the science, social studies, or math curriculum. List possible thematic connections you could make between these books and other curricular areas.

THE THEORY AND RESEARCH BASE FOR READING AND RESPONDING TO LITERATURE FOR CHILDREN

The key word in this chapter title and section heading is *responding*. Most inquiries into literature for children in the 1980s and early 1990s emphasize children's responses. Response-oriented researchers focus on what individuals say or write about a literary passage, giving secondary attention to the work itself. These researchers concentrate primarily on readers' reactions to what they read. Response-oriented researchers have distinctive views about comprehension of literary texts and the instructional practices that promote comprehension.

Current conceptions of literary response began with the work of Louise Rosenblatt (Beach & Hynds, 1991), who published her first major work on literary response in 1938 (Rosenblatt, 1983). Rosenblatt suggests that authors, like painters and sculptors, elicit aesthetic responses from their patrons. Students can focus on the quality of these experiences as much on the contents of the object that stimulated them.

According to this view, reading results in a mental construction invented by readers with input from others. Readers do not uncover the meaning that resides in a literary work; readers construct individual, perhaps idiosyncratic, meanings in response to a work. What readers bring to a page—their stances toward literature, thoughts, feelings, predispositions, and ways of thinking—are central to the reading transaction.

Literary responses are subject to many influences. As readers process text, they produce momentary understandings that change as the text unfolds (Langer, 1992). These understandings may come from individual solitary thought, or they may be evoked socially. Indeed, readers shape their responses in part according to the social norms and standards of their interpretive communities (Bleich, 1978; Fish, 1980). School classrooms are major interpretive communities, having authority over what counts as reading.

Influences on literary response are illustrated further by studies showing effects for reader, text, and context (Martinez & Roser, 1991). Readers at different age levels respond to literature differently (Galda, 1990). For instance, young children's interpretations of thematic aspects of literature are less sophisticated than older students' interpretations. Intermediate students tend to generalize what story characters have learned, whereas primary students tend to offer specifics embedded within a story. Readers' preferred response styles also affect their interpretations (Galda, 1990). Some students focus on plot, and other stress characters' feelings, personalities, and motives.

The text being read also affects readers' responses. To illustrate, stories that offer rich, nuanced worlds with several minor characters and events can evoke in-depth responses better than superficial stories (Galda, 1990). Informational books surpass storybooks in influencing students to discuss topics, speculate, rely on peer information, and consider related topics (Leal, 1992).

The instructional context of school is another influence on response (Many & Wiseman, 1992; Purves, 1981). When classroom interpretive communities are decentralized, students tend to produce alternate critical interpretations of texts (Hickman, 1983). However, most classrooms still adhere to traditional views of authority and are characterized by teacher-led recitations of factual information lifted from texts (Weinstein, 1991).

Finally, culture affects response to text. Readers who find material unfamiliar due to cultural differences often produce limited responses (Reynolds, Taylor, Steffensen, Shirey, & Anderson, 1982; Steffensen, Joag-Dev, & Anderson, 1979). Instructional practices that conflict with cultural expectations also shape literary response (Barrera, 1992). Students who expect authoritarian statements often become confused and anxious during leaderless discussions.

Although literary response researchers emphasize readers' articulated statements about their literary experiences, unarticulated experiences also merit consideration. In a position paper outlining the goals of the National Reading Research Center, Alvermann and Guthrie (1993) proposed study of literary engagement, sustained meaningful attention to print. Engagement is a means to an end as well as an end; it predicts academic success and is a desirable outcome by itself. In a study of readers who lose themselves in books, Nell (1988) described engaged reading as something done for its own sake. This type of response is a "flow experience" wherein individuals find reading intrinsically motivating and totally absorbing, and the experience is its own reward.

A response-centered approach to literature seeks to engage students with books and the community of readers around them. It seeks to help students articulate and refine their responses by promoting explorations of multiple interpretations. The major roles of teachers are to help plan the sequence of readings, set the tone for responding to them, and encourage students to explore the range of possible responses. Two instructional practices commonly associated with this approach involve response journals and discussions.

In a response-centered approach to literature, students maintain response journals while reading, recording their responses at intervals such as every day or every chapter (Hancock, 1992). Students respond freely in these journals, although some teachers prompt responses with generic questions such as "Are you like any character in the story?" and "What was your first reaction to this story?" (Kelly & Farnan, 1991, p. 284).

Wollman-Bonilla (1989) found that many of her students' spontaneous comments fell into five broad categories:

(a) *opinions about plot episodes and characters,*

(b) *direct expressions of personal engagement ranging from enthusiastic appreciation to placing the book within the framework of the child's life and concerns,*

(c) *discussion of the author's style, language, and techniques,*

(d) *reflections on the reading process and on expectations for narrative texts, and*

(e) *questions about vocabulary, language, or plot. (p. 118)*

Students' entries in their response journals can serve as the basis for discussion when students gather in small groups to compare their responses to what they have read. In these discussions, termed "grand conversations" by Eeds and Wells (1989), students might share personal events related to a passage, question what they read, and report what they liked about the author's writing. When discussing stories independently in literature groups, students can engage the text at high levels of thinking, construct multiple meanings for it, and participate in conversations that have a natural structure (Eeds & Wells, 1989; Leal, 1992). Students can record and explore the insights gained from such discussions in additional response journal entries.

Integrated approaches to instruction are associated with responses to literature. Reading materials frequently are organized by genre or theme, and students investigate selected topics. Teachers act as guides, inviting students to explore subject matter and their responses to it.

Huck, Hepler, and Hickman (1987) identify numerous personal and educational values for children that result from immersion in literature. In the compendium on children's literature, they cite studies by others that they used to extract these *personal values* for children: pleasure, narrative thought, developed imagination, vicarious experiences, and insights and understanding of human actions and interactions. The studies documented these *educational values:* enhanced language development, positive effect on reading aloud, understanding story structure, developing oral reading fluency, models for children's writing, learning about the world, and discovering our heritage of literature. These days, teachers do not need to work so hard justifying real literature in the classroom reading program, but if there are challenges, we can point to many studies that support a strong literature base in classrooms.

LOOKING BACK

This chapter presented a rationale and a plan for using children's literature in the classroom. Various genres of literature and ways to respond to literature were described and a variety of ways to think about the many ways and places literature might be part of the elementary curriculum were discussed. The six key ideas in this chapter are:

1. A diverse world of literature exists for children.
2. Engaging children with literature promotes many outcomes.
3. Teachers can vary in their classroom use of literature.
4. Immersing children in literature takes many forms.
5. Children can respond to literature in a variety of ways.
6. Literature enriches the content areas across the curriculum.

ADD TO YOUR JOURNAL

 Are you a reader? A reader is not just someone who can read; a reader is someone who chooses to read—who reads a chapter or two of a good book before turning off the light and looks forward to that week at the beach partly because of the sustained reading time it will permit. If you are a reader, how did that happen? Did you have teachers who read to you? Did you get to choose some of your own books to read in school? Did you participate in any literature response activities? If you are not a reader, what can you do to assure that the children you teach have the opportunities in your classroom to become readers? What will be the role of literature in your classroom? Will you get off the reading railroad with the SomeLit teachers, the LottaLit teachers, or the AllLit teachers? How often will you read to your students and what will you read to them? How much time will you provide for them to read materials of their own choosing? What kinds of response activities will you engage them in? Think about the potential of books to enrich people's lives—throughout their lives—in a variety of ways and decide what role books will play in your instruction.

REFERENCES

Alvermann, D. E. (1991). The discussion web: A graphic aid for learning across the curriculum. *The Reading Teacher, 45,* 92–99.

Alvermann, D. E., & Guthrie, J. T. (1993). *Themes and directions of the National Reading Research Center* (Perspectives in Reading Research No. 1). Athens, GA: National Reading Research Center.

Applebee, A. (1978). *A child's concept of story.* Chicago: University of Chicago Press.

Barrera, R. B. (1992). The culture gap in literature-based literacy instruction. *Education and Urban Society, 24,* 227–243.

Beach, R., & Hynds, S. (1991). Research on response to literature. In R. Barr, M. Kamil, P. B. Mosenthal, & P. D. Pearson (Eds.), *Handbook of reading research* (Vol. 2, pp. 453–488). White Plains, NY: Longman.

Bleich, D. (1978). *Subjective criticism.* Baltimore, MD: Johns Hopkins University Press.

Cullinan, B. E., Harwood, K. T., & Galda, L. (1983). The reader and the story: Comprehension and response. *Journal of Research and Development in Education, 16*(3), 29–38.

Currel, D. (1980). *Learning with puppets.* New York; Play, Inc.

Eeds, M., & Wells, D. (1989). Grand conversations: An exploration of meaning construction in literature study groups. *Research in the Teaching of English, 23,* 4–29.

Fish, S. (1980). *Is there a text in this class? The authority of interpretive communities.* Cambridge, MA: Harvard University Press.

Galda, L. (1990). A longitudinal study of the spectator stance as a function of age and genre. *Research in the Teaching of English, 24,* 261–278.

Hancock, M. R. (1992). Literature response journals: Insights beyond the printed page. *Language Arts, 69,* 36–42.

Hickman, J. (1983). Everything considered: Response to literature in an elementary school setting. *Journal of Research and Development in Education, 16,* 8–13.

Huck, C. S., Hepler, S., & Hickman, J. (1987). *Children's literature in the elementray school* (4th ed.). New York: Holt, Rinehart, & Winston.

Hunt, L. C. (1971). Six steps to the individualized reading program (IRP). *Elementary English, 48,* 27–32.

Kelly, P. R., & Farnan, N. (1991). Promoting critical thinking through response logs: A reader-response approach with fourth-graders. In J. Zutell & S. McCormick (Eds.), *Learner factors/teacher factors: Issues in literacy research and instruction* (Fortieth Yearbook of the National Reading Conference) (pp. 277–284). Chicago: National Reading Conference.

Kuenzer, K. (1978). Junior Great Books: An interpretive reading program. *School Library Journal, 24*(2), 32–34.

Langer, J. A. (1992). Rethinking literature instruction. In J. A. Langer (Ed.), *Literature instruction: A focus on student response* (pp. 35–53). Urbana, IL: National Council of Teachers of English.

Leal, D. (1992). The nature of talk about three types of text during peer group discussions. *Journal of Reading Behavior, 24,* 313–338.

Many, J., & Wiseman, D. (1992). The effect of teaching approach on third grade students' response to literature. *Journal of Reading Behavior, 24,* 265–287.

Martinez, M. G., & Roser, N. L. (1991). Children's responses to literature. In J. Flood, J. M. Jensen, D. Lapp, & J. R. Squire (Eds.), *Handbook of research on teaching the English language arts* (pp. 643–654). New York: Macmillan.

Moore, J. C., Jones, C. J., & Miller, D. C. (1980). What do we know after a decade of sustained silent reading? *The Reading Teacher, 33,* 445–450.

Nell, V. (1988). *Lost in a book: The psychology of reading for pleasure.* New Haven, CT: Yale University Press.

Purves, A. L. (1981). *Reading and literature: American achievement in international perspective.* Urbana, IL: National Council of Teachers of English.

Reynolds, R. E., Taylor, M. A., Steffensen, M. S., Shirey, L. S., & Anderson, R. C. (1982). Cultural schemata and reading comprehension. *Reading Research Quarterly, 17,* 353–366.

Rosenblatt, L. (1983). *Literature as exploration* (4th ed.). New York: Modern Language Association.

Routman, R. (1991). *Invitations.* Portsmouth, NH: Heinemann.

Sloyer, S. (1982). *Readers theater: Story dramatization in the classroom.* Urbana, IL: National Council of Teachers of English.

Steffensen, M. S., Joag-Dev, C., & Anderson, R. C. (1979). A cross-cultural perspective on reading comprehension. *Reading Research Quarterly, 15,* 10–29.

Sudduth, P. (1989). Introducing response logs to poor readers. *The Reading Teacher, 42,* 452–454.

Weinstein, C. S. (1991). The classroom as a social context for learning. In R. Rosenzweig & L. W. Porter (Eds.), *Annual review of psychology* (Vol. 42, pp. 493–525). Palo Alto, CA: Annual Reviews.

Western, L. E. (1980). A comparative study of literature through folk tale variants. *Language Arts, 57,* 395–402, 439.

Wollman-Bonilla, J. E. (1989). Reading journals: Invitations to participate in literature. *The Reading Teacher, 43,* 112–120.

Worthy, M. J., & Bloodgood, J. W. (1993). Enhancing reading instruction through Cinderella tales. *The Reading Teacher, 46,* 290–301.

Young, T. A., & Vardell, S. (1993). Weaving readers theatre and nonfiction into the curriculum. *The Reading Teacher, 46,* 396–406.

Children's Books/Materials Cited

Alice's Adventures in Wonderland, by Lewis Carroll, Franklin Watt, 1966.

"April Rain Song" in *The Dream Keeper and Other Poems,* by Langston Hughes, Alfred Knopf, 1932.

Bears, by Ian Stirling, Sierra Club Books for Children, 1992.

Charlotte's Web, by E. B. White, Harper & Row, 1952.

Coral Reef, by Michael George, Creative Education, 1992.

Dad's Diet, by Barbara Comber, Ashton Scholastic, 1987.

Dinosaur Valley, by Mitsuhira Kurokawa, Chronical Books, 1992.

Doomsday Book, by Connie Willis, Bantam, 1992.

Dove Isabeau, by Jane Yolen, Harcourt Brace Jovanovich, 1989.

"The Elephant's Child" in *Just So Stories,* by Rudyard Kipling, Doubleday, 1952.

Exactly the Opposite, by Tana Hoban, Greenwillow, 1990.

Frederick, by Leo Lionni, Pantheon, 1967.

Frog and Toad Together, by Arnold Lobel, Harper & Row, 1972.

Grandfather's Journey, by Allen Say, Houghton Mifflin, 1993.

The Handmade Alphabet, by Laura Rankin, Dial Books, 1991.

How Many Spots Does a Leopard Have? and Other Tales, by Julius Lester, Scholastic, 1989.

Jumanji, by Chris Van Allsburg, Houghton Mifflin, 1981.

Kitchen Fun for Kids: Healthy Recipes and Nutrition Facts for 7- to 12-year-old Cooks, by Michael F. Jacobson and Laura Hill, Henry Holt, 1991.

The Magic School Bus on the Ocean Floor, by Joanna Cole, Scholastic, 1992.

Meanwhile Back at the Ranch, by Trinka Hakes Noble, Dial Books, 1987.

Nature Crafts, by Sabine Lohf, Children's Press, 1990.

Number the Stars, by Lois Lowry, Houghton Mifflin, 1989.

Of Colors and Things, by Tana Hoban, Greenwillow, 1989.

Ouch! A Book about Cuts, Scratches, and Scrapes, by Melvin Berger, Lodestar, 1991.

Papier-Mâché Project Book, by Marion Elliot, Chartwell Books, 1992.

Polar Express, by Chris Van Allsburg, Clarion Books, 1991.

The Rainbabies, by Laura Krauss Melmed, Lothrop, Lee, & Shepherd, 1992.

Robots: Your High-Tech World, by Gloria Skurzynski, Bradbury Press, 1990.

Roll of Thunder, Hear My Cry, by Mildred Taylor, Dial Books, 1976.

Sarah, Plain and Tall, by Patricia MacLachlan, Harper & Row, 1985.

Stellaluna, by Janell Cannon, Harcourt Brace Jovanovich, 1993.

The Stinky Cheese Man and Other Fairly Stupid Tales, by Jon Scieszka and Lane Smith, Viking, 1992.

Stone Fox, by John Gardiner, Harper & Row, 1980.

Ten, Nine, Eight, by Molly Bang, Greenwillow, 1989.

This Time of Darkness, by H. M. Hoover, Viking, 1980.

The Three Little Javelinas, by Susan Lowell, Northland Publishing, 1992.

The Three Little Pigs, by Paul Galdone, Scholastic, 1970.

The Three Little Pigs, by Margot Zemach, Sunburst Books, 1990.

Three Little Pigs and the Big Bad Wolf, by Glen Rounds, Trumpet Club, 1992.

The Three Little Wolves and the Big Bad Pig, by Eugene Trivizas, Macmillan, 1993.

The True Story of the Three Little Pigs, by Jon Scieszka and Lane Smith, Viking, 1989.

Tuesday, by David Wiesner, Clarion Books, 1991.

Turn Homeward, Hannalee, by P. Beatty, Morrow, 1984.

Two Bad Ants, by Chris Van Allsburg, Houghton Mifflin, 1988.

The Very Hungry Caterpillar, by Eric Carle, Putnam, 1989.

War of the Worlds, by H. G. Wells, Watermill Press, 1980.

Where the Wild Things Are, by Maurice Sendak, Harper & Row, 1963.

Why Do Volcanoes Erupt: Questions about Our Unique Planet Answered by Dr. Philip Whitfield with the Natural History Museum, by Viking Pengiun, 1990.

Winnie-the-Pooh, by A. A. Milne, Dutton, 1926.

A Wrinkle in Time, by Madeleine L'Engle, Farrar, Straus, & Giroux, 1962.

ADDITIONAL READINGS

There is a large variety of sources for topic-related books. Here are a few of the best currently available.

Heltshe, M. A., & Kirchner, A. B. (1991). *Multicultural explorations: Joyous journeys with books.* Englewood, CO: Teacher Ideas Press.

Kobrin, B. (1988). *Eye openers! How to choose and use children's books about real people, places, and things.* New York: Penguin.

Not too many years ago, teachers who wanted to take a book and spin off interesting activities had to make up almost all the activities. Today, literature spin-offs are very popular. Here are a few of the best books currently available.

Butzow, C. M., & Butzow, J. W. (1989). *Science through children's literature.* Englewood, CO: Teacher Ideas Press.

Fredricks, A. D. (1991). *Social studies through children's literature.* Englewood, CO: Teacher Ideas Press.

Griffiths, R., & Clyne, M. (1991). *Books you can count on.* Portsmouth, NH: Heinemann.

McElmeel, S. L. (1991). *Adventures with social studies (through literature).* Englewood, CO: Teacher Ideas Press.

Rommell, C. A. (1991). *Integrating beginning math and literature.* Nashville, TN: Incentive Publications.

Multicultural Literature

Crawford, L. W. (1993). *Language and literacy learning in multicultural classrooms*. Boston: Allyn & Bacon.

Harris, V. J. (Ed.). (1992). *Teaching multicultural literature in grades K–8*. Norwood, MA: Christopher Gordon.

Easy-to-Read Books

Fielding, L., & Roller, C. (1992). Making difficult books accessible and easy books acceptable. *The Reading Teacher, 45,* 678–685.

Pilla, M. L. (1990). *The best high/low books for reluctant readers*. Englewood, CO: Libraries Unlimited.

Picture Books

Cianciolo, P. (1981). *Picture books for children* (2nd ed.). Chicago: American Library Association.

Danielson, K. E. (1992). Picture books to use with older students. *Journal of Reading, 35,* 652–654.

Freeman, E. B., & Person, D. G. (Eds.). (1992). *Using nonfiction trade books in the elementary classroom: From ants to zeppelins*. Urbana, IL: National Council of Teachers of English.

Lima, C. W. (1986). *A to zoo: Subject access to children's picture books* (3rd ed.). New York: R. R. Bowker.

Poetry

Brewton, J. E. (Comp.). (1983). *Index to poetry for children and young people, 1976–1981*. Bronx, NY: H. W. Wilson.

Harms, J. M., & Lettow, L. J. (1991). Recent poetry for children. *The Reading Teacher, 45,* 274–279.

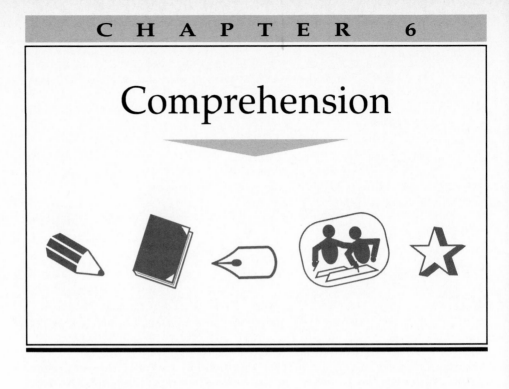

CHAPTER 6

Comprehension

LOOKING AHEAD

Reading comprehension requires much on the part of students. Readers actively think about what is on the page and what they already know, and this thinking is colored by interest in reading about the topic. Teachers develop students' reading comprehension proficiencies by planning and implementing various activities throughout the school day. Teachers provide students with time and motivation for individual reading and for exploring information in subject-matter materials. One activity, comprehension strategy lessons, is designed to teach students directly how to comprehend. Knowing the principles of effective comprehension strategy lessons informs decisions about how to guide and support children's comprehension.

Say the following words silently or aloud:

nonverbal	randomized
blocked	presentations
experiments	verbal
strategy	dyslexics
normals	stimulus
predict	hemispheric
structural	atypical
laterality	strategical

You probably were able to pronounce all of these words, but read the following paragraph containing the same words to see how well you understand it:

The experiments employed randomized or blocked presentations of verbal and nonverbal materials to determine whether previously reported differences between dyslexics and normals were due to structural hemispheric differences or to strategical processing differences. The results indicate that if dyslexics are unable to predict the nature of the stimulus, then they behave as normal readers. Their atypical laterality emerges only when they adopt a strategy in anticipation of a specific type of stimulus. (Underwood & Boot, 1986, p. 219)

Did the click of comprehension occur as you read this paragraph? Could you retell it in your own words to a friend? Could you give examples that illustrate what the authors were explaining? Although word identification is important, we hope this exercise convinces you that for readers to comprehend, they must do much more than simply pronounce printed words and listen to what they are saying. Furthermore, as noted in Chapter 5, "Reading and Responding to Literature for Children," response-oriented educators concentrate on readers' aesthetic reactions to literary texts, giving secondary attention to readers' learning of text contents. But as the above example shows, readers' grasp of text contents is also a compelling concern. Educators who share this concern concentrate on reading comprehension, giving secondary attention to literary response. We include chapters on literary response and learning from text in this book because both aspects of reading deserve classroom attention.

This chapter on comprehension contains four key ideas:

1. Reading comprehension requires interactions among word identification, prior knowledge, comprehension strategies, and interest.
2. Comprehension can be developed in the content areas across the curriculum.
3. Comprehension strategy lessons engage students before, during, and after reading.
4. Study strategies can be developed in the content areas across the curriculum.

READING COMPREHENSION REQUIRES INTERACTIONS AMONG WORD IDENTIFICATION, PRIOR KNOWLEDGE, COMPREHENSION STRATEGIES, AND INTEREST

Reading comprehension is an incredibly complex process. Comprehending is practically synonymous with thinking, and the act of thinking has mystified scholars since antiquity. How is meaning obtained? If readers form mental images, are they of different intensities? Does the process of responding to literary texts differ from learning from informational texts? These questions, and countless others, remain to be answered about the reading comprehension process.

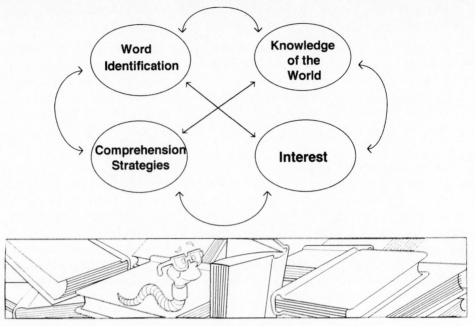

FIGURE 6.1   Interactive Nature of Reading Comprehension

Although a complete version of the reading comprehension process is not available, a general explanation is this: *Reading comprehension results from an interaction among word identification, prior knowledge, comprehension strategies, and interest.*

Comprehension occurs as the result of an interaction (Rumelhart, 1985). This means that forces act upon one another; one force influences another, and the second force then doubles back to influence the first. For example, when readers pick up a book, their interest in the topic influences the words they identify. The identified words, in turn, interest the readers in some way. This interactive cycle then continues forward. Figure 6.1 contains a model of the comprehension process that emphasizes its interactive nature. The two-way arrows indicate that readers continually move from one component to another in a flexible sequence.

Comprehension is an interactive process of at least four major components. However, each component is described most clearly one at a time. What follows is a description of each one.

Word Identification

Chapter 3 presents a thorough view of word identification, so only one additional point is made here: Word identification is both a cause and an effect of comprehension (Goodman, 1984). It helps cause comprehension by signaling certain thoughts. If you saw the following symbols, you would not be able to comprehend the message they represent:

{ + #@)*#&##$

However, if you knew the code, you would have little trouble with this message. The code is simple:

Coded Symbol	Letter
)	a
#	e
{	i
&	d
$	p
*	r
@	s
+	v

Working back from these symbols gives the trite message: *Rivers are deep.* This demonstration shows that word identification helps cause comprehension. Readers need to identify words to derive meaning from print. However, this role of word identification probably seems obvious to you.

The effect of comprehension on word identification is not so obvious. Nevertheless, readers who derive meaning from print are better able to identify words as they progress through a passage. To appreciate this phenomenon, read the following short paragraph:

> The hunter set his trap and began moving away. He did not get far when he heard a sudden metallic snap. He knew he had caught something. He quickly returned to his _____ to see what he had.

Did you mentally produce the word *trap* when you came to the blank in the paragraph? If so, you were correct, because *trap* was the deleted word. Even though absolutely no printed symbols were included in the space, you no doubt were able to identify the word that fit. Your understanding of the paragraph enabled you to identify a word despite the fact that the word was not even spelled out for you. Your comprehension helped cause your word identification.

The positive effect that comprehension has on word identification is important to remember. This effect necessitates an instructional program that balances attention to words as well as attention to ideas to produce the best possible readers. Emphasizing one of these aspects of reading at the expense of the other is counterproductive because the two work together.

Prior Knowledge

Along with word identification, comprehension depends in part on how knowledgeable readers are about the contents of the passage being read (Anderson & Pearson, 1984). Think about the difficulty you had with the passage presented earlier about the experiments. To understand the passage, you needed to know about specific concepts such as *blocked presentations* of materials, the difference between *verbal* and *nonverbal* materials, and *laterality*. You also needed to have some general knowledge about the type of research being reported. Knowing that psychological studies frequently present tasks to different groups of readers to determine their intellectual differences would have provided some perspective for interpreting this particular study.

As Chapter 4 indicated, prior knowledge is important because writers assume that their readers share certain understandings. To illustrate, the authors of the experiments passage assumed that their readers already knew about the general features of the study they reported. This assumption justifies the authors' not explaining most of the technical terms. Similarly, writers of general materials do not explain every term they use. If a travelogue writer for a popular magazine were describing a trip to southern California, he or she would not explain concepts such as *airplane, freeway, ocean, Hollywood,* or *Beverly Hills.* The author would assume that readers could connect prior knowledge with these words, so they would not be explained. Literate Americans know terms such as *antibody, Genghis Khan, melody,* and *zodiac.* Failure to know these and other terms limits one's comprehension.

Having knowledge of the world is essential for comprehension, but it is useless if it is not connected to the passage being read. Readers need to know something about what they are reading; they also need to realize when their knowledge fits the particular passage they are reading. To appreciate this point, read the following sentence:

The notes were sour because the seams split.

This sentence probably seemed incomprehensible. Individual words made sense, but they most likely did not hang together. You might be able to repeat the sentence verbatim, but you would be only parroting sounds. However, if you knew that the sentence was about bagpipes, you would have thought it quite comprehensible. Knowing that this particular sentence is about bagpipes is just as important as knowing about bagpipes in the first place; connecting knowledge of the world to a passage is just as important as having knowledge of the world (Bransford & McCarrel, 1974).

In brief, prior knowledge is crucial for comprehension. Students require a great deal of information before they can understand what is presented in books. Students also require the ability to call up what they know and connect it to the upcoming ideas in a passage. Simply having knowledge of the world is not enough; readers need to activate and apply it when they read.

Comprehension Strategies

Word identification and prior knowledge are only part of the comprehension process; comprehension strategies also are crucial (Paris, Wasik, & Turner, 1991). Strategies are tactics, or procedures, that are employed to achieve certain goals. To appreciate the role of strategies, solve the following word puzzle:

$$\frac{0}{\text{B.A.}}$$
M.A.
Ph.D.

Readers who are familiar with this type of puzzle have no difficulty determining that this one stands for *three degrees below zero.* However, if you did not already know what the puzzle represented, and if you did not know how to figure it out, you would be stuck. You might ask someone, "How do you do these puzzles? What's the trick?" You would be wanting some word-puzzle strategies. An astute friend might explain his or her tactics this way: "First, look at the puzzle and come up with one directional word like *over, through,* or *between.* Then say that word along with what the other words and letters represent. Keep combining these words in different order until you produce a well-known saying." With this strategy for solving word puzzles, you would be able to figure out that *you just me* represents *just between you and me* and *side side* stands for *side by side.* After a while, you would not need to think about the word-puzzle strategy when you met unfamiliar puzzles because you would apply it automatically. In fact, this process might become so automatic that you might be unable to describe the strategy if someone asked you about it.

Comprehension strategies are like word-puzzle strategies in that they provide tactics to derive meaning. Sometimes children have to think explicitly about a strategy in order to apply it, and sometimes children apply it automatically. Whatever the case, comprehension strategies are considerably more numerous and complex than word-puzzle strategies. Some of the comprehension strategies frequently listed in school curriculum guides, published instructional materials, and professional articles are as follows:

Calling up relevant background knowledge

Predicting what the passage will contain

Focusing on important ideas

Following story structures (e.g., setting, goal, outcome)

Following expository structures (e.g., cause-effect, comparison-contrast, topic-detail)

Noting the author's purpose

Monitoring understanding

Distinguishing facts from opinions

Evaluating passage contents

Good readers perform the strategies listed above as well as the ones presented in Chapter 1. A major instructional decision is to determine which strategies students need to understand the passage they are reading currently as well as strategies they will need in the future. Many teachers select strategies from lists provided by their schools to address their students' needs. Then they teach strategy lessons involving many of the lesson-planning features presented in this chapter.

Interest

As we noted in Chapter 1, reading is feeling. Among other things, this means that interest influences readers' comprehension. Different readers will come away from an identical passage with different understandings partially because their interest in the topic varies (Baldwin, Peleg-Bruckner, & McClintock, 1985; Wade & Adams, 1990).

Interest attracts readers to certain materials. Students who are particularly interested in animals or superheroes will tend to understand passages about those topics better than students who are more interested in romantic fiction or biographies. Even within a particular type of literature, some passages exert a greater attraction than others. Everyone has favorite reading materials. Some materials engage readers' attention and cause them to become concerned with the contents. For instance, readers tend to identify emotionally with some story characters more than others, and this identification influences the message readers take from the passage. It seems clear that teachers should consider the role of interest when attending to students' reading comprehension.

FOR CHILDREN WITH SPECIAL NEEDS—BALANCED INSTRUCTION

The four aspects of reading comprehension described in this section apply to all readers. Good and poor readers mix words, prior knowledge, comprehension strategies, and interest to construct meaning. However, children with special needs sometimes receive an instructional diet consisting mainly of word identification and comprehension strategies. This can be counterproductive. Remember that all readers—including children with special needs—require attention to their prior knowledge and their interest to fully develop as the best possible readers.

COMPREHENSION CAN BE DEVELOPED IN THE CONTENT AREAS ACROSS THE CURRICULUM

To help students become proficient with the dynamics of reading comprehension, teachers engage readers with passages from a curricular topic such as ecology or friendship, or they use children's books, such as *Charlotte's Web* or *Roll of Thunder, Hear My Cry*, that are not necessarily embedded in a cross-curricular topic. The key words distinguishing these practices are (a) *theme-based* and (b) *literature-based*.

Theme-Based Teaching

Theme-based teaching of comprehension involves materials that relate to units of content. These units often are based on ideas or blocks of subject matter such as space, friends, and patterns. They typically last from a few days to a few weeks.

When you explore subjects with your students, you have countless opportunities to extend their reading and language abilities (Fulwiler & Young, 1982). For example, during the study of the weather, your class can read newspaper weather reports, listen to radio announcements, talk about how rain occurs, draw pictures of various cloud formations, and write about experiences during various types of weather disturbances. You can use the textbook along with informational trade books, Weather Service brochures, and pamphlets. Charts can be developed to show wind currents and pressure systems. Maps that indicate weather patterns can be interpreted, and tables that report the temperatures of various cities can be consulted. Experiments with water evaporation can be conducted and reported. Filmstrips and movies that explain weather changes can be watched and then discussed or written about. As students develop understandings of facts and ideas related to a topic, they also develop abilities to read and write about facts and ideas.

Several approaches for using varied reading materials during content-area instruction have been designed since the turn of this century when John Dewey advocated such a procedure (Joyce & Weil, 1992). In general, these approaches are based on investigations, exploring a variety of information sources, and composing and sharing what was discovered (Atwell, 1987; Harste & Short, 1988). For example, your students might investigate how mountains were formed, how many kinds of animals there are, or what people are depended on in a community. Information about such topics then can be obtained from a great assortment of materials: textbooks written at easier and more difficult levels, trade books, supplemental reading books, magazine features, pamphlets and brochures, newspaper articles, encyclopedias, and kits. Additionally, films, filmstrips, records, pictures and photographs, guest speakers, and field trips can be used as references. The curriculum web presented in Chapter 5 is an excellent device for organizing materials related to different topics or questions. Single- and multiple-purpose units presented below are good ways to organize these classroom investigations.

SINGLE-PURPOSE UNITS   Having the whole class pursue one specific purpose is a good way to organize classroom investigations. In this approach, you begin by introducing a topic for study and then presenting whatever you have available to develop basic concepts related to that topic. Concrete objects, pictures, movies, and discussion can be helpful here. Next, one specific purpose for a group investigation is set. Students then work with a variety of printed materials and other matter as they attempt to satisfy that purpose. As your class gathers information, a group project is constructed to report the information they locate. For example, in Chapter 14 Ms. Maverick conducts a unit of study on the state in which she and the children live. To guide her students through this unit, she posts a large blank map of the state and encourages children to designate areas on it that they have visited or else know about. Some children talk to their parents about places in the state, some recall places on their own, and some read the literature provided by the state for information. Learning about their state provides direction and motivates students to read and learn about one specific topic while pursuing numerous materials. Filling in the blank map is the group project that allows students to report their information in a structured manner.

If you were studying reptiles, you might ask children to go through all available materials to satisfy three purposes: (1) list reptiles, (2) describe reptiles, and (3) describe the areas where each reptile is found. These purposes enable you to differentiate the materials that your children are using, but it keeps everyone on the same track.

Some structure might be added by telling your students how to describe their reptiles. For instance, you could tell them to draw their reptiles and to indicate each animal's size, color, and whether it is dangerous or not. Additional information could be gathered, but those three things provide specific ways to describe a reptile. As in the case of the state map, a group product such as a chart or bulletin board of reptiles can be constructed so that students share with the class what they have been reading and learning on their own.

MULTIPLE-PURPOSE UNITS   The second general way to organize classroom investigations involves each student or small groups of students pursuing multiple purposes. This approach provides greater independence than when students pursue a common question.

It seems best to allow students to embark gradually on individual or small-group research projects while the class pursues one specific topic. This means that you begin an overall topic just as you would if you intended to maintain only a few questions at a time. Then you encourage children to look into related areas. To return to our reptiles example, you may be presenting whole-class activities such as movies, filmstrips, discussions, and comprehension lessons about these cold-blooded creatures. Students also may have time each day to search library books, encyclopedias, and articles for the names, descriptions, and habitats of various reptiles. If crocodiles or rattlesnakes have caught their fancy, you could help the children form some specific questions about them and suggest how to organize and report the information that is located. (The lessons you do as a whole class on comprehension strategies and on writing, which we discuss in the next chapter, will come in handy as these students work independently.)

You can encourage individual and small-group unit activities after a whole-group project. For instance, after listing reptiles, describing them, and classifying them according to where they live, the following individual and small-group projects might be undertaken: create a poster describing one reptile in detail, write a story about a friendly lizard, draw a map that shows where reptiles are found, draw an illustration of a snake that emphasizes its scales, and describe various dinosaurs. As you can see, these projects all deal with one general topic, but students choose the aspects of that topic to explore.

Literature-Based Teaching

Literature-based teaching calls for students to interact with extended pieces of text. Students read complete separate books rather than abridged excerpts of books contained in anthologies. To be sure, book lengths correspond to children's sophistication. Children typically begin with short books containing more pictures than print before progressing to books containing chapters with no illustrations.

The essential element of literature-based teaching is students' engagement with "real books," although many other instructional features are associated with this practice. The classroom organization relative to the reading material varies among whole-class, small-group, or individual. The entire class might move through a single book title, responding at designated points. Small groups or pairs of students might meet several times a week to discuss a particular novel, complete study questions, and confer with their teacher. And each student might have his or her own title and set of response guidelines.

As Chapter 5 noted, literature-based classrooms typically contain a wide variety of materials. Class sets of materials are found in these classrooms along with books borrowed from the school library. Children also have access to the larger collection in the school library. Literature-based teachers read aloud to the class every day, and students often discuss their responses to what they have heard. Materials selected for the read-alouds often are ones that would challenge the reading—but not the listening—capacities of the class. Additionally, response to literature takes many forms. Students react to their reading and expand the meanings they construct through many modes. They may write, tape-record, illustrate, or construct responses to what they have read.

As you and your students explore thematic- and literature-based units of study, you will discover that your students would benefit from instruction in particular comprehension strategies. With this information you can plan strategy lessons for the class or small groups (Porter, 1990). Count on presenting about one strategy lesson per week. The next section details how to plan and implement these lessons.

LISTEN, LOOK, AND LEARN

 Observe a class for about three days. Note the type of unit being followed during literacy instruction. Is it centered about a theme or a piece of literature? If there is no central theme or piece of literature underlying the unit, what ties the lessons together conceptually?

COMPREHENSION STRATEGY LESSONS ENGAGE STUDENTS BEFORE, DURING, AND AFTER READING

Comprehension strategy lessons include planned straightforward descriptions of how to comprehend specific aspects of reading passages. These lessons emphasize the ideas contained in a passage along with the ways students can go about understanding those ideas. Students come to understand and remember the contents of a passage while learning strategies to acquire the content.

Comprehension strategy lessons occur during three time frames—before, during, and after reading. It is important to realize that the preparation done with students before reading is as important as the extension activities that occur after reading.

To present comprehension strategy lessons, we wrote a model plan that accompanies a folktale. The steps of this lesson apply to all strategies and passages, but the specifics of the plan presented here apply only to one comprehension strategy and passage.

One of our lesson plan features is that the actual wording for the lessons (i.e., a script) is provided. The point to remember about the script is that it is a model for teachers to follow. The lesson plan script presented here is intended to demonstrate the types of things teachers might say when conducting a lesson; the script is not meant to be followed verbatim.

Before reading the following model, you need some additional perspective. First, the following is a lesson *plan;* it is a bare-bones framework designed to start actual lessons. If the dialogue between teachers and students during a comprehension lesson were tape-recorded and reported here, much more would be presented. Another piece of additional perspective is that lessons take time. Steps 1 and 2 might be accomplished on a Monday, Step 3 on a Tuesday, and so on. The following lesson plan does not indicate which steps should be presented on which day. Finally, the wording for this model lesson plan is presented three ways: (1) directions to the teacher are in italic print—*like this;* (2) the actual words suggested for teachers to say to students are in regular print—like this; and (3) the expected responses from students are included in brackets—[like this]. What follows is a model comprehension strategy lesson plan and corresponding story. In the section following this one, we explain more about the special features of each step.

Model Comprehension Strategy Lesson Plan *for* The Farmer's Crowded House

This comprehension strategy lesson guides students reading through a story they enjoy and that makes them think. The strategy, finding a central story problem and its solution, is an appropriate one to teach using this story. It is also a strategy that will help students comprehend many of the stories they will read in the future.

BEFORE READING

Step 1. Introduce the Strategy   Today we are going to learn how to find a central story problem and its solution. A central story problem is the difficulty that the main character faces. The solution is what the character does to take care of the problem.

Looking for the problem and solution in stories is helpful. When you learn the problem and solution of a story, you are able to categorize characters' actions according to whether they were part of the problem or part of the solution. You are able to organize the story. In addition, every story has a problem and a solution, so you know you can expect them when reading stories.

Think of the story of THE THREE LITTLE PIGS. The central story problem, the difficulty that pig number three faced, was the big bad wolf trying to eat him. Pig number three did not solve his problem by getting angry with his brothers. The problem was still there after pig number three got angry. And pig number three did not solve his problem only by building a house of bricks. Pig number three solved his problem by building a house of bricks and then cooking the wolf when it came down the chimney. After cooking the wolf, pig number three did not face a problem anymore.

What were the problem and solution in SLEEPING BEAUTY? [The evil Witch cast a spell on Sleeping Beauty, but the Prince killed the Witch and woke Sleeping Beauty with a kiss.] What were the problem and solution in SNOW WHITE? [The evil stepmother was jealous of Snow White, so she had Snow White eat a poisoned apple that caused her to sleep. The Prince came and kissed Snow White and woke her.]

Step 2. Activate Prior Knowledge and Teach Specific Vocabulary The story we will read today is titled THE FARMER'S CROWDED HOUSE. Like all stories, it has a central problem and a solution. We will be finding them soon. But first, here is some information about the story.

THE FARMER'S CROWDED HOUSE is a folktale. This means it began when people told stories aloud rather than writing them. Folktales are meant to entertain people and present a lesson about life at the same time.

THE FARMER'S CROWDED HOUSE contains these words that you should know:

CROWDED: The title of this story suggests that a farmer had a house that was crowded. This means that the house was filled. Think of the times you have been in a crowded place. Tell us about being crowded and what you did about it. *Have a few students share their experiences being crowded in places such as their homes, cars, school assemblies, and shopping malls.*

MISERABLE: The base word of MISERABLE is MISERY. People who are miserable, who have a lot of misery, are very uncomfortable. In this story the farmer is miserable because his house is too crowded. Who can tell about a time when you were miserable? *Have a few students share their experiences.*

WISE MAN: A wise man is someone who is very knowledgeable about life. Listen to this description: "My father was a very wise man. He could listen to a problem and do the right thing to solve it. If my brother and I fought over who could have a toy, my father would take it away for a week. We soon learned to stop fighting over toys." Why was the speaker's father a wise man? [He solved problems well. For instance, he took away toys if two children were fighting over the same one.] The farmer in this story talks with a wise man about his crowded house.

MANSION: Here is a picture of a mansion. As you can see, it is a house. It is a special type of house because it is especially large and well built. The farmer's crowded house is not a mansion.

Advice: Let's say you have a problem and don't know how to solve it. A friend keeps borrowing your things and not returning them. You might ask someone what they suggest you do. You ask someone for advice. In this story, the farmer asks the wise man for advice about what to do with his crowded house.

Step 3. Engage Students in the Purpose Now get ready to read THE FARMER'S CROWDED HOUSE. Remember, this is a story, so it has a problem and a solution. Based on the title of the story and what I've said, what do you think the story problem is? [The farmer has a crowded house.] What should you know at the end of the story? [How the farmer solved the problem of his crowded house.] Read to learn how the farmer solves his problem.

THE FARMER'S CROWDED HOUSE

Once there was a farmer who lived with his wife and their ten children in a very small farmhouse. The farmer and his family were miserable. They were always bumping into each other and getting in each other's way. When the children stayed inside on rainy days, they fought all the time. The farmer's wife was always shooing children out of the kitchen so she could cook. The farmer had no place to sit quietly when he came in from work.

The farmer finally could stand it no longer. He said to his wife, "Today I am going into the village to talk with the wise man about our crowded house. He will know what to do."

DURING READING

Step 4. Monitor Comprehension during Reading (Optional) So far, what do you know about how the farmer solved his problem? [So far all we know is that he went to talk with a wise man.] Please read the next two pages to learn more about how the farmer solved his problem.

So the farmer walked to the village and told the wise man his problem. The wise man listened and then asked, "How many animals do you have?"

"I have ten chickens, eight pigs, six goats, four donkeys, two cows, and one horse," replied the farmer.

"Good," said the wise man, "go home and move all your animals inside your house. Come back and talk with me in one week."

The farmer returned to his family and told them to gather together the chickens, pigs, goats, donkeys, cows, and horse and bring them inside the house. When this was done, the house became more crowded than ever. The children fought all the time, even when it was not raining. The farmer and his family ate their meals off the cow's back because they could not reach the kitchen table. After a week the farmer returned to the wise man.

"The animals take too much room!" cried the farmer. "We are too crowded!"

The wise man answered, "Now go home, move the animals back into the farmyard, and come see me again in one week."

The farmer did as he was told. When he returned to the wise man one week later, he exclaimed, "Our house seems like a mansion now that the animals are gone! I will never complain again about our crowded house. Thank you for your advice."

AFTER READING

Step 5. Monitor Accomplishment of the Purpose How was the farmer's problem solved? [Following the advice of the wise man, the farmer and his family lived with all the animals in the house for one week. When the animals were put back outside, the house did not seem crowded.]

Step 6. Elicit Additional Responses Did you like this story? Why? *Have students freely express and support their opinions.*
   How else might the farmer have solved his problem? *List possible solutions.* Which solution would be best? *Discuss choices and point out the consensus if one emerges.*
   Remember I said that advice is what people suggest you do about a problem. What was the advice that was given in this story? [To move the farm animals into the house for a week and then move them out.]

Step 7. Extend the Comprehension Strategy I would like you to write a folktale like THE FARMER'S CROWDED HOUSE. However, your story should have a different problem and solution. You may read your stories to each other when finished. What possible problems might you write about? *List possible problems.* How might you solve these problems? *List possible solutions.*
   Remember, all stories have problems and solutions. Looking for them when you read helps you understand.

The seven steps of a comprehension strategy lesson plan can be applied to any passage. Once you learn this pattern, you can develop lessons for chapters of paperback novels and passages contained in basal reader series, subject-matter textbooks, library books, and magazines.
   As noted earlier, the pattern of a comprehension lesson plan consists of three time frames, before, during, and after reading. Teachers prepare students for a selection before they read it, guide students during the reading, and follow up afterward. In addition, the three time frames of comprehension lessons are broken down into seven steps. Figure 6.2 on page 173 contains a list of guidelines pertaining to each of the seven steps of comprehension lesson plans; the guidelines are explained in the next section.

FOR CHILDREN WITH SPECIAL NEEDS— LISTENING/READING TRANSFER LESSONS

Many years ago Cunningham (1975) designed listening/reading transfer lessons to help children do the same kind of thinking while reading that they do while listening. When reading, children must simultaneously identify words and think about meaning. When listening, however, children can devote all their attention to thinking about meaning.

Listening/reading transfer lessons can be used to teach any comprehension strategy. Imagine, for example, that a passage you have to share with your children is rich in figurative language. This passage could provide a great opportunity to help children understand how authors use such language to make stories come alive.

To begin the lesson, alert the students to the prevalence of figurative language in everyday speech. You might say something like:

> My son David has just turned fourteen and his stomach is a *bottomless pit*. He comes to every meal as *hungry as a bear* and gobbles down three helpings of everything. In spite of all he eats, he stays *thin as a rail*.

Using a real-world example such as this one helps children identify figurative language and realize that it plays an important role in daily communications. Note the examples of figurative language and have students focus on it during the next stage of the lesson.

Read the story to the children, stopping when appropriate to identify the language and discuss how vividly it communicates ideas. If the selection you are going to have the children read is a long story or a chapter book, you could use the first part of the story or the first chapter of the chapter book for the listening part of your listening/reading transfer lesson. This has the added advantage of getting your children into the story or book, pronouncing the character names, and establishing the setting and problem. The first part of a story or book can be difficult to get into, so reading the first part to reluctant readers is a way to help them become less reluctant.

Many times, however, the selection you are going to have the children read is fairly short. In these cases, you will need a similar passage to read aloud to them first in order to conduct the listening portion of the lesson.

Once you have completed the listening portion, have the children read and do the same thing while reading that they did while listening. Say something like:

> When you listened to me read, you found many examples of figurative language and you used this language to enjoy and understand more clearly what the author was saying. Expressions such as "scared stiff," "stubborn as a mule," and "lightning fast" helped you form vivid pictures in your mind. When you are reading to yourself, you are going to find many more expressions that will make the words come alive for you. Be on the lookout for these expressions and notice how they help you form clear mental images. After you have all read it, you can point out some examples of figurative language and how that language makes the story come alive. Try to do the exact same kind of thinking and visualizing while you read as you did while you listened.

Once the children have read, identified examples of figurative language, and explained how this language helped the story come alive, conclude the lesson by again pointing out that we do the same kind of thinking when reading as we do when listening. You might also suggest that they experiment with figurative language in their own writing to show how this process is similar.

Listening/reading transfer lessons can be used to teach any comprehension strategy. To do this, you plan parallel lessons as shown above. In the first lesson the children listen and in the second lesson they read. To ensure the maximum amount of transfer, be sure to emphasize the message that "we do the same kind of thinking when reading and listening." Children think all the time. Your job is to help them get in the habit of using their thinking strategies when they read. Many applications of listening/reading transfer lessons will help your children capitalize on what they already have.

Comprehension Strategy Lesson Plan Steps

The same steps followed in the model comprehension strategy for *The Farmer's Crowded House* can be followed in any comprehension strategy lesson.

BEFORE READING

Step 1. Introduce the Strategy The comprehension strategy presented in the model lesson was relevant. Determining the central story problem and solution is part of the organize thinking process that will be described in Chapter 7.

Step 1: **Introduce the Strategy**
  Teach only strategies that are relevant.
  Include the what, why, when, and how.
  Demonstrate the strategy with easily understood passages.
Step 2: **Activate Prior Knowledge and Teach Specific Vocabulary**
  Decide what background knowledge and word meanings to teach by considering
    what students need to know to fulfill their purpose.
  Teach no more than 10 new vocabulary words for any one selection.
  Tap thinking processes when teaching vocabulary.
  Relate new vocabulary with the contents of the selection.
Step 3: **Engage Students in the Purpose**
  Establish one clearly stated purpose for reading.
  The purpose should reflect the strategy modeled in Step 1.
  The purpose should require that students read and think about the entire selection.
Step 4: **(Optional) Monitor Comprehension During Reading**
  Monitor comprehension during reading only when students are having difficulty
    reading for the stated purpose.
  Elaborate on the comprehension strategy as students need help.
Step 5: **Monitor Accomplishment of the Purpose**
  Determine if students have fulfilled their purpose for reading and elaborate on
    comprehension strategy if needed.
Step 6: **Elicit Additional Responses**
  Encourage a variety of thinking processes while having students respond freely to
    the selection.
  Review vocabulary by relating word meanings to the context of the selection.
Step 7: **Extend the Comprehension Strategy**
  Follow up the comprehension strategy by assessing students' proficiencies and
    decide if more instruction and practice are needed.
  Remind students when and why the comprehension strategy is helpful.

FIGURE 6.2 Comprehension Strategy Lesson Plan Guidelines

Organizing information according to events related to the problem and to the solution is superior to simply listing events or discussing answers to various questions (Armbruster, Anderson, & Ostertag, 1987).

Determining the relevance of the comprehension strategy to be taught is important because comprehension strategies frequently are presented as irrelevant, isolated skills. Using "main idea" as an example, Duffy and Roehler (1986) put it this way:

> *Main idea is often presented as a task of reading paragraphs and selecting the best title. With diligent teaching, students often become quite good at this. However, they probably never use it when actually reading, since real readers seldom read to select appropriate titles for the paragraphs they read. Instead, students learn an isolated exercise which has little, if any, relevance to the task of making sense out of text. (p. 415)*

Before introducing comprehension strategies, study the ones that your school district curriculum guide presents. If the basal reader teacher's manual is the guide for your reading curriculum, examine each strategy and the way it is presented before you teach it. After all, determining main ideas seems to be an appropriate strategy; however, producing brief, capsule statements that summarize passages is much more sensible than selecting from three choices a title that fits best. Ask yourself, "Will this strategy and the way it is presented be useful in other school subjects as well as outside of school?" If the answer is yes, teach it as thoroughly as possible. If the answer is no, recast the strategy so that it is relevant, or substitute another one in its place.

The introduction of the strategy in the model lesson contained answers to the questions *what*, *why*, *when*, and *how* relative to the strategy. For example, the answer to *what* is the strategy was answered as follows: "Today we are going to learn how to find the central story problem and its solution. The central story problem is the difficulty that the main character faced. The solution is what the character did to take care of his or her problem." If you reread Step 1, you will see that information also was given about *why* the strategy should be used, *when* to use it, and *how* to go about doing it. This is essential information.

During the presentation of how to perform the strategy, the lesson called for the teacher first to demonstrate the strategy. He or she made public the reasoning that went into determining the story problem and solution. Alternative problems and solutions were posed and rejected until acceptable ones were formed. During this part of the lesson the teacher assumed the role of a coach who says, "Watch how I do this and listen to what I say about it because you're going to be doing the same thing." Also note that the demonstration was done with a familiar, easily understood, brief story (*The Three Little Pigs*) so the students could focus on the strategy rather than on the contents of the demonstration passage. Familiar stories are not always needed, but the demonstration should be done with easily understood, brief ones. Finally, it is important to realize that the students practiced the strategy with some similar stories (*Sleeping Beauty* and *Snow White*) before applying it to the main selection.

In sum, the following guidelines, which are listed in Figure 6.2, apply to Step 1:

1. Teach only strategies that are relevant.
2. Include the *what, why, when,* and *how* of comprehension strategies.
3. Demonstrate the strategy when explaining how to do it.
4. Use easily understood passages when demonstrating a strategy.

Step 2. Activate Prior Knowledge and Teach Specific Vocabulary   Step 2 of a comprehension lesson plan is designed to teach students general background along with certain words and their meanings. As mentioned earlier in this chapter, readers require knowledge of the world. To decide the particular background knowledge and word meanings to teach, you need to know the passage to be read and the purpose to be met. Then ask yourself, "What do my students need to know to fulfill this purpose?"

To determine the problem and solution of *The Farmer's Crowded House,* students would need to realize that the story was a folktale. Knowing that *The Farmer's Crowded House* allowed unusual happenings would help them accept the idea of a farmer going to a designated "wise man" who, in turn, suggested moving animals into the house. Students who expected only realistic stories probably would be confused by these events.

Only five words and their meanings were presented in the model lesson. We recommend thoroughly teaching no more than 10 words during each lesson. Teaching a few words well seems to be better than teaching many words superficially.

To select the words to be taught, decide which ones your students probably do not know well and are the most important for fulfilling their purpose for reading. We selected *crowded, miserable, wise man, mansion,* and *advice* because they met this criterion. Limit the words to be taught by holding them to the criterion of being unfamiliar yet important for understanding the passage.

Various thinking processes were tapped to teach the five words that were selected. Two very powerful thinking processes, calling up and connecting, were used to teach *crowded* ("Think of the times you were in a crowded place"). Connecting was used with *advice* ("Let's say you have a problem and you don't know how to solve it. A friend keeps borrowing your things and not returning them. You might ask someone what they suggest you do. You ask for advice"). To teach *mansion,* imaging was tapped ("Here is a picture of a mansion") along with organizing ("It is a house. It is a special type of house because it is especially large and well built"). When first presenting vocabulary, calling up, connecting, imaging, and organizing are the four thinking processes that should be tapped regularly because they are most feasible and powerful.

Students did not use their dictionaries or glossaries to look up the meanings of the five words introduced in *The Farmer's Crowded House.* Such an activity keeps students busy, but it results in little long-term retention of word meanings. Dictionaries are best used as resources to check meanings and to clarify or embellish word meanings already known. For instance, if students wanted to know more about why a mansion was a special house, teachers might have students locate the word in a dictionary and discuss the meanings that were provided. Young students require initial instruction in how to use dictionaries and glossaries.

Finally, as each word was introduced in Step 2 it was tied to the contents of the story. This practice is designed to promote students' predictions about a passage, and it seeks to develop interest. Students learn vocabulary and what to expect from a passage simultaneously.

The guidelines for this step are summarized as follows:

1. Decide the background knowledge and word meanings to teach by determining what students need to know to fulfill their purpose for reading.
2. Teach only about 10 new vocabulary terms for each passage.
3. Tap essential thinking processes when teaching vocabulary.
4. Use dictionaries and glossaries to confirm or clarify word meanings.
5. Relate new vocabulary with the contents of the upcoming selection.

Step 3. Engage Students in the Purpose　　The purpose set in Step 3 was a single, clearly stated reason for reading ("Read to learn how the farmer solves his problem"). Setting a purpose, monitoring students' performance, and guiding students to acceptable performance are designed to teach students to focus their attention. No one can absorb all of the information and gain all of the insights possible from a passage, so purposes allow students to be selective. Helping students become selective during these lessons is meant to develop selective readers in the future.

Another characteristic of the purpose set in Step 3 is that it was based on the comprehension strategy introduced in Step 1. Students were taught how to determine story problems and solutions, so the reason for reading was to determine a story solution. Connecting Steps 1 and 3 allows students to apply the strategies that are introduced.

A third characteristic of the Step 3 reading purpose is that it focused on implied information that was obtained only from reading the entire selection. Stated simply, students would need to read between the lines, and they would need to read the whole story to fulfill the purpose. Setting this type of reading purpose is important because it promotes a full range of thinking processes. A purpose that called for finding a specific fact from the passage would promote only superficial scanning. A purpose that called for an entirely creative response (e.g., "If you were a farmer who lived in a crowded house, how would you solve your problem?") would not compel students to read the passage carefully. Students with a broad purpose that taps implied information can monitor their comprehension readily throughout the passage. Students continually can ask themselves, "How did the farmer solve his problem?" Teachers can ask students this question after each page of text if so desired. Students direct their attention meaningfully when reading for broad implied purposes.

To summarize, three guidelines relative to setting purposes were presented here:

1. Establish one clearly stated purpose for reading.
2. Establish a purpose that reflects the comprehension strategy introduced in Step 1.
3. Establish a purpose that focuses on implied information that is obtained only from reading an entire selection.

DURING READING

Step 4. Monitor Comprehension (Optional)   Monitoring comprehension in Step 4 provides extra guidance for students who need support beyond what is given before and after reading. However, interrupting students during their reading might disrupt their concentration, so this step is optional; it should be used judiciously.

The comprehension check in Step 4 reflects the purpose set earlier. Note that the question asked during Step 4 of the model comprehension lesson ("What did the farmer do to solve his problem?") reflected the purpose that was established in Step 3 ("Read to learn how the farmer solved his problem").

During this step, teachers can further explain comprehension strategies in response to students' performance. For example, a student participating in the model comprehension lesson might report confidently that the farmer's visit with the wise man was the solution to the problem. A teacher then could inform this student that story characters frequently try solutions that do not work, and they sometimes try something that eventually will lead to a solution. Because of this, students might be told that only tentative statements about solutions are appropriate, and completely reading a passage is typically needed before one can know the overall solution.

When monitoring comprehension, you can help students apply a comprehension strategy by adjusting your instruction to accommodate the difficulty particular students have. This extra guidance is given in response to students' answers, comments, and questions. Students seldom catch on to a teacher's instruction immediately. Thus, teachers prompt students with comments (e.g., "Tell me more about . . .") to determine the extent of their understanding. When teachers honor students' responses during the comprehension checks (e.g., "I see how you might think that, but try looking at it this way"), students are encouraged to share their thinking.

To recapitulate, three guidelines are offered for Step 4:

1. Monitor comprehension during reading only with students who require extra guidance.
2. Monitor comprehension by determining how well students are fulfilling their purpose for reading.

3. Elaborate on comprehension strategies in response to students' perfomance.

AFTER READING

Step 5. Monitor Accomplishment of the Purpose After reading, the purpose set beforehand is followed up before any other activities are begun. This follow-up is identical to the comprehension check during reading (Step 4) because the follow-up question is the same one asked during reading, and both questions reflect the reading purpose.

Another similarity between Steps 4 and 5 is that teachers clear up misconceptions and further explain comprehension strategies in response to students' performance. During both steps teachers often have students orally read portions of a passage to support their responses, and teachers resolve difficulties students might have fulfilling the purpose.

This brief explanation boils down to two statements:

1. Determine whether or not students fulfilled their purpose for reading.
2. Elaborate on comprehension strategies in response to students' performance.

Step 6. Elicit Additional Responses Responses not related directly to the purpose for reading are elicited in Step 6 of a comprehension lesson plan. Group interaction is especially important during this step to demonstrate different perspectives that could be taken with a passage. Higher-order questions frequently are asked ("How else might the farmer have solved his problem?"), and students' responses are developed. Students are encouraged to share their personal responses to the selection ("Did you like the story? Why?"). As students share their responses, connections with a passage can emerge ("I knew a family who lived in a crowded house, and they solved their problem by moving"). Students can ask their own questions ("If a real farmer today had a problem, where would he go for advice?"). The full range of thinking processes is encouraged during this step.

An important part of Step 6 is to review some of the vocabulary presented earlier. After reading, students have additonal context in which to develop word meanings, so this context should be exploited ("Remember, I said that advice is what people suggest you do about a problem. What was the advice that was given in this story?"). Students might compare what they knew about the meaning of a word before reading the passage with what they know after reading. Such a comparison can demonstrate the value of context in determining the meanings of words.

Curriculum guides, suggestions for teaching novels, and basal reader materials often contain numerous questions to accompany reading selections. It is important to realize that all such questions do not need to be asked during Step 6 or any other step. These questions are suggestions for teachers to select or reject. If appropriate purposes for reading are established, and if students accomplish the purpose, the additional questions usually become redundant. However, if a question happens to tap an important understanding that does not surface during Steps 4 or 5, ask it.

To summarize, three guidelines apply to Step 6:

1. Encourage as many thinking processes as possible when having students respond freely to passages.
2. Review selected vocabulary terms by noting them in the context of the reading selection.
3. Ask only questions that tap important understandings not elicited in Steps 4 and 5.

Step 7. Extend the Comprehension Strategy   In Step 7 students practice the comprehension strategy that was introduced and then applied to a selection. This practice is provided to review the strategy, generate additional insights about it, and integrate it into students' daily functioning. At the same time, you can assess how each student performs the follow-up task to determine who is proficient with the strategy and who is not. Reteaching is needed for students who did not learn the strategy.

The model lesson plan extension consisted of a writing task that paralleled the reading task. Both tasks concerned problems, which was the subject of the story. In the model follow-up, students were to write rather than read a story. To be sure, composing an original story problem and solution differs from comprehending those of an author, so these activities might not seem to match. However, composing and comprehending have many similarities (Tierney & Shanahan, 1991), and one value of writing is that it can generate insights into the components of the comprehension process.

Another logical extension would be to compare other passages containing clear problems and solutions. Collections of short stories, novels, picture books, and plays could be tapped. Students also might note the problem-solution structure of past readings as well as movies and television shows. Comparing the various problems and solutions could be done in students' journals, through formal writing, during cooperative group discussions, or as a whole class. Students could work individually or as a group. Such student-centered activities provide learners with choices, opportunities to collaborate, and connections. Students reflect on the relevance of the strategy.

Finally, the closing comments in the model comprehension lesson consisted of a reminder about the strategy ("Remember, all stories have problems and solutions. Looking for them when you read helps you understand and remember stories"). Information is given about when to apply the strategy and why it is helpful. Students are reminded about what was presented to them. Three guidelines were described in this section:

1. Follow up strategies to provide practice, assess students' proficiencies, and teach again if needed.
2. Match extension activities with what was taught.
3. Remind students about *when* and *why* strategies are helpful.

FOR CHILDREN WITH SPECIAL NEEDS—STORY MAPS

Story maps draw children's attention to the structural elements of stories. Stories have characters and a setting. The characters ususally have some goal they want to achieve or some problem they need to resolve. The events in the story typically lead to some solution or resolution. Sometimes stories have implicit morals or themes.

Here is a story map based on a model created by Isabel Beck (Macon, Bewell, & Vogt, 1991):

Main Characters

Setting (Time and Place)

Problem or Goal

    Event 1

    Event 2

    Event 3

    Event 4

    Event 5

    Event 6

Solution

Story Theme or Moral

Here is the story map from above filled in for *The Three Little Pigs*:

Main Characters: Mother pig, three little pigs, big bad wolf.

Setting (Time and Place): Woods, make-believe time and place.

Problem or Goal: Pigs wanted to be independent and have own house.

    Event 1: Mother pig sends three little pigs out to build their own houses.

    Event 2: First little pig gets some straw and builds a straw house. Big bad wolf blows the straw house down.

    Event 3: Second little pig gets some sticks and builds a stick house. Big bad wolf blows the stick house down.

    Event 4: Third little pig gets some bricks and builds a brick house. Big bad wolf cannot blow the brick house down.

    Event 5: Big bad wolf runs off into woods (or gets scalded coming down the chimney—depending on how "violent" the version of the story is).

Solution: Pigs live happily ever after in strong brick house.

Story Theme or Moral: Hard work pays off in the end!

For readers having trouble comprehending, it is not enough to simply distribute story maps and have children complete them. After reading a story, display the map on an overhead projector and complete it with the students as your interactive audience. Express your thinking processes aloud as you complete the map so the children understand what you are thinking. Such thinking aloud by a teacher provides the expert model many special-needs children require.

Once children understand the story map elements, they can complete such maps in small groups and eventually on their own. It is important to help children see that the map is a device to help them determine and remember important elements in a story.

A Call to Action

In closing this somewhat long section on comprehension strategy lessons, we wish to stress two points that are part of a call to action. These points involve the plans teachers make about their instruction. One is concerned with control of curriculum resources and the other involves metacognition.

CONTROL OF CURRICULUM RESOURCES Suggestions for comprehension strategy lessons abound in resources such as curriculum guides, published units for novels, and basal reader materials. But what if your curriculum resources violate the guidelines presented here? What if your resources activate no prior knowledge but present 35 new words for each passage? What if your resources contain on each page five or six comprehension questions that do not relate to the purpose for reading? What if your resources include activities that do not extend the strategy that was presented? Teachers often feel pressured to follow curriculum resources, yet such resources were not designed to be followed word for word. Curriculum resources are best used to guide, not dictate, instruction.

You can refine a program. If your curriculum resources do not introduce strategies before expecting students to apply them, introduce the strategies. Teach general background and emphasize only about 10 vocabulary terms if your curriculum resources do not provide for this. Ask only the questions that relate to the purpose for reading before asking unrelated questions. If needed, redesign the curriculum resources to match the strategy that was presented. Refine your comprehension lesson plans to fit your students and your conception of appropriate instruction.

METACOGNITION Another important point about the strategies that are presented during comprehension lessons is that they need to be applied throughout a school day. Applying strategies to materials is important because performing a strategy when directed by teachers and performing it without teachers' directions are two separate concerns. Research in metacognition (Paris, Wasik, & Turner, 1991) clearly indicates that knowing *when* to perform strategies is a characteristic of proficient readers. Students might reread a difficult section of a passage when their teacher tells them to do so, but these same students might seldom reread difficult sections when on their own. Students might form mental images when so instructed by their teacher, but they might never form images when reading by themselves. Independent application of strategies is the goal of reading instruction.

The distinction between using strategies only when told to and using them independently is referred to as being skillful versus being strategic. Skillful students do well when someone tells them to perform a particular strategy (e.g., "Find the main ideas of the next 10 paragraphs"); strategic readers are skillful, and they independently apply their skills when needed. Strategic readers know *when* to note main ideas or problems and solutions.

Several techniques are available for developing strategic readers. The conversation between teachers and students when checking comprehension and following up on the reading purpose is a good time to help students learn when and why certain strategies are appropriate. Another way to help students become strategic readers is to assign a reading passage and then ask the students what they should do in order to understand it. The few minutes spent brainstorming strategies that probably are needed for comprehending a particular passage is time well spent. Strategic reading, along with other important literacy outcomes, develops especially well when students use reading and writing to explore topics across the curriculum.

FOR CHILDREN WITH SPECIAL NEEDS—QARS

QARs (Raphael, 1982) stands for Question-Answer Relationships. QARs help children learn that much of the information they gain from reading is not "right there" on the page. If you have ever had a child leave a question unanswered and then protest, "I couldn't find the answer—it didn't say!" you will appreciate the value of teaching children to use the QAR strategy. In QAR children learn that there are three basic types of questions:

1. Right There questions
2. Think and Search questions
3. On My Own questions

To teach children about the three types of questions, write a paragraph or two about one of the children in your class, such as:

> The morning got off to a bad start when David turned off his alarm clock and rolled over and went back to sleep. He barely made the bus and he had to sit next to Jennifer! When David got to school, he realized that he had forgotten his lunch money and his homework! He borrowed lunch money from Jennifer and had to do his homework over again during the after-lunch recess! The long day finally ended and David boarded the bus to go home. "One down, four to go," he thought as the bus slowly made its way to his street.

Ask the children two questions that are explicitly answered in the paragraph:

Who did David sit next to on the bus?

What two important things had David forgotten?

The children should be able to find the answers to these literal questions, and you can easily illustrate why this type of question is labeled "Right There."

Next, ask two questions that do not have answers right there but have clues to appropriate responses. Explain to the children that they will be able to answer these questions only if they search for clues in the passage and think about what would make sense:

What were the other children doing while David did his homework over?

On what day of the week did this story take place?

Help the children realize that you must Think and Search for clues in order to answer these questions. Since it was recess time, the other children were probably outside playing. Because David said, "One down, four to go" as he was riding home, it was probably Monday, leaving four more days of the school week. The children should conclude that you can find support for answers to these questions, but you cannot find the answers stated right there on the page.

Finally, ask two questions that do not necessarily have a right answer, such as:

What will David do when his alarm goes off on Tuesday morning?

If David's mother asks him, "What kind of day did you have?" what words might he use to describe his day?

Help children to see that there are many possible answers to these questions and that the answers come not from the story but from their own experiences and their own thinking. We label these questions "On My Own."

Once children understand the differences between the three types of question-answer relationships, use all three types to guide the reading of selections. Do not label the questions but have the students decide which type of question each is after they answer them. When students are able to distinguish the three types of questions, have them work together in groups to make up questions of each type to ask other groups of students.

QARs can be used with both stories and informational text. Their value lies in the message their regular use conveys to children. Reading is not just saying words and looking for answers that are right there. Reading is also searching for clues and thinking about what the clues lead to, and reading is using your own ideas and experiences to make predictions, generalizations, and evaluations.

TRY IT OUT

 Plan and deliver a comprehension strategy lesson plan. Select one of the strategies listed in Figure 6.2 and prepare a seven-step lesson for teaching it to students. Presenting a lesson to actual elementary students is best, but presenting one to your classmates in a role-playing microteaching format can be an alternative. Obtain feedback from your students about the strengths and limitations of the lesson, and, if possible, present a revised version of it to a second set of students. Be sure to use materials appropriate for the students' reading proficiencies.

STUDY STRATEGIES CAN BE DEVELOPED IN THE CONTENT AREAS ACROSS THE CURRICULUM

Study strategies are another aspect of literacy that students readily develop when reading across the curriculum. Study strategies differ only slightly from comprehension strategies. Whereas reading comprehension strategies enable readers to understand printed information, study strategies enable readers to understand and *remember* printed information (Devine, 1991). Study strategies enable long-term learning from text. The distinction between comprehension and study strategies is clear when you listen to jokes. Have you ever heard a good joke, laughed at the punch line, and then failed to remember the joke when you wanted to tell it later? You understood the joke, but you didn't learn it. Your comprehension strategies were successful, but your study strategies were either nonexistent or unsuccessful.

When you want to learn jokes—or any other verbal message—you can employ several strategies. You can tell yourself to think about the joke, making a conscious decision to learn. After hearing a joke, you can review it to be sure you remember it correctly. You might form a mental image of the characters and actions in the joke. You might select key words to be a reminder of the entire joke. You might think of similar jokes and mentally attach the new one to the old ones. If you're really serious about remembering the joke, you might write it down. Indeed, you might perform all of these strategies, only a few of them, or others in order to learn the new information.

Teachers who wish to teach students how to learn information encountered across the curriculum present several study strategies. Some of the strategies are described in basal reader series and language arts textbooks, and some content-area textbooks present strategies for learning from text. Some of the study strategies frequently listed are as follows:

Previewing a passage

Establishing a purpose for learning

Asking and answering one's own questions

Summarizing

Graphically organizing information (e.g., web, outline, time line)

Maintaining a learning log

Taking notes

Orally reviewing content with others

Producing word study cards

To describe how these strategies can be taught, we focus here on note taking.

As a complex study strategy, note-taking cannot be taught in one or two sessions. Students need a variety of experiences and clear guidance. Modeling is perhaps the essential element in teaching this strategy. As reading passages come up during content lessons, occasionally "walk" students through the process of taking notes with the aid of a listening guide. In such a "walk through," you provide a rough outline of the passage that omits selected details and/or major points. Your students have a copy of the outline at their desks, and you have one on an overhead transparency. You then read aloud brief portions of the passage, and students follow along in their text. The length of the portions depends on factors such as your students' attention span, background, reading ability, and interest. After reaching a logical stopping point, stop and fill in your outline guide on an overhead projector with its light off. Next, turn on the overhead projector light and explain what you have written. This enables your class to see what good notes are like. Then turn off the projector light and read the next portion of text to your class as they read along. Have your students write their own notes, and then compare what they have written with what you have written. This read-compose-compare prodcedure continues throughout the passage.

The modeling format described here should be mixed with opportunities to compose notes independently so that your students do not come to overdepend on your help. Furthermore, the amount of structure provided by the listening guide is to be faded out with time. This means that you provide most of the information in an outline at first but gradually remove more and more of the points during the year until your class begins with practically a blank page. Finally, the rough outline you provide as a listening guide during this activity need not follow the rigid format of traditional outlining. For instance, during a unit on volcanoes students might investigate what magma produces. As Figure 6.3 shows, this information could be graphically organized three ways, through an outline, a data chart, and a web. Moreover, ideas about whether magma is helpful or hurtful could be listed in a T-diagram as Figure 6.4 shows.

You can present study strategies in much the same way as you present comprehension strategies. Tie them into the content of the material students are using. Show students how the strategies facilitate their grasp of the material. Help students understand what the strategies are, why they are helpful, how they work, and when to use them.

An important point about comprehension and study strategies involves their complexity. Both rely on higher-order thinking. The processes in determining problem-solution story structures, connecting known information with passage contents, taking notes, and graphically organizing ideas cannot be reduced to a fixed series of steps that always produce the same results. Long division can be presented as an invariant routine, but comprehension and study strategies cannot. These strategies require countless decisions about the relative importance of ideas and their relationships. Due to the complexity of strategies, do not expect students to become adept with them after one or two experiences. Students require many opportunities to apply and refine strategies to their reading, to integrate strategies into their repertoires. Students need much support when

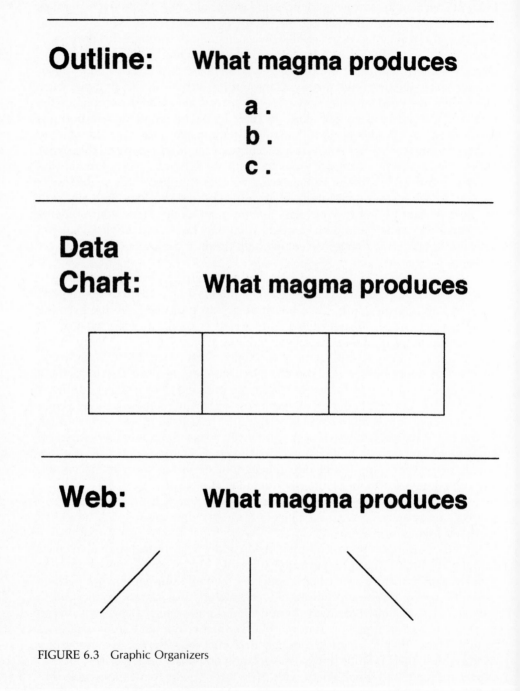

Outline: **What magma produces**

        a .
        b .
        c .

Data
Chart: **What magma produces**

Web: **What magma produces**

FIGURE 6.3   Graphic Organizers

Is magma helpful or hurtful?

Helpful   ## Hurtful

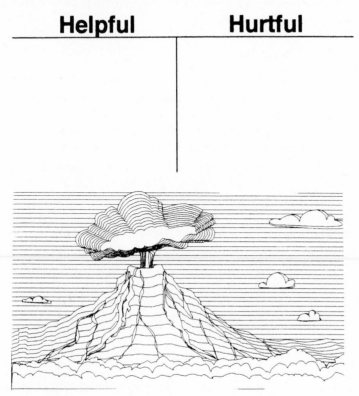

FIGURE 6.4   T-Diagram

strategies are first introduced and a gradual reduction of support over time. Students need supportive instructional settings to gain control of comprehension and study strategies.

FOR CHILDREN WITH SPECIAL NEEDS—RECIPROCAL TEACHING

Reciprocal teaching (Palincsar & Brown, 1986) is a highly regarded technique for teaching students an independent study system. The technique is titled *reciprocal* because teachers and students alternate in a give-and-take, back-and-forth dialogue. Teachers introduce this technique by stopping at designated points in a text to share their thinking about the passage and elicit students' responses to particular types of inquiries. Students act like apprentices during these introductory lessons, eventually assuming the teacher's role and taking turns leading their own discussions with a partner.

Reciprocal teaching is centered about four study strategies: summarizing, questioning, clarifying, and predicting. Teachers—and later students—begin a reciprocal teaching session by summarizng a passage, asking questions to check understandings of it, clarifying difficult concepts, and predicting what will be encountered next. This four-step process continues throughout a passage, with extensive teacher-student or student-student conversations about the contents. The following exemplifies a reciprocal teaching exchange with a section entitled "Troubled Children in Troubled Schools."

> TEACHER [summarizing]: This section talked about how children who grew up to commit crimes are almost always children who had troubled experiences in school. Many children learn in school that they are second rate.
>
> TEACHER [questioning]: I wonder what statistics there are to support this. Do adult criminals have worse school records than noncriminals?
>
> STUDENT [clarifying]: The passage doesn't say. We would have to look somewhere else. Besides, the point here is that criminals don't just start out as adults; they get started when they are young.
>
> STUDENT [predicting]: The title of the next section is "How Schools Have Changed." It probably will tell how schools are more dangerous now compared to 10 years ago.

The reciprocal teaching exchange presented above is very brief. It illustrates thought processes associated with each study strategy, but it only minimally represents the interactions that occur in full-blown discussions. Teachers and students might have extensive back-and forth discussions before agreeing on a statement of the summary. In addition, the sample above shows only a reciprocal teaching cycle with the introductory teacher-student role; it does not show teacher-student roles reversed or a cycle with student-student roles.

THE THEORY AND RESEARCH BASE FOR READING COMPREHENSION INSTRUCTION

Since the late 1970s researchers and theorists have concentrated enormous amounts of attention on reading comprehension. As with any body of knowledge, the amount that is known reveals the even larger amount that is not known. Nevertheless, this research and theory have produced some commonly accepted generalizations, three of which correspond to the three key ideas of this chapter.

Comprehension Is an Active Process

In order to construct meaning from print, readers manipulate vast stores of knowledge, strategies, and dispositions. Proficient readers interact and transact with the words on the page to derive a message. As noted in Chapter 1, readers' thinking can be categorized among strategies such as calling up prior knowlege, connecting new ideas with preexisting ones, and evaluating the ideas contained in the text.

Many authorities (e.g., Flood & Lapp, 1991; Paris, Wasik, & Turner, 1991) allocate strategies to three stages of the reading act, before, during, and after, as follows:

Before Reading/Preparing to Read
Preview
Build background/activate prior knowledge
Set purpose

During Reading/Constructing Meaning while Reading
Check understanding
Monitor comprehension
Integrate
Identify main ideas
Make inferences
Inspect text already read

After Reading/Reviewing and Reflecting
Culminate strategies begun earlier
Summarize
Evaluate
Apply

Students Benefit from Guided Instruction in Comprehension Strategies

Research reviews by Tierney and Cunningham (1984), Haller, Child, and Walberg (1988), and Pearson and Fielding (1991), among others, have demonstrated effects for directly guiding children to comprehension strategies such as the ones listed above. Teachers typically play a central role in guiding instruction and deciding what strategies to teach, when to teach them, and how well they were learned. The comprehension lesson presented in this chapter exemplifies guided instruction.

Children seem to benefit from this direct guided approach as long as teachers explain the strategies in a sensible, meaningful, and compelling manner; present the strategy's components in a step-by-step manner; and indicate when the strategies are appropriate to use. Moreover, guided strategy instruction with perhaps the most consistent support involves control of text structure (Pearson & Fielding, 1991). Students typically benefit from learning to recognize how authors relate ideas (e.g., problem-solution, comparison-contrast, cause-effect) and how to graphically represent those relationships (e.g., web, data chart, time line).

Students Benefit from Process-Oriented Approaches to Comprehension Instruction

Students also acquire comprehension strategies by reading widely, having a passion for the ideas and enjoyment they obtain from reading, and responding to what they read within a community of like-minded peers. They acquire strategies when they take the lead in deciding what to read and what to do with the ideas stimulated by their reading. When students realize that they are having difficulty making sense of an idea, they seek help from their teachers or classmates, who might suggest specific comprehension strategies. Teachers who provide an instructional environment that supports this form of instruction are following a process-oriented approach.

Applebee (1991), Jensen (1989), and Short and Pierce (1990), among others, have described process-oriented classrooms that promote students' understanding of texts. The teachers in these classrooms follow a constructivist orientation, viewing learning as an active personal endeavor strongly affected by social dynamics. Teachers working wihtin a constructivist process-oriented framework emphasize student inquiries into topics of study. They foster student ownership of literacy tasks, encouraging students to establish their own purposes for reading. They also foster collaboration, having students work together and with the teacher in risk-free settings.

This chapter emphasizes guided instruction in comprehension strategies, detailing the specifics of comprehension strategy lessons. Chapter 5, "Reading and Responding to Literature for Children," tends more toward a process-oriented approach to comprehension instruction.

LOOKING BACK

Comprehension is a complex process that requires readers to juggle many sources of information. Students learn to control this process during many encounters with print inside and outside classrooms. Teachers plan and implement comprehension lessons to directly teach students to control their comprehension. Teachers also capitalize on explorations of subject matter topics to develop students' comprehension and study strategies. This chapter presents this information under four key ideas:

1. Reading comprehension results from an interaction among word identification, prior knowledge, comprehension strategies, and interest.
2. Literacy can be developed in the content areas across the curriculum.
3. Comprehension strategy lessons engage students before, during, and after reading.

4. Study strategies can be developed in the content areas across the curriculum.

ADD TO YOUR JOURNAL

 This chapter presents four aspects of reading comprehension. Do you think anything else belongs in a description of the dynamics of reading comprehension? What else do you think might be involved in the process of constructing meaning from print?

The seven steps of comprehension lesson plans present a rather detailed view of lesson planning. Compare this lesson format with others you have encountered. What is the same; what is different? How might you combine their positive features?

Call up your elementary school experiences with reading across the curriculum. What attention to your reading and writing during subject matter study do you recall? How do you intend to incorporate literacy instruction with subject matter study?

REFERENCES

Anderson, R. C., & Pearson, P. D. (1984). A schema-theoretic view of basic reading processes in reading comprehension. In P. D. Pearson (Ed.), *Handbook of reading research* (pp. 255–291). White Plains, NY: Longman.

Applebee, A. N. (1991). Environments for language teaching and learning: Contemporary issues and future directions. In J. Flood, J. M. Jensen, D. Lapp, & J. R. Squire (Eds.), *Handbook of research on teaching the English language arts* (pp. 549–556). New York: Macmillan.

Armbruster, B. B., Anderson, T. H., & Ostertag, J. (1987). Does text structure/summarization instruction facilitate learning from expository text? *Reading Research Quarterly, 22,* 331–346.

Atwell, N. (1987). *In the middle.* Portsmouth, NH: Heinemann.

Baldwin, R. S., Peleg-Bruckner, Z., & McClintock, A. H. (1985). Effects of topic interest and prior knowledge on reading comprehension. *Reading Research Quarterly, 20,* 497–504.

Bransford, J. D., & McCarrel, N. S. (1974). A sketch of a cognitive approach to comprehension. In W. B. Weimer & D. S. Palermo (Eds.), *Cognition and the symbolic processes* (pp. 189–229). Hillsdale, NJ: Erlbaum.

Cunningham, P. M. (1975). Transferring comprehension from listening to reading. *The Reading Teacher, 29,* 169–172.

Devine, T. G. (1991). Studying: Skills, strategies, and systems. In J. Flood, J. M. Jensen, D. Lapp, & J. R. Squire (Eds.), *Handbook of research on teaching the English language arts* (pp. 743–753). New York: Macmillan.

Duffy, G. G., & Roehler, L. R. (1986). Teaching reading skills as strategies. *The Reading Teacher, 40,* 414–418.

Flood, J., & Lapp, D. (1991). Reading comprehension instruction. In J. Flood, J. M. Jensen, D. Lapp, & J. R. Squire (Eds.), *Handbook of research on teaching the English language arts* (pp. 732–742). New York: Macmillan.

Fulwiler, T., & Young, A. (1982). *Language connections: Writing and reading across the curriculum.* Urbana, IL: National Council of Teachers of English.

Goodman, K. S. (1984). Unity in reading. In A. C. Purves & O. Niles (Eds.), *Becoming readers in a complex society* (Eighty-third Yearbook of the National Society for the Study of Education) (pp. 79–114). Chicago: National Society for the Study of Education.

Haller, E. P., Child, D. A., & Walberg, H. J. (1988). Can comprehension be taught? A quantitative synthesis of "metacognitive" studies. *Educational Researcher, 17,* 5–8.

Harste, J. C., & Short, K. G. (1988). *Creating classrooms for authors.* Portsmouth, NH: Heinemann.

Jensen, J. M. (1989). *Stories to grow on.* Portsmouth, NH: Heinemann.

Joyce, B., & Weil, M. (1992). *Models of teaching* (4th ed.). Englewood Cliffs, NJ: Prentice-Hall.

Macon J. M., Bewell, D., & Vogt, M. (1991). *Responses to literature.* Newark, DE: International Reading Association.

Palincsar, A. S., & Brown, A. L. (1986). Interactive teaching to promote independent learning from text. *The Reading Teacher, 39,* 771–777.

Paris, S. G., Wasik, B. A., & Turner, J. C. (1991). The development of strategic readers. In R. Barr, M. L. Kamil, P. B. Mosenthal, & P. D. Pearson (Eds.), *Handbook of reading research* (Vol. 2, pp. 609–640). New York: Longman.

Pearson, P. D., & Fielding, L. (1991). Comprehension instruction. In R. Barr, M. L. Kamil, P. B. Mosenthal, & P. D. Pearson (Eds.), *Handbook of reading research* (Vol. 2, pp. 815–860). White Plains, NY: Longman.

Porter, C. (1990). Student-created units: Choice, collaboration, and connections. In K. G. Short & K. M. Pierce (Eds.), *Talking about books.* Portsmouth, NH: Heinemann.

Raphael, T. (1982). Question-answering strategies for children. *The Reading Teacher, 39,* 186–190.

Rumelhart, D. E. (1985). Toward an interactive model of reading. In H. Singer & R. B. Ruddell (Eds.), *Theoretical models and processes of reading* (3rd ed., pp. 722–750). Newark, DE: International Reading Association.

Short, K. G., & Pierce, K. M. (1990). *Talking about books.* Portsmouth, NH: Heinemann.

Tierney, R. J., & Cunningham, J. W. (1984). Research on teaching comprehension. In P. D. Pearson (Ed.), *Handbook of reading research* (pp. 609–655). New York: Longman.

Tierney, R. J., & Shanahan, T. (1991). Research on the reading-writing relationship: Interactions, transactions, and outcomes. In R. Barr, M. L. Kamil, P. B. Mosenthal, & P. D. Pearson (Eds.), *Handbook of reading research* (Vol. 2, pp. 246–280). White Plains, NY: Longman.

Underwood, G., & Boot, D. (1986). Hemispheric asymmetries in developmental dyslexia: Cerebral structure or attentional strategies? *Journal of Reading Behavior, 18,* 219–228.

Wade, S. E., & Adams, R. B. (1990). Effects of importance and interest on recall of biographical text. *Journal of Reading Behavior, 22,* 331–353.

ADDITIONAL READINGS

A good introduction to teaching text structure is in the following.

Armbruster, B. B., Anderson, T. H., & Ostertag, J. (1989). Teaching text structure to improve reading and writing. *The Reading Teacher, 43,* 130–137.

These two articles on how to teach comprehension strategies offer additional perspectives.

Pressley, M., El-Dinary, P. B., & Gaskins, I. W. (1992). Beyond direct explanation: Transactional instruction of reading comprehension strategies. *Elementary School Journal, 92,* 513–555.

Rosenshine, B., & Meister, C. (1992). The use of scaffolds for teaching higher-level cognitive strategies. *Educational Leadership, 50,* 26–33.

Consult these three references for additional views on how to present inquiry and integrated units of instruction.

Gamberg, R., Kwak, W., Hutchings, M., & Altheim, J., with Edwards, G. (1988). *Learning and loving it: Theme studies in the classroom.* Portsmouth, NH: Heinemann.

Jacobs, H. H. (Ed.). (1989). *Interdisciplinary curriculum: Design and implementation.* Alexandria, VA: Association for Supervision and Curriculum Development.

Porter, C. (1990). Student-created units: Choice, collaboration, and connections. In K. G. Short & K. M. Pierce (Eds.), *Talking about books.* Portsmouth, NH: Heinemann.

Special-needs children can be accommodated in literature-based units, as the following article explains.

Bartley, N. (1993). Literature-based integrated language instruction and the language-deficient student. *Reading Research and Instruction, 32,* 31–37.

A good overview of study skills instruction is presented in this monograph.

Gall, M. D., Gall, J. P., Jacobsen, D. R., & Bullock, T. L. (1990). *Tools for learning: A guide to teaching study skills.* Alexandria, VA: Association for Supervision and Curriculum Development.

Writing

LOOKING AHEAD

No area of the elementary school curriculum has undergone more change than how children are taught to write. The process approach to teaching writing has spread until it is now widely used. This chapter helps teachers understand how elementary schools can teach both process writing and focused writing as well as how traditional concerns with writing mechanics and usage can also be met.

Back when they were first called "The Three R's," *reading* usually meant oral reading, *arithmetic* meant computation, and *writing* meant handwriting. In recent decades, reading has increasingly come to include and emphasize silent reading comprehension, arithmetic to include and emphasize problem solving, and writing to include and emphasize composition. Still, until the recent process writing revolution, the focus in writing instruction was more on spelling, mechanics, and usage than the ability to organize and express ideas.

Contemporary society increasingly communicates through writing. Listen to those who work in large businesses or agencies today. Their constant complaint seems to be the amount of paperwork they must do. Some of that paperwork is the completion of simple forms, but more and more it also consists of writing memoranda, reports, brochures, and business letters. Word processing is ubiquitous, and almost everyone appears to want or need to leave "a paper trail" in his or her wake.

Like the learning of reading and mathematics, learning to write takes several years of good instruction, each of which builds on what was previously learned. In this chapter, we present to you a balanced approach to help children become writers through the elementary school years. The key ideas in this chapter are:

1. All students need to engage in process writing.
2. Students need to learn to produce many different types of writing.
3. Students learn conventions by applying them in their own writing.
4. Students profit from writing in the content areas across the curriculum.

ALL STUDENTS NEED TO ENGAGE IN PROCESS WRITING

Since the late 1970s, there has been a steady and dramatic increase in elementary classrooms of what is often called the *process approach to teaching writing.* Other names for this same approach include writing process approach; natural process mode of teaching writing; writers' workshop; journal writing; and writing workshop. Whichever label is used, process writing programs are characterized by their adherence to several principles and their inclusion of several components.

Children Choose Their Own Topics

From the very first day of a process writing program, individual children have the responsibility of deciding what topics they will write about and how they will approach them. This is an essential characteristic of process writing for three main reasons. First, children the world over acquire the ability to listen and speak by trying to communicate with others in their homes and surroundings. No infant is taught how to listen or speak in a direct fashion, but he or she acquires oral language ability by actually participating in communication acts. Every language user begins by wanting to make others understand. Having something to say serves as the motivation for acquiring the ability to say it. Success in communicating is the reward for trying to learn how to do it. The inability to make oneself understood provides the incentive for trying to improve in language development. Consequently, when children are introduced to writing, it does them little good for someone else to tell them what to write about. That destroys their motivation to do the hard, sometimes frustrating, work of trying to be understood by others.

Second, people communicate best when they have knowledge of the topic they are speaking or writing about. When students choose the topic of their writing, they almost always choose something from their experience. When provided a topic by someone else, they often lose the advantage their prior knowledge of a personally chosen topic would have given them.

Third, process writing is an area where we can take advantage of an excellent opportunity to utilize the multicultural backgrounds and perspectives of an increasingly diverse student population. When students write mainly about topics we provide them, we miss that opportunity.

Children Share Their Writing with Other Students

Once individual students are writing several times a week about topics of their own choosing in their own ways, it is an essential characteristic of a process writing program that the students share what they have written with each other. If the chief motivation for learning to write is to communicate with others, the writer must have a supportive audience who reads or listens to what was written. Process writing programs use other students rather than the teacher as that audience. Writers must understand and be able to relate to their audiences. A child writer is more likely to understand children and be more able to relate to other children than to an adult, particularly a teacher who is responsible for grading and discipline. When the teacher is the only one who reads or hears student writing, much less sharing goes on and it is often delayed. If sharing is to have maximum value for establishing writing as communication, the amount of sharing must be substantial and come soon after pieces are written. Having students regularly share their writing with each other is the best way to achieve substantial and timely communication through writing.

For sharing to play its role in helping children develop as writers, the children must respond as readers and listeners, not teachers or critics. They must respond to the ideas of what is written, not its form, and positively, rather than negatively. Fortunately, having students choose their own topics for writing and approaching those topics in their own way make it much more likely that sharing can be kept positive and centered on ideas. When a group of students is given a topic for writing, the content of the different papers will tend to be somewhat similar. This similarity of content causes students to focus more on the lower-level form of a piece of writing when it is shared. However, when the topic of each piece of writing is different, children are more likely to concentrate on the ideas when a piece is shared.

In addition, when students all write on the same topic, their differences in writing ability become obvious to all. This fact usually results in more negative comments on the writing of the students whose abilities are less well developed. In our experience, children seem quite tolerant of major differences in sophistication between two pieces of writing by two different children as long as those two pieces address different topics in different ways.

As children improve in their willingness and ability to express their ideas in writing, sharing serves an additional role. These shared writings become models for other children to follow and adapt as they make decisions and solve problems about what they want to say and how they want to say it.

Teachers Teach Minilessons

As long as they are careful not to intimidate students with their sophistication or quantity of writing, teachers can also provide modeling to children by sharing what they write. When teachers plan aloud what they are going to write and then actually write it on the overhead projector while students watch and read what is being written, that kind of teacher sharing is called a *writing minilesson*. Minilessons are extremely valuable tools for showing children how to think of a topic and how to go about deciding the way one approaches writing about a topic one has chosen. When a writing minilesson is followed immediately by a time of student writing, the teacher can often see students improve in the use of whatever planning or writing strategies the teacher modeled during that minilesson. Of course, teachers can also write while the children are writing and occasionally share what they have written during sharing time afterward. The emphasis during sharing time, though, must be on the children sharing their writing with each other.

Children Invent Spellings

The most controversial feature of process writing is that students must invent spellings (guess how to spell words) while writing. It is feared by some that students who invent spellings will develop bad habits and fail to discover the importance of correct spelling. Both concerns are legitimate, but overstated. If process writing is seen as the way we *introduce* writing to children, the tolerance for incorrect spellings in children's writing is as natural and harmless as our tolerance for the beginning speech patterns of two-year-olds. Invented spelling has two main values that make it an essential component of a process writing program. Its greatest value is that it enables children to write before they have mastered spelling. If children who have not learned to spell well are held account-able for correct spellings on their first drafts, they will write very little and will write it very slowly. They will resist writing words unless they are sure how to spell them correctly. They will wait to write a word until the teacher or another child tells them how to spell it. If you try to get them to use a dictionary instead of asking you, writing must be postponed until children have learned alphabetization and the other skills necessary to use one efficiently. Without invented spelling, beginning writers will not write enough for a process writing program to succeed.

A less well understood value of invented spelling is that it is an important activity to help children develop the phonological skills on which later phonics and spelling abilities are based. When children are encouraged and required to guess how to spell words, they must listen for the sounds of the words in order and represent those sounds as best they can with letters. This process requires them to focus on letter-sound relationships in an intense way and provides them with an excellent application activity for any phonics they are learning elsewhere during the day. And their attempted spellings reveal to the teacher how well they are progressing in their acquisition of sound-letter knowledge.

Three practices mitigate against children having any long-term problems re-sulting from invented spelling. (1) Teachers can place the most frequent and least phonetic words on the wall so children can see them from wherever they sit in the room. This "word wall" eventually becomes internalized by students as they refer to it during writing, so they learn to spell the most frequent words correctly without having to interrupt their writing to ask someone or consult a dictionary. (2) Teachers of process writing can also require students to have correct spellings in any final drafts they "publish," for example, those displayed on a bulletin board in the hall or sent home with them. This practice teaches the importance of correct spelling without requiring it on first drafts, which would reduce the amount and enjoyment of writing itself. (3) Teachers can teach conventional spellings at a separate time during the school day and expect that students will eventually spell those words correctly in their first drafts without being told to do so. (See Chapter 3, "Word Fluency: Decoding and Spelling.")

Children Revise Some of What They Have Written

In a process writing program, at first, children write several times a week on topics of their own choosing and share what they have written by reading it aloud to the class, a sharing group, or another student. During sharing (sometimes called *peer conferencing*), teachers help students be content oriented and positive in their comments about each other's writing. After several weeks of this kind of writing and sharing, children's apprehensions and negative associations with writing diminish or even disappear. They look forward to writing and sharing what they have written.

When writing has become a regular, positive occurrence for students, process writing teachers begin having students do some targeted rewriting of selected first drafts. The impetus for students to rewrite at first is usually that they are going to write a "book." Having students rework and extend a first draft, illustrate it, and bind it with the teacher's help makes writing incredibly exciting for children and gives them a purpose for working hard on what they have written. Actually, it is the several phases of publishing a piece of writing that gives the *process* approach its name (Dyson & Freedman, 1991).

As each student plans first drafts, writes first drafts, and selects a first draft from his or her working portfolio to revise for publication, the teacher does very little other than to encourage, to model, and to help students be open and positive toward each other's efforts. Once a student has selected a first draft to revise, however, the teacher's guidance becomes much more important. Even if revisions are to be based on suggestions made during peer conferences, the teacher needs to be involved to maximize the feeling of accomplishment that the student achieves from the publication. It is usually a good idea for the teacher to read the draft each student has selected and then meet individually with that child for a few minutes to help the child develop a plan and reasonable expectations for what the published piece will be like. If a book is going to be produced by the child, will the book have illustrations? Who will do them? What size will they be? Will they be drawn or colored? Will the illustrations be done first? Will the book be bound? Will there be a dedication? Who will copy the text onto the book pages, the student or the teacher? Whether or not the published draft will have illustrations or take the form of a book, will the spelling, capitalization, punctuation, and so forth have to meet certain standards? What are they? Will it be the student's responsibility to meet those standards or will the teacher make any required corrections that only need be copied?

Obviously, the teacher must carefully oversee this process to maximize both students' learning and students' feelings of success. Assessment of student writing is the crucial factor in guiding how the teacher will use revision and editing to help each student improve. (See Chapter 8, "Diagnosis and Assessment.")

Why Process Writing Is Essential

Traditionally, prior to the late 1970s, students did very little writing other than copying or responding to short-answer questions until they wrote their first report in social studies, science, or health, around the fourth grade. Even that first report was often largely copied from an encyclopedia. What little "creative writing" was done in elementary school was often on a voluntary basis, as part of a writing contest or during leisure time. Those students who most needed writing opportunities were, of course, the least likely to volunteer. Does the contrast between this tradition and the process writing approach mean that process writing is new? Not really.

Most of the children who became good writers in the traditional elementary school had engaged in something like process writing at home. Perhaps a chalkboard or marker board was purchased for the child when he or she was about three years old. The letters of the alphabet were probably displayed at the top of that board. Perhaps magnetic letters were purchased and placed on the front of the refrigerator so the child could manipulate them. Alphabet blocks and even soup were probably also made available to the child.

From age two, the child was probably allowed to mark on paper with pens, pencils, or crayons as long as he or she did not write on floors or walls. At age three or four, the child was probably taught how to print his or her first name. Since the parents often wrote letters and shopping lists, the child pretended to write letters and shopping lists as well.

As these children received formal handwriting, reading, phonics, and spelling instruction in the primary grades, they gradually incorporated some of what they were learning in their "play" writing at home. Perhaps they were often encouraged to write an occasional letter to Santa Claus or Grandma or a friend who had moved away. Perhaps they were then encouraged to put foods or things they needed for school "on the list." Perhaps they made a birthday list or Christmas list of presents they wanted to receive.

Without necessarily intending to do so, many families provided and still provide occasional "process writing" experiences over a five- or six-year period for their children. During these experiences, children are usually permitted to "write" without the parents caring whether they spell words correctly or make their letters just so. Unlined paper and colored writing implements are used without penalty. Communication and enjoyment are the only important features of most of these out-of-school writing activities.

The growth of the process writing approach in schools over the last decade and a half is based on two basic insights. First, if some children are already doing process writing at home (including invented spelling), it cannot hurt them to do more at school. Second, if some children have not been doing process writing at home, they may never learn to write well without it.

Indeed, it has been our experience that even students in fourth or fifth grade who have not engaged in regular process writing before will demonstrate the same growth in willingness and ability to write from regular process writing as do kindergartners and first graders.

Establishing a Process Writing Program in Your Classroom

It is not difficult to establish a process writing program in your classroom, if:

1. you are committed and patient;
2. you encourage and eventually require invented spellings;
3. you do not correct or grade first drafts;
4. you encourage and eventually require sharing; and
5. you insist that students respond positively to each other's writing.

THE FOUR STEPS   Early in kindergarten or first grade, many teachers teach students "the four steps": draw a picture, write something, write your name, copy or stamp the date (Fisher, 1991). At first, the teacher carries out a minilesson to model the four steps. Using an overhead projector placed on the floor so as not to obstruct anyone's view of the screen, the teacher actually does the four steps while the children sit together on a rug and watch. The teacher is careful to draw a very simple and primitive picture that will not intimidate the children into thinking they must be artistic. While drawing, the teacher tells them what he or she is trying to draw. Then the teacher prints something about the picture (e.g., "This is my new car" or "I went to see a baseball game") while saying it out loud. There are no lines on the acetate for the teacher to write on. At this point, the teacher explains to the students that, since they have not been taught how to write yet, they may just write some letters they know. The children are told that whatever they write will be okay. Some teachers model for the children what their writing might look like. Then the teacher writes his or her name. Again, the children are told that it is all right if they cannot write their names; they should just put some letters they think might be in their names. Finally, the teacher copies the date (e.g., 9/10) off the chalkboard. Immediately after this minilesson, the children are given paper and writing implements and encouraged to do the four steps at their seats. The teacher walks around the room encouraging children to do whatever they can. This minilesson, followed by having students do the four steps, is repeated every day in an atmosphere of patience and encouragement until all students are attempting to do the four steps.

SUSTAINED SILENT WRITING   When children come to second grade or higher and have not engaged in much process writing before, the teacher often uses Sustained Silent Writing (SSW) as the means of getting students to write regularly without fear of failure or fixation on form. This same method is sometimes called Can't Stop Writing. The children are given a minute or two of quiet time to think individually of what they want to write about. Then, using a kitchen timer with its face turned away, the teacher sets an amount of time during which everyone, including the teacher, must write without interrupting anyone. At first, most teachers set the timer for three minutes. When the timer bell rings, students are allowed to finish the sentence they are writing and then they must stop.

Teachers often introduce students to SSW by modeling it in a minilesson. They first do a teacher think-aloud to model their choice of a topic (e.g., "Let's see . . . what have I seen in the last day or two that was interesting? Oh, I know. On the way home yesterday, I saw firefighters trying to put out a fire in a field. I think I'll write about that"). They pick up the kitchen timer, set it for three minutes, and write on the overhead while the children sit and watch. While teachers write, they are careful to keep it simple and to write slowly so they do not intimidate the students with their superior writing facility. They do not talk while they write, so the students try to read what the teacher is writing while it is being written. When the timer bell rings, teachers finish the sentence they are writing and stop. They then read aloud to the children what they have written. If the children want to talk positively about the ideas briefly, teachers permit that discussion.

Immediately following this minilesson, the children are given a minute or two to think individually about what they want to write about, and then three minutes of SSW occurs for the entire class, including the teacher. SSW is done regularly until all the children are sustaining their writing for three minutes. Gradually a minute is added to this time until children are able to sustain their writing for six or seven minutes. Once children are writing willingly and enjoying it for six or seven minutes or longer, SSW has probably outlived its usefulness. Rather than a means to get students comfortable just writing to their own topics with invented spelling, timing actually becomes counterproductive. How long will it take to increase a class's SSW from three to six or seven minutes? It depends on how much writing the students did the prior year.

Of course, it is not always possible to determine how much the children have engaged in regular process writing in previous years, especially the prior year, so it is a good idea to monitor carefully. If children moan when it is writing time, complain that they can't think of anything to write about, and ask you to spell words for them, they are almost certainly not ready to write longer. If children seem familiar with writing, write without asking you for topics or spellings, and some even complain that they want more time to write, a minute should be added to the timer. In short, SSW may be used for a few weeks or a few months, depending on what the students seem to need.

INVENTED SPELLING   Invented spelling is always encouraged from the beginning in a process writing program. Before students write on the first day, they are told that their papers will not be corrected or graded for spelling. They are told that if they share what they have written, they will do so by reading it aloud. A few days into the program, the teacher does a minilesson before students write in which she or he models invented spelling (sometimes called "ear spelling") for the children. Whenever children ask how to spell a word, they are told "to write down any letters you hear." The teacher may do a guided invented spelling lesson in which the students guess several different ways a given word might be spelled before finding out how it is spelled correctly.

SHARING   From the beginning of a process writing program, children are also invited to volunteer to share what they have written. Usually the student who has just shared is allowed to call on two or three children to make a comment or ask a question about what they have just read or heard shared. The teacher is always prepared to guide and encourage positive responses about the content of what was shared. As voluntary sharing increases, the teacher may eventually choose an equitable way of having students take turns sharing, if that becomes necessary.

BOOK PUBLISHING   Once these components of a process writing program are operating smoothly, it is easy to get the students to select a piece of writing from their writing folder that they want to turn into a "book." Each day for a while, the children move through the stages of book publishing: conferencing with one or more other students, rewriting, conferencing with the teacher, illustrating, copying or having the teacher copy their writing onto the illustrated pages, making a dedication page, creating a cover, and binding the cover and pages together into a book. These stages are usually conducted in centers or at stations. When a child has published a book, the child shares that book with the entire class from "the Author's Chair."

GRADES   If children must be graded, we recommend that they be given a single grade for reading/language arts. However, if children in a process writing program receive a separate grade on their report cards for writing, their grade can be based on two factors. (1) Their grade can reflect their progress in terms of their willingness to write during writing time, their willingness to invent spellings, their willingness to share, and their effort when preparing a "book" for publication. This factor has nothing at all to do with what they write, only with their participation and cooperation in the program itself. The rationale is simple: Children must be actively involved in the process writing program to benefit from it, and parents can be informed whether children are so involved. (2) Their grade can also be based on the quality of their final drafts, to the extent that their contributions to that draft can be clearly differentiated from yours. Here the distinction in grades should not be between pass and fail but between satisfactory and excellent. The rationale: All children who are actively involved in a process writing program should make satisfactory progress or the program should be modified until they do.

FOR CHILDREN WITH SPECIAL NEEDS— DIALOGUE JOURNALS

While process writing is generally successful with the widest range of students, some teachers use dialogue journals with children who can write some but who are reluctant to share what they have written with others. In a dialogue journal the child turns in the journal to the teacher after each first draft. The teacher writes a simple, personal response to what the child has written after the child's draft. When the child writes next time, he or she can write on a new subject or can, in turn, respond to what the teacher wrote. This dialogue in writing between teacher and child can do wonders in motivating a child to write and in teaching that child the true nature of writing as communication.

STUDENTS NEED TO LEARN TO PRODUCE MANY DIFFERENT TYPES OF WRITING

Over the years in our work with teachers and schools, we have found it useful to draw a distinction between process writing, as discussed above, and what we call *focused writing*. You should be aware, however, that much of what we call focused writing is included under process writing by those who use that term more broadly than we do.

There are a number of important distinctions between process writing as we have so far delineated it and what we refer to as focused writing. In process writing, students choose their own topics and how to address them; in focused writing, the teacher gives the class a writing prompt that constrains their writing in one or more ways. In process writing, the time before students begin a first draft is spent on individual planning—deciding what to write about and how; in focused writing, students also do some individual planning, but, depending on the prompt, students may additionally be taught background knowledge for the topic, the role, and/or the audience, as well as for the form (type of writing). They may also be guided to do some inquiry or research on the topic before writing about it. In process writing, there is an emphasis on having students revise what they have written in order to improve it; in focused writing, students sometimes revise, but there is more of an emphasis on having students evaluate what they have written in order to do better on their next first draft of that type of writing.

There are also important differences between focused writing and traditional school writing (how writing was generally taught, when it was taught, before 1970). In traditional school writing, students were given a writing assignment and allowed to ask some questions about it; in focused writing, for each prompt, the teacher guides students through a planned, prewriting phase. In traditional school writing, the emphasis was usually on mechanics and usage; in focused writing, mechanics and usage have value, but the emphasis is always on the ideas and type of writing. In traditional school writing, students were often taught about a particular form by examining a good example of it; in focused writing, students examine good models but are also taught how to do a particular form by being put in a writing situation that naturally elicits that type of writing. The prompt, and any inquiry or research they do, are designed to help students develop the strategies a particular type of writing requires. In traditional school writing, students learned about a type of writing, tried to produce a piece of that type, and were graded on it; in focused writing, students do a large number of pieces of a type of writing and self-evaluate how well they did on each one until they become successful at composing that type of writing.

Both process and focused writing are crucial if most students are going to learn to write well. Used regularly over several years, focused writing activities are particularly helpful to students in learning to produce many different types of writing.

A Lesson Framework for Focused Writing

While focused writing activities can vary significantly, each one can be seen as an instance of a general lesson framework with mandatory and optional phases and steps:

Focused Writing Lesson Framework
   I. Focused Prewriting Phase
       Step 1. Teach or review background knowledge for the prompt
       Step 2. Present the prompt
       Step 3. Have students engage in inquiry or research (Optional)
       Step 4. Have students individually plan their writing
   II. Writing Phase
       Step 5. Have students produce a first (and possibly final) draft
   III. Sharing Phase (Optional)
       Step 6. Have each student share the draft with at least one other
               student

The heart of a focused writing lesson is the prompt. Constructing a good writing prompt is the first thing a teacher does when planning a focused writing lesson. The prompt that will be given to the students in Step 2 of the lesson determines what background knowledge needs to be built in Step 1, and what inquiry or research—if any—students will do in Step 3. The writing prompt is simply a brief, written statement of the writing assignment. If it is not written down so the students can refer to it while planning and writing, it is not a prompt.

Your ability to construct good writing prompts will come from practice, trial and error, and understanding your particular class of students. It will also help you to think critically about each prompt you construct if you *analyze* it before using it in a focused writing lesson. Analyzing a prompt consists of breaking it down into its elements.

A writing prompt may have as many as four elements:

audience = to whom the writing should seem to be directed
role = who should seem to be "speaking" the words
topic = what the piece of writing should be about; its content
type of writing = the general form the piece of writing should take

Since the main goal of the focused writing approach is teaching students how to produce different types of writing, the most important aspect of the prompts used in the approach will be the element that specifies or implies the type of writing students are to do.

A writing prompt may also contain specifications as to how long the piece of writing must be or can be, and when it is due, but these are not considered elements of the prompt. These specifications may be written at the end of the prompt or simply told to the students. Students are often informed as to what will be done with the drafts after they are finished, that is, shared, taken up and graded, self-evaluated, and/or filed in a working portfolio, but that information is not considered an element of the prompt either. It may also be written at the end of the prompt or told to the students. The prompt itself, the four elements combined in a brief paragraph, must always be written and made accessible to the students during planning and writing.

Imagine that you have constructed the following prompt for your fourth-grade class:

Pretend you are a fourth-grade teacher. Write a business letter to the director of the state's history museum. Ask him or her when the museum is open for visitors and how to schedule a visit for a class.

audience = the director of the state's history museum
role = a fourth-grade teacher
topic = asking when the museum is open for visitors and how to schedule a visit for a class
type of writing = a business letter

When analyzing a prompt, try to put every important word in one of the four elements. Do not put any word from the prompt in more than one element. If one or more of the elements are not specified in the prompt, just leave them blank. Since the students will never see the elements broken out separately, it is not necessary to word the elements in complete sentences.

After you have broken a prompt into its elements, you can readily see which elements you need to build background for and whether you want to have students do inquiry or research on the topic, role, or audience. If it appears that a lot of background building may be necessary on concepts that are not really your focus, you may want to modify those elements to make the prompt more targeted to your objectives for the students.

In the sample prompt, above, both the state's history museum and the concept of a visit to the state capital could require some background building or research, depending on how much you think your students already know about one or both. Certainly, the teacher would have to provide students with the name and address of the director of the state's history museum. The emphasis in the background building step (Step 1), however, should be on the form of a business letter. The best tack to take would probably be to display or distribute a model of a business letter that the students could follow when formatting their letters. This model should *not* be a letter to the director of the state's history museum. We want the children to apply the model when writing, not merely to copy down its formatting.

This sample prompt would probably work best if students were also guided through an inquiry step (Step 3) in which they worked together in pairs or small groups to examine a couple of sample business letters that asked for information. By discussing how two or three different letter writers went about asking for information, they could decide how they might go about asking for information in their letters.

Consider a second sample prompt for a third-grade class:

> Pretend you are your mother or father [or . . . if someone in the class lives with another kind of caretaker]. Tell a story about what it was like when you were in the third grade.

audience	=
role	= your mother or father
topic	= what it was like when you were in the third grade
type of writing	= a story

This lesson will probably require background building on what a story is, depending on how elaborate you want their stories to be. By "story" you may just mean "an interesting event." Letting them see or hear a couple of "stories" like those you have in mind would be helpful. Providing two or three models and helping students think about them is always a good way to build background for a particular form you are teaching children how to produce.

Let's say your Step 1 also has the students brainstorm interesting things that they have done or that have happened this year in third grade. In Step 2, you present the prompt and allow students to ask questions and make comments. A few of the children may already know some stories about their parents' childhood experiences, and you may choose to allow a few of those to be told. In Step 3, you first put the students together in small groups to plan an interview they will use to get one of their parents to tell them about what third grade was like for them. During or after this inquiry activity, you have each student make a copy of the interview that the small group composes. Then you assign students to complete their interview (conduct their research) by a certain day. On that day, students could carry out Step 4 of the lesson in class by individually webbing the story each intends to write. At this point in the lesson, you could refer them to the prompt and remind them to tell the story in the first person. In Step 5, they would write their stories at the same time in class, at different times during the school day, or at home. If you have a Step 6 in this lesson, children would share their stories in pairs, small groups, or as a whole class.

Analyzing each prompt you have constructed should stimulate this kind of decision making before you teach the focused writing lesson containing that prompt. A good prompt and good decisions about what to do at each of the four mandatory steps and two optional steps, if anything, make for a successful focused writing lesson. The more focused writing lessons you teach, the better you and your students will become at doing them.

TRY IT OUT

Plan a focused writing lesson for a particular grade level of students. Come up with a prompt, considering audience, role, topic, and type of writing. Then decide what you will do for all six steps of your lesson.

Once you become proficient at crafting good prompts and teaching successful focused writing lessons based on those prompts, you have a powerful tool to help your students learn how to produce any type of writing you need or want to teach them. There is tremendous flexibility in the focused writing lesson framework. Step 1, for example, could consist of an entire reading/literature lesson that would ordinarily stand alone. Now, however, you could integrate writing and reading by using that lesson as the background knowledge step of a focused writing lesson in which your students learn to produce the type of writing exmplified by that piece of literature. Moreover, during Step 3, the students could work together in inquiry groups to discuss what about that piece of literature made it so interesting, beautiful, inspiring, gripping, or whatever. In Step 4, they could be led to plan individually what each would do to make his or her attempt at that type of writing interesting, beautiful, inspiring, gripping, or whatever.

Developing a Writing Scale

No single focused writing lesson ever teaches students how to produce a particular type of writing. A series of focused writing lessons, all specifying or eliciting the same form, has a better chance of teaching students how to achieve that form. However, the combination of teaching a series of focused writing lessons on the same form *and* teaching students to self-evaluate their writing with a writing scale developed for that form is the most effective means of teaching students how to produce a particular type of writing.

A writing scale is a list of rules or questions to answer that students are taught how to use to evaluate their own papers. A writing scale for a type of writing has a list of questions to answer that focus on the key features of that form. Developing a writing scale for a type of writing is tantamount to making explicit what you, as the teacher, look for in deciding whether a particular piece of student writing is a good example of an assigned or elicited form. Providing students with a writing scale based on a type of writing is the only way to effectively teach them to self-evaluate their writings as instances of that type of writing. Through this self-evaluation, they will eventually internalize a sense of that form. See Figures 7.1, 7.2, and 7.3 for samples of different types of writing.

The first criterion or question on a form-based writing scale should help students learn to address the prompt when there is one. Here is a question that gets at whether the student's paper addresses the prompt for each type of writing:

1. Does the paper have the same topic as the prompt?

The second criterion or question on a form-based writing scale should probably deal with the unity of the writing. Every kind of writing has a subject that needs to be maintained throughout the piece. Here are second questions that get at the unity of the piece that students can be taught to answer about each of three types of writing:

2. Is the paper clearly about just one character, person, place, or event? [narrative writing]
2. Is the paper clearly about just one person, place, thing, or feeling? [descriptive writing]
2. Is the paper clearly arguing for just one opinion? [persuasive writing]

When students become able to produce first drafts that consistently allow their readers to be able to answer "yes" to both of these questions, they have learned how to address the prompt and maintain unity of subject in the particular type of writing they are learning.

The trickiest part of developing a form-based writing scale is formulating questions that get at the basic structure of ideas in that form. Here are possible third and fourth questions for each of the three examples we are using:

3. Does the paper tell exactly what happened?
3. Does the paper talk about several major features of the person, place, thing, or feeling?
3. Are there at least three different reasons given to support the opinion?
4. Is it clear what happened first, what happened after that, and what happened last?
4. Is there a good explanation of each major feature?
4. Are the reasons good ones that might convince the readers?

Once students come to understand the basic logic of a form, their chief failing in carrying out that form is usually the lack of elaboration. Here is the fifth question for each of the three examples that helps students gradually improve their elaboration:

5. Are there enough details to help readers clearly imagine each thing that

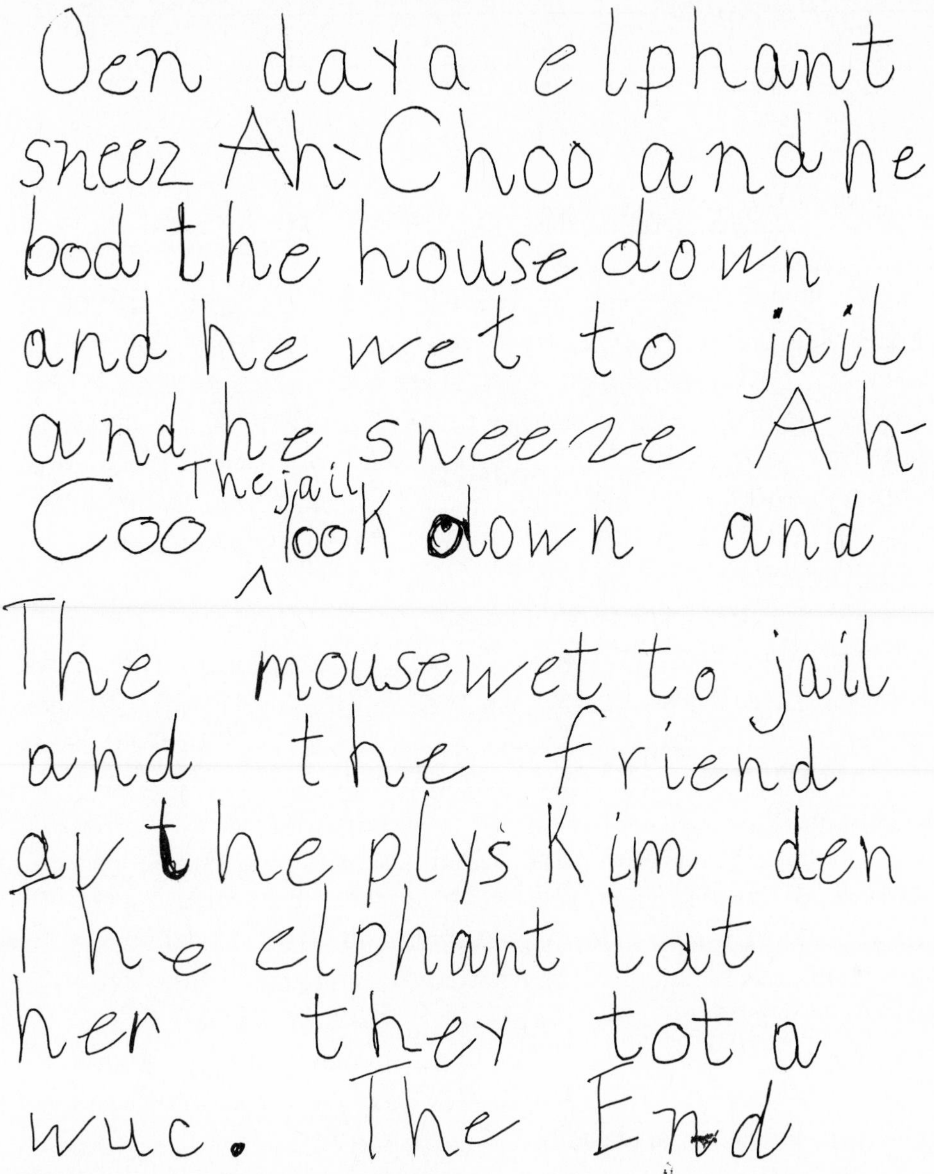

Oen day a elphant sneez Ah-Choo and he bod the house down and he wet to jail and he sneeze Ah-Coo The jail look down and
^
The mousewet to jail and the friend ay the plys Kim den The elphant Lat her they tot a wuc. The End

FIGURE 7.1 First-Grade Narrative Writing

happened? Are we helped to see, hear, smell, taste, and feel in our minds?

5. Are there enough details to help readers clearly imagine the person, place, thing, or feeling? Are we helped to see, hear, smell, taste, and feel in our minds?

5. Is each reason supported and explained well?

Why Rock and Roll is better than Classical Music

In my opinion Rock and Roll is far better than Classical music in many ways. The first being Rock 'n' Roll is simpler and therefore easier to hum while walking around. Take Beethovens 5th sympony da da da da dé, chang, da da dé da dang, and so forth. Now take Louie, Louie na na na na na na na na na na and you could go on like that forever, or at least until you remember a new song.

The second reason is Rock 'n' Roll is more up-beat. Compare Hayden's <u>Suprise Symphony</u> to Pink Floyd's <u>Another Brick In the Wall</u>. Suprise Symphony ta ta ta ta ta ta taaa, ta ta ta ta ta ta taaa. Another Brick in the Wall, na na na na na na na na. Rock obviosouly rolls faster.

The third and final reason in this essay (though I could go on) is instruments and vocals. In Rock and Roll you have electric guitars!, keyboards!, and a drum set! In classical you have violins, cellos, double bassoons and about 500 types of drums. Now to vocals, Rock 'n' Roll has quick, snappy words that alot of the time rhyme, Classical has no vocals, Case closed.

FIGURE 7.2 Fifth-Grade Persuasive Writing

Finally, every form-based writing scale needs to have some questions that get students to self-evaluate how well they carry out that type of writing. We can use the same questions for all three examples:

6. Does the paper have a good beginning, or does it "start in the middle"?
7. Does the paper have a good ending, or does it "leave us hanging"?
8. Does each sentence nicely connect to the next one, or do we sometimes have to say "huh?"

My Dog, Poco
by Maria Martinez

My dog's name is Poco because he is little. He is a Chihuahua. The top of his ears don't come up to my knees. We have to be careful not to step on him! He is little but he is quick and he is loud! Poco is white and pink all over. His nose is black. Poco likes to eat table scraps. He also eats Alpo.

FIGURE 7.3   Third-Grade Descriptive Writing

Our form-based writing scale for narrative, descriptive, or persuasive writing would consist of the corresponding eight questions. A form-based writing scale for any other type of writing that intermediate elementary students might be taught to write would probably be similar.

At first, students should be given only the first question to answer about a draft, and they should probably answer it for each other's drafts. The teacher should not add the second question to the writing scale until the class is comfortable answering the first question. After the second question is added, it must not be assumed that the first question was mastered. Now students should use both questions to evaluate each other's or their own drafts. Eventually, students will be able to self-evaluate their drafts using all the questions on the scale. When you respond to the form of a student's draft, you should use the same questions on the writing scale that the students are currently using. Occasionally having students rewrite a paper to get "yes" for all the questions on the writing scale to that point helps them understand and internalize the characteristics of that type of writing.

When students engaged in focused writing are graded on writing, that grade should be based on pieces of writing done in class in response to new prompts. Children should be allowed ample time to plan and write during these "tests," because quality of writing is not a function of time spent writing. Some great writers have been very prolific; others have labored long to produce a little. The grade each paper receives should be based on (1) its conformity to the prompt, (2) its consistency with the form-based writing scale, and, possibly, (3) its correct spelling of the words on the wall.

It is not a mystery why students generally did not learn how to produce many different types of writing from traditional writing instruction. Most of them had not previously engaged in two or three years of process writing. Most of them did not attempt each form often enough. When they attempted a form, they did not write to a well-crafted prompt, and they were not systematically taught how to evaluate their own attempts at a form by answering a limited set of clearly stated questions. They rarely if ever revised, and when they did so, they did not revise to improve their papers relative to a form-based writing scale.

FOR CHILDREN WITH SPECIAL NEEDS—
ADAPTING WRITING SCALES

 Sometimes it is necessary for a teacher with a wide range of children to add new questions to the form-based writing scale, even though one or two students are really not ready for them to be added. When this happens, it is important and easy for the teacher to require some children to evaluate or revise their papers based on the specific questions the teacher knows they can handle. For example, if the teacher has five questions on the writing scale, that teacher may require one or two students to use the first three questions on the writing scale while most students will be required to use all five.

STUDENTS LEARN CONVENTIONS BY
APPLYING THEM IN THEIR OWN WRITING

Back when elementary students did very little writing other than copying or responding to short-answer questions, they were taught writing rules in isolated exercises from the language book or on worksheets. There were probably several reasons that this practice persisted. Traditional standardized and teacher-made language tests assessed writing rules in isolation from writing. Because many students have trouble transferring what they have learned to new situations, experienced teachers usually have their teaching activities resemble the test the students will be given. Traditional teachers tended to teach writing rules in isolation, at least in part because they tested them in isolation. This tendency increased when teachers were held accountable for student performance on tests. In addition, behaviorism used to be the worldview of most educators and, to behaviorists, all learning was habit formation. Teachers taught children writing rules before letting them write much, in part because they did not want them developing bad habits. Finally, since teachers had been taught writing rules in isolation when they were children, they in turn taught them in isolation, out of tradition.

Of course, teaching writing conventions in isolation was an unsuccessful practice, as indicated by middle and high school students' writing. Their lack of proficiency in capitalization, punctuation, formatting (margins, placement of headings, indentation, etc.), and usage (subject-verb agreement, consistency of tenses, pronoun-antecedent agreement, knowledge of verb conjugations, etc.) was the constant complaint of middle and high school teachers and administrators. The solution? More isolated work on mechanics and usage, but no more writing. Isolated work on mechanics and usage in writing became the modern equivalent of bleeding: When the patient died it was *in spite of* being bled, and when the patient recovered it was *because of* being bled. When most students did not become proficient at writing by the rules, it was assumed that they had been hopeless anyway or that even more isolated work should have been done. When some students did become proficient at writing by the rules, the isolated work was credited with their success. In other words, the more isolated teaching of mechanics and usage elementary teachers did, the more they were criticized for not having done enough!

As writing tests were developed that required students to actually write, as behaviorism gave way to cognitivism, and as dissatisfaction with traditional educational achievements grew, more and more educators began to face what the research had always indicated: Teaching writing mechanics and usage in isolation does not work for most students. Today, the most successful teachers of writing emphasize ideas and type of writing over mechanics and usage, while using writing scales and other supports to help students gradually learn mechanics and usage rules through applying them in their writing.

Writing Rules on the Wall

When a teacher is establishing a process writing program in his or her classroom, that teacher's goals are to get the students to write regularly about their own topics in their own ways, to invent spellings while writing, and to respond positively to the ideas of each other's writings while sharing. In kindergarten, achieving these three goals for all students will probably take the entire year. In first grade, depending on how much process writing the children did in kindergarten, achieving these three goals for all students may take as long as the entire first semester. Beyond first grade, regardless of how much process writing students have done previously, it is important to establish at least six weeks of process writing early in the year, because it builds an atmosphere of trust and a supportive relationship between the students and the current teacher.

Once children are writing regularly, usually generating a reasonable quantity of writing, inventing spellings, and sharing appropriately, in first grade or above, many teachers begin helping them apply a few basic mechanics rules in their writing. Sometimes teachers call the writing scale consisting of these rules a *writing checklist*. Because we advocate that this writing scale be posted so all children can see it from anywhere in the classroom, we call it *writing rules on the wall*.

Sometimes the first rule or two on the wall chart do not deal with mechanics or usage, but communicate to the children the more basic notion that what they write should have a message:

Every sentence should make sense.
Every sentence should keep to the topic.

When the writing scale on the wall consists of either or both of these two rules, the word *sentence* should be not interpreted strictly or grammatically. At this stage, if it makes any sense when read aloud, it's a sentence! The second of these rules requires a loose understanding of *topic* as "what the paper is about." Most teachers find that these two rules are unnecessary to post, because most students who write and share regularly will automatically apply them without being told to do so. Teachers monitor the sharing that students are doing to determine if either or both of these rules will be necessary to post when the first writing rule is placed on the wall.

The first (or next) rule on the wall is often:

Every sentence should begin with a capital letter.

Again, if it makes sense when shared, it's a sentence.

As with all writing scales, no new rules are added until most students consistently apply those already posted. When a new rule is added, it is taught to the students in several ways. Most teachers like to post the first or new rule on the wall and then immediately teach a minilesson focusing on that new rule.

A rule-based minilesson proceeds by having the teacher write a brief piece on the overhead projector while students watch and read along. The teacher purposely writes in such a way that there are a number of opportunities to apply the new rule on the wall. The first few times, the teacher applies the rule correctly but then makes sure to violate (fail to apply) the new rule several times by the end of the composition. After writing, the teacher asks the children to help determine whether the teacher kept the new rule throughout. As a child points out an error on this new rule, the teacher asks someone to say what should have been written or lets the child correct the error on the overhead. At the end of this minilesson, the children immediately write on topics of their choosing. The teacher reminds them of the new rule as they begin writing.

The same rule may be modeled in several minilessons, if necessary. After students have written several times with the new posted rule, they practice proofreading their own or each other's papers for all the posted rules, including the new one. Some of the times that students proofread for the writing rules on the wall, they also correct their papers for those rules and the teacher takes up the papers to check them for those rules. Many teachers have children skip every other line when writing to make it easier for children to correct errors when editing.

After students become consistent in beginning their sentences with capital letters, they are ready to learn to put appropriate punctuation at the end of their sentences. Only two rules, taught one at time, are necessary:

Every question should end with a question mark.
Sentences that are not questions should end with a period or an
exclamation point.

The first rule requires a question mark after a question. The second of these two rules lets students decide whether a sentence should have a period or an exclamation point. Exclamation is really in the mind of the writer rather than the teacher.

While using minilessons, proofreading practice, and editing practice to teach the rules on the wall, teachers also use other activities and exercises to help students understand and remember a rule. These other activities and exercises will be effective, however, only if they simplify rather than complicate the rule, and if they do not take much time away from that spent applying the rule in actual writing. An example of such a helpful exercise would be one that helps the students learn to determine whether a sentence is a question or not. (See Figure 7.4.)

? ? ? Question or Not **? ? ?**

1. On one side of the chalkboard, write four different questions. End each one with a question mark. Above these questions write *Questions*. On the other side of the chalkboard, write four sentences that are not questions. End each one with a period. Above these sentences write *Not Questions*.

2. In the middle of the chalkboard, write a sentence. Do not put a period or question mark at the end of the sentence.

3. Have a volunteer read the questions aloud and then read the "mystery sentence" aloud. Have the volunteer read the nonquestions aloud and then read the mystery sentence aloud. Have the volunteer decide whether the mystery sentence sounds more like the questions or more like the nonquestions and put a question mark or a period at the end of the mystery sentence. If the student is correct, the teacher should say so; if the student is incorrect, the teacher should read all the sentences aloud and explain to the students why the answer was incorrect.

4. Repeat Steps 2 and 3 with different sentences and volunteers until the students seem to be catching on.

5. Have each student tear a piece of paper in half and write a large dark question mark on one half and a large dark period on the other.

6. In the middle of the chalkboard, write a sentence. Do not put a period or question mark at the end of the sentence.

7. Tell the students to read the mystery sentence to themselves, then read the questions and nonquestions to themselves and decide whether the mystery sentence needs a question mark or a period at the end. When they have had enough time say "Ready, set, show!" When you say "Show!" each student should hold up either the question mark or the period to indicate his or her choice. Pick someone who made the right choice to come to the board and place the correct ending punctuation on the mystery sentence.

8. Repeat Steps 6 and 7 until almost everyone gets it right every time. Gradually decrease the time students have to make their choices.

FIGURE 7.4 Question or Not

From the time a process writing program is well established, this method of teaching writing rules on the wall gradually helps students learn to apply the basic mechanics and usage conventions of writing. When they are used in the intermediate grades, it may or may not be necessary to include basic mechanics rules like the five discussed above.

Beyond these basic three to five rules, a number of other writing rules will probably be important enough to teach by the end of fifth grade:

Every sentence should be a complete sentence.

Indent the beginning of every paragraph.

Combine short, choppy sentences.

Do not use run-on sentences.

Use commas after the first words in a series.

Punctuate quotations correctly.

Use *I* and *me*, *we* and *us*, *he* and *him*, *she* and *her*, and *they* and *them* correctly. (This rule could be broken out into five separate ones, if necessary.)

Do not use double negatives.

Both the subject and verb of a sentence should be singular, or both should be plural.

Use the correct form of every regular verb.

Both a pronoun and the noun it stands for should be singular, or both should be plural.

Obviously, some of these more sophisticated writing rules require an extended period of time to teach students to apply them. In the case of usage rules such as pronoun case or subject-verb agreement, the students will probably benefit from wall charts they can refer to for help to decide how to write or edit a particular construction. For an example of one of these wall charts, see Figure 7.5.

Some rules are difficult for children to apply because they lack a prerequisite ability. Children above first grade often write in run-on sentences because they are trying to produce longer sentences. They compose run-on sentences because that is the only way they know how to produce longer sentences. Putting a rule on the wall that says "Do not use run-on sentences" is really telling such children to produce short, choppy sentences. Many of them will refuse to do that because they associate it with being younger. Sentence-combining activities can teach such children how to achieve longer sentences without making them run on. The wise teacher will try to figure out why children are having trouble applying a rule and will try to teach them any prerequisite abilities they lack.

If children in a process writing program receive a separate grade for writing, their application of the writing rules on the wall can be considered in their grades. Students' willingness to proofread and correct their papers for the rules on the wall constitutes an aspect of their overall involvement in the process writing program. Students' ability to apply the rules on the wall in their final drafts also constitutes an aspect of the overall quality of those drafts.

Mount five charts on the wall or bulletin board on which you have written four forms (present, past, past perfect, and future tense) of regular verbs (as many as each chart will hold). The five charts should be in this order with these titles: I   he she or it   you   we   they

I
help, helped, have helped, will help
talk, talked, have talked, will talk
he, she, or it
helps, helped, has helped, will help
talks, talked, has talked, will talk
you
help, helped, have helped, will help
talk, talked, have talked, will talk
we
help, helped, have helped, will help
talk, talked, have talked, will talk
they
help, helped, have helped, will help
talk, talked, have talked, will talk

Steps:

1. Write a sentence in the middle of the chalkboard that has present, past, future, or past perfect time and uses one of the verbs from the regular verb tables mounted on the wall or bulletin board. Leave the verb out of the sentence and replace it with a long blank. The blank should always be the same length so the children cannot tell what the right answer might be from looking at how long the blank is. Put the first person singular present tense form of the verb in parentheses at the beginning of the sentence. Two examples are:

(help) Next week at this time, Maria and David _____ me move.

(talk) She _____ loud because her father is hard of hearing.

2. Have each student copy the sentence from the board (without the verb in parentheses) and fill in the blank with the correct verb form. Allow them to use the charts to decide which form to use.
3. Have a student volunteer read his or her completed sentence aloud and then have him or her explain the reason for using that verb form. If the student is right, say so; if the student is wrong, explain why the student is wrong.
4. Repeat these steps with other sentences.
5. When almost all students are successfully using the correct verb tense, add this rule to your list of writing rules on the wall: "Every sentence must have the correct verb tense,"
6. Have your students use the regular verb tables to proofread for regular verb tense errors in their or another student's writing.

FIGURE 7.5   Regular Verb Tables

If children engaged in focused writing receive a separate grade for writing, their application of the writing rules on the wall can also be considered in their grades. If students are to be held accountable for applying the rules on the wall when taking a writing "test," they must be told so in advance. It will then be up to them whether they want to be concerned with those rules on the first draft or to leave themselves time to proofread and edit their first drafts before handing them in.

Whether they are engaged in process or focused writing, children must not be graded in such a way that they lose sight of what is most important in writing. Mechanics and usage should always be less important than the ideas and type of writing. If a grading system is giving children a different idea, it must be modified or that grading system is undermining the entire writing program.

Even though the ideas and type of writing continue to be the main emphases of the writing program, mechanics and usage conventions can be successfully taught to children through the systematic use of writing rules on the wall, rule-based minilessons, supporting exercises and wall charts, and proofreading and editing practice.

DO IT TOGETHER

 Meet with three or four of your peers and call up your memories of writing. Did you engage in process writing as well as some focused writing lessons? Were you taught the rules in ways that you could apply to your own writing? Was writing something you looked forward to or dreaded? Summarize the collective experiences of your group with writing and compare what you experienced to what you have read so far in this chapter.

STUDENTS PROFIT FROM WRITING IN THE CONTENT AREAS ACROSS THE CURRICULUM

Whether students are involved in process writing or focused writing, as we have distinguished them, they receive additional benefits from engaging in that same kind of writing across the curriculum. Not only do the increased opportunities to write in different contexts help children learn to write better, but writing also helps children learn more social studies, science, health, and literature. Teachers at upper levels of schooling have always recognized that writing is the best means to get students to think about whatever they are learning. In recent years, educators have realized that the same holds true for content learning in the elementary grades.

Again it should be noted that many teachers naturally extend writing into all content areas without making a distinction between that writing and what the students have been doing previously. The distinction between *writing* and *writing across the curriculum*, like that between process and focused writing, has been useful for us in helping teachers. Many teachers of writing, perhaps most, refer to it all as process writing.

Process Writing in the Content Areas

While some students in a process writing program may naturally choose to write about what they are learning in science, social studies, health, or reading/literature, it is not likely they will. Consequently, a teacher often needs to make a modification in process writing when using it to elicit student writing in a content area. Specifically, when they engage in process writing across the curriculum:

Children choose their own subtopics.

When writing across the curriculum, individual children still have the responsibility of deciding what they will write about and how they will approach it, with one exception: Each must choose a topic having to do with the particular content area in which the writing occurs (e.g., science). Once students are comfortable with process writing, it is not difficult to get them to do process writing across the curriculum. After a particularly interesting or stimulating experience during a content subject, the teacher can readily say something like "That was amazing. Now, I would like for you to write what you think about that."

Otherwise, when they engage in process writing in the content areas across the curriculum:

Children still share their writing with other students.

Children still invent spellings.

Children still revise some of what they have written.

Teachers still do not correct or grade first drafts.

The major application of the process writing approach to curricular areas takes the form of *learning logs*. Learning logs are a type of journal writing in which students summarize what they have learned and how they feel about it. Children can keep learning logs in any subject and can add to their logs daily, weekly, or after the teacher completes a unit. Sometimes, the teacher responds in writing to a student's learning log entry, making the learning log into a dialogue journal. If so, the teacher always responds positively to the ideas, rather than negatively to the form, and no grade is given. The purpose of the teacher's written response is to help students think more and more deeply about what they are learning. (For examples of entries in learning logs, see Figures 7.6 through 7.9.)

During process writing across the curriculum, teachers should leave on the wall any writing rules, words, and other supports that they use during writing/language arts time. However, children should not spend time during science, social studies, or health proofreading or editing their papers or journals. The students' concern and attention in process writing across the curriculum should always be exclusively on content. The only grade a piece of process writing in a content area ever receives should be based solely on the content of a final draft.

that if
they
stinged
you
it wuld
put posion
in to you

I.

FIGURE 7.6   First-Grade Science Learning Log

Process writing across the curriculum increases the quantity and variety of process writing that students do. It also encourages students to monitor and evaluate what they are learning in their content subjects, and to think interpretively about that new learning.

Focused Writing in the Content Areas

After students have engaged in process writing across the curriculum for an extended period of time, they are ready to benefit also from focused writing across the curriculum. The main difference between focused writing and focused writing across the curriculum is that the former concentrates on teaching students to do one or more types of writing, while the latter focuses on specific subject matter. The increased structure of focused writing across the curriculum can help students better learn social studies, science, health, or literature.

9-9-93

Venus ♀
☆ Venus has very strong surface winds and heavy cloud cover
☆ no natural sattaliets
☆ Surface temperature 470°C
☆ Venus often reffered to as a star
★ Venus is earth's twin in many ways
☆ Mass of Venus is close to that of earth
★ Venus surface a scorched desert
☆ Temprature can melt lead
☆ Clouds are made of sulfuric acid
☆ Atmosphere traps heat like a greenhouse
☆ Atmosphere is 90 times that of earth and could crush a human explorer
☆ Harshest planet known to humans
☆ Air In Venus is 97% carbondioxide
☆ Venus' clouds are freezing cold
☆ Venus rocks glow red at night
☆ Revolution time is 225 earth days
☆ 4 levels of clouds
☆ Rotation 243 earth days

FIGURE 7.7   Fifth-Grade Science Learning Log

A CONTENT WRITING LESSON FRAMEWORK   Exactly the same focused writing lesson framework can be used when focusing student writing in a content area. What differences there are lie in how the steps of a lesson are carried out.

The background-building step (Step 1) of a focused writing lesson almost always focuses on the type of writing that will be specified in the prompt when it is presented in Step 2; Step 1 of a content writing lesson almost always focuses

Community Helpers

polce man protects the city.
fire man puts
out fires.

mail man delivers
mail.

FIGURE 7.8 First-Grade Social Studies Learning Log

on building background for the role, audience, and/or topic that will be specified in the prompt. The prompt (Step 2) and inquiry/research (Step 3), if any, of a focused writing lesson are designed to enable the students to be successful at producing the type of writing specified in the prompt; the prompt and Step 3, if any, of a content writing lesson are designed to enable the students to be successful at understanding and interpreting the content they are writing about.

As with focused writing lessons, planning good prompts is the key to having

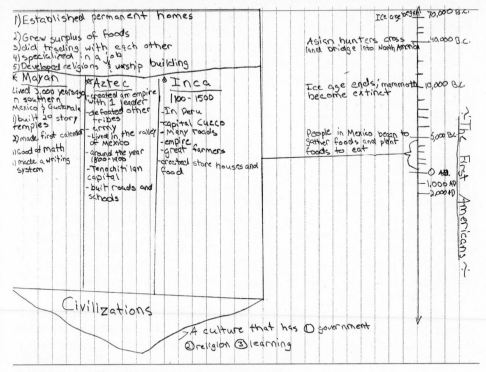

1) Established permanent homes

2) Grew surplus of foods
3) did treeding with each other
4) specialized in a job
5) Developed religions & worship building

Mayan
Lived 3,000 years ago
in southern
Mexico & Guatemala
1) built 2 story
temples
2) made first calendar
3) Good at math
4) made a writing
system

Aztec
-created an empire
with 1 leader
-defeated other
tribes
-army
-Lived in the valley
of Mexico
-around the year
1800-1900
-Tenochtitlan
capital
-built roads and
schools

Inca
1100 - 1500

-In Peru
-capital Cuzco
-Many roads
-empire
-great farmers
-created store houses and
food

Ice age began 70,000 B.C.

Asian hunters cross — 40,000 B.C.
land bridge into North America

Ice age ends; mammoths 10,000 B.C.
become extinct

People in Mexico began to — 5,000 B.C.
gather foods and plant
foods to eat

0 A.D.
-1,000 AD
-2,000 AD

The First Americans

Civilizations
→ A culture that has ① government
② religion ③ learning

FIGURE 7.9 Fifth-Grade Social Studies Learning Log

effective content writing lessons. This ability comes only with effort and experience but is helped by analyzing a prompt before using it with students.

Imagine that you have constructed the following prompt for your fourth-grade social studies class:

> Pretend that you are President Abraham Lincoln. Write a speech for fourth graders explaining why no one should have slaves.

audience	= fourth graders
role	= President Abraham Lincoln
topic	= why no one should have slaves
type of writing	= a speech that explains

In this sample prompt, both President Lincoln and the topic of slavery could require background building or research, depending on how much you have previously taught your students about one or both. If you are more interested in students' affective responses to slavery at this point, you might read them a book or story or show them a video about life as a slave before teaching this particular lesson. If you are more interested in students' knowledge about the institution of slavery, you might have them take notes from encyclopedias during Step 3 and then allow them to use these notes during Steps 4 and 5.

For this example, students should need very little, if any, background built about the nature of a speech or lecture. The emphasis of this lesson is on the content, not on teaching students how to compose a speech.

Here is a sample prompt for a content writing lesson in science:

Why do bees fly from flower to flower? Does this help or hurt flowers? How?

audience	=
role	=
topic	= why bees fly from flower to flower and how this helps flowers
type of writing	=

This second sample prompt is very assumptive. It assumes that students have been regularly sharing what they have written with each other so that they have developed a sense of the audience as their peers rather than you, the teacher. If not, a number of students will probably be pretty sketchy about what they write, and when you ask them why, they will reply that you already knew the answers! The sharing phase of a focused/content writing lesson is optional only if students have done enough sharing previously to develop a sense of the audience as their peers.

Of course, this second sample prompt also assumes that students have done enough process writing and focused writing to have developed their own voice (self as role). Knowledge of the topic is probably too involved to be developed in Step 1. Either this writing lesson should follow a study of cross-pollination in plants or it should require research on that topic in Step 3. The second sample prompt is fine, but it assumes a lot of previous experience with writing and also either assumes knowledge of the topic or requires a research step.

As with process writing, the students' concern and attention in focused writing across the curriculum should always be exclusively on the content. The only grade a piece of focused writing in a content area ever receives should be based solely on its content.

Again, the flexibility of the focused writing lesson used across the curriculum should be noted. For example, a focused writing lesson can be taught both for its own sake and to prepare students to read a particular piece of literature in a subsequent reading lesson. Specifically, to heighten students' understanding and interest, they could write to a prompt that elicits persuasive writing from them before reading a piece of persuasive writing during literature class. Focused writing lessons can serve as content writing lessons in a great variety of ways: preceding the reading of literature and integrated with it, following the reading of literature and integrated with it, or in any of several roles in a thematic unit.

LISTEN, LOOK, AND LEARN

 Interview a teacher you respect about his or her writing program. Ask questions that will help you determine if process writing, focused writing, or traditional writing are used regularly. Remember that people use other terms for these types of writing, so phrase your questions so that you can determine what kind of writing is actually being done and how often. See if you can determine whether process writing or focused writing are being used to support learning in different content areas. Ask to see some first-draft and published writing samples. Summarize what you learned from your interview. What changes would you make in the writing program if you were the teacher?

THE THEORY AND RESEARCH BASE FOR WRITING INSTRUCTION

Most of the research on writing over the past 25 years has been in three areas: the uses of writing—emphasizing how literacy functions in various communities and cultures; the processes of writing—emphasizing how writers actually write; and the development of writing—emphasizing how writers mature and progress over time, both overall and in particular aspects (Dyson & Freedman, 1991). This third area includes writing instructional research but has concentrated more on stages writers may move through in their writing and writing-skills development. This complex body of research on writing is probably best reflected and applied in the excellent and highly influential books on teaching writing published by Heinemann, including Atwell (1990), Calkins (1994), Graves (1983), Newkirk (1989), and others.

While there have been many classroom applications of the research on writing, these applications have generally stressed four components. Because one of the major areas of recent writing research has focused on how literacy functions in various communities, applications of this writing research are usually marked by *authentic writing* and *collaboration*. Because research has also focused on how writers write, classroom applications are usually marked by an emphasis on *process* rather than product. And, because the third major area of research has focused on how writers develop, applications usually emphasize stages that children move through while involved in a writing program. The most common aspect of student writing that teachers examine from a developmental perspective is *invented spelling*.

The notion that children's writing in school should generally be authentic follows largely from research on the role of writing in various communities (e.g., Heath, 1983) and as engaged in spontaneously by children (Dyson, 1985). Writing is said to be authentic when it is done for real purposes. When authenticity is a component of the writing program, children choose their own topics, write to communicate with others and for enjoyment, and write across the curriculum. Isolated writing skills instruction and artificial writing assignments are kept to a minimum.

The research on the uses of writing has also led to the insight that communities often collaborate when planning to write, when writing, or when responding to what has been written. Real writers who function well in communities ordinarily produce "reader-based" rather than "writer-based" prose (Flower, 1979/1990). Sharing writing with other students and peer conferencing, along with training in responding positively to ideas rather than negatively to form, are the means teachers usually employ to achieve the collaboration that, in turn, helps writers become more reader based. By these means, the teacher attempts to establish a community of writers in the classroom.

The process (or processes) of writing, on the part of both adults and children, has probably been the major focus of the research on writing since 1970. How writers actually write, rather than how they should, has served as the impetus for the process writing revolution. Eliminating standards for first-draft writing and regularly involving students in revising what they have written are the two means teachers usually employ to involve students in the writing process. In combination with the other components that follow from recent writing research, process writing has represented a concerted effort to help children become and see themselves as authors.

Since the pioneering work of Read (1971) and Beers and Henderson (1977), young children's incorrect attempts to spell words while writing have been recognized as powerful indicators of their developing phonemic awareness and knowledge of sound-letter relationships (Adams, 1990; Henderson, 1990). The research on spelling indicates that invented spelling is an important part of an effective spelling and phonics program in the primary grades. Spelling is not merely right or wrong. Students' incorrect spellings can be studied for what they indicate about the development of students' awareness of sound-letter relationships and phonemic sequencing (Gentry & Gillet, 1993). This work does not, however, suggest that correct spelling has no place in these same grades. On the contrary, Clarke's study (1988) suggests that the combination of invented spelling and correct spelling is what helps children most.

Research on writing instruction prior to the 1970s was largely limited to studies of the efficacy of formal grammar instruction. Formal grammar instruction has traditionally consisted of teaching children to identify the parts of speech; to determine whether a sentence is simple, compound, or complex; to diagram or otherwise identify the function of each word, phrase, or clause in a sentence (e.g., subject, indirect object); to state rules for capitalization and punctuation; to conjugate regular and irregular verbs, especially *to be*; and so on. From as early as 1903 (Palmer, 1975), a number of researchers compared groups of students taught grammar with groups not taught grammar on the correctness of their writing. There were also a number of studies during this era that examined the correlation between students' knowledge of traditional, formal grammar and the correctness of their writing. Braddock, Lloyd-Jones, and Schoer (1963) summarized all of the research to that point:

> In view of the widespread agreement of research studies based upon many types of students and teachers, the conclusion can be stated in strong and unqualified terms: the teaching of formal grammar has a negligible or, because it usually displaces some instruction and practice in actual composition, even a harmful effect on the improvement of writing. (pp. 37–38)

Others summarizing those same studies, along with the research conducted since 1963, including attempts to teach newer grammars such as structural or transformational, have agreed with Braddock et al. (Hillocks, 1986; Linden &

Whimbey, 1990; Palmer, 1975). It can now be stated in no uncertain terms that grammar instruction of the kind we all experienced does not teach students how to write "grammatically" (i.e., conventionally correctly). Common sense should have told us what this body of research has repeatedly confirmed. We do not expect children to learn to play the piano by learning rules or memorizing the names of the parts of it. We do not expect children to learn to swim or ride a bicycle properly without actually engaging in those activities. Why did we think we could teach children to write conventionally correctly from instruction that involved little or no actual composition?

So, if formal grammar instruction has been a failure because it is taught separately from writing, how can students be taught to write mechanically correctly while they are learning to write? The traditional approach was to assign an occasional piece of writing, mark errors on students' papers, and return those papers with a grade that reflected the number of errors made. In his landmark overview of research on teaching writing, Hillocks (1986) summarizes the research on this practice:

> *Teacher comment [written on students' compositions] has little impact on student writing. None of the studies of teacher comment . . . show statistically significant differences in the quality of writing between experimental and control groups. Indeed, several show no pre-to-post gains for any groups, regardless of the type of comment. [emphasis is the author's] (p. 165)*

Teachers who wish to increase student ability to write mechanically correctly will not rely on either formal grammar instruction or marking errors on student papers. These two methods have nothing but tradition to support them.

The major examination of writing instructional research was conducted by Hillocks (1986). His meta-analysis did not focus on formal grammar instruction or on the uses, processes, or development of writers through stages. Rather, he synthesized the best available research on how to teach writing, including how to teach students to write mechanically correctly. The distinction in this chapter between process, focused, and traditional writing is similar to Hillocks's distinction between the natural process, environmental, and traditional modes of writing instruction. The use in this chapter of form-based writing scales and writing rules on the wall is based on his discussion of the research on teaching students to evaluate their own writing with writing scales.

The research on writing supports a balanced program that begins with process writing, gradually incorporates a writing scale for conventions, moves into focused writing, uses form-based writing scales, and extends writing across the curriculum.

LOOKING BACK

A balanced writing program for the elementary school begins with process writing, extends process writing across the curriculum, builds on process writing with focused writing, and extends focused writing across the curriculum. From the time children become comfortable writing and sharing what they have written, conventional spelling, mechanics, and usage are supported with wall charts and gradually taught by having students learn to apply them a little at a time in their writing. The four key ideas in this chapter were:

1. All students need to engage in process writing.
2. Students need to learn to produce many different types of writing.
3. Students learn conventions by applying them in their own writing.
4. Students profit from writing in the content areas across the curriculum.

ADD TO YOUR JOURNAL

 In this chapter, process and focused writing instruction have been contrasted with each other and with traditional writing instruction. What was your experience with these different approaches? Compose a brief memoir of your development as a writer. Describe particularly the writing experiences and instruction you remember having at home and in elementary school. How did you feel about the kind and amount of writing instruction you received? How do you feel about it now? When you teach writing in an elementary classroom, how do you intend to go about it?

REFERENCES

Adams, M. J. (1990). *Beginning to read: Thinking and learning about print*. Cambridge, MA: MIT Press.

Atwell, N. (1990). *Coming to know: Writing to learn in the intermediate grades*. Portsmouth, NH: Heinemann.

Beers, J. W., & Henderson, E. H. (1977). A study of developing orthographic concepts among first graders. *Research in the Teaching of English, 11*, 133–148.

Braddock, R., Lloyd-Jones, R., & Schoer, L. (1963). *Research in written composition*. Champaign, IL: National Council of Teachers of English.

Calkins, L. M. (1994). *The art of teaching writing* (2nd ed.). Portsmouth, NH: Heinemann.

Clarke, L. K. (1988). Invented versus traditional spelling in first graders' writings: Effects on learning to spell and read. *Research in the Teaching of English, 22*, 281–309.

Dyson, A. H. (1985). Research currents: Writing and the social lives of children. *Language Arts, 62*, 632–639.

Dyson, A. H., & Freedman, S. W. (1991). Writing. In J. Flood, J. M. Jeusen, D. Lapp, & J. R. Squire (Eds.), *Handbook of research on teaching the language arts* (pp. 754–774). New York: Macmillan.

Fisher, B. (1991). Getting started with writing. *Teaching K–8*, 49–51.

Flower, L. (1979/1990). Writer-based prose: A cognitive basis for problems in writing. *College English, 41*, 19–37. Reprinted in T. Newkirk (Ed.), *To compose* (pp. 125–152). Portsmouth, NH: Heinemann.

Gentry, J. R., & Gillet, J. W. (1993). *Teaching kids to spell*. Portsmouth, NH: Heinemann.

Graves, D. H. (1983). *Writing: Teachers and children at work*. Portsmouth, NH: Heinemann.

Heath, S. B. (1983). *Ways with words: Language, life, and work in communities and classrooms*. Cambridge: Cambridge University Press.

Henderson, E. H. (1990). *Teaching spelling* (2nd ed.). Boston: Houghton Mifflin.

Hillocks, G., Jr. (1986). *Research on written composition: New directions for teaching.* Urbana, IL: ERIC Clearinghouse on Reading and Communication Skills; National Conference on Research in English.

Linden, M. J., & Whimbey, A. (1990). *Why Johnny can't write.* Hillsdale, NJ: Erlbaum.

Newkirk, T. (1989). *More than stories: The range of children's writing.* Portsmouth, NH: Heinemann.

Palmer, W. S. (1975). Research on grammar: A review of some pertinent investigations. *The High School Journal, 58,* 252–258.

Read, C. (1971). Pre-school children's knowledge of English phonology. *Harvard Educational Review, 41,* 1–34.

ADDITIONAL READINGS

These books have excellent suggestions for setting up process writing in classrooms.

Bromley, K. (1994). Journaling: Engagements in reading, writing, and thinking. New York: Scholastic.

Fiderer, A. (1994). Teaching writing: A workshop approach. New York: Scholastic.

Routman, R. (1988). *Transitions.* Portsmouth, NH: Heinemann.

Routman, R. (1991). *Invitations.* Portsmouth, NH: Heinemann.

Suggestions for writing in the content areas across the curriculum can be found in these books and articles.

Atwell, N. (Ed.). (1990). *Coming to know: Writing to learn in the intermediate grades.* Portsmouth, NH: Heinemann.

Cudd, E. T. (1989). Research and report writing in the elementary grades. *The Reading Teacher, 43,* 268–269.

Cudd, E. T., & Roberts, L. (1989). Using writing to enhance content area learning in the primary grades. *The Reading Teacher, 43,* 393–404.

Ways to integrate reading, literature, and writing are the topics of these two excellent journal articles.

Shanahan, T. (1988). The reading-writing relationship: Seven instructional principles. *The Reading Teacher, 41,* 636–647.

Walmsley, S. A., & Walp, T. (1990). Integrating literature and composing into the language arts curriculum. *Elementary School Journal, 90,* 251–274.

Classroom Diagnosis and Assessment of Reading and Writing

LOOKING AHEAD

All children are different, as we noted in Chapter 1. They have different interests and abilities. They learn at different rates and in different ways. In this chapter you will find out how to diagnose the different abilities of children and how to assess their progress toward becoming literate. To teach anything, teachers must have some knowledge about what learners already know and can do. Deciding how much learners know or at what stage of learning they are is referred to as *diagnosis.* Each day, teachers diagnose the abilities, attitudes, and prior knowledge of their class as a whole and individual students within that class. Based on this diagnosis, they make decisions about where to begin instruction and how to pace that instruction.

Once some diagnosis is made and instruction is begun, teachers constantly monitor how well students are progressing toward meeting particular goals the teachers have set. This monitoring of instructional progress is referred to as *assessment.* Some people think of assessment and testing as being synonymous. But testing is only one means of assessing progress. Teachers assess when they observe how children respond to a question, complete an assignment, or carry out an experiment or project. Teachers assess when they have a conference with students or parents about how the students or parents perceive progress. Teachers may use anecdotal records and checklists to help them assess the progress that particular children are making. In this chapter you will learn how to teach different children by making diagnosis and assessment an ongoing part of daily instruction. Four key ideas about diagnosis and assessment are presented:

1. Assessment must be both reliable and valid.
2. Portfolio assessment is authentic, follows from, and leads to instruction.
3. Anecdotal records, running records, and observation are authentic, follow from, and lead to instruction.
4. Assessment should include attitudes and interests.

ASSESSMENT MUST BE BOTH RELIABLE AND VALID

A person is said to be reliable if that person can be depended on, time and time again, to do whatever he or she is expected to do. J. C. Nunnally (1967) stated that "reliability concerns the extent to which measurements are *repeatable*" (p. 172). An assessment measure is said to be reliable if it can be depended on, time and time again, to do what it is expected to do. If a measure is very reliable, it will yield approximately the same results today as it will tomorrow or next week. You can rely on the consistency of the response. A scale is a reliable indicator of your weight if, when you neither gain nor lose pounds, it indicates the same weight each time you weigh yourself.

Test makers achieve reliability in a number of ways, one of which is by including many different items to measure each ability. A student may miss one of the items because of confusion, inattention, or fatigue but may get most of the other items correct. Another student may correctly guess the answer to an item but show the true deficiency by responding incorrectly to the remainder of the items. The scores of both students will be fairly reliable if there are a number of items testing the same ability, because judgment is not likely to be made based on one chance mistake or guess.

Teachers achieve reliability in a similar manner. Judgments are never based on one observation or on one test item. Rather, teachers make decisions based on several observations or testings. In addition, once decisions are made, teachers continue to observe, evaluate, and constantly rethink their decisions based on new information.

The concept of validity is somewhat harder to explain than the concept of reliability. Nunnally (1967) stated that "in a very general sense, a measuring instrument is valid if it does what it is intended to do." Validity of measurement refers to the match between the concept or skill to be measured and the means by which it is measured. A measure is valid to the extent that it measures what it was intended to measure. This distinction may seem academic and superfluous since we ought to be able to assume that any instrument will measure what it is intended to measure. This assumption, however, is often questionable. An example should clarify both the meaning of validity and the difficulty of achieving it.

Imagine, for example, that a reading skill important for beginning readers is associating consonant letters such as *b*, *m*, and *s* and the sounds commonly associated with these letters. Creating a valid test of this knowledge would appear to be simple. One could create a test that contained some pictures and ask students to write the letter they thought the picture began with. Is this a valid measure of their knowledge? When the tests have been scored, will the teacher know which students have this initial consonant knowledge and which don't? The answer is "perhaps." Imagine, for example, that some students don't know, or can't remember the names for, or have different names for some of the pictures. A student who looks at a picture of a dog, calls it a puppy, and writes the letter *p* under the picture has the wrong answer and the right knowledge. Imagine another child who writes the letter *b* under the picture thinking that he or she has made the letter *d*. This student, too, has marked the test item incorrectly but has the knowledge that the test was designed to evaluate. Another student may be able to spell *dog* and thus will write the letter *d* under the picture. If this response was generated by a memorized spelling, the correct response does not indicate that the child has achieved the desired letter-sound associations. To create a valid test of students' consonant letter-sound knowledge, the test creator would have to be sure that most of the stimulus pictures were familiar to the children, called by the desired name, and not familiar enough to have their spellings memorized. Moreover, even this test would be valid only if students can write all their consonants correctly.

There is, however, a much more serious problem with the test procedure just described. This problem is related to the issue of why it is desirable for students to be able to associate consonant letters with sounds. This knowledge, in and of itself, is useless. It becomes useful only when the student can *use* this knowledge and the context of what is being read to decode an unfamiliar word. What we really want students to do is to *apply* their knowledge of letter-sound relationships as they read. The previously described test procedure is aimed at testing the student's letter-sound association knowledge, not the application of this knowledge in real reading. So if the desired skill is the ability to use this knowledge in reading, how can this skill be measured validly? The answer to this question is obvious and simple. Put the children in a "real" reading situation in which they demonstrate their ability.

Imagine that you want to know which students have learned consonant letter-sound associations and can apply them as they are reading. How would you find this out? You would probably carry out a lesson that looked like this:

Boys and girls, this morning I put some sentences on the board. While I wasn't looking, a leprechaun sneaked in and covered up some of my words with these shamrocks. He must want us to play a guessing game since this is St. Patrick's Day, a special day for leprechauns. Let's read each sentence together, saying "blank" when we come to the covered words. Then let's guess which word the leprechaun covered up. [Students read the first sentence and make four or five guesses for the word.] We certainly have a lot of guesses. How can we decide which is right? Yes, we could uncover the whole word, but look here: the shamrocks are cut so that the left corner of each comes off. The leprechaun must want us to have some extra clues. Let's tear the left corner off. [Corner is torn off revealing the initial consonant of the word.] Aha! He did give us some extra clues. Now, which of our guesses are still possible? Yes, that word begins with an *l* so it could be *lake* but not *pond, ocean,* or *river.* Let's try the rest of them in the same way. First, we will guess without any clues about how the word begins. Then we will make new guesses based on the clue our leprechaun left us.

The lesson continues, and once the sentences on the board are completed, each child is given a duplicated sheet on which you have written three sentences. Each sentence has a word with a shamrock drawn over all but the initial consonant. Tell students that the leprechaun left them each a surprise (leprechaun picture to color and puzzle are at the bottom of each sheet). Then ask students to read each sentence, saying ''blank'' when they come to the shamrock and trying to figure out what will go in that blank that makes sense and begins with the clue left by the leprechaun. When they think they know what goes in the blank, they can come up and whisper read the sentences to you, and then, telling no one else what their guess was, they can color the leprechaun and complete the puzzle. As the children whisper in your ear, you will make notes about two abilities, the ability to use context to come up with a response that makes sense and the ability to use initial consonant letter-sound associations to figure out unknown words.

Because these observations occur as a natural part of the lesson, children are able to demonstrate their true ability unconfounded by the anxiety, panic, and inability to understand directions that often result from the awareness that one is taking a test. Because you have structured the observations so that decisions are based on the correct or incorrect response of the children, you view these responses in an objective, unbiased way. Because these observations are conducted in the context of ''real reading,'' you can observe not only whether students have learned certain associations but also whether they can apply what they have learned as they read. You have achieved validity by objectively measuring what you chose to measure in a context that simulates as closely as possible the tasks children are actually required to perform as they read. You will achieve reliability if you make tentative decisions about how well different children are learning to use context and initial consonant letter-sound knowledge based on the three sentences read to you but suspend judgment in any final sense until you have had a chance to observe the children's responses for another day or two.

Standardized, Group Tests

When most people think of diagnosis and assessment, they think of standardized, group tests—the kind you probably remember taking throughout your K–12 experience. In this chapter, we present diagnosis and assessment as an ongoing and continuous part of teaching. How do standardized, group tests fit into this scheme?

Except as a screening device, standardized, group tests have *no* place in diagnosis and assessment of individuals. Standardized reading tests may tell you how well groups of children are achieving. They do not tell you very much about individual children even though, unfortunately, they do print out scores for individual children. How can this be? If a child scores 44th percentile on a standardized reading achievement test, what does that mean? Does that mean this child is a better reader than a child who scores 14th percentile? Probably. Does that mean that a child who scores 74th percentile is a better reader than this child? Probably. Does that mean this child is a better reader than a child who scores 40th percentile? Possibly, but almost as probably not. There is quite a good chance that the child who scores 40th percentile is a better reader than the child who scores 44th!

All tests have what is called "standard error." *Standard error* is the term used to describe how much the child's true score is apt to vary from the test score. Standard error comes from sources such as the fact that some children get really "up" for tests and perform much better for the test than they ever could on a day-in, day-out basis, whereas other children panic and don't do nearly as well as they do on a day-in, day-out basis. Standard error also exists because some children don't feel well on the day of the test. Moreover, some test-wise children make great guesses. Others are easily frustrated and quit when they get to a hard item. Finally, some children are just lucky. All standardized tests have a standard error, and the test manual will tell you how much the standard error is for each part of the test.

Standardized, group tests are developed to be reliable for a group of students. Give a standardized test, as directed, to a group of 30 or more students who are the kind of students the test was designed for, and the average score of those 30 children will be highly reliable. The problem is that the score of any one of those students will not be reliable: That's what the standard error of measurement is telling you. On a highly reliable test, for every child in a group who scores better than he or she should, another child out of the group is likely to score worse than he or she should, so it evens out. The problem is that the teacher wants to diagnose and assess each individual student, and it is impossible to know whether an individual student scored above or below the true score (what the child's score would have been on a perfect test) and by how much. Each child's true score will fall within the range described by the child's actual score plus or minus the standard error of measurement 68 percent of the time. To be 95 percent sure the child's true score lies within a certain range, you have to add two standard errors of measurement to the child's actual score to get the top of the range and subtract two standard errors to get the bottom of the range. If one child had a particularly bad day and another a good one, four standard errors could separate their actual scores when their true scores are the same!

And what about the validity of standardized, group tests? Let's say schools gave every child 30 different forms of the standardized reading test each spring (no doubt dramatically increasing the burnout rates for teachers, children, and parents!). Each child's average score across the 30 testings would certainly have a standard error that approached zero. What would each child's highly dependable average score mean? It would tell you how well the child could and would do on the kind of reading task the test employed. The question is, how much is the test's reading task like the reading tasks you had your children engage in during the year (curricular validity), and how much is it like the reading tasks your children are apt to engage in outside of school over the years to come (authenticity)? To the extent that the reading test has your children do tasks that resemble your instruction and your long-term goals for them, you will probably think it yields valid scores. Otherwise, you will probably conclude that the test lacks validity.

These same problems exist with statewide writing tests. Such tests usually require students all over the state to write at one time to the same prompt. Again, looking at the average score of a large number of students on this writing test will tell you with reliability how well that group as a whole did on the test. However, anyone who has been involved in administering these tests will know that an excellent writer can often score very poorly on these tests and that a mediocre writer can sometimes do quite well. It seems to matter a lot how much an individual child knows or cares about the subject matter of the prompt. Other factors such as sickness, test anxiety, test wiseness, student frustration, and so on also play their customary roles. Moreover, the test is usually scored on the basis of whether a student's writing product conforms to a kind of formulaic writing. Children who were taught to write to the formula sometimes do better than children who were involved in a more authentic writing program. Still, these tests represent progress over an era when "writing" was tested without the children actually doing any writing.

Most schools and school districts administer standardized, group tests and use them to evaluate the reading and writing abilities of their students in general, or even classroom by classroom. The best standardized tests are reliable enough to be used in that way, but their validity is often questionable. Sadly, many schools also make decisions about individual child placement in special programs or even promotion/retention based on a single score on a standardized, group test. Experienced teachers have learned, however, that such tests of reading or writing really tell them almost nothing of value about their individual students or how to teach them better. In the remainder of this chapter, we show a variety of ways that you can more reliably and validly diagnose and assess the students in your classroom.

PORTFOLIO ASSESSMENT IS AUTHENTIC, FOLLOWS FROM, AND LEADS TO INSTRUCTION

In spite of the halo that standardized, group tests of reading and writing still wear for many politicians and educational administrators, we have seen that their reliability for individual students is low and that the validity of their scores, even for groups, is questionable. How, then, is a teacher to assess student learning? There is only one solution to the lack of reliability of a single score for an individual student: Base the assessment of each student's ability to do something on multiple indicators. Fortunately, each child attends school for at least six hours most days for nine or more months. That amount of time provides the teacher with ample opportunity to gather a great number of indications of a student's ability in any academic area of interest. Reliability of estimates of individual student ability may be an insoluble problem for schools, school districts, states, and nations, but it is a problem that each teacher can solve in his or her own classroom. A teacher who withholds judgment about a student's ability until having several measures of that ability will improve on the reliability of the best standardized, group test.

So, the teacher whose judgments of children's reading and writing are each based on a number of indicators can make reliable assessments of individuals, but will they also be valid? Today, tests or other measures are usually considered valid if they faithfully assess what students were taught. The principle is straightforward: Diagnosis and assessment should follow from and lead to instruction. If students will not engage in the instructional activities of their classroom, if they engage in them but do not do them well, or if they do them well but do not improve in their performance over time, they are apparently not learning from those activities. If we are evaluating students' learning, it seems reasonable to report their degree of engagement, success, and achievement with the activities that compose the heart of the instructional program. If we are diagnosing students, we should do so to find out how to modify our instruction to increase student engagement, success, or achievement with instructional activities. By this principle, any measure is valid if it faithfully follows from and leads to actual instructional activities.

This principle of assessing students based on their engagement, success, and achievement with actual instructional activities interacts with the concept of *authentic* assessment. As we have seen, authentic assessment determines how well students are progressing toward the long-term goals of schooling. Consequently, assessment that follows from and leads to instruction will be authentic only if that instruction is authentic. In other words, authentic assessment of reading or writing will measure student engagement, success, and/or achievement on reading or writing tasks that resemble those our schools are preparing children to do later on in life. The use of portfolios enables teachers to have student assessments that are authentic and that follow from and lead to instruction.

A *portfolio* is a collection of student work. The idea of a student portfolio comes from the practice of painters, photographers, architects, interior designers, and other individuals who maintain an assemblage of their work as a means of demonstrating their professional ability and accomplishments.

When teachers use student portfolios to diagnose or evaluate reading or writing, they maximize the reliability and validity of those assessments. If done well, portfolio assessment is reliable for individual students because the teacher bases each judgment on multiple indicators. It is also valid because the teacher bases each judgment on how well students perform on the actual activities being used to teach them reading or writing. There are at least four types of portfolios that a teacher may choose to use when diagnosing or assessing each student's reading or writing: working, showcase, growth, and cumulative portfolios.

Working Portfolios

A working portfolio is simply all the student's work of a particular kind (e.g., process writing). Neither the teacher nor the student has screened the samples that are placed in a working portfolio. As long as the student is at least temporarily finished with a piece of work, it is dated and placed in the working portfolio for that kind of work. For example, if students write a first draft two or three times a week, that draft is filed in the student's working portfolio for writing as soon as the student finishes writing or sharing it. Of course, the teacher or the student may later select a first draft from the working portfolio to confer about, or for the student to proofread, edit, and/or revise. When additional work on the piece is completed, all subsequent drafts are also dated and filed along with the first draft in the working portfolio. For another example, the teacher may have each student record an oral reading each week. The same cassette tape could be used for each child. Each oral reading sample should begin with the date. By listening to the tape, the teacher can readily hear children's improvement or lack thereof in their oral reading as long as the passages are of comparable difficulty and length. The tape itself could stand alone as the oral reading portfolio for that child, or it could become one item in the child's more diverse reading portfolio.

The chief characteristic of a working portfolio is its completeness and lack of selectivity. It is the student's working portfolio that provides the samples from which the student will choose that which he or she places in a showcase portfolio.

Showcase Portfolios

Tierney, Carter, and Desai (1991) have eloquently argued the advantages of having students develop a sense of ownership over their own portfolios. Involving them in evaluating their own progress and accomplishments builds students' independence, increases their motivation to work and learn, and helps them develop insights about reading or writing that cannot be taught directly. The purposes of a showcase portfolio are to grant students ownership and involve them in self-assessment.

While the teacher may set a minimum and/or maximum number of samples or items that the student must choose, the student independently selects and periodically updates the pieces of work that go into that student's showcase portfolio of reading or writing. It is the process of student selection rather than the particular products chosen by the student that has instructional value. As students examine all their dated work in order to choose a few samples, their sense of themselves as readers or writers is fostered in a powerful and personal way. They develop pride and ownership over their work as they remember the occasions when the work was produced. Examining their work in order cannot fail to show them that they are improving and learning.

The instructional value of having students maintain showcase portfolios is enhanced by having them caption the pieces they select and allowing them to share their showcase portfolios with the class. When professional photographers and others put together their showcase portfolios, they generally caption each piece in the portfolio with a brief statement that explains why that piece was selected, or what is special, important, or unique about it. Teachers often require students to use one side of a 3×5 lined index card to caption each piece of work chosen for his or her showcase portfolios. Teachers may guide the captioning process somewhat by suggesting that students begin their captions with "I chose this piece because . . ." or "When I did this piece, I was trying to. . . ."

Several approaches to the sharing of showcase portfolios can be taken. Each week, for example, one of the students in the class could be "Reader" or "Writer" of the Week. A bulletin board could be made with the student's photograph and various biographical or personal facts on it. Books that the child has read or previously published could also be affixed to this bulletin board. One day during the week, time could be set aside for the child to share his or her showcase portfolio with the class, explaining why each piece was chosen and what the child hopes to accomplish in the future. By the end of the school year, every child in the class could have had one week each semester devoted to his or her work.

For showcase portfolios to provide their potential benefits to students, adequate time must be set aside for students to select, caption, and share. These processes must be conducted in a truly student-centered manner. Teachers should also be careful not to base report card grades on showcase portfolios. Few students in elementary school are sophisticated enough to choose work that will maximize their grades or otherwise put their best foot forward to an adult audience. Showcase portfolios are designed to help children learn to self-assess, not to grade them on how well they are able to self-assess. When elementary students are to be graded, it is the responsibility of the teacher, not the children, to select the work that most fairly and accurately determines those grades. This point leads us to a discussion of the third type of portfolios.

Growth Portfolios

What does a teacher want more than anything else for his or her students? Growth. Every literacy teacher wants students to grow in their willingness to read and write, their effort to read and write well, their enjoyment of reading and writing, and their ability to read and write. Portfolios have the potential to help teachers reliably and validly assess growth on all of these dimensions. Teachers can also analyze samples to diagnose why more growth has probably not occurred and what might be done about it.

A growth portfolio is the collection of student work samples and other items that a teacher selects or elicits in order to conduct the diagnosis or assessment the teacher has decided to perform. First, the teacher selects samples for a student's growth portfolio from the student's working and showcase portfolios. The teacher may also elicit new work from or administer special tasks to the student for the growth portfolio in order to answer specific diagnostic or assessment questions. The chief characteristic of a growth portfolio is that items are selected or elicited to shed light on specific aspects of reading or writing learning and development. For example, a teacher concerned with student improvement in focused writing could choose to compare writing samples done several months apart in response to similar prompts on the same topic. Teachers sometimes design parallel prompts to contrast student growth in producing a type of writing such as a story, biography, letter, or description. For another example, a child's growth portfolio in reading or writing may contain three or four dated entries from that child's reader-response journal on poetry.

Instead of captioning each piece of work in a growth portfolio, most teachers write a narrative description of the child's strengths, weaknesses, and changes as manifested by the samples. This description can be shared with the child or with parents during a conference to inform them of progress and to get their input on future goals. If necessary, the teacher can assign a grade or grades to one or more aspects of the growth portfolio and justify the evaluation by referring to specifics in the samples.

Cumulative Portfolios

Cumulative portfolios are growth portfolios that reveal progress over the years. In a school that maintains cumulative portfolios for students in one or more areas, teachers usually agree on the amount and kinds of items to be included. Sometimes groups of teachers design parallel reading or writing situations to highlight certain facts of long-term growth in literacy. Some schools encourage each student to help the teacher decide on some of the work that will be placed in the student's cumulative portfolio. The cumulative portfolio can be a real source of pride and accomplishment on the part of an upper elementary student who can readily discern the tremendous progress he or she has made over the years.

TRY IT OUT

 Find one child who writes regularly and work with that child to assemble showcase, growth, and cumulative portfolios in writing. Be sure to let the child select what will go into the showcase portfolio and have the child caption those pieces. You should decide what will go into the growth portfolio and write a narrative description of what you included and what it demonstrates about the child's writing development. You and the child might work together to decide what will go into the cumulative portfolio in writing.

ANECDOTAL RECORDS, RUNNING RECORDS, AND OBSERVATION ARE AUTHENTIC, FOLLOW FROM, AND LEAD TO INSTRUCTION

In addition to portfolios, today's teachers also use anecdotal records, running records, and observation to diagnose and evaluate their students. Like portfolios, these methods accomplish reliability for individual student assessments by basing each judgment about a child on multiple indications. They accomplish validity by basing each judgment on the child's engagement, success, or achievement with the actual instructional activities in the classroom. If the literacy instruction in the classroom is authentic, these approaches to assessment will also be authentic. Some teachers broaden the concept of portfolio to include anecdotal records, running records, and records of observation. If so, a child's growth and cumulative portfolios in reading or writing would contain those kinds of records as well. Because many teachers restrict portfolios to student work samples, we have chosen to discuss anecdotal records, running records, and observation separately. You, of course, are free to combine all these kinds of classroom diagnosis and assessment into diversified portfolios of reading and writing.

Anecdotal Records

Children in elementary school learn very little from passively listening to the teacher talk to the entire class for more than a few minutes. Elementary students learn best by being actively engaged in worthwhile and appropriate tasks for most of their instructional time. A classroom where the children are active rather than passive much of the time has an additional advantage: Teachers who use observation to diagnose and assess their students have much more to observe.

Anecdotal records are the written records that teachers keep on individual children based on their ongoing observation of and interaction with them. A classroom in which children are involved in comprehension lessons, self-selected reading, responding to what they have read, discussing what they have read, writing, inventing spellings, inquiring, researching, writing about what they have read, sharing what they have written, proofreading, editing, and revising what they have written, making words, using wall charts that support their reading and writing, and so on provide the teacher with hundreds of opportunities each day to form or modify judgments about how individual students are learning. Unfortunately, no teacher can systematically, objectively process this wealth of information. Fortunately, because there is so much of it, sampling from it in a systematic and objective manner will still provide a rich portrait of each child across the weeks and months.

Why is it necessary to keep timely, written records of a teacher's observations of each child? There are several reasons. First, experienced teachers know that, without keeping written records, they will remember very little of all they witness. For some children, they will remember almost nothing. Second, we all have personalities and preferences that match us better with some students than others. We may naturally respond better to girls than boys, or vice versa. We may interact more with children who are highly verbal than those who are quiet. Unless we keep systematic written records of some kind, it will be very difficult for us to observe every student enough to maintain a truly reliable and valid assessment of that child's engagement, success, and achievement with each major type of instructional activity. Third, because anecdotal records are written, we can sit in a quiet place and examine what we have observed about a single child and decide what we want to observe in the future to round out our developing picture of that student.

There are probably a large number of ways that a teacher can efficiently record and update written observations about individual students. Here is the one we have found to be the most practical.

Any school supply or office supply store sells file folder labels by the sheet. Each label is "sticky," so the user types or writes on a label, peels it off the sheet, and affixes it to the tab of the file folder being labeled. These sheets of file folder labels are also perfect for recording brief comments about children's understanding and engagement, success, or achievement with instructional activities.

The teacher places one or more sheets of file folder labels on a clipboard that he or she carries. When interacting with or observing students, the teacher will occasionally witness a significant indicator of the child's learning or lack thereof. It is quick, easy, and unobtrusive to record the child's nickname, the date, and a brief comment on one of the file folder labels on the sheet in the clipboard. After school, the teacher takes a few minutes and affixes each label used that day to a page for that subject in the child's anecdotal records folder.

When planning an instructional day, the teacher will often analyze the anecdotal records for two or three of the children. At this pace, every student's anecdotal records can be analyzed every two weeks. The analysis of a child's anecdotal records consists of determining how much support there is in the folder for evaluative statements that would be written in a narrative description of the child's learning or shared with a parent at a conference. It is during this analysis that the teacher often realizes that he or she has not actually recorded enough observations about how well the child is doing in some important area of the literacy program. When this occurs, the teacher writes the child's nickname or initials on one of the file folder labels on the sheet in the clipboard along with a one- or two-word description of the observation needed for that child. While moving through the school day, the teacher then has several labels on the sheet that remind him or her to obtain particular observations of certain children.

If anecdotal records are collected regularly and systematically, and if they consist of objective and specific descriptions of children's engagement, success, or achievement with actual instructional activities, there is no more reliable or valid means of diagnosing or evaluating students' ongoing learning. These records can then serve to support any summative statements that the teacher needs or cares to make to anyone about the child's progress.

Running Records

A running record is a particular method of transcribing a child's oral reading of a passage in a book (Clay, 1993a). Using a sheet of lined paper, the teacher places a check on the line for every word the child reads correctly from a corresponding line in the book. Every time the child begins reading a new line in the book, the teacher uses a new line on the paper to record the reading. When a child reads the page differently than you expect, that *miscue* is recorded so that the quality of the miscue can later be analyzed.

There are various systems for recording miscues. When a word is skipped or omitted by the child, we write the word on the line and then circle it. When the child inserts a word, we write a + followed by the word that was added. When a word is not decoded accurately or when another word is substituted for it, we write the word from the book with what the child said written above it. If a child goes back and successfully corrects a miscue, we leave the miscue marked as it is but place a check over it. The child's dialect is usually ignored when marking miscues. If a child reads a word the way he or she would have pronounced it in conversation, the child has read the word correctly.

This simple system of recording an individual student's oral reading has lots of advantages. The teacher does not need a copy of the passage the child is reading in order to mark miscues. The teacher can readily see how accurately the child reads the passage and can reconstruct the child's miscues sufficiently to determine what strategies the child uses when reading orally.

Running records must be modified when used with older and more sophisticated oral readers. The same system of marking miscues can be used, but the teacher will need a copy of whatever the child is reading from. When there are a number of words per line and a number of lines per page, it becomes very difficult to keep up with where the child is unless one has a copy of the passage to mark on. As we said above, the term *running record* is usually restricted to miscues recorded using lined paper and pen or pencil. When a copy of the passage is used to record miscues, the procedure is often called "taking an *oral reading protocol.*" For clarity and simplicity, we refer to both procedures as a running record.

When running records are taken regularly and analyzed carefully, they indicate two important factors: a student's reading instructional level and a student's reading strategies.

READING INSTRUCTIONAL LEVEL   A child's reading instructional level is simply the level of difficulty of material that the child will most benefit from reading. Over the years, research, common sense, and professional experience have shown that children learn to read better only by reading material that is neither too difficult nor too easy for them. One of the best ways to decide whether material is at that level of appropriateness for a child is to take one or more running records of that child reading orally from that material. Again, several systems exist for deciding which miscues to count as errors. Today, almost all reading authorities count any miscue that does not change meaning (e.g., saying "little" when the book said "small") as if it were read correctly. Why? These are the kinds of miscues good readers make. When a child makes a non-meaning-changing miscue, that is a good sign, not a bad sign.

A miscue that changes meaning is counted as an error. A miscue that changes meaning but is successfully corrected is counted as half an error. Why? It was an error, but it is good that the reader corrected it. So it is half good and half bad.

The number of errors that a child made on a selection is counted as all the meaning-changing miscues that were not corrected plus half the ones that were corrected. This number of errors is interpreted as a percentage of the words read (i.e., number of errors per hundred words). Traditionally, children were considered at instructional level if they made 3 to 5 errors per hundred words. Research suggests that 3 errors per hundred words is the number of oral reading errors that predicts the greatest growth in reading (Cunningham, 1985). Reading Recovery allows children to make as many as 10 errors per hundred words in a new book (Clay, 1993b), but the error rate can be that high only because the child is going to read that book at least four or five times. By the last time a child in Reading Recovery reads a particular book, the child will make no more than 3 to 5 errors (Askew, 1993). For situations in which children will read a selection only once, 3 to 5 errors as the indication of instructional level seems prudent. Certainly, children who are going to be the best readers will invariably read that well in the material the teacher gives them.

It should be noted that a running record can indicate only the highest level that a student's reading instructional level can be. For students who read better orally than they comprehend, their reading instructional level will actually be lower than a running record would indicate. The greatest growth in reading occurs when children read material on which they can answer 80 percent or more of the comprehension questions a teacher later asks (Cunningham, 1985). Using both running records and measures of reading comprehension on graded passages to determine a student's reading instructional level is called an *informal reading inventory*. A number of published informal reading inventories exist for teachers to use in estimating the reading instructional level of individual children. Of course, they yield only an estimate, since the passages they contain may not really represent the literature you want your children to read. It is the ability of children to read the materials they actually read in your class that determines whether or not they are reading at instructional level.

MISCUE ANALYSIS AND READING STRATEGIES   When a child is reading from material in which he or she makes no more than 10 errors per hundred words, the miscues the child makes can provide a window through which the teacher can examine some of the child's reading strategies. If the selection is harder than that for the child, *miscue analysis* reveals very little about the child's strategies.

While systems of varying complexity have been developed for analyzing miscues, a few aspects of oral reading miscues are most helpful to consider. It is generally possible to classify a student as tending toward one of these three reading strategies:

Context-only strategy—The student makes several meaning-changing miscues that are successfully corrected. The student also makes several non-meaning-changing miscues. Few, if any, of the student's miscues have the same initial letter or onset of the original word.

Decoding strategy—The student makes several meaning-changing miscues that are not corrected. Many of the student's miscues have most of the letter-sounds of the original word.

Balanced strategy—The student makes few meaning-changing miscues and corrects almost all of the ones that were made. Several of the student's non-meaning-changing miscues have the same onset as the original word.

Students with a context-only strategy should be helped to use the onset of the word along with context to decode an unknown word while reading. They probably also need systematic decoding instruction. Students with a decoding strategy should be helped to monitor what they are reading and to self-correct when it does not sound right or make sense. They probably also need to do more self-selected reading.

Running records provide an excellent indication of whether students are reading literature or other material at instructional level and are developing a balanced reading strategy. Students who consistently read in material harder than their instructional level or who maintain a context-only or a decoding strategy cannot be expected to improve much in reading over the long term.

TRY IT OUT

 Have a child select a piece to read to you. Do a running record as the child reads, and then analyze the results. Was the selection read at the child's instructional level? Which of the three reading strategies was the child using? What might the child need to do in order to continue to become a better reader? What else would you need to do to diagnose this child's reading?

Observation

Teachers can use portfolios, anecdotal records, and running records, as well as tests, to diagnose and evaluate their students in reading and writing. Most of the time, though, teachers assess their students by simply watching them and listening to them. Experienced teachers have learned "to have eyes in the back of their heads." They have learned to withhold judgment until a pattern emerges for a child in a particular area. Most important, they have learned to avoid prejudice. If children are to behave or learn better than they have in the past, we must truly see what they actually are doing, not allow ourselves to see only what we expect to see.

In our experience, the best teachers are constantly monitoring the learning of all the students. No child "falls through the cracks." The lesson frameworks, methods, and activities described throughout this book will work only for teachers who observe students carefully and make fine adjustments to maximize the effectiveness of instruction. Recipelike lessons and teacher's manuals cannot be made teacherproof. No such script can tell a teacher when to speed up, when to slow down, when to reteach, or when to move on. It cannot tell a teacher when more or better examples are needed or how much repetition to provide. The ability to reliably, validly, and objectively observe students may be the single most important ability in teaching. Certainly, teaching cannot succeed without it.

Are good observers of children born or made? We believe they are made. Our evidence? The best observers are almost always teachers with several years' experience, and few new teachers, whatever their potential, are very good at it. What can teachers with little or no experience do to improve their ability to observe children accurately and efficiently? Use portfolio assessment, keep anecdotal records, and take running records. Because these methods of diagnosis and evaluation provide a fine-grained analysis of a child's development in reading or writing, a teacher learns a tremendous amount about both assessment and literacy from doing them. The more one uses portfolios, anecdotal records, and running records, the better one's powers of observation of children become.

LISTEN, LOOK, AND LEARN

Interview a classroom teacher you respect about how that teacher diagnoses and assesses students' needs and abilities in reading and writing. What kind of observational records are kept? Are portfolios part of the assessment? Are the children learning how to self-assess their progress? Good assessment and diagnosis take time and must be done efficiently. Try to determine not only how the teacher carries out reading and writing assessment but when the assessment is done. Having read this chapter so far, can you think of any assessment or diagnostic components the teacher might add or some ways to be more efficient?

ASSESSMENT SHOULD INCLUDE ATTITUDES AND INTERESTS

One of the dilemmas of teaching is that there are so many different things to keep up with and attend to that teachers are always in danger of losing sight of the forest for the trees. In reading, the trees are all of the various skills and strategies we want students to learn how to perform. The forest is real reading. Although we do need to diagnose and assess students' progress toward becoming able readers, we should not lose sight of our ultimate goal—producing people who find pleasure in reading and who turn to reading for information and entertainment.

Results from a 1983 survey by the Book Industry Study Group (Lehr, 1985) indicated that an overwhelming majority of Americans not only can but do read. According to their survey, 96 percent of the U.S. population aged 16 and older read books, magazines, or newspapers. Fifty-six percent of these adults read books. A larger percentage read newspapers and magazines.

Although the results of the overall survey were encouraging, the results for young adults aged 16 to 21 were discouraging. Only 63 percent of the 16- to 21-year-olds surveyed reported that they were readers. This number represented a 12 percent decline from 1978, when 75 percent of this age group reported that they were readers. Achievement-test scores indicating how well children and young adults read generally rose from 1978 to 1983. The combined achievement-test scores and results of the BISG surveys indicate that students were reading better but liking it less.

Throughout this book, we have emphasized that reading is affective. The way you feel about what you read and what you do during reading instruction matters. If students read well but don't choose to read, we have not accomplished what we want to accomplish. We have suggested numerous activities and ways of organizing for instruction that should produce students who like to read and read for information and pleasure. We cannot, however, take it for granted that this will occur and should demonstrate our concern with reading attitudes by periodically assessing how our students feel about reading. Here are some suggestions for monitoring the progress your students are making toward becoming lifelong readers.

Assess Attitudes and Interests at the Beginning of the Year

Early in the year, try to determine what your students like to read and how they feel about reading. You may want to make a homework assignment for everyone to bring to school on a specified day, "The three best books you read all summer." Encourage the students to go back to the library to check out a book previously read. Even if they can no longer find the book, ask them to tell why they thought it was such a good book. Young children should bring favorite books they like to have read to them. When the children bring their books, let each child tell why he or she liked the books. You may want them to do this book sharing in small groups. As they share, note the titles of the books they bring and their reasons for liking them. This will tell you what current reading interests you should encourage and also where you need to try to broaden interests.

You may have some children who don't bring three books or who bring books but don't really have anything to say about them and may not have really read or liked the books. This tells you a lot about the current interests and attitudes of these children and lets you know that all of the efforts you plan to make to encourage and support reading are truly important and needed.

You might want to follow up this "best-books" assignment with another homework assignment to bring in magazines and parts of the newspaper they read. Again, follow up this assignment with group sharing and make notes about what each child brought (or didn't bring). Record your results on a "Beginning Interests and Attitudes Summary" such as that shown in Figure 8.1. In addition to noting what each child shared, summarize the interests of the class by noting which topics and types of books were shared most. You have now diagnosed

Children's Names	Books Shared	Magazines/ Newspapers	Current Interest (none, little, some, much)
Carol	Ramona the Pest Charlotte's Web	none	some
Sheryll	3 Bobbsey Twins mysteries	none	some
Sue Ann	Whales Dinosaurs Runaway Horse	U.S.A Today	much
Travis	none	Sports page	little
Ray	none	Fishing	little
David	3 Star Trek books	Sports Illustrated	some
Jason	Cannonball Death at High Noon Dirty Dozen	Time	some

Topics of interest to many children:

Sports, fantasy

Types of books read:

✓Realistic fiction   ✓Science fiction   Historical fiction
✓Mystery   Myths/legends   Folk/fairy tales
Fantasy   Biography   Autobiography
✓Informational   Other _____

FIGURE 8.1 Sample Form: Beginning Interests and Attitudes Summary

your students' entering interests and attitudes toward reading and can plan how much and what kinds of motivational activities you will do.

Assess Periodically Your Efforts to Improve Attitudes and Broaden Interests

Just as with any kind of assessment, your assessment of reading interests and attitudes should follow from and lead to instruction. By linking your assessment directly to your instruction, you ensure that your assessment is valid. By assessing interests and attitudes on a regular schedule, you get a more reliable indicator than if you assess only once or twice a year. Also, as in any assessment, you can use a variety of methods to assess interests and attitudes. One of the best methods of assessing is to observe what your students actually do. Figure 8.2 is an example of a checklist you might use to observe systematically the growth in reading attitudes. To make this less of a burden, you might fill out

Child's Name_____   Date____

Across the last two weeks, has the child:

	Yes	No
1. Seemed happy when engaged in reading ?	____	____
2. Seemed happy when engaged in writing?	____	____
3. Talked about reading at home?	____	____
4. Talked about writing at home?	____	____
5. Brought a book from home to share with the class?	____	____
6. Checked out and read books from the library?	____	____
7. Read a piece of writing to the class?	____	____
8. Published a piece of writing?	____	____
9. Shown enthusiasm during a reading conference?	____	____
10. Shown enthusiasm during a writing conference?	____	____
11. Chosen to read rather than engage in another pleasurable activity?	____	____
12. Chosen to write rather than engage in another pleasurable activity?	____	____

FIGURE 8.2   Sample Form: Observation Checklist to Assess Literacy Attitudes

one of these checklists each week for a fourth of your class. At the end of the month, you will have observed and focused on the reading attitudes of everyone. If you do this all year, you should have eight or nine indicators of reading attitude throughout the year and should be able to document which students have better attitudes at the end of the year than they did at the beginning.

In addition to diagnosis by observation, you may want to interview students or have students fill out a short form indicating how they feel about reading. Figure 8.3 is an example of a form students might fill out to indicate their attitudes toward reading. Although it is probably too optimistic to expect everyone to rank reading at the top of his or her list, it is reasonable to expect reading not to be at the bottom and to move up as the year goes on.

In addition to making observations, you might periodically ask students what they are interested in, what they are reading about, and what they think they would like to read about. You can construct an interest inventory that lets you know which children are apt to like which books.

It is a rainy Saturday afternoon. Your friends are all gone for the day. The television is at the repair shop. List in order from "most like" to "least like" what you would do at home by yourself on a rainy afternoon. Pick from the activities at the bottom or make up some of your own.

1.   6.

2.   7.

3.   8.

4.   9.

5.   10.

Listen to a game on the radio
Put a puzzle together
Make a model car or plane
Cook something
Read a good book
Write in my journal
Read a magazine
Write a story or poem
Draw or paint a picture
Take a nap
Read part of the newspaper
Write a letter to a friend
Listen to music
Clean out my closet
Sew, knit, or crochet
Listen to a story tape or record

FIGURE 8.3   Sample Form: What I Like to Do

THE THEORY AND RESEARCH BASE FOR CLASSROOM DIAGNOSIS AND ASSESSMENT OF READING AND WRITING

Psychometrics is the science of measuring mental abilities, processes, and states. Of course, that definition includes measuring the relative strengths and weaknesses within a student's overall profile of reading or writing capabilities (diagnosis). It also includes measuring how well a student reads or writes at a particular point in time (assessment). From its beginnings a century or so ago, psychometrics has gradually given us a sophisticated body of theory and research on scientific concepts of measurement. Any teacher would certainly benefit from an increased knowledge of psychometrics, especially a practical understanding of the notions of validity and reliability in educational tests and measurement. We began this chapter with an overview of those important evaluative concepts. A more in-depth study of educational psychometrics can be gained from reading such basic textbooks as Kubiszyn and Borich (1992).

While psychometrics has developed into a science with much to teach us, most educational applications of psychometrics have been in the production of standardized tests of various kinds. These tests have generally been used in what Calfee and Hiebert (1991) call "externally mandated assessments": Federal, state, or local agencies, laws, or pressures, acting from without, compel schools and teachers to administer certain assessments in certain ways at certain times. The value of these "high-stakes tests" remains a matter of considerable controversy, but there seems to be a consensus among literacy educators that "internal assessment" (Calfee & Hiebert, 1991) holds much more promise for helping teachers improve student learning of literacy.

Other terms for internal assessment include *curriculum-based assessment* (Fuchs & Fuchs, 1989), *assessment designed for instruction* (Calfee & Hiebert, 1991), *constructive evaluation* (Johnston, 1992), and *teacher-directed assessment* (Calfee & Hiebert, 1991). These various terms, and others like them, all imply that successful teachers of reading and writing evaluate their students continually in order to modify how they are teaching them. In addition, these terms imply that, whatever their value, externally mandated assessments can never be as useful to teachers as quality assessments they administer and interpret for their own instructional purposes. Developing the ability to direct their own assessment is probably one of the most valuable professional skills teachers of literacy can acquire.

Actually, the notion of teacher-directed assessment has a long history in reading education. The individual informal reading inventory, administered and interpreted (and even constructed) by the teacher, was advocated some 50 years ago by Betts (1946). Today, there are a number of commercially available informal reading inventories for teachers to select from (Burns & Roe, 1993; Ekwall & Shanker, 1993; Flynt & Cooter, 1993; Johns, 1994; Leslie & Caldwell, 1990; Silvaroli, 1989; Stieglitz, 1992; Woods & Moe, 1989). Each of these inventories relies on teachers to decide when and whom they will test, how they will score the various subtests, and how they will interpret those scores. In this chapter, we emphasized *running records* (Clay, 1993a), the contemporary approach to doing the oral reading error/miscue analysis part of an informal reading inventory.

Likewise, in writing education, there has been for several decades a tradition of teacher-directed assessment. Teachers of writing have been taught to achieve reliability and validity of assessment through either analytical or holistic scoring of student papers (Spandel, 1990). In our "Writing" chapter (Chapter 7), the discussion of writing scales as an evaluative tool subsumes both analytical and holistic systems for scoring writing. Rule-based writing scales are equivalent to analytic scoring systems used by students; form-based writing scales are equivalent to holistic scoring systems used by students. Teachers who use writing scales typically assess student writing in their growth and cumulative portfolios with regard to the criteria on one or the other of the two kinds of writing scales.

A separate but related movement in recent theory and research on educational measurement has argued for more authentic measurement practices, both in externally mandated and teacher-directed assessment. "The aim of authentic assessment is to assess many different kinds of literacy abilities in contexts that closely resemble the actual situations in which those abilities are used"(Valencia, Hiebert, & Afflerbach, 1994, p. 9). It may be said that the move toward more authentic assessment involves increasing teacher-directed assessment and making externally mandated, high-stakes tests more like teacher-directed assessment.

In addition to running records, the two major types of authentic, teacher-directed evaluation discussed in the literature on literacy assessment have been portfolios (Jordan, 1994) and observation (Goodman, 1994).

LOOKING BACK

If all children were alike, or could be taught as if they were, this chapter would not have been written. While both teacher-made and commercially available tests have long been the mainstays of assessment, the past decade or so has seen unprecedented progress in the development of other assessment methods. These new methods supplement or even supplant traditional tests because they provide ongoing assessment of student learning, they are more reliable and valid for individual students, they are concerned with a broader range of learning that includes application and attitudes, they permit student self-assessment, and they train teachers to be better observers of student behavior. The four key ideas of this chapter were:

1. Assessment must be both reliable and valid.
2. Portfolio assessment is authentic, follows from, and leads to instruction.
3. Anecdotal records, running records, and observation are authentic, follow from, and lead to instruction.
4. Assessment should include attitudes and interests.

ADD TO YOUR JOURNAL

What experience have you had working with children? Have you taught for several years? Do you have children of your own? Have you student-taught? Have you visited classrooms, been a counselor at a summer camp, taught Sunday School, or been a lifeguard? What do these experiences tell you about the need to observe children carefully? Can engagement, success, and achievement with instructional activities, as well as attitudes and interests, be observed? What do you remember about how your literacy abilities and interests were assessed? Make a plan for classroom assessment of literacy based on your experiences and on what you have learned in this chapter.

REFERENCES

Askew, B. J. (1993). The effect of multiple readings on the behaviors of children and teachers in an early intervention program. *Reading and Writing Quarterly, 9*, 307–315.

Betts, E. A. (1946). *Foundations of reading instruction*. New York: American Book Co.

Burns, P. C., & Roe, B. D. (1993). *Burns/Roe informal reading inventory: Preprimer to twelfth grade* (4th ed.). Boston: Houghton Mifflin.

Calfee, R., & Hiebert, E. (1991). Classroom assessment of reading. In R. Barr, M. L. Kamil, P. B. Mosenthal, & P. D. Pearson (Eds.), *Handbook of reading research* (Vol. 2, pp. 281–309). White Plains, NY: Longman.

Clay, M. M. (1993a). *An observation survey: Of early literacy achievement*. Portsmouth, NH: Heinemann.

Clay, M. M. (1993b). *Reading Recovery: A guidebook for teachers in training*. Portsmouth, NH: Heinemann.

Cunningham, J. W. (1985). Three recommendations to improve comprehension teaching. In J. Osborn, P. T. Wilson, & R. C. Anderson (Eds.), *Reading education: Foundations for a literate America*. Lexington, MA: D. C. Heath, Lexington Books Division.

Ekwall, E. E., & Shanker, J. L. (1993). *Ekwall/Shanker reading inventory* (3rd ed.). Boston: Allyn & Bacon.

Flynt, E. S., & Cooter, R. B., Jr. (1993). *Flynt-Cooter reading inventory for the classroom*. Scottsdale, AZ: Gorsuch Scarisbrick.

Fuchs, L. S., & Fuchs, D. (1989). Curriculum-based assessment. In C. Reynolds & R. R. Kamphaus (Eds.), *Handbook of psychological and educational assessment of children: Vol. 1. Intelligence and achievement*. New York: Guilford.

Goodman, Y. M. (1994). Observation. In A. C. Purves (Ed.), *Encyclopedia of English studies and language arts* (A Project of the National Council of Teachers of English). New York: Scholastic.

Johns, J. L. (1994). *Basic reading inventory: Pre-primer through grade ten* (6th ed.). Dubuque, IA: Kendall/Hunt.

Johnston, P. H. (1992). *Constructive evaluation of literate activity*. White Plains, NY: Longman.

Jordan, S. (1994). Portfolio assessment. In A. C. Purves (Ed.), *Encyclopedia of English studies and language arts* (A Project of the National Council of Teachers of English). New York: Scholastic.

Kubiszyn, T., & Borich, G. (1992). *Educational testing and measurement: Classroom application and practice* (4th ed.). New York: HarperCollins.

Lehr, F. (1985). A portrait of the American as reader. *Journal of Reading, 29,* 170–171.

Leslie, L., & Caldwell, J. (1990). *Qualitative reading inventory.* Glenview, IL: Scott, Foresman.

Nunnally, J. C. (1967). *Psychometric theory* (p. 172). New York: McGraw-Hill.

Silvaroli, N. J. (1989). *Classroom reading inventory* (6th ed.). Dubuque, IA: William C. Brown.

Spandel, V. (1990). *Creating writers: Linking assessment and writing instruction.* White Plains, NY: Longman.

Stieglitz, E. L. (1992). *The Stieglitz informal reading inventory: Assessing reading behaviors from emergent to advanced levels.* Boston: Allyn & Bacon.

Tierney, R. J., Carter, M. A., & Desai, L. E. (1991). *Portfolio assessment in the reading-writing classroom.* Norwood, MA: Christopher-Gordon.

Valencia, S. W., Hiebert, E. H., & Afflerbach, P. P. (1994). *Authentic reading assessment: Practices and possibilities.* Newark, DE: International Reading Association.

Woods, M. L., & Moe, A. J. (1989). *Analytical reading inventory* (4th ed.). Columbus, OH: Merrill.

ADDITIONAL READINGS

These books have lots of practical suggestions for portfolio and other authentic assessment devices.

Batzle, J. (1992). *Portfolio assessment and evaluation: Developing and using portfolios in the classroom.* Cypress, CA: Creative Teaching Press.

DeFina, A. A. (1992). *Portfolio assessment: Getting started.* New York: Scholastic.

Graves, D. H., & Sustein, B. S. (Eds.). (1992). *Portfolio portraits.* Portsmouth, NH: Heinemann.

Harp, B. (Ed.). (1993). *Assessment and evaluation in whole language programs.* Norwood, MA: Christopher Gordon.

Jasmine, J. (1993). *Portfolios and other assessments.* Huntington Beach, CA: Teacher Created Materials.

For detailed examples of running records and a wealth of other excellent diagnosis by observation instruments, see these two recent books by Marie Clay.

Clay, M. M. (1993). *An observation survey: Of early literacy achievement.* Portsmouth, NH: Heinemann.

Clay, M. M. (1993). *Reading Recovery: A guidebook for teachers in training.* Portsmouth, NH: Heinemann.

This article contains a wonderfully practical attitudes survey using the popular Garfield character:

McKenna, M. C., & Kear, D. J. (1990). Measuring attitude toward reading: A new tool for teachers. *The Reading Teacher, 43,* 626–639.

Outcomes Based Education (OBE) is possible only if we have reliable and valid measures of important outcomes. This issue of *Educational Leadership* is devoted to a discussion of some of the real-world difficulties of measuring outcomes.

Educational Leadership, 51 (March 1994).

A critique of the assessment procedures used in Chapter One and other special programs along with suggestions for needed changes are found in this thought-provoking article.

O'Neal, S. F. (1994). Students will string five, one-inch beads in one minute or less, or why assessment for special programs must change. *Language Arts, 70,* 602–610.

Organizing and Planning Successful Instruction

LOOKING AHEAD

Classrooms are complex environments in which one teacher and 20 to 30 children must carry out a variety of activities. There is always too much to be done and not enough space or time in which to do it. The fact that all children are different and come with their own personalities and learning preferences/difficulties further complicates the orchestration. Being a successful teacher requires a high level of knowledge of literacy development and instruction as well as an unswerving commitment to and caring for children. In addition to knowledge and commitment, however, successful teachers must be good planners and organizers. In this chapter, we will help you think about the "nitty-gritty" issues of planning and organizing that sometimes make or break a teacher.

In the previous chapters, you have learned many important concepts about children and about the different dimensions of teaching them to read and write. You have learned that reading and writing are language and thinking and that how children feel about reading and writing is related to how well they accomplish these important goals. You have learned how important it is to foster emergent literacy and to get all children off to a successful start on their literacy journey. You know that reading and writing fluency are dependent upon a strong base of word and topical knowledge and that quantity reading and writing contribute to increasing both word and topical knowledge. You have learned many strategies for helping students become better comprehenders and writers and a variety of ways to assess and evaluate how well individual children are progressing and what kinds of individual adaptations are needed by which children. You have been introduced to the wonderful world of literature that exists for children and know that literature can enrich your teaching and not only in the language arts but throughout the day and across the curriculum.

These key ideas fleshed out in the previous chapters provide you with the major concepts and teaching strategies you need to create a classroom in which a variety of different children make steady progress toward the critical goal of becoming literate adults. To make all this work, however, you must develop some critical planning and organization strategies. Beginning and veteran teachers alike report that classroom organization and management issues often get in the way of their accomplishing the goals they know they should and could accomplish. Research (Evertson, Emmer, Sanford, & Clements, 1983; Brophy & Good, 1985; Doyle, 1985) demonstrates that there are certain characteristics of well-organized classrooms. These characteristics relate to the important issues of planning, classroom arrangement, time, adaptations for children with special needs, and discipline. The key ideas in this chapter are:

1. Successful teachers do yearly, unit, weekly, and daily planning.
2. Successful teachers make the best possible arrangement of classroom space.
3. Successful teachers make the best possible use of the time available.
4. Successful teachers make special provisions for children with special needs.
5. Successful teachers have good discipline.

SUCCESSFUL TEACHERS DO YEARLY, UNIT, WEEKLY, AND DAILY PLANNING

Planning is at the heart of successful teaching. Planning is thinking ahead, setting goals, and determining how much time you can allot to various activities. Successful teachers plan on at least four different levels—yearly, unit, weekly, daily—and each level of planning serves an important function. Planning at any of these levels requires that teachers observe their children analytically and make plans that consider their unique talents, needs, and interests.

Planning the Year

One of the most rejuvenating parts of teaching is that every year, you get to start again! Most of us are convinced that "next year will be the best year ever!" Most teachers do a lot of thinking and planning between the time one year's class leaves for the summer and the next year's class arrives in the fall. Veteran teachers evaluate how well certain strategies, units, activities, and so on worked and plan to modify some, continue others in pretty much the same form, and drastically overhaul or dump others. Beginning teachers—or teachers who change grade levels—also engage in yearly planning and goal setting. The plans and goals of beginning teachers may have to be adjusted more quickly and more frequently, but having some idea where you are going is still preferable to the aimless day-by-day, minute-by-minute existence some beginning teachers complain characterized their first year of teaching.

There are, of course, a variety of ways to approach the yearly planning, and the approach you take will vary depending on your own learning style and your level of experience. Here are some possibilities for you to consider in making your own yearly plans.

LIST IN SIMPLE LANGUAGE YOUR MOST IMPORTANT LITERACY GOALS FOR YOUR STUDENTS   What do you want your students to do, think, feel, and experience related to reading and writing? This is the time to think about the big, important, obvious (and consequently often overlooked) goals:

They should come to see books and reading as enjoyable.

They should learn to use informational books to find out answers to questions they have and things they wonder about.

They should learn to love poetry.

They should all publish some books.

They should learn how to read their social studies books.

They should read a variety of genres and come to know lots of different authors.

They should learn to revise and edit their own writing.

This is just a sampling of the big goals teachers might have, and what these goals are will depend on your own experience, your view of literacy, and your teaching situation. The important thing is not that the list be perfect or complete but that it exist. In teaching, it is very easy to lose sight of the forest for the trees; one leading reading educator/professor who took off a year to teach in an elementary classroom and get back in daily contact with kids put it this way: "When you're up to your neck in alligators, it is hard to remember that you came in to drain the swamp!"

Your big goals will help you make the thousands of little decisions about time, materials, and so forth. Many teachers write their big goals on a large index card and tape it to a prominent spot on their desks. A quick glance at these goals is sometimes enough to help you get back on track.

LOOK THROUGH WHATEVER CURRICULUM GUIDES/PLANS YOUR SCHOOL USES   Once you know what your personal goals for your students are, it is time to find out what goals your school or school system has set. Although there is a lot of variety across the different schools, most school systems and some states have written down somewhere the major topics, concepts, strategies, and so on that students should experience at each grade level. Curriculum guides can be very helpful, if they are relatively short, practical, and up to date—or not helpful, if they are long, detailed, and out of date. But, helpful or not, if they exist, you need to know about them and consider them in your long-range planning. Once you find them and look through them, you will need to decide how much your instruction should reflect the established goals. In the fortunate event that your goals and teaching beliefs match much of what you find in the guides, your planning will be much easier. If you don't agree with what you find, ask another teacher you respect and trust (diplomatically!) how closely he or she follows the guide. (If that teacher's response is "What guide? I don't remember us having a language arts guide," you can probably put the guide back where you found it!)

PERUSE ALL THE MATERIALS/BOOKS/TEACHING AIDS YOU HAVE AVAILABLE   This is a big job and not one you will be able to do thoroughly and carefully. But at least you should know what materials you have and how much you can use them to support your own goals and those you developed based on the curriculum guides. Once again, if your materials support the kind of literacy program you believe in, you are in luck! If not, you will need to ask your trusted friend how closely you are expected to stick to what is in the books and where other materials can be found.

LIST THE BIG TOPICS/GOALS/STRATEGIES YOU WILL FOCUS ON AND MAKE SOME INITIAL TIME ALLOCATIONS   The issue of time—the fact that there is never enough of it and how to use it as wisely as possible—is so important that it gets its very own key idea later in this chapter. Right now you are not setting a schedule or deciding minute-by-minute allocations, but you should decide such things as these:

> How much time to give to each subject area you have to teach
> What integration you could do across subject areas so that you can "kill two birds with one stone"
> How many weeks you can spend on each topic—science, health, social studies, math—allotting more time to more important topics but making sure you won't have six critical topics left over for May!

Yearly planning includes deciding what your important goals are, what school system and state goals are, what materials you have available, and then coming up with some time allocation decisions so that you have some initial plan for the impossible task of getting it all done. Teachers who plan how they will do it all don't always meet all the various goals, but they come much closer than teachers who don't know all the big things they need to try to accomplish in one short year.

Planning Topical and Thematic Units

After yearly planning, the next biggest chunk of planning most teachers do is planning certain units of instruction. This is usually a year-long process in which teachers look at what needs to be taught and consider how to use the time and resources available to accomplish a variety of goals for a variety of students. Units can take a variety of forms. Sometimes, units are topically arranged. This is often the case in the content areas where energy or Australia or drugs might be the unit focus. Literacy units are also sometimes organized around a topic. Students in first grade might spend a few weeks reading lots of bear books—both fiction and nonfiction—while older students might spend time reading a variety of stories and books related to the Old West. Literacy units sometimes revolve around a particular author such as Eric Carle or Katherine Patterson, a particular theme such as courage or ethnic differences/similarities, or a particular genre such as mysteries, poetry, or historical fiction. In addition to reading that supports the focus of the unit, writing helps students focus on the unit. Students might write about a particularly courageous person they have known, write a poem in the style of a poet being studied, or write a mystery for classmates to solve.

Sometimes literacy units revolve around particular strategies. Students might read lots of different stories and use these to discuss story elements such as setting, character, story problem, or theme. Students might then compose stories and work on these story elements in their own writing. Students might read informational texts and learn how to sort out the main ideas from the details and perhaps how to web or outline the most important ideas. The writing component of this informational text structure unit would teach students how to write well-formed paragraphs and eventually how to combine these into longer informational pieces.

In many classrooms today, unit planning cuts across the curriculum. Teachers planning a science, health, or social studies unit find materials for the students to read and identify writing tasks that not only help the children learn the science information but also provide real purposes for reading and writing. Sometimes, teachers begin the unit with the literature they want children to read and then see how that literature leads students into discoveries in other parts of the curriculum.

Unit planning varies greatly according to the focus of the unit, the needs of the students, and the purposes and beliefs of the teacher. Good unit planning, however, requires that the teacher list the major goals for the unit, provide for a variety of materials and activities within the unit that will meet the needs and abilities of a wide range of children, and plan some assessment activities that will allow both students and teacher to see how much was learned.

Weekly and Daily Planning

Most schools require that teachers have weekly plans, and some schools require that these plans be turned in to the office before teachers leave on Friday afternoon! Some schools require that plans be written in a specific format and other schools leave it to each teacher to determine how best to write down these plans. (Check with your trusted, respected teacher friend!) Generally, beginning teachers need to write down more detailed plans than do veteran teachers who "carry all that wealth of information around in their heads."

Weekly planning is a much easier task when it has been preceded by some yearly and unit planning. The time allocations across the week should reflect those you decided based on a careful consideration of important goals and topics during yearly planning. A three-week unit on mysteries might involve the whole class of students in reading and discussing the same mystery the first week, choosing one of three mysteries to read and discuss in a literature circle the second week, and collaboratively writing mysteries the third week. If you have two weeks to do a science unit on energy, the first week might be spent on sharing beginning information and ideas together as a whole class, and the second week might be spent having the students do experiments and gather information in small groups. The final day would be spent in having children share what they learned and assessing with them the success of the unit.

Weekly planning also requires that the time you decided should be given to recurring activities actually occur. If children are going to write something every day, when is this going to happen? If children are going to engage in self-selected reading every day, when is this going to happen? If you believe you should read aloud to children several times during the day, when is this going to occur?

Daily planning usually involves looking at what got accomplished—and what didn't get accomplished—today and then adjusting tomorrow's plan based on your evaluation of today. Often teachers include the children in daily planning. Many teachers sit down with the children during the last 15 minutes of each day and have a class meeting in which they discuss a variety of things, including a look back at what the class, small groups, and individuals accomplished and a preview of what the class will be trying to accomplish tomorrow. Teachers who include the students in planning—including some weekly and unit planning as the year goes on—find that children are more motivated to meet the goals and accomplish the tasks when they have some say in determining what those goals and tasks will be and how and when they will get done.

SUCCESSFUL TEACHERS MAKE THE BEST POSSIBLE ARRANGEMENT OF CLASSROOM SPACE

In the old days desks were screwed to the floors in straight rows. A raised platform and podium distinguished the teacher space from the pupil space. This classroom arrangement was conducive to teacher lectures, pupil recitations, and whole-class instruction. Currently, most classrooms have furniture that can be moved, and most classrooms are arranged so that a variety of activities can go on throughout the school day. In the old days, the teaching materials consisted of textbooks for each subject, notebooks, and pens. Classrooms of today have a variety of teaching materials. The effective elementary teacher knows that the arrangement of classroom space, furnishings, and materials can support or detract from good reading instruction. Although there are other considerations beyond supporting reading instruction that must be kept in mind when arranging your classroom, here are some arrangement suggestions that most teachers agree are crucial to successful reading instruction.

Arrange Space for Working with a Group

Regardless of whether you have your class divided into reading groups or call children together for other kinds of groups, you will need a space where you can work with your groups. Ideally, this space would have a chalkboard on which you and the children could write. If not, you will want to provide chart paper or an overhead projector and screen, because being able to write words and sentences and have the children *watch* you as you write are essential to good reading instruction. This space may have a carpet on which the children (and you, occasionally) sit. Alternatively, you may have chairs that stay in this small-group space, or children may carry their chairs with them to the group. Regardless of what the children are seated on, they should be seated in a half-circle or horseshoe arrangement with their backs to the rest of the class. Seated this way, they can (1) all see what the teacher is writing, (2) face each other as they are responding and discussing, and (3) not be distracted by what the children elsewhere in the class are doing. The teacher would then be facing the small group and the rest of the class and would have better control of the children not in the group. To make efficient use of the limited time available for small-group instruction, a box of supplies (scrap paper, index cards, markers, scissors, etc.) would be kept handy for use only in this area. Teacher's manuals and other instructional materials needed for reading would also be stored in this area.

Arrange Space for Learning Centers

Learning centers are areas of the classroom in which children can carry out a variety of activities. There are many kinds of learning centers. Some have structured activities and directions for students to follow. Others are more exploratory and contain a variety of materials that children can do a variety of things with. Many classrooms have a library center, a cozy place containing books and magazines in which children can read individually or with a friend. A writing center is also common in many elementary classrooms. In addition to having a variety of different kinds and shapes of paper and writing implements (markers, pens, etc.), the writing center may contain models for different types of writing, pictures to stimulate writing, staplers, paste, art materials, and other materials for bookmaking. Some classrooms have a research center in which children use encyclopedias and other sources to look up information. A message center in which children can write messages to each other and put them in each other's mailboxes is always popular with children. Listening centers and computer centers are common in elementary classrooms today. There are many types of centers and ways to organize and make space for them. You will find many examples as you read Chapters 10 to 15.

Arrange Space for Whole-Class Teaching

Occasionally, you will be doing instruction that will include the whole class. The ideal whole-class seating arrangement is one in which (1) all children can easily see you and the largest blackboard; (2) you can maintain eye contact with all children as you move around and position yourself next to various children; and (3) the children all face one another and thus can easily hear one another and interact in a discussion. This ideal arrangement would probably be an open rectangle or horseshoe in which the children's desks or tables are all along the outside and that is open to the area where the chalkboard is located. This would leave a large open area in the center, which could be used for various activities and might contain a table on which needed supplies are kept and completed papers are filed. In this ideal arrangement, you would have good attention and interaction when desired because everyone is looking at everyone else and you can move easily around the group and still maintain eye contact with all children. Troublesome children can be placed at either open end of the rectangle or horseshoe, and a better behaved child can be seated next to them. Thus while not isolated from the other children, they have fewer opportunities for creating disturbances, and since they will be seated at the front, they will be close to the teacher working from the chalkboard area. (This assumes, unfortunately, only two troublesome children per classroom!) If the children in the different reading groups are not seated next to one another, there are empty spaces throughout the seating area when any group is with the teacher. It is easier to work quietly and not be distracted when you are not too close to lots of other people.

In many classrooms there is not enough room to make one large horseshoe or rectangle and have room leftover for anything else. If this is your situation, you may want to make two horseshoes or rectangles, a smaller one inside the larger one. This arrangement keeps the advantage of all children being able to see the teacher and the chalkboard and allows the teacher easy movement to all children. You do, however, lose the important advantage of all children being able to maintain eye contact with one another. (The children on the inner horseshoe or rectangle can't see the children on the outer one; the children on the outer one can see only the backs of the inner horseshoe or rectangle children.) Also, the children cannot hear each other as well. Some teachers solve this problem by having a "discussion-time arrangement" for which the children on the inner horseshoe or rectangle bring chairs along the front open area and, with their backs to the chalkboard, face all of the children in the outer horseshoe or rectangle. This creates a supportive discussion arrangement with a minimum of movement and hassle.

Have a Place for Everything

Having a place for everything and teaching the children to put everything in its place are not easy tasks, but they are of crucial importance. In classrooms in which teachers are free to spend a good portion of their time working uninterruptedly with individuals and small groups, the children know where to get what is needed and that they must put things where they belong afterward. Your major task in considering room arrangement is that you must establish where needed materials can be put so that they are accessible to the children and easily put away. Some teachers keep a box of needed supplies handy for each small group of children who are seated near one another. Along with containing supplies such as pencils, erasers, scissors, and paper, the box often contains worksheets and assignments for the children who share the box. Finished work may be filed in folders kept in the box. A child is assigned each week to make sure that all supplies are returned and to check to see that papers are filed in the right folders.

Labeling everything goes a long way toward solving the keeping-up-with-materials problem. Many teachers hang shoebags on bulletin boards, walls, or doors and label the pockets of the shoebags according to what is in there and what should be returned there. Pictures of what belongs where along with the word labels help very young children to be responsible workers. Parts of games or puzzles should always be numbered or color coded so that their replacement is as simple as possible.

In spite of all your organizing and labeling, people will find things during the day and not know where to put them. Thus every classroom needs a "Where Does This Thing Go?" box. Objects, papers, and game and puzzle pieces whose place cannot be located easily are placed in this box. At the end of each day, the teacher and children clean out the box and jointly decide where the things go. All of this organizing, arranging, and labeling takes a large initial investment of time and energy from the teacher and the children, but the long-term gain in teacher energy and time as well as independence and responsibility for the children make it a wise investment.

LISTEN, LOOK, AND LEARN

 Visit several classrooms or watch a videotape of some classrooms in action. Think about the main points discussed in this section and evaluate the various classroom arrangements you see. Is there a place for the teacher to meet with groups that meets the criteria listed here? Is there space for learning centers? Can the teacher carry out some whole-class instruction effectively? Are supplies available where the children can get them and put them back? What seems to work best? What would you change? Write a summary of what you observed and then describe your ideal classroom arrangement. Draw and label various areas in the classroom.

SUCCESSFUL TEACHERS MAKE THE BEST POSSIBLE USE OF THE TIME AVAILABLE

Making the best use of the teaching time you have is a large part of what you must do if you are going to effectively teach children to read. The other time variable teachers must consider is what is happening during the time children are not working with the teacher.

Observational research unfortunately has indicated that children spend 30 to 70 percent of the designated reading time doing independent seatwork. Most students spend more time working alone during reading time than they do working with the teacher. This seatwork most often involves workbooks or ditto sheets. Seatwork in classrooms should serve both a managerial and an instructional function. The managerial reason seatwork exists is to keep the rest of the class busy while the teacher works with small groups of individuals. The instructional function should be to make the best use of children's time when they are not working directly with the teacher. In spite of the fact that in most classes children are reading at different levels, many seatwork assignments are made to the whole class. It is no surprise that low-achieving students have difficulty completing seatwork and often don't turn it in (Anderson, Brubaker, Alleman-Brooks, & Duffy, 1985; Thurlow, Graden, Yseldyke, & Algozzine, 1984).

In *Becoming a Nation of Readers,* a report of the Commission on Reading appointed by the National Academy of Education (Anderson, Hiebert, Scott, & Wilkinson, 1985), research-based recommendations were made for improving reading instruction in America. Three of these recommendations relate directly to the seatwork issue: (1) Children should spend less time completing workbooks and skills sheets. (2) Children should spend more time in independent reading. (3) Children should spend more time writing. To increase the possibility that the time children are not working with the teacher will be well spent, we make the following suggestions for seatwork time.

Maximize Real Reading and Writing Time

Real reading and writing are activities that might occur outside of a school setting. *Real reading* means that students are reading books, magazines, and a variety of other real materials. *Real writing* is not copying or filling in a blank or completing a workbook page; rather, it is writing a letter or a story or a newspaper advertisement. There are a variety of ways to structure the real reading and writing students should do during seatwork time.

Many teachers have a reading center into which they schedule children or children can choose to go. The reading center should not be empty during reading time. Children should be encouraged to read there by themselves or with a friend. To keep records, each child might "log in and out" and just jot down a sentence or two about what they did there.

A center of informational books and magazines related to something being studied in one of the content areas is also a popular place in many classrooms. Often, teachers just want children to spend a specified amount of time there reading in whatever sources they choose. To structure this a little more, some teachers post a "What Did You Learn?" chart on which each child lists one thing learned and signs his or her name. Teachers sometimes post lists of questions that children can try to answer. As students find an answer, they write it along with the source in which they found it and their name and drop it into the answer box. At a specified time, the answers are removed and sorted by question and shared with the whole class.

Listening centers in which children can listen to books are popular centers in classrooms. Children who listen to favorite books read aloud often learn to read

Newspapers provide a wonderful source of authentic reading materials. This newspaper board changes as children express interest in certain current events. The teacher and the students in this classroom both brought newspaper articles related to the Winter Olympics.

these books on their own. Some teachers include in the listening center a writing or art activity that children complete to follow up the listening activity.

Some teachers have students write in a journal each day. A topic may be assigned, or children may choose their own topic. A length of time to write or an amount of page space may be specified. Teachers check the journals to see that the writing is being done but do not grade or correct each day's writing.

A writing center is a popular place in many classrooms. Children may be scheduled there or may choose to go there. Many classes have a message center where children can write notes to each other without getting into trouble. They put these notes in each other's mailboxes, and at a specified time, there is a mail call.

Writing can also be used to follow up or prepare for something that is happening in one of the content areas. Students might all be assigned to write one real-world multiplication problem for the others to solve at math time. Data from a science experiment conducted the day before might be used by students to make a chart or a graph. Students might write a riddle about one of the states they are studying and share it during social studies time.

Reading, listening, and writing activities should be a part of each child's daily work. Unlike the time for traditional worksheet activities, time spent in reading, listening, and writing has been shown to contribute to growth in reading ability. In addition, reading, listening, and writing are more interesting, enjoyable, and intrinsically motivating than worksheet work. Teachers will spend some of their time structuring these activities but will spend less time "staying behind" the students to make sure they do them and less time grading worksheets.

Minimize the Number of Worksheets

To learn from a worksheet activity, children must be able to complete the activity with a high success rate and must need to work on the skill or strategy being practiced. The need for a high success rate and for children to be practicing skills they actually need practice on leads to one inevitable conclusion. Worksheet assignments should be made sparingly.

When worksheet assignments are made, they should be closely related to something students have been working on. Make clear not only what the students are to do but also why they are doing it and how it will help them be better readers. Completed worksheets should not be turned in and graded. Rather, children should bring their completed worksheets back to the group. The teacher should lead the group as each child checks his or her own worksheet. Not only should answers be given but the reasoning behind the answer should also be explained. Children who have made mistakes should fix them before turning the worksheet in. This procedure will ensure a high success rate for all students and will increase the possibility that children will learn as they complete and check their worksheets.

Let Children Teach Each Other

The old saying that "two heads are better than one" has been proven true in classrooms. A whole body of research under the heading of "cooperative learning" demonstrates that when children work together on something, all children learn more (Johnson & Johnson, 1985). There are many opportunities in every classroom every day for children to work together on something. Sometimes, the teacher may assign the groups and assign specific duties for the different members of the groups. At other times, teachers may let the children choose a subject or activity of interest, and the groups will be formed by children who chose the same thing. Groups can research questions, share and respond to each other's writing, prepare a play for the class, make a mural, or do any number of other activities. When the teacher structures the classroom so that working together in school is as normal as it is in real life, there are many "little teachers" in the class.

Children can work together on many of the activities already suggested. Children like to read to each other in a reading center or to read each other's writing in a writing center. Young children enjoy partner reading in which they take turns reading or rereading the pages of a favorite book. Children can work together in research groups to find information and plan how to make reports.

Children can even do worksheets together. Assign two children of similar ability who like working together to be worksheet partners. To be sure that both children are working and thinking, assign one partner to be the "thinker" and the other partner to be the "writer." The thinker's job is to read each question and tell what he or she thinks the answer is. The writer's job is to write the answer if the writer agrees and to explain to the thinker why the answer is wrong and what the right answer would be if the writer does not agree. If they cannot reach agreement on the correct answer, they write both answers with their initials next to them. As you can imagine, a lot of learning goes on as the two children try to convince each other why their answer is correct. If they cannot reach agreement, they are eager to bring their worksheet to the group to see who was right. The next day the children switch roles. The thinker becomes the writer and the writer becomes the thinker.

Make and Post a Schedule

To make the best use of instructional time, teachers and children must know what is to be accomplished and the approximate time in which it should be accomplished. Certain activities (an opening-together time, break time, story time) will probably occur at the same time and for approximately the same duration every day. Other activities may vary from day to day. The important point is that the teacher and children have a clear notion of what is going to happen and when so that they can plan ahead. Students can't behave responsibly and go to the restroom or sharpen their pencils *before* their teacher meets with their group if they don't know when the teacher is going to meet with the group. It is very frustrating for children to get started in an activity and be abruptly called away from that activity to meet in a small group or with the whole class. So a schedule should be posted and gone over together each morning. Many teachers make a changeable schedule by cutting slots in a piece of poster board and inserting in the appropriate time slots strips of paper that indicate what will be happening when. Standard activities that occur at the same time each day can be permanently written on the poster board and the others inserted at the beginning of each day.

Give Students Think Time

Thinking requires time. The average time most teachers pause after asking a question and before calling on someone to answer is one second. One second is probably sufficient to respond to a factual, recall question such as "Who was president during the Civil War?" But five seconds is probably the minimum time required for consideration of questions such as "Was Abraham Lincoln considered by his contemporaries to be a great president?" or "How could history have been changed if Abraham Lincoln had not been assassinated?" Many teachers find that they can greatly increase the inferential and evaluative thinking abilities of their students by simply prefacing an appropriate question with comments like the following: "This next question requires you to think about what you read. The book didn't answer this question directly. So after I ask the question, I am going to count slowly and silently to five and only when I nod my head to show I have counted off five seconds do I want to see any hands raised. Remember, this is a thinking question, and so I want each of you to take five seconds of think time. I won't call on anyone whose hand is raised before I nod my head."

Think time saves time because all children have a few seconds to consider the question, and thus more children are actively engaged in learning as you are engaged in teaching. Time is also saved because the responses you get after five seconds of think time are better, and children are able to think at higher levels without the teacher feeling as if he or she is "pulling teeth."

Use Every-Pupil-Response Activities to Increase Engagement

Imagine that you are meeting with a group of children who have read an informational text about insects before coming to the group. You want to establish quickly what factual information was provided about insects and then move on to helping the children choose an insect about which they want to learn more. You could tell the children to "listen as I describe some feature of some of the insects you have just read about. Raise your hand if you can tell me what insect I am describing." Then you could describe various insects and call on children who volunteer to demonstrate that they have comprehended what they read. Now, consider another way of accomplishing the same goal of reviewing the literal information contained in the text about insects.

Have each child tear a sheet of paper into eight pieces. The children will use them to make response cards. Tell the children, "On each card, I want you to write the name of one of the insects we have read about. When you have your cards made, I will describe an insect, and when I give the signal, show me the card that has the name of the insect you think I am describing." As you describe each insect, all children in the group listen and shuffle through their cards so that when you say "Ready, Set, Show!" they can display the name of the described insect.

How does this every-pupil-response activity make maximum use of instructional time? In the "raise your hands and I will call on you" mode, each child gets to respond once or twice, and since children know that when they have "had their turn" you probably will call on someone else for a while, they are apt to stop thinking. Children who are not very confident, able, or assertive may never try to have their turn and may never be thinking. Every-pupil-response activities increase the attention and number of responses made by each pupil. Thus, although the amount of time you are teaching has not increased, the amount of time that each pupil is actively thinking and learning may have tripled or quadrupled. Furthermore, if you told the children *before* they read the story the nature of the every-pupil-response activity they were going to engage in after reading (and maybe even had them make the cards with the insects' names on them), they would probably have read the story more actively in an attempt to be sure they could make the appropriate responses. Thus, you have actually increased their learning even when they were reading the story on their own.

SUCCESSFUL TEACHERS MAKE SPECIAL PROVISIONS FOR CHILDREN WITH SPECIAL NEEDS

We have a lot of trouble with the term *special children* because it is our fundamental belief that all children are special and because those children designated by school systems as special often don't really get the special treatment they need and deserve. We also have a lot of difficulty with labels given to special children. The term *learning disabled*, for example, is a catchall term that means there is a large discrepancy between the child's achievement and that child's perceived ability. In most states, a 15-point discrepancy is required—14 points and you are not learning disabled, 15 and you are! Often the diagnosis of learning disabled hinges on one answer to one test question! The same holds true of other categories. In most states, children must have a tested IQ of less than 70 to be categorized as EMH—Educably Mentally Handicapped. Test 69 and you are, test 70 and you aren't! Gifted programs often have an IQ cutoff, too. In some communities, parents take their children to private practice psychologists and have them tested three or four times, hoping to achieve the magic number and have their child classified "gifted." (We have no examples of parents paying a private psychologist to test their child three or four times and get that child classified EMH.) ADD (Attention Deficit Disorder) is the newest "special" classification. Before this was added, these children were often referred to as immature, late bloomers, or "squirmers."

There is currently great concern within the educational community about the testing, arbitrary cutoffs, and categories that funding for special education requires. Perhaps, in the future, we will have less rigidity and more flexibility to use the money and special teachers we have in ways that we as professional teachers believe will better meet the needs of all the different and special children we teach. Meanwhile, teachers must do a lot of paperwork to get children referred, wait a long time for the results, and then hope that something will be done to truly help the child!

While we quibble with how children are categorized and with the arbitrariness of the services they receive or don't receive, we know that there are children out there who do need some additional support if they are going to achieve the highest levels of literacy possible for them. Throughout this book, we have included boxes with special activities for children with special needs. The narrative chapters tell about children with special needs, and the teachers in those chapters show a variety of ways of adapting instruction and providing support for these children. In addition to the specific suggestions already included, we have some general suggestions you might want to consider when you are planning and organizing your instruction.

Collaborate with Special Teachers

When two teachers working with the same children have little shared knowledge of each other's instruction, it is unlikely that the children are participating in the most coherent and supportive instructional environment. Developing shared knowledge of instructional practices in classroom and specialist teachers is a good starting point for enhancing a sense of shared responsibility.

There are several activities that can be used to develop shared knowledge and foster collaboration. In some schools, children head off to their special instruction with a traveling notebook around their necks. The notebook can be just a simple spiral-bound notepad with a string run through the spiral binding and looped over a child's neck as he or she leaves for special programs instruction. In the notebook the classroom teacher simply notes the classroom material being used and the focus of the lesson that day. In addition, the classroom teacher might jot a comment about the child's performance (e.g., Tim had difficulty following the story line) or a particular skill or strategy felt to need additional attention (e.g., Tim has real difficulty with long words. He seems not to know how to break them down into more manageable components). The special program teacher jots notes back to the classroom teacher and returns the notebook with the child after their instructional session. The point is that the notes do not have to be long or complicated, especially if they are jotted down regularly.

Another activity is sharing lesson plans. In some schools, the classroom teacher shares lesson plans for reading and language arts with the special program teacher, who uses that as one source of information in planning instruction. Even better than simply sharing the plans is to sit together and jointly create the lessons to be offered in both situations. Of course, this requires time for both teachers to meet, but in some schools that recognize how crucial classroom and special teacher collaboration is, joint planning time is being built into the schedule.

In an increasing number of schools, special program teachers provide their instructional support in the regular classroom rather than in a location down the hall. The fundamental goal of these "in-class" instructional support models is to improve classroom instruction through developing shared knowledge and creating more coherent instructional interventions. In addition, students should lose less instructional time in transition from one setting to another.

Consider Your Children with Special Needs When Making Your Schedule

One of the government regulations that teachers find most irrational is that the special instruction children get cannot "supplant" classroom instruction. This regulation was well intended and really means that classroom teachers have the major responsibility for the instruction of all children and that children with special needs cannot be given all the instruction they need in the 45 to 60 minutes they are with a special teacher. Children who have trouble learning to read and write need *more*, not less, instruction in reading and writing. The best instructional program for them will be one in which the classroom teacher and the special teacher collaborate to decide who will provide what and share their knowledge of the changing needs of each child. Special children make the most progress when the classroom teacher and the special teacher both provide high-quality, coordinated instruction.

But time does not stop when the special children leave. Something will happen in the classroom that the special child will miss, and that reality cannot be changed—even by federal regulations! Classroom teachers usually cannot control when the special children leave—although there is a laudable movement in many schools to have all special children in one classroom go to special teachers during the same time period so that the classroom teacher doesn't have children coming and going all day and has substantial blocks of teaching time with all the children present. Classroom teachers can decide what part of the curriculum the special child can most afford to miss and schedule that when the special child is out. If a child is a very poor reader and writer, perhaps French is not currently critical to that child's academic development. Social studies instruction is important for children but is probably less important than developing fluent reading and writing abilities. Children who are designated as "gifted" are usually exceptionally good readers and perhaps could afford to miss some of the comprehension/word lessons that the teacher feels most students need.

In some schools, special teachers stagger their schedule for working with children so that the children don't miss the same block of time each day. In other schools, the classroom teacher makes the adjustment. There are a variety of ways to make sure that special children get the most coordinated instruction in their areas of greatest need. The first step toward providing what they need is to face the fact that if they leave your room, they will miss something. Then you can work together with the special teacher and decide what they can most afford to miss.

Alternatives for Children Who Don't Qualify for Special Instruction

Not all children who need special instruction get it. Some children don't qualify; some parents won't sign the forms; some special teachers are not very good teachers. In addition to providing as much quality instruction as you possibly can, there are people besides you who can help. First, think about the children in your classroom. Does the child who needs help have a friend who is more able and who would help the child by reading some difficult assignments to him or her or by acting as a scribe to write down the ideas this child has but finds difficult to get down? In classrooms where there are a variety of cooperative learning arrangements, it is much easier to make adaptations for children because working together and teaching each other is a normal part of the classroom routine.

Next, consider volunteers—older children, parents, senior citizens. In many schools, the oldest children in the school volunteer a half hour each day in a younger grade. In some schools, parents who bring their children to school or who pick them up stay an extra half hour or come a half hour early and provide individual attention to children who need it. These volunteers can provide some valuable instruction by providing simple activities such as listening to a child reread a familiar book, helping the child write a story, or supporting a child's writing on a computer. Computers offer some wonderful opportunities for special children who have coordination problems or are terrible spellers. When equipped with spelling checks and other writing-support programs, special children can often produce writing they can be proud of.

Special children can be the helpers as well as the ones being helped. When older children read regularly to kindergartners or first graders, they have a legitimate excuse for reading and rereading "easy" books. Older children who help younger children practice their math facts usually get some practice themselves. Older children who know how to write on the computer can teach younger children how to do this and increase their fluency with the computer at the same time.

In the previous chapter on diagnosis and assessment, you learned some ways to determine what children are learning and what particular needs individual children might have. Once you know this, you think about what you can do to meet these needs and then consider what other people and computer resources might support your instruction.

Use the Widest Variety of Materials You Can Obtain

All children are really special and they have a wide range of reading and writing interests and abilities. If almost all the materials available are at or close to grade level, students whose literacy levels are below level will not be able to find books and other resources with which they can be successful. Likewise, more advanced students will not be challenged to make the most of their literacy abilities. Classrooms in which the whole range of special children is successful are classrooms in which teachers make available to their students the widest, broadest assortment of diverse learning resources.

LISTEN, LOOK, AND LEARN

 Interview a teacher you respect about how the needs of all the children are met. Make a list of the children with special needs and what their special needs and talents are. Find out if they get any services from a special teacher and how the special teacher and the classroom teacher collaborate to ensure a coordinated literacy program. Try to determine what adjustments the classroom teacher makes for children and how a variety of materials fits into the overall plan.

SUCCESSFUL TEACHERS HAVE GOOD DISCIPLINE

Classroom discipline is the major problem faced by beginning teachers (Veenan, 1984). Even experienced teachers find it difficult to establish and maintain an orderly classroom. Teachers who have orderly classrooms spend time in the first weeks of school setting up rules, procedures, and routines that help them prevent discipline problems. The most effective teachers often seem to have no discipline problems. In reality, they have structured their classrooms so that discipline problems seldom occur, and they deal quickly and quietly with those that do occur. The following recommendations will help you prevent discipline problems.

Evaluate the Classroom Instruction

There is no way to separate instruction from discipline. Classrooms in which there is a good balanced program of literacy instruction will have better-behaved children. Regardless of who the children are, they need to spend much of their time in authentic reading and writing activities. They need time to interact and cooperate with each other. They need to have available a wide range of materials with which they can find success. Teachers who are observant of their children and who adjust instruction to suit the needs and interests of those children have better discipline. In a sense, everything that has been described in this book so far has been directly related to the question of classroom discipline. Good, varied, balanced, sensitive classroom instruction is the most important variable. Once this is in place as well as possible, the remaining recommendations can further support smooth-running classrooms.

Have a Limited Number of Reasonable Rules

Orderly classrooms have rules. These rules are usually posted and gone over at the beginning of the year. Each day, the children read the rules and talk about why that rule is important to getting along in the classroom. Some teachers allow the children to help come up with the rules. It is important that the number of rules be limited—five or six seems to be ideal—and that the rules be reasonable. "No talking at any time" is not a reasonable rule. Many teachers have a "No Talking" and a "Quiet Talking" sign that they display on the chalkboard. The "No Talking" sign is put up when the teacher needs the full attention of the entire class, when the children are taking a test, or when the classroom has gotten too noisy and needs a quiet-down time. The "Quiet Talking" sign is displayed the rest of the time. The rule about talking in that classroom is to "follow the talking signs." Another teacher's talking rule is to "listen when I am talking; talk quietly at other times." This is also a reasonable talking rule and can be enforced consistently. The problem with absolute rules such as "no talking at any time" is that they are unreasonable, and thus the children cannot follow them, and the teacher cannot consistently enforce them.

Once the rules are established, the teacher must consistently enforce them. Here the key word is *consistently*. *Consistently* means "every time for every student." In classes in which teachers have good discipline, teachers consistently enforce the rules. They stop whatever they are doing to remind a child of the rule and why it is important. They may also tell a child what consequence will ensue if the rule is broken again.

As much as possible, consequences should follow naturally from the rule. Children who are talking too loudly and are reminded that quiet talk is required so that the teacher can teach the reading group should be separated, and the privilege of talking should be withdrawn for those children for a specified period.

"I'm sorry," the teacher tells them. "But you can no longer work together on this. You were disturbing me and others and continued after I reminded you. Go to your own desks and finish this alone. Tomorrow, we will see if you can work together without disturbing others."

All teachers have rules. Teachers who have orderly classrooms expend a lot of time and effort in the first few weeks making sure that the rules are reasonable and that the children understand them. They then take the time to stop, explain, and enforce the rules each time they are broken. Children in these classes soon learn that they must follow the rules.

Establish Routines

In every classroom, pencils need to be sharpened, and the children need to go to the restroom. These constantly recurring activities are not what schooling is all about, but they must be carried out efficiently and unobtrusively and with as little teacher direction as possible so that the teaching and learning that schooling is all about can occur. There are still a few schools in which children are lined up all at the same time and walked down to the boys' and girls' restrooms! In most schools, however, teachers recognize that this practice is degrading, wasteful of children's and teachers' time, and not very effective. Regardless of what time your schedule indicates they should all go to the restrooms, someone will need (or say they need—and how can you tell?) to visit the restroom at other times. If the procedure for going to the restroom is to interrupt the teacher and ask permission, not much reading instruction is going to happen. Activities such as pencil sharpening and going to the restroom are considered to be routines, and children should learn to carry them out in a routine, unobtrusive way.

Many teachers routinize going to the restroom by hanging somewhere in the room a chart that says "Boys" and one that says "Girls." In a pocket created by stapling a strip of paper along the bottom of each chart are cards on which each child's name is written. When a child needs to go to the restroom, that child looks at the chart to see if there is a card displayed in the slot where children put their cards when they are in the restroom. If there is no card there, the child knows there are no other children out of the room and, after placing his or her name card in the appropriate slot, goes to the restroom. Upon returning, the child removes the name card from the slot and places it back in the pocket at the bottom of the chart.

Pencil sharpening can also be routinized. Most teachers allow children to go to the pencil sharpener as long as there is no one there or they are not in a group that is supposed to be attending to the teacher. (Going to the restroom also should not take place when the group is working with the teacher, except in dire emergencies. Children who know when they will be with the teacher will plan ahead and go to the restroom during their independent working time.)

Some teachers are disturbed by the noise made by the pencil sharpener when they are working with a small group. This is especially true in classrooms in which the pencil sharpener is permanently attached very near to the only feasible small-group working area. If you do not want children going to the pencil sharpener during small-group time, provide a store of pencils they can borrow and then replace when they have had a chance to sharpen theirs. If you have a box of supplies for children sitting near one another to share, "loan" pencils could be a part of this box. There are also small, inexpensive, quiet little pencil sharpeners that might be included in the supply box and that would also minimize the pencil-sharpening hassle.

Pencil sharpening and restroom going have been used as two examples of everyday events that occur in classrooms and that should be routinized. Anything that goes on regularly and that is apt to require teacher time and energy should be routinized. Other examples of situations needing routines include learning to walk quietly, to close the door without a bang, to carry chairs and slide them in and out quietly, and to get the teacher's attention without shouting. These things can all be routinized if the teacher and children figure out a reasonable, workable system and then practice the system until everyone understands what is expected. All routines should be role-played by children and teacher when they are first begun so that there is no doubt that *all* children understand the procedure.

Let the Children Share the Work and Responsibility

One of the questions a successful teacher continually asks is, "Could one of the children do this?" Often, the answer is, "Absolutely!" When one of us was a first-year, first-grade teacher, she had a terrible time remembering to send the milk and lunch count to the office. Every morning at 9:15, the intercom would come on, and an impatient voice would inform the teacher that they were waiting for *her* count. Frantically, she would interrupt her teaching and get a count, which often was incorrect, since it was done so hurriedly. This occurrence created problems later in the day at snack and lunch time, and the teacher was often at odds with the lunchroom staff as well as the office staff. Try as she did to remember, this beleaguered beginning teacher would always get caught up in greeting the children and trying to get her instruction under way quickly (she had been taught that every minute counts), and, most mornings, the click of the intercom coming on would remind her and set in motion the frantic, inaccurate count. One morning Eric, who was an extremely precocious first grader, said, "Teacher, why can't I just take the count every morning as the children come in and then you wouldn't have to get so upset and get yelled at by the office lady and the lunchroom lady?" "Eric, do you think you would be able to do that?" asked the hopeful but dubious young teacher. "Oh, sure, no problem," replied the confident and concerned young Eric. Thereafter, every morning Eric sat at a table by the door, and as the children entered, they told him if they were buying milk and/or lunch. Eric made a tally mark next to a dittoed sheet containing each child's name and milk and lunch columns. He then added up the tally marks, wrote the *correct* numbers on the slip, handed it to the teacher to sign, and took it to the office. The first graders, their teacher, the "office lady," and the "lunchroom lady" lived more happily ever after. The teacher also learned that there were many jobs the children could do better than she and that the children derived a lot of pride, identity, and satisfaction out of doing them.

In classes that function smoothly and in which a lot gets accomplished, the teacher and everyone else is working hard. In classes in which the functioning is rocky and rough, and not enough seems to be getting done, the teacher is usually found to be trying to do everything. Some jobs (cleaning the chalkboard, keeping up with materials, being in charge of a center, for example) can be done by everyone in the class, and well-organized teachers keep a large job chart posted, rotate jobs every week or two, and make sure the jobs get done. The children feel proud of their accomplishments. Other jobs are beyond the talents and capabilities of most but not of some children. Is there a tall child who is the only one who can open and close the windows? Is there an Eric who even in the first grade can take care of the lunch count? Is there a person who is such a good leader and so well liked and respected by all that he or she could be substitute teacher and keep order without bullying the other children whenever the teacher has to leave the room momentarily?

In addition to all of the help the teacher now has in keeping the classroom running smoothly, sharing the work and responsibility with the children has an important bonus. The children who work to keep the classroom orderly and interesting feel more pride and ownership in *their* classroom. Because they work in it, it belongs to them. Because it belongs to them, they will care for it and take better care of it.

Think Positively

In any classroom at any time, there are positive things going on and children behaving in positive ways; there are also negative things going on and children behaving in negative ways. Successful teachers deal with the negative things, but they focus on the positive things. If your students were asked to clear their desks and get ready to listen and discuss, and 24 of them have done so and 2 of them have not, that is a 24 to 2 positive ratio. Show children that you appreciate their quick responses to your directions. Statements such as "Billy sure is ready to go today. He had his desk cleared before I finished telling everyone to," or "I asked all of you to clear your desks, and 24 of the 26 of you did. What a good class I have!" focus on the positive things children do and show them you appreciate their quick compliance while suggesting to the 2 who didn't comply that you noticed and expect them to.

One third-grade teacher we know kept a dittoed list of all of her students' names in her top desk drawer. At the end of each day, she reflected for a few minutes about what nice things she had said to whom during the day. As she remembered positive interactions, she put a check mark next to that child's name in the appropriate dated column. "Let's see, I told Carol she wrote a great story, and I told Bill I had seen his picture in the paper, and I told Jill and Carrie they had made the best bulletin board ever." After several days, when she noticed some children with no check marks next to their names, she contrived to find some positive things to say to them. (There is *something* positive about every child, although with some, you may have to stretch it: "I love the color blue in your shirt." "You have the biggest freckles I have ever seen!")

Another teacher divided her bulletin board into enough spaces to display *every* child's work. Each child had a yarned-off and labeled space on that bulletin board on which something (work, story, art, etc.) that the child had done was displayed. Sometimes the teacher chose what to display; sometimes she let the children choose. Regardless, that bulletin board said, "This room belongs to every one of you. You can all do some things well, and these things are worthy of being put on display." The children in this room, knowing that some things would be displayed, developed pride in their achievements and took more care with their work.

Many successful teachers send "brag notes" home. Throughout the day, they take a few minutes to write a note to the parents of some child, telling the parents why the child should be praised.

> Dear Mr. and Mrs. Jones,
>
> You should be so proud of Billy. He has been paying such good attention during reading group, and I am seeing real progress in his reading. I shall let you know how he continues to grow. Meanwhile, if you choose to, you could let Billy have a special treat or extra privilege this weekend in recognition of his good attention and growth.
>
> Sincerely,

Unlike the teacher notes many of us remember from our childhoods, brag notes are always positive, and because they are, they get home!

Distinguish between Normal Behavior and Discipline Problems

Even in the smoothest-running classrooms, things will not always go right. Teachers and children have their bad days. Three rainy days in a row will have you all wondering if you can survive another rainy day. When you are disturbed at something your students are doing or something that is not going well, ask yourself: "Is that normal?" If you are out of the classroom for a few minutes and upon your return find some children "messing around" and talking and laughing instead of working away diligently, is that normal? Would the same thing happen in a university class if the professor left the room momentarily? The answer is probably yes. If so, the teacher should respond by getting the children back on track but should *not* act as if they are bad. If you decide that what is occurring is normal (what any group of people, children or adults, might do in similar circumstances), simply get everyone back on track with a firm but not angry attitude. The teacher who returns and finds some children not working might simply flip the lights to get their attention and then cheerfully announce, "Okay, you've had your unscheduled break. Now, the old ogre is back, so it's back to the grindstone." The teacher would then wait until everyone had settled down again before resuming small-group or individual instruction.

If, on the other hand, the teacher returned to find a fistfight in progress, that is not normal and should be dealt with differently. The participants involved might be taken from the room and dealt with by the teacher and/or principal, parents might be called, and privileges would certainly be revoked. Since a fistfight is not what you should expect from a group left unattended for a few minutes, the teacher has a right and a duty to feel angry and to punish the offenders.

If in the heat of a two-team vocabulary contest the participants or spectators get a little noisy and carried away (as might the participants and spectators at a close basketball game), that's normal. The teacher doesn't let it continue because order and relative quiet are important to learning in school settings, but the teacher gets everyone calmed down without getting angry or acting as though they are bad or abnormal. On the other hand, fights or verbal abuse are not tolerated at basketball games and should be seriously dealt with if they occur as part of classroom contests.

Good teachers ask themselves, "Is that normal?" Often the answer is yes, and then, although it may still need to be curtailed, it is not a discipline problem. By asking that question, teachers have fewer discipline problems with which to deal, and the ones they have are clearly not normal and need to be dealt with.

Get Help with Severe Discipline Problems

Doing all of the things suggested in this chapter will dramatically reduce the number of severe discipline problems you might have to deal with. Most children will behave most of the time if they know what is expected, if they are given worthwhile tasks they can accomplish with a high success rate, and if the classroom climate is one that is fair, consistent, and positive. Occasionally, however, you will have a student who will not cooperate. When this happens, you need help. Consider the following possibilities for finding a way to handle a child with a severe discipline problem.

TALK TO THE CHILD   This may seem obvious, but it is often overlooked. When you have a student who cannot or will not follow the rules, start your search for help with that child. Arrange a time when you and the child will not be interrupted—perhaps you could have lunch together in your room or you could talk before or after school. Explain to the child exactly what he or she is doing that is a problem and ask the child to explain "his side of the story." Listen sympathetically to any ideas the child might have about being treated unfairly and so on. Then explain that you realize why he or she might feel this way. Try to show the child that you are on his or her side. But make sure the child understands that the problem behaviors have to stop because they are interfering with the learning of the whole class. Try to get the child to come up with a plan for dealing with anger or a problem before the problem occurs. Perhaps there is a place in the classroom where the child could work alone if the need is felt for the child to be away from the rest of the class for a while. Some young children find it impossible to behave if they are more than three feet away from the teacher. Such children could be your shadow for a week. These children would do their seatwork while sitting next to you in reading groups, erase the board as you write on it, and turn the pages as you read a book.

Although we don't think it is a good idea to have tangible reward systems for most children, some children need such a system to help them begin to learn how to behave and control their behavior. You might offer to take a child someplace special or to let him or her do something special when the child has cooperated and followed the rules for an entire morning.

Children who constantly disrupt classrooms often have emotional problems. They feel neglected, betrayed, angry. Taking the time to talk with a child and listen to what he or she feels is a step toward solving the problem. Letting a child know you care and want to help him or her fit into the classroom is often an important first step in solving the problem.

IF TALKING TO THE CHILD DOES NOT RESULT IN A SATISFACTORY SOLUTION, TALK TO THE PARENTS   Often the parents of difficult children are hard to contact. Sometimes, home visits or calls to them at work are necessary. When you do contact the parents, emphasize that you are concerned about their child. Explain exactly what the child does that is disruptive and help them to understand that if the child continues to behave in this way, there will be serious difficulties in school. Listen to the parents' side of the story. Ask them if they have ideas about how to help the child behave better. Work with them to make a plan. The most important information you can convey to parents is your concern for their child. Even busy, harried parents love their children and will work with you if they sense that you have the best interests of their child at heart.

ASK ANOTHER TEACHER FOR HELP   Pick a teacher whose classroom climate you respect. Explain to that teacher exactly what problems the child creates. Listen to the teacher's advice, and do your best to implement it if it makes sense.

ASK YOUR PRINCIPAL, GUIDANCE COUNSELOR, OR SCHOOL PSYCHOLOGIST FOR HELP   Some children's problems cannot be solved by the classroom teacher. When you have done everything you need to do and sought help from the child, the child's parents, and a mentor-teacher and still are having severe discipline problems, you need and deserve the help of some other professionals. Most schools have someone who can help you deal with severe discipline problems. Good teachers know when a problem is beyond their abilities and resources and ask for professional help with students when they need it.

DO IT TOGETHER

Talk with your peers about discipline. Pool your knowledge about classes in which everyone behaved and classes in which the students were unmanageable. Consider the issues of good instruction, reasonable rules, and routines. Think about whether or not the students in the classroom had a sense of it being "theirs." Think about teachers with positive attitudes and those with negative attitudes. Write a group summary comparing your collective experience with discipline in a variety of classrooms and what you have learned in this section of the chapter.

LOOKING BACK

Successful teachers carry out many important roles. Two of the most critical involve planning and organizing. The five key ideas in this chapter are:

1. Successful teachers do yearly, unit, weekly, and daily planning.
2. Successful teachers make the best possible arrangement of classroom space.
3. Successful teachers make the best possible use of the time available.
4. Successful teachers make special provisions for children with special needs.
5. Successful teachers have good discipline.

ADD TO YOUR JOURNAL

As you write, try to connect your own experiences with classrooms you have been in to what you have learned in this chapter. Try to form images of these classrooms and teachers. Do you remember teachers who were good planners, in which you had a clear sense of the direction in which you should be going, and other classes where teachers rushed through the last half of the course during May? Describe a classroom arrangement you have experienced that meets the criteria set forth in this chapter. Evaluate our suggestions for making the best possible use of your teaching time. Think about children with special needs you have known. In what classrooms were these needs more closely met? What adjustments did the best teachers make? Finally, think about discipline. Evaluate our suggestions for good discipline and decide how well they would work in your classroom.

REFERENCES

Anderson, L. M., Brubaker, N. L., Alleman-Brooks, J., & Duffy, G. G. (1985). A qualitative study of seatwork in first-grade classrooms. *Elementary School Journal, 86,* 123–140.

Anderson, R. C., Hiebert, E. H., Scott, J. A., & Wilkinson, I. A. G. (1985). *Becoming a nation of readers.* Washington, DC: National Institute of Education.

Brophy, J., & Good, T. (1985). Teacher behavior and student achievement. In M. Wittrock (Ed.), *Third handbook of research on teaching.* New York: Macmillan.

Doyle, W. (1985). Classroom organization and management. In M. C. Wittrock (Ed.), *Third handbook of research on teaching.* New York: Macmillan.

Evertson, C. M., Emmer, E. T., Sanford, J. P., & Clements, B. S. (1983). Improving classroom management: An experiment in elementary classrooms. *Elementary School Journal, 84,* 173–188.

Johnson, D. W., & Johnson, R. T. (1985). Cooperative learning and adaptive education. In M. C. Wang & H. J. Walberg (Eds.), *Adapting instruction to individual differences.* Berkeley, CA: McCutchan.

Thurlow, M., Graden, J., Yseldyke, J., & Algozzine, R. (1984). Student reading during class: The lost activity in reading instruction. *Journal of Educational Research, 77,* 267–272.

Veenan, S. (1984). Perceived problems of beginning teachers. *Review of Educational Research, 54,* 143–178.

ADDITIONAL READINGS

These books offer concrete suggestions for planning thematic units.

Eisele, B. (1991). *Managing the whole language classroom.* Cypress, CA: Creative Teaching Press.

Fredericks, A. (1993). *Thematic units.* New York: HarperCollins.

These books are excellent sources of information for organizing classrooms for balanced literacy instruction.

McVitty, W. (Ed.). (1986). *Getting it together: Organizing the reading-writing classroom.* Portsmouth, NH: Heinemann.

Routman, R. (1988). *Transitions.* Portsmouth, NH: Heinemann.

Routman, R. (1991). *Invitations.* Portsmouth, NH: Heinemann.

These books are excellent sources of information for preventing discipline problems.

Gathercoal, F. (1993). *Judicious discipline.* San Francisco: Caddo Gap Press.

Wong, H. K., & Wong, R. T. (1994). *The first days of school.* Sunnyvale, CA: Wong Publications.

This book is a good source of authentic, holistic reading and writing activities for children with special needs.

Rhodes, L. K., & Dudley-Marling, C. (1988). *Readers and writers with a difference: A holistic approach to teaching learning disabled and remedial students.* Portsmouth, NH: Heinemann.

PART II

. . . In ELEMENTARY CLASSROOMS

Miss Launch: Kindergarten

THE PARENT MEETING

Over at last! Miss Launch glanced at her watch and noted with surprise that it was only 9:00 P.M. It seemed much later to her. As she moved about the room collecting materials and getting out other supplies for the next day, she thought over her first parent meeting in this new school. The previous school where she had taught kindergarten for three years had not held these meetings, and she had *not* looked forward to this one!

She had talked to them for approximately half an hour, and then some parents had asked questions. To her surprise, many parents had stayed longer for a private chat. But now, even they had gone, leaving her to her reflections.

She knew that this should be one of the most important encounters she would have with parents this year, and that this meeting would set the tone for all future parental cooperation. Mr. Topps had also told her to relax—these meetings went much more smoothly if they were informal and casual. To Miss Launch, with her penchant for food, that meant cookies and coffee!

While the parents were assembling in the classroom, she had announced that refreshments were in the rear of the room as was a sign-in sheet for their names. She would need to contact absent parents at a later time to discuss her kindergarten program with them.

Miss Launch firmly believed kindergarten to be an essential and integral part of the total school program. She had told the parents that kindergarten was *not* play time for which she was the baby-sitter. Further, she had emphasized that the foundation for all future school success was laid in kindergarten.

She had outlined some of the experiences that the children would have in her room and the reasons for them. This had been an important part of her presentation, for she wanted and needed parental support and cooperation. She had pointed out to the parents the various centers for learning. In addition to providing the traditional block, art, and house corners she had included other areas that she felt would enhance the educational program for the children. There was an animals area, an area for puppets and plays, one for reading, and a things-to-do corner that would include activities ranging from math, to science, to cooking and other topics. Much of the learning would take place in these centers.

Centers

Learning, however, would also occur outside of the classroom. Miss Launch had told the parents that she had planned two field trips a month to various places in the school and community. Follow-up activities for these field trips would include making thank-you cards, drawing pictures, and having shared writing/language experience.

Direct Experience

Miss Launch also had informed the parents of her concern with oral language development. She said that there would be many and varied opportunities for the children to talk. One of the mothers questioned why talking was important.

"Miss Launch, I don't know much about how they do school now, but when I was in school they didn't take learnin' time for talkin'. I don't see how that can help Chip learn to read! Readin' and talkin' are two different things as I see it!"

Integrated Language Arts

Miss Launch had replied calmly to Mrs. Moppet. "Not so different as you might think! Children are already speaking many thousands of words when they enter kindergarten. They will be able to read all of those words within the next few years. In addition, they will be reading other words that they do *not* yet know. But almost without exception, those new words they will learn to read will also be words that they have used in speech. If they do not learn to *say* new words, or if they do not learn to use old words in new ways, then they will read only at the level at which they now speak. That is why I do so much with oral language development. In reading I want to build from what the children know to what they need to know. That is another reason, by the way, for the two monthly field trips. Not only will the children become more familiar with their community, but these trips will also expose them to new words and new ideas that they will need later for reading."

Meaning Vocabulary

She had gone on to say that there would be much dramatization and storytelling. Some of the children's stories would be written on chart paper, some might appear in individual storybooks, and still others might become part of one of the classroom books of original stories. Each day, before the children left, she would sit with them and discuss all the activities engaged in that day. She felt this discussion would help them develop a sense of sequence, the recognition of main ideas, and a memory for things they had accomplished, all important requisites for reading. Besides, she had said, when parents ask children what they had done in school all day, she wanted to prevent the old "Oh, nothing!" response that children often give!

Miss Launch explained that she wanted to give the children many experiences in identifying, sorting, and classifying. These activities help children develop vocabulary and see conceptual relationships. They would work with letters, colors, numbers, their own names, and myriad other concepts that would help them build the foundation for success in reading.

Meaning Vocabulary

She planned to read to the children a great deal, and she expected them to "read" to her. For some children this reading would consist of picture interpretation, while for others, actual words would be read. Everyone would be reading during their classroom SQUIRT (*Sustained QUIet Reading Time*) period. They would all start out reading for three minutes. By the end of the school year they would be able to read silently for much longer. She had also planned many literature response activities for the children. These activities would be extensions of stories read to them, and they would be tied into other classroom activities such as music, art, and cooking.

Teacher Read-Aloud

Literature Response Activity

Miss Launch indicated that she would use a variety of techniques to prepare children for the very important idea that one reads with the expectation of understanding what is read. They would construct charts of their animals' activities, of the weather, and of other things they knew about or could observe. They would be dictating stories and "reading" them to one another and to her. They would cook in the classroom and follow simple recipes. While she did not believe that kindergarten is the place to establish reading groups and use commercial reading programs, she did believe that each child should have constant exposure to things that can be read.

Emergent Literacy

Miss Launch told them that she would read to the children to develop their listening skills. ("Good luck," she heard Butch's mother mutter.) During these listening lessons she would model for the children her thinking processes as a reader. While reading good children's books, she would model how to call up, connect, organize, monitor, predict, image, generalize, apply, and evaluate. She showed them a copy of a Big Book of a nursery rhyme she would be reading to the children the first week of school. Parents exclaimed over the size and joined in as she modeled how she would do these shared book readings with the children. Even parents in the back row could see the words as she pointed to them.

Thinking Processes

MISS LAUNCH: Children first of all need to develop a desire and purpose for reading. Reading is a difficult task at best, but without proper motivation, it is even more so. We're all going to read, read, read in this class and not just during SQUIRT. I will read to the children and they will "read" to me and to one another. Even if they're only reading pictures, they are still acquiring abilities they will need to be good readers. They can determine the sequence of story events, what the important ideas in the story are, and what might happen next in the story. We will write and, I hope, receive letters. We will label things around the classroom and set up a post office for messages. We'll make books of all kinds—some will have only pictures like Mercer Mayer's "Frog" books, and others will have words. We'll follow recipes for purposeful reading. In addition, we'll be working with rhyming patterns and the shapes of letters. As I said earlier, I feel that a firm background of oral language is

Balanced Literacy Programs

the most important contribution I can make to your child's future success in reading, so I will do much with that. I have lots more planned, but I hope that you have the general idea.

Horace's mother held up her hand. "Could you explain that in a little more detail, Miss Launch? I'm not quite sure that I understand what our children will be doing."

MISS LAUNCH: It seems that children who are ready to begin reading have certain characteristics. They know why people read and write, they have a broad background of knowledge and concepts, they know that words are made up of sounds and they know some letter names and sounds, they know how print works and how we describe print, they know 20 to 30 sight words, and they want to learn how to read and write. Children are at all different places with these knowings; I'll be working to make sure I develop them during the school year. To do so, I'll focus my instruction around four key ideas: read to and talk with children, use shared book experiences such as I modeled earlier, use language experience and shared writing, and all children will begin to write in a journal the first week of school. Those first writings may be only pictures, but I want to develop the idea that we can communicate our ideas to others with written symbols.

MR. MARTIN: You've mentioned cooking in kindergarten a couple of times now, and I can't for the life of me figure out what cooking has to do with reading and writing. Can you explain it to me?

MISS LAUNCH: Would you believe that it's really because I like to eat? [Chuckles around the room] Actually, I can justify it educationally, though I must admit that I enjoy the food too! [Chuckles again] Cooking in this room will be done for several reasons. First, since children eat what they prepare, they learn that it is important to follow directions carefully; second, the food produced is the incentive to do the work well, so there is meaning to doing it; third, there is always more language produced as we discuss why a particular sequence is necessary and why certain ingredients are added, what they do together; and fourth, new concepts are observed and dealt with, such as the evaporation of liquid, or the nature of change as we observe it with popcorn. And, maybe **Attitudes** I should add a fifth one—because it's fun, and if learning can result from an enjoyable activity as well as it can from a pencil and paper task, well, I'm all for it!

MRS. SMITH: My friend's son was in kindergarten last year, and he had all kinds of those papers done with purple ink and he had a reading readiness workbook too. I think that with those you can tell what children are learning.

MISS LAUNCH: I feel that workbooks and ditto papers stifle creativity and encourage conformity. And not only that, they do not necessarily teach the important things that children need to know. It's very important to instill an interest in reading and a desire to learn how to read. The best way to do that is with books—lots and lots of books! I assure you, however, that I will know **Assessment** what your children are learning. I use charts to keep track of children's progress with learnings that are important. I keep anecodotal records on children. I also keep portfolios of children's productions, such as their writing, so that I can observe vocabulary and language understandings. These are the ways that give me the greatest possible information about your children.

Miss Launch then explained that there would be at least two parent conferences this year, and that at the end of the year parents would receive a written appraisal of their child's performance in various areas.

MR. GRAHAM: I have no questions as such, but I just want you to know that I am amazed that so much can be done with kindergartners! You have a very ambitious year mapped out! Is there anything we can do to help you?

MISS LAUNCH: Is there ever! Thanks so much for asking, because my next statement was to be a pitch to solicit your help. I can use parents and other relatives to help with taping stories, typing books children write, field trips, cooking, and all sorts of things. I'll be sending a request-for-help letter home soon, giving you the opportunity to volunteer. Some of the jobs can be done at home so that even if you don't have a lot of time, you can still help me out. As to all that the children can do, I have found that many adults tend to underestimate the capabilities of children, and for that reason we do not help them to attain their full potential. I hope to help them do so without the attendant pressure that we sometimes place on children.

As Miss Launch evaluated the evening, she found that the meeting had gone rather well. Many of the parents had remarked to her that they were pleased that the emphasis would be on learning through creative means. She was certain that she would have a great deal of support from the parents whenever she might need it. She hoped she had convinced them that kindergarten was "real school." Oh, well, if not now, then by the end of the year they would be aware of it! She glanced around the room. Yes, all was in readiness for tomorrow morning. She allowed herself the luxury of a stretch and a yawn; then, she turned off the lights and left for home.

MONTHLY LOGS

September

September is always a bit of a shock to my system. Each year I am taken aback at how small and shy the entering kindergartners are. I quickly realize that I am using the children of the previous spring as my criteria. How much they do grow and change in one year's time! It always takes so long to deal with some of the school socialization processes—such as how to use the water fountain and what "line up" means! Those can be difficult areas for children to deal with for the first time. Fortunately, most of them are already "housebroken"!

Starting the year is the difficult task, and as I look over the list of all I have set out to accomplish, I wonder somewhat at my audacity. This year I am going to make much more of a concerted effort to systematically teach children about language and the reasons for reading. I know that a certain road is paved with

Phonological Awareness

good intentions and that if I don't structure myself, I will probably not do all that I now plan to. Therefore, I have taped a list of factors inside my plan book so that I will be reminded to include specific activities for these factors as I do my planning.

Emergent Literacy

The Seven Critical Knowings

1. Children know why people read and write.
2. Children have a broad background of knowledge and concepts.
3. Children know that words are made up of sounds.
4. Children know some letter names and sounds.
5. Children know print conventions and jargon.
6. Children know 20 to 30 concrete words.
7. Children want to learn how to read and write.

Classroom Instruction to Accomplish the Knowings

Read to and talk with children.

Use shared book experiences.

Use shared writing and language experience.

Have children writing regularly.

My group of 25 includes some very interesting people; I can tell already! The list of children follows:

Alex	Daphne	Mike
Alexander	Hilda	Mitch
Anthony	Horace	Mort
Betty	Jeff	Pat
Butch	Joyce	Paul
Carl	Larry	Rita
Chip	Mandy	Roberta
Daisy	Manuel	Steve
Danielle		

Children with Special Needs

One child was so withdrawn that I was immediately aware that his problem was more than fear of coming to school for the first time. Paul wouldn't speak to me or any of the others for three class sessions, and then he merely uttered his name in a group game. When this happened, we were so excited that we gave him a "silent cheer" (that is, we raised our hands into the air, shook them up and down, and formed our mouths as though we were cheering). Paul cried often during those first two weeks, but they were strange, silent tears that rolled down his cheeks. There was no sobbing or screaming—just a sad, sad look and those tears running down his cheeks. (I have asked the school social worker to investigate the home situation. Something is drastically wrong; perhaps we can discover what it is and then remedy the situation.) Alex and Daphne began to sniffle when they saw this (tears are among the most contagious of childhood afflictions), but Hilda simply told them to be quiet, that she had looked around and it was obvious that there was nothing to be afraid of! The sniffling subsided, but Paul continued his silent crying despite all my efforts to comfort or distract him.

I was reading recently about allowing children to have notebooks from the first day of kindergarten and first grade. There are lots of articles available now on "invented spelling." The idea is that by allowing children to have their own writing utensils and paper from an early age, we encourage them to view writing and reading as important activities, and that children will practice both reading and writing so that they get better at it. Another major point that was made was that children know a lot more about words and letters than most adults realize. By letting them do a lot of writing, we allow them to explore letters and words as we focus on what they can do. If, for example, a child writes:

Invented Spelling

Midg nm Sm

we can tell that child knows, among other things, that letters go from left to right when words are made, that many sounds have been matched with their letter forms, that letters are grouped to make words, and that there is an understanding that words are written so that others can read them. Clearly there are many things still to learn; however, it is easier to teach from a base of what is known and introduce the new information.

I explained to the children that they would make an entry every other day each week. Sometimes I will give them a stimulus related to a book we're reading, and other times I will ask them to put in their own ideas. I will encourage them to attempt writing words from their own knowledge, words around the room, and words they use invented spellings for. I want them to view writing as a very important part of our school day and to see that words are how we communicate with others.

Process Writing

I read to the children every day, and sometimes the whole morning is built around one book. First the story is read to them, and then we do other activities to tie the book into the other curricular areas. As an example, one of the first books I read to them was Mirra Ginsburg's *Mushroom in the Rain* (1974). After reading it, we talked about their favorite parts of the story and they drew with crayons or painted at the easel the one thing they had enjoyed the most. We hung these up and let children tell what the part was and why they had chosen it. The fox section was the most popular of all, for children like to be scared just a little. Then we dramatized the story by playing the parts of the various animals. When I asked the children what we could use for a mushroom, they cleverly decided to use an umbrella that they would open out more and more as the various animals came under! In addition, we counted the number of animals in the book. We looked for certain colors ("Find all the red things on this page"). We made up a song that we could sing to the tune of "Are You Sleeping?":

Content Area Integration

Is it raining,
Is it raining,
Little Ant?
Little Ant?

Hurry to the mushroom!
Hurry to the mushroom!
Drip, drop, drip.
Drip, drop, drip.

Is it raining,
Is it raining,
Butterfly?
Butterfly? (etc., for all the animals up through the rabbit. Then:)

Here comes Foxy!
Here comes Foxy!
Poor Rabbit! (two times)
"No, he is not here, Sir." (two times)
"Go away." (two times)

See the rainbow. (two times)
In the sky. (two times)
Now the sun is shining. (two times)
Warm and bright. (two times)

We tested the hypothesis that mushrooms grow in the rain and we planned additional adventures for the characters in the book. We talked about who else might have come to the mushroom, what might happen next, where Ant would go when the rain finally stopped, and what other scary things might happen to the other animals. After we did a lap story with *Mushroom in the Rain*, I placed the characters, props, and the book in the puppets and plays center so they can retell the story individually or in small groups over and over.

Focused Writing
In their journals, they drew a picture about another animal that might try to get under the mushroom. I encouraged them to write a word or more on their paper that would tell others about their idea. Then I had them think of a sentence to dictate about their picture, and I circulated among their work tables, writing sentences for them on the page. I can really see how it might help to have a parent volunteer help me with this part! Chip seemed not ever to have seen a crayon, and so Danielle helped him learn how to hold it and mark with it. Paul could not come with an animal to draw or a word to say. Larry wrote his own sentence!

(An elephant tried to get under the mushroom.)

Scheduling
We have established a daily pattern or schedule. Establishing a routine that children can depend upon is a critical aspect of school. The morning is mainly spent on math and language arts, so I have only three hours in which to do a lot of things. The morning schedule is:

8:30 Attendance, sharing, read a story or poem
9:00 Work time—centers, SQUIRT, oral language lessons, etc.
10:00 Physical education—outside if possible

10:15 Snack and story

10:30 Work time

11:15 Group together for review of work sessions

During the third week, at work time the children were to find pictures of red things in magazines and catalogs. Larry, who is already reading, I've discovered, found the word *red* also. We pasted the things they found on a chart labeled "Red Things." Most of the children could already identify the colors without help, but some could not. I paired Joyce (who could) and Chip (who couldn't) so she could help him find red things. Daisy, Jeff, Paul, and Butch also worked with other children to find red objects. **Meaning Vocabulary**

Also during work time, I've been having the children practice their phone numbers and addresses. It is essential that they learn those as soon as possible, so that if they should ever get lost, they can be reunited with parents quickly. As Chip has no phone, he has learned the phone number of a neighbor. We'll practice dialing their numbers on toy telephones.

We began the first field trips of the year right in our own school area. It is important for children to become oriented to the building, the grounds, and the personnel as soon as possible. The first day the children came to school, we spent part of the morning walking through those parts of the building we *had* to know—the restrooms, the office, and the janitor's room—so that *when* (not *if*, but when) a child throws up I can stay with the child while someone else asks the janitor to bring a mop. We have our own kindergarten-sized playground equipment, and that also had to be shown. We went to the office on subsequent days and met the secretary, Mrs. Mainstay, and the principal, Mr. Topps. I prepared for these trips by first going there myself and making sure that someone who knew precisely what it was I wanted children to learn about that particular place would be on hand. I prepared the children by telling them the highlights of each place, alerting them to what to look and listen for, and urging them to try to remember everything so that we could talk and make up a story when we got back to the room. Upon our return, I asked them to tell what we had seen and done. As each child made a contribution, I wrote it down on chart paper with the child's name after it, so that he or she could see the very words contributed. Then I cut the words apart and with the children's help, I glued them back on another piece of paper in the proper order of occurrence. Finally I read it all back to them and they agreed that they had done a fine job! **Direct Experience**

Language Experience

Our cooking experience for September came near the end of the last week in the month. I began by talking with children about one of their favorite foods: peanut butter! "Yippee Skippy," they yelled. I asked them what they thought peanut butter might be made from. They all guessed, with no trouble, the main ingredient. "What else?" I queried. They said that there was nothing else because that's why they called it peanut butter. After all, they reasoned, butter was only made of butter and hot dogs were made of hot dogs! Oh, boy! it's going to be a long year! I reached into the bag next to me and took out two peanuts in the shell. Some of the children were clearly fascinated, since they thought peanuts came in cans. They watched me shell the peanuts (two nuts to a shell, we noted) and place them in a little ceramic bowl. I then began to mash the peanuts with **Direct Experience** a pestle and showed the results periodically. When I had the four peanuts pretty well mashed, I showed the bowl to each child. "Does that look like what you put on your crackers?" I asked. They all agreed that it did not, and we discussed why.

"It's too dry looking," said Larry. "Maybe they call it peanut butter because they put butter into it."

"Good guess," I responded. "You're right that it does need something greasy in it. The recipe I have says that we just put plain oil into the mashed peanuts, add a little salt, mix it up, and spread it on crackers or bread." Then I asked if they would each like to make their own peanut butter to have at snack time. They were, to put it mildly, agreeable to the suggestion. We made a recipe chart for the cooking area and I put them into pairs to work on their peanut butter during the morning work time. I paired them so that more independent and mature children would work with those who needed help. Larry and Paul were put together and did a really nice job. Here is the recipe chart that the children dictated.

Shared Writing

How to Make Peanut Butter for Two People:
We Need:
10 peanuts for each person
1 teaspoon of oil
1 sprinkle of salt

We Do:
Count out 20 peanuts.
Take the peanuts out of the shells.
Mash the peanuts in the bowl.
Measure 1 teaspoon of oil.
Put the oil into the bowl.
Mix the oil and peanuts together.
Add salt.
Mix everything together.
Put the peanut butter on a cracker.

In the cooking center I placed five-by-eight-inch index cards with the directions done in pictures so children could go through the steps more easily. In addition, I color-coded the measuring cups and spoons so that I could use the matching color on my direction cards. As a backup to ensure accurate measures, I also drew around the outside of the teaspoon so the children could lay the spoon on top of the drawing to see if it matched before pouring the oil. These individual and paired cooking experiences work very well in the beginning.

October

October is over—I didn't think Halloween would *ever* arrive, and neither did the children! Every day they asked if it were here yet! Well, at least I was able to channel some of that interest toward school activities. Many of the books I selected to read to them and ones they chose themselves were about Halloween, witches, or monsters. One of my favorites, *Where the Wild Things Are* (Sendak, 1963), was one of those with which we did literature response activities. The children made monster masks and we had a "wild things" parade. We also had a word gathering for scary words—I asked them to tell me all of the scary things they could think of. Since this was our first word gathering, the children had trouble getting started. After only a few suggestions by other children everyone joined in. Even Paul gave me one—*night*. When they started to bog down, having given me several words and phrases, I asked them for scary colors, then for scary smells, sounds, and looks. This is their completed list. Frederick the mouse (Lionni, 1970), the original word gatherer, would be very pleased with this compilation.

Literature
Response
Activity

Meaning
Vocabulary

Scary Things

blood	monster	bad dream	nightmare
howl	bloody	black cat	Boo!
ghost	scream	witch	mummy
giant	storm	red	fire
dogs	growl	night	orange
purple	blue	scared	afraid

something touching me in the dark

when my night light burns out

footsteps in the dark

my mom's closet without the light on

my window with the curtains open

noises outside in the dark

After we had completed the list, I read the words back to the children, running my hand under each word or phrase as I said it so that they would have more opportunity to observe left-to-right progression with the return sweep to the next line. "Now," I told them, "we are going to write a poem!" I had read many poems to them and they did enjoy poetry. Now it was our turn to produce. I used a concrete format since it is the simplest one I know. I drew a random number and arrangement of lines on the chalkboard and the children helped me to fill them in with words and phrases. To show them what I wanted us to do, I had them count the number of lines I had drawn and I told them that I was going to use some of the words from our scary things chart to help me make up the poem. There would be only 1 word written on each line, so since we had counted 21 lines, I needed to write 21 words. This is what they saw:

Shared Reading

____ ____

____ ____ ____ ____ ____ ____

____ ____

____ ____ ____ ____ ____

____ ____

____ ____ ____ ____

The children were intrigued, particularly when they saw me begin to write words on each of the lines. This is my finished poem:

I felt
something touching me in the dark.
I knew
my window curtains were open.
I screamed.
Bad dream go away.

Concepts about Print

We counted the number of words that were on each of the lines. Mort pointed out that the first line in the second row had nine words on it! At that point we talked about how some words have one letter (pointing out "I" in the poem) and that some words have more than one letter. The word *something* has nine letters. I wrote *Mort* on the board. "What is that word?" I asked. He did know his name and told me that it said *Mort*. "This is one word and that word is your name. But your name has four letters in it." Of course, it was necessary to do the same with the names of several other children, since all of them wanted their names written. But it was also important to count the letters in the names of several children in order to show children the concept of *letter* versus *word* in lots of examples. Obviously they didn't all get it this time around, but with lots of examples throughout the year they should all have the idea by the time they hit first grade (I hope!). With a little help, this is what the class was able to come up with:

ONE NIGHT
Black cat scream, black cat howl!
Why do you make that noise?
Growl, purr, growl, purr
Dog and cat
fight.

Individual Differences

I copied both my poem and their poem onto sheets of chart paper and hung them near the scary things chart. I find it fascinating that Danielle will steer her wheelchair over and pore over the poems with Roberta and Alex. They seem fascinated with the idea that there is one word on each of the lines and they try to count how many letters are in each of the words. Occasionally Mort will wander over and watch them for a while. I heard him say, "But how do you *know* which ones are words and which ones are letters? I don't get it. I think you're making it all up." Clearly, there is a range of abilities within *this* classroom!

We also did a concrete poem on the color black. First we had a word gathering of black words, sounds, and smells to get them prepared.

BLACK
Black, black is the night,
blacker than black
is
my window.

While we were gathering black words (which was, of course, the color chart they were working on that week), a discussion took place. The children were coming up with all kinds of black things, when Butch contributed three words: *Joyce, Danielle,* and *Jeff.* Some of the children turned around and looked at those children as if they had never seen them before. Others started murmuring—this *was* a revelation!

Larry said, "No, I don't agree. They are called blacks, but I think they are actually more brown."

The three were asked what color *they* thought they were. Joyce said, "Well, what color do you think *you* are?" There was a general comparing of arms, but little agreement. Finally Jeff said proudly, "Well, I don't care what color I look like, I'm black." So his name went up on the chart and though he tried to hide it from them, he smiled! Later I saw him tracing out the letters of his name on the chart. He was the only child to get listed on the chart!

By now I had labeled a lot of things around the room: window, door, mirror, desk, table, chair. Children seem to enjoy finding labeled objects that have letters like those in their names. I was working with each of the children so that they would recognize their own names. I wrote each name about three inches high on unlined paper. I then took each child's hand and traced over the name with two fingers. All the time we did that, I said the name over and over with the child. Then, after we had done that a few times, I let them go to the chalkboard where they could write it, using the paper as a model. I stayed with each child until the name was mastered and then went to work with the next one. With that technique, almost all of the children can recognize their names when they see them in manuscript writing, and several can write their own names without looking at a model. As a further incentive, I labeled the bulletin board with their names and then asked them to make a picture of themselves and tell me where to hang it. Mort, Paul, and Daisy were the only three who needed extra help. Mort got confused because of all the names that began with *M*, as did Daisy with three *D* names. Paul just didn't have a clue! Another activity they like is to dip their one-inch brushes into clear water and write on the board with those. They have fun, they learn, there is no erasing to do, and at the end, the chalkboard is clean!

I also have the alphabet spread out around the walls of the room, and I have placed the color words and the names of all of the children by the first letter of the words. I wrote each color word and name on a sentence strip made of colored tagboard. They are large enough to read from anywhere in the room. There is plenty of space too to add other words to the wall as we go through the year.

Another popular "hangout" is the "Words We Know" bulletin board. Children have been bringing in words from advertisements that they can read. Of course, if "the golden arches" are missing, Betty can't really say, "McDonald's." Nevertheless, being able to read the word with the logo is a beginning step for successful later reading. They love bringing in words, which they share with the class during our morning opening time, pinning them to the bulletin board. I've had to place some restrictions on them, however, ever since Butch brought in the beer ad. They must show the word to me first; I decide if they can share it with

Concrete Words

Word Wall

Concrete Words

others. Along with this, the children are making their own *Words I Know* books by pasting logos and words to pages. I often see them reading their books to other children.

Parent Involvement

Here's a copy of the letter that the parents received from me at the beginning of October to solicit help. Parental response to the letter was overwhelming. For the most part, parents want to be involved in their children's education and will volunteer if there is something specific that they feel confident in doing. In some cases, parents prefer to or *must* do things at home. For example, Chip's mother must stay home to take care of an elderly aunt and uncle who live with them. She thus offered to cut out things for me if I would send the materials to her, since they don't have any magazines or newspapers. *Where* it's done matters not to me! I'm just delighted that parents are willing to do it at all!

Dear Parents,

As I told you at our September parent meeting, I am most eager to provide your children with a year full of good learning experiences. In order to give them the kind of program I have envisioned, I am asking for your help in many ways. Would you please put a check mark beside those things which you would be willing to do for us this year. The space for "other" is one in which you might suggest to me any possible aid or special talent you would like to contribute.

Thank you so much for your prompt attention to this matter. Your children and I will gain much from your participation in their education.

Sincerely,
Helen Launch

· ·

Please detach here and return.

I would be willing to help in the following ways:
____ helping in class one hour a week
____ typing at home (or school)
____ cutting out paper at home (or school)
____ transporting children for field trips
____ helping with the cooking projects at school
____ donating scrap materials (cloth, pretty paper, etc.)
____ tape-recording stories, music, etc.
____ making puppets
____ contributing art materials
____ contributing materials for house corner
____ contributing books, records, pictures, etc.
____ contributing scatter rugs, pillows for floor, etc.
____ other:

Name: _____
Telephone: _____

Our two field trips this month were to those places that supply us with food—the store and the farm. I had gone to these places prior to the children's visit, and I made extensive notes to myself about the kinds of things I wanted them to notice and learn about. I spend a lot of time listing for myself what concepts and vocabulary I anticipate will be developed. After each visit, then, we make charts of things seen and learned.

Direct Experience

Since the store didn't open until 9:00 A.M., I made arrangements for the manager to show us around at 8:45. I planned to spend half an hour there so the children would be able to observe some shoppers, but the store wouldn't be too crowded. I prepared the children for this trip by discussing with them the various services and goods the store has to offer. Daisy was the greatest contributor, for she had spent a good bit of time in stores with her mother. I put down things the children said, so after the trip they could look at their list and add to it. From the amended list we made up a story about the store that hung on the bulletin board surrounded by all of the children's pictures. Here it is:

Language Experience

We went to the store. (Daphne)

We saw lots and lots of food. (Daisy)

The fruits and vegetables are called *produce*. (Larry)

We saw lots of meat. (Chip)

There were sweet things to eat. (Carl)

The store man showed us many things. (Pat)

We had fun and learned a lot. (Rita)

My mother and Larry's mother drove. (Roberta)

In addition the children drew pictures and wrote thank-you letters that I mailed to "the store man" along with a copy of their story and a personal note of thanks from me. Some of the children were even able to write a few real words.

Focused Writing

We did the same kinds of activities for our visit to the farm. So many children do not associate the farm with the store that I made a special effort to talk about where butter, milk, meat, and vegetables come from. When I first asked them where milk comes from, Butch replied, "From the carton." But where did the milk for the carton come from, I persisted. Jeff told me that it came from the store! In the whole group, only four—Larry (no surprise!), Steve and Anthony (the science buffs), and Daphne (who lives on a farm)—knew that cows are milked and that is the source of milk.

Meaning Vocabulary

A concern I have when taking my children on these trips is that the guide speak loudly enough for all to hear. Because I prepare them so well for their trips, they have plenty of questions to ask and are willing to listen to the answers, but too often the guide is not prepared to wait until they are all quiet and close enough to hear, or careful to speak loud enough to overcome background noises.

We received several pumpkins from both the farm and the store, so it seemed only reasonable to try out some of the recipe and craft ideas in *The All-Around Pumpkin Book* by Margery Cuyler (1980). Following her directions, we cooked

Direct Experience

pieces of pumpkin and put the peeled, softened pumpkin meat through a sieve to make pumpkin sauce. Two of their favorite recipes were roasted pumpkin seeds and pumpkin milk (believe it or not!). Here's the adapted recipe for pumpkin milk, which they did in groups of six:

Pumpkin Milk
We Need:
2 cups of plain yogurt
3/4 cup pumpkin sauce
4 tablespoons honey
1 1/2 teaspoons nutmeg
1 1/2 cups milk
2 tablespoons wheat germ

We Do:
Put everything in the blender and turn it on.
Turn the blender on whip.
When it is all mixed up it will be all orange.
Turn off the blender and pour the pumpkin milk into 6 glasses.

I thought it turned out remarkably well. All the children except Anthony tried it. However, I was a bit chagrined to overhear Butch muttering, "I'd rather have some coffee."

November

Finally! Colors are finished! Our room looks like a rainbow gone crazy. Because Joyce and Danielle had finally declared themselves brown, I changed the order to the colors we were working on. We did brown the first week of November, and their names were the first words put on the chart. They helped me spell them, too, which made it even more important to them. We did purple and white things during the second and third weeks, which led to further discussion among the children of which ones were white. Some decided they were pink, some orange, and some light brown. Mike (of course!) declared himself purple and used some of the finger paints to prove his point. What an unexpected way to have gotten into such a serious issue—I think the children have a better idea now of how complicated the notion of skin color is.

Larry is able to read a great many of the things we have listed on our charts. I'm amazed that he can read so well. He often chooses the reading corner in which to spend his free time.

Centers   The reading corner is furnished with an old bucket seat from the car of a friend of mine. (My friends are well trained—they never throw any unusual items away without checking with me first. Over the years I have asked them for odd items, from popsicle sticks to eggshells.) The children love the car seat—two can sit together cozily, reading or looking at books. There also is a small rug, some pillows donated by parents, and a small table with three chairs.

A shelf contains a variety of books, ranging from those with pictures only to those with quite a long story line. The children choose books they want me to read to them, and often we do literature response activities with these books.

The blocks area is another one that the children enjoy and use frequently. It lends itself to all sorts of language experiences as the children build and discuss what they have done and why. Sometimes they ask me to write signs for them or write down stories that the constructions trigger. By the end of November we had enough of those stories to make a book, which we placed in the reading corner. The children were really pleased that I valued their work enough to put a cover around it and give it a title. Nearly everyone in the class had contributed something to the book, and even those who hadn't had worked in the block corner and could enjoy the stories and illustrations.

The art area has paint, easels, clay, crayons, colored chalk, *lots* of paper, odds and ends for constructions, and various other materials for artwork. I have a section of the bulletin board reserved for paintings and a small table nearby for displaying constructions. Very often, artwork acts as a stimulus for story writing. One of the children might ask me to write down his story about the horse he or a classmate had made of clay. I am often asked to label their work; not only is there further language concept development, but this labeling also seems to add value to the work.

I have never called the house corner the doll corner or dollhouse as some of my colleagues do, for lots of boys don't want to play there if it has that name. They learn too soon to shun the so-called feminine playthings. By calling it the house corner there is a greater opportunity to draw boys in. They experiment with all sorts of housekeeping experiences, even arguing over whose turn it is to vacuum the floor. Of course, they get real cooking and dishwashing experiences from the cooking sessions we have.

It has been another busy month, of course, with the field trips as well as some of the activities that I have been doing with the children to help develop visual discrimination of letters. We have learned to play some new games. I wrote out six copies each of the capital forms *P*, *H*, *A*, and *R*. I made each one about six inches high so that the children could readily see them from across the room. They are on sheets of oak-tag and covered with clear plastic adhesive paper so that they are durable. The first game was one that the whole class played together. I shuffled the cards and dealt out one to each of the children. I told them to find the other children who had the same letter shape. When two children got together they had to stay together while searching for other children who matched them. If they thought that they had found one that was a match, they carefully looked at the parts to see if they were correct. After all groups had been formed with no leftovers, I checked them: Perfect the first time, just as I had known it would be, for the abler ones helped those who could not yet match! (I had set the timer for three minutes. They enjoyed the timing—it gives games a little added excitement.)

Letter Names

It was interesting to observe the differences among the children as they formed their groups. Paul stayed put and was found by Mandy and Horace, who also had *P*s. They dragged him along with them until they found or were found by

Individual Differences

the other *P*s. Daisy dashed wildly around the room, ostensibly looking for the other *A*s, but in fact making it only more difficult for them to track her down. Mort sat in a chair, apparently not wanting to exhaust himself, being fully confident that the *H*s would get to him in time. Chip and Manuel held hands and went from group to group checking the letters, even though Chip was an *A* and Manuel an *R*. I suppose they just needed the extra confidence that they gave one another. The children begged to do it again, so we shuffled the cards and went through the same process. This time, Hilda tried to organize the thing a little more by shouting out, "A! A! A!" apparently as a clue to those who might know the name of the letter. Larry formed his hand into the letter *P* and said "Do you look like this?" Ingenious children I have!

For another game I used the same cards and placed three cards of the same letter on the chalkboard tray with one that was different. I arranged the cards like this for ease the first time: *A A A P*. I then asked Rita to come find the ones that were the same. She chose the first three. "Terrific! Let's all give Rita a silent cheer!" (The silent cheer is a good reward for children and it's also easy on the teacher's eardrums.) I continued the game with other children, making the letter combinations harder or easier depending on a child's capabilities. I then put the cards into the things-to-do center and suggested that they were available to play with.

Language Experience

For the time being, every time we do a language experience story, I underline each word as I read back the completed story to the children to emphasize the concept of a word. Our latest one dealt with one of our more disastrous cooking experiences!

We had a messy time cooking today. (Anthony)
We made cranberry-orange relish to take to our Thanksgiving dinner with the first graders. (Danielle)
We got juice and seeds all over the floor. (Alex)
It tasted yucky. (Butch)
Nobody wanted to eat any but Miss Launch. (Carl)

Concepts about Print

We continue the quest to distinguish between letters and words, as well as trying to emphasize the return sweep to the next line of print. Paul, Mort, Daisy, and Chip are still unable to figure out how children like Roberta, Danielle, and Larry can always tell which marks mean words and which ones mean letters. Most of the group are able to figure out questions such as "How many words are in the first sentence?" if they can come up to the chart and put a finger on each word in the sentence as they count. The story here allowed me to get into another concept with them. Danielle's sentence continued onto another line. When I asked, "How many words are in Danielle's sentence?" most of the children said 12. A few, Betty and Larry and some others, disagreed. There were 15 words, they contended. Alexander, who thought he had finally caught Larry in an error, volunteered to come to the chart and check it out. It took a lot of convincing, with Danielle chiming in for support, to try to convince some of them that Danielle's sentence was indeed 15 words long. Eventually, I know, all of them will understand the difference between words and letters, but for now. . . .

Self-Selected Reading

This month I began SQUIRT. Most of the teachers in this school set aside a time period during which the children and the teacher silently read in materials of their own choice. I explained to the class that I was going to set our timer for three minutes and during that three minutes everyone was to be looking at a book. We went to the school library to select books just for SQUIRT. I aided some in their selections so that Larry, Roberta, and Danielle had books they could read and Paul and Daisy had some bright picture books on topics they found interesting (a children's cookbook for Daisy!). At SQUIRT time it all went rather well, considering that this was a first for them. After it was over, I pulled aside the children who had had an especially difficult time sitting with a book for three whole minutes. We discussed again how they could look at the pictures to try to figure out what the story was about or to try to name the colors they saw on the pages, or how they could go through and think of the names of as many things as possible on each page. I encouraged these children to try to decide if they liked the book enough to want me to read it to the whole class. I had to do this several times with various children in the room (not always the same ones), but by the end of the month the children really could sit still with a book for three minutes. Mr. Topps was really pleased when he came into the classroom to read with us!

Parent Involvement

Daphne's grandparents, with whom she lives, are farmers. In fact, it was their farm we had visited in October. They told me that they very much enjoyed having the children come to the farm and that they felt somewhat guilty that they did not have enough time to come to the school and volunteer some of their time. Despite my protest that it was fine, they insisted that they wanted to help out in some way. Could I use two bushels of apples from their orchard? I love questions like that!

Need I tell you that every one of our cooking activities for the month of November involved apples? I did have to alter the cooking plan that I had made for the year, but it was worth it. One of their very favorite recipes came from *The Taming of the C.A.N.D.Y. Monster* (Lansky, 1978).

Candy Apples
We Need:
1 apple for each person
1 popsicle stick for each person
A bowl of honey
Toasted wheat germ on waxed paper
We Do:
Pull the stem off your apple.
Push the stick in where you took out the stem.
Dip the apple in the bowl of honey and turn it 2 times.
Hold the apple over the bowl of honey until it stops dripping.
Roll the apple in the wheat germ and eat it up!

December

Despite the holiday rush and clamor, we did manage to accomplish some things this month. It does seem to me, though, that the break can't come a minute too soon, for we have been in a holiday whirl since Halloween!

Comprehension Strategy Lesson

I have quite a collection of books without words or with only a few words that I have been using with children in small groups. I use these books to encourage them to discuss what they are seeing in the story and to help them develop the story line as it occurs. The first books I used were *Flicks* (de Paola, 1983) and *The Elephant's Nest* (Burton, 1979). These books each contain several very short stories. I had a small group consisting of Butch, Alexander, Betty, Anthony, Jeff, and Hilda do the story "The Big Pocket" with me. First I told them that we were going to look at a book that had no words but had some stories in it. "How can there be a story without any words?" asked Hilda. "Stories have words." I assured her that it would all come clear. I showed them the title page (Hilda said, "Ah ha! I knew there would be words!") and then turned to the next page, which showed a kangaroo with babies jumping out of her pocket. At the end of the four pages, there are four babies who have leaped out. I did not try to tell the story to them; rather as I showed each page I asked them to tell us what was happening. Before I would turn to the next page I asked them to predict what might be coming up next. After seeing three kangaroo babies hop out of the pocket they readily guessed that another would jump out on the next page. When I asked my same question at the end of the fourth page, they thought they had the pattern. "Another one will jump out," they told me.

What a surprise it was when the baby elephant jumped out of the mother kangaroo's pocket! They immediately guessed, in response to my question of "What will happen next?" that there would be a total of four elephants jumping out of her pocket. But the next page showed a baby giraffe climbing out of the kangaroo's pocket. They were surprised to find during the course of the story that the parents of the giraffe and the elephant came by to pick them up and take them home. We continued the free-flowing discussion through the examination of all the pictures in that story. "Now, we are going back to the beginning of the story and this time you are going to tell me what is happening in the story."

They wanted to go ahead of the pictures we were looking at, but I would not let them do that. I wanted them to listen to one another and stay with what was on each page. The next day I called the same group to me, showed them the book, and asked them to review by telling the story with me again. After this retelling (which went better than the others), I told them that now we were going to tell the story with the tape recorder on, and every time we finished with one page, someone would ring the bell as a turn-page signal. The upshot of it all was that I prepared a written test to go along with the book and the tape-recorded story and placed it all in a learning center. I've done quite a few of the wordless books this way and are they ever popular!

Routines

A device I started this month to help the children identify their own names and also to help develop responsibility is a *job chart*. There are always many tasks to be done in a classroom, and by this time of the year I try to involve the children even more than previously. There are enough jobs for everyone, even though several children have the same job simultaneously, as the cleaners do. So that children have a variety of jobs during the year, the job assignments rotate weekly. There are jobs that can be done by the children only if their teacher instructs them. For instance, they must be told how much water to give the plants. One tip that I found helpful was to color-code plants to soup cans used for watering. I draw a line inside the soup can with permanent marker to indicate how much water is needed for a plant. A small square of color on the plant container that matches the line drawn in the can will clue children so that they will have a hard time going wrong. I learned, however, that with a color-blind child like Butch, you may have a drowned cactus and a droopy ivy! Using this kind of a coding system is the beginning of learning to follow "written" instructions. Though no words are used, children learn to decode the meaning of the symbol being used (in this case, color) in order to follow some specific instructions.

Here is the job chart for one week. Every week new assignments are made:

Water plants	Chip	Paul	Anthony		
Room cleaners	Betty	Butch	Daisy	Rita	Hilda
Messengers	Manuel	Daphne	Alexander		
Mail	Larry and Danielle (they knew all of the names)				
Line leader	Mort				
Group work leaders	Roberta	Horace	Carl	Alex	
Feed animals	Pat	Mike	Steve		
Special helpers	Mitch	Joyce	Mandy	Jeff	

We did another very easy poetry format this month. First, I asked the children it they knew what opposites were. Horace volunteered. "That's when my mom puts money into the bank." **Meaning Vocabulary**

"Pretty good guess," I replied. "That is called a *de*posit."

Larry said, "You know, they're words that mean just the different thing, just the, well, *opposite*, like hot and cold, wet and dry, up and down."

"Very good, Larry. Can you think of any other opposites, children?" They came up with several pairs: warm and cool, summer and winter, big and little. I asked them to choose a pair so that we could make up a poem. They chose up and down. I told them that this time we would start and end the poem with those words and fill in with others. We would put the words in one long column, one word per line. There was an uneven number of words, for the middle word, the transition word, had to have something to do with both of the opposites. Together we talked for a short time about some possible words for the slots in the poem. I chose from among their ideas to complete the poem that follows: **Shared Writing**

Up	(Larry)
Sky,	(Joyce)
Clouds,	(Pat)
Flying,	(Mike)
Swing,	(Hilda)
Falling,	(Butch)
Dirt,	(Mitch)
Rocks,	(Steve)
Down.	(Larry)

I read their poem to them, phrasing it to make the most of the poetic elements. Notice that the middle word is the one where the transition is made between the opposites. The words from the top to the middle build images for the top word; the words from the middle down build images for the bottom word.

This month we did one of our recipes as a chart very much like the ones that are in some of the children's cookbooks that I showed to the class. They had almost all seen their mothers' cookbooks, but they had not really noticed how the recipes were written. The form we now use includes the headings *Ingredients*, *Utensils*, and *Preparation* (written with numbered steps). The recipe was for "Happy Holidays Egg Cones," a kind of egg salad that we scooped into ice cream cones. Recipes certainly help work on the essential thinking processes as we *connect* new and old cooking experiences; *review* how to prepare the food; *apply* skills as we cook different recipes; *image* how this might look, taste, feel, or smell; *organize* the directions in a logical sequence; *predict* what might be added next or what step to do next; *monitor* if the directions or proportions make sense ($\frac{1}{2}$ teaspoon or $\frac{1}{2}$ cup oil?), and *evaluate* the product.

Thinking Processes

This was one of our better experiences this year. The children learned so many things while putting together this recipe. For example, we looked at raw eggs and hard-cooked eggs and talked about how the cooking changed them from a liquid to a solid. We measured the water after the first batch of eggs had finished cooking. Evaporation was discussed when they noticed much of the water gone. This recipe format allowed the introduction of quite a few new words, such as *ingredients*. There was much more measuring than in other recipes we had tried. All in all, it did go well. It amazes me to realize the number of concepts being developed. I guess they are ready for recipes that involve heat cooking now.

Meaning Vocabulary

January

The children seemed really glad to be back at school—two weeks is a long time to be away. I find, too, that they have become bored at home and come to miss the routine we have so carefully established. Furthermore, most of them are anxious to share their holiday "goodies" with the other children. Pat got her wish and received some new books, which she assured me she could read. I asked her to bring them in and show them to us and perhaps read them to the class. Pat brought in a predictable language book, *The Napping House* (Wood,

Predictable Books

1986), that she had received for Christmas. First she read it to me, and then I let her read it to her small group.

Reading to others is one of the favorite activities of the children. It works this way: When one of the children indicates to me, as Pat did, that there is a book she would like to share with her group, I ask the group leader to get the group together. (Group leaders are appointed each month and are listed on the job chart.) The group leader informs the others in the group when they are to work together, and is also responsible for this work being turned in to me. In addition, the group leader must get the group together for special things, such as when a member of the group wants to read to them. At an appointed time the group meets and listens to the story. Most often the children "read" pictures to one another and make up a story. This story, while generally plausible, is often quite different from the original.

Children are getting the idea that what is in books should make sense to them and to others. By "pretend reading" the books over and over, many of them are even able to identify some of the words that occur over and over. Certainly the motivation of reading to their peers has helped some of the children to become more interested in reading and in words. They also are becoming exposed to a variety of book types. Anthony always brings a science book to class, so the children are learning about all sorts of real things in an expository format and not just listening to stories.

Direct Experience

There was a flood of stories from the children after our field trip to the fire station this month. *Now* everyone wants to be a firefighter! They tell gory stories about how brave firefighters save helpless women and little babies—the influence of television, I think, for the fire chief certainly did nothing that would have aroused such stories.

Our second trip, a visit to a restaurant, couldn't compare with the excitement of the trip to the fire station. The children were fascinated with the huge appliances in the kitchen, and informed the chef that they too were cooks. He asked them what they could cook and they proceeded to catalogue our entire year of cooking for him, complete with the description of the mess we had with the cranberry-orange relish!

Self-Selected Reading

SQUIRT too continues to roll along smoothly. We are up to five minutes of reading time, now. We will hold at that level for a while, since Butch and Mort are at the upper limit of their ability to sit still. Larry and Danielle, however, continue to read after the class time is up. They both are reading almost a book a day. Danielle's father told me that he thinks Danielle is such a good reader because she was in the hospital for so long after the car accident in which she was hurt and her mother was killed. Her father, the nurses, and all her visitors read constantly to her, and had her try to guess about story events, and sat beside her so that she would always see the words as they were reading.

Children with Special Needs

I am still having problems with Alexander. He often removes his hearing aid so that he can get out of work by claiming he doesn't know what to do! And of all the children, he is one of the most in need of the language activities we do. He still doesn't talk in sentences; mostly he grunts and points. I suspect he can understand more than he appears to because his mother told me that they communicate this way at home often. He points and she fetches! He is really getting to be a pill! He is so low in language because he missed so many important concepts since his hearing loss wasn't discovered until two years ago! He really has the language development of a three-year-old child. Even Paul may be ahead in this area!

I've been working hard also on visual discrimination. They really have become quite good at matching letters to one another and at being able to tell which letters are different in a row of letters. Now I will put up four words on the chalktray and they have to locate the different one and group the three that are alike to one side. I also will write selected words from our language experience charts on cards and put these cards in the chalktray. Putting my hand underneath the word *snail* on the chart, I will say, "Carl, this word is *snail*. Can you find another word that says *snail* in the chalktray? If you can, bring it here and we'll check it letter for letter." Carl, finding the word, brings it to the chart and we check first by counting how many letters are in the card he has brought and comparing that to the number of letters in the word on the chart. Next I have him check to see if the first letter looks like the first letter of the chart word; then we check the second letter, and so on. If each letter matches the letters on the chart word and all are in the same order, ta da, a match! Hooray for Carl!

Phonological Awareness

Sometimes, after I write a language experience chart, I tell the children that I am going to cover up the chart with another sheet of paper and we're going to play the "How Many Words?" game. I peek at the first sentence so that I can say it aloud to the children. As I read it to them, they are to clap with each word I say so that they can tell me how many words are in a sentence. They tell me the number (or numbers!) and I remove the paper covering so that we can count the number of words. Then I clap with them so that they have a model for what we are doing, and we do another sentence on the chart the same way.

I have also been doing a lot with listening to tell if two words are the same or different. Earlier in the year I used only two words that were very different to help them get the idea of same and different. For example, back in the fall, I would say, "Listen and tell me if I am saying the same word or if I am saying two different words." Then I would use pairs like *Hilda Hilda, Carl Anthony, story chair,* and *door lights.* With such dissimilar word choices for the "different" category, the children quickly advanced so that I could use words that were different but began or ended with the same letter. That has been tougher. Rhyming words seem particularly hard for them to label as different, so that is what we are working on right now. I will say, "Listen to these words and tell me if they are the same or different: *chair pear, juice juice, cook look, cup cup, paste paste, dot hot, cream dream, fix mix.*" If we keep plugging away, I guess they will all eventually get it. Some, of course, understand well the learnings just described. By working with small groups, I can adjust my instruction accordingly.

Shared Reading

I have been having so much fun with Big Books! Every week this year I have been sharing an enlarged-print book with the children. I began in September with familiar songs and nursery rhymes, and I am now using storybooks. As I think back on the experiences, one particularly memorable book comes to mind. I had made a book of Little Miss Muffet by using shapes to represent the characters and props: Miss Muffet was a red circle, the tuffet was a green square, the curds and whey were a yellow triangle, and the spider was a black rectangle. The book had five pages with the appropriate shapes on each page. Here's what page 3 looked like:

Predictable Books

Along came a spider

I wrote the lines of the rhyme in very large print so that children could read the book from about 12 feet away. I used white cardboard that was 18 by 24 inches. After gluing on the shapes, I laminated the book for durability.

I had also cut out pieces of felt using the same shapes so that I could retell the story on the flannel board and show children how the spider moved beside her and how Miss Muffet ran away. In addition, I had duplicated the pages so that the children could create their own small book by pasting on the appropriate shapes as we went through the story page by page. Children helped one another at each table, and I had a mother-helper in that day too. In about 45 minutes, I had gone over the story with the Big Book several times, as children joined in, and with the flannel board once, and all of the children had completed their own books. They then went to Mrs. Wright's room to read to the children there.

Literature Response Activity

Other creations like that took much less time. Now they know the process, and it really goes much faster to make the small books. I guess we must have made a half dozen or so by now. The parents really love them!

I think that Big Books and the journal writing have totally changed the way I view beginning reading instruction. Everyone can have success, and I can tell so much more easily who is acquiring which of the critical knowings.

Their favorite Big Book this month was *Brown Bear, Brown Bear* (Martin, 1970). I introduced it in the usual way by showing the cover and having them predict what the story might be about. I asked them to image with me as I conjured up the bear lumbering through the forest, lifting his nose to sniff for honey. Then I began to read the story in a fluent and expressive way. I told children that this was my turn to read, and they should not try to join in with the reading yet. They were to listen to the story first. I read each page of the book, pausing to

Predictable Books

allow them to comment on the pictures and the story line. I used a pointer to touch each word as I said it. The second time I read it, I invited children to join in when they could. By the third reading, nearly everyone was chiming in. The fourth time I asked them to try to read it without my help, and I had to step in only a few times to help them.

Shared Reading After we read the book together for three days (the other two days took much less time), I gave the children small copies that they read together in pairs. They love this part the most! They really feel like readers as they go off together to a special corner and read with a friend. I have put capable and less capable children together so that the modeling continues for those who need it. They continue to read the book with their partner until they feel very comfortable with it. At that point they read it to me, and if they do well (which means they sound fluent, not that each word is necessarily perfect), they may check the book out to take home to read to their parents and others.

Jeff burned himself during a cooking adventure the other day, so I took him over to the plant shelf, broke off a piece of a leaf, and rubbed the cut end of the leaf over the burned area. Immediately a crowd grew around the scene, fascinated children observing that the juice of the plant had made the burn feel better. "What is that?" "How did you know to do that, Miss Launch?" "Wow! Magic!"

Ah ha! The teachable moment my college teachers were always talking about! "Let's sit down and do a chart about this plant," I suggested. "Plants are really wonderful things. Not only do they look nice in our room, but some of them can be used for food, some for medicine, and some to make clothes and houses. What are some questions you have about this plant?" For the next five minutes they asked questions and I wrote those questions on the chart.

Student Research Some of their questions were related to the name and characteristics of the plant (color, size, etc.), some dealt with the care of the plant, and some concerned with how new plants were grown. After all their questions were on the chart, I cut them apart and we grouped them according to the type of question they had. Based on this grouping, I sent Danielle, Paul, and Horace to the library to bring back books on plants. I sent a note with them to Miss Page, the librarian, telling her we were trying to get information about the aloe plant. With books before us, we came up with the following chart about aloe plants.

Language Experience *The Aloe Plant*

Our plant's name is "aloe vera." (Anthony)

Aloe vera means "true aloe" because there are more than one kind of aloe. (Larry)

Aloe vera is a succulent because it has fat leaves and likes water. (Danielle)

It can grow one or two feet. (Paul)

It is all green. (Chip)

It likes lots of light. (Carl)

You can make new plants by planting the baby shoots called suckers. (Steve)

Aloe is special because it can help the burn places on you. (Jeff)

I was impressed with how much they really got into the aloe plant. Now they keep asking me if the other plants we have are special in any way. We may be making our own book about our classroom plants.

Another really successful cooking experience was tied to one of the many books I read to the children each week. I had brought in several versions of the old story "Stone Soup," and we compared how the stories were alike and how they were different. After those discussions, I told them that we were going to make some stone soup in the slow cooker. Their reactions ranged from Butch's "Yuk!" to Hilda's "How fascinating!" Everyone was told to bring in a vegetable, any vegetable, the next day.

Literature Response Activity

"But what do we need, Miss Launch? How can we cook if we don't know what we need?" asked a worried Betty.

"Well, in the book they didn't have a recipe. They just put in whatever was brought to them." That, clearly, was not very satisfying to Betty.

The next day most of the children had remembered to bring in a vegetable and Daisy brought a loaf of Italian bread! Oh, well, it should go well with the soup! Next we went out to the playground and each person was to find one small stone to put in the soup. Alex was appalled! "But they're dirty. People have been walking on them and I even saw Mort and Butch spitting on the rocks!" "Yuk too," I thought, though I dared not show it! "We will carefully wash each rock in hot, soapy water so that they are nice and clean for the soup," I told him.

And wash we did. The rocks were then placed in the bottom of the slow cooker and I added 12 cups of water and 12 beef bouillon cubes. Joyce's job was to turn the cooker to high heat.

We began role-playing the story with three children pretending to wonder what else they could put in the soup and how good it would be if only there were a carrot or two. We went through each of the vegetables the class had brought in this way. Whoever had brought the vegetable had to wash it and cut it into pieces to put it into the soup. I helped cut off the tops and bad places, but the children did most of the work. When all the veggies had been added, we put on the lid of the slow cooker and left it until nearly time to go home. Daphne gave it a stir with a big wooden spoon and put the lid on one more time. I took it home with me to continue cooking and brought it back for snack time. Needless to say, the soup was pretty good, much to Alex's amazement. Daisy's bread was just the right touch and all of the children plan to make stone soup at home with their mother's help.

February

Our poetry writing is coming along so well! I read Mary O'Neill's *Hailstones and Halibut Bones* (1990) to the children and discussed with them that O'Neill thought colors could represent things and feelings as well as thoughts. Then we did a poetry format (again as a group) that has this configuration:

Shared Writing

I feel _____

I see _____

I hear _____

I smell _____

I taste _____

I feel _____

The unifying factor here is the repetition of the phrase "I feel." To help the children recognize the five senses the poem deals with, I told them that I would give them several days to work on a collage of pictures from magazines, newspapers, and other sources that portray the five senses. They were to find as many pictures as they could that would finish the phrases I listed. It was a messy assignment, but the children helped to create several poems and collages. In addition the children were proud because the collages described *them* as individuals. I had the children work individually on this project, so I did have to help out some of the more unsure children such as Paul and Chip. Paul struggled—with my help—to find one example for each phrase; Chip kept asking the others to save any pictures of peanuts that they found for him—he wanted to finish each phrase the same way! When some of the children wondered if they could finish the phrase with just one word or a picture, I told them that they could. Others complained that they couldn't do that—they needed to say more! I told them that the only rule was that they finished the phrases, no matter how many words they used.

Process Writing The writing notebooks are, all in all, rather successful. Each child has a notebook and I ask them each to write in their notebooks for a while during their

Individual Differences work time. Some of the children still draw, but even Paul has gotten to the point where he will, if I remind him, go to one of the bulletin boards and copy down words he sees there. There is no spacing between words, he hasn't a clue what he is writing, and he frequently leaves out letters from the words he is copying. Hilda, on the other hand, has become so intrigued with her notebook that I have trouble getting her to work in the math center or go to recess! She carries it everywhere. She is attempting to write about the people around her and is learning more about letters and words with each page she fills!

Publishing Last month's interest in the plants did indeed result in a book we made for the classroom and the school library about the plants we have. Steve, who has a remarkable eye for drawing nature objects, did the illustrations. Actually, he did the outlines in pencil and then he asked certain students to do the coloring in. We made one book for our room and another for the library, since Miss Page had been so helpful when we requested information. That interest in a book on our plants caused Mitch to suggest that we make a book about the animals we have in our room. We went through the same process: What are the questions we have about our animals and how can we organize those questions?

I suggested that the first page in our book ought to be about how the animals are alike and how they are different. That way, I told them, we help people get ready to pay attention to what we want them to know. I also suggested that I work with small groups of children, one group for each animal, and one group to do the page where we compare the animals. They were agreeable, naturally, so I assigned children to groups and then pulled a piece of paper out of a box with the name of the section each group would work on. Here are the groups:

Guinea Pig	Guppies	Turtle
Alex	Betty	Alexander
Butch	Daisy	Joyce
Anthony	Hilda	Horace
Danielle	Manuel	Pat
Rita	Mort	Steve

Snail	Introduction
Carl	Chip
Jeff	Daphne
Larry	Mandy
Mike	Mitch
Paul	Roberta

It took most of the month to meet with each group, call up what they already knew, make connections about the similarities among the animals, look at and read reference materials, observe and make notes about the animals, review information, and organize it. When I told Mr. Topps that we were working on a massive project, he suggested that we duplicate the pages so that we could make enough copies for all the children to take home. Terrific! Here is what the introduction finally looked like:

THE ANIMALS IN OUR ROOM

We have many animals in our room. It is too hard to count them all because the guppies won't hold still. Besides, they keep having babies. We have four kinds of animals. We have two guinea pigs, one turtle, fourteen snails, and a lot of guppies.

Guppies are the littlest animal we have except for some of the baby snails. The next biggest animals are the snails. Our turtle is the next biggest animal, but he is much smaller than our guinea pigs.

Some of our animals have legs and some do not. Some of our animals have fur. Some of our animals have shells. Some of our animals have scaly bodies.

All of our animals need air, just like us. But the guppies and snails get their air from the water! The guinea pigs would die if they tried to breathe in the water.

All of the animals have to eat food, but their food is real different. People could not eat guppy food and guppies might get sick if they ate people food. Guinea pigs like vegetables even more than we do!

If you like to read about animals, you will like this book. It tells about all of our animals.

This month was our turn to schedule the school computers in the library. **Computers** Many of the classes have their own computers, but additional ones can be scheduled through Miss Page. There are several games they like to play on the computer. I'm just sorry there aren't more of the better quality materials for young children. There really are very few pieces of software that do what I want to do with the knowings. But this period will accomplish the goal of helping them feel comfortable with computers.

I have been doing some interesting kinds of listening comprehension lessons with the children recently. Sue Port, the curriculum supervisor, was in last month and complimented me on the way I asked children to use the essential thinking processes as I read through a story. She really liked relating the listening to those processes. But, she said, what about Paul and Chip and some of the others who never contributed to the discussion? It was clear that children like Larry and Danielle were dominating the discussions. I told her that this had concerned me too. "Give me a week," she said. "I've got an idea for another way to use those thinking processes that I'd like you to try out."

Think Links   Well! Sue Port's idea has revolutionized my classroom listening lessons. She told me that she wanted to try out a "Think Link." In Think Links the teacher models what she is thinking about by talking through the story, stopping at appropriate places to tell children which of the essential thinking processes were triggered by the text. In this way, children like Paul and Chip can get an insight into *how* people think, not just *what* they think. She asked if she could model a story with my class.

Sue Port began her lesson by telling the children that when they went on to first grade, people were going to be asking them to tell about things they were reading. She wanted to show them how she understood things she was reading by reading a story and telling them what her mind was thinking about throughout. She showed them the cover of *Swimmy* (Lionni, 1970) and said:

> This book is called *Swimmy*, and it is by Leo Lionni. I know that I am probably going to like this book because I have liked other books by him. If I went into the library and found this book, I might pick it up and look at the cover and think, "Hmmm. *Swimmy*. I see a fish on the cover and since fish swim, I'll bet that's the name of the fish in this story. I wonder where the fish lives. Maybe a river. Maybe a lake. Maybe this fish lives in the ocean. Maybe Swimmy is a pet. I don't know yet if the fish is a girl or boy. I'd guess, though, that it's a make-believe story because Lionni writes a lot of make-believe stories."

She continued to go through each page of the book with the children, talking about "what is going on in my mind" as she read the text and looked at the pictures. I was particularly intrigued by her imaging with the children, because I had found that to be the hardest of the essential thinking processes for me to use with children. After reading about Swimmy's family being eaten and Swimmy going off on his own, she said:

> I can just see Swimmy gliding through the water, slowly, sadly. His little tail is hardly swishing at all. Close your eyes. Can you see him swimming? Ooooh! The water is getting colder as he goes deeper. I'm shivering as I feel that cold water all around his body. Can you feel it? Close your eyes. Feel that cold water. Are you shivering?

The children responded so well to what she was doing. Mike even said, "So that's how Larry knows so much! His brain is thinking of stuff!" As we talked later, Sue told me that she did not cover all of the thinking processes because not all of them were appropriate for that story. In fact, she really spent most of her Think Link on imaging and predicting, because the story fit those two quite well.

After she left, I dug out some stories I had planned to use with the children and developed a skeleton of a Think Link for several of them. I plan to do Think Links once a week.

The favorite cooking experience this month was making whole-wheat pretzels. Children shaped the dough into letter names they knew and baked them. What fun and what motivation! Even Mort seemed to want to learn some more letters so he could make more pretzels.

March

An odd thing has been happening to me recently. I noticed that I don't even look at my knowings in the front of my plan book anymore. It has become so automatic to think of everything we do in terms of my knowings that I was well into the preparation of the cards for a game when it suddenly occurred to me that this simple game was facilitating some of my seven ingredients. In fact, all around me are opportunities to exploit learning!

I started this month with a game that the children really enjoyed. I told the children that we would be playing a game that might take all morning to finish, but that it didn't matter because they could play the game while they worked.

Surprise, surprise! Each child was going to have the picture of an animal pinned on his or her back, and they were to guess the animal. They could ask only two questions of each classmate, and the questions could only be answered yes or no. The purpose of this restriction was to encourage a maximum use of language on the part of the one guessing and to discourage unnecessary hints and clues. The children seemed very excited by the idea and were ready to begin immediately! I reminded them that they were to continue their work while trying to guess and that it would be a good idea to think carefully before asking questions so that the questions wouldn't be wasted. I gave the following demonstration: "Mandy, will you please pin the picture of an animal to my back?" She did so, and I turned so that my back—and the picture—were toward the children. There was much giggling from some of the children.

"Okay. Steve, do I have hair? No? Hmmmm. Steve, do I have six legs? No? Thank you. Let's see now—Rita, do I have wings? No. All right, do I have scales? Ah ha! Now we're getting someplace. Mandy, do people catch me to eat? No, that means that I'm not a fish. Do I crawl? I thought I might. Horace, am I a snake?"

The children were amazed that I guessed the animal so quickly. I explained that animals are in groups and that I was trying to find which group my animal was in. One large group that includes bears, cats, dogs, beavers, and people was the one I was asking about first—they all have fur or hair. When I knew

Thinking Processes

that the animal didn't have fur or hair, I knew that it had to be an insect or an amphibian (living both on land and in water) or a bird or a reptile (an animal with scales). "Listen carefully" was my last injunction before pinning on the animals. And the game was on! Larry, Hilda, Roberta, and Steve guessed theirs rather quickly, for they had paid attention to what was told to them and tried logically to figure out what to ask next. Daisy used up all her questions by running from person to person asking questions like "Am I a deer? Am I a goat?" rather than trying to find the category and proceed logically. It took most of the children the entire morning to determine what they were. Paul managed to find out that he was a dog, though his guess was based on luck rather than system. Mitch never figured his out because he kept trying to start arguments with those who answered his questions. He wanted so much to own a horse that he was convinced that a horse must be the animal pictured on his back. Whenever the children would give him an answer that didn't fit his mind-set, he would argue with them, insisting that they must be wrong! Carl guessed "deer" fairly early, partially, I think, because he likes deer so much. And so it went—an interesting exercise for the children. They've already asked to play it again soon.

So many things are going on with this particular activity. Children are engaging in an identifying-sorting-classifying game that helps to develop further their understanding of animals and animal characteristics. They are developing logical thinking processes as they work on this background information. I think I'll do this again next week with forms of transportation or foods.

Letter Names   The children have been working all year on matching uppercase letters to uppercase letters, and recently they have been matching lowercase letters to lowercase letters. At last we're ready to begin matching upper- and lowercase letters. One of my tricks is to tell them that while they were outside an elf came in and mixed up all those nice letters we had been playing with—could anyone help us to get them straightened out again? Of course, there are always several volunteers! We concentrate on three pairs at a time, which is a workable number for them. Also, I always begin with those upper- and lowercase letters that tend to resemble one another except for size (such as *Ss*) to further ensure success.

I also play a game of "Memory" with the letters that we are currently working on. I shuffle the six letter-cards and place them face down in a two-by-three array. The children take turns selecting two of the letter cards to be revealed. They are then turned over. If they match, they keep the cards. If they do not match, the cards are turned back over to be chosen at a later time by someone who can remember the position of the letters.

Another game for group work after all of the upper- and lowercase letters have been studied is a game like "Go Fish." We have two different groups of cards, one each for upper- and lowercase. The cards are shuffled together, and three cards are dealt to each player. If the player has a match of letter forms, the cards are put on the table. After everyone is given a chance to do this, the player to the left of the dealer asks another player if he or she has a particular letter. If the answer is yes, the card must be relinquished. The player continues to ask for cards until he is told to "Go Fish" by a player who doesn't have the card asked for. The first player then picks a card from the remainder of the deck, which has been placed in the center of the playing area. The first player to have all his or her cards matched and on the table is the winner.

An individual activity for matching is played with the bottom of an old ditto master box. All 26 letters of the alphabet, uppercase form, are written on the bottom of the box. The lowercase forms are on separate cards that can be placed over the uppercase forms. In the lid of the box is the answer key showing which forms match, so that children can check their own work and correct errors immediately.

I have begun to check letter name knowledge with the children too. I have been calling them to me one at a time and showing letter cards with both the upper- and lowercase on the same card and asking the children to name the letter. I use a system of putting the known and the unknown in separate piles. Later, then, I write down on that child's card which letters he or she still doesn't know so that I can begin direct instruction. Up to this point, the letter names that the children have learned have been through exposure to lists of their classmates' names, letters and words they have matched on the chart stories, and writing in their notebooks. Eleven of the alphabet letters were easily learned by most of the children just because those letters begin the names of the 25 children. Paul is the only child who knows only two letters: *P* and *C* (for Paul and Carl). Larry, Danielle, Pat, Roberta, Hilda, Joyce, and Mandy can name all the letters. Rita, Betty, Horace, Alex, Steve, and Anthony know most of the letter names with the exception of the less frequent ones like *Q*, *U*, *V*, *X*, *Y*, and *Z*, at least in the words we have been using. The other children are at varying points in the number of letters they can name.

I used to begin in September to teach the names of the letters to the kindergartners in my class. Boy, what a frustrating experience both for them and for me! Trying to associate the names of the letters with those funny-shaped symbols that could be called different things depending on how they were turned (*b*, *d*, *p*, and *q*) drove them and me buggy! When I tried to make it easy on myself by teaching everybody every letter, starting with *Aa*, many of the children were terrifically bored and an equal number just couldn't quite get it. I began to notice that on their own many children would go to one of the labels on objects in the room or to the list of children's names and ask someone what the name of the letter was. It occurred to me that such opportunities could be expanded and encouraged without actually trying to teach the names of letters until later in the year. I find that by starting now to assess where the children are in letter name knowledge, I still have plenty of time to teach the names of the letters to those who can learn them. Even if I began teaching them systematically to Paul in September, I cannot imagine that he would be further ahead in the number known. I am convinced that by now he would have a real sense of failure because of his inability to learn the letters, had I taught them. As it is, now he doesn't know them all, but at least he is receptive to learning them.

Anthony's mother has been riding me all year about making sure that I am teaching the children all they need to know to go into first grade. She and I have had a few points of departure this year in our assessments of his abilities.

Assessment

He is her brilliant, only child and she wants to make certain that he will be ready to attend M.I.T. when the time comes! She has been taking books home from the school she teaches in for him to read with her. No wonder he is so intractable some mornings. She had told me that they have one hour of reading every night, and that she has been having him copy the words he doesn't know over and over. I told her that he had many opportunities and materials to explore and read at school. However, since he is so focused on science she feels that we are not providing enough science stuff here. I haven't been able to budge her or she me. Oh, well!

Self-Selected Reading

Things are not going badly at all. SQUIRT is up to seven minutes and the children are still writing in their notebooks. Some of the children have been going through the collection of recipes we have made this year and copying those recipes into their notebooks. Other students have been writing stories about events in their lives. Steve and Anthony have been trying some science experiments and writing down what they do and how it turns out (I am unable to read most of it, but they generously share what their markings mean).

The third graders from Mrs. Wise's class have been writing books for the children as well as coming down to take dictation so that the kindergartners can get *their* stories into print as well. The third graders have been studying bookbinding and have made some very handsome books for the children to take home or to put in our classroom library. To thank them for all their help, we invited them to come help us eat the peanut butter cookies we made. However, we bought our peanut butter. Do you know how long it takes to *make* three cups of peanut butter?

April

Spring, spring, spring!!! I love it. We've been outside a lot lately, which has been good for the children as well as for me. We do some of our work out there when we can, such as our lesson with rhyming words for which I use one of my favorite books, *The Hungry Thing* (Slepian & Seidler, 1971). The children in the book meet the Hungry Thing and find that he will eat only silly rhymes for real words, so that if they want to feed him "noodles," they tell him he is eating "foodles"; "soup with a cracker" is "boop with a smacker," and so on. As we read the story, the children try to guess what the Hungry Thing is eating throughout the book. When we finish the book I tell them it is our turn to feed the Hungry Thing. I tell them to think of their favorite food and then to try to find a silly rhyme for it so that the Hungry Thing will eat it. It's fun to play with words, and if children realize this when they are small, I think they will be more likely to enjoy words as they grow up.

Phonological Awareness

Shared Writing

The poetry we composed this month used an "I wish" format. I told the children that they were to think of four different things they wished for. The poem was to have lines beginning with the words *I wish,* but the first and the last lines were to be identical. Here is the large-group poem that we did before breaking up into small groups for more poetry writing using this format.

I wish spring was here. (Steve)
I wish that the sun was warm. (Manuel)
I wish that the frogs would make noises. (Butch)
I wish I could go out without my coat. (Alex)
I wish spring was here. (Steve)

The children have been creating greeting cards all year long, but some of the birthday cards for Jeff were just too much! Someone got the notion that even if he couldn't give Jeff a present, he could *wish* to give him a present. I don't know who began it, but children began to write things such as "I wish you could have this" with their invented spellings. Some children became the "experts" at the table, offering their help to those who wanted to write messages. In walking around later, I noticed that they were cutting pictures out of our catalogues and magazines. The picture of a bike, swimming pool, motorcycle, or some other luxury would appear at the bottom of the written message, which was then passed over to Jeff for his birthday. Jeff was grinning from ear to ear all day long!

Focused Writing

Each of these activities has children using whole words, but I find that they are increasing in their ability to name the letters and are becoming quite proficient with rhyming games. All around the four walls of the classroom are the upper- and lowercase alphabet letters to which I have added a picture for consonants and the names of various children and classroom pets where they are appropriate. I decided not to put pictures up for the vowels since the vowel sounds are so variable and I would need so many for each chart. Occasionally I will put up some highly interesting word (such as *cookie*) from our language experience stories. I have also added a "silly sentence" for each of the consonants. For example, by *Mm* I have written "My mom makes marshmallow munchies" and by *Ss*, "Steve saw seven silly seals." They like to play with the sentences as tongue twisters, and these also help children begin to associate a sound with a letter form in a more natural way than practicing on worksheets.

Letter Sounds

Also I am still trying to help the children develop their reasoning and questioning abilities by such things as the "feely" box. I have constructed the feely box by cutting a hole in one end of a shoebox and attaching to the hole a sock with the toe end cut off. I placed a comb in the box and permitted the children to reach in through the sock and into the box where they could feel the object but not see it. Each child was permitted a few seconds to feel the object and then report what the object might be. I changed the objects frequently so that the children would have many opportunities to use the sense of touch. The next project was somewhat harder for the children, for I had arranged the experiences in order of difficulty. This time a single child would feel the object, describe it in three different ways, and then guess what it was. The third kind of experience was to let a child see an object, describe it to the other children, and let *them* guess what was being described. The fourth task was even more complicated, for this time the child felt an object, described it to the other children, and they had to guess what it was that he or she had felt. Occasionally, as a variation, I would let several children feel the same object so that they could help one

Thinking Processes

another with the description. The rest of the group had to try to guess what it was that was being felt. This worked out very well, particularly when Paul, Chip, or Joyce, who have a great deal of difficulty verbalizing, described the object. However, it is obviously easier for the group if the clues are clearly stated, a skill these three were unable to demonstrate yet.

The three gained from listening to the descriptions given by the more verbal children, however, for they experienced the same object and could compare their own perceptions with what was being said. The fifth task with the feely box was to have a child feel an object and then give a one-word clue, and so on. A particularly interesting game was one that took place this week. Steve reached into the box and felt the object. He said, "Prickly." There were guesses of *porcupine, cactus,* and *pins.* The next clue was, "Woody." The children were stumped for a moment, until Larry guessed that it might be a plank from the workshop. The next clue: "Tree." Something from a tree that is wooden and prickly?

"Oh, I know, I know!" exclaimed Hilda, who had been putting all the clues together. "It's bark from the tree!" She sat back smug and confident.

"No, that's not it. 'Seeds.' "

The crestfallen Hilda began muttering, "Seeds? Seeds. Seeds! It's a pine cone! Am I right this time, Steve?" Steve's nod reassured her that her deduction skills had been well utilized.

The most difficult of all was the last project—identifying the object within a wrapped box by asking questions of me. They found this to be a very challenging task. They knew that it could not be a chair, for instance, for the package would not accommodate that large an object. The questioning techniques of the children had increased with the readiness activities that they had been doing for the few weeks prior to this exercise, and they did guess that the object was a shoe. I got the idea for this project from one of the other kindergarten teachers at a recent meeting. The teacher said she had presented a wrapped package to the children for them to determine the contents. The task was too difficult for them because they had not had exercises leading up to this game. As a result, the children were unable to figure out what was in the box, the teacher was frustrated and embarrassed, and she had tried to figure out what had gone wrong. She concluded that the activity was incomplete and useless until she set up the other activities.

We went back to some individual recipes this month for a change. The children made "Ants on a Log" by cutting celery using a premeasured length and then filling the hole with peanut butter and putting on the ants (raisins). A great snack and E A S Y, even for Paul at this point.

May

Direct Experience We had two really nice field trips this month. The trips were preceded, as usual, with a listing of words they could think of that were associated with the location. We also generated questions for the inevitable question period guides always have. Afterward, we did a whole-group language experience lesson and some children dictated or wrote individual remembrances. Same old stuff we always do prior to and following these trips, but such activities are crucial to concept development.

The first was a day trip to the zoo with the children as well as many parents. They took sack lunches. Everyone returned exhausted but exhilarated (and only a few of the children got sick on the bus).

For the last field trip, I asked the two first-grade teachers if they would permit our children to visit their rooms to acquaint them with the teachers and also to give them some idea of what they could expect to see in first grade. Both teachers agreed and gave the children a fine overview of the first-grade program. Mrs. Wright had one of her students act as guide around the room, and she had others who explained the various things that they were working on. The kindergartners were quite impressed with the "big" first graders who were so helpful to them, and all of them said that they wanted to be in Mrs. Wright's room next year.

After the children had finished their tour, I asked them how they would feel about doing something similar for the kindergarten class who would be arriving next fall.

"You mean you're going to have *more* kids here? I thought you just taught us," said Daphne.

"Now you know that there is going to be another group here. Remember the recent kindergarten round-up?"

"Yes, but we thought . . . I thought . . . I mean . . ."

"I will remember all of you. You don't have to worry about that. We care about one another, and when we care about people, we don't forget them. But you can't stay with me forever. You are ready to go on and learn more. You don't want to do the same things again. First grade is so exciting! You'll love it, but remember to say hello to me once in a while! But you still haven't answered. Shall we do something for the next kindergarten class like what the first graders did?" Amid cries of "Yes! Yes!" there was one, Larry, who commented that that would be difficult, since we didn't know who the children would be.

"How about this?" I began, and outlined the plan for creating a mural depicting the various kindergarten activities. The children would put it up on the bulletin board and leave it there. When fall came the new students would see some work done by "big" kindergartners telling them what to expect. The children loved the idea, and so did I. One of my pet peeves has always been that I begin the school year without any artwork from children on the walls—now there will be.

SQUIRT has been highly successful this year. We're up to eight minutes a day as a class. However, some children continue reading after the timer rings. Mandy told me that she enjoys the idea of everyone reading at the same time. **Self-Selected Reading**

I dragged out a bedsheet from which I made a replica of a computer keyboard. **Computers**
I put it on the floor, and we played games of hopping from letter to letter to spell our own names and other words from the words on the walls. They need to become somewhat familiar with the keyboard because I know that the teachers

in this school do a lot with computers. At least they'll have some idea of where the letters are when they sit down to work on the computer next year.

Predictable Books

The Big Books continue to be popular reading material with the children, and their favorite Big Books are the ones we made that were parallel to stories read in class. We wrote a version of *The Three Little Kittens* called *The Three Little Goats* who had lost their boats. They came up with some very nice ideas. I put it on the large cardboard and let the children illustrate the book. They worked in small groups so that every child got to add something to the book. We went through the same process with their book that we had done with the others, practicing it together before they read it to a partner. Although we had no small versions, the children seemed to love lying on the floor, turning the Big Book pages. Some children did, however, make their own copies to take home, laboriously copying the words from the Big Book.

Think Links

I have found that I can do Think Links almost without thinking. It seems very easy to me now to examine a book for which one of the thinking processes can be highlighted and then to talk my way through the book. I have also found that by varying the kinds of materials I read—magazine articles with animal facts, social studies books, poems, and stories—I have thoroughly covered all of the thinking processes by this time. By now I have begun asking the children at several points to tell me what they are thinking and what caused them to have that thought. Even Chip and Alex are doing well with this now. Daisy is still too scattered with all of her thinking to be able to explain her ideas clearly.

I did decide to risk making a meal at school and it actually came off well! I had considered an early lunch for them to prepare, but I decided after one of our book sessions that nothing would do but to fix breakfast. The impetus for this decision, as you might have guessed, was Dr. Seuss's *Green Eggs and Ham* (1960)! The room was set up in stations for the big event. There was the measuring and mixing area, the scrambled eggs area, the toast area, the juice and milk area, and the cleanup area. Five children were in each of the areas, with clearly defined responsibilities.

Literature Response Activity

The scrambled egg recipe was quite easy, although it did involve some high-level counting skills. For each person to be served, they measured and mixed: 1 egg, 1 tbsp. milk, and 2 tsp. diced ham. When it was all mixed together, they added the special ingredient: $1/2$ tsp. blue food coloring! (We had quite a discussion about what color we should add to the yellow eggs.) The eggs were cooked in three electric skillets at the scrambled eggs area. Many cries of "Yuk!" and "Gross!" were heard and brought others to the scrambled eggs area to exclaim anew at the mess they saw before them.

Meanwhile, the people in "juice and milk" were pouring out servings into paper cups and the people in "toast" were making four slices at a time. After the toast came out of the appliance, they used a plastic glass and pressed the top into the slice of toast, cutting out a circle. They made two heaps of toast: circles and slices with holes. The cleanup people, who would not have anything to do until after the breakfast was over, came to the toast area and placed one circle and one slice on each one of the paper plates. They carried the plates to "scrambled eggs," where a spoonful of green eggs and ham was put into the hole of the bread slice. They got their beverages and then their plates, and we all ate heartily! I didn't think Chip would ever stop eating, and I was sure that Daisy wouldn't, though she informed us that she had a huge breakfast before arriving at school! Even Mort seemed to show a flicker of interest—I suppose because it was not our normal routine (he seems so bored by routine).

My routine, lately, has involved sorting out materials and tossing away some of the accumulation. In doing so, I came across my very tattered copy of the critical knowings. I looked over the list yet again and thought back over all the activities I had been led to do using those seven factors as my guideline. I did indeed have children using shared book experiences and lots of writing. They dictated all sorts of language experiences to me. I read to them and talked with them a lot. Many of the activities, such as the writing notebooks, fulfilled several of my goals at the same time. I wonder if it is possible to delineate all of the learnings that occurred in this room this year, or is there such an interaction of children, needs, and knowings that it would not be possible to construct two-dimensionally? I think I'll leave that one for contemplation at my beach retreat this summer!

THE CURRICULUM COMMITTEE

Miss Launch sat at the large, oval table, trying to restrain herself from tapping her pencil on the tabletop. She had been sitting at this table every week for the last three months. Miss Launch had been very quiet during these meetings, feeling that as the newcomer she should allow those who had been with the school system longer to do most of the talking.

As nearly as she could tell, the group of kindergarten teachers, all of those who taught in the school system, were divided into three general groups. Miss Launch felt sorry for Sue Port, the curriculum supervisor, who had to chair the meetings. She had always found Ms. Port very facilitative and helpful. But these meetings must surely be a strain on her good nature!

"All right, people," interrupted Ms. Port, "let's try to get some consensus on this matter. Let me summarize what we have all agreed on!" There was general laughter around the room, since they all knew that this would be a short summary!

"Our curriculum guide is fifteen years old and though it has some good aspects to it, it seems that some of the information and guidelines are outdated. It also seems that the guide is better the longer you have taught! This indicates to us that the guide is not very helpful to beginning teachers, since more experienced teachers have to fill in with materials and knowledge they already possess—not a problem for them, but it surely is to some others. The feeling among many of you is that you like the, shall we say, vagueness of the present guide since it allows a lot of freedom for individual teaching styles. But there is no choice, which is what I've been trying to get through to you these past many weeks; we are mandated by the school board to produce a new curriculum guide by the end of the summer. Frankly, I'm getting worried! I see three factions in this group. Let me outline them for you so that we can try to bring this together today.

"We have one group of teachers who would like us to purchase one or more of the kits on the market. This group argues that the kits are complete with materials, teacher's guide, and objectives. I brought a few examples of kits today so that we could examine them more closely.

"Another group seems to want to develop a new curriculum guide that will be a kind of super teacher's manual and to meet through the summer over salad lunches to put together the materials you'll need for the first few weeks. We would then meet regularly during the school year to produce additional materials and to add to the teacher's manual based on the actual teaching done with it.

"The third group is inclined to forget the whole thing"—she paused as laughter interrupted—"but knowing we can't, they would like us to add a couple of things to the old guide and then ignore it so that they can continue teaching as they have always done."

"Wow," thought Miss Launch, "she's not pulling any punches today!"

"That's not quite fair," spoke up the most vocal member of the third group. "We have been teaching for a long time and nobody seems to have complained about what we've been doing. Why change now just to be changing? I know for sure that I can do a better job with the children I teach than if you made me use one of those kits over there! Those kits don't contain all the aspects that I deal with in my program."

"You know, Willa," said Ms. Port, "you just might be able to pull off the greatest program in the world. However, much as I'd like to think it, this school system just is not filled with Willa Tichners. What about some of our teachers who just got out of college? What about teachers like Helen Launch who came to this school system from another, very different one? Don't we owe those people a chance to share in your expertise?

"One problem we face is that we have to have some consistency within our school system so that kindergarten means essentially the same thing no matter where one goes. Why, even within the same school I've noted great differences, substantive differences, in the kindergarten program. Another fact to face is that the instruction in kindergarten should help to facilitate the child's beginning reading experiences, not hinder them. If we have some common goals toward which we are all working, then we should be facilitating beginning reading. Right now, we only hope we are. We have some ideas about specific teaching emphases based on our experiences with the spring kindergarten screening we do. However, I've always felt *that* information is somewhat suspect because the situation in which the children are assessed is so strange to them. They are taken into a big room, the cafeteria or gym, and meet with many different people to perform many different tasks. You all know how hard it is to get a five-year-old to perform on command! So we know if they can see or hear, but I wonder how much valid information we get on their academic knowledge.

"I'm open to suggestion as to where we go from here. Yes, Helen, is that your hand I see?"

"Well, I've kept rather quiet through all of these discussions, but I wonder if

I might be able to offer, just as a starting point, the guidelines I used to help me teach this year. Maybe we could look at the kits up there using these objectives, so that at least we would all be talking about the same things."

With Ms. Port's encouragement, Miss Launch put the seven critical knowings on the chalkboard in the room and then sat down and discussed each of them briefly. She noticed murmurs and nods of agreement among teachers from all three factions. No one could argue against any of them, since they did seem to be essential to beginning reading success. However, the discussion did turn lively when they began to examine the kits, using the knowings as guidelines!

"Hey, where are all the books? If we are to encourage children to read and listen to a variety of materials, and to immerse them in books so that they develop a desire to learn to read, then we're going to need more books than the five they have in this kit. Five books is an insult! Why put in any?"

"Look how flimsy all this stuff is! My kids would have these thin cardboard pictures destroyed in a week, even though they're pretty careful. And those puppets! Do you believe they are trying to pawn those off for classroom use? I give them three days!"

"Speaking of the pictures, just look at them closely. What's that a picture of? A dog? A beagle? A puppy? Pet? Stuffed animal? It's really hard to tell. The pictures are small and not very clear, too much distraction in them."

"Listen to this manual, you guys. This whole kit as well as the other two really hit phonics hard! These are not whole-language kits like their ads say; they're phonics stuff! And it's not even as good as the phonics materials I make on my own; this is too hard for my students and they need a lot more repetition than these kits provide for. It says here we can 'add additional materials' from our own sources, if necessary! I thought this was supposed to be complete?"

These comments continued for some minutes as the teachers found that even with their aura of professionalism, the kits were not complete sets of materials that would make teaching a breeze for the school year, and more important, they didn't even come close to providing for all the learnings that adherence to Miss Launch's seven knowings called for. Ultimately, it was clear to Ms. Port that the consensus had indeed been found. Though much discussion about the details of pulling off the new curriculum guide remained to be gone through, basically the teachers agreed that Miss Launch's seven knowings should be the core of the new curriculum guide. They realized that they could produce their own curriculum, which would be much more complete than the kits they could purchase for the same money.

Miss Launch and Ms. Port left the room together, the last of the group to trail out. "Thank you for your help today," said Ms. Port. "I think they see now that good learning and teaching can't be totally packaged nor can it exist without structure. That was the breakthrough today. You've left your mark on this school system. I'm glad you're one of us!"

Miss Launch waved to the departing back of the smiling Ms. Port, marveling at what she had just said. "Me? I left a mark? I'm just trying to teach some kids the best way I know how."

ADD TO YOUR JOURNAL

Think back to when you were in kindergarten and to any kindergartens you have observed or taught in. Compare what you experienced with what you read in Miss Launch's journal. Think about the seven critical knowings: (1) what reading and writing are for; (2) background knowledge and concepts; (3) phonological awareness; (4) some letter names and sounds; (5) print conventions and jargon; (6) 20 to 30 concrete words; and (7) desire to learn to read and write. How well did Miss Launch develop each? How did her multifaceted curriculum—reading to children, shared reading, shared writing, language experience, writing, field trips, cooking, centers, games, and so forth—support the development of these critical understandings? How does Miss Launch's style match your style? What parts of her program and style would you like to make our own and which things would you change? If you were suddenly transported into Miss Launch's classroom to teach this class of children, what would you do the same and what would you do differently?

Children's Books/Materials Cited

The All-Around Pumpkin Book, by M. Cuyler, Scholastic, 1980.
Brown Bear, Brown Bear, What Do You See? by Bill Martin, Holt, Rinehart, & Winston, 1970.
The Elephant's Nest, by M. R. Burton, Harcourt Brace Jovanovich, 1979.
Flicks, by Tomie de Paola, Harcourt Brace Jovanovich, 1983.
Frederick, by Leo Lionni, Knopf/Pantheon, 1970.
Green Eggs and Ham, by Dr. Seuss, Random House, 1960.
Hailstones and Halibut Bones, by Mary O'Neill, Doubleday, 1990.
The Hungry Thing, by J. B. Slepian & A. G. Seidler, Scholastic, 1971.
Mushroom in the Rain, by Mirra Ginsburg, Scholastic, 1974.
The Napping House, by A. Wood, Harcourt Brace Jovanovich, 1986.
Swimmy, by Leo Lionni, Knopf Books for Young Readers, 1970.
The Taming of the C.A.N.D.Y. Monster, by V. Lansky, Book Peddlers, 1978.
Where the Wild Things Are, by Maurice Sendak, HarperCollins, 1963.

Mrs. Wright: First Grade

THE PARENT MEETING

Mrs. Wright sat in her first-grade classroom awaiting the arrival of the parents for their orientation meeting. She remembered how nervous she had been at her first parent meeting years ago and, while there was still a little nervous flutter in her stomach, she had learned to approach these meetings with confidence. "The parents all want the best for their children," she reminded herself, "and I have learned so much since that first year about how to teach them." Mrs. Wright felt particularly confident and excited about this year because last year she had phased in a four-block approach to reading and writing that had resulted in accelerated progress for both her top and her bottom students. She had worked out the "bugs" in this combination approach and was beginning this year with a clear sense of how she would organize and what she might accomplish. Tonight, she hoped to explain to the parents, in simple terms, what this four-block approach was and how it would benefit all their children.

The first parents began to arrive and Mrs. Wright rose to greet them and make sure they all put on name tags. She recognized several parents whose older children she had taught and chatted with them for a minute about how these children were doing. As the parents introduced themselves and put on their name tags, she found herself noticing how like and unlike some of their children they were. Daphne's grandmother was there, and Mrs. Wright understood where Daphne got her nurturing, caretaking ways from. Chip's grandfather came and he, just like Chip, was clean and presentable but dressed in old, threadbare clothes. Mike's father came and paced around restlessly, and Mrs. Wright could picture his constantly-in-motion son. Betty and Roberta's mother came, and Mrs. Wright could account for Betty's neat, orderly, pleasing style. She wondered if Roberta took after her father! Thinking about what different personalities these twins had reaffirmed Mrs. Wright's belief that children come with their own personalities and do not all learn in the same way.

Individual Differences

When everyone appeared to be there—Paul, Butch, and Alexander, three of her students she was most concerned about, had no parent or other relative present—Mrs. Wright began the meeting.

"I am just delighted that you took time out from your hectic schedules to be here tonight. School has been in session only a week but your children and I are already hard at work here in our classroom. My goal is that all your children will learn to read and write and do math and learn more about the world in which we live. Accomplishing this with a diverse class of twenty-five children will take all our best efforts. Your making the effort to be here tonight lets me know that your children and the school have your support, and I will do my very best to teach all your children and keep you informed of their progress.

Scheduling

"In this classroom, time is like money. There is never enough of it and you have to think carefully about what you are going to do with it if you want the best return. I would like you to look at our schedule, which is posted on this chart, and when I explain to you what happens during each of these blocks of time, I think you will understand all we have to accomplish and how hard we will be working each day.

First-Grade Schedule

8:30– 8:45	Morning Meeting/Planning for the day
8:45– 9:20	Writers' Workshop
9:20– 9:50	Working with Words
9:50–10:10	Break/Recess
10:10–10:45	Guided Reading Lessons
10:45–11:30	Math
11:30–12:00	Lunch
12:00–12:15	Rest/Quiet Time
12:15– 1:00	Science or Social Studies Unit
1:00– 1:30	Specials—P. E., Music, Library, Spanish
1:30– 2:00	Teacher Read-Aloud/SQUIRT
2:00– 2:15	Summary/Review/Prepare to go home
2:15– 2:45/3:00	Centers

Pointing to each of the time slots, Mrs. Wright explained what happened in each of these and what they were intended to accomplish.

"Although some children are in the room earlier, we start our official day at eight-thirty. The children check in when they arrive and indicate their lunch choices, so we don't waste time with attendance and so forth. In the first fifteen minutes, I try to accomplish a number of goals. We always do some activities with our calendar, determining what day and month it is, counting the number of days to certain special days, and so on. This may seem simple enough to you, but many first-grade children are still unsure of important time concepts like days of the week, months, and seasons. We then look at our daily schedule and we move the hands of this big clock to show what time we will do each activity. If there are any changes in our normal schedule, I point these out to the children and write them on a Post-it note that I attach to our schedule. Starting out each morning by orienting ourselves in this way helps the children have a real sense of orderliness and allays any fears they might have that we might forget one of the important parts of the day like recess or lunch or centers! It also gives us lots of opportunities to use math in real situations as we count days, months, and so on and work with the important first-grade math concept of telling time. We usually end this opening meeting by singing a favorite song, reciting a favorite rhyme, and doing a favorite finger play.

"At eight-forty-five, we begin Writers' Workshop. Daily writing is a very important part of how children learn to write, and writing is also a major way in which children become readers. Each day, I write something while the children watch me write. Then the children write. Right now, we are in what I call the 'driting' stage. The children both draw and write, often intermixing the two. I model this for them by drawing something each day and writing a little something to go with my drawing. Here is the driting I did this morning. [Mrs. Wright put a large piece of drawing paper with a drawing and a few word labels on the board. Parents chuckled when they saw her artwork!]

Process Writing

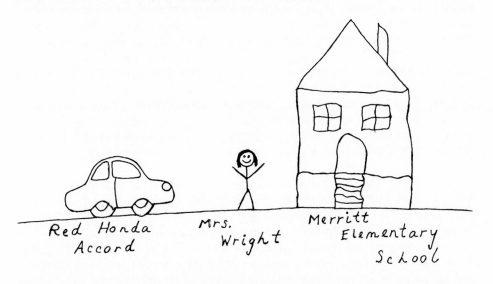

"As you can tell, my drawing skills are limited, but I try to turn this disadvantage into an advantage. My children never tell me that they can't draw because they know that they can all do as well—and many better—than I do.

"After I draw and write a few words and tell the children about my driting, they all get a piece of drawing paper and they 'drite' something they want to tell about. I go around and encourage them but I don't spell or write words for them. If they want to write a word, I encourage them to put down all the letters they hear and write it just so that they can remember what they want to tell about."

At this point, Mrs. Wright was interrupted by Roberta and Betty's mother, who said, "Mrs. Wright, this is something I have been worrying about. Betty told me that she wouldn't write because she can't spell all the words, and Roberta says that it doesn't matter if you spell them right as long as you know what you are saying. They are always fussing about this when they come home with their driting and I don't know what to tell them. I always spell words for them at home. How are they going to learn to spell if no one spells words for them?"

Several parents were nodding their heads in agreement and Mrs. Wright realized she would have to try to convince them that invented spelling was an important part of learning to spell correctly.

Invented Spelling

"I know that for many of you, letting the children spell words by putting down the letters they hear seems strange. That is certainly not the way things were done when I was in school and not the way I taught just a few years ago. But research has shown that children who are encouraged to put down the letters they hear as they are writing write more and better pieces and become better at sounding out words when they are reading. Think about it—if your child is trying to write *motorcycle* and says *motorcycle* slowly, listening for the sounds in *motorcycle*, he might end up writing **morsk**, which is not *motorcycle* but does have many of the letters heard in *motorcycle*. The difficulty with teaching children to use phonics to figure out words is not in teaching them the sounds made by letters but in actually getting them to use what they know about letters and sounds when they are reading and writing. Children who invent spell as they write are using the phonics they are learning, and both the research and my experience during the last few years confirm that they write more and become better at figuring out how to read and spell unknown words. I can assure you that your children will not spell *motorcycle* **morsk** forever. There is a problem with children invent spelling the high-frequency words like *they*, *was*, and *want*, however. Let me finish talking about our Writers' Workshop and then when we get to our Words block, you will see how we are going to handle that problem."

Mrs. Wright quickly finished talking about Writers' Workshop, saying less than she had intended, realizing that time was marching on and she wasn't even halfway through the morning yet!

"After the children finish their driting, we go around and let each child show and tell about what he or she drew and/or wrote. We will continue in the driting stage for several more weeks. Meanwhile, during the Words block, children will be learning to read some words and we will be doing some handwriting instruction. When most of the children know some words and can make most to the letters, we will move to writing on this paper I call half-and-half paper. [Mrs. Wright held up a piece of paper with drawing space on the top and writing lines on the bottom.] I will continue to model for the children, but now I will write a sentence or two first and then do a little drawing at the top. When the children do their writing, I will ask them to write a sentence or two or a few words first and then draw. When almost all the children are able to write something readable, we will move to our writing notebooks. In my newsletter to you, I will announce that we are about to graduate to writing notebooks—a very advanced stage—and ask you to send a notebook like this one [Mrs. Wright held up a 70-sheet spiral-bound notebook]. Once the children start writing in their notebooks, we will begin our editing and publishing process. Every three or four weeks, your child will pick one piece to publish. I will work with your child to edit that piece and at that point we will fix the spelling. Your children will publish in various forms, including these books that they are so proud of. Here is one written by a child who moved unexpectedly last year and left this behind."

Publishing

Mrs. Wright passed around the book, and she could tell that the parents were impressed and that their fears about spelling were starting to be allayed. She then explained the major goals for the Working with Words block.

"At about nine-twenty each morning, we devote approximately thirty minutes to making sure your children are learning to read and spell the most common words and to developing their phonics and spelling skills so that they become increasingly more able to read and spell new words. If you look here above the alphabet letters [Mrs. Wright pointed to the space above the chalkboard], you will see the beginning of our word wall. Currently, as many of you have heard, we are adding the name of one of your children each day. Of course, all your children want their names up first, so to be fair I have all their names written on different colored paper scraps in this box. Each morning, at the beginning of our Words block, I close my eyes and reach in and pull one out. That child becomes our special child for the day and the name gets added to the wall. As you can see, Horace, Manuel, Paul, Daphne, and Roberta were the lucky five whose names came out first, but in twenty more days, everyone's name will be up there and they will all have been special for a day. Perhaps you know that our first social studies unit focuses on the idea that everyone is special and different and that we should celebrate these differences.

Word Wall

"Jumping ahead to our twelve-fifteen to one o'clock social studies/science time slot, we read many books and do other activities during that time to develop the notion that we are all different and special, and one thing we do each day is to interview the special child whose name was added to the word wall and do a shared writing chart based on that interview. Once we get all the names up here, we will begin adding those common, hard-to-spell words I mentioned earlier, including *they*, *were*, and *want*. We will add five words each Monday and we will spend our entire thirty minutes of Words time on Monday working with those five words. We will use them in sentences and have a handwriting lesson on them. On the other days, Tuesday, Wednesday, Thursday, and Friday, we will spend about eight minutes at the beginning of each Words block practicing how to spell these important words. When the children tell you that they are chanting words and learning to be cheerleaders, they are referring to our daily word wall practice. I pick five words each day and the children chant them cheerleader style several times and then write them. You will be hearing more about our word wall because it is an important part of our total reading and writing program. Word wall is the main way I have of making sure your children can read and spell what we used to call 'sight words.' When children are writing, they know that they should spell words with whatever letters they know unless it is a word wall word. Your children will get tired of hearing me say, 'If it's on our word wall, we have to spell it correctly!'

Decoding
Spelling

Letter Sounds

"As I said, word wall takes all our thirty minutes of Words block on Monday when we add the five new words, but only about eight minutes on the other days. We devote the remaining twenty-two minutes to activities that teach phonics and spelling. [Mrs. Wright noticed some relieved faces and reminded herself that first-grade parents always need to be reassured that their children are learning phonics!] Currently, we are working with the sounds of the initial letters. If your children told you that *R* is their *running* letter and they ate raisins today because *raisins* begins with an *R*, you know that we are beginning our phonics instruction. The concept that words have beginning, middle, and ending sounds and that letters 'make' these sounds is a very difficult one for young children, and I try to make it as concrete as possible by giving them an action and a food for each letter. I have duplicated for you the action and food we are going to do for each letter. One way you could help is by donating one of the foods on the list. We ate raisins today and tomorrow we will all drink milk as we try to get a handle on the sound of *M*. There is no particular order in which the letters need to be taught, so I try to begin with letters that begin children's names that are already on the wall and to make the first letters taught very different in appearance and sound. By the end of this week, your children should be able to tell you that *R* is the *running* and *raisins* letter and the first letter in Roberta's name, that *M* is the *marching* and *milk* letter and the first letter in Manuel's name, and that D is the *dancing* and *donuts* letter and the first letter in Daphne's name. It is too bad that I don't have children's names for all the beginning letters! Here is a list of the actions and foods that you might use to remind your children when they are reading or writing and can't remember the letter that goes with a particular sound. I have tried to make the foods as healthful as possible. Let me know at the end of the meeting if you would be willing to donate one of these and we will talk about when we will need it.

"Many of your children already know some of these letter sounds, but they are so important that I like to spend the first four or five weeks making sure that almost everyone knows them. Once they have learned these, we will do many activities during the Words block that focus on the vowel spelling patterns. As you know, the vowels in English have more than one common sound and have different spellings. The *o*, for example, has the sounds you hear in *box* and *boat*. Perhaps you remember that we used to call these the 'short' and 'long' sounds. But *o* in combination with other letters represents many more than just two sounds. Think about *port* and *joy* and *cloud*. Then think about the fact that *boat* and *vote* rhyme but have different spelling patterns. The vowel sound spelled *o-y* in *joy* is spelled *o-i* in *soil*. The Sound spelled *o-u* in *cloud* is spelled *o-w* in *cow*."

Mrs. Wright had been writing these words on the board as she said them and

Mrs. Wright's Action and Food List

b	bounce	bananas
c	catch	cookies
d	dance	donuts
f	fall	fish (we will do this on a day when fish is on our lunch menu)
g	gallop	gum (sugarless!)
h	hop	hamburgers (lunch menu)
j	jump	Jell-O
k	kick	Kool-Aid
l	laugh	lemonade
m	march	milk
n	nod	noodles (lunch menu)
p	paint	pizza (lunch menu)
r	run	raisins
s	sit	salad (lunch menu)
t	talk	toast
v	vacuum	vegetables (assorted, raw)
w	walk	watermelon
y	yawn	yogurt
z	zip	zucchini bread
ch	cheer	Cheerios
sh	shiver	sherbet
th	think	three thin things

you could tell from looking at the faces of the parents that most of them had never thought about how complicated a spelling system English has.

"The ability to figure out how to read or spell a word you have never seen before is a critical skill in becoming a good independent reader, and we will spend most of our Words block every day helping children to learn these spelling patterns and how to use the patterns in words they know to help them figure out how to spell and read new words, but because English is a complex language, this will not happen overnight. We will make charts of rhyming words and I will include some of these in my newsletters to you. We will also do an activity called Making Words a couple of times a week. The children will be bringing home some Making Words strips and challenging you to see how many words you can make from the letters on the strip. Be sure to encourage and praise them for their growing spelling and phonics skills and be patient with us. By the end of the year, most of your children will be spelling simple words well and able to figure out almost any regular one-syllable word."

Mrs. Wright glanced up at the clock and realized she had less than ten minutes to explain the rest of the day. Quickly, she moved through the other time slots.

Guided Reading
Shared Reading

"After our Words block, we have our break/recess time. Fortunately, you all know what happens in the twenty minutes. Then we have our guided reading lessons. At this point, we are doing shared reading with Big Books such as these. (Mrs. Wright quickly showed them *Mrs. Wishy Washy* and *The Very Hungry Caterpillar*.) We read the book together and do many activities related to the book. In October, we will begin reading in our basal series. (Mrs. Wright held up three preprimers.) These are the books adopted by the school system and we will read these as well as good stories from other basals and real books whenever I can get my hands on enough copies."

At this point, Steve's father raised his hand and asked, "How will you do three reading groups in thirty-five minutes?"

Mrs. Wright hadn't intended to go into this tonight, but the question had been asked.

"I won't have three reading groups. Reading groups are another mainstay of our school days that have been seriously questioned in recent years. The children who are put in the bottom group in first grade almost always remain in the bottom group throughout elementary school and almost never reach the point where they can read on grade level. Three groups is also a problem for children in the top group. You wouldn't believe how much difference there is between children in a top reading group. Some are just a little faster and further along than average readers, while others read at second- or third-grade level at the beginning of first grade. For truly top children, just putting them in a book a little above grade level doesn't even begin to meet their needs. The other problem with ability groups is what you pointed out—you can't do three reading groups in thirty-five minutes. If I were to put your children in three groups, I wouldn't really be meeting the needs of my most advanced readers or of those who need a lot more practice. I also wouldn't be able to give thirty-five minutes each day to writing, which is an approach to reading, thirty minutes to the Words block, and thirty minutes here (Mrs. Wright pointed to the 1:30–2:00 time slot) to the critically important Teacher Read-Aloud/SQUIRT time. As many of you know, Merritt Elementary has always emphasized that we need to teach children to read and be sure that they do read, and so each class schedules time each day

Self-Selected
Reading

for SQUIRT—which stands for Sustained QUIet Reading Time. I must admit that it is not really quiet because children mumble to themselves while reading for most of first grade before they actually get the idea of what it means to read silently—'in your mind.' But we do take thirty minutes each day for enjoying real books. At this time of the year, I usually read to the children for about twenty minutes and they read to themselves for about ten minutes, but by February I hope to have that time divided more evenly so that the children are reading books of their own choosing for about fifteen minutes each day.

Teacher Read-Aloud

"Having three groups is an attempt to meet the needs of the whole range of diverse children that are found in any classroom. Unfortunately, it doesn't meet the needs very well, and doing three groups takes most of the reading/language arts teaching time. My instruction in reading takes place in all four blocks: the Writing block, the Working with Words block, the Guided Reading block, and the Teacher Read-Aloud/SQUIRT block. These blocks represent the competing methods that people are always arguing about—what is the 'best method.' My experience with the four blocks last year and the experience and research of others who have organized this way show that all children do not learn in the same way. We need a variety of methods going on simultaneously if we are to teach all children successfully. Think about two sisters you have known, born to the same family, growing up in the same house. Have you ever said, 'How can two sisters be so different?'"

Individual Differences

At this point, Roberta and Betty's mother piped up with, "Maybe the sisters are even twins—born within minutes of each other!"

The group of parents, many of whom knew Betty and Roberta, broke into laughter, and the point that not all children learn in the same way was brought home to everyone.

Mrs. Wright summed up. "Children come to us at all different levels of beginning reading and writing knowledge. They all have unique personalities and learning preferences. My instruction is called multimethod because children can learn to read in any of the four blocks. It is called multilevel because we don't stick with just first-grade–level materials. During writing and SQUIRT, there is no limit to how high the children can move. The Guided Reading block is the hardest one to make multilevel because whatever we are all going to read has a level—which is too hard for some and too easy for others. I make this block multilevel by not sticking with the same level of material all week and by having the children sometimes read with partners. Sometimes, I form flexible groups that meet for a few days or a week to read a particular story or book, and these groups might find the more advanced readers reading something challenging together and the children who need more easy reading, reading something easy together. Last year was the first year I organized my language and reading instruction into the four blocks, and I have to tell you that the children who would have been in the bottom group made much more progress than in previous years and that children who would have been in the top group really moved ahead."

Balanced Literacy Programs

Just then Mr. Topps popped his head in the door. A glance at the clock told Mrs. Wright that she was now 10 minutes over and that all the other classes were probably already assembling in the cafeteria for refreshments and the general meeting.

"Let me assure you that I do a somewhat better job of sticking to my schedule and giving the four blocks fairly equal amounts of time when I am teaching than I have done here tonight. I know that a lot of this is new to you and I intend to communicate with you regularly. Your children will be bringing home books they can read and their own published writing, as well as other samples of what they are doing. I will send a newsletter home every few weeks letting you know about all our exciting activities and plans. If I have any particular concerns about any area of your child's development, I will call you and I trust that you will call me if you have any concerns. Please let me know if you can bring any of the foods on the list. I look forward to seeing you all at parent conference time in eight more weeks and want to remind you that visitors and volunteers are always welcome in this school and in my class."

Parent Involvement

As the parents left, several offered to send food and several others said they would love to come and see how "this four-block thing" worked. Mrs. Wright suggested that they wait a few weeks until she and the children could get the routines better established and then just send her a note telling her when they would like to come. She warned them, however, that there were never enough hands to help or ears to listen to children read and that when they came, she would probably put them right to work!

MONTHLY LOGS

September

Now I know why October is my favorite month—all month long I celebrate my survival of September! My supervising teacher from long-ago student-teaching days used to say, "I could teach first grade until I am eighty if someone would teach the first four weeks for me." Of course, that was in the days before there was kindergarten. Now, most of the children have been to kindergarten and know something about lining up and listening. I got my group this year from Miss Launch.

Individual Differences

They are as ready and eager as a motley crew of six-year-olds can be. And a motley crew they are. I am most worried about Paul. It is a rare day on which Paul doesn't return to his seat, put his head on his desk, and sob. I have tried to contact his parents but there appears to be no father at home and his mother works odd hours. Miss Grant, the social worker, says his home situation is awful, so I will continue to do what I can for him here. Daisy needs to be put on a diet! Her mother will be in next week for a conference. I wonder if I'll broach the subject to her. I guess it depends on her overall reactions to the other concerns I have about Daisy. I'd like to say, "Your daughter is a spoiled, selfish child," but I'll restrain myself!

Poor Chip! I have managed to stop most of the taunts and snickers directed at his tattered clothes, but I know Butch and Mort still bother him on the playground. He goes his own way, however, and pays as little attention to them as possible. I do admire the child.

Last Friday he contributed to a language experience chart. We were talking about fishing and Chip's sentence was, "You fry them up and they sure good." Joyce wanted to correct his sentence and I informed her that that was Chip's way of saying it and that was the way I was going to write it!

Larry, Danielle, Roberta, and Pat are reading! Miss Launch tells me that Larry and Danielle were reading when they came to kindergarten and that Roberta and Pat learned during the year. Larry has more general knowledge than anyone else. He is always adding some little-known (to the other children) fact to our stories. The others listen in awe and amazement. Yesterday Hilda said, "Larry, how do you know that?" He responded, "I read it in a book," as if that were the most natural thing in the world, and I guess it is for him.

Alexander has a hard time sometimes dealing with me and the other children. The hearing aid he wears is supposed to give him enough hearing capacity to function normally if he is seated close to you, but his oral language and listening abilities are like those of a four-year-old. Miss Launch says I should have seen him when he came to kindergarten last year. He could hardly talk and wouldn't listen. Apparently, they didn't discover his hearing problem until he was over two years old and had yet to say "mama" or "daddy"! I have assigned Steve to be his buddy for the time being and have talked with the children about what an important invention hearing aids are. One hundred years ago, Alexander would not have been able to hear at all! We try to treat Alexander as special and lucky, but he still gets frustrated sometimes and lashes out at us. Once in a while, I think he pretends (or chooses) not to hear—usually when I say, "Time to clean up," or, "Where is your paper?" It is hard to know what to do. I want to treat him as normal, but he does need special consideration, yet I can't let him get out of things, using his handicap as an excuse. Mr. Lang, the speech and hearings specialist, will work with Alexander on Wednesdays and Fridays. I think I will ask him for advice.

Children with Special Needs

We have made good progress this year into our four-block instruction. We are still using drawing paper for our Writers' Workshop but I think we will move to the half-and-half paper by the middle of October. Almost all the children are adding some letters and words to their drawings now, and Larry, Danielle, Roberta, Pat, and Hilda are often writing sentences along the bottom of their drawing paper. Even the children who are further behind have the idea of what reading and writing are and are adding some labels to their drawings. All but four of the children's names are now up on the wall, and the children often draw pictures of themselves and other classmates and write the classmates' names next to their pictures. They also draw their pets and usually can spell their pets' names.

We are about finished learning actions and eating foods to go with the letters. Connecting the letter names and sounds with children's names, actions, and foods seems to be really helping my slower children. We were reading together in one of our alphabet books the other day and the children couldn't remember that the animal was a porcupine. As they were trying to think what that strange-looking animal was called, Daisy piped up and said, "I don't know what it is but it begins like pizza!"

Letter Names Letter Sounds

"And Paul," chimed in Chip.

"And paint," added Butch, acting out the painting action as he said it!

We have read lots of alphabet books this month. It is truly amazing to me how many different and fascinating alphabet books there are. The children particularly enjoyed the illustrations in *The Icky Bug Alphabet Book* by Jerry Pallotta, the singable rhymes in *ABC Bunny* by Wanda Gag, and finding the hidden animals in *Alphabeasts: A Hide and Seek Alphabet Book* by Durga Bernhard. I even found two alphabet books that tied in with our I Am Special social studies unit. *Ashanti to Zulu: African Traditions* by Margaret Musgrove allowed us to think about how special each of our heritages and traditions is, and *The Hand Made Alphabet* by Laura Rankin shows children how to finger spell the letters along with some great pictures of objects beginning with those letters.

Language Experience

Individual Differences

In addition to interviewing the special child each day and then writing a language experience chart telling what was special about that child, I read them a book almost every day about a child and we talked about what was special about the child in the book. We read a wide variety of books and talked about some of the things that make each person special and how the same things that make you special are problems at times. They enjoyed old favorites like *The Hundred Dresses* by Eleanor Estes as well as some new books including *I Hate English* by Ellen Levine, in which a Chinese girl, Mei Mei, tries to cope with life in a new country, a new school, and a new language. We also read some books in which animal characters had special characteristics, including *The Biggest Nose* by Kathy Caple, in which an elephant is being teased by her hippo friend about having such a big nose! The elephant feels self-conscious until she realizes that her hippo friend has such a big mouth! My children are very aware of how they are physically different from one another, and talking about the differences is easier sometimes when characters in the book are humorous, lovable animals.

Predictable Books

I have read several predictable Big Books with the children during our Guided Reading block time, including *Ten, Nine, Eight* by Molly Bang, which portrays beautifully the relationship between an African-American girl and her father. In addition to fitting into our I Am Special unit, this counting book tied in with our math!

Self-Selected Reading

We have moved much more quickly than in past years into sustaining individual reading for 10 minutes. I think that is because I didn't take for granted that children knew how to enjoy books before they could actually read them. In the past, I have noticed my children with the fewest literacy experiences at home having great trouble settling down with a book. They would keep picking books up, flipping through them, and putting them back. I didn't mind that they weren't reading the books but they weren't even really looking at them. This year it occurred to me that maybe they didn't know how you could enjoy a

Teacher Modeling

book even when you couldn't read it! I decided that some modeling and direct experience were called for. About the third week of school, as I sat down to read to them before their SQUIRT time, I picked up a copy of *Are You My Mother?*—a book I had already read to them several times and one many of them had at home.

"You know," I began, "there is more than just one way to read a book. Usually, when I read to you, I read by saying all these words." I pointed to the words and read a few pages. "Saying all the words is one way to read, but there is another way to read. Let me show you how my son, David, used to read *Are You My Mother?* when he was just starting first grade."

I then unzipped my magic bag (this is a big canvas bag I carry around with me all the time. I call it my magic bag because I often keep things hidden in it and surprise the children with them when I pull them out! The children are always asking, "Got anything magic in that bag today?") and pulled out my son's favorite teddy bear and introduced Bare Bear to the class.

"Now, when my son David was just your age, he loved his Bare Bear and he loved *Are You My Mother?* Every night, I would read him two books and he would always choose *Are You My Mother?* first. After I read to him, I would let him have ten minutes to look at his books before he had to turn his light out and go to sleep. I would go to the kitchen to clean-up the dishes and I could hear him reading *Are You My Mother?* to Bare Bear. This is how he read it."

I then read *Are You My Mother?* to them the way a young child pretends to read a memorized book. The children watched in amazement. When I finished, I asked them if I had read it the way I usually read to them by saying all the words, and got them to explain that I knew the story so well I could tell it and repeat the familiar parts:

> *"Are you my mother?" the baby bird asked the cow.*
> *"I am not your mother. I am a cow."*

Then I asked, "How many of you have a favorite book at home that someone has read to you over and over again and you can pretend read that book to a little brother or sister or to your favorite stuffed animal?" Several hands went up and I let the children tell me the title of the book they could pretend read. I then invited them to bring these books the next day and show us how they could pretend to read the book. Betty asked if she could bring her Kitty that she read to. I asked if Kitty was stuffed or alive. Betty looked horrified and said, "Kitty's not alive. I couldn't bring a live cat to school!" Her twin (in name only), Roberta, chimed in with, "I bet I could!"

The next day Betty, Roberta, Harriet, Steve, and Anthony proudly walked in with books and stuffed animals. At Teacher Read-Aloud/SQUIRT time, they "read" their books to their animals and to us. Betty "read" *The Gingerbread Man*, Roberta "read" *Where the Wild Things Are*, Harriet "read" *Goodnight Moon*, Steve "read" *Over in the Meadow*, and Anthony "read" *Where's Spot?* On the following day, several more children brought in their favorite predictable books and "read" them to us. By the end of the week, all my children knew that there were two ways you could read a book. You could say all the words or you could retell the story of a favorite book, making up parts and saying the repeated parts you knew.

Last week, I introduced the third way we read books. Out of my magic bag, I pulled a whole stack of books about airplanes. I explained to the children that when David was their age, he loved airplanes. He wanted to be a pilot when he grew up or the owner of an international airline! He was always checking books about airplanes out of the library and I bought him many airplane books with great pictures. I then proceeded to show them how David "read" the airplane books, not by saying the words and not by pretending to read them. I showed them that most of the books had a lot of writing and that David would have to be at least 10 or 11 before he could even begin to read these books. There was also too much writing in these books to remember what the book said and pretend you were reading it. David read these books by talking to himself about the pictures. I then went through several of the airplane books with the children and, making no pretense at reading the words, I talked about the pictures as if I were a six-year-old.

Oh, look at that old airplane. Hard to believe that anyone would fly in something that rickety looking!

What a neat fighter jet! I bet that one can go a thousand miles per hour!

The children joined in and helped me talk about the pictures. After looking at several of the airplane books, I asked the children if any of them had books at home that they couldn't read or pretend read but that had lots of wonderful pictures that they loved to look at and talk to themselves about. Several children volunteered that they had such books, and on the next several days they brought these books in and "read" them to us by talking about the pictures. Mitch brought in some books about trucks. He wants to be a truck driver like his father when he grows up. Steve brought in some books with all different kinds of plants in them. Larry surprised us all by bringing in a bunch of books about different countries and talking about the pictures and where he planned to travel when he was grown up.

"But, Larry," Hilda asked, "you can read! Why don't you just read the books instead of talking to yourself about the pictures?"

"I like the pictures," Larry explained. "That is a lot of words," he pointed out—pointing to the words on one of the pages!

"Even when you can read," I explained, "there are books you like to enjoy just by looking at them and talking to yourself about the pictures."

Now everyone in my class knows that there are three ways to read books and the difference at SQUIRT time is incredible. Even Paul, who doesn't participate in much of anything, ponders over the pictures in informational books and sometimes mumbles to himself. Most of my other children are pretend reading some favorite books and some, of course, are really reading some of the books. I wish I had realized years ago that some children couldn't settle in with a book because they knew they couldn't read it and that is all they had ever seen anyone do with a book! Now that all the children know three ways to read and that all those ways are acceptable (how could they not be acceptable if geniuses like Larry and my son, David, did them?), they are all eager readers and we are having no trouble with 10 minutes of SQUIRT time.

Next month will be a busy month. We will start writing on half-and-half paper, add high-frequency words to our word wall, and begin the first preprimer in our basal series. In our social studies/science time, we will do a unit on fall, spend some time discussing Halloween customs, and learn more about families around the world. Good thing October has 31 days!

October

To most first graders, Halloween is second only to Christmas in generating excitement and distractions. I try to capitalize on their excitement and channel their energies. Our unit at the beginning of the month was on families. We extended the I Am Special unit from September into a Families are Different and Special unit. The children talked about their families, but I was careful not to ask for too specific information. Fewer than half my class live in a family that contains both the father and the mother they were born to. We defined a family as the people you live with who love you and each other, and we defined an extended family as including all your relatives. We brought in pictures of our families and talked about how families have to work together, do fun things together, and sometimes they don't all get along perfectly! Paul had very little to say during the unit but he did listen and seemed comforted to know that all families have problems they have to work through.

Unit Teaching

We read the Big Book *Families Are Different* by Nina Pelligrini, which explores all kinds of different families all held together "with a special kind of glue called love." I read them a number of books that featured various family groups, including *The Mother's Day Mice, A Perfect Father's Day*, and *The Wednesday Surprise*, all by Eve Bunting, who treats the issue of different families with extreme sensitivity. I also read them *Fly Away Home*, Bunting's story of a boy and his dad who live in an airport while looking for a real home.

In addition to our family unit, we spent some of our afternoon science/social studies time learning about the seasons, particularly fall, and this past week we have done many Halloween activities. In addition to reading numerous Halloween stories and nonfiction books about Halloween customs, I read them a newspaper article about children being hurt on Halloween and we made up a list of Halloween safety rules. We carved a jack-o'-lantern and then wrote down in sequence the steps we had gone through to carve it. We also planned our Halloween party and made a list of what was needed and who would bring each item. All these activities happened during our science/social studies slot but involved a lot of talking, reading, and writing. If you look at our schedule, we have only 130 minutes of our time specifically devoted to reading/language arts, but when you consider how much we do during our unit time, we actually are getting a lot more time each day for these critical areas.

Content Area Integration

Our Writers' Workshop is moving right along. We are now using half-and-half paper and pencils to write with instead of drawing paper and crayons. I have made a transparency with lines like the bottom of the handwriting paper and left a little drawing space at the top. Each day, for our minilesson at the beginning of the Writing block, I sit down at the overhead and write two or three sentences and then draw a picture to go with them. Before I write, I think aloud about the topic I might write about:

Process Writing

> Let's see, what will I write about today? I could write about seeing Anthony and his baby sister at the grocery store last night. She is so cute! I could write about what a time we had yesterday getting George back into his cage after someone left the door open! I know what I'll write about!

By thinking aloud about a few topics that I don't write about, the children are reminded about some things they may want to write about. I don't write about running into Anthony and his baby sister, but he might! I don't write about trying to recapture our pet gerbil, but many of the children involved in the chase yesterday are reminded of this and they might choose to write about it.

When I do write, I don't say the words as I am writing them. You will be amazed at how closely the children watch me write and how hard they try to figure out and anticipate what I will write when I am not saying it as I write it.

Teacher Modeling

I do say a few words aloud, however. Each day in my writing I invent spell a few words. I tell the children that this is how I used to spell the big words when I was their age and each day I invent spell a few words—saying the word very slowly and putting down some letters I hear. I also remind them that they will need to write many words that aren't on our word wall yet and that they can't spell yet and that they should put down the letters they hear just as I do when I write the big words in my story.

I write all kinds of different things. On some days I write something related to what we are learning in science and social studies. Other days, I write about something that happened in our classroom. Sometimes, I write about something special that will happen that day or that week. I tell about children's lost teeth, new baby sisters or brothers, accidents, and upcoming birthdays. The children are always eager to see "what she will write today"! Probably their favorite thing for me to write is what I call the "When I Was Your Age" tales. Here is one I wrote just before Halloween.

The children love my "When I Was Your Age" tales and are always asking me if they are all true! It is a little hard even for me to imagine my middle-aged self going door to door in a fairy princess costume and craving Tootsie Rolls!

Individual Differences

I take no more than eight minutes to write and then read aloud my piece to make sure it makes sense. Then the children all get their half-and-half paper and I give them about 15 minutes to write and draw. Some of my more advanced children, including Larry, Pat, Danielle, Steve, and Betty, are writing some fairly lengthy pieces, often continuing a story on the back of their papers and taking several days to complete one story. Other children are just getting a few words down. Paul wouldn't write anything for several days and now seems to be copying the names of the children from the word wall! Alexander is the other one who writes almost nothing. With his hearing loss, I am not sure he can hear any of the sounds in the words he might write. Mostly, he is still drawing. Mike is a surprise! He writes up a storm, putting a letter or two for each word and with no spaces between the words. No one else but Mike can read it, of course, but he draws wonderful monster pictures and when he shares, he tells all about the monsters, and I guess that is what he is trying to write with his collection of letters. At any rate, the children all love his stories and I see monster stories being written by other children. It is funny how these writing crazes catch on with six-year-olds. I worry about some of my children who just "go through the motions" during writing time. Mort, particularly, is always sitting there looking pained, and when I ask what he is thinking about writing, he just responds, "I don't really care!"

When I was your age, I loved
Halloween. I went trick or
treating dressed as a fairy
prinses. My favrit candy was
Tootsie Rolls.

Finally, all the names are on the word wall, including mine and George's (our
gerbil), which the children insisted had to be there. Once we got the names
up, I added five words last week—*boy, girl, friend, like, is*—and five more this
week—*play, school, good, come, go.* I added these words first because they are
some of the words used in the first preprimer we began this month and they
are more concrete than the abstract connecting words such as *with, of,* and *they.*
They are also words children use a great deal in their writing. I try to make sure

Word Wall

that the first words begin with different letters and are different lengths. I use the scraps from the construction paper drawer, write the words with a thick permanent black marker, and then cut around their shape so that the length and shape become quite distinctive. I use whatever colors are big enough except that I do make sure to put those easily confused words on different colors. *With* is on blue, so when I get ready to add *will, went,* and *want,* I will make sure I use different colors. The different colors and shapes make for an interesting display and help my slower children differentiate the confusable words.

On Monday, when I put the new words up, we do a lot with them, count the number of letters, use them in sentences, compare them to other words on the wall, and do a handwriting lesson with them. On the other days, I call out any five words from across the wall—including a name or two each day. I point to each word and when all their eyes are glued to the word, we clap and chant it three times and then they write it on handwriting paper as I write it on the board. When they have written all five words, they take out their red checking pens and check each word by making the shape around the word with their red pen. I do the same with my words on the board. Making the shape helps to emphasize which are the tall letters and which go below the line. Most children have written them as best they can, but if they do find something not correct when they are checking, they just go over that part with their red pen. The children are becoming better at their handwriting, but there are still huge differences in their ability to control those pencils and get them to do what they want them to do. I know that handwriting develops with practice, along with maturity and development—especially for my young boys—so I accept whatever they can do, as long as they appear to be making a good effort.

Decoding   We have actions and food for all the initial consonants and *ch, sh,* and *th.* We are now using our 20 to 22 remaining minutes of Tuesday, Wednesday, Thursday, and Friday Words time to collect rhyming words. I have read them lots of *Hop on Pop* and *The Cat in the Hat* type books and then we list on a chart a lot of words that rhyme. Our *Cat in the Hat* chart had *a-t* words all lined up with the *at* underlined in each. I do include words that begin with the blends and we say them slowly, listening for the sounds of both beginning letters.

This week, we made charts of words that rhymed with Halloween words. We chose the words *cat, witch, moon, trick, treat,* and *owl.* We used our rhyming **Shared Writing** word charts to write a group poem. I made up the first sentence of each couplet and the children composed the second. In several cases, we had several suggested second lines. We wrote them all down and decided as we wrote the poem which choice we liked best. Here is the final version.

Guided Reading   Our Guided Reading block is going pretty well. We are now halfway through the first preprimer. I begin this block with the whole class gathered on the rug and introduce the story first. We always begin each story by looking at the pictures and talking about the meaning. As we turn each page, I ask questions such as:

What do you see in the picture?
What do you think is happening?

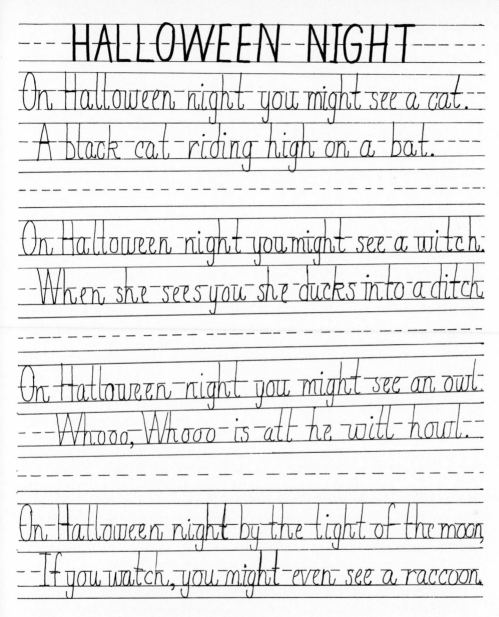

HALLOWEEN NIGHT

On Halloween night you might see a cat.
A black cat riding high on a bat.

On Halloween night you might see a witch.
When she sees you she ducks into a ditch

On Halloween night you might see an owl.
Whooo, Whooo is all he will howl.

On Halloween night by the light of the moon,
If you watch, you might even see a raccoon.

Why do you think everyone looks so mad?
What is that big brown animal called?

I usually lead them to look through the whole story with me and we talk about what we see in the pictures, naming the characters, animals, objects, places, and so on. We predict what might happen next and speculate about what is happening based just on the pictures.

After looking at the pictures one time and focusing only on meaning, we then look through the pages a second time, but this time I write an important word or two for each page on the board. They use what they know about letters and sounds and word length along with the picture on each page to try to figure out the word I have written. These words are not very difficult to figure out when you use all the clues you have. Once they have figured out the word, I have them search the page and put their finger on the word when they find it. This vocabulary introduction works well for the picturable words—*kangaroo, babies, pouch*—but, of course, doesn't work for other words.

High-Frequency Words

I introduce the other words by writing some patterned sentences on the board using the names of my children and the word I want to draw their attention to. For the word *is*, for example, I wrote these simple sentences:

> Mandy *is* a girl.
> Mitch *is* a boy.
> George *is* a gerbil.

Because they know each other's names and because they love to have things written about them, they pay close attention and can more easily learn an abstract word like *is*. I then send them on an *is* hunt in the story they are going to read. They move their fingers along the line of print and try to count how many times they see the word *is*. I introduce a few more high-frequency abstract words in the same way, and these words are likely candidates to be added to the word wall next week.

Next, the children and I read the story. Sometimes we read it together, with everyone chiming in, still sitting there on the rug. After we have read each page, we talk about what we found out and add that to the meaning gained from looking at the pictures. On other days, we don't read it together first but I send them off to read it with their partners. I have assigned all the children a reading partner, pairing up students who are a little weaker with friendly, helpful children who can help them but not do it for them. (I have paired Daphne with Paul and have quietly asked her to just read the story to him and let him read if he wants. She is such a little dear. She leads Paul off somewhere quiet and reads with him the way a mother would to a little child!) The children know that they and their partner should take turns reading pages and that they should give each other clues when they get to words they don't know:

> "Remember the name of that animal who has the babies in her pouch."
> "It's that little word she used in the sentences about Mandy, Mitch, and George."

After they do partner reading, we gather together again for just a few minutes and talk about the story, using "what else did we learn from reading the words that we couldn't figure out from just the pictures?"

We usually spend two days on a story. If we partner read the first day, we often read it chorally the second day and then do some comprehension-oriented follow-up such as acting the story out or talking about the order in which things happened or discussing the characters, setting, problem, and solution.

So far, the Guided Reading lessons are going well. Even though the stories are much too simple for my readers like Larry, Danielle, and Pat, they seem to enjoy talking about them and reading with their partners. I would worry about their not being on the level they need to be on if this were my total reading program. But my observations of them during the Writing block, the SQUIRT time, and our science/social studies unit time assure me that they are working up to their advanced levels for a large part of the day. Once we get further along in our guided reading, however, I do plan to have my more advanced children do some reading together in higher-level materials from time to time.

Balanced Literacy Programs

November

Thanksgiving took much of our attention this month. I have always enjoyed all the holidays, and one of the fringe benefits of teaching first grade is that all the traditional holiday songs and activities are fresh and new to the children and I get into the holiday spirit right along with them. We did many Thanksgiving activities and read Thanksgiving stories as well as some nonfiction books describing the first Thanksgiving and the early days of our country.

Our Writers' Workshop is moving along very well. I plan to ask all the parents to send spiral notebooks next month so that we can start writing in our notebooks. I came up with an ingenious plan to limit the amount of time we spend sharing each day. At the beginning of the year, we had time for everyone to share because they were writing just a little and they could show their driting and tell about it. Now that they are writing longer pieces, however, it was taking 20 minutes each day for them all to share. This cut into our Words block time and put us about 10 minutes behind schedule every day. In addition, as what they were sharing got longer, the children were not able to sit and be good listeners for everyone's piece!

Process Writing

I have designated all the children as days of the week. I did this arbitrarily but with an eye to having some of the most prolific and reluctant writers spread across the days. Each day, we end the writing block with an Author's Chair and the designated children get to sit in the rocking chair and read one piece they have written since the last time they shared. After they share their piece, they call on one person to tell them something they liked about their piece. This is working out quite well. With the exception of Paul and sometimes Joyce, the children are all eager to read on their special day. The listeners listen better when they are listening to only five authors. Here are the designations:

Author's Chair

Monday	*Tuesday*	*Wednesday*	*Thursday*	*Friday*
Joyce	Daisy	Larry	Rita	Mitch
Alex	Butch	Carl	Mort	Hilda
Danielle	Anthony	Betty	Horace	Manuel
Jeff	Chip	Paul	Pat	Mandy
Mike	Daphne	Alexander	Steve	Roberta

I have also extended this "Day of the Week" idea to other areas. The children whose day it is pass out and pick up things whenever that service is needed.

Routines

They lead the line and get to do whatever other special things need doing. This has certainly cut down on the "But I never get to do . . ." and the occasional "You always let her do everything!"

Anecdotal Records

I am also using these designations to do my anecdotal records on children. Last year, we moved to a report card/conference system that really stresses using portfolios and regular comments to monitor and demonstrate progress. I have an anecdotal record sheet for each child, and I was walking around with 25 sheets on my clipboard and never able to pull out the right sheet at the right moment. Now, each morning I put on my clipboard only the sheets for the children whose day it is. I begin writing comments when they share in the Author's Chair and then I glance at their writing, which they hand to me after they read. I continue to note how they do with our Word block activities and I make sure to have them read a little bit to me during our Guided Reading lesson. During SQUIRT time, I have the children come on their designated day and read to me—in whichever of the three ways we read—two pages from a book they select. I write down the title of the book, which way they are reading it, and a comment about their comprehension, enjoyment, fluency, and so on. Since I carry around these sheets with me anyway, I am making some notes about their math skills, their contributions during our science/social studies unit time, and a note about what they choose to do during center time. By the time I got to report cards and conferences this month, I had a great deal of information about each and every child. This "Day of the Week" system is so simple I can't figure out why I didn't think of it earlier.

Teacher Modeling

We now have 30 words on our word wall in addition to the names. The children are continuing to respond well to our daily look, chant, and write practice and they are obviously using the word wall when they are writing. As I write each day, in addition to modeling the invented spelling of a few big words, I also model looking up at the word wall and finding a word there that I need in my writing. As I do that, I think aloud, "If it's on our word wall, I have to spell it correctly!"

Content Area Integration

In addition to our word wall, which has high-frequency words, I am doing content boards related to our science or social studies theme. Along with pictures, I put important words children might need in their writing. Our Thanksgiving board has Thanksgiving pictures and the words *Thanksgiving, thankful, turkey, feast, Pilgrims, Indians, corn,* and *food.* Between the high-frequency words now on our wall and the content words, even children who can't (or won't) use invented spelling can do some writing. Last week Alexander wrote:

I like Thanksgiving. It is fun. I have a feast. I eat good food.

While this is hardly an award-winning piece, for Alexander, who still has not learned how you separate words into sounds and will not attempt invented spelling, his ability to write something is remarkable. He is pleased with himself, too, and I think he now has a strategy for writing. With the word wall, the content boards, and their growing awareness of letter-sound patterns, all my children can and do write.

Context/ Cross-Checking

We are continuing to work on rhyming words, and our room is now filled

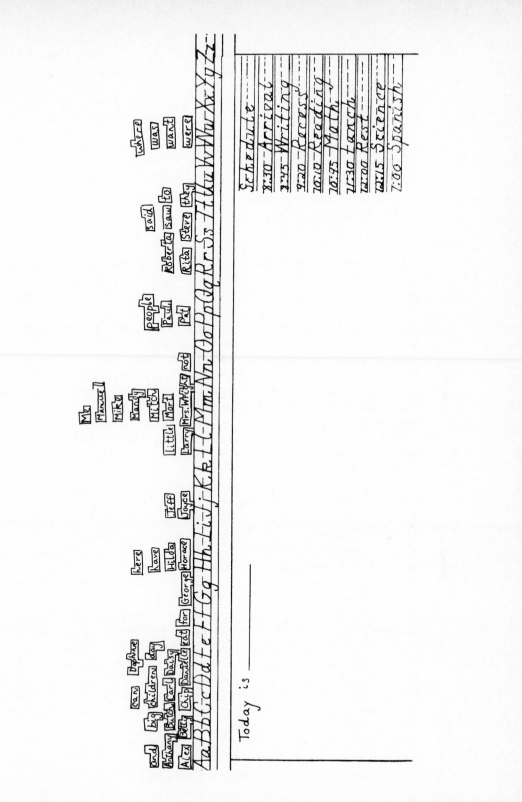

Word Wall

and   earn   Daphne
Anthony big children Ray
Alex Bitty Carl Daisy
            eat for George Horace
                 here
                 have
                 Hilda

Jeff
Joyce

Mr.
Manuel
Niko
Marly
MiTch
little Mort
Larry Mrs. Wicket not

people
Paul
Pat

sad
Roberta saw to
Rita Steve they

where
was
want
were

Aa Bb Cc Dd Ee Ff Gg Hh Ii Jj Kk Ll Mm Nn Oo Pp Qq Rr Ss Tt Uu Vv Ww Xx Yy Zz

Today is _____

Schedule
8:30 Arrival
8:45 Writing
9:20 Recess
10:10 Reading
10:45 Math
11:30 Lunch
12:00 Rest
12:15 Science
1:00 Spanish

349

with charts of rhymes. In addition, I have come up with a little activity that helps them apply their knowledge of initial letters and sounds. To prepare for this activity I write four or five sentences using my children's names in each and cover up an important word in each sentence. Here are the sentences I used this week. (The food word in each sentence is covered with two Post-it notes so that the children cannot read it.)

Butch likes to eat hamburgers.
Mitch likes to eat cheeseburgers.
Paul likes to eat spaghetti.
Mrs. Wright likes to eat lasagna.
George likes to eat carrots.

The children see the sentences when they first come in the morning and they immediately begin trying to guess the word hidden under the Post-it notes. (I put these high up on the board so they can't peek under!) Once we finish our word wall review, we begin to guess what each person likes to eat. I write several possibilities they suggest on the board and then we observe that "the word can be lots of different foods when you can't see any letters." I then remove the Post-it note that covers the first letter or letters (all letters before the vowel). We then cross out any guesses that don't begin correctly, observing that the guesses made sense but didn't begin with the right letters. Next, we guess some more things that both make sense and begin with the revealed letters, and then reveal the whole word.

We do sentences like this one or two days a week and my children are becoming very good at realizing that when you come to a word you don't know, you can make a real good guess if you think of something that makes sense and starts with the right letters.

We are reading in the second preprimer of our adopted series now. Before beginning this book, I had the children I was most worried about—Paul, Mike, Alexander, Mitch, Daisy, Mort, and Chip—read a few pages in the first story to me. I took a running record as they were doing this and then I had them **Individual** retell what they remembered. Using the 90 percent word accuracy criteria, Mort **Differences** and Chip just made it. Alexander, Mitch, and Jeff were less than 90 percent but better than 80 percent. All five of them had good comprehension although it was hard to tell with Mort because he was so bored by the whole process, he didn't tell me much! Paul, Mike, and Daisy, however, were not even close. They are reading with us in the second preprimer but I am doing some individual work with them, rereading the first preprimer. I have scheduled each of them for 10 minutes with me. Paul is always here when I come to open up the room so I have my 10 minutes with him first thing. I take Mike during the after-lunch quiet time because Mike can't sit quietly under any circumstances, and I read with Daisy for 10 minutes during centers.

Fluency I am doing repeated readings with them with the preprimer we have already read and discussed. Each day, when it is time to read with one of them, we set the timer for 10 minutes and, beginning on the first page each day, we see how far we can read in 10 minutes. They read to me and if they miss or don't know a word, I help them. Then I model fluent reading of the page and they read it fluently, without error, before going on to the next page. We continue reading until they get stuck, then I help them, model fluent reading, and have them reread the page. When the timer signals the end of the 10 minutes, we note down the page on which we stopped. On the first day, Mike got to page 5 in 10 minutes. Starting again on page 1 the next day, he got to page 9. On the third day, he got to page 15. When he got to page 20, I stopped beginning on the first page each day but did back up about 10 pages, beginning with the story that began on page 10.

This is working exceptionally well for Mike. He is much less distractible when I have just him to focus on, and he loves trying to beat the clock and seeing the progress he is making on his pages-read chart. Daisy is making some progress but she doesn't particularly like giving up 10 minutes of her center time, so she is not always very cooperative. Paul is sporadic. Some days, he does quite well, and other days, he won't read at all. I try to talk to him and assure him that he is making progress and I give him a hug and tell him I love him! Some mornings, if he can't read, I just rock him and talk to him the way you would a crying two-year-old. I have yet to see his mother, but Miss Grant tells me the home situation is pitiful—whatever that means! I have referred him for psychological evaluation but I don't know what they will tell me that will help! It just isn't right that children should be so emotionally upset and we can do so little for them! I have always found this the most frustrating thing about teaching first grade!

Children with Special Needs

December

Finally—two weeks' vacation! Am I ever ready for it after this month. Every year I forget what a fevered state my little ones get into as they await the big day. Of course, much of what we do this month is related to the holidays. This year we celebrated Christmas, Hanukkah, and Kwanzaa! We read books, of course, including *A Picture Book of Hanukkah* by David Adler, *My First Kwanzaa Book* by Deborah Newton Chocolate, and *Happy Christmas, Gemma* by Sarah Hayes. Joyce's mother came and talked to us about the Kwanzaa celebrations they were taking part in. Mort's mom came and talked to us about their Hanukkah customs. I thought Mort might perk up with his mother here but he was his typical uninterested, "Who cares?" self. I talked briefly with his mother about his apathy and she says he is the same way at home and she doesn't know how to motivate him either!

Multicultural Awareness

Our Writing and Words blocks are moving along nicely. Of course, I put some holiday boards up in our room with words attached to them, enabling the children to write their letters to Santa, and so forth. Butch and Hilda insist that there is no such thing as Santa and they tease some of the others about this. Yesterday, Butch had Rita in tears and I decided to try to call a halt to it. I told them that I didn't know for sure that there was a Santa Claus but that someone always left presents under my tree. Larry refuses to comment on the subject but he wears a knowing look.

**Running
Records**

We did manage to finish our second preprimer this month and again I had the children who are borderline read to me a few pages from the third preprimer and I took a running record. All but Daisy, Paul, Mike, and Chip could read with at least 90 percent word accuracy. Mort read well but I couldn't get him to tell me enough to be sure his comprehension is adequate. Chip was close enough and tries hard enough that I think he will be okay. I had Daisy, Paul, and Mike read to me the first selection in the second preprimer—the one we just finished. Daisy and Mike read it with better than 90 percent word accuracy. Paul didn't meet the criteria but he could read some and he told me what was happening in the story and seemed to enjoy it. I plan to continue my 10-minute timed repeated readings with Paul, Daisy, and Mike in the second preprimer as they, along with the rest of us, read the third preprimer together in January.

**Children with
Special Needs**

I did get the psychological report back on Paul. He doesn't qualify for anything! His IQ is well below average but not low enough for him to be classified EMH. Of course, his IQ is too low for him to be classified as learning disabled. Although he has many emotional problems, he is not severely enough disturbed to meet the criteria for the emotionally disturbed class. The report recommended that he be given individualized instruction on his level and that adjustments be made for his slow learning rate and his periods of inattention. I will continue to work with him, but it is frustrating that more can't be done. So often with a child like Paul, you know he needs help but he doesn't fit anywhere! Thank goodness for Daphne. I told the class that we would change reading partners when we began the second preprimer. Daphne approached me quietly that morning and asked to be able to keep Paul! "He reads a little with me and I think I am helping him. Can I still be his partner?"

**Teacher
Read-Aloud**

Our afternoon Teacher Read-Aloud/SQUIRT time is going exceptionally well. For many years now, I have suggested to parents that if they wanted to send me a holiday gift, they could donate an "easy-to-read" book to our classroom library. I have stressed that I didn't expect a gift but that if they wanted to buy something I would really appreciate, we could never have too many copies of the *Clifford* books; *One Fish, Two Fish, Red Fish, Blue Fish; Robert the Rose Horse;* or *The Gingerbread Man.* By now I have multiple copies of many of these easy-to-read classics. This month, I began reading them to the children. As I read, I made a tape of the reading. I signaled the children and they clapped their hands when it was time to turn each page. They also joined me in saying any repeated refrains—"Run, run, as fast as you can. You can't catch me. I'm the gingerbread man!"

Once I had read this book and made the tape, I pulled out my many copies of the book. The children were delighted and I distributed the books to them for their SQUIRT time. (I started this on Monday so, of course, Monday children got first choice of the books.)

The next day, I read another easy-to-read favorite of which I had multiple copies, making the tape with the children's help. Again, I let the children choose copies of the book read on the previous day and today's book. The Tuesday children got first choice today. By the end of the week, I had read aloud and made tapes of five easy-to-read books of which I had multiple copies. These books are out for all the children now and many children are amazed to find that they can really read them. I overheard Roberta remark that she was reading these books, not just pretend reading! That, of course, was my plan. By now most of them know enough to really read some of these old favorites, and they are delighted with their newfound ability! It is one thing to be able to read in a "schoolbook" like a preprimer, but a real book that you can buy in a store or get through the book club—that's reading!

Of course, I put the tape I made, along with multiple copies of the book, in our listening center. Each day from 2:15 to 2:45/3:00 (children leave on buses at staggered times), we have our center time. I started this many years ago when I realized that things would go well in our classroom for almost all day and then fall apart in the last 30 minutes. It was almost always during this last half hour that arguments would occur between the children, and I often found myself losing my composure and yelling at someone! Yelling is not my style and, after the children left, I would feel terrible and berate myself for not handling the situation better. "We were having such a nice day," I would think, "until it all fell apart at the end!"

Centers

After many years of teaching, I decided that neither the children nor I could give learning the kind of attention required by any subject after 2:15. I had been doing some center activities in the morning on certain days and I just decided to pretend the day ended at 2:15—get the children all ready to go, notes distributed, book bags on desks, and so forth, and then children could go to the centers. This is a very nice way to end the day. The children all look forward to it and because they get to choose what they want to do and don't have to attend to me or each other, there is almost no fussing or squabbling. (Mike does still have some problem during center time, but I give him one warning and then send him back to his seat, and he is learning some self-control!) I enjoy this time because I get to circulate and talk with the children individually, a luxury that I seldom have at any other time when I try to keep up with 25 children!

Some centers stay with us all the time and some centers change as we work on different projects. We have a center board in our room, and the number of clothespins there indicates how many children can go to each center at one time. Each day at 2:15, the children choose their centers. We do this by days of the week. On Thursday, the Thursday children go first to claim their clothespins, followed by the Wednesday, Tuesday, Monday, and Friday children. The Friday children who choose last on Thursday don't complain, though, because they know that they will choose first on Friday! Children can change centers if there is a clothespin available indicating space in the center they want to go to.

Each day I put two of the tapes we made and several copies of the easy-to-read books in the listening center. This has become a very popular center and is almost always chosen first. The children love hearing me read the books with themselves clapping to turn pages and joining in for repeated refrains.

Other popular centers this month have been the art center, in which I have put old greeting cards and the materials for making greeting cards, and the

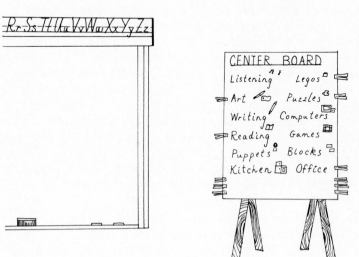

writing center, which has, among other things, stationery on which to write to Santa and catalogues of many of the items on their wish lists! I was delighted to see many of the children going off to find a copy of one of their favorite books so that they could copy its title on their list. Invented spelling is fine, but when it comes to someone knowing exactly which book you are hoping to find among your holiday presents, better make sure you spell it right!

January

January is always one of my very favorite teaching months, and this year has been no exception. The fall is wonderfully exciting with all the big holidays but exhausting too as I get to know a new class of children and get them smoothly into reading and writing and the routines they need to follow. But when we come back after the holidays, they and I are rested, eager, and ready to move!

Unit Teaching We did a big science unit on animals this month. Children love animals and we took a trip to the zoo. This was a major adventure because the zoo is two hours away. The bus rolled out of our parking lot here at 8:00 and we returned about 6:00. I always do this trip on a Friday so that I have the weekend to recover. It was worth it, however. Most of my children had never seen any animals except for pets and some farm animals—tigers, lions, bears, kangaroos, and penguins were just pictures in books and images from TV! Of course, we did a lot of research and reading and looking at videos before we went, and since we have come back, many of the children have started writing about various animals.

Our Writers' Workshop is moving along quite well. The children are all writing in their notebooks now. On Fridays, I let them select one piece they have written and draw a picture to go with it, but on the rest of the days, they are spending their full 15 minutes writing. I still do a minilesson each morning, but I am writing slightly longer pieces, just as they are. I have begun our editing checklist. **Editing** As I was getting ready to write one morning, I told the children that now that they were all real writers—writing in their writing notebooks every day—they would need to learn how to help each other edit their pieces. We talked about editors and publishing books and how every book that I had read to them or that they had read had been written by an author, but the author had an editor's help to make the book as exciting and easy to read as possible. I told them a little about publishing companies and how books got published and the many different people who are involved in the publishing of a book. I then wrote on a half sheet of chart paper:

Our Editor's Checklist

1. Do all the sentences make sense?

I explained to the children that one thing editors always read for is to make sure that all the sentences make sense. Sometimes, writers leave out words or forget to finish a sentence and then the sentences don't make sense. "Each day, after I write my piece, you can be my editors and help me decide if all my sentences make sense." I then wrote a piece and purposely left out a few words. The children who were, as always, reading along as I wrote and often anticipating my next word, noticed my mistakes immediately. When I finished writing, I said, "Now let's read my piece together and see if all my sentences make sense." The children and I read one sentence at a time, and when we got to the sentences where I had left a word out, we decided that the sentence didn't make sense because my mind had gotten ahead of my marker and I had left out some words. I wrote the words in with a different-colored marker and thanked the children for their good editing help. I then had a child come and draw a happy face on my paper because although my sentences didn't all make sense when I first wrote them, I checked for that and fixed them.

After I wrote my piece, the children all went off to their own writing. When the 15 minutes of allotted writing time was up, I rang my little bell and then walked up and pointed to the Editor's Checklist we had just begun. "Be your own editor now. Read your paper and see if all your sentences make sense. If you didn't finish a sentence or left a word out, take your red pen and fix it." I watched as the children did their best to see if their sentences made sense and noticed a few writing something with their red pens. After just a minute, I said, "Good. Now, use your red pen to draw yourself a little happy face to show you checked your sentences for making sense."

Every day after that when I wrote I would leave a word or two out or not finish the sentence. The children delight in being my editor and helping me make all my sentences make sense. Every day, when their writing time is up,

I point to the checklist and they read their own sentences for sense. They don't find every problem but they all know what they are trying to do and I have noticed almost everyone picking up the red pen and glancing up at the checklist as soon as I ring the bell to signal the end of writing time. I am about to add to our checklist a second thing to read for. I will add:

2. Do all the sentences start with capital letters?

Once I add that, I will begin some sentences with lowercase letters and let them help me edit for sentences both making sense and beginning with capital letters. Of course, they will read their own piece for these two things also. We will then be to the "two–happy-face" editing stage.

Our writing is going so well that next month we are going to start publishing some pieces. I have some volunteer parents making some blank books and I hope that by the end of February all my writers will be published authors!

Word Wall

The Words block is going well. I add five high-frequency words each week to our word wall. We continue to use our Monday Words time for making sure we know how to use these words and for handwriting lessons, and we do about eight minutes of looking, chanting, and writing practice each day. Many of my children are learning to spell these words. My slower children still have to find them to write them but they have all learned to read them. Paul and Daisy are the only two who cannot read almost every word up there.

Making Words

I continue to do some work with rhyming words and, one day a week, I do the Post-it–covered word sentences they enjoy so much, in which they practice using the context, beginning letters, and word length to figure out unknown words. I also began this month our Making Words lessons. Making Words is a manipulative hands-on activity through which children learn how letters go together to make words. I usually do two Making Words lessons each week. For the first five lessons, I gave the children only one vowel. Here is how the very first Making Words lesson went.

I did the first lesson on a Tuesday. The letters for this first lesson were *u, k, n, r, s,* and *t.* I have made letter cards with the lowercase letter on one side and the capital letter on the other side for all the letters. The vowel letters are written with a permanent red marker and they are stored in red plastic cups, one for each vowel. The consonants are written with a blue marker and stored in blue plastic cups. The Tuesday children each had a cup and went around and gave one letter to each child. Meanwhile, I passed out holders made by cutting file folders in half and folding up and stapling the bottom inch. The children all had their little letter cards in front of their holders, and I had big letter cards in the pocket chart.

I began the lesson by making sure the children had and could name all their letters. I held up the *u* card from the pocket chart and had them hold up their *u*. I told them that the *u* was red because it was the vowel, that every word needed at least one vowel and that because their only vowel today was the *u*, they would need it for every word. I then held up the other letters, named each, and had the children hold up and name theirs. I told them that we would use these letters to make lots of words and that at the end of the lesson, we would make a word that used all six letters. I then wrote a 2 on the board and told them that the first word would use only two letters. I asked them to take two letters and make *us*. I had them say the word *us* and watched as they decided how to spell *us*. I then asked Mike, who had made *us* correctly with his little letters, to come up and make it with the pocket chart letters. I then put the word *us*, which I had written on an index card, along the top of the pocket chart.

Next, I crossed out the 2 on the board and wrote a 3. I had the children hold up three fingers and told them that the next word would take three letters. I asked them to take three letters and make *run*. Again, I watched and sent someone who had made it correctly to make it with the pocket chart letters. I placed the word *run* next to *us* along the top of the pocket chart. "Change the first letter in *run* and you can change your *run* into *sun*." They made two more three-letter words, *nut* and *rut*, and then I crossed out the 3, wrote a 4 on the board, and said, "If you add a letter to *rut* you can change your *rut* into *ruts*. After it rains, my driveway has lots of ruts in it."

Once a child had come and made *ruts* with the big letters, I said, "Now, this is a real magic trick. Don't take any of the letters in *ruts* out of your holder and don't add any. Just change around where the letters are, and you can change your *ruts* into *rust*. Say *rust*. When we leave things made of metal out in the rain, they might rust." The children seemed amazed to discover that just changing the position of those last two letters could change *ruts* to *rust*!

We then made two more four-letter words, *tusk* and *stun*.

I crossed out the 4, wrote a 5, and said, "Now we are going to make a five-letter word. Take five letters and make *trunk*. We have been studying about animals and we know that an elephant has a trunk. Say *trunk* slowly and listen to where you hear all those letters."

At the beginning of the lesson, when we were making *us* and *run* and changing *run* to *sun*, I had been monitoring my slower children and sending them to make the word with the pocket chart letters, but the lesson had now moved to a challenging stage, and I was watching to see how Danielle and Pat were going to spell *trunk*. Pat got it spelled correctly, and as she did so, she also realized what word you could make with all the letters. "If you put the *s* on *trunk*, you have *trunks*," she exclaimed. "That's exactly right," I said. I then had her make *trunk* with the pocket chart letters, asked everyone to make sure they had made it right with their little letters, and let her show how adding the *s* made the word *trunks*.

Next, I had the children close their folders with the word *trunk* still in them and directed their attention to the words on index cards I had been placing along the top of the pocket chart. I had them read the words with me and talk about what we changed to make them:

us run sun nut rut ruts rust tusk stun trunk trunks

I then placed the words *run*, *sun*, and *stun* together and helped the children to know that they all had *un* at the end and they all rhymed. We did the same with the rhyming words *nut* and *rut*. Finally, we said all the words and noticed that they all had just the vowel *u* and that the *u* had the same sound in all the words. I left the words we had made in the pocket chart and asked the children who had passed out letters to pick up the same letters.

That afternoon when the children were getting ready to go home, I gave them a take-home strip. The strip had the letters *u k n r s t*. Most children immediately recognized that these were the letters they had used to make words. "For homework," I said, "take this strip home and cut it up and see if some adult in your family can figure out what word you can make from all these letters. Don't tell them right away that the word is *trunks* but see if they can figure it out. Then, show them all the other words you made from just these six letters." Once again we read the words lined up in the pocket chart, and I could tell that the children were going to enjoy seeing if they could stump their parents!

We did several other lessons this month with just one vowel. From the letters *i, g, n, p, r,* and *s,* we made the words *in, pin, pig, rip, rips, nips, spin, pins, sing, ring,* and *spring*. From the letters *o, g, n, r, s,* and *t,* we made *so, no, go, got, rot, not, song, sort, rots, snort,* and *strong*. From the letters *e, d, p, n, s,* and *s,* we made *Ed, Ned, end, pen, den, pens, dens, send, spend,* and *spends*. From the letters *a, h, l, p, s,* and *s,* we made *Al, pal, lap, sap, has, ash, sash, pass, pals, slap, slaps,* and *splash*.

The children enjoy manipulating the letters to make words. Even Paul stays with us most days for the easier words in the lesson. My whiz kids love trying to figure out the word that can be made with all the letters. Making Words, when you always start with easy words and end up with a big word made from all the letters, is truly a multilevel activity. The parents tell me that their children love bringing home their Making Words strips and often stumping them about what word can be made with all the letters.

February

As this anonymous valentine shows, the children are becoming independent writers as well as independent readers! In addition to all the Valentine's Day excitement, we have done units this month on African Americans in celebration of Black History Month and we have learned about our nation's presidents, including Abraham Lincoln and George Washington. I read several biographies to them, including *If You Grew Up with Abraham Lincoln* by Ann McGovern, *If You Grew Up with George Washington* by Ruth Belov Gross, and *A Picture Book of Martin Luther King* by David Adler. We have talked about biographies and autobiographies. The children are fascinated with the idea of autobiographies and with it being such a huge word!

Multicultural Awareness

I have modeled how you write biographies during some of my minilessons, and last week, when I wrote a "When I Was Your Age" tale telling about my first-grade boyfriend and the valentine I made for him, Larry observed, "If these 'When I Was Your Age' stories are true, you are really writing your autobiography!" I had never really thought about that before, but I had to admit that I was at least writing the six-year-old part of my autobiography! At any rate, many of the children are into writing biographies and autobiographies!

Publishing

We have published one set of books and the children are thrilled. Before we

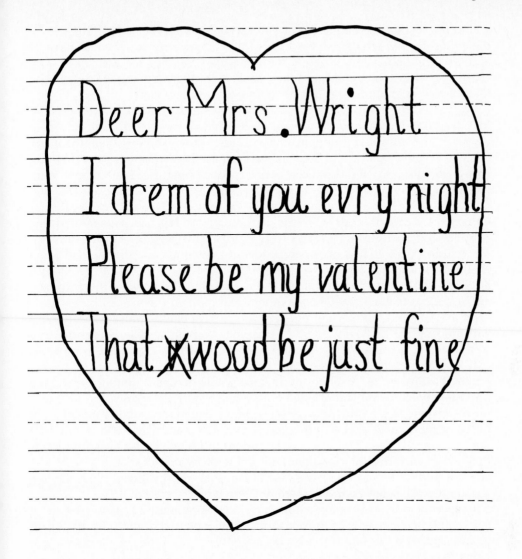

Deer Mrs. Wright
I drem of you evry night
Please be my valentine
That ✗wood be just fine

began, I showed them the book made last year by Jonathan, a boy in my room who moved and forgot to take his book. I read the book to them, beginning with the dedication page *(Dedicated to Mrs. Wright and all the people in my class),* reading the story about a soccer match between Jonathan's team and his cousin's team, talking about the illustrations that Jonathan had done to accompany his writing, and ending with the "About the Author" page on which I had written:

Jonathan Marr is seven years old and is in the first grade at Merritt Elementary School. He loves to read and write and play soccer. This book tells the true story of his soccer team's biggest victory!

I then explained how Jonathan and my other first graders last year had made the books. "They couldn't all make books at once," I explained, "because, as you know, books need editors and you can help each other edit, but I will be the editor-in-chief who approves final copy!" No editor-in-chief could have 25 authors in the publishing stage at the same time! Because we had talked a lot about publishing companies and how books got published, the children knew that a book takes a lot of work after the first draft is written.

I explained how I had helped Jonathan's class and would help their class so that everyone would publish a book by the end of the month, but only one-third of the class would be publishing at a time. I then showed them the blank books that some parents had helped me assemble. The books were spiral-bound with covers made from half sheets of construction paper. Inside each book were half sheets of ditto paper. The first page of each book had a place for the title, author, and date. The second page said "Dedicated to" and had several lines on which the author could write the dedication. The last page said "About the Author" and had lines on which I would write something about each of them. The middle pages all had two writing lines at the bottom and the top half blank for the illustration. I showed the children that the parents had made books with 8, 12, 16, and 20 pages and reminded them that some books were much shorter and some books much longer than others. We counted the pages in Jonathan's book and realized that he had published a 12-page book! "Most of your books will probably be 12 pages, too," I remarked, "but some may be shorter and some longer!" I could see by the looks on Larry's, Steve's, and Roberta's faces that they already had long books in mind!

I then explained to the children how we would go about getting everyone a published book by the end of the month. I had arbitrarily divided the class into thirds, making sure to put my weakest writers—Paul, Daisy, and Alexander—in different thirds and my best writers—Larry, Hilda, and Pat—also in different thirds. I wanted Paul, Daisy, and Alexander in different cycles because I knew they would each require a lot of individual attention, and I wanted Larry, Hilda, and Pat in different cycles so they could help me edit! I showed them the list, and there were some grumblings from children who were not going to be first, but I told them that everyone would have their turn and that those publishing later would have more time to work on a really good first draft. Roberta chimed in and said, "I don't care if I'm in the last group. I need the time because I am going to write a really long book!"

Finally, I explained how we would make each book. The children who were in the first group had to decide by tomorrow which first draft they wanted to make into a book. We would work together to help each writer make the meaning clear and the book as interesting and exciting as possible. Then children would work with partners to do a first editing. I would do a final editing, and the children would copy their piece into their book and do the illustrations. "By the end of the month, if we all work hard together, you will all have a published book like Jonathan's!"

It was easier said than done, but we did do it! For the rest of the month, we continued beginning Writers' Workshop with my minilesson and ending it with the children whose day it was sharing in the Author's Chair, but during the 15 to 20 minutes of writing time, two-thirds of the class were writing in their notebooks while I helped the other third edit and publish.

On the first publishing day, I sat down with Paul, Daphne, Pat, Rita, Horace, Danielle, Jeff, and Mike. I had each person read the piece he or she wanted to publish, and after they read, I and the other children made comments. As in Author's Chair sharing, we always bgan by telling the writer one thing we liked. Next, however, I modeled helping the author make the piece as clear and exciting as possible by comments such as, "Daphne, I loved your story about your grandmother and I know she will love reading this book. You say she is very nice to you. Tell me some of the nice things she does."

Daphne had many examples of her grandmother's love and caring, and I suggested that she address these to her story. I told her to write these on another sheet of paper and then, when we edited, we would figure out where they should be inserted.

As each child read, I tried to listen for anything that was unclear or something that could be added to make the book more interesting and I suggested this. I also invited the suggestions of the other writers, and some of them had good comments. In the time we had that first day, five of the eight children read their first-draft pieces and listened to our comments on meaning. We finished this on the second day. I knew that Paul would not share his with the group and so I got him to tell me ahead of time what he wanted to publish and then I explained this to the group. They were very supportive and said Paul's book about George, our gerbil, was going to be terrific! On the third day, the children worked on adding or changing anything they wanted to do based on our comments. They then chose someone to help them read their piece for the two things on our Editor's Checklist: Do all the sentences make sense, and do they all begin with capital letters?

While they did this, I worked with Paul. I explained that I wanted him to have a great book about George the gerbil and I got him to tell me what he wanted to say. I then wrote his sentences on a clean sheet of paper and let him choose an 8-page book. I had him read his simple sentences to me several times and made sure he understood that he would copy them in his book and then illustrate them. I asked him who he wanted to dedicate the book to and helped him write *My Mom* on the "Dedicated to" page.

By the fourth day, Paul was working on his book and I was ready to play editor-in-chief for my other writers. I talked with them first and helped them decide how many pages they needed in their book and about how much would go on each page. They wrote the page number on their first draft in red pen above what they thought would fit on each page. I told them that the sentences wouldn't all fit exactly on each page and that it would be fine for sentences to go over to the next page. By knowing approximately what was going on each page, the children could begin their illustrations while I was helping each child edit. For the next three days, I worked with each child individually to edit his or her piece. I helped them fix up sentences that didn't make sense. I inserted needed punctuation and wrote the correct spelling of words above their invented spelling. After my editing, they copied their writing into their books and did their illustrations.

Seven days after I began with this first group, I had the second group sitting with me and reading their chosen piece so that we could give them feedback on their message. Children from the first group finished up their illustrations and then went back to their writing notebook first-draft writing. I helped Alexander, who was in this group, just as I had helped Paul, and he got a nice book written about his dog.

By the time I got to the final third, they were ready to go. The children who had already published had shared their books when it was their day in the Author's Chair, and the last third had a better idea than the others about what they were trying to accomplish. They worked hard, and by the very last day in February, all 25 of my children were published authors. I have put their published books in special baskets in our classroom reading center, and these are very popular choices for reading during SQUIRT.

The children are already asking me when they can do another book! We are going to take a few weeks just for first drafts at the beginning of March and then we will begin another book publishing cycle. This is a lot of work but the pride they take in their books and their clear sense that they are all real writers now makes it worth all the time and trouble!

Work in the other blocks has also moved along this month. We now have 65 words on the wall besides our names. We continue to do work with rhyming patterns, Post-it note sentences, and Making Words lessons.

Guided Reading

We are now reading in the adopted primer for some of our Guided Reading lessons. On Thursdays and Fridays, however, I am using some flexible groups to provide more challenging reading for my better readers and easier reading for my children who still need lots of easy reading. I introduce the books to all the children, explaining that I didn't have enough copies of any of the books for all to read them, but that after each group had read them, I would put them out for everyone to share. They are in four sharing groups and, most days, they read the book by themselves or with a friend for the first 15 minutes and then get together as a small group and read and talk about it.

Fortunately, I was able to order some six-pack copies of some *Sunshine* and *Story Box* books. I am using the easiest levels of these books with Paul, Daisy, Mike, Chip, and Alexander. Mort, Jeff, Carl, Butch, Manuel, and Alex are reading books that are a little harder. Horace, Betty, Daphne, Mandy, Mitch, Anthony, and Joyce are reading the highest-level books in these series, which are on a good solid first-reader level. Larry, Steve, Pat, Roberta, Rita, Hilda, and Danielle are reading multiple copies of chapter books, including Arnold Lobel's *Frog and Toad* books and James Marshall's *George and Martha* books. Thursday's and Friday's Guided Reading block is a four-ring circus, but the children are clearly enjoying the books, and along with the comprehension-oriented guidance I give them during their primer-level reading on Monday, Tuesday, and Wednesday, I know they are all moving ahead in their ability to read independently.

Self-Selected Reading

Their burgeoning independent reading ability is really showing up during our afternoon Read-Aloud/SQUIRT time. I am reading to them from more advanced books for 15 minutes and they are reading on their own for the remaining 15 minutes. Even Mike is getting to the point where he actually settles down and reads most days! Now if I could just find something to motivate Mort and captivate Daisy!

March

We did a science unit on weather this month. We read two terrific Big Books, *What Will the Weather Be Like Today?* by Paul Rogers and *Caps, Hats, Socks, and Mittens* by Louisa Borden. I also read many other books to them. Their two favorites were both about snow—*The Snowy Day* by Ezra Jack Keats and *White Snow, Bright Snow* by Alvin Tresselt.

We are up to the three–happy-face stage of our Editor's Checklist with the addition of:

3. Do all the sentences have . ? or ! at the end?

Now in my writing, I make all kinds of mistakes. I leave a word out, resulting in a sentence that doesn't make sense. I begin sentences with lowercase letters and sometimes stick a capital right in the middle of a word. I sometimes write a whole piece of four or five sentences without a single ending punctuation mark. The children are getting good at seeing my mistakes and helping me edit. At the end of their writing time each day, I remind them to read their sentences for sense, beginning capitals, and ending punctuation and to give themselves three happy faces.

We are halfway through our second book publishing cycle. The third that had to wait 'til last to make their first books went first this time and the first third has to wait until last. This publishing has gone much more smoothly because we all learned so much the first time through. They are producing some really terrific books. We should be able to get one more publishing cycle in and then they will all have three published books to take home for the summer!

My children are getting so fast at chanting and writing their five words each day that I have added an "on the back" activity. After they have written the five called-out words on the front and checked them by tracing around them, I have them turn their papers over and we do an activity on the back. At least one day a week, I have them write their word wall word with an ending. I always preface this with "Sometimes when you're writing, . . ." because I really stress that the word wall is not there just so we can chant and write the words during our daily word wall practice but to help us when we are writing.

Last Tuesday, I had called out the five words: *play, go, come, give,* and *want.* When they turned their papers over, I said, "Lots of times when you are writing, you need to write a word that is on our wall but you need to add an ending. What if you were writing *I was playing baseball,* how would you spell *playing*? I got them to tell me that you would spell playing *p-l-a-y-i-n-g* and then to write it on their papers. I continued, having them write *wanting, going, coming,* and *giving,* making sure they told me about dropping the *e* before adding *ing* before writing the last two.

On Wednesday, I called out the five words: *house, look, thing, those,* and *saw.* When they turned their papers over, I said, "Lots of times when you are writing, you need to spell a word that is not on our word wall, but if you can think of a word that is on our word wall that rhymes with the word you want to write, you might be able to use that word to help you spell your word. What if you

Unit Teaching

Editing

Publishing

Word Wall

were writing a story about a mouse, which word from the wall will help you spell *mouse?* I had the children tell me that "since *house* is spelled *h-o-u-s-e, mouse* is probably spelled *m-o-u-s-e.*" They wrote *mouse* on the back of their papers and I continued in the same manner. What if you were writing about a crook? A rose? Some string? A house of straw? For each word, I had them tell me the word wall word that rhymed and how that might help them spell the word they needed and then spell it aloud before writing it. These on-the-back activities are taking only about two minutes each and are giving me a lot of good spelling practice beyond just the word wall words.

Guided Reading

We are finishing the primer in our Guided Reading block and have continued our small-group reading of multiple copies of easier or more challenging books on Thursdays and Fridays. This is working out remarkably well and I plan to continue this as we read in our adopted basal first reader during April and May. Reading the chapter books has given the highest readers a lot of confidence, and I see many of them spending most of the SQUIRT time reading chapter books in the afternoons. Sometimes they are rereading the ones they read earlier during Guided Reading and sometimes they are reading new ones. Actually, many of my children are rereading during SQUIRT the books we read during Guided Reading, as well as their old favorites that we earlier made tapes of. I forget from year to year what absolute delight children take in being able to "really read!" and how much they enjoy reading books again and again, for the sheer pleasure of doing it!

Decoding

This month, I have made a special effort to get my children actually using the letter-sound knowledge they have when they are reading. When they write, they have to represent the word in some way, so they do use their letter-sound knowledge to invent spell. But getting them to look at the letters and use what they know to figure out a word in reading is harder.

Teacher Modeling

I do several things to help them learn to apply their phonics skills. One thing I do is to model for them how I would decode an unknown word. I do this most often during the afternoon science and social studies time because that is when I am most often introducing words to the whole class and having them do some reading in their science and social studies books.

This month our science unit was on weather. I wrote sentences on the board one at a time, underlining the words I wanted to introduce. I told the students that the underlined words were words they didn't know but that if they used the letter sounds they knew and made sure the words made sense, they would be able to figure them out.

I read the first sentence and stopped when I got to the underlined word, *hot.* I then thought aloud, "Hmm, if I didn't know this word, how could I figure it out? I know that *h* usually has the sound it has in *hamburger* and *house.* I know that *n-o-t* spells *not* and *l-o-t* spells *lot. H-o-t* should be a rhyming word—*hot!* Yes, hot makes sense because it is a kind of weather."

I then had children read the other sentences, led them to figure out the underlined words, and helped them to explain how they might have figured it out. *Cold* was decoded based on the rhyming word *old.* The children knew the words *rain* and *sun* and pronounced "rainy" and "sunny" so that they sounded right in the sentence. *Storms* was decoded because "it starts with *st,* has *ms* at

_A a B b C c D d E e F f G g H h I i J j K k L l M m N n O o P p Q q R r S s T t U u V v W w X x Y y Z z_

Today is ————————

Sometimes the weather is <u>hot</u>.
Sometimes the weather is <u>cold</u>.
Some days are <u>rainy</u>.
Some days are <u>sunny</u>.
Some days we have bad <u>storms</u>.
On <u>stormy</u> days, we see
<u>lightning</u> and hear <u>thunder</u>.

the end, and makes sense because storms are bad." _Stormy_ was difficult, but when I pointed out how _rain_ and _sun_ became _rainy_ and _sunny_, most of the children understood it. _Lightning_ was decoded because "you see lightning on stormy days, and it has _light_ as the first part." _Thunder_ "begins with _th_ and ends like _her_, and you hear thunder in storms."

Next, I had the children read part of the weather chapter in their science books. I told them that there would be several new words they would have to figure out and reminded them of what they could do when they came to a word they didn't know. After they had read, I let several children write words on the board that they had figured out in their reading and explain how they had figured them out.

On the following morning, I gave each child a yellow index card and asked all of the children to try to find a word somewhere in their reading that day that they didn't know. They should write that word on the yellow card and then use the card to mark the page on which they found the word. At the end of the day, each child who found a word came to the board, wrote that word on the board, read the sentence in which the child had found the word, and tried to explain how he or she had figured it out. The children really seemed to like doing this, so I designated Wednesdays as official "word-busting" days. Every Wednesday the children get their yellow cards and are on the lookout for one new word they can figure out. I hope their enthusiasm stays high.

April

All year I have been concerned with providing direct experiences to promote concept development and increase the depth and breadth of my children's meaning vocabulary store. Whenever possible, I bring real objects into the classroom

**Direct
Experience**

and encourage them to bring objects in. We not only name each object, we also describe and classify it and decide which attributes it shares with other objects and how it is different from other objects. Often these objects relate to the science or social studies unit we are studying, and in addition to talking about these objects, we write about them in group-experience stories. I also use many films, filmstrips, picture books, and pictures to provide the students with visual experience with words and concepts for which we don't have real objects readily available. Years ago, I started a picture file for one of my methods courses and I have added to it ever since. Currently my picture file categories include: food, animals, plants, clothes, occupations, vehicles, holidays, city life, South America, Asia, Africa, United States, famous people, tools and utensils, and a huge and disorderly miscellaneous category. I have laminated with clear adhesive plastic most of the pictures I have collected and I find it an invaluable resource in concept and meaning vocabulary development.

Meaning Vocabulary

I also do many categorization activities with my children to help them clarify and extend meanings for words. One I particularly enjoy doing is a list, group, and label lesson originated by Taba (1967) for use in the social studies curricula. To do a list, group, and label lesson, you begin by asking children a question that will elicit many responses. Last week, as we were beginning our science unit on nutrition, I asked the children to list all the foods they could think of. As they named various foods, I wrote these food words on the board. From time to time, I stopped to read what was already listed on the board and encouraged them to think of more foods. Finally, when we had filled almost the whole board, I said, "Let's just have Mike, Roberta, and Horace tell me their foods since they have their hands up. We will then have the whole board full of food." I then reread the whole list, letting the children read along with me if they desired. I then left the list on the board for the next day.

On the following afternoon, I pointed to our list of foods and told the children that I was going to read the list again and that this time they should listen and think, "Are there any foods on the list that seem to go together in some way?" I then read the entire list and asked if anyone had a group of foods that seemed to go together.

Mitch said that cake, cookies, chocolate pie, ice cream, and gingerbread went together. I wrote these five on a sheet of chart paper and asked him why he had put these foods together. He said, "Because you eat them all after the meal." I then asked him if he could think of a name or label for his group. He hesitated a moment and then said, "Desserts."

Steve put mushrooms, grapes, berries, rhubarb, and nuts together. I listed these five foods on the chart paper and asked him why he had put those particular foods together. He said it was because they all grew wild. I then asked him if he could give a name or label to that group. After some hesitation, he said, "Things that Grow Wild."

Chip put peanuts, chocolate candy, hamburgers, potato chips, soda, oranges, and tomatoes together. I listed them and in response to my "why" question, he said, "Because they are my favorite things to eat." When I asked him to give a name or label to this group, he couldn't. I said that that was fine, that we couldn't always think of names for groups, and went on to the next child.

While doing these lessons, I accept every child's response. During the listing process, everyone usually contributes something, but I call on the children with smaller vocabularies first so that they have a chance to contribute. I usually save the grouping and labeling steps for the next day so that the lessons don't take more than 25 minutes. When we form groups, each child who wants to organize a group tells me why those particular things are grouped together and then attempts to give a label to that group. This labeling step is difficult for many of my children, and if they can't do it, I simply accept that and go on to the next volunteer.

As you can see, the children have different categories and different reasons for grouping things together. Therefore, no child is allowed to add anything to another child's group. I also write the name of the child who labeled a group under that group. Objects from the list can be used over and over again as different children make groups. The children enjoy these lessons, and I can see that they have had an effect on their vocabulary and categorization skills.

We are through with our second book publishing cycle and everyone is going to publish one more book in May. The children are even more excited about this last book, and those children who have been in the second publishing third each time have already informed me that it is their turn to be first! I have added the fourth and final thing to our Editor's Checklist:

Editing

4. Do all the people and place names and I start with a capital?

I continue to write each day and the children help me fix my piece using the four items on the checklist. I have been amazed at how well all my children are writing. When I think back to my early teaching days when I thought that children had to be able to read well before they could write independently, I am appalled! It is perfectly clear that with word wall and content board support plus encouragement and modeling of invented spelling, all children can write and, for many of them, writing is their major avenue to reading. I consider all four blocks—Writing, Words, Guided Reading, and Teacher Read-Aloud/ SQUIRT—equally important, but I must admit that Writing is the block in which many of my lowest and highest achievers seem to make the most progress.

We now have 110 high-frequency words on the word wall, in addition to the **Word Wall** names. I am not going to add any more words this year because I want to use May to really help them consolidate their knowledge of these critical words. I am doing daily practice with the words. On Mondays we are making up sentences, using only words on the wall or on our content word boards. This is quite a challenging task but the children are enjoying it. After they make up the sentence, I locate all the words and we all write the sentence. We are trying to make up big "fancy" sentences and they are very clever at combining the words. Here are the three sentences they composed last Monday using the word wall and our nutrition board. (The underlined words are attached to our nutrition board. The others are on the word wall.)

Vegetables are very very good for you.
People should not eat too much junk food.
People should eat some cereals and grains.

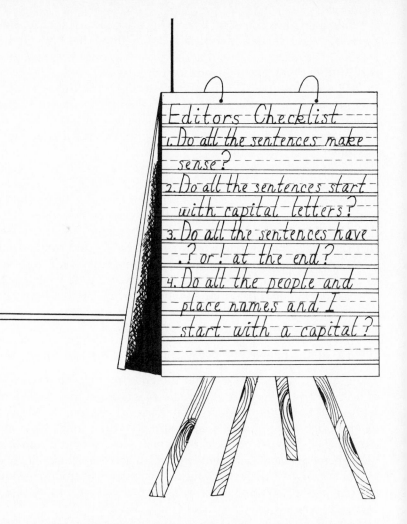

Editors Checklist
1. Do all the sentences make sense?
2. Do all the sentences start with capital letters?
3. Do all the sentences have . ? or ! at the end?
4. Do all the people and place names and I start with a capital?

I am continuing to do an "on-the-back" activity after we chant and write five words on Tuesday through Friday. In addition to adding endings to our wall words and spelling rhyming words, we have written some compound words—*boyfriend, girlfriend, playhouse, without, cannot, someone, something, somewhere, everything, seesaw,* and so forth. The children are very impressed with their ability to spell such big words! I am also occasionally having them put the five words they wrote on the front in alphabetical order on the back as we begin to learn some alphabetizing/dictionary skills.

Making Words   We are continuing to do Making Words lessons at least twice a week. Whenever possible, I tie these into our science/social studies units or what we are reading during Guided Reading. This month we did three lessons in which the last word connected to nutrition. From the letters *a, o, c, r, r, s,* and *t,* we made the words *car, cat, rat, rot, cot, coat, cost, star, oats, coats, coast, roast, actor,* and *carrots.* We then sorted out the rhyming words and also the words that had *oa.* From the letters *a, e, o, g, n, r,* and *s,* we made *or, oar, ore, nor, Ron, ran, rag, sag, gas, nose, rose, sore, soar, snore,* and *oranges.* We sorted out the homophones *or, oar, ore* and *sore, soar* and talked about their meanings and the fact that the *or, oar,* and *ore* patterns sounded alike. We also sorted the other rhyming words.

The word that no one could figure out was the word that can be made from the letters *a, a, e, o, l, m,* and *t.* They noticed immediately that they had more red letters—vowels—than blue letters and this had never happened before. I began by having them take three letters and make *eat.* Then I told them that they could just change their letters around and that, like magic, these same three letters could spell *ate.* When they had accomplished that trick, I told them that the same three letters in different places would spell the word *tea.* While they were still marveling at three words they knew spelled with the same three letters, I had them add a letter to *tea* and turn it into *team,* and then move the same four letters around to spell *tame, meat,* and *mate.* After changing *mate* to *late* and *late* to *lame,* I had them move the letters in *lame* around to spell *meal* and then *male.* The children are really getting the idea that where you put letters makes a big difference in what word you spell, and this lesson with so many "turn-around" words made a big impression on them. We finished up the lesson by spelling *mole* and *motel* and then, since no one had figured out the word that could be made with all the letters (and most of my children were convinced that there was no such word!), I got to show them how all their letters could be used to spell *oatmeal!* They hate it when I stump them like this, and I don't get to do it very often. We then sorted the words into those in which the *e* and *a* were right together and those in which the *a* was followed by a consonant and then the *e,* and talked about these two important spelling patterns. Most of my children's invented spelling in their writing is showing the benefit of our making and sorting words. They now know that you have to listen for what you hear but that it often takes more letters than you hear to spell words in English.

We are reading in the first reader of our adopted series now along with easier and more challenging books in sharing groups on Thursday and Friday. I had each of them come and read to me a few pages of a story toward the end of their first reader, and all but Paul, Daisy, Mike, Butch, and Alexander met or exceeded the 90 percent word identification criteria I use when I make running records of their reading. I then had these five read to me from a primer story they had not read before and all but Paul were successful with that. While I would love to have them all reading at or above grade level at the end of the year, I know that not everyone can accomplish that in one year's time. I am delighted that Daisy, Mike, and Alexander have moved as far as they have and even Paul is not a nonreader. When he is having an "alert" day, he can read preprimer material independently.

Guided Reading

Running Records

I am also glad that all my children see themselves as readers and writers! That is one of the main benefits of not putting them in fixed ability groups and giving them multiple opportunities to read and write. The discouraged, defeated attitude that has taken hold by this time in the year for children in the bottom group is not evident in my lowest children. I just hope they can make some more progress next month, and I am going to do my best to encourage their parents to take them to the library and read with them this summer. I know Mike's mother will try. I am not sure about Butch's, Alexander's, or Daisy's parents, and I have yet to meet Paul's mother. I am also going to encourage Chip's and Carl's parents to make library trips and books a regular part of their summer. They are about on grade level now, but they probably won't be if they don't look at a book for three months!

May

Well, the year is almost over. Just one more week of school for the children and lots of report writing and finishing up for me. I always feel a little sad during the last weeks of school—so much yet undone. All in all, this has been an exceptionally good year. The children have all learned to read and write and do math and I know they know a lot more about the world we live in than they did when they entered this classroom in September.

Unit Teaching

We finished the year with a social studies unit on friends and a science unit on water. I like to do the friends unit at the end of the year because by now the children have so many friends here at school and they also have friends in their neighborhoods and in the places they will visit this summer. We talk about what it means to be a friend and how most of us have friends who have moved away or whom we see only at certain times of the year. We locate on the map the places they will visit this summer as well as places where some of their friends have moved to. I modeled writing letters to some friends during my minilessons and I did a few "When I Was Your Age" tales, in which I wrote about my friends when I was in first grade. Of course, we read some books about friends and reread some of their old favorite *Frog and Toad* and *George and Martha* stories.

Content Area Integration

Our water unit was, as always, a lot of fun. Many of the children will vacation near some kind of water this summer and the rest will spend some time at the community pool. We did lots of experiments with water, learned about water pollution and the need for water conservation, and realized how critical and huge a part water plays in our everyday lives. We read books about the ocean and other bodies of water and enjoyed some more of the Jerry Pallotta alphabet books, including *The Ocean Alphabet Book* and *The Underwater Alphabet Book*. By far, the children's favorite book this month was *The Magic School Bus at the Waterworks*. Like the other books in Joanna Cole and Bruce Degan's science series, this book finds Mrs. Frizzle and her class taking an incredible journey—this time right through the town's waterworks! The children marveled at what they found on this journey! They remarked longingly, "Wouldn't it be wonderful if we could really go inside things like they can on *The Magic School Bus!*"

Fortunately, Ms. Maverick's class had foreseen the popularity of *The Magic School Bus* books and had ordered many copies of each title for their annual end-of-the-year book fair. My class was one of the first to go, and they bought up all the copies of *The Magic School Bus at the Waterworks* and a lot of the other titles. This book fair is a super idea but I worry about the children who can't scrape together any money. Paul surprised me by bringing five dollars, which he spent with great care. Daisy had money but wouldn't spend it. The others teased her, saying that she was probably going to spend it all on candy! Chip was the only one who didn't bring any money, but I had anticipated that and had hired him to stay after school for several nights and help me do some of the end-of-the-year packing up, and then I paid him with books he had selected.

Last week, we had an experience in here! Sue Port came and asked me if I would spend a half day with all the first-grade teachers in the school system and explain to them my four-block approach to reading and writing. I protested that I couldn't possibly explain this in just a few hours' time, but she persisted. Then she had this brainstorm! "How about if I send our central office media person to make some videotapes of what is happening in here? That way, you could show them what is happening and the teachers would really understand what a lively, varied day the children have and how well they are all reading and writing!" Before I could convince her that I didn't want someone in my room taping everything we did during these last hectic days, she had bustled off to "set it up"!

The next morning Miss Media arrived and she stayed for three days! Of course, the children were beside themselves on the first day and I didn't think we would get any good tape. But on the second and third days, they settled down and started ignoring the camera—as did I—and, while I haven't looked at it all yet, I do think we will have some parts that really do show what is happening and how well the children are reading and writing. On the third day, Miss Media had each child bring a book he or she wanted to read and the last book he or she authored, and each child read a few pages of the favorite book and the entire authored book for the camera. This part we did watch together as a class, and the children all did remarkably well. The books Danielle, Pat, and Larry read parts of were chapter books usually read by fourth graders. Mike's authored collection of monster stories is extraordinarily clever! Even Paul had one of the *Sunshine* readers he enjoyed reading and could read the book he wrote. I hate to admit it, but Sue was right. I am going to pick portions to show each block, as well as the children reading and writing. The fact that my top children and bottom children are reading and writing better than anyone could expect them to is undeniable when you see them doing it. While I don't enjoy talking to groups of my peers, particularly other teachers I work with, I think I might actually look forward to this presentation!

THE FIRST-GRADE MEETING

Sue Port called the meeting to order and introduced Mrs. Wright. "To most of you, Freida Wright needs no introduction. Freida has taught at Merritt Elementary School for more years than she likes to admit to. Freida has served on and, at times, chaired your grade-level curriculum committees. Freida is, and has been for many years, an outstanding first-grade teacher, who uses all means at her disposal to get children off to a terrific start. Last year, Freida began implementing what she calls her four-block approach to reading and writing. She had read about this approach to organizing beginning reading instruction, and the idea that children do not all learn in the same way and that multiple methods were needed if all children were going to succeed was one she had believed in for many years. Another part of this organizational plan she agreed with was not putting children in reading groups. Reading groups have been our major way of dealing with the differences children at entering literacy levels bring with them to school, but the effectiveness of reading groups has been seriously questioned in recent years. I don't want to take any more of Freida's precious time because, knowing Freida, I am sure she has this planned down to the minute, but I do want you to know that I have been impressed with what I have seen in Freida's classroom in the past two years and it is at my insistence that she is here to share with you today."

The assembled teachers clapped in a restrained, polite way as Freida rose to speak. The anticipation she had felt earlier began to turn to anxiety as she looked out at the somewhat skeptical faces of some of her colleagues. She began by telling them that she felt a little uneasy talking to them about first grade. She knew most of them and knew that they were all terrific first-grade teachers.

"If you had asked me two years ago to honestly tell you how good a job I thought I was doing as a first-grade teacher, I would have told you that there were things I would like to change—mostly things about some of the kids (some teachers nodded and laughed in agreement, and Mrs. Wright began to relax a little!), but that all in all I thought I was doing as well as you could, considering the wide range of children we have at Merritt and the lack of home support many of the children we teach today have. Two years ago this summer, however, I read these two articles, which Sue has had duplicated for you to take with you (Cunningham, Hall, & Defee, 1991; Cunningham, 1991), and I got excited by what I read. A lot of what was in the articles I was already doing, but the teachers who developed the four-block approach had put components together in what looked to me like a very workable, practical way. Last year, I tried out some of the parts of this approach and this year, I jumped in feet first! I am the same teacher, teaching in the same school, teaching the same variety of children, using the same materials, working as hard as I always work, and my children—particularly the ones at the very bottom and the ones at the very top—are reading and writing much better than they have in all the other years. Since there are no other changes except for this new way of dividing up my time and organizing my day, I have to assume that this approach is just better suited to the varied needs of my children. Let me begin at the end and show you some of my children reading and writing."

Mrs. Wright switched on the VCR and there on camera was Chip. Chip read a few pages from a *Curious George* book he had selected and then read and showed the illustrations of his last published book. Daisy was next to read, followed by Alexander, Mike, and finally Paul. When these five children had all read from selected books and their own published books, Mrs. Wright paused the tape and said, "Now I know that many of you are thinking these children are not unusually good readers and writers for the end of first grade, but these are my five lowest children. Chip can almost read a first reader with 90 percent word accuracy and good comprehension. Daisy, Alexander, and Mike are on a good solid primer level, and Paul is my lowest but he can read preprimer independently and he can read the three books he has authored."

Mrs. Wright could tell that most of the teachers were looking at this reading and writing of these five children differently when they realized they were the below-level readers. Mrs. Wright then fast-forwarded through the rest of the class reading and writing, stopping once or twice so that the teachers knew that these children all read easily at first-grade level or above. She showed the tape at normal speed once again while Larry, Danielle, Pat, and Steve read aloud. All four of these children had chosen to read a couple of pages of chapter books usually read by fourth or fifth graders. The published books they shared also demonstrated writing abilities way beyond that of average first graders.

When she stopped the tape, the teachers were all abuzz, talking to each other. Mrs. Wright mouthed a "thank you" to Sue for insisting on the three days of taping and on having all the children read for the tape. The teachers now had all kinds of questions:

Was Mrs. Wright sure that this was a normal class at the beginning of the year?

How far had she taken those last four students in their basal series?

How could a student like Paul write a book like the one he wrote?

Wasn't there a single child who was still a virtual nonreader/nonwriter?

Mrs. Wright laughed at this question and said, "I didn't hide any children or ask any of their parents to keep them home when the visitors came like I hear used to happen in the old days."

Mrs. Wright then showed the teachers her daily schedule and showed clips of each of the four blocks. As she went through, she reminded the teachers that they were seeing the last few days of school and that although she had done all four blocks from the beginning of school, what she and the children did in those blocks looked quite different in September and even in February from what they were seeing at the end of May.

She showed some tape of the writing block and of her minilesson in which she wrote while the children watched. The teachers expressed amazement that she didn't say the words while she was writing them, but she had them focus on the children and it was obvious that the children were all trying their best to read what she was writing. She also pointed out to the teachers that in her minilesson she always looked for a word or two on the word wall, looked pleased to find it there, and commented, "If it's on our word wall, we have to spell it correctly!"

When she got to the point where she invent spelled a couple of big words, saying the words slowly and writing down the letters you could hear, she could tell from the shaking heads that some teachers didn't think a teacher should ever spell a word wrong. Leaving out some ending punctuation and capital letters did not please some either! As soon as Mrs. Wright finished writing, she pointed to the Editor's Checklist:

Editor's Checklist

Do all the sentences make sense?

Do all the sentences start with capital letters?

Do all the sentences have . ? or ! at the end?

Do all the people and place names and I start with a capital?

She took a different-colored marker and the children helped her read for each item on the checklist and fix each and then draw a happy face. In addition she asked them which words she had invent spelled and she underlined these, remarking that she would have to find the correct spelling for these words if this were the piece she chose to publish.

Next, the tape showed the children writing. Most children were writing in their notebooks, but a few were finishing up the copying and illustrating of their final first-grade published books. When Mrs. Wright rang the bell to signal the end of the writing time, five children lined up and read their chosen piece in the Author's Chair. Each child who read chose one child from the audience to tell something he or she liked about the piece.

Mrs. Wright stopped the tape and there were a slew of questions!

How did she get them started writing?

Did she give them a topic for writing?

How did they know how to choose a topic?

How did she have time to help them all edit and publish?

Who made all the blank books?

Mrs. Wright tried to answer the questions, and then Sue Port jumped in to announce that it was time for a break and that after the break, she wanted Mrs. Wright to show tapes of the other blocks. "I know that you all still have questions about the writing and you will have questions about the other blocks, but we will have only an hour left and I want you to get an overview of all four blocks. When we end this afternoon, I am going to ask you to write down the questions you still have and then I will see what we can plan before the start of the next school year to help provide answers to your questions."

The teachers talked to each other and asked Mrs. Wright individual questions throughout the break, and Mrs. Wright was amazed at their enthusiasm. After the break, she did a whirlwind tour of the other blocks. She showed the word wall and explained about putting the names up one each day and having one child be the special child for the day. She told them how she had added five high-frequency words each week and explained that they took all the Monday Words time to work with and practice handwriting with the five new words. On the other days, five words were reviewed. The teachers watched the children clap and chant and write the words and then get out their red pens to trace around and check them. Then the children turned their papers over and Mrs. Wright led them to use their word wall words to spell rhyming words on the back. The tape then focused on their content board, which at this point had pictures of water and water words, and Mrs. Wright explained that between the word wall and the content boards, even children like Alexander, who couldn't invent spell, were able to write.

Next they watched a Making Words lesson in which the children used the letters *a, e, h, l, s,* and *w* to make the words *we, he, she, sea, was, saw, law, slaw, heal, seal, sale,* and *leash.* The teachers were amazed when Mrs. Wright got to the end of the lesson and asked, "Has anyone figured out what word we can make with all these letters?" At least a dozen hands went up from children who (unlike many of the teachers watching) had figured out that these letters could spell *whales*—an animal they were studying about as part of their water unit. Mrs. Wright then led the children to sort the words into patterns, those ending with just an *e,* the *ea* words, the *a—e* words, and the *aw* words.

The teachers again had all kinds of questions about the word wall and Making Words lesson, but Sue insisted that they write down their questions and pushed Mrs. Wright forward to show some of the Guided Reading block. Mrs. Wright showed part of Wednesday's lesson in which they were all introduced to a selection in the adopted first reader and then read it with reading partners, as well as part of Thursday's lesson in which they were reading in the *Sunshine* readers or chapter books and then meeting together in a sharing group.

Finally, Mrs. Wright showed just a little snippet of the Teacher Read-Aloud/ SQUIRT block. The teachers were all amazed at the ability of all the children to sit and sustain their reading for 15 minutes, and Mrs. Wright explained about the three ways to read books that she had modeled and had children model with books from home at the beginning of the year.

The meeting was running a few minutes over, and Mrs. Wright knew that many of the teachers had to rush off to pick up their own children from day care. She summed up, however, by telling the teachers what she had learned during the last two years.

"Remember in your education courses, when you were taking an essay exam, no matter what the question was, you knew you should always get the words *individual differences* in the answer somewhere if you wanted an A?" The teachers all chuckled and Mrs. Wright knew they had all had this universal experience.

Individual Differences

"Well, what I learned is that individual differences are really true—not just something we should give lip service to. The differences in the levels are the obvious ones, but there are also differences in the way children learn and respond—personality differences, I guess you would call them. This year, I taught two twins—born within minutes of each other, raised in the same environment—and the two girls are as different as night and day! Not different in their ability—they are both smart girls—but different in how they approach things, in the amount of structure/freedom they need, and so on."

The nods of the teachers assured Mrs. Wright that all the teachers knew these learning style/personality differences were a reality of teaching. "The four blocks—Writing, Words, Guided Reading, and Teacher Read-Aloud/ SQUIRT—are like four roads, four ways to get there. The reason I think my children—particularly the top and the bottom children—are reading and writing

Balanced Literacy Programs

so much better is that regardless of how they learn best, that method is present in our classroom for some consistent part of every day. The four-block approach is a multimethod and a multilevel approach. The four blocks represent different methods, and within each block there are a variety of levels on which children can operate. I don't have time to discuss this now, but the multilevel concept is critical when you have the differences we always have at Merritt. The Writing and SQUIRT time are naturally multilevel, but I have had to work to make the Words block and the Guided Reading block multilevel."

Sue hurriedly brought the meeting to a close, thanking Mrs. Wright and reminding the teachers to pick up their articles and leave their questions with her. Some teachers hurried off, but many others stayed and talked 'til late in the afternoon. Mrs. Wright could sense their genuine interest, and she reminded herself that most teachers work hard and want the very best for their children. "It's not that we don't care enough or that we don't do enough. It's just that the differences in learning style and entering level make it so complex to get it all organized," she assured them.

As the teachers left, many of them exchanged phone numbers and agreed to meet for a few potluck lunches over the summer and make plans for next year. Sue was beaming as she walked Freida to her car. "You see," she said, "those teachers know a good thing when they see it and next year, I will arrange for them to come and visit your class and you can be their support as they move into this! Now aren't you glad I made you do this and sent Miss Media to tape for three days in your class?" Mrs. Wright smiled and said, "I'm glad it went well and I'm glad they are enthusiastic, but I am going to have to decide how I feel about the rest of it!" Sue assured her that she would be there to help and that Freida would love her new leadership role!

ADD TO YOUR JOURNAL

 Think back to when you were in first grade and to any first grades you have observed or taught in. Compare what you experienced with what you read in Mrs. Wright's journal. Does it make sense to you that because children have different personalities and don't all learn in the same way, beginning reading and writing should be provided using a number of different methods? Compare Mrs. Wright's approach—to meet the various entering literacy levels of the children by providing multimethod, multilevel instruction—with ability grouping. Just as children have different ways in which they most comfortably learn, teachers have different styles. How does Mrs. Wright's style match your style? What parts of her program and style would you like to make your own and which things would you change? If you were suddenly transported into Mrs. Wright's classroom to teach this class of children, what would you do the same and what would you do differently?

REFERENCES

Cunningham, P. M. (1991). Research Directions: Multimethod, multilevel literacy instruction in first grade. *Language Arts, 68,* 578–584.

Cunningham, P. M., Hall, D. P., & Defee, M. (1991). Non-ability grouped, multilevel instruction: A year in a first-grade classroom. *The Reading Teacher, 44,* 566–571.

Taba, H. (1967). *Teachers' handbook for elementary social studies.* Palo Alto, CA: Addison-Wesley.

Children's Books/Materials Cited

ABC Bunny, by Wanda Gag, Putnam, 1978.

Alphabeasts: A Hide and Seek Alphabet Book, by Durga Bernhard, Holiday, 1992.

Are You My Mother? by P. D. Eastman, Random House, 1960.

Ashanti to Zulu: African Traditions, by Margaret Musgrove, Puffin Books, 1980.

The Biggest Nose, by Kathy Caple, Houghton Mifflin, 1985.

Caps, Hats, Socks, and Mittens, by Louisa Borden, Scholastic, 1989.

The Cat in the Hat, by Dr. Seuss, Random House, 1987.

Clifford books, by N. Bridwell, Scholastic, various years.

Curious George books, by Margaret & H. A. Rey, Houghton Mifflin, various years.

Families Are Different, by Nina Pelligrini, Scholastic, 1992.

Fly Away Home, by Eve Bunting, Houghton Mifflin, 1993.

Frog and Toad books, by Arnold Lobel, HarperCollins, various years.

George and Martha books, by James Marshall, Sandpiper, various years.

The Gingerbread Man, by Karen Schmidt, Scholastic, 1986.

Goodnight Moon, by Margaret Wise Brown, Holt, Rinehart, & Winston, 1969.

The Hand Made Alphabet, by Laura Rankin, Dial, 1991.

Happy Christmas, Gemma, by Sarah Hayes, Morrow, 1992.

Hop on Pop, by Dr. Seuss, Random House, 1987.

The Hundred Dresses, by Eleanor Estes, Scholastic, 1980.

The Icky Bug Alphabet Book, by Jerry Pallotta, Charlesbridge Publishers, 1992.

I Hate English, by Ellen Levine, Scholastic, 1989.

If You Grew Up with Abraham Lincoln, by Ann McGovern, Scholastic, 1992.

If You Grew Up with George Washington, by Ruth Belov Gross, Scholastic, 1993.

The Magic School Bus at the Waterworks, by Joanna Cole & Bruce Degan, Scholastic, 1988.

The Mother's Day Mice, by Eve Bunting, Ticknor & Fields, 1988.

Mrs. Wishy Washy, by Joy Cowley, Wright, 1989.

My First Kwanzaa Book, by Deborah Newton Chocolate, Cartwheel, 1990.

The Ocean Alphabet Book, by Jerry Pallotta, Charlesbridge Publishers, 1989.

One Fish, Two Fish, Red Fish, Blue Fish, by Dr. Seuss, Random House, 1987.

Over in the Meadow, by Olive A. Wadsworth, Scholastic, 1990.

A Perfect Father's Day, by Eve Bunting, Houghton Mifflin, 1993.

A Picture Book of Hanukkah, by David Adler, Holiday, 1982.

A Picture Book of Martin Luther King, by David Adler, Holiday, 1989.

Robert the Rose Horse, by Joan Heilbroner, Random House, 1962.

The Snowy Day, by Ezra Jack Keats, Puffin Books, 1976.

Sunshine and *Story Box* books, Wright Group, various years.

Ten, Nine, Eight, by Molly Bang, Morrow, 1991.

The Underwater Alphabet Book, by Jerry Pallotta, Charlesbridge Publishers, 1991.

The Very Hungry Caterpillar, by Eric Carle, Putnam, 1986.
The Wednesday Surprise, by Eve Bunting, Houghton Mifflin, 1990.
What Will the Weather Be Like Today? by Paul Rogers, Scholastic, 1992.
Where the Wild Things Are, by Maurice Sendak, HarperCollins, 1988.
Where's Spot? by Eric Hill, Putnam, 1987.
White Snow, Bright Snow, by Alvin Tresselt, Morrow, 1988.

Miss Nouveau: Second Grade

THE PARENT MEETING

Miss Nouveau arrived at the school two hours before her 7:30 P.M. parent meeting was scheduled to begin. Frankly, she was nervous and dreaded having to face all the parents in a large group. But at least, she thought, Mr. Topps would be there to help. He had generously offered to come to her meeting in case she needed help answering questions about schoolwide policies she might not even know about yet.

She was looking over her new bulletin board when Mr. Topps arrived at 7:15 P.M. He told her that it was lovely and that the fall theme she had chosen brightened the room. She didn't tell Mr. Topps that she had been working on that bulletin board for two weeks, sometimes until 2:00 A.M. She wanted him and the parents to think that she was efficient and organized.

Miss Nouveau had made name tags for all of the parents to wear. In that way she could easily identify each parent, and she would know from the leftover name tags who had been unable to attend. When all of the parents had had a cup of coffee and were seated, Mr. Topps, as had been agreed earlier, introduced her to the group.

"As you all know," he began, "I am Mr. Topps. I especially wanted to come this evening to introduce your child's teacher to you. Miss Nouveau comes to us this year as a first-year teacher. She did exceptionally well both at the university and during her student teaching, so that when this position opened up last spring, I was delighted to have her among the applicants for the job. I know that you will be as happy with her as we are. If there is anything that you would like either of us to do, do not hesitate to call. Now, let's hear from Miss Nouveau."

"Thank you, Mr. Topps. This is an exciting moment for me. All my life I have dreamed of being an elementary school teacher.

"I want to explain to you the kind of program that I have planned for this school year. You see here on this table the reading books that your children will be using. It is the *Reading Can Be Fun* series published by Basic Publishing Company. In addition to reading these books, your children will be working with these workbooks. When they are not with me in one of the three reading groups, they will be at their seats doing follow-up skills in workbooks or other assignments that reinforce the basal's skill development program or reading a book from the library shelf over there. My assignment of the children into these three groups has been based on the results of a test that accompanies the reading series called an Informal Reading Inventory (IRI). It measures your child's performance in oral reading and comprehension." Miss Nouveau, relieved that *that* was over, hurried on to a topic she knew more about.

"You know that physical factors are quite important in determining how well your children do in school. You can be most helpful in seeing to it that your children get to bed by 8:30 at night, that they come to school after having had a nutritious breakfast, and that they play out in the fresh air for a while every day after school. I intend to emphasize these basic health habits with the children this year. We will be studying nutrition, the value of recreation, and the importance of adequate rest. Starting on Monday, I am going to ask you to send a snack to school with your child. We will have snack time every morning in order to help keep the energy level of the children high. The school nurse will test vision and hearing in October, and if there are any problems, I will be in touch with you."

Miss Nouveau looked at her watch and saw that what she had planned to take 30 minutes had consumed only 15 minutes of time, so she asked Mr. Topps if there was anything he would like to add. There was not. The time had come for the part of the meeting that she had been dreading. She turned back to the parents and asked, "Are there any questions?"

All over the room, hands shot up. She called on Mrs. Moore first.

"You will be using the same set of books for all of the children? How can you do this? Aren't they at different reading levels?"

Miss Nouveau replied, "Yes, they are at three different levels. Some of them are reading below grade level and they are reading in this first reader or 1^2 book; most of them are reading right on grade level and they are in this 2^1 book; however, some of them are reading above grade level and they are reading from this 2^2 book." She smiled proudly! "The difference in instruction among the three groups will be not only the book they're using and the pace at which they move through the books, but also the amount and kinds of material covered."

Mrs. Penn raised her hand to ask, "Why are you using *this* particular series?"

Mr. Topps intervened. "If I may, I would like to answer that one, Miss Nouveau, since the decision was made before you were hired. You see, Mrs. Penn, the teachers in this school who use basals met together last spring and selected this series from among the six state-approved adoptions. Most of the teachers at that meeting felt that this series allowed for the most flexibility while still retaining the structure and sequential development of skills that is a strong point of the basal reader approach."

Another hand went up, and Miss Nouveau called upon Mr. Tomás. "When the kids aren't with you, how will they know what to do? Won't they just waste time and not do their work?"

"I take time every morning to explain to the children what they are to do on their work papers. You see, they all do the same ones, so I can give those instructions to everyone. In their reading groups, they have been told what they need to do in their workbooks. They do have instructions, and they know what to do. But sometimes some children don't complete their work. When this happens, they just have more to do the next day."

Mrs. Penn glanced over at Mr. Topps for his reaction. Had he pressed his fingertips to his forehead because of a headache?

With all of the questions answered, Miss Nouveau thanked them for coming. She started to gather up some of her materials when she noticed Mrs. Penn at her elbow.

"Miss Nouveau, I just want to offer to help you in any way that I can. I used to be a teacher, so I think that I might be of some help to you. *Please* feel free to call on me. I really enjoy helping out, and I know what a difficult task you have."

"Oh, thank you, but I'm sure that won't be necessary. I think that I have things pretty much under control now. But I do appreciate your offer. I will call for help if I need it."

"Fine. Good evening. It was lovely meeting with you this evening."

Mrs. Penn and Mrs. Middleman left the room together. They were talking quietly, but Miss Nouveau heard some of what was said.

MRS. MIDDLEMAN: Isn't she a dear little thing? So cute! And just look at that lovely bulletin board. My, she certainly is creative.

MRS. PENN: Yes, she is. But you know, I always rather like to see the children's work up on the bulletin board. It's not as pretty or tidy but there's something wonderful about your own child's work displayed. Mrs. Wright did so much of that last year.

Miss Nouveau was crestfallen. All of that work, and they would rather see things that the children had done! "Maybe I should think about having the children do something to put up. Oh, but it will be so messy!"

MONTHLY LOGS

September

My major premise is wrong! I thought that all children loved to read or that at the very least they were eager to learn. How wrong! How wrong! I just can't understand it. Butch sits in his seat (sometimes) just waiting out the day. If I ask him to do one of the assignments, he just looks at me and asks, "Why?"

"So that when you grow up you'll be able to read. You need to be a good reader to get a job."

"Oh yeah," he replied. "Well, my dad, he don't read so good, but he makes two hundred bucks a week!" That sounds like a great deal of money to a seven-year-old, but if only he knew!

One of the most frightening aspects of this teaching business is the weight of responsibility one feels. I was so excited to have my own classroom assigned to me and spent a lot of time here this summer getting my room ready for the first days of school. But the full realization of the responsibility didn't hit me until I saw the first children come into the room—my room—*our* room.

I fervently hope that I will never again live through a day like the first day of school. The children were quite well behaved (I suppose the novelty of returning to school) and I had prepared an excess of material for them, just in case. I had enough for two days—so I thought! By noon, I had used up everything I had planned for the first day. They worked so much more quickly than I ever imagined! By lunch time I was rattled. What to do? That afternoon I used up the next day's lessons!

Another horrible feeling of incompetence came when I realized that I had to put these children into reading groups. How many *is* a group? Grouping had been talked about in my undergraduate reading course, but I now realized I really didn't have a well-defined idea of how to go about it.

Assessment I gave all the children the IRI that accompanies the series. It wasn't easy to get it done because the other children were so noisy and interrupted me so often. I think also that it was too much to try to do it all in two days. Next year (if I am alive and teaching!), I will spread it out across a week so that the children have to work independently for only a little while.

By the time of the parent meeting, I did have my groups formed, though that had not been as easy as I felt it would be. Larry gives every indication of being an extremely bright child, yet when I was scoring his IRI, I was amazed at the number of errors he made in oral reading. Instead of "He could not get the car to start," Larry read, "He couldn't get the car started." Yet with all of those errors, his comprehension remained high! As a matter of fact, he did amazingly well, answering every question asked of him without error. I put him into the middle group anyway, because the requirements for the IRI include both oral reading and comprehension. I thought Mort would do better, too, but he was so inattentive that he made all kinds of silly mistakes.

Daisy and Mike didn't really meet the 90 percent oral reading accuracy criterion for the first reader but I didn't think I could manage another group so I put them there and I will send extra work home with them. Paul wouldn't read for me! I pleaded, threatened, and bribed, but he steadfastly refused. I put him in the lowest group but I don't know where he belongs. He won't read aloud or do his workbook. He is not mean and behaves; he just won't do anything. I must talk to Mrs. Wright about him.

Grouping I assigned children to reading groups and let them choose a group name. For some of the groups this took a long time, but eventually all three groups were named. Some things do puzzle me about these groups. Why are the Butterflies all girls and why is there only one girl in the Monsters? I wonder if there's any significance to that?

Monsters		Astronauts		Butterflies
Mike	Chip	Horace	Mitch	Mandy
Daisy	Mort	Daphne	Manuel	Pat
Paul		Betty	Joyce	Roberta
Butch		Steve	Larry	Rita
Carl		Alex	Anthony	Hilda
Alexander		Jeff		Danielle

One thing that really concerns me is the name of one group. I tried to get them to change the name, but Mike, the leader in the group, convinced the others that they should keep it. I just hope that no one thinks that *I* named them! (They certainly chose a descriptive name!)

When the groups begin to work each morning, they can see the order of their assignments on the chalkboard. The first thing that each child must do is work on the writing lesson that I placed on the board. Children need this practice in handwriting and it keeps them busy until they come to their reading group. If they finish that and their other work, they are permitted to choose a book from the library shelf to read quietly at their seats. The reading group order changes every week so that I do not always see the Monsters after recess when they are so excited! Here is this week's schedule:

Scheduling

Monsters	Astronauts	Butterflies
copying and	reading group	workbook
ditto sheets	workbook	copying and
reading group	copying and	ditto sheets
workbook	ditto sheets	reading group

I haven't written a time schedule for them, for I find that I'm never quite sure when I will be done with one reading group and ready to call another, or how long it will take a group of children to finish their workbook assignments.

Discipline

I've been having trouble with some of the children not finishing their work. At the beginning of the month, they all worked so hard and cooperated with me very well, but as time went by, I found they didn't maintain that attitude. Roberta, for instance, says the workbook is stupid. When she refused to do it, I had no choice but to move her into the middle group where the work is easier. Last week I began keeping those children who didn't complete their work in at recess, so that they could finish what had been assigned. They were not permitted to go out unless all of their work was finished. So on Monday and Tuesday, I had Mort, Mitch, Mike, Daisy, Paul, Jeff, Butch, and Roberta stay in and finish work. On Wednesday, Daisy, Butch, and Mitch didn't have to stay in, because they finished their work. I thought my system was working until I checked over their work. I found it had been done very carelessly and that it needed to be done over again. By Wednesday, I noticed that Carl, too, dawdled over his work and seemed delighted when I told him that he would have to stay in. Thursday, the same children were told to stay in to work when I suddenly realized, after looking at my planbook, that I had to go outside since it was my day to supervise the playground! I got chills thinking what this group of children might do if left unsupervised in the classroom, so I did what I thought it best to do—I marched them down to the office and told them to sit on the bench and do their work there. From what Mrs. Mainstay told me later, there was little work accomplished. Mr. Topps came down to talk to me after school, as he does nearly every afternoon, and suggested that I might be able to find another solution for this problem. He reminded me of my own statement at the parent meeting that children require recreation and fresh air. I thought hard about it all night, and decided that any work left undone at the end of the week would be sent home with the children to be completed over the weekend. That should take care of that problem!

I've had to send a note home to the parents about our morning snack time. It never occurred to me that there might be problems, but several children bring nothing. I don't know whether Chip, Paul, and Jeff forgot to bring something, but they look hungrily at the other children who do bring snacks. And Daisy! The first day she brought three cupcakes, a bag of potato chips, and a can of cola (warm)! The rest of that first week was just as bad, so I have written to the parents asking them to please send snacks like fruits, vegetables, peanut butter and crackers, cheese, and so on.

Self-Selected Reading

SQUIRT is such a neat idea! I usually have the children reading for five minutes a day when we do it. At first I read along with them as Mr. Topps told me I must, but I am getting so far behind on grading all of these assignments that I'm sure it won't matter if once in a while I check a few papers while they read. I always make sure that the children do the reading. Sometimes, however, I get so involved with my work that they read for eight or nine minutes. I am usually reminded by my clock-watchers that we have gone past the five-minute mark. Other days, we read for only three minutes. I figure that makes up for it, and besides there are so many things that we have to get done!

October

If only I can survive until January! I student taught during the winter quarter last year, and if we can only get to January I'll know what to do! Why did everything look so easy when my supervising teacher did it? Either I am doing something wrong or else I have a really rough group of children. I always wanted to teach second grade because the children are still so cute and they already know how to read. That seemed like the perfect grade to me, but how different it really is! Some of them can't read and some of them are definitely not in the "cute" category!

Discipline

This class makes me wonder about the first-grade experience that they had. Whenever I walk by Mrs. Wright's classroom, it *appears* that she has good discipline, but I wonder if she does really. If she had good control of her class, how could a class like this one be giving me so much trouble? I know that Mrs. Wright is an excellent teacher—listening to the reading of Pat and Rita convinces me of that—but perhaps she is just not a disciplinarian. Well, whatever the reason, I've really had to crack down on these kids. I've started putting much longer writing assignments on the chalkboard just to keep the children from running around the room. That should keep them sitting a little longer! The problem with the added material is that they take less time to copy it than it takes me to think it up and carefully write it on the chalkboard.

Another thing we have been having trouble with is going to the bathroom **Routines** and getting drinks of water. Every morning at 10:10 we go to the restrooms and water fountain. The teacher under whom I did student teaching called this "watering" the children. I give the children five minutes in the restrooms, which should be adequate time for them without allowing too much extra time for "messing around." Obviously, for some of the children five minutes is several too many!

And the pencil sharpening! At the end of the day I require the children to turn in their pencils that need sharpening. After they leave I sharpen the pencils. Yuk! But what else can I do? They would probably be at the pencil sharpener all day long if I let *them* do it.

Mr. Topps observed me during October. In spite of everything he did to help, I'm afraid I was a miserable failure. He spoke with me privately after school early in the month and explained that he had waited to observe me until I had had a chance to get acclimated to my students and the school. He assured me that he was observing me to help me improve rather than to evaluate me. "Most low teacher evaluations result from poor supervision!" he said with some fervor.

He asked me to pick the day and the lesson that he would observe, and he encouraged me to choose what would best display my strengths as a teacher. Little did he suspect that I had none!

When he entered the room at exactly the time I had asked him to, I had done my best to prepare the students and me for an effective and well-conducted lesson. I had chosen to teach the lesson from the basal teacher's manual to my top group, the Butterflies. "Surely," I reasoned, "following the lesson plan from the *approved* material with my brightest and best-behaved students will make for a satisfactory lesson."

Actually, the lesson was the best one I had taught this year. The students really did try to make me look good in front of Mr. Topps. That's what is so sad. My very best lesson was a failure! Of course, Mr. Topps encouraged me when he talked to me later about the observation. He complimented my degree of preparation and the behavior of the students, but then he asked me about Larry. "Do you have Larry working independently because he is so far ahead of the others?"

"Why, no," I admitted. "He is in my second group."

"But, Miss Nouveau, Larry reads better than all of the students in our entire school except for a handful of fifth graders." His kind eyes looked concerned.

When I sat unable to speak for several seconds, he quietly changed the subject. (The next day I transferred Larry from the Astronauts to the Butterflies. He does seem able to keep up.)

Then the ax fell. I had wondered why my top group had been getting steadily **Oral Reading** worse at reading aloud during reading group time. Well, Mr. Topps explained to me why they had become worse. Rather, he explained how to get them to do better. "Miss Nouveau, there is just one area I want you to work on before my next observation. You obviously want your students in the top reading group to read well orally since you devote so much of your lesson to that. Let me give you some suggestions for improving oral reading, and you let me know when you want me to come back to see you lead these same students through another oral-reading lesson.

"You've already done the most important single thing to help those students read well orally; you've placed them in a book that allows all of them to have high success. Now there are just two suggestions I have for you. I would appreciate it if you would try them and let me know how they work for you. Are you willing to do that?"

Of course, I said I would. He was being so kind, I must have really been a disaster!

"The first suggestion," he continued, "is that you do not ask these students to read anything out loud that they have not first read to themselves. Oral reading is always better if students have read the material silently first."

"But I don't have enough time now," I blurted out before I could stop myself. "And besides, if they don't read aloud, how will I know they read it?"

Mr. Topps agreed that these were problems. He recommended that I have the Butterflies read orally only two days a week. He also suggested that I have them read the basal selection at their seats independently while I work with another group. "Introduce the words and do the other things to prepare them for comprehension and then send them back to their seats to read it to themselves. The next time they come to reading group, do your comprehension follow-up based on their silent reading rather than on their oral reading, as you do now. Since you have them all in a high-success book, you can use their performance on your comprehension activities to determine whether or not they read the selection. After your comprehension activities are over, you can do your oral-reading lesson with that selection."

"The second suggestion," Mr. Topps smiled, "is simpler than the first but even stranger, I'm afraid. Whenever a student is reading aloud, have the others close their books. They can hold their places with an index card or strip of paper. You might even close your book too! You'll find that you pay more attention to the quality of expression and the sense of what is being read and less to minor errors when you do that."

After I left his office, I considered the two suggestions. That certainly wasn't the way I was taught, and that certainly wasn't the way my supervising teacher did it when I student taught. Surely, it wasn't necessary to go through all that, I thought. Still, I knew I should try it just so I could tell him it doesn't work and is a lot of trouble to boot.

Imagine my surprise when I did what he said and saw major improvement in the Butterflies' oral reading in just a week's time. Just the other day, at my invitation, he came back to observe me teach them another reading lesson. This time things went great and he was glowing in his praise for me and them.

In addition to everything that has been happening within the room, they tested the children's vision and hearing this month. I was convinced that Mort had an auditory problem, for he seems to be tuned out a lot of the time. He doesn't hear me when I call on him and when he does hear, he doesn't follow through on what I ask him to do. His hearing screening was normal, however. I guess he just doesn't pay attention. Jeff, Mandy, Larry, and Manuel were referred to optometrists. Butch, I discovered, is color-blind. No wonder he couldn't do the work papers that required him to color according to the directions given at the top. I hate to admit this, but I had him do them over three times before I finally gave up on him in disgust!

SQUIRT is not going very well. Sometimes I have them read for 10 or 15 minutes. Butch and Mitch say they hate SQUIRT and have become very rambunctious during this time. I had been told about SQUIRT when I first came to Merritt and had heard that almost all the teachers did it and that the children loved it. That's certainly not the way a lot of my children feel about it. I don't think it's as great as it's cracked up to be but I sure can get a lot of grading done while they read.

Children with Special Needs

Self-Selected Reading

November

Butch, unable to complete his daily work, has been the bane of my existence lately. Two weeks ago he had accumulated so many work papers that by Thursday evening I could see that he would have a lot to do for the coming weekend. That Friday morning he arrived at school with a cast on his left arm, and I'm ashamed to admit that my first reaction was, "Oh, thank goodness it's his left arm. He can still do his work!" He came into the room grinning and showing off his autographed cast. During work time, I noticed that he wasn't working. I told him that he had better do some of his work or he would have even more to take home that evening. He simply looked up at me and said, "I can't. My arm's broke."

"Yes, I know it's broken, but that's only your left arm. You can still use your right one."

He grinned and said, "Yeah, but I'm left-handed." Oh no! I had never noticed—I had never thought to notice handedness before. I glanced around the room and saw that no one else was left-handed. There must be a conspiracy against me!

How is Butch going to do his work? I finally decided to let him do what he could (circling answers, and so forth) and paired him with Larry or Pat to do the rest of his work. He thoroughly enjoys having secretarial help. Sometimes I wonder—is it really broken?

Poor Paul! It has been most frustrating and amazing to discover that he is not eligible for special education. Mrs. Wright referred him for testing last year, but his IQ was too high for him to be considered mentally handicapped and too low for him to be considered learning disabled. Even his emotional characteristics fall in the low–normal range. Mr. Topps had the school psychologist come out to observe him in my classroom during November, but she agreed that his

Children with Special Needs

occasional emotional withdrawals and lackadaisical behavior were unusual but insufficiently serious for him to be classified as emotionally disturbed. I just never dreamed that students like Butch, Mike, Daisy, and Paul are not special-education students. I guess I always thought that anyone who was below average was exceptional.

I think I should resign at Christmas. I'm not doing these children any good and they are not doing any good for me. I go home every night at 6:00 or 6:30 simply exhausted. Even then I take work home with me so that I don't get to bed until after midnight. I barely can make it to school by 8:00 the next morning; I haven't been to a movie or on a date for weeks. I had no idea that teaching would be so difficult and so depressing. I thought that children were lovable, but I have found I cannot bear to be around some of them. I must be an ogre not to be able to love them all.

I have been talking quite a bit with Mr. Topps recently, and he has been making some very positive suggestions. He tells me that I shouldn't quit, but that instead I should talk with Mrs. Wise or some of the other teachers to get some ideas. He has also continued to help me improve my reading instruction. During November he watched me teach a reading lesson to the Astronauts. Amazingly, having them read a selection silently before reading it orally and having all other students but the one reading aloud close their books helps the middle group even more than it did the top group. In a faculty meeting, Mr. Topps even used me as an example of a teacher who is really seeing improvement in reading. I appreciate his not mentioning that this improvement has totally eluded the Monsters. Maybe I should try the same two suggestions with them. The situation there can't get any worse!

Two of the children have started wearing glasses this month. Larry came in with his first and all of the children wanted to get them! Mr. Topps told me that Jeff, whom I had referred for further testing, had not yet been to the eye doctor. When I questioned him about it, Mr. Topps indicated that Jeff's family couldn't afford the glasses. I was appalled! A child not able to get the glasses he needs! I remembered something in my notes from college and checked them when I got home that night. One of my professors had indicated that service organizations often provide funds for schoolchildren to get glasses or other medical attention. I got the phone number of the local organization from Mr. Topps and called that night to explain the situation. The club president was very helpful and told me that his organization would be glad to help Jeff get his glasses. I also discovered that his organization acted as a collection agency for old pairs of glasses that people don't use. They take these glasses to eye doctors who are able to reuse the frames and regrind the lenses to provide glasses more cheaply for those who need them. I told him that in return for helping Jeff, I wanted to do something to help his group, so my class and I began canvassing our neighborhoods to collect old pairs of glasses for the service organization. I dittoed a sheet for people whom the children contacted so that the youngsters wouldn't have to remember all the details about why they were asking for glasses. They handed a sheet to whoever answered the door and asked if they had any old glasses to contribute. My kids collected 15 pairs of glasses! Boy, was I proud of them!

The workbooks are still causing me some problems. They take up so much time and I have to grade them all at night. Four pages per child is a lot of work for me to correct in addition to all the dittos they do. I sat down one night to try to find a solution, and I thought about it for a long time. Why is it that the workbooks are provided with these basal reading programs? I came to the conclusion that the authors wanted to provide practice for some of the skills they had introduced. Well, some of my groups already know some of the skills, so I have taken a chance and decided to skip some of the pages if everyone in the group can already do them. I hope that is okay. Somehow it doesn't seem right to have those unfinished pages.

I have also begun letting the middle and top groups work on their workbook **Partners** pages in pairs. Two children work together to come up with their best responses. We then go over these responses together when they come to the group. During reading group we check the pages and analyze why an answer is right or wrong. I also have them explain the reasoning behind wrong answers. Sometimes their reasoning leads them to an answer that is wrong according to the workbook key but makes much more sense from a child's point of view.

I have tentatively moved Mort from the low group into the middle group. He is the best comprehender in the Monsters and I have noticed that when he makes oral reading errors, they are usually "smart errors" like reading *can't* for *cannot*, or *little* for *small*. I learned in my undergraduate reading course that all good readers have an eye-voice span and that their eyes are out ahead of their voices. I never thought that this could apply to a second grader. I think, however, that this must be why he didn't meet the 90 percent word identification criterion at the 2^1 level on the IRI, and I am just sure he can read as well as several in the middle group.

Nevertheless, I am still discouraged about the conflict between what I had hoped to accomplish this year and what I am actually accomplishing. I am rapidly coming to the conclusion that a job as a waitress might not be so bad after all! Or maybe I can try to support myself with my writing. Since I love to write children's stories, I might be able to sell some of them for publication. I will talk with Mrs. Wise and see what she suggests, for I have found her name to be quite descriptive of her ability to analyze a situation.

December

At the beginning of this month, we stopped SQUIRT. It seemed obvious to me **Self-Selected** that it just couldn't work. I had forgotten about Mr. Topps, however. He has a **Reading** schedule of when the different classes do SQUIRT so that he can come and read along with the different classes from time to time. He thinks it is particularly important that the boys see reading as something that adult males do. About a week after we had quit, he walked in at what had been our SQUIRT time and sat down and opened up his book. He noticed, of course, that no one was reading or ready to read and looked perplexed. "Did I get your schedule mixed up with someone else's, Miss Nouveau?" he asked kindly.

"Oh, no," I replied, "We're just running a little behind. Come on, boys and girls. Get your books out."

"But why?" asked Alex, "You said we wouldn't have SQUIRT anymore."

Mr. Topps said, "Oh, is there a problem, Miss Nouveau? Maybe I can help. Let's chat after school." Then he sat down in a chair and began to read as if nothing were out of the ordinary. Of course, the children and I began to read too. We read for eight minutes, and Mr. Topps signaled me at that point that we should stop. I told the children to put away their books and return to work.

After school, clutching my keys, I knocked on the open door to Mr. Topp's office. He looked up and said, "You didn't have to come up here, Norma. I would have come to your room on my way home later this afternoon."

"Well," I replied, "I would rather get it over with now. I know that I'm a disappointment to you—I am to myself. Would you like me to resign now or wait until Christmas?"

"Who said anything about resigning? I think you have the wrong notion about my role in this school. I want to help you because I remember well the agonies of *my* first year as a teacher! Now, what seems to be the problem with SQUIRT?"

"The children are restless and bored with it. Maybe second graders are just too young, or perhaps this particular group of children is just too undisciplined. Anyway, I can't seem to control them."

"We know they aren't too young, Norma. They have been involved in SQUIRT since kindergarten. While I do agree that you have an unusual class, I have seen SQUIRT used with enough classes to know that it will work with your class, too. Let me just run through some of the hazards that one might encounter when using SQUIRT; perhaps being aware of some of these might prove useful to you in organizing the program. First of all, and probably most important, children must know that we adults value reading. That is why I circulate among the various classes as often as I can and read with the classes during SQUIRT.

Teacher Modeling

"Until you get it going well, you need to read also to model for your children that adults enjoy reading. Once all your children are able to sustain their reading for ten minutes, you may want to do as Mrs. Wright does and spend a few minutes each day with different children bringing books they choose to read to you so that you can have a personal book conference with them and steer them toward other books they might enjoy. But, for right now, you need to get them back reading and that means two things—limiting the amount of time they read and modeling enjoyment from reading by reading your book instead of correcting papers!

"Today, they read for eight minutes. Of course, my being in the room might have made a difference." ("It sure did to me," thought Miss Nouveau.) "Why don't you back up to six minutes and then increase the time gradually a minute at a time as they get used to settling down and sustaining their reading. I will try to come to your room more often in the next few weeks at SQUIRT time to impress upon all the children how important we believe it is to take time out to just read and enjoy books every day!

"And please don't think of resigning. I've been really pleased to note your enthusiasm, sincerity, and dedication. I think you have already worked out some difficult problems for yourself. I have a great deal of confidence in you, Miss Nouveau!"

Wow! Maybe things will get better for me. I think I had better call Ms. Port and ask her for some suggestions. And Mrs. Wise has always been most helpful.

I have tried, up to this point, to write in my journal at the end of each week so that I could keep up with what was happening, but since my chat with Mr. Topps, so many things have been happening that the weeks rushed by until the holidays gave me a chance to sit down at home and continue my journal. I am so excited by the changes that I have made and the ones I am going to make! I called Ms. Port the evening after I had talked with Mr. Topps. She told me that she had been planning to come and see me that week.

Ms. Port and I talked for almost two hours one afternoon early in the month. At first, I was afraid to tell her about all the problems I was having. But she asked me about my groups and my schedule and before I knew it, I had told her everything about how I couldn't get everything done even when I kept my groups for 45 minutes, and how the children didn't do their seatwork and workbook pages, and the parents complained when I sent them home with too much homework every night. I told her about the Monsters. "Heavens, my dear, you don't call them that, do you?" she inquired.

"Well, yes, I do. But I didn't name them. I learned in my college reading class that you should let them choose their name. No one ever told me they might choose such a descriptive name."

Ms. Port suggested that I refer to them by using the name of one of the children in the group. "You might choose the natural leader in the group or, on the other hand, you might choose a quiet child and call the group by his or her name."

"I think I would rather call it Paul's group than Mike's group," I replied. "Mike already thinks he is in charge of the group. And actually, neither Mike, nor Paul, nor Daisy belong in that group. I think Mike and Daisy belong in the primer and Paul probably could read the primer on a good day and nothing at all on a bad day. I know I should have another group for these three. But, how would I ever find time to meet with them? I am worried about Carl, too. He is with the Monsters (Ms. Port flinched and I quickly corrected that to Paul's group!) but I think he could read with the Astronauts, which is Alexander's group." Ms. Port suggested that I let Carl read with both groups for a while and see if he could, indeed, catch up with and function well in the 2^1 book. "Now, why didn't I think of that?" I asked aloud.

"Because, my dear," Ms. Port replied, "when we are under a lot of pressure and feeling anxious, we don't think very well. That is often the sad dilemma of the beginning teacher." Ms. Port suggested that I needed to do some things with the whole class, some things with individuals, and some with my groups. "Take writing and listening, for example. You can often teach those with the whole class." Ms. Port must have realized from the expression on my face that I wasn't teaching those and that the thought of something else to try to fit in was overwhelming because she hurriedly went on, "You are meeting with your groups every day. Perhaps you could meet with them three days a week and use the other two days for whole-class and individual instruction."

"I wish I could," I responded, "but as it is, it takes me a week to read one story with each group and do everything in the teacher's manual. At that rate, we will just finish the books if I don't miss a day."

Ms. Port then picked up the teacher's manual and a red pen. She went through a lesson plan and circled the things in red that had to be done for each story. "The most important part of reading is reading," she lectured. "Having the children read the story silently and then having a follow-up comprehension-oriented discussion is the essential thing. These other activities are helpful suggestions for you to use when you and the children need them." As we looked at the manual, Miss Port helped me to see that sometimes, if the topic was familiar to the children (which it almost always is to the Butterflies, I mean Danielle's group), you didn't need to introduce all the new vocabulary words. She also pointed out how I could decide if the children need to work on a particular skill and do that skill's lesson only with the groups or children in a group who needed it.

"But what if I'm not sure?" I asked.

"Then you do a quick diagnosis at the beginning of the lesson and decide," she responded. "Freida Wright is a master teacher when it comes to using every-pupil-response cards to determine what children know and don't know. You should talk to her about that. Or, better yet, I will come and keep your class one morning and let you go and observe her. I think you will find she knows many tricks of the trade that will help you."

"I never thought of that either," I responded. "I would love to watch both Mrs. Wright and Mrs. Wise."

And that's how it came to be that Ms. Port took my class on two mornings and I spent a morning in Mrs. Wright's class and a morning in Mrs. Wise's class. I can't begin to list here all the things I learned, but I can see now where many of my problems were coming from and I think I know how to begin to solve them. I have already solved the pencil sharpening and bathroom problem, again thanks to Ms. Port. As she was preparing to leave that afternoon after our long talk, I picked up a stack of pencils and began my nightly routine of pencil sharpening. Ms. Port paid no attention to me until I was working on my eighth pencil, when she turned to me and said, "Good grief, you use a lot of pencils! What do you do—chew off the points?"

"Oh, these aren't mine. I sharpen the children's pencils."

"*You* sharpen? Do they all have broken arms? My dear, your time is more valuable than that! Let the children sharpen their own. I know—you're afraid that they'll stand there all day just sharpening and not have any pencil left. Yes, that will happen at first, especially since you have made it such a high priority. They think it must be something pretty special if you always do it. But they'll soon tire of it, and will sharpen only when they need to. You know, one of the best ways to ward off trouble is to create a routine. If things get bad, just make a routine like having them sign a sheet of paper every time they use the sharpener, or putting a ticket on your desk. Children will soon tire of the extra step and you can see more clearly who is still a problem. Now that we're on the subject of management, how do you handle the bathroom situation?"

I explained to her about the "watering" procedure, and my general dissatisfaction with it, primarily because some of the children claimed they didn't have "to go" when we went! But later, they needed to go by themselves.

"Then why don't you just let them go when they need to? How would you like someone to tell you when to go to the restroom? Try this. Have a symbol for the boys and one for the girls in the chalkboard tray. Whenever a child wishes to use the restroom, he or she comes to the front, picks up the symbol, places it on his or her desk, and goes to the restroom alone. The child returns the symbol to the chalkboard tray when he or she returns. When the symbol is in the tray, one child may go to the restroom; when it is missing, the next child must wait. Now at first, there will be problems, for going to the restroom alone will seem to be a big deal. But again, as with the pencil sharpening, the novelty will wear off if you don't make a fuss."

So far, so good. The children went through the stage that Ms. Port predicted and are now settled down into this new set of routines. Without her warning of what to expect, however, I think that I would have chucked the whole thing when the negative behavior increased temporarily.

I was quite eager for the holidays to begin! Not, as originally, so that I could escape from here but so that I could have some uninterrupted time to plan how I would begin the new year. I want to make a new schedule and look through the books I got at the faculty Christmas party. Each teacher was to bring an "idea" book for another teacher. Mrs. Wise drew my name and she gave me an excellent book that explains how to do story drama to improve listening and reading comprehension. I also got two unexpected presents. Mrs. Wright gave me a timer. She says it is her most valuable teaching resource. I can see why she says that, having watched her teach. Mr. Topps also gave me an unexpected gift—a copy of the latest best-seller. "This book is totally worthless," he announced, "and your homework over the break is to relax and not think about school long enough to read this." Never in my wildest dreams did I think I would ever have a principal like Mr. Topps!

Why, he even sent me a "Christmas letter":

Dear Norma,
As you take a well-deserved rest, I just wanted to tell you how glad we are that you have joined our faculty this year. I know you are discouraged at times, but almost all new teachers have a similar experience. Teaching is at once the most challenging and most rewarding profession there is. I appreciate your willingness to take counsel and to try suggestions. You have improved so much in how you teach reading that teachers with many years' experience could benefit from watching you!

The coming months and years will continue to be a time of growth for you. As you contemplate the changes you will make, please don't change these things:

Having a well-stocked library shelf for independent reading

Your emphasis on students' nutrition, recreation, and adequate rest

A schedule that has you work with your reading groups in a different order each day

Using an IRI to determine basal reader placements
Teaching small groups
Skipping work pages students do not need
Being so dedicated and conscientious

Merry Christmas!
I. B. Topps

Maybe, just maybe, I'm going to be a good teacher someday after all!

January

I always thought that if I could survive until January, I could make it. This turns out to be true but not for the reasons I had thought. I student taught last year starting in January and I figured when I got to January, I could pull out my student-teaching lesson plans! I did pull them out but they weren't very relevant to this class. Many of my children read much better than the children in the class in which I student taught, and then there are always Mike, Paul, and Daisy! Besides, the children in my student-teaching classroom had had an excellent teacher prior to January and these children have had me! I'm getting better, however. Those visits to Mrs. Wright's and Mrs. Wise's classrooms and my several long chats with Mr. Topps and Ms. Port have really helped. I now have

Scheduling   a new schedule that I have posted, and each morning, first thing, the children and I look at the schedule and decide who is going to be where doing what when! I couldn't possibly keep on schedule, however, were it not for the timer Mrs. Wright gave me for Christmas. I carry it around with me and use it to keep my groups to 25 minutes, to see who can get their old places cleaned up and get to their new places in the 5-minute transition time, and to time SQUIRT and snack time. It is so much a part of me, I feel like I am missing something when I leave for home and do not have it in my hand.

I had such success improving the reading of Larry's group and then Mitch's group in the fall that this month I thought I would finally make a major shift in the way I taught Daisy's group. What a disaster! First, they didn't want to do anything differently. I can't imagine why, since they always complained about the way we had been doing things. They wouldn't first read the material silently no matter how many times I sent them back to their seats to do it! It worked with the top two groups, why not them? I went to Mr. Topps for help.

"I have been waiting for you to try the suggestions I gave you with your bottom group. I'm glad you have. I believe there are two reasons you aren't having the same success. First and most important, you have students in Paul's group who cannot read in the first reader with high success. I haven't said anything to you about it because I knew you were changing as much as you could, but the students who are overplaced in that bottom group will not improve in reading no matter what you do until they are given material to read that they can identify almost all of the words in."

So I admitted to him that I had been aware for some time that Paul, Daisy, and Mike really belong in the primer. Then I asked him the question that had been in my mind for months. "Mr. Topps, if Mrs. Wright is such a good teacher, and I know she is, why do I have 6 students out of 25 who read below grade level in the second grade? Actually, I have 7 if you count Carl who is borderline."

He answered me without hesitation, "Norma, if you had the experience I've had, you would know how wonderful a job Freida did last year with this group of students. I have seen schools where only a little more than half of the second graders could read proficiently in the primer at the beginning of the year. You have no one reading below the primer. You have only 3 students out of 25 who read below the first reader!

"Frieda Wright," he continued with pride, "succeeds so completely precisely because she does not expect every student in first grade to read at grade level by the end of the year. If she taught as if every student were average or above, the six worst readers in your room would all read somewhere in the preprimers. They would have fallen behind by Thanksgiving and would have wasted the rest of first grade by doing things they were not ready to learn to do. Every child makes as much progress as he or she is able to do. Someday, you'll be able to say the same thing about your students."

Whew! I quickly asked him for the second reason I was having trouble teaching Daisy's group to improve their reading. He explained that they had to be taught how to read silently. "Although students can read orally before they can read silently, they never become really good at reading until they are able to read the material silently. Daisy and Paul's group needs to learn how to read silently."

I left his office armed with two additional suggestions for teaching my low group. I had to teach them to read silently, and somehow I had to get Daisy, Mike, and Paul in an easier book! I wonder if Ms. Port has anything else to do besides help me?

Once in a while, I have children come to the reading group who I suspect haven't read the story. I try to encourage them to do it and I don't let them participate in our group's activities if they indicate by their responses to comprehension questions or in oral reading that they haven't read the story silently. Last week, I had to send Roberta (who is now back in the top group where she belongs) to her seat during group time to read a story she hadn't read. When I questioned her about it she protested, "It was a dumb sissie story." I told her I was sorry she didn't like it but that she had a responsibility to her group to come prepared. I then sent her to her seat to read the story while I did some story dramatization with her group. Roberta, who loves to act in stories, was furious, but she hasn't come to reading group unprepared since. I have also had some trouble with Alexander's not reading his stories and I have him sit with me in the group area while I meet with Paul's group until he has his story read. He is not too happy about this and promises to read his stories faithfully if I will let him sit at his seat like everyone else in his group.

Discipline

We began SQUIRT again after the holidays, every day, right after lunch. I now get my children settled with their books before we set the timer and I am forcing myself to be a good model and read too. (It's not that I don't like to read, because I do. It's all those papers to grade and lessons to plan!) We started with 5 minutes again and I made a SQUIRT chart. It is hanging at the front of

Self-Selected Reading

the room and is a long sheet of paper marked off in days and months. Along the side, the minutes are marked off in 7- to 15-minute segments. Each day we color our bar graph to show how many minutes we are reading. In just this one month, our bar graph shows that we have increased a minute at a time from 6 minutes to 10 minutes. The children are already begging to go to 11 minutes. They love to see the bar graph growing. I am going to increase the time very gradually, however, so that we don't have the trouble we had before.

Though my classroom control techniques are improving, and it is so much easier to accomplish our work, there are still problems. I hate to sound like a fishwife yelling at the children, but sometimes that seems to be the only way to deal with a situation. In extreme cases, I send a child to stand facing the chalkboard for a period of time. Unfortunately, the last child I had do that was Mike. He was to stand there quietly until I told him he could return to his seat. I sat down with a reading group, my back to Mike, and worked with them until I noticed children giggling and pointing to the spot behind me where I had positioned Mike. I turned around and saw that he was imitating a monkey for the benefit of the other children.

That afternoon, I talked to Mrs. Wise and, of course, I ended up telling her my latest "Mike story." She said that after hearing about Mike all year she was considering retiring a year early so that she wouldn't have to spend her last teaching year with Mike! I was horrified to think that someone like Mrs. Wise would worry about discipline and told her so. She responded, "You are going to worry about discipline for as long as you teach. I have to run out early this afternoon and haven't helped you much with your problems. Why don't you come over and have dinner with me tomorrow night. We can have a long, uninterrupted chat then." Of course I accepted. We had a lovely, relaxed dinner during which she steered me away from school topics whenever I brought them up. As we were stacking the dishes, she told me that she knew I wanted to discuss school but that her own philosophy of life prevented her from doing so. "We live with school so much of our lives as it is that I force myself to forget it, or at least not discuss it, during dinner. There are so many disturbing things about school that they can ruin your digestion!"

Why, I could hardly believe that this woman with more than 20 years of teaching experience could still have troubles in school! That made me feel better.

After dinner, though, we did talk. She suggested that I find a book at the primer level and that one day each week, I assign Paul's group a story to read silently at their seats from this easier book.

"That's a marvelous idea," I responded. "It will also be good for Paul, Daisy, and Mike, who really should be reading in a primer all the time."

"In that case," she suggested, "why not meet with them another day each week and do some instruction in the primer-level book." I told her I would love to but I couldn't imagine when I could do it. I showed her my schedule (which I had in my car. I keep all my teaching stuff in the car. At least I am never idle in traffic jams!) and she suggested that perhaps I could let Danielle's group go to the library one day each week during their group time.

"Miss Page is always willing to help the children and she especially loves to introduce the precocious ones to the wonders of reference books." I could then use that time to meet with Paul, Daisy, and Mike. I will talk to Miss Page about this tomorrow.

We talked about discipline, too, and particularly about Mike. Mrs. Wise seems to think I am handling him about as well as he can be handled! "Make sure he knows the rules. Withdraw privileges as necessary. Keep giving him chances to be responsible and show him he will not get the best of you," she advised. "Some children are difficult and we must continue to be firm and fair with them. No system will work for everyone but it sounds like what you are doing is working quite well for most of your children most of the time. You are having a good year for a first-year teacher."

Discipline

As I was trying to absorb the fact that Mrs. Wise seemed to have such faith in me, the doorbell rang. Mrs. Wise went to answer it and I gathered up my things. Mrs. Wise then returned with her neighbor, a new doctoral student at the university. She introduced me to Mr. Horatio Flame, who said, "Just call me Red." We chatted for quite a while and I got home much later than I usually do on a school night. As I was driving home I realized that we had talked for over an hour about things other than teaching. What a wonderful feeling! Red seems like a really nice guy. I wonder why he just happened to drop in like that. Surely, it was just a coincidence that he came while I was there.

February

As you can see by my schedule, there have been some changes made! Each morning, I start the day by reading aloud to the whole class. This was one of the things I knew was important but never found time to do. I decided that if I did it first thing, it would get done! Mrs. Wise has convinced me that if I teach these children to read and they never do read, I have wasted all that effort! The first two books I read to them were *Miss Nelson Is Missing* and *Miss Nelson Is Back* by Harry Allard. After reading the books, we discussed them and I had to admit to feeling like Miss Nelson sometimes. "I wonder if there is a Viola Swamp living anywhere in this area," I mused aloud. "Don't get any ideas, Miss Nouveau," Horace pleaded! "We're being much better than we were! Aren't we?" Carl suggested. "There aren't really mean teachers like Viola Swamp," Roberta declared!

Scheduling

Teacher Read-Aloud

The book clearly made an impression on them and I have been tempted to buy a black wig! Rita found another Miss Nelson book—*Miss Nelson Has a Field Day*—at the public library and brought it in for me to read. Many of the children are now reading the Miss Nelson books on their own during SQUIRT time.

At 8:50, we do our daily words on the wall practice, an idea I discovered while visiting in Mrs. Wright's classroom. Each Monday, I add five new words. I choose the words by looking for the words they commonly misspell in their writing. I also let children suggest some words they would like to learn to spell. Each day, I call out five of the words from the wall and they chant them and

Word Wall

	8:30–8:50	8:50–9:00	9:00–9:25	9:30–9:55	TRANSITION	10:00	10:15–10:40	TRANSITION	10:45–11:10
Monday	READ TO WHOLE CLASS	WORDS ON THE WALL	Meet Mike's group Larry's group—centers Horace's group—seatwork	Meet Larry's group Mike's group—seatwork Horace's group—centers	TRANSITION	SNACK	WHOLE CLASS WRITING	TRANSITION	Meet Horace's group Mike's group—centers Larry's group—seatwork
Tuesday	→	→	Same as Monday	Same as Monday except Larry's group—lib.	→	→	WRITING	→	Same as Monday
Wednesday	→	→	Children choose which of four groups they want to work with, prepare story dramatization, choral reading, play, pictures, or other story-response activities for Friday →		→	→	→	→	→
Thursday	→	→		Meet, Paul Daisy, Mike	→	→	Same as Monday	→	Same as Monday Whole-class listening comprehension activity
Friday	→	→	Children share response activities from Thursday's groups		→	→	→	→	Children choose favorite story for editing and rewriting and/or art

then write them. I have them check the words themselves, just like Mrs. Wright, but some—Butch, Mike, Alexander, Daisy—in particular don't check them very carefully. Other children want me to take their papers up and give them a grade every day. I have told them that not everything needs a grade, but they still want me to give grades. I suppose that is because up until now I have been grading everything they do and so I have set this trap for myself!

It was Red (who knows nothing about teaching, thank goodness) who came up with the brilliant idea. "Why not have five checkers in a box," he suggested one night as I was telling him my problem while he was, as usual, whomping me at checkers, "four red ones and one black one. When the children have finished and exchanged and checked their words, let one child close her eyes and pick a checker. If a red checker comes out, this was only for practice. If the black one comes out, however, this was 'the real thing' and you can collect them, verify that they are correctly checked, and record them in your grade book." I told Red he would be a wonderful teacher, he is so creative, but he declares he hasn't "the stomach for it."

Grading

At any rate, we now use his checkers system. It is super! All the children, including Mike, put forth their best efforts each day because they never know when it will count. They love to have the black checker come out because, if they try, they can do well and this helps their grades. I am going to try this system in the afternoon when we practice addition and subtraction facts. Each day, we will have a five-minute timed practice, exchange and check papers, and then see if it counts or not by having a blindfolded child select a checker. This will give the children the practice they need without putting an impossible grading burden on me.

On Mondays, Tuesdays, and Wednesdays, I meet with my three reading groups. (Except that on Tuesdays, Larry's group goes to the library and works with Miss Page while I give special instruction at the primer level to Mike, Daisy, and Paul). I meet Mike's group first and then have their seatwork time immediately following. They have their center time after snack time and I check to see that they have the work done reasonably well or they don't go to the centers! The children in Horace's group are more dependable, so I have them do their seatwork first, then go to centers, and then meet with me. I don't have time to check and make sure they all have their work done before they go to centers, but I do suspend their center time for the following day if they are not getting their seatwork done. Mort, however, must check with me each day before going to centers. He simply won't do his work without this immediate consequence. Larry's group always does the work. (Except for Roberta, who is too smart for her own good. I check with her first thing in the morning before her group goes to centers.) Larry's group begins the morning in centers, then meets with me or Miss Page, and then has time to prepare for the next day's group. This system is working so well, I can't believe it. I thought I didn't have time to have centers, but now I can see I don't have time not to. I assign a reasonable amount of work, mostly preparation for silent reading of and follow-up to stories, to each group and they spend a part of each morning with me, part doing seatwork, and part in the centers.

Centers   My centers are quite simple. I have a math center in which I have collected a lot of math manipulatives, an art center in which I put a different art medium each week, a game center in which I put a different game (Candyland, Old Maid, or Chutes and Ladders, for example) each week, a listening-viewing center in which I set up some tape-filmstrips Miss Page suggested the children might enjoy, and a classroom library. The children choose which three of the centers they would like to go to and sign up for them on Monday. They go to a different center on Monday, Tuesday, and Wednesday, and thus can go to three of the five. The current complaint is that they can't go to all five centers!

Process Writing   At 10:15 each day, we have our writing time. One thing I noticed in both Mrs. Wright's and Mrs. Wise's classrooms is that the children write every day—and the first graders are even beginning to publish books. Mrs. Wright told me that everyone had published three books last year. I asked my children about their books and the next day, many of them proudly brought in their books to show me. Even Paul, who rarely brings anything from or says anything about home, brought three books he had published. He even read them to me, with fluency and confidence! That afternoon, I asked Mrs. Wright how children like Paul could write books, and she explained about how she divided the class into thirds for publishing purposes and put one of the three lowest children in each third. She then explained how she did the editing and publishing and how she let Paul tell her what he meant to write and she wrote it for him to copy into his book! I am beginning to understand why everyone thinks Mrs. Wright is such a savvy lady!

I have gotten all the children to bring in writing notebooks and we are writing each day. I do a minilesson like Mrs. Wright does and try to write about varied topics. Mike was the one who asked me to write a "When I Was Your Age" tale. When I admitted that I didn't know what that was, the class was amazed! They told me all about when Mrs. Wright was in the first grade, how she liked to dress up as a fairy princess at Halloween and about her boyfriend in first grade. I must have looked a bit incredulous because Betty quickly explained that Mrs. Wright never really told them if the tales were all true or some were made up. Harriet volunteered that if they were true, Mrs. Wright was writing part of her autobiography. The children all nodded and I was once again amazed at how much they knew!

So I wrote my first "When I Was Your Age" tale! I invented the spelling of a few big words, saying them aloud slowly just as I had seen Mrs. Wright do, and I looked up occasionally on the word wall. I didn't read what I was writing otherwise, and the children had all eyes glued to the screen as I wrote.

When I was in the second grade, I loved school. My teacher's name was Mrs. Hope and I thought she was the most butiful lady in the world. I only got in trouble once and that was when Billy Higginbopper kept teasing me because I was so tall and skinny and had so many freckles. I didn't mean to knock him down but I was so mad. When he fell, he hurt his arm and had to go to the hospitell. It was a terrible, no good, very bad day!

Editing   "Is that really true?" they all asked, when I had finished. I just smiled and sent them off to do their writing.

We have begun the Editor's Checklist again. Mrs. Wright suggested that I add the items to check for gradually and remind the children to read their papers for each thing when their writing time was up. We have the first three items that they learned last year and I will add the final review item next month. Then, I will try to add a few new ones before the end of the year. Editing

We haven't begun publishing yet but I hope that by the end of the year, the children will all have a couple of books they wrote in second grade to add to their first-grade collection. I am so grateful to Ms. Port for arranging for my visits to Mrs. Wright and Mrs. Wise. I can't imagine that all that "know-how" was right here in this very building and, had it not been for Ms. Port, I might never have realized it!

March

We had parent-teacher conferences early in March. Everyone except Paul and Jeff had a parent (or other relative) come. I was so much more at ease because I knew I was doing a better job. I wasn't on the defensive waiting for them to ask me something I didn't know or expecting them to attack me for something I wasn't doing. Rather, I was relaxed (relatively!) and we had good conversations about their children. Most of the parents expressed their pleasure at what I was doing with their children. I think this may have been a reflection of how relieved they were that things have gotten much better as the year has gone on. Mike's mother is quite worried about him and says she can hardly handle him at home. I told her that he is making some progress and seems to be able to learn when he settles down long enough. I suggested that she read some easy-to-read books at home with Mike each night and let him chime in when he knows a word. She said she would try but that she practically had to "rope" him to get him settled down long enough to eat, never mind anything else. When she left, I thought, "I shall be more patient with Mike. I imagine that that woman must deal with his energy for as many waking hours as I do each day, and all day on Saturdays, Sundays, and holidays." Parent Involvement

Many parents expressed their pleasure with the writing their children were doing. Mandy's mother declared that Mandy has decided to become a writer and keeps a writing notebook at home in which she writes faithfully. She told me that the children liked writing each day and especially like my pulling the popsicle sticks out of the hat to see which children get to read their stories. (This was Red's solution to the problem of everyone wanting to read and not enough time.) When the timer signals the end of the 10-minute writing time, the children who wish to read their story put the popsicle stick with their name on it in a special container. I pull the popsicle sticks out and those children whose names come out get to read their stories. The children love the drama of wondering whose stick will come out and are very good listeners as they know we will get to pull more sticks in the allotted time if I don't have to interrupt constantly and ask them to be good listeners. Routines

Thanks to Ms. Port, I have now learned how to get Paul's group to read silently. When I called her a month or so ago and told her that the silent reading just wouldn't work for my six poorest readers, she told me she would get back to me. One day a few weeks later she arrived at my room after school and taught me how to teach a comprehension strategy lesson. Students like Mike, Daisy, and Paul have to have a very particular kind of comprehension lesson if they are to learn how to read silently with understanding.

She went on to explain the seven steps of a comprehension strategy lesson and gave lots of examples so I could plan and teach one myself. She suggested that I try it with my top two groups first before using it with my bottom two groups. "They will like and profit from it, too," she said.

Even the first comprehension strategy lesson I taught to Paul's group went surprisingly well. The third one was truly wonderful. It went like this. I started out by introducing the strategy I was going to teach to them that day (Step 1). I had chosen to teach them *to follow the sequence of a story*. Remembering some warnings that Ms. Port had given, I did not rush this introduction. We spent enough time here for the students to connect with the concept of story sequence. I told them that most stories would be hard to understand and impossible to enjoy if we confused the order in which the main actions take place. Their faces revealed that my telling had failed to impress them. So I told them the story of "The Three Billy Goats Gruff." I had the biggest billy goat cross the bridge first and kill the troll; then I had the middle billy goat start to cross the bridge. Daisy seemed to wake up. "No, no, Miss Nouveau, that's not right. You can't have the biggest billy goat cross first! That messes up the whole story."

Then I started to tell them the story of "The Three Bears." When I started out with the part where the bears returned home to find their house in disarray, everyone protested. I had prepared sentence strips, each of which had a major event from the story. I laid them out in front of Paul's group on the table and let them take turns organizing the strips into the right order. Even Paul took a turn, although Daisy tried to tell him what to do at each decision point. I put a stop to that. They were all able to organize correctly the events of this simple, familiar story. I then told them again how important getting things in the right order was to understanding and enjoying a story. They were with me now. I told them that as stories get harder, it gets more difficult to figure out which things happen first, next, and last. I told them that grown-ups who are good readers follow or monitor the order that actions happen in a story, and if they become confused about the order, they reread and think until their confusion is ended. I told them that I wanted them to learn to follow the order that things happen in every story they read or hear.

I then attempted to prepare them to understand the particular story I had chosen to use with them to teach them the comprehension strategy of following story sequence (Step 2). The story was in the primer that I use with Paul's group. It is a modern retelling of the Aesop's fable "The Wind and the Sun." To complete this step, I followed the basal teacher's manual suggestions for teaching general background knowledge and specific passage vocabulary. These suggestions helped the students to call up what they already knew as well as to learn new background information.

Following Step 2, I set a purpose for reading that clearly reflected the comprehension strategy I was teaching (Step 3). Before the lesson, I had determined what I thought were the five major events of "The Wind and the Sun":

The wind blew the boy's hat off.
The wind blew the boy's balloon into a tree.
The wind gave up trying to get the boy to take off his jacket.
The sun made the boy hot.
The boy took off his jacket.

I had written these five major events in a random order on a piece of chart paper. At this point, I taped the chart paper to the chalkboard with masking tape. I read the five events aloud as they followed along, and then explained that all events were right but that they were not in the right order. I explained to them that when finished reading, they would have to close their books, and then we would decide as a group how to put these events in the right order.

While they read to themselves (Step 4), I walked around the room and helped the other students with their seatwork. Ms. Port had said they would read to themselves if I gave them enough preparation before reading and if I gave them only one clear purpose for reading, but it still had to happen for me to believe it! They all moved their lips slightly, but you have to crawl before you can walk. When I saw that they were all finished, I returned and had them close their books. They then attempted to put the events in order as a group (Step 5). When Daisy and Mike disagreed and starting fussing, I allowed them to open their books to prove which of those two events went first. When that dispute was settled, they all closed their books again. When they were right, I praised them. When they were wrong or disagreed, I encouraged them by saying that they would be able to get it right by returning to the book and thinking about the sequence while they reviewed part of it. Before long, they had put the five events in the right order.

We then talked about the story, how they liked it, and why they thought the author might have written it (Step 6). This discussion was loose and "student centered," as one of my education professors used to call it.

At this point in the lesson, I had them turn to several pages in the workbook that had sequence as the focus (Step 7). After introducing the workbook activities, I sent them to their seats to complete the pages. For the first time this year, they went without complaining about either the lesson or the assignment.

I am going to plan a comprehension strategy lesson for each story I teach in either Paul's group or Butch's group. Next year, I will have all of these lessons already planned! Of course, I can hope I won't have any below-average students next year, and I can also hope someone will give me a million dollars!

I have read many books aloud this month. In addition to my read-aloud time first thing in the morning, I have discovered that there is a veritable treasure trove of informational books that build important science and social studies concepts. This month our science unit was on space and the solar system. We read several wonderful books by Jeanne Bendick, including *The Planets: Neighbors*

Content Area Integration

in Space; The Sun: Our Very Own Star; and *The Stars: Lights in the Night Sky.* Steve brought in a marvelous book, *The Magic School Bus Lost in the Solar System*, by Joanna Cole. As soon as the children saw it, they started chattering about Miss Frizzle's trip to the waterworks. When they discovered that I didn't know any of the Magic School Bus books, they insisted on going to Mrs. Wright's room right then and there and borrowing *The Magic School Bus at the Waterworks*, which we read and enjoyed again. It is amazing what a lasting effect a truly great informational book has on their retention of information!

Unit Teaching
In social studies, as part of our continuing study of communities, we are doing a unit on Native Americans. Again there are many wonderful, sensitive books that portray how different groups of Native Americans live today and in the past. The children especially enjoyed Ann McGovern's *If You Lived with the Sioux Indians* and Mary Perrine's *Nannabah's Friend*. I even found a book that connected up to both the science and social studies units. *They Dance in the Sky* by Jean Guard and Ray Wiliamson recounts the myths and stories told about the constellations by various Native American tribes.

Red, who is working to put himself through his doctoral program, has offered to come to school early next month to show the children the muscial instruments that he plays. He is the leader of a rock band that he calls "Red and the Flamers." I know that Mike and many of the others will be enthralled with his presentation as well as his personality, which matches his gorgeous, curly auburn hair. I realize how busy he is—and am delighted he is willing to talk to the class.

April

Red's appearance was enormously successful! We discussed rock bands, and I was amazed at how knowledgeable these young children are about rock groups. Mike was fascinated with the drums. Red had brought an amplifier along as well, and we caught Butch just in time; he had plugged in the electric guitar and was ready to strum—full blast!

Language Experience
After Red left, I had the children tell me about his visit and I wrote what they told me on chart paper. We read it over together, cut apart some of the sentences, and relocated them in the correct order of occurrence. Here is what they came up with.

Mr. Flame of "Red and the Flamers" came to our class. (Alex)

It was really cool, man! (Mike)

He showed a variety of instruments. (Larry)

Some of us danced when he played. (Rita)

I almost played the electric guitar. (Butch)

He asked Miss Nouveau for an aspirin before he left. (Mandy)

Fluency
I have begun doing imitative reading with Paul's group. Imitative reading is a fancy name for having the children read a story enough times so that they can read it easily and fluently, "like a good reader." One day, Ms. Port was visiting our school. That afternoon, she popped into my room with some easy-

to-read books and tapes. She then explained to me that I should let each child in Paul's group pick one of these easy-to-read books and sign up for a time each day to listen to the book. The child was to listen to the book until he or she could read the book without the aid of the tape recording. Then, the child would sign up to read the book to me and, assuming that the child could indeed read the book well, that child could choose another book-tape combination.

So far, so good! Chip has read four of the easy-to-read books. He listens to them at his signed-up time each day and then will often come in first thing in the morning or stay a little late in the afternoon to listen to them. I am keeping a chart of the books they have read. Daisy is not happy with me, however. She listens to the book-tape one time and then signs up to read it to me. Of course, she can't, and I send her back with instructions to listen to it at least two more times before she signs up to read to me again. Mike's mother has bought him a tape recorder and he takes his book-tape home every night. Even he seems pleased that he can easily read, cover-to-cover, three books and seems motivated to read some more. If Chip had a tape recorder at home, there would be no stopping him! Imitative reading is an important addition to my oral reading instruction for Paul's group and for Chip. I think that by listening to the tape of the easy-to-read book often enough, they get to the point where they can easily identify the words and anticipate what is coming next and they have, probably for the first time, the experience of reading like a good reader. I am going to start my word-by-word readers right off next year with imitative reading.

This month the children got into mysteries. I started them off, I guess, by reading *Nate the Great* by Marjorie Weinman Sharmot, *Encyclopedia Brown Sets the Pace* by Donald Sobol, and *Two Bad Ants* by Chris Von Allsburg. The children quickly began finding mysteries, including more *Nate the Great* and *Encyclopedia Brown* mysteries and the reissued *Boxcar Mysteries* series. Now almost everyone is into the mystery craze, and several children, including Hilda and Butch, have declared their intention to be detectives or spies when they grow up!

We read books related to our science unit on plants, including a beautifully illustrated plant alphabet book, *Allison's Zinnia* by Anita Lobel. I even found some books to integrate with math this month. We are doing a unit on counting and big numbers and the children were fascinated by David Schwartz's *How Much is a Million?* and Mitsumasa Anno's *Anno's Counting Book* and *Anno's Mysterious Multiplying Jar*.

Content Area Integration

We have finished our first publishing cycle and although it did not go as smoothly as Mrs. Wright had made it sound, we did it and the children all have books they are very proud of. Mrs. Wright was so pleased when I showed her the books that she brought her first graders over and we had an authors' party. We put the children together into mixed groups of first and second graders and let them read their books to each other. My children all behaved very well and seemed determined to be more "mature" than the first graders. I was amazed to see how little the first graders are and how well they can write. My children have not gone as far in writing this year as those first graders have, but knowing what I know now, at the beginning of next year I should be able to pick up right where Mrs. Wright left off. The first graders seemed delighted to be "up in

Publishing

second grade," and as many of them left, they gave me a hug and said, "See you next year!" The true rewards of teaching!

May

I can't believe this year is coming to an end. We have had a busy last month. I wanted the children to have two published books from second grade so we did another publishing cycle. This one was easier!

I read them some of the *Amelia Bedelia* books, which appealed greatly to their seven-year-old silliness. That got them started on lots of other word play, joke, and riddle books. We also read books connected to our final combined science/

Content Area Integration

social studies unit on the environment and what various communities can do to help clean up and maintain a healthy environment. After reading *The Empty Lot* by Dale Fife, we took a walking field trip to a nearby empty lot and discovered that our empty lot was also teeming with animal life. The children also loved *When the Woods Hum* by Joanne Ryder and *The Great Kopak Tree* by Lynne Cherry.

Self-Selected Reading

We had to add to our SQUIRT chart, for we have reached 16 minutes of SQUIRT time! I never thought last fall that I would be here in May, and I probably wouldn't have been if Mr. Topps and the others hadn't helped me isolate my problems and correct them. I certainly never thought that I would see my class sitting still and reading attentively for 16 straight minutes and liking it! In some ways it has been a long year, but in others it has been too short. How I wish I could have begun my current reading program earlier!

Focused Writing

Anticipating next year and the first day of school (it just has to be better!), I asked the children to think back over the year and all of the things we have done. I wrote their comments on the chalkboard and we filled it in no time! I had no idea that we had done so many things or that the children could remember them.

The next instructions that I gave them were to pretend that they were their own desk. As the desk, they were to write a letter to whoever would be sitting in that seat next year. They were to give the new second graders an idea about what to expect during the new school year. We would leave the letters in the desks and surprise the new children with them in the fall. The children seemed excited about the project and eagerly began to write. Here is a copy of the letter that Roberta wrote:

> Hi, Kid,
> You're pretty lucky to be starting second grade already. And boy, will you have fun. Especially sitting at this desk. This is where Roberta Marie Smith sat last year, and she had fun. This year you will learn to read harder books and you'll do your workbook (if you're better than Roberta). Have a good time, kid, 'cause it won't last long. Soon you'll have to go to the third grade where they really have hard work to do! Maybe I can ask Roberta's desk in third grade to write to you, too.
>
> Love,
> Clarence, your desk

We have added to the supply of books this year with children's paperbacks. The children and I receive brochures every month from two companies that publish inexpensive, high-quality children's books. The children take their individual brochures home and bring back the completed order forms with the necessary money. I mail these and add the bonus books, 1 of which we get for each 10 books the children order. Then we all eagerly await the arrival of our new books. In this way, I have added about 25 new books to our classroom library.

All in all, it has turned out to be a very good year for me and, I think, for **Discipline** almost all my children. Most of my discipline problems have lessened as I established some routines and began to give the children interesting and varied things to do that they can do. The new seating arrangement, a group-meeting place, and the timer have really helped, too. I still have some days when I wonder why I ever wanted to be a teacher. Mike is most difficult to handle and my promises to myself to be firm and patient with him just seem to dissolve when I am faced with one of his regular disruptions. He tells me they are moving right after school is out. Some third-grade teacher somewhere will have her hands full next year. I am sorry he is moving because I am sure Mrs. Wise would be able to calm him down. Paul is another one of my failures. He seems to be perking up and making some progress and then he goes into a somber, detached state during which he might as well not be here. I don't know what is going to happen to him. And Daisy—I never thought I would teach a child and not come to love that child but I can't find anything lovable about Daisy. Maybe Mrs. Wise can get through to her, too. I have such faith in that lady. I would never have made it through the year without her.

I *have* made it through the year, however, and I will be ready for next year. I told Mrs. Wright the other day that if I learned as much every year I taught as I have this first year, I would never have to fear getting stale and bored. She said that teaching was many things, some positive and some not so positive, but that she had never found it to be boring. Red says that one thing he learned this year was that in teaching, there are so many intriguing problems to be solved! I guess that if I can continue to view my crises as "intriguing problems to be solved" I will someday be a good, capable, creative teacher.

THE STUDENT TEACHING SEMINAR

Miss Nouveau, veteran of one year in the classroom, had been asked by Dr. Link to talk with her student teachers at their weekly seminar. At first, she had protested that she was the last person who should be asked. After all, she was still learning herself, and she didn't think she had anything of significance to contribute.

Dr. Link explained that several students in the class had asked her to find a first-year teacher who would talk to them. They wanted to know what it was *really* like when one started teaching. While teachers like Mrs. Wise could contribute a great deal to the seminar, they had been teaching too long to focus honestly on the first year of teaching. And, she added, she had been observing Miss Nouveau's progress throughout the year and was pleased with the growth that had been taking place. Miss Nouveau finally consented to address the class. "But," she cautioned, "I'm not promising that it will be any good."

"If you just tell them what you have lived through this past year," Dr. Link replied, "they will be more than satisfied."

And that, she resolved, was precisely what she would do. These students would find out the real truth from her before they had to live through it themselves! She requested that they meet in her room.

The afternoon of the seminar, Miss Nouveau stood at the back of her room while Dr. Link greeted the carefree students. After Dr. Link had introduced her, she began her talk by saying, "This year I have worked harder than I ever dreamed I would have to, and even so, things have gone well only at times." She then related the inaccurate judgments, errors in placement, discipline problems, and poor assignments she had made. As she spoke, she noted looks of disbelief turning to looks of pity and fear as she related anecdote after anecdote. Not wanting to discourage them, however, Miss Nouveau then began to relate the positive things that had happened to her and the consequent changes she had made in her program especially since Christmas. When she finished, several hands went up for questions.

"If you knew you weren't doing very well in October, how come you kept right on doing things wrong? I mean, if *I* were doing something I knew was wrong, I wouldn't just keep on!"

"Well," answered Miss Nouveau with a smile, "maybe you would and maybe you wouldn't. I would have thought that same way a year ago, but it's so different when you're actually there day after day with the children and you know you're totally responsible for their instruction. There's neither the opportunity nor the knowledge to do it any other way! I was fortunate, though, to be in a school with a principal who cared, other teachers who helped me, and an elementary supervisor who showed me alternatives. Though they were all as busy as I was, they gave freely of their time and advice. If it hadn't been for them, I know I would have resigned at Christmas."

"What would have helped you, though, before you got to your first year of teaching?" another student asked.

"If only I had been given more experience in classrooms prior to my student teaching, then I could have spent student teaching time learning more about classroom management. The better prepared you are when you enter your student teaching, the better you will be at the end of it. Also, if my reading/language arts course had been more practical, I would have been better prepared to teach the children."

Another student raised his hand to ask, "Could you just summarize for us a few of the most important things that you learned this year?"

Miss Nouveau thought for a moment before replying, "I suppose that one of the most important things I learned was how to get kids to the bathroom." The class exploded into laughter. "You laugh! But when it happens to you, it won't be so funny!" She smiled at them and began again. "Another thing was locating the school storeroom. It's often a gold mine of books and materials just lying there, gathering dust. Also, I learned that I must have some time for myself. One reason I was so depressed last fall, I'm sure, was that I had no time to do things that I had always done and that I enjoyed doing. I regret very much some of the things I did this year, and if I could be granted one wish it would be that I could repeat this school year knowing at the beginning what I know now!"

"How are you going to start next year, since obviously you won't repeat what has been done?"

"I thought you might ask that," responded Miss Nouveau confidently. "As a matter of fact, I have given a lot of thought to that and I think I am prepared to get next year off to a better start. I will begin the year right off with my horseshoe seating arrangement. I even know from watching the first graders which children will get the ends of the horseshoe! I will give an IRI to all the children but I will count only errors that change the meaning and that way will not penalize fluent readers like Larry for having their eyes out ahead of their voices as all good readers do. I will form my reading groups according to the instructional levels I find and I will make sure that the lowest group spends some time in an instructional-level book and some time in an independent-level book each week.

Assessment

"When I meet with my groups, I will make sure that they have purposeful silent reading. I will not do oral reading unless the students have read the material silently first and all the other students have their books closed. I will try to remember to use every-pupil-response activities whenever possible, both because they help to keep the children involved and attentive and because they allow me to diagnose in an informal, ongoing manner who is learning what (and who is not!). Never again will I make the mistake of trying to do everything in the teacher's manual. Rather, I will pick those activities that a particular group needs and can profit from at that time. Since I will be timing my groups for 25 minutes each day, I will have to decide which things the children need to be with me to do, which they can do independently before and after meeting with me, and which to leave out altogether.

Oral Reading

"Finally, I shall balance my day and instruction with whole-group, small-group, and individual instruction. I will also remember that reading instruction does not go on solely when the children are reading their basal reader. I will read to the children each day and have them write each day. I will do regular listening comprehension lessons. I even hope to help them become better readers during science and social studies as they read informational text."

Balanced Literacy Programs

As Miss Nouveau paused to catch her breath, Dr. Link interrupted to say that she regretted having to announce that the seminar time was up. Miss Nouveau and most of the students turned in astonishment to view the clock and confirm that indeed an entire hour had fled past. "Just like teaching," observed Miss Nouveau, "when you are thinking about what you have to say and do, it seems like there is an enormous amount of time to fill. But, when you start doing it, there is never enough time." The students chuckled. A few stayed afterward to talk privately with Miss Nouveau. Dr. Link looked on proudly!

ADD TO YOUR JOURNAL

 Miss Nouveau got off to a rocky start her first year of teaching, but most of us do. Teaching is an extremely complex job and no one can be completely prepared ahead of time. Because beginning teachers are under such stress and pressure, they often do not see things as clearly as they would if they were less stressed! Anxiety reduces your ability to think and problem solve. Also remember that having gone through kindergarten and first grade with this class of children, you have a lot more knowledge about these children and have had more vicarious teaching experience than Miss Nouveau had. So, without being too hard on her, analyze her first year of teaching and compare it with your own first year if you have already taught, or think ahead to your first year if you are preparing to teach. What could Miss Nouveau have done differently earlier? What were her smartest moves from December on? What have you learned from reading about Miss Nouveau that you wished you had known before you started teaching or that you will remember and apply when you do begin teaching?

Children's Books/Materials Cited

Allison's Zinnia, by Anita Lobel, Greenwillow, 1990.
Amelia Bedelia books by Peggy Parish, HarperCollins, various dates.
Anno's Counting Book, by Mitsumasa Anno, HarperCollins, 1986.
Anno's Mysterious Multiplying Jar, by Mitsumasa Anno, Philomel, 1983.
Boxcar Mysteries series, by Gertrude Warner, Whitman, various years.
The Empty Lot, by Dale Fife, Little, Brown, 1991.
Encyclopedia Brown Sets the Pace, by Donald Sobol, Scholastic, 1989.
The Great Kopak Tree, by Lynne Cherry, Harcourt Brace Jovanovich, 1990.
How Much Is a Million? by David Schwartz, Scholastic, 1986.
If You Lived with the Sioux Indians, by Ann McGovern, Scholastic, 1984.
The Magic School Bus at the Waterworks, by Joanna Cole, Scholastic, 1988.
The Magic School Bus Lost in the Solar System, by Joanna Cole, Scholastic, 1992.
Miss Nelson Has a Field Day, by Harry Allard, Houghton Mifflin, 1988.
Miss Nelson Is Back, by Harry Allard, Houghton Mifflin, 1988.
Miss Nelson Is Missing, by Harry Allard, Houghton Mifflin, 1987.
Nannabah's Friend, by Mary Perrine, Houghton Mifflin, 1989.
Nate the Great, by Marjorie Weinman Sharmot, Dell, 1977.
The Planets: Neighbors in Space, by Jeanne Bendick, Millbrook, 1991.
The Stars: Lights in the Night Sky, by Jeanne Bendick, Millbrook, 1991.
The Sun: Our Very Own Star, by Jeanne Bendick, Millbrook, 1991.
They Dance in the Sky, by Jean Guard & Ray Williamson, Houghton Mifflin, 1992.
Two Bad Ants, by Chris Von Allsburg, Houghton Mifflin, 1988.
When the Woods Hum, by Joanne Ryder, Morrow Junior Books, 1991.

CHAPTER 13

Mrs. Wise: Third Grade

THE PARENT MEETING

Mrs. Wise walked around the room, carefully placing materials for the parents to examine when they arrived for the meeting later that evening. She went about the task methodically, for she had been having parent meetings for most of her 28 years as a teacher, long before they became an "in" thing to do. As a matter of fact, she was the one who had suggested to Mr. Topps, some 10 years before, that these meetings become a regular part of the school routine. She had also initiated the parent conferences that everyone now held twice yearly. There were those who called her an innovator and those who said it was amazing that a woman of her years could be so up-to-date! Mrs. Wise chuckled over that one! She told them all that it had nothing to do with innovation or age—she simply knew what her children needed and how *she* could best teach them.

She was always exhilarated by these meetings, as she was by the parent conferences. It was astonishing how much one could learn about a child in half-hour conferences with the parents. She made the parents feel relaxed by sitting in a chair beside them rather than in the more formal position behind the desk. She had acquired a knack for knowing what to say and how to say it that helped put parents at their ease and yet elicited from them the maximum amount of information about the child. Tonight, however, she was to meet the parents en masse. She enjoyed explaining what she and their children were going to be doing, for she loved teaching. She was not looking forward to the day in the near future when she would be retiring.

Shortly before 7:00 P.M., the parents began to arrive. Mrs. Wise didn't begin the meeting until 7:05, however, for long years of experience had taught her that many parents would arrive late no matter when the meeting was to begin.

"Hello. Some of you I know quite well because I have had other children of yours. Some of you are new to me as I am to you. I certainly hope that we will become well acquainted this year. I want to urge you *all* to come visit the classroom. I have only two requirements: (1) that you let me know in advance when you want to come, so that I can let you know whether or not it is convenient, and (2) that you plan to stay at least an hour, so that the children will settle down and forget that you are here so that you can really see the program. I warn you! You may be put to work though. Any extra hands in my class can and probably will be used. Just ask Mr. Topps! I'm sure that is why he has been avoiding my classroom for the last couple of years!"

She paused for breath and to let the laughter die down. "We, at this school, decided many years ago that we felt strongly enough about the place of children's literature and children's writing in the curriculum that we would make a concerted effort to incorporate them into our classrooms. I have developed my entire reading and language arts program around books for children and children's own writings. In order to make reading and writing situations as natural as possible, I have implemented a literature-based program. Let me explain to you how it works.

"As you look around the room, you see that I am fortunate enough to have hundreds and hundreds of books that are part of our permanent classroom collection. I have been collecting these books for years. I get them from a variety of sources. My friends know never to throw out a book without checking with me first. Across the years, parents—including some of you—have given me children's books, which I add to our collection. I haunt flea markets, yard sales, and bookstores, and I must admit that I have bought a lot of the books in this room with my own money. Don't feel too sorry for me, though, because I love books and I enjoy reading them myself and then sharing them with the children. Some people shop for clothes, I shop for books!

"In the last few years, I haven't had to buy too many books using my own money. The school system has finally come to realize that children who love reading become good readers and that immersing children in lots of wonderful books is an investment that pays off. Every year now, I am allotted quite a substantial sum of money to buy books. Of course, since I had stocked myself so well to start with, I didn't need all the single copies of books that many other teachers needed. I have used almost all my funds to buy multiple copies of books, and it is these books that I use for reading lessons and that the children will be discussing in their literature response groups. I also used some of my book money to buy us a brand new set of *World Book* encyclopedias and to get classroom subscriptions to several magazines for children. This year we will be getting *Cricket, Sports Illustrated for Kids, Penny Power, Ranger Rick, 3-2-1 Contact,* and *Kid City.*

"In addition to all the books and magazines that reside permanently in this room, the children and I make good and frequent use of the school library, the public library, and even, when we need some hard-to-find things, the university library. My sister teaches there and she and I have spent some wonderful afternoons hunting for information I need for one of my units.

"The books that you see in this room are my reading program. I know that some teachers use basal readers for part of their program, and I have used them in the past, but I have so many wonderful books—including multiple copies of lots of the best books—that I don't see any need for the children to read anything but the real thing. Don't worry, however, that I won't be teaching your children the strategies that are outlined in the basal reader and that they need to become independent readers. When you have taught 28 years, taken as many reading courses and workshops as I have, and used as many different basals over the years, you learn what the critical reading strategies are and how to help children develop these. I will be doing short minilessons with the children several times a week, and in these minilessons I will teach them the comprehension strategies they need. They will then apply these strategies to the books they are reading and I will make sure the strategies get followed up in the literature response groups and in individual conferences.

"For most of the year, expect that your child will be reading at least two books at a time. During our Readers' Workshop each morning, the children are given books to read. It is these books that I use to make sure that the children are reading a wide variety of literature, applying the reading strategies I teach them, and it is these books that they are discussing in their literature study groups. Sometimes I assign the book and sometimes I let them choose from four or five titles, but what they read during Readers' Workshop is determined by me with some input from the children.

Guided Reading

"Equally important is our afternoon self-selected reading time. Each day, when we come back from lunch, we settle down for some self-selected reading time. Your children are all used to having this time every day—you may have heard it called SQUIRT in some other classrooms. I call it self-selected reading because I put the emphasis on the children choosing. I make no demands on them during this time except that they are quietly reading something of their own choosing. While they read, I have individual conferences with the children about their reading. The children sign up when they want to conference with me, and if I check my records and I haven't conferenced with a particular child for two weeks, I sign that child up for a conference. On Friday afternoons, we take our after-lunch time to share what we have been reading in small groups."

Self-Selected Reading

Mrs. Wise glanced up at the clock and frowned. "Just like during the day here, there is never enough time to do everything as thoroughly as you would like to. We have to be in the cafeteria in ten minutes for the schoolwide PTA organizational meeting, so just let me explain two other critical components of our language arts program.

"Each morning, in addition to our Readers' Workshop, we have Writers' Workshop. Most of you know that we do process writing here at Merritt and that your children do lots of first-draft writing and publish some pieces. This

Process Writing

year, since most of your children have some facility with writing, we will work more on revising and polishing first drafts so that their writing becomes more conventional.

Focused Writing

"In addition to process writing in which the children choose their own topics, as the year goes on, we will take several weeks of time during which I will teach them how to write specific things. In these focused writing lessons, I often use what they are reading as springboards to writing. Reading and writing support one another. When children write about what they are reading, they have a wealth of information and ideas to draw from. Writing also increases their comprehension and enjoyment of reading because as they write, they must think about and decide how they feel about various aspects of their reading.

Decoding Spelling

"Finally, we will spend some time each day in activities designed to move them along in their word and spelling knowledge. Like most of the other teachers, I have a word wall on which I put the words I see commonly misspelled in their writing. We add five words each week and practice spelling these when we have a few minutes between activities. As you see, the words I have put up already—*friends*, *because*, *would*, *people*, *to/too/two*, *their/there*, *don't*—are words some adults still have trouble spelling and using correctly. We will also be doing lots of word sorting, which will increase their knowledge of how to spell many words.

"Most of you have already sent the three notebooks your children need. I know three is a lot, but one is for their first-draft writing, one is their literature response log, and the other is their word book in which they sort words and put the words they find that fit certain patterns. All three of these notebooks are critical to our program and we will use them all year. If you have a problem getting the notebooks right now, let me know. I do have a few squirreled away.

"We have to move to the cafeteria now, but I will answer any questions you have if you walk with me to the cafeteria or if you stay a few minutes afterward. I can't really answer questions about your individual children yet because I am just beginning to get to know them and to assess their reading and writing interests and levels. I will have a lot more to tell you about each of your children when we have our conference in October. Remember that I consider this our classroom—mine and your children's and yours—and I hope that you will all schedule some time to come and see how hard we work and how much we love it once we get up and running in a few weeks!"

MONTHLY LOGS

September

Now that this busy summer is over, climaxed by Norma Nouveau's marriage in August, I'm ready to begin my last year of teaching. I've been around a long time—I've seen fads come and go in education, and I have observed the cyclical nature of these fads—the whole-word approach, phonics, altered alphabets, and others. I am, I suppose, reluctant to change, but the program that I have developed for my students is one that I am comfortable with and one that has proven itself to me. I don't need to constantly search and try out new methods. Years ago I read about individualizing instruction through children's literature, and this is the technique I have continued to use, though with modifications.

I always assess the children before I begin instruction as well as doing ongoing assessment. So many teachers have indicated to me that they could not carry through with the literature-based curriculum plans that they had established. With further questioning, I often discover that either they have not assessed the children to see what they know and what they need to know so that they can plan intelligently or they have simply taken the same old material and put the children through it at different rates. Both of these are contrary to the nature and spirit of a literature-based curriculum.

There are as many systems as there are teachers who use literature. The system that I have used for years with my students is one that allows me more control. And, in the beginning of the year, there is more teacher control than there is at the end. When children first come into my room, they have often been through a basal reading program that is highly structured and sequenced. One of the most difficult tasks I face, therefore, is weaning them away from an overdependence upon the teacher for instruction.

These children have had fewer problems adapting to my program than some classes. Norma Flame did an excellent job with them toward the end of the year.

As part of my initial assessment, I like to give the children an interest inventory **Assessment** as well. As a matter of fact, that is one of the papers that they find in the folders on the first day. I walk around the room while they are working on it so that I can identify those children who are unable to read the inventory and therefore need to have someone read it to them. I soon discovered that children like Larry, Pat, Hilda, and Roberta were quite willing to be amanuenses for children such as Butch, Chip, and Paul. They were a great help. Questions such as "You are going to be living all alone on the moon for one year. You can take only a few things with you. What three things will you take?" and "I sometimes feel ____" produce many clues to the needs, perceptions, and values of children. With some of this information in mind, I can help the children to find reading materials that will be both interesting and informative.

I have finished administering the IRIs (Informal Reading Inventory) to all the children. I always wait until we are a couple of weeks into the school year before giving these because some of my children haven't cracked a book all summer and if I test them before they get back into reading, I will get levels that are lower than their actual levels.

I have used a variety of commercially published IRIs over the years. Currently, I am using the *Basic Reading Inventory* (Johns, 1993). One of its advantages is that it has four passages at each level. While for most children, one passage at a level is enough, some children have borderline scores or huge discrepancies between their word identification score and their comprehension score. When this happens, I have the child read a second—and sometimes a third—passage at that level to try to get the most reliable indicator of that child's reading level that I can.

I tested two children each day during their afternoon self-selected reading time. I began with a passage I thought might be on their level based on their records from previous years. I then moved up or down a level until I found the level at which their word identification dropped below 90 to 95 percent or their comprehension dropped below 70 percent. Their instructional level is the highest level at which they can read with at least 90 percent identification accuracy and 70 percent comprehension.

Individual Differences

As happens every year, I have a wide range of reading levels in my classroom, with a few children still reading at first- or second-grade levels and many reading well above third-grade level. Here are the September instructional levels for my children according to the results of the IRI.

Alex	4th
Alexander	3rd
Anthony	4th
Betty	5th
Butch	2nd
Carl	3rd
Chip	2nd
Daisy	First Reader
Danielle	6th
Daphne	5th
Hilda	7th
Horace	5th
Jeff	3rd
Joyce	3rd
Larry	8th +
Mandy	6th
Manuel	3rd
Mitch	3rd
Mort	2nd
Pat	6th
Paul	Primer/First Reader?
Rita	6th
Roberta	6th
Steve	4th

This is about the range I usually get, with a few more children at sixth and seventh grades and of course Larry, who read the highest passage I had—eighth grade—with no problem at all. I was pleased to have only five children reading below grade level and three of them are only one year behind. I have lots of good easy books, so finding things for Chip, Mort, and Butch to read during Readers' Workshop won't be any problem. I will have to include some extra easy books from time to time to accommodate Daisy and Paul. I am not really sure how well Paul reads. I tested him on three different days on all four primer and first-reader passages and his performance was very erratic. His word identification is pretty good for sight words and he did use some letter-sound knowledge and context to figure out some words on one of the passages. On another passage, however, he seemed unable to do anything with words he didn't immediately recognize. His comprehension was also erratic, and I am not sure he was telling me everything he knew in answer to the questions. I am sure he can read primer level and he can read some first-reader material—probably depending on the topic and what kind of day he is having.

I am going to steer both Paul and Daisy to some of my very easy books for their self-selected reading and conference with them for a few minutes at least twice a week. I need to partner them up with someone for some of the Readers' **Partners** Workshop selections. Finding a partner for Paul won't be hard. Daphne has already let me know that she "helps Paul," and Horace is very kind to him also. Daisy, however, is so difficult to get along with that I may have to pay someone to be her partner!

While the IRI scores give me an initial picture of how well my children read, I use running records throughout the year to help me determine if a particular book is at the appropriate difficulty level for a particular child and what reading strategies the child is using. I do these running records during our individual conferences during self-selected reading, and based on these regular observations, I know how each child is growing and what particular reading strategies to emphasize.

I have also gotten my first writing sample to put in each student's growth portfolio. This growth portfolio is part of what I use to determine how the **Portfolios** children are growing and developing in their reading and writing strategies as the year goes on. I include many different samples of their process writing on their self-selected topics—both first drafts and published pieces. I do however think it is very informative to be able to look at each child's effort to write to the same task. To do this, I give them basically the same task to write about at the beginning, middle, and end of the school year. This year, I had them describe what they liked best about Merritt Elementary School. We talked a little about Merritt Elementary. Most of the children have been here since kindergarten and they enjoyed reminiscing about lots of the fun things they had done here. I then asked them to imagine that someone new had moved into their neighborhood and to think about what they would tell that person about Merritt Elementary. Their writing task was to describe Merritt Elementary and tell as much as they could about it—emphasizing the things they liked best about school. I gave them as much time as they wanted to write a first draft. I have copied and dated this first draft and put it in their growth portfolios. Next week, I am going to put them in small groups to share their Merritt Elementary pieces and then ask them to revise the pieces in whatever way they choose to—and can. Finally, I will review the items on the Editor's Checklist they began last year with Miss Nouveau, have them edit their own pieces using this checklist, and have them write a final draft. I will put this final draft in their growth portfolios along with the copy of their first draft and I will have a very good idea of their writing abilities—including first draft, revision, and editing. By looking at what they can do now, I will know what kind of minilessons to teach during process writing, when to begin some more structured guided writing lessons, and what to work on with individual children during writing conferences.

In January, when they have forgotten what they wrote in September, I will once again ask them to describe Merritt Elementary, particularly the things they like best about it, and go through the same first draft, small group sharing/ revision, and editing process. I will do this one more time in May. It is amazing how much growth you can see in their writing when you have them write about something they know a lot about at three different points in the year, using the same procedure to get the samples. One of the most difficult things about teaching children to write better is that, because writing is such a complex process, even when there is a lot of growth in their writing, third graders still have a long way to go. When you look at these three writing samples along with the writing they select for their showcase portfolio, you can see and document how far they have come.

Self-Selected Reading
Self-selected reading is going well. This is always easy to start at Merritt because the children expect to have part of their day devoted to "just reading." We have just gotten started with our Readers' Workshop and Writers' Workshop. Next month, we will do our first big word sort and begin hunting for words. Most of my previous classes have really enjoyed these word activities and I think this group will too.

October

October is always one of my favorite teaching months. I have set up all the routines and done the initial asessment and we can get down to really doing things. I also like the fact that we have four weeks of uninterrupted teaching time. Holidays and vacations are fine but they do interrupt the teaching flow.

Process Writing
Writers' Workshop is going quite well. I begin each day with a short 5- to 6-minute minilesson in which I write something and then do a little editing on it. I have added—one thing at a time—the conventions Miss Nouveau had on their Editor's Checklist last year and will begin next month to add some new ones. Most of the children have published one piece and my most prolific writers—Hilda, Pat, Danielle, and Steve—have already published two.

Publishing
When the children are ready to publish, they sign up with me for an initial conference. I check to see that they have three good first drafts (*good*, of course, is a relative term—good for Joyce would not be good for Daphne, and three pieces that show some effort are good for Daisy or Paul) and I talk with them about which one they plan to publish and how they want to publish it. Some children love to copy their first drafts into spiral-bound books and add illustrations, others like to use the word processing software along with the clip art, still others like to write it out, scroll-like, on long butcher paper. Once they have my okay to publish, they select two friends and read their draft to them. The friends know that they are to comment on what they like and make suggestions that will make the piece better. (Better is defined as clearer, more interesting,

more exciting, more suspenseful!) Often, the friends make suggestions about illustrations or particular clip art that would enhance the writing.

The writer then revises the chosen piece for meaning, using the friends' suggestions if the writer thinks they are good ideas. I require that they write in their first-draft notebooks on every other line so some revision can be done on the blank lines, and I spend more time in these conferences with children at both ends of the ability continuum.

Revising

My Readers' Workshops are organized around three kinds of units—author units, genre units, and topic/theme units. This year I decided to start with an author unit. I like to start with something of high interest to the children and something quite easy to read so that they can learn how to write in their literature logs and how to discuss in their literature response groups. I have always found that almost all the children love Beverly Cleary books. Many of her books are quite easy to read, but even better readers enjoy and empathize with Ramona, Beezus, Henry, and the rest of the gang. I began the unit by putting out all the Beverly Cleary books I could find and talking with the children about them. Many of the children had already read some of her books and they talked about the characters—Ribsy included—like they were old friends. I told them that we were going to spend a few weeks reading and rereading these Beverly Cleary books and they all seemed delighted at the prospect. I showed them that I had enough copies of *Henry Huggins* so that everyone could read this one and that when we finished this, they would get to choose the next Beverly Cleary book they wanted to read.

Guided Reading

Next, I distributed the books and told them to read only the first chapter. I told them that they could read by themselves or with a friend and that when everyone had finished we would make our first entries into our literature response logs. The children grabbed their books and went off to read. Many of the children partnered up and, as I had expected, Daphne grabbed Paul and took him off with her. No one grabbed Daisy, so once they all got settled, I went over and read the chapter with her, taking turns reading the pages and helping her use word identification strategies—pictures, context, spelling patterns, and so forth on her pages. She did quite well and clearly loved the individual attention!

When I saw that some of the children had finished, I told them to take a piece of scrap paper and write down a few of the important things that had happened so they would be ready to help us write our response log entry. When Daisy and I finished, I went over to the overhead and asked the children who were through to join me, indicating to the others that they should join us when they finished. The children and I discussed the first chapter informally as other children joined the group, and when almost everyone was there I showed them how we would write in our response logs.

Literature Journals

Using the overhead, I wrote at the top of the page the book title and then the chapter title and pages we had read. I then began a sentence about the main character by writing:

Teacher Modeling

Henry Huggins is

The children told me lots of things about Henry and then, working together, we constructed a sentence about Henry, which I wrote on the transparency. Next, I wrote this sentence beginning:

Henry wants to

Again, the children shared ideas and came up with a sentence to describe Henry's problem and I wrote this. Finally, I wrote:

I think Henry will

The children had lot of predictions about what would happen next. I listened but didn't write any of these down. When they had shared their predictions, I had them return to their desks, get out their brand-new literature response logs, and write the book and chapter title and pages to head their first page as I had. I then had them copy the *Henry Huggins is* and *Henry wants to* sentences that we had composed. Finally, I asked them to write their own ending to the *I think Henry will* sentence.

We continued these procedures through this whole first book, working together as a class to discuss the chapter read and then jointly composing a sentence or two that summed up some major points from the chapter and finishing by having the children copy our class-composed sentences and make their own predictions for the next day.

By the time the children finished the book, they all understood how our response logs would work and were getting very good at summarizing one or two important events and making a prediction. I did have to collect the books each time they finished reading and make them pledge on their honor not to read ahead! They are so eager to have their predictions be right that they will cheat if you let them!

When we had finished reading *Henry Huggins* together, I showed them six other Beverly Cleary books of which I had six to eight copies of each. I read them a little bit of each book and then had them write down on a slip of paper their first, second, and third choice of which book they wanted to read. Several children complained that they wanted to read them all, but I reminded them that time and books were always limited and that they would have to choose! I did tell them that after we finished reading and discussing these books, they could choose to read the ones they hadn't read during Readers' Workshop, at home or during self-selected reading time.

Looking at their choices, I formed them into five groups with four to six children in each group. I tried to put a mix of children in each group and I assigned Chip, Butch, Mort, Daisy, and Paul to the easiest book they had chosen. Daphne put her three choices down but also wrote on her choice sheet,

I would like to read the same book Paul reads if you have enough. I like to help him.

What an angel she is!

The procedure we used for the second Beverly Cleary book was basically the same as the one we used for *Henry Huggins* except that the children got together in their response groups, discussed the story, and jointly composed two or three sentences summing up what happened. Each child then returned to his or her desk and wrote what he or she liked best about the part read that day and made a "secret" prediction for the next day.

When we finished all the books, we had a Beverly Cleary party! I pretended to be Beverly—the guest of honor—and the children told me what they liked and asked me lots of questions. This unit was a big hit with the children. Many of them (including Daisy!) are currently reading all the Beverly Cleary books their group didn't read. I was just thinking that I would start next year off with this same author unit and then I remembered I won't be starting next year off with any unit! I'll be retired! I have real mixed emotions about that, but there is so much traveling and other projects I want to do that I can't do just in the summers!

November

A new student has arrived—Tanana—and I am afraid that she will have some rather severe adjustment problems. Tanana is an Eskimo child and is so accustomed to wilderness and freedom that she must be finding her new life here rather confining. I have asked two of the girls, Daphne and Betty, to be her special friends until she becomes acclimatized. Those two girls are very outgoing and friendly, and will help Tanana feel at home here.

Whenever a new student moves in, I give him or her a few weeks to adjust to us and then I do the same kind of assessment I did with all the children at the beginning of the year. I could tell right away that my interest inventory was not going to mean much to a child from a culture as different as Tanana's, so rather than have her fill that out I talked with her and wrote down some of the things she liked to do, and I put out a variety of books and had her pick the three books she would most like to read or have read to her. I got a writing sample from her by asking her to describe the school she had gone to in Alaska. I gave her the IRI, and her word identification is much higher than her comprehension. I am sure that this is because comprehension is so prior-knowledge dependent and Tanana just doesn't know a lot of the things all children growing up here would know. She could pass the comprehension criteria on the first reader passages but not on the second-grade passages. I think, however, that her reading level will quickly get to at least third-grade level as she learns more about our culture and language.

> *Assessment*

When Tanana arrived, I decided to focus our Readers' Workshop on the topic Other Times and Places. I had several good books set in earlier years of this country as well as books set in other countries, and with Tanana's arrival, I took advantage of the chance to help children think about how people lived in other times and places. Together, we read Cynthia Rylant's *When I Was Young in the Mountains* and Karen Ackerman's *Song and Dance Man*, and then the children chose from a variety of books that take place in other times and places. I formed groups, trying once again to give everyone their first, second, or third choices and to assign my lowest readers to the easiest book they had chosen. I put

> **Guided Reading**

Daphne, Tanana, and Paul in the same group, and Daphne read the chapters of their books with both of them. I told her she had found her calling and asked her if she was planning to be a teacher when she grew up, and she just smiled happily and nodded!

Literature Journals

I once again modeled for them how to respond in their literature response logs. I used sentence frames that lead them to compare and contrast life then and now and make decisions about what would be better or worse. I also included a sentence frame to get them to make their own personal response to what they were learning:

*The most fascinating thing I learned today was*_____

To connect reading and writing, I tied in some focused writing lessons on descriptive paragraphs with this theme. I used the books we were reading to point out examples of some good descriptive paragraphs. We talked about the words authors used to let us see and feel what the faraway and long-ago places were like. I then wrote a paragraph describing the farthest-away place I have been—the coral reef in Australia! (The children were fascinated with the notion that it had taken 18 hours on the airplane to get there and with the notion that day here was night there and vice versa. I brought in some books and other literature I had picked up in Australia, and these are very popular reading materials during self-selected reading.) I then had the children talk about the farthest place they had been and write descriptive paragraphs that would make that place come alive for those of us who hadn't been there.

Focused Writing

Having written about what they knew firsthand, I had them work in their response groups to collaboratively write descriptive paragraphs about some of the settings for the books their groups were reading. We took a week off from our process writing to do these teacher-guided lessons on descriptive paragraphs. We are now back to process writing and I can already see the insights they gained about descriptive writing being used in the self-selected topic writing of many of my children.

Word Sorting

We have also gotten started into our word sorts, which I use to move them forward in their knowledge of spelling/decoding patterns. I make these word sorts multilevel by including a variety of spelling patterns used in short and long words. For the first sort, I used common spelling patterns for the vowel *u*. I gave the children a sort sheet and I made a transparency from this sort sheet to use with my overhead.

OTHER	u	ue	u-e	ur	sure	ture
	us	sue	use	burn	insure	nature

Forming the tops of the columns were the major spelling patterns represented by *u* along with an example word for each. The first day we used this sort sheet, I had the children fold their sheets so that they couldn't see the last two columns—*sure* and *ture*. (I covered those columns on my transparency also.) I then showed them 15 to 20 words that had the vowel *u*. As I showed them each word, they pronounced it and then wrote it in the column they thought it belonged in. When they had had a chance to write it on their sheets, I let them tell me which column to write it in on my transparency. At the end of that first lesson, our sort sheets looked like this.

OTHER	u us	ue sue	u-e use	ur burn	sure insure	ture nature
menu	run	true	mule	turn		
	must	blue	mute	urban		
	snub	due	cute	turtle		
	runt		amuse			
	strum					
	bus					

On the second day, we used the same sheet again and kept the last two columns covered. We sorted another 15 to 20 words into the first five columns. Some of these words had more than one syllable and I had to remind the children that it was the syllable that had the *u* that we were focusing on. I also had to remind them that it had to have the same spelling pattern and the same pronunciation as the model word that headed each column.

On the third day, I had them open their sheets and I uncovered my transparency so that all columns were visible. This is what the sheets looked like at the end of the third day.

OTHER	u us	ue sue	u-e use	ur burn	sure insure	ture nature
menu	run	true	mule	turn	measure	creature
tuna	must	blue	mute	urban	assure	picture
	snub	due	cute	turtle	treasure	mixture
	runt	statue	amuse	return	pleasure	mature
	strum	value	reuse	hurt	pressure	adventure
	bus	rescue	compute			
	minus	continue				
	numbers					
	sunset					
	summer					
	submarines					

The first three days of our sorting activities are usually devoted to reading sorts—that is, we pronounce the words before asking the children to decide which column they belong in. On the fourth day, I do a blind sort. The children get a new sorting sheet just like the one they used the first three days and I use a new transparency. I use the same words we have used on the first three days, but on the fourth day, I say the word but do not show it (thus the name—blind sort). The students put their finger on the column to show where they think it should be written. I then show them the word, and they write it and I write it. On Friday, we do a blind writing sort. I say the word and they have to try to write it in the correct column before I show it to them. This is the hardest one of all, but having worked with these words on the previous four days, most of the children are able to write the word in the correct column.

At the end of the fifth day, I have the children use two facing pages in their word sort notebooks and set up the columns as they were on their sheets. They then pick one or two of the words we sorted and write these in the correct columns. Their sorting notebooks are now set up for the best part of word sorting—the hunt. The children have one week to find other words that fit the patterns and write them into their own sorting notebooks. They can find words anywhere—around the room, on signs, or in books they are reading for Readers' Workshop, self-selected reading, and even science, social studies, and math. They do this hunting on their own and are all eager to have lots of words—especially big words—to contribute to our final sort.

For the final sort, I put a huge piece of butcher paper all the way across the chalkboard. I set up the columns as they were set up on the original sort sheets—using a different-colored permanent marker for each. We then go around the room, letting the children have a turn coming up and writing one word in its correct column, pronouncing that word, and for obscure words, using it in a sentence. We keep going around until we run out of words or space on our sort mural. Usually, we fill up the easy columns—*u* as in *us*, *ur* as in *turn*—but have space left on the more difficult ones. I hang the mural along the back wall, and children can continue to write in the correct columns the words they find.

We do a sort like this about every three weeks. We spend the first week together working through the five-day cycle (reading sort, blind sort, blind writing sort), the next week hunting, and the last week experiencing the delight of finding a few more words to fit the pattern. The children responded quite enthusiastically to this sort, and I am going to do one more before the Christmas break.

December

We have done plays this month! Children love plays, and there are many good holiday plays as well as others that children enjoy acting out, so that December is the perfect month for plays. We began by choosing some plays already written as plays and later in the month made up some plays based on award-winning books.

The children in my class decided to go on a hunt for books that had been awarded one of the two major awards in children's literature. I was reading *The Whipping Boy* (Fleischman, 1986) to them when I happened to mention that this book was a Newbery winner. "A new berry winner?" asked Carl. "Why? Because of all the fruit he eats?"

I explained then about John Newbery and the award that had been established in his honor for books of high literary quality. While I was on the subject, I also told them of the Caldecott award, which was established in Randolph Caldecott's honor to recognize superior illustrations in children's books. As I was doing so, I was reminded of something I had read that stated perhaps we ought to have a "Caldebery" or a "Newcott" award for the books that *children* like, for the other awards are selected by adults who think they can choose books that children will enjoy most. Very often the best books are chosen, but it is also true that many times children prefer the runners-up, or even books not nominated, more than the winners of the Newbery and Caldecott awards. Lots of states have developed "children's choice" awards, and I have served on the International Reading Association's "Children's Choices" committee for two years.

The children decided that they would very much like to see how many award-winning books our school possessed. I told them that I would provide them with a list of all of the winners and runners-up since the time that the awards began. With this list in hand, the children decided that it would be easier if they divided into groups that could check the books in the different classrooms and the library.

Literature
Response
Activity

I arranged with the other teachers to have my children—in groups of two or three—come to their room and see how many of the books we had and then borrow them for a week or two.

A young woman walked into the midst of all this confusion as the children were organizing the books that they had gathered. There were books on the floor, on tables, desks, window sills, and in boxes—what a mess! Mr. Topps told me that she had introduced herself to him and that she had asked to meet me. It seems that Miss Yung is to be my student teacher next quarter. At least she will be if the mess didn't scare her off! I had forgotten she was coming! I gave her some packets of materials that I had prepared for substitutes and explained my goals, policies, and program. I also told her that I hoped she had a strong background in children's literature and suggested some children's books she might read during the Christmas vacation. She went over to a group of children and started helping.

After we had finished with that project, some of the children were talking about several of the books that they had discovered. The ones that especially intrigued them were the Caldecott winners. Mandy said, "You know, I always thought that those were just books for little kids. But some of them are so interesting!"

Daphne asked, "Couldn't we make plays out of those and give them to the other classes for a Christmas present?'' Cries of ''Yeah! Yeah!'' rang through the room. Mort was the only dissenter.

''Why not a Hanukkah present?'' he inquired.

''Well, let's make it a Happy Holidays present,'' I mediated. This was accepted and we set to work. Each group devised a play for one of the kindergarten, first-, or second-grade classes. They became as excited about this as they were about the approaching holiday season, so that December became a little harried!

Another helpful holiday deed was sending volunteers from my class to Helen Launch's kindergarten room to write down the children's dictated letters to Santa. I don't know if it's just the thought of Santa's coming or if there really is a change occurring, but both Butch and Mitch have been extremely helpful and kind this month. I *fervently* hope that it will last!

January

Well, my expectations about this term's student teacher seem to be supported by her deeds. Vera Yung is a most eager young woman, staying late in the afternoon to complete a bulletin board or game that she is making for the children. The children have, for the most part, become quite attached to her. Her special friend seems to be Joyce. Joyce and Vera Yung talk at great length on the playground, and I have noticed that Joyce is beginning to get really involved with her work. She doesn't need to be reminded to do it and even seeks extra things to do now. Part of the reason might be that Vera Yung had discovered Joyce's interest in witchcraft and the supernatural, and that she has been bringing some of Zilpha Keatley Snyder's books for Joyce to read. She especially enjoyed *The Egypt Game* (1967) and *The Changeling* (1970). Right now she is reading *Below the Root* (1975), a book that I found fascinating. Joyce is really growing up!

We have had an unusually busy month. Readers' Workshop focused on folklore. I chose this genre to study partly because I have always loved fairy tales, folktales, and legends and partly because there are so many wonderful things for the children to read that cut across all the reading levels. I have versions of some of the fairy tales as well as *Pecos Bill* and *Babe the Blue Ox* tales that are easy enough for everyone but Paul to read independently, so I could have Chip, Daisy, Butch, and the other low readers read by themselves rather than with a partner. I am always concerned that children develop independent silent reading ability during this third-grade year, and this folktale unit provided the children with lots of easy choices.

I steered my super readers—Larry, Pat, Danielle, and others—in the direction of myths. I read *Hades and Persephone* to the whole class and talked with them about Greece and Greek mythology. The children were amazed to discover that at the time these myths were first told, most people believed that they were true. After I finished reading this, I showed them some of the other myth stories of which I had multiple copies and, as I had expected, my most sophisticated readers gravitated to the myths when making choices of what to read for their literature response groups.

I included many folktales from other countries in this unit. Unfortunately, I don't have many multiple copies of the folktales from other countries, so I did most of these by reading them to the whole class. For some, I read the entire book, but for many others, I just read the first chapter or story in a collection and then made these books available during self-selected reading. The ones the children liked best were *Sedna, an Eskimo Legend*, which I hunted up in honor of Tanana; *Why the Sun and the Moon Live in the Sky*, an African tale; and *Bawshou Rescues the Sun*, a Chinese tale.

Multicultural Awareness

Since many of the folktales and myths have clear problem-solution structures, I decided that this was a good time to teach the children to create story maps. There are many different ways of creating story maps, but all help children to follow the story by drawing their attention to the elements that all good stories share. Stories have characters and they happen in a particular place and time that we call the setting. In most stories, the characters have some goal they want to achieve or some problem they need to resolve. The events in the story lead to some kind of solution or resolution. Sometimes, stories have implicit morals or themes that we hope children will learn from.

Story Maps

There are many different kinds of story maps. I like this one I adapted from Isabel Beck (Macon, Bewell, & Vogt, 1991).

Main Characters

Setting (Time and Place)

Problem or Goal

Event 1

Event 2

Event 3

Event 4

Event 5

Event 6

Solution

Story Theme or Moral

For our first story map experience, I chose *The Three Little Pigs*. The children and I retold and acted out this favorite story, and then we worked together to fill out this story map. Here is that story map filled in for *The Three Little Pigs*.

Main Characters *Mother Pig, three little pigs, big bad wolf*

Setting (Time and Place) *Woods, make-believe time and place*

Problem/Goal *Pigs wanted to be independent and have their own houses.*

    Event 1 *Mother Pig sends three little pigs out to build their own houses.*

    Event 2 *First little pig gets some straw and builds a straw house. Big bad wolf blows the straw house down.*

    Event 3 *Second little pig gets some sticks and builds a stick house. Big bad wolf blows the stick house down.*

    Event 4 *Third little pig gets some bricks and builds a brick house. Big bad wolf cannot blow the brick house down.*

    Event 5 *Big bad wolf gets scalded coming down the chimney of the brick house.*

Solution *Pigs live happily ever after in strong brick house.*

Story Theme or Moral *Hard work pays off in the end!*

We completed three more story maps together after watching the videos of *Snow White and the Seven Dwarfs, Beauty and the Beast,* and *Aladdin.* We also read several book versions of the tales on which these movies were based and discussed how they were different and the same. The children could not believe that there were no dwarfs named Sleepy and Doc in the original *Snow White.*

Once we had done these four story maps together, the groups had no trouble completing story maps for the tales and myths they were reading. For the most part, they completed these collaboratively and then each child wrote his or her own story map in the literature response journal.

Because the children had so enjoyed doing the plays in December and since folktales and myths just "beg" to be performed, I ended the unit by letting each group act out one of the pieces they had read. I showed them some wonderful books I bought last summer (*Overhead Transparencies for Creative Dramatics* by Creative Teaching Press), which had on transparency important scenery from some of the myths and tales they had been reading. When projected from the back of the room, these colored transparencies transformed our room into the dark woods through which Red Riding Hood walked or a square in ancient Greece. In addition to this instant transparency scenery, the books of transparencies contain simple headband patterns that make acting out a story a snap. Since I had planned this creative reenactment response culmination to the unit, I made sure that at least two of the stories that each group had read were ones for which I had scenery and headbands. I didn't require the groups to restrict their choice of which one to act out to only those, but they all chose a piece that had these accoutrements.

Literature Response Activity

The reenactments were a big success, and we had a special evening performance for parents before one of our schoolwide PTA meetings. We also sent performing troupes to the younger grades. Miss Yung was a tremendous help to me this month and she had a great time. I hope I didn't overwhelm her, however. As I was pulling out books and videos and the transparency books, she kept saying, "Where do you get all this stuff? I have never seen anyone with so many different things and ideas. How will I ever have what I need next year?"

In her notebook she has pages and pages full of things she needs and wants. I, on the other hand, am wondering what I am going to do with it all—28 years of accumulated stuff is a lot of stuff! I think I will box some of it up and send it off with Vera when she leaves at the end of March. I hate to part with it, but it won't be of any use to anyone in my attic—and, come to think of it, my attic is already full!

February

Another exciting month! This month I used the broad umbrella of animals as the organizing theme for our Readers' Workshop. We read both fiction and nonfiction books, including such favorites as *Charlotte's Web* and some of the *Winnie-the-Pooh* stories. We discussed how you could tell if a book was a story or informational, and I tried to get all the children to read some of each type. We made webs for the different animals different groups were reading about and included the factual information we found in informational books. We also decided that even in a clearly fictitious animal story, there were some things that were true. Spiders do spin webs and bears do like honey. When reading animal stories, the children sometimes argued about which characteristics were true of the animals, and I helped them look up the animal in question in various reference books to resolve the disputes. We discovered some wonderful authors

Guided Reading

of animal informational books. The children were entranced with Dorothy Hinshaw Patent's books—especially *Buffalo* and *Gray Wolf, Red Wolf.* They also enjoyed the books of Carol Carrick, who writes fiction with realistic depictions of animals as well as informational books, including Mitch's favorite, *Sand Tiger Shark.*

Focused Writing

Once we got lots of animal webs made, I used these to teach some guided writing lessons on writing reports. The children and I had read several books on whales and jointly constructed the web. I then showed them how we could take this information and write a report on whales. I modeled for them how to write an introductory paragraph about whales, then to use the information from the different spokes of the web to write descriptive paragraphs, and finally how to write a concluding paragraph. The children and I jointly constructed each paragraph—they gave me suggestions and then I put the sentences together in a cohesive way. It took us several days to turn our whale web into this report. Steve—who is our resident nature expert and quite an artist—drew the whale illustrations.

Once we had done our whale reports together, the groups picked one of the animals they had been reading about and webbing and wrote reports based on their webs. They are getting quite good at writing collaboratively, probably because we do a lot of it as a class. They pick someone "who writes real nice" to do the actual writing, but they all add their ideas. I have them use the Editor's Checklist to proofread their reports, and they are getting much better at finding and fixing those things we have been working on all year.

Realizing that "time is marching on," I decided that I needed to move them toward more independence in their writing. After the groups collaboratively wrote their reports on an animal, we constructed as a class several webs about animals commonly kept as pets—dogs, cats, gerbils. (They told me all about George in first grade and wanted to go get him and bring him for a visit. Steve informed them that George had been dead for over a year and many were devastated when they realized that their first-grade pet was no longer with us. Steve volunteered to ask Mrs. Wright if we could borrow Samantha—but they didn't want "just any old gerbil.")

Publishing

I then had each child choose one of these pets and write a report using the web and the format we had used as a whole class and in their response groups. After writing their report, they shared in small groups, got suggestions for revision, then picked a friend to help them edit, and finally brought their paragraph to me or Miss Yung—joint editors-in-chief. They are now typing their individual reports on the computers and we are compiling a class book on animals. Many of them have chosen their animal reports as one of the pieces to go in their showcase portfolios, and I have noticed lots more animal reports being written now that we are back to self-selected topic process writing for a few weeks.

Miss Yung has been invaluable to me this month. We have done a lot of team teaching and our styles mesh wonderfully. She is, however, much more organized than I am and has come up with a very clever way of keeping anecdotal records on the children. I have a folder for each child with divisions for the major areas in which I write comments on a regular basis. I always note in this folder what the children bring to read to me from their self-selected reading as well as some observations on what strategies they are using well and which strategies I need to help them develop. I also make some notes immediately after each writing conference. In addition, I sit down each afternoon for a few minutes and sift through my folders, remembering what I observed the children doing as they read and wrote throughout the day, and make some notes based on these remembrances.

Miss Yung, observing me do this each afternoon, would always ask how I could remember all this. I told her that it is hard to remember when you are just starting teaching because you have so many things to think about at one time but that with experience, she would find that she too could sift through the folders at the end of the day and remember specific observations she had made about different children as the day progressed. Not willing to wait for experience, Miss Yung has come up with a simple system. She walks around all day with a clipboard on which she has attached one sheet of file folder labels. As she observes children, she puts the child's initials and the date on one of the labels and then writes down what she wants to note in the folder. At the end of the day, she peels all the labels off the sheet and puts them on the right child's folder. She also notices which children she hasn't made any observations about in several days and puts their initials on a label on the sheet she will use the next day. (Some quiet children like Rita and Manuel just don't get noticed unless you decide to notice them!)

Between writing observations down immediately after each reading and writing conference and the labels that are always there to record observations at any time of the day, you don't have to try to remember what you saw the different children doing. In fact, I realize as I watch her with her clipboard and labels that I am probably not as good at remembering as I think I am. She will be doing almost all the teaching next month, but when I get back into it in April and May, I think I will get myself a clipboard and sheet of labels! I told both Vera and Dr. Link, her supervisor, that I intended to do this, and Vera expressed delight and amazement that she had been able to teach me something! Dr. Link said that the best teachers were also lifelong learners, and they both tried to talk me out of retirement! "It's too late," I said, "I've got travel plans made and it's time to make way for the Vera Yungs of the world!"

March

Vera Yung has become invaluable to me and the students, and I told Dr. Link that I was not going to let her go! She laughed at me, of course, and said that if I felt that strongly, perhaps I would be willing to recommend her for my position, which would become vacant with my retirement this June. I assured her that I would certainly do that, for Vera has been the *best* student teacher I have ever had. She is so creative, willing, and sympathetic to the students! And yet she doesn't let that sympathy interfere with providing them the best possible instruction: She feels quite sad about Chip's home situation, but it is one that we can do nothing about, since his family is too proud to accept welfare. But, we can't let that interfere with doing what we can for him: providing him with the best possible education.

Vera has become a real expert at managing her time. With both of us working, team-teaching style, we can accomplish even more, so I was reluctant to give her the experience that she needed in handling the entire day by herself. But I did allow her two weeks, of course, so that she had a small taste of what it would be like to be totally responsible for a class.

Publishing   During those two weeks—her last two weeks with us—she had the children making "shape books." Chip made a "hand book" in the shape of a large hand. The illustrations were photos made with an inexpensive Polaroid camera as well as others cut out from magazines. All were pictures of hands doing various things. The illustrations were labeled with descriptions of the hands' actions. One picture had a man's hands playing a piano, and the sentence said, "Hands can make music." Another showed a lady cuddling a baby, and was titled "Hands can love you, too." Horace made a "foot book" using the same technique. Several other children found shape books to be an entertaining exercise.

Another project of hers was the long-awaited poetry unit. I knew that these children had had quite a lot of exposure to poetry. They had had much poetry read to them, and they had, in turn, created many poems of their own. I knew that they were ripe for the kinds of activities that Vera had in mind for them.

She began the poetry unit by reading to the children from Mary O'Neill's beautiful *Hailstones and Halibut Bones* (1961), a collection of poems about colors. After reading a couple of her favorites and one of mine ("What is Purple?"), she discussed with them the fact that Mary O'Neill is saying that colors are not only things but also feelings, moods, smells, and sounds. Then she took a stack of colored construction paper from her table and asked the children to form groups of five or six and told them that each group would receive one color sheet. They were then to list all the things that the color could be, feel like, smell like, sound like, or make them feel like within the five minutes that the timer would be set for. They began to discuss furiously and to list all of these qualities while she sat calmly reading more of the book (presenting all the while a good model for the children). When the timer rang, there were groans of "Oh no! Not yet! Let us put down some more." She asked each group to choose someone who could read the completed list to the rest of the class. One that I thought was particularly good was this one by Rita, Jeff, Manuel, Mort, Pat, and Steve. Their color was white:

lacy snowflakes	glaring light	refrigerator door
frosty window pane	anger	fear
unfriendly	coldness	sweet apple inside
crunchy ice cube	fluffy whipped cream	winter morning breath
hot mashed potatoes	a story before it's written	clouds above

She told the children that poetry creates images and that those images do not need to be done with rhymes. She said that she was sure that the children could create a poem from what they had listed. She said, "Let me see if *I* can try to make one." And this is it:

Lacy snowflakes
Against my window pane
Fluffy whipped cream
Coldness from clouds above.

The children were enthralled, as was I, with this creation. Immediately, each group set to work to create a poem. Vera had explained to me that she wanted the children to have many experiences in writing group poems before they attempted to write individual ones. She told me that she had come to love poetry only within the last few years, that she had dreaded and hated it before. She was sure that that was because of the way in which her teachers had dealt with it—not as something to be loved, treasured, and enjoyed, but rather as something to be analyzed, dissected, and criticized. She had vowed that she would do her best to help her students learn to enjoy poetry at an early age. A format that she used with them involved the "diamante" form that Iris Tiedt (1970) had developed. It is as follows:

noun
adjective, adjective
participle, participle, participle
noun,   noun,   noun,   noun
participle, participle, participle
adjective, adjective
noun

The first and last words are to be opposites, and images build on the first noun through the two nouns in the middle. The transition is made here to building images for the last noun. The poem below is one written by the class.

Father
Strong, kind
Working, resting, loving
Bed, baby, boy, Mommie
Working, working, working,
Tired, busy
Mother.

She also had the children complete the following phrases, and with the unifying factor of "The year" repeated at the end of the poem, she found that even the less capable children could produce a poem they were pleased with.

The year . . .
The fall . . .
The winter . . .
The spring . . .
The summer . . .
The year . . .

I knew that the poetry unit had been successful when I noticed that the previously untouched poetry books in the class library became the most demanded ones and when poetry began to appear in their writing notebooks. The children recited poetry to one another at the playground! If only they keep this enthusiasm!

April

My, how the time is passing now. With April over, only one more full month of school remains. I always begin to panic at this time of the year, wondering if I will accomplish all that needs to be done. Oh well, done or not, the year *will* end! I've started to go through my file cabinets so that I won't be here all summer, trying to move out of this room. One accumulates a lot in 28 years.

While cleaning, I came upon the file folder for literature-based curriculum compiled the year that I first began to become discontented with what I had been doing and was searching for something more satisfying for myself and the children. I had read a lot of articles in my professional journals, attended workshops, and taken courses at the university. I tried, then, to put all of the information together in a way that I could deal with it. I thought that I was ready after we returned from our Easter break (in March of that year). There was still enough time to work out some of the problems and to give it a fair try, realizing that if it didn't work, I wouldn't have wasted an entire year of the children's time.

For the rest of that year, I used trade books for most of my reading instruction and began doing Readers' Workshops. The children responded well but I had very few books of which I had multiple copies and no whole-class sets of books. I used what I had here plus what I could check out from the school, public, and university libraries and we got through the year, but I couldn't offer children very much choice, and just gathering up the books took a huge chunk of my time.

The second year, I used basals and trade books, alternating which we would read in. I had purchased some multiple copies of trade books and the school purchased some more that could be checked out from the library. Gradually, I got to the point where I am today. My reading program is totally literature based and I give the children complete freedom in what they read for self-selected reading and a lot of choice in what they select to read and discuss in their literature response groups. I have some selections that we all read and a lot of pieces that I read to the whole class. I make sure to include lots of variety in topics, authors, and genres so that my children all get a fairly balanced reading diet.

Our topic this month was sports! In talking with the children and looking at their interest inventories, I realized that sports is one topic almost all my children are interested in. Many of them play sports—baseball, soccer, tennis—and with the university so close, lots of my children go to basketball and football games. There is also a lot of excitement and interest this year in the upcoming Olympics. I included stories in which children play sports, including *Thank You, Jackie*

Robinson by Barbara Cohen, *Never Say Quit* by Bill Wallace, and *Scoop Snoops* by Constance Hiser. I also included biographies of sports heroes. They read about some of the old pros but seemed to enjoy most the *Sports Shots Books,* which chronicle the lives and careers of modern heroes, Michael Jordan, Wayne Gretzky, and Joe Montana. Of course, we used reference books such as *Amazing but True Sports Stories* and *Inside Pro Football.* Both this year's and the back issues of *Sports Illustrated for Kids* were great references.

I also used the sports theme for several guided writing lessons. The students remembered writing their animal reports and compiling them into a class book. This month, they all became sports reporters. We watched together a video of a championship basketball game and then worked collaboratively to write up the game for *Sports Illustrated for Kids.* I told the class that reporters were always given a limited amount of space and so we had to limit our article but make it exciting at the same time. When we had finished our class-composed article, the children chose another sport for which I had a game or match on video—baseball, football, tennis, soccer, swimming, or gymnastics—and worked in groups to write an article describing that. **Focused Writing**

We completed two fairly sophisticated word sorts this month. For the first one, we worked with some common endings and suffixes and emphasized the spelling changes that occur when these endings are added. I gave the students their sort sheets and on the first day, I had them fold their papers so that we were sorting only words that had no ending or words that ended in *en, er,* or *est.* We had previously sorted words with endings that needed no spelling changes. All the words I gave them for this sort required that they make some change in the root word before adding the ending. On the next two days, I included more *en, er,* and *est* words and others that ended in *ment, less,* or *ness.* Following our usual procedures, I gave them a clean sort sheet on Thursday and did a blind reading sort, followed by the hardest task of all on Friday—a blind writing sort in which they had to decide where to write the word and write it before I showed them the word. The following week they hunted words that fit these patterns and wrote them in their word sort notebooks. These words are harder to find than the ones sorted by vowel patterns that we did earlier in the year and they had a hard time filling up the butcher paper columns during our culminating sort. Roberta and Horace teamed up together and figured out that if you started with words ending in *y,* you could get a lot of words to add. Their list included many *nasty, nastier, nastiest, nastiness/silly, sillier, silliest, silliness* combinations. Hilda complained that this wasn't fair because they surely had not found all those words in their reading. Roberta picked up the dictionary and claimed that she had been reading it! **Word Sorting**

No Ending	en(e)	er(y-i)	est(y-i)	ment	less	ness(y-i)
sun	*sweeten*	*sunnier*	*meanest*	*agreement*	*winless*	*greediness*

The other sort we did was also a challenge. We sorted for words that ended in *el, le,* and *al* along with words that ended in *able* and *ible.* The children were frustrated by the fact that you couldn't tell by hearing these words which way the end would be spelled. I pointed out that with some words, you can't be sure which way it will be spelled, you just have to write it and see if it looks right and sometimes use the dictionary to check.

Other	el	le	al		able	able	ible
	label	*turtle*	*general*		*table*	*notable*	*edible*

Portfolios

The children have begun compiling their showcase portfolios. We are having our first show for parents in mid-May and the children all want to put their best foot forward. I have limited them to five pieces each—and they must include at least one piece in which they have written in response to something they read. For each piece they select, they are writing a brief description on an index card indicating why they chose this piece and what they were trying to do with it. Some of my most prolific writers are having a terrible time deciding which five to include, while Daisy, Mort, and Chip are complaining, "You mean we have to find five things we are proud of and want everyone to read? That's too many!" I am taking them on a field trip to the university next month and one of the things we will go to is an artist's showing. I hope that will help them understand what our showing is all about.

May

I always have approach-avoidance conflicts at the end of the school year but this month has been especially emotional. It is strange, but I can picture in my mind and name almost all the children in the first class I taught 28 years ago (yegads, I am getting old—most of them are almost 40!) and I am sure I will always remember this class. These last few weeks, as they have been assembling their showcase portfolios and I have been selecting samples from their growth portfolios to put in their cumulative portfolios, I kept thinking that they were the best class I had ever had—I wouldn't have believed it at the beginning of the year, but I think I will even have fond memories of Mort and Daisy!

Assessment

It was apparent from looking at their beginning-of-the-year, midyear, and end-of-the-year writing samples in which they described Merritt Elementary and told about what they liked best that they have all shown tremendous growth in both their first-draft writing ability and their ability to revise and edit a piece of writing. The growth was most striking for the students who came in furthest behind. Paul can write coherent pieces now. While these pieces are short and not terribly interesting, they do say something and hold together and he is able to improve them a little when he edits and revises. Daisy, Butch, Chip, Joyce, and Jeff have all shown marked increases in their writing ability. Tanana is writing more and is willing to write, but her language is still quite immature and often her sentences don't sound quite right.

I did not give end-of-the-year IRIs to all the children because I could tell from my observations of them during Readers' Workshop and from my running records taken during self-selected reading conferences that they were growing in both their ability to read and respond and in the breadth of their reading interests. I did give IRIs to my lowest children, however, because I wanted to see how far they had come.

Paul, who entered reading at either primer or first-reader level, can read most material at second-grade level if he is having an "alert" day. Daisy and Butch have each gained about a year's growth—they were a year behind, reading at second-grade level, while they now read at third-grade level. Of course, that still puts them one year behind when they go to fourth grade next year, but they did make a full year's growth. Chip and Mort, who read at second-grade level at the beginning of the year, tested fourth-grade level. I am so proud of them—Chip didn't surprise me, because he is a real worker and he really got into books this year. Mort did surprise me. His daily work and attitude didn't show much improvement. If he applied himself, he could probably be a very good student! Tanana's instructional level tested third grade and again her word identification was much better than her comprehension. She has shown amazing growth, however, and I know that with Ms. Maverick's integrated knowledge-building curriculum in fourth grade, she will continue to grow in her knowledge of the world and consequently her comprehension will improve.

I am delighted with the growth shown by my very best students. Larry, Hilda, Danielle, Pat, Mandy, and Roberta have become quite sophisticated readers and writers. They have all broadened greatly what they like to read about and the different types of writing they can do. They are confident in their abilities and—except for Roberta, who is still too bossy—they are very helpful to the other children in literature response groups and in revising/editing conferences. Ever since I started to organize the classroom around literature and writing and include many multilevel activities, I have noticed remarkable growth for the children on the two ends of the continuum. I am not sure that the way I teach makes much of a difference for the Mitches and Carls in the world, but I know that it makes a difference for the children who come to me reading and writing substantially below or above where you would expect third graders to be.

We finished up the year with "Your Choice" Readers' Workshops. I put out all the multiple copies of books that we hadn't used yet and let children choose from them all and then formed literature response groups based on their choices. They decided what they would write in the literature response logs and completed these individually before going to their discussion groups. Because I modeled for them so many different ways of responding, the children had no trouble thinking of what they wanted to say. As I circulated among the groups, I saw children with their logs open and heard them reading some statements such as:

Literature Journals

I think the funniest part was when the dog got into the game.

I didn't think she should have told her mother what had happened when her friends had sworn her to secrecy.

I know what is probably going to happen next. They are going to lose the game and the coach will quit.

Hearing my readers make statements like this on their own convinces me that they have learned how you think about and respond to what you are reading. Since they are so in the habit of thinking this way, I bet they will continue to do this even if no one makes them write their responses down. Literature response logs are not so much for me to know what they are thinking as they are to help them clarify for themselves what they are thinking.

THE THIRD-GRADE MEETING

Mrs. Wise smiled as Sue Port departed. There were many teachers who felt considerable fear of that small but dynamic Ms. Port whenever she entered their classrooms. Not Mrs. Wise! She remembered when Ms. Port had been *her* student teacher some 14 or 15 years ago. It was on Mrs. Wise's recommendation that the school system had hired Sue and had later promoted her to the position of curriculum supervisor. Now Mrs. Wise was smiling, for she had just been asked if she would present the program for the final meeting of the third-grade teachers. "My valedictory," she thought, "Oh, well. I suppose they had to ask me now, since I won't be here next year. I was hoping, though, that I could get away without even attending, let alone being the program!" After 28 years of these meetings, she was *ready* to retire; she had often said that the meetings were things she would never miss about school!

But now to plan what to do! She began by going through some of the materials that she had selected for this final meeting, dragging out samples of books that she had used during this past year. She had asked to have the meeting in her own room so that she would not have to transport all of her paraphernalia across town to the room in the administration building where these meetings were usually held. Here she would show the other teachers the learning centers that occupy the children's time, as well as the card catalogue system that the children had devised. She sat down to plan the meeting for the following week.

One week later, Mrs. Wise was completely organized and ready for the meeting. She greeted the teachers who entered her room and then began the meeting by expressing her pleasure at seeing all her old friends and acknowledging her sincere delight at the interest they had shown in her program. She told them that she was eager to share with them the kind of program that she had been using for many years. Some of those present had visited her classroom in the past and she invited them to make any comments that they felt were pertinent.

"Knowing me, you can expect to see a lot of books this afternoon." As she said this, she reached down and opened two large boxes, which were indeed full of books! As she talked about her AllLit classroom, she pulled out books to illustrate what she had read to the children, which books the whole class had read, and the kind of books she had let them choose from to read and discuss in their literature response groups. She showed them Jeff's literature response log (Jeff had been in the hospital the last week of school so Mrs. Wise was using a lot of his things to demonstrate what the children did and then was going to drop everything off at his house after the meeting) and showed how she structured their responses early in the year but how they were able to independently write their own personal responses by the end of the year.

She also had Jeff's writing notebook, his word sort notebook, and the five pieces he had selected for his showcase portfolio. She showed them these also as she explained about how she did both process writing and guided writing lessons to move all the students forward in their writing ability.

On transparency, she had some of the webs the groups had made from which they wrote their animal reports, along with the transparencies she used for the word sorts they did. She also had brought along the class book they made on animals and the butcher paper sheet on which they had accumulated their words from their last word sort.

As Mrs. Wise was showing them all these things and describing what they did, she could see some agitated faces. She stopped talking once she had shown them all the main things and said, "Now, this is what I wanted to show you. What else would you like to know?"

A lot of hands went up and Mrs. Wise called on a young teacher she had not seen before. This teacher said, "Mrs. Wise, I am awed by what you have shown us but I wouldn't have any idea how to do this. Where do you get all the books, and how do you decide what they should read and write, and how do you know who is doing what?"

Mrs. Wise could see that a lot of the more experienced teachers were thinking this too and they all looked relieved that it was one of the beginning teachers who had asked the question—she wasn't supposed to know everything!

Mrs. Wise smiled and told them about how she had begun gradually and only after several years of transition had accumulated the knowledge, organization, and books to allow her to do an AllLit classroom. She talked about buying books with her own money in the old days but bragged about Mr. Topps and Merritt Elementary's decision to put more of their funds into classroom libraries and to let the teachers decide what they needed.

She also talked about her assessment system and showed them the IRI and interest inventory she gave at the beginning of each year along with the repeated Merritt Elementary School writing prompt. She showed them the folder she kept on each child in which she kept her running records and observations after each reading and writing conference. She showed them her clipboard with file folder labels and told them how she used these to record her observations and then moved them to the appropriate folders. She could tell that everyone was impressed by this simple solution to the difficult-to-manage anecdotal record system, and then she told them that it was Vera Yung, her student teacher, who had thought of this. (At the mention of Vera, the young teacher whose question had instigated this explanation looked first amazed and then delighted. After the meeting, she explained to Mrs. Wise that Vera was her sorority sister, that she had no idea she had been Mrs. Wise's student teacher, and that she was going to call her this summer and "pick her brain.")

Mrs. Wise went on to tell them about the three kinds of portfolios she used—growth portfolios that contained samples she had chosen and in which she kept her anecdotal records, showcase portfolios that the children put together

Assessment

to demonstrate their literacy prowess, and cumulative portfolios that contained the samples each teacher selected to move with the child from year to year.

The teachers had other questions, mainly about what she did "with the low kids" and "how she challenged the high ones." This gave Mrs. Wise a chance to explain why she believed her approach to literacy was most beneficial to the low and high achievers. "For an average child like Jeff," she mentioned, pointing to his samples that had been passed around for the teachers to look at, "I'm not sure my AllLit classroom really matters, but I can tell you that for students like Daisy and Chip on one end and Larry and Hilda on the other, the multilevel instruction, the cooperative learning, and the amount of choice I give them makes a world of difference."

A hand went up and Agatha Nostic said, "Now, Beatrice, are you telling us this Jeff was just one of your average children?"

"As average as they come," responded Mrs. Wise. "He tested third-grade level on the beginning-of-the-year IRI and I have his initial writing sample here, which is actually a little below average in many ways for the beginning of third grade. If I were going to pick one of my kids to have his appendix out so that I could show off his things here at this meeting, it surely wouldn't have been Jeff!"

Mrs. Wise glanced up at the clock and then summed up what she did and how it fit her philosophy of teaching. "I have probably been teaching third grade longer than anyone in this room—even you, Agatha—and I have tried about every fad that came along and jumped on a lot of the bandwagons and taught a lot of 'new and improved' basal reading series. After all these years, I am sure of just a few things. Children are all different and they have different interests, attitudes, home experiences, and reading and writing abilities. Some children need more structure and instruction. Some children really thrive in situations where they can work with partners and small groups. All children profit from being immersed in a wide variety of wonderful books and being given a lot of time and support to write. The program I have developed has structure and instruction. We do things to build word knowledge—primarily our word wall and word sorting. I teach them reading and writing strategies through the mini-lessons I do at the beginning of Readers' and Writers' Workshops. In addition to teaching, however, I give them time to do the activities I want them to value and I let them make lots of choices of what they will read and write."

Mrs. Wise paused to notice the nods of agreement around the room. She had had the feeling when she began that some of these teachers were not very sympathetic to what she was doing, but now there was a noticeable change. Several of the teachers wanted to know how to begin her program.

She began to gather up her materials, preparatory to leaving the meeting, when Sue Port, with a grin on her face, told her to sit down, for the best part of the meeting was yet to come. And through the door, borne by two of her oldest friends, came a cake of mammoth proportions. The inscription read "Good-bye, Mrs. Wise. We will miss you." She was stunned and unable to speak for a moment, but one of her friends thought she heard her mutter under her breath, "I'd rather have a martini!"

Individual Differences

Balanced Literacy Programs

ADD TO YOUR JOURNAL

What do you think of Mrs. Wise's AllLit classroom? Would you like to be a student in her room? Can you see yourself teaching the way Mrs. Wise teaches? What about her approach to diagnosis and assessment? Do you think she knows her students better than she would if she based her assessment on tests? Mrs. Wise does have all those years of experience and all those wonderful books. What parts of her program could you use if you were just starting out teaching and you didn't have all the books?

REFERENCES

Johns, J. L. (1993). *Basic reading inventory*, 5th ed. Dubuque, IA: Kendall/Hunt.

Macon, J. M., Bewell, D., & Vogt, M. (1991). *Responses to literature*. Newark, DE: International Reading Association.

Tiedt, I. (1970). Exploring poetry patterns. *Elementary English, 47,* 1083–1084.

Children's Books/Materials Cited

Amazing but True Sports Stories, by Phyllis Hollander & Zander Hollander, Scholastic, 1986.

Below the Root, by Z. K. Snyder, Atheneum, 1975.

Buffalo: The American Bison Today, by Dorothy Hinshaw Patent, Ticknor & Fields, 1986.

The Changeling, by Z. K. Snyder, Atheneum, 1970.

Charlotte's Web, by E. B. White, HarperCollins, 1974.

A Convention of Delegates, by D. J. Hautly, Atheneum, 1987.

Cricket magazine.

The Egypt Game, by Z. K. Snyder, Atheneum, 1967.

Gray Wolf, Red Wolf, by Dorothy Hinshaw Patent, Houghton Mifflin, 1990.

Hailstones and Halibut Bones, by M. O'Neill, Doubleday, 1961.

Henry Huggins and other books, by Beverly Cleary, Avon, various years.

Inside Pro Football, Scholastic, 1992.

Kid City magazine.

Never Say Quit, by Bill Wallace, Scholastic, 1992.

Overhead Transparencies for Creative Dramatics, by Creative Teaching Press, 1987.

Pecos Bill.

Penny Power magazine.

Ranger Rick magazine.

Sand Tiger Shark, by Carol Carrick, Houghton Mifflin, 1991.

Scoop Snoops, by Constance Hiser, Scholastic, 1986.

Sedna, an Eskimo Legend.

Snow White.

Song and Dance Man, by Karen Ackerman, Knopf, 1992.

Sports Illustrated for Kids magazine.

Sports Shots Books, Scholastic, 1990.

Thank You, Jackie Robinson, by Barbara Cohen, Scholastic, 1989.

The Three Little Pigs.

3-2-1 Contact magazine.

The Whipping Boy, by S. Fleischman, Greenwillow, 1986.

When I Was Young in the Mountains, by Cynthia Rylant, Dutton Children's Books, 1982.

Why the Sun and the Moon Live in the Sky, by Elphinstone Dayrell, Houghton Mifflin, 1990.

Winnie-the-Pooh stories by A. A. Milne, Dell, 1987.

World Book Encyclopedia.

Ms. Maverick:
Fourth Grade

THE PARENT MEETING

Ms. Maverick greeted most of the parents by name as they entered the door of her fourth-grade classroom. Five years before, she had known no one and had missed the easy familiarity she had established with the residents of the small mountain community where she had taught during her first three years.

"Welcome," she began. "As most of you know from our annual book fairs, I am Ms. Maverick. I am pleased to see so many parents here tonight. Usually, there is a tremendous turnout of parents for the kindergarten and first-grade meetings, but attendance decreases as the grade level of the children increases. You are to be commended for your continuing interest in the education of your children.

"Tonight, rather than talk at you about the reading program we pursue in this room, I am going to engage your participation in a learning activity similar to many of the lessons your children will be participating in. I would like you now to think back on all your activities over the past week and to try to remember all the things you had to read in order to get along in your daily lives. You see, reading is such a constant activity that often we read without realizing it. We are aware that we are cooking or traveling or working without realizing that reading is an integral part of all these activities. Tonight, I want you to tell me all the things you have read this week that were not books or magazines and, as you list these things for me, I will write them up here on the board."

At first there was silence as the parents adjusted their expectations to include their active participation in the meeting and began to think about what they had read that was neither a book nor a magazine. Mrs. Penn broke the silence by volunteering that she had read a map to get over to the state capital for a special meeting of a citizen's action group. Ms. Maverick wrote *map* on the board and then waited. Mr. Moore said that he had read the revised criminal rights statutes that had come in the mail to the police department. Mrs. Smith said that she had read the electric bill. Everyone groaned, the group relaxed, and suggestions came faster than Ms. Maverick could record them: *traffic signs, clocks, patterns, exit signs, blueprints, phone books, letters, sales ads, the dials on the stove, directions on a varnish can.* In 10 minutes, Ms. Maverick had the board filled and the parents had "experienced" reading as a survival skill.

"You know, I have always been a reader and thought how unfortunate people were who couldn't read," Mrs. Penn volunteered. "But I never realized how downright impossible it would be to get along in the world if I couldn't read."

Daphne's grandmother recounted, "Once I was in the grocery store and a man came up to me with a can of soup in his hand and asked me what kind it was. I just assumed he had left his spectacles at home, but perhaps he couldn't read the label. They don't put pictures on the can the way they used to, you know." Her husband added, "You can't be a successful farmer these days if you don't know how to read!"

Ms. Maverick agreed. "That's right, there are very few jobs you could hold these days that don't require some reading ability. So often, wanting the best for our children, we point out to them that they must do well in school if they want to grow up to be lawyers or doctors. Many children, however, aspire to the 'exciting' occupations: They want to be truck drivers, police officers, medical technicians, beauticians. Little do they realize the reading demands of these jobs.

"My most important reading goal for your children is that they experience reading as a survival skill. To accomplish this, I do exercises with them like the one I just did with you tonight. I also provide them with 'real-world' reading materials. I have some of these 'real-world' materials displayed here on this table and I will be encouraging the children to bring in reading material they find of interest."

The parents looked over to the table and saw displayed there two daily newspapers, several different magazines, a driver's license manual, maps, menus, pamphlets, telephone books, catalogues, games, and directions for constructing various objects.

"For the final part of my 'reading is real' scenario, I plan to invite people engaged in various jobs to come in and talk with my children about what they must read to do well in their jobs. I haven't done this before, but I think it will make a more lasting impression if the children hear people explain the reading needs of their jobs. This is one area in which I am seeking your help this year. I won't ask you to volunteer now, but if you could spare a half hour to come and talk to the children about your job and its reading demands, please stay a minute after the meeting and leave me your name and the best time for you to come."

Ms. Maverick looked at the clock and realized that she had already used most of her meeting time. ("This is a consistent problem in an activity approach to learning," she thought. "It always takes more time.") She then hurried on to explain the other three components of her reading program.

"Tonight I have spent most of my time trying to make real for you the 'reading is real' component of my four-pronged approach to reading. The other three components are equally important. Each day in this classroom we take time out for me to read aloud to your children and for your children to read books of their own choosing. I try to read a great variety of books, including old favorites such as these [Ms. Maverick held up copies of *Charlotte's Web* by E. B. White, *The Borrowers* by Mary Norton, and *Little House on the Prairie* by Laura Ingalls Wilder] and contemporary fiction such as these [Ms. Maverick held up copies of *Tales of a Fourth Grade Nothing* by Judy Blume, *Fourth Grade Is a Jinx* by Colleen O'Shaughnessy McKenna, and *Anatasia on Her Own* by Lois Lowry]. In addition to fiction, we read many wonderful informational books as part of our units. Here are just a few of the resources we will be using in the next several months as we study about our own state. [Ms. Maverick held up reference books such as *Fabulous Facts about the 50 States* by Wilma Ross and several books just about the state they live in.] During their daily SQUIRT time, the children read books of their own choosing, and I find that when I read such a variety of books to them, they broaden their own personal reading choices. I was pleased to notice that, after four years here, your children are used to settling down for their daily SQUIRT time. We are having 15 minutes of SQUIRT time now and I hope that, by increasing this time gradually, they will be able to sustain their reading for 25 minutes by the end of the year.

"The third part of my reading approach is what I call my 'integrated curriculum block.' I do not separate the subjects so that math is taught for 45 minutes, followed by 45 minutes of reading, language, science, and social studies. It seems so much more economical to spend the reading, language, and math time engaged in reading, writing, and doing math problems that relate to the real-world topics of social studies and science. So each morning from 9:00 to 11:00 we have our block time. During this time we are practicing our language and math skills as we investigate a topic from the social studies or science curriculum. **Content Area Integration**

"For the next several months, we will be busy finding out about our state, which is the major social studies topic in fourth grade. We will be reading from all kinds of sources to find out more about the history, geography, politics, and economics of our state. During this morning block time, I will be especially concerned with improving your children's comprehension and helping them build rich concepts and increase their meaning vocabulary stores.

"The final part of the reading approach is our afternoon skills time. Each afternoon from 1:15 to 2:00 the children work with me or in small groups on those skills they most need to master. During this time we work not only on reading skills but also on the other language skills and basic math skills. By the time children reach fourth grade, there are great differences among them. During this afternoon skills time, I work with each child to focus on his or her own individual needs." **Individual Differences**

Ms. Maverick finished her last sentence hurriedly and apologized for going over the allotted 30 minutes. She thanked them for coming and said that she would answer any questions they might have individually if they would stay for a moment after the others left. She reminded them that she really hoped some of them would come and talk with her class about the reading needs of their jobs and also asked for volunteers to drive the class on field trips.

Parent Involvement

To her surprise, she had six volunteers to come and speak to her class. Mr. Perkins, who was a truck driver, said he had come to five of these meetings over the years and that this was the most interesting one he could remember. He said he would be glad to come and bring all his maps, routing sheets, and delivery orders. Mr. Moore, the chief of police, also volunteered, as did Mr. Smith, who worked for the gas and electric company. Mrs. Tomás said that she and her husband ran a diner and that one of them would come. She apologized for Mr. Tomás's absence. "Someone has to be there all the time, you know, so we just take turns coming to these meetings. This year it's my turn."

Mandy's parents, both of whom were musicians, volunteered to come together. The last to leave was Steve's mother. She said she didn't usually like to talk in front of groups of people but that she had never thought of how important reading was before. Since she is a waitress, she could bring the menus and order pads from her restaurant and let the children pretend to be either waitresses or waiters and customers. That way she could help and wouldn't need to talk too much! Ms. Maverick assured her that that would be delightful and signed her up for the following Tuesday!

MONTHLY LOGS

September

What an unusual class of children this is! I thought that over the eight years I have taught I had seen every possible combination of children, but this class disproves that theory. Of course, I expect to find great differences among children by the time they get to fourth grade, but I have never before seen the range represented by the span between Paul, who reads almost nothing, and Larry, who qualitatively reads almost as well as I do and quantitatively reads more than I do. Then there are the personality differences. Roberta cannot do the right thing no matter how hard she tries, and Betty, her twin sister, can't do anything wrong. Joyce and Hilda are both very capable and intelligent but they are so independent.

I am pleased, however, with the adjustments most of the children have made to my program. I always enjoy getting Mrs. Wise's children because they have had so much experience working together in groups. It is still a shock to me to see someone else teaching in her room next door.

I am especially pleased with Daisy. According to her records, she just never got anything done. She is working now, although I think she is doing it for me rather than for herself. Each time she does anything, she comes to me for approval. I pat her on the head because I want her to establish the habit of sitting down and accomplishing something, but I am trying to help her develop some internal feedback. Yesterday she brought me a picture she had painted. I said, "Yes, it is lovely. Didn't it feel good to do it?" I have a feeling this is going to be a yearlong process, however; I have seldom seen a child with so little intrinsic motivation. For the moment, I am thankful that she is working for whatever reason. Paul is the weakest reader in the class. I must work individually with him during the afternoon time.

Mort is a pill! If I hear that child sigh and say, "Well, it doesn't matter. I don't care," one more time I may lose my composure and shake him! Except I know it wouldn't do any good. Yesterday I said to him, "Mort, what do you do when you go home after school?"

He replied, "Oh, mostly I just sit around and get bored. Sometimes I watch television." As far as I can tell he has no friends, no interests, and no aspirations! I guess I should think of him as "a real challenge."

While we have not actually begun the unit on our state this month, we have done some readiness activities in preparation for this unit. One of the concepts that is very difficult for young children to grasp is the notion of time and sequence. Last year I had my class construct a time line showing the important events in our state and their corresponding dates. While the children learned from this activity, it was very difficult for them to conceptualize the differences in time. Last year's class never understood that the spaces between the depicted events were proportional to the actual time elapsed between these events.

Graphic Organizers

In order to provide readiness for the state time line and to help the children apply time passage and sequence to their own lives, I had the children make a time line depicting the important events in their lives. I began by having the children put their chairs in a circle and asking them to call up the important things that had happened in their lives. The children were all eager to respond and everyone had something to share, since the subject was one they all knew lots about. Rita recalled her first trip to the library when the librarian told her she was too young to have a library card. Tanana remembered moving to our state and how scared she was when she first came to Mrs. Wise's classroom. Larry recalled the first Hardy Boys book he had read. When all the children had contributed something to the discussion, I suggested that we might create some "life lines" to show all the important events that had already taken place in their lives. I showed them how we could use string and little slips of paper with words and illustrations to depict our individual histories.

The children were most enthusiastic, so we began right then. I gave each of the children a long sheet of paper and asked them to put their birthdate in the top left corner and the current date in the bottom left corner. Although many of the children knew the month and day on which they were born, only Larry, Pat, and Hilda knew the year of their birth. I then asked the others how they thought they could figure out the year in which they were born. After some discussion, they worked out the mechanics of subtracting how old they were from the current date and filled in the year on the chart they were making. In the meantime, I modeled by making my chart on the board. Next to my birthdate,

I wrote "Ms. Maverick was born" and next to the current date, I wrote, "Ms. Maverick is helping her children to make their own life lines." The children then followed my example and put appropriate entries next to their own names.

They then listed the important events in their lives. I told them not to worry too much at this point about the date or the order but just try to get down about 8 to 10 events. Most children had no trouble at all listing a dozen events. Paul, however, needed a great deal of help with this and I fear his life line represents my thinking more than his. When the children had finished listing the events, I asked them how they thought we could find out the approximate date of each event. Several suggested their parents kept lists of everything and that if they could take the charts home that night, they could fill in many of the dates. The others suggested they could fill in by knowing in what order things happened in relation to the events with known dates.

The next day they returned with dates and many more events filled in on their charts. We then cut the charts and organized the events into the proper order. Next began the construction of the actual life lines. Since all of the children in the class were either 8 or 9 years old, we decided to cut the strings either 9 or 10 feet long. In that way, each foot could represent a year. Any events that happened in the same year would be placed close to one another. If there were a year or two in which no events occurred, that would be represented by the unfilled space for that year. We also agreed that since we were going to hang these around the room for others to read, we should try to spell the words correctly and to use readable handwriting. Each child then measured and cut his or her string and marked it off in one-foot lengths. They also cut and measured strips of colored paper to three-by-six-inch dimensions. While the children were doing this, I acted as editor, helping children correct the spelling and punctuation on their charted events so that they could copy them correctly on their life line slips.

Somehow, it all got done! The children illustrated the events and taped the slips to the strings. Those who finished first helped the others. The life lines now hang below the windows and the chalkboards, and whenever the children have a spare moment, they can be seen reading their own or someone else's life history. This activity, which started out as readiness for our state's time line, had value in and of itself. The children helped one another and learned more about one another. They learned that we share many common experiences and that other experiences are unique to each individual. They do seem to have a better sense of time sequence and proportion, and they have certainly practiced their math, reading, and writing skills. I will do this again next year!

Concept Development— Maps

The other readiness activity this month was constructing a map of the school. We will do a lot of work with maps when we begin the actual study of our state next month, and for many children this is their first exposure to maps. I wanted them to connect maps to their own life space before asking them to generalize to the less tangible world outside. After a discussion about maps and what would be involved in constructing a map of our school, we walked around the whole building to observe what we would include in our map. The children suggested, and I listed on the board, all the things we might want to include in a map of our school. I then grouped the children in pairs and each pair took responsibility for going to a particular classroom or area of the building, measuring that area, and constructing that part of the map. When all the children reassembled with their measurements, we measured the total length and width of the building and then decided what proportion of that length and width the various rooms comprised. For a while, it looked as if we had a lot less total space in what we had measured than what there actually was in the building. Larry was the one who realized we had forgotten to consider the space taken up by the hallways! After measuring these, we were able to decide on a scale. Each pair of children cut from colored paper the model for the room or area they had measured and labeled it appropriately. We then pasted the individual rooms on a piece of appropriately sized poster board and, six days after we started, had our map of the school. Well, actually, we had it for only a day or two before it was commandeered! Mr. Topps noticed it when he came in to read with our class during SQUIRT time and remarked that we had done a first-rate job and that this map was just the thing he needed to hang outside the office so that visitors could find their way around. He asked if he could "borrow" it for a while. The children all autographed it, and it now hangs outside the office.

Cooperative Learning

October

We are now off and running on our state unit. Each unit actually has three overlapping phases. At the beginning, I provide the children with a great deal of input from many different sources. During most of this first phase we work together as a whole class, building some interest and motivation for the unit, becoming familiar with new and specialized vocabulary terms, and discovering enough information so that we can begin to raise some questions to which we can seek answers. During the second phase of the unit, while we continue many whole-class activities, the children are also doing extensive reading, listening, and viewing, either individually or in small groups. Finally, they engage in several culminating activities that help them to organize and synthesize the information gained during the unit.

Unit Teaching

Throughout the unit, we do a variety of activities designed to foster concept development and to increase the store of words for which they have rich meanings. As much as possible, I try to provide direct experience for concept and meaning vocabulary development. We take field trips to the source of real places, objects, people, and events, and the children and I are always on the lookout for things to bring into the classroom that will make new words and unfamiliar concepts real to us. Of course, we cannot go to see everything or bring it into the classroom, so I rely on pictures, filmstrips, and other visual aids to provide indirect experience. When I introduce new vocabulary to the children, I always try to put these words in topical word sets. During our state unit, I will begin topical word sets for maps, state government, and places to visit. These topical word sets become part of our wall vocabulary. The children learn to read and spell them as well as develop rich meanings for them.

Meaning Vocabulary

My kickoff motivator for this unit was a large white outline map of our state, which I had drawn by projecting the image of an overhead transparency map onto the bulletin board at the rear of the room. After tracing the projected image, I cut along the outline and stapled the giant white map to the red-backed bulletin board. I did this all late one night so that the children's attention would be drawn immediately to the giant blank white map against the bright red background. Of course, they noticed it immediately and were intrigued by its size and blankness. Several correctly guessed that it was an outline map of our state. I had the children move their chairs closer to the board and began to lead them in a discussion of our state. Little by little, in response to their comments and questions, I wrote the name of a particular landmark in its proper location. I let the children help me decide where these landmarks should go by consulting several maps that I spread out on the floor as we talked. At the end of this initial motivating session we had (1) located our town, the state capital, several other cities, lakes, and rivers, (2) talked about what went on at the capital and began to use words such as *governor, lieutenant governor, legislators, laws,* and *taxes,* (3) used directional words such as *north, south, east,* and *west* and noted these directions above, below, and on the appropriate sides of our map, and (4) begun to discuss various places that the children had lived, visited, or had some other connection with.

I told them that as we studied our state we would use again and again many of the words we had used in our talk. They would need to be able to read the words in order to find out more about our state and they would need to be able to spell them in order to be able to write about it. Mitch, Jeff, and Daisy didn't look too happy at the thought of additional work, so I smiled reassuringly as I picked up a black marker and several half sheets of different colored construction paper and let them help me remember the "special" words we had used that morning. I then let them watch me print these words on the colored slips of paper. As I was doing so, I remarked about the relative length and distinct features of the words, pronounced the words carefully, and had the children pronounce each word after me. I then had Mitch climb on a chair and tape the words to the wall above the bulletin board. I noted that we had 11 words to start with and that we would add more as we continued to study about our state. I then prepared the children for our following morning's activities by showing them a little color-headed pin and a triangular shaped slip of paper. On the triangular slip, I printed in tiny letters

Ms. Maverick
was born
here

and pinned this slip to our map high in the northwestern corner. Next to the pinned flag I wrote the name of the community in which I was born. The children were fascinated and all wanted to make little flags. I assured them that that was tomorrow's activity and that, in the meantime, they should look at the maps and try to figure out places they had been to or knew of to put flags on them. I also suggested that they talk with their parents and perhaps even look at a map with them to determine such family history information as their parents' birthplaces, where aunts and uncles lived, and the names and locations of places they had visited. For the rest of the day, there was always someone at the back of the room looking at our giant map and investigating the smaller ones that I had placed on a table under the bulletin board.

The next day the children came bursting into the room loaded with maps and family histories they had brought from home. We immediately gathered in the back of the room and the children began to spread out their maps, sharing the information they had with one another and trying to locate the places they wanted to flag on our giant map. While still giant, our map was no longer blank. It was covered with place-names and flags, all of which the children had some personal affiliation with. We even have a flag marking the city to which Mike had moved. Mrs. Flame would be happy to see that. She still worries about how Mike is doing. We also added the names of several neighboring towns and a few lakes and rivers to our wall vocabulary, which now has 18 words.

Parent Involvement

The interest and excitement generated by the giant map motivator has grown throughout this month as have the number of words in our wall vocabulary. We now have 32 words up there and as I use these words again and again in different contexts, I try to remember to point to the words and remind the children of the other contexts in which we used them. We take five minutes each morning to practice spelling the words in our wall vocabulary. Each child takes out a sheet of paper and numbers it from 1 to 10. I then call out 10 of the words on the wall. As I call each word, the children are allowed and, indeed, encouraged to look up at the wall and find the word and then write it on their papers. The trick to this technique is that they can't actually copy the words, since they must look up and then down at their papers and then up again. In order to do this they have to be trying to take a mental image of the word and then reproduce this mental image. When all 10 words have been called out, the children check their own papers by chanting the spelling of each word. Most days, all the children get 9 or 10 right and because they are so successful at it, they love to do it. The other day during recess it rained and when they were trying to decide on an indoor game, Horace suggested that we do the spelling words again! I couldn't believe it, but that's what they "played," with Horace being the teacher and calling out the words. From now on, once the children are very familiar with the words, as they are now, I shall let the children take turns "being teacher" and calling out the words. Strange—I always think I am allowing the children as much participation as possible and then discover something else that I am doing that the children could do with benefit.

Meaning Vocabulary

I have done several whole-class comprehension lessons this month. Through these lessons, I help them increase their knowledge about our state and work on increasing their vocabularies and improving their comprehension skills at the same time. To do these lessons, I select part of a newspaper or magazine article or a short selection from a book and type it on my computer in large print. I then run the typed sheet through the machine in the office to make a transpar-

Comprehension Strategy Lesson

ency. Using my overhead projector for group comprehension lessons has several advantages: If the passage I select is unusually difficult to read, I can change a few of the words or omit sections to make it more readable. I don't waste a lot of paper making 25 copies of the same thing, and I can focus the attention of the children where I want it. I do, however, always show the children the source of the original article so that they know that what they are reading is "something real."

Meaning Vocabulary

I begin my preparation for the lesson by identifying any words or concepts I think will present difficulty for many of my children. I make a distinction between unknown words and unfamiliar concepts. In the first directed reading lesson, for example, the subject was "things to do in our state." I had taken this article from the magazine section of the Sunday newspaper. Two concepts that I thought would not be familiar to most of my children were *rapids* and *currents*. In both cases, most of my children would probably be able to identify the words but would not have a meaning for those words appropriate to the particular contexts in which they were being used. The word *current* they might associate with the term *current events*, and for *rapids*, while they might have the concept of speed, they would probably not readily associate this concept with fast-moving water.

In addition to the two relatively unfamiliar concepts, *current* and *rapids*, I also identified several words for which most of my children would have listening-meaning concepts but would not be able to identify in print. These unknown words for the "things to do in our state" selection included *reflection* and *parachute*. In both cases, I was quite sure that the children would have a concept for these words once they were able to identify them but doubted that the "big word decoding skills" of most of my children would allow them to figure out the pronunciation of these familiar concepts but unknown words.

Having identified several unfamiliar concepts and unknown words, I then decided what to do about them. Sometimes, I build meanings for unfamiliar concepts or tell them the pronunciation of unknown words before they read the story. More often, however, I alert the children to the existence of these unfamiliar concepts or unknown words, and challenge them to see if they can figure out what a word is or what the concept means as they read the selection. This encourages the children to use the context to figure out the meaning and/or pronunciation of words. This is what I did with *current, rapids, reflection,* and *parachute*. I wrote these four words on the board and asked a volunteer to pronounce *current* and *rapids*. Betty gladly pronounced them. I then asked them if anyone could give me a meaning for *current* or *rapids*. Manuel suggested that current has something to do with electricity and Steve said that it means "like in 'current events.'" For *rapids*, Roberta said that "without the *s* it means fast." I told them that the definitions they had given were right but that, as I hoped they knew, words have many different meanings and that the words *current* and *rapids* in the selection we were about to read had meanings different from the ones they knew. I then told them that, as they were reading the selection, I wanted them to see if they could figure out what these different meanings might be. I hinted to them that the other words and sentences near the words *current* and *rapids* would give them the clues they needed to solve the mystery.

To add another element of mystery, I pointed to *reflection* and *parachute* and told the children *not* to pronounce the words. I told them that these two words were different from *current* and *rapids* in that they knew what these second two words meant but hadn't yet learned to identify them in print. I suggested that as with *current* and *rapids*, the words close to *reflection* and *parachute* would allow them to solve the mystery. Once the children had read the selection, they explained what they thought *current* and *rapids* meant in this context, identified the other words that had let them figure that out, and compared these meanings for the words with the meanings they already knew. Many of the children had also figured out the unknown words, *reflection* and *parachute*, and explained which other words had led them to solve the mystery.

Having identified and decided what to do about any unknown words or unfamiliar concepts, I then decided for what purpose I was going to have the children read the selection. In a comprehension strategy lesson, my goal is always that the children are better at reading for a specific purpose after reading the selection than they were prior to reading the selection. Sometimes I work on improving their literal comprehension. I may decide that after reading the selection, we will put the events of the selection in order, or that we will read in order to answer the fact questions: Who? What? When? Where? How? For other selections, I may decide that we will work on being able to state main ideas in our own words.

I teach many lessons designed to sharpen the children's inferential comprehension ability. In these lessons, I show them only a portion of the text and ask them to predict what will happen next. I write these predictions on the board and let the children vote to decide which one they consider most likely to occur. I then display enough of the text so that they can check their predictions. Finally, I ask the children who made the correct prediction to read me the words in the passage that allowed them to make the correct prediction. In this way, the children who are not very good at inferring see that inferences are based on something that is directly stated in the text.

The first year I taught, I referred to inferential comprehension as "reading between the lines." One day, I watched one boy squinting at his book and then peering over the shoulder of the boy in front of him who could "read between the lines." It suddenly occurred to me that, from a child's vantage point, it was conceivable that he believed that there was something between the lines that he couldn't see or that was only between the lines of other people's books. Since then I have stopped using that particular phrase. I have begun to ask those who can make inferences to point out the words in the text on which they based their inferences. This allows the children who can't make inferences to begin to observe the way the process works in the minds of those who can.

Finally, I teach some lessons designed to help children become more critical readers. During these lessons, I ask the children to read in order to make judgments or evaluations, and I stress that their judgments are decided on the basis of their own value systems and that there are no right or wrong answers to these judgment questions.

For the "things to do in our state" lesson, I decided to focus the children's attention on the main ideas of each paragraph. I displayed only the portion of the text that mentioned a particular place and asked the children to read so that when they finished they could tell me in a sentence what the main attraction was at each place. First, I let the children read silently. When most appeared to have finished, I let a volunteer read the section aloud. In this way, Paul and others whose reading skills are still limited could get the content of the selection and participate in the comprehension activity.

After each section was read silently and then orally, I asked a child to tell me in one sentence what the main thing was that people went there to see. I then made a list on the board that gave each place-name and the sentence describing its main attraction. When we had completed reading about the eight places, I read over the list I had made on the board and pointed out to the children that, in addition to being the main attraction, these sentences were also the main ideas of each paragraph. Main ideas, like main attractions, are the most important ideas (attractions); the ideas (attractions) most people would like to remember after reading (visiting) a paragraph (place). While we will continue to work on identifying and stating main ideas all year, this lesson was a good one to begin with because it helped to make the concept of main idea a little more concrete.

As a follow-up to this directed reading lesson, I put the children in eight cooperative groups. Each group was to make a little flag for one of the eight places we had read about, write the place-name and the main attraction on the flag, locate the place using the ever-growing supply of maps we now had in the room, and pin the flag to our giant map, which was no longer blank.

Direct Experience We have taken two field trips this month. For the first, we went to visit the local newspaper. I bring daily copies of both the local and capital newspapers to school each morning, and since we began the unit on our state, the children have become quite interested in them. Before we took the field trip, I had the children put their chairs in a circle and we began to talk about the local newspaper and to formulate some questions to ask Ms. Daley, the editor. I listed these questions on a large sheet of chart paper and, on our return, we checked the chart to see how many of our questions had been answered.

We then got out a local map and looked at the various routes we could take to get from our school to the newspaper office. We tried to decide which route would be the shortest and which would be the quickest. Since there was much disagreement about the best route, I asked the children how we might plan an experiment to find out. After much discussion, the following plan was arrived

Parent Involvement at. Each of the four cars (Mrs. Penn, Mrs. Smith, and Daphne's grandfather had volunteered to drive) would take a different route. One person in each car would be responsible for writing down the beginning and ending mileage. Another person would time the trips. The other riders in the car would keep track of the number of lights, stop signs, intersections, and so on. It was agreed, of course, that each driver would drive carefully and obey all speed limits.

Finally, Friday arrived! The four cars set out at the same time. Mrs. Smith arrived first, but Mrs. Penn had taken the shortest route. I, of course, arrived last and my passengers were not too pleased about that, especially Butch!

The receptionist took us on a tour around the buildings and then took us to

Ms. Daley's office. The children behaved very well and, because they had discussed and planned before coming, asked some very good questions. I was just beginning to relax and pat myself on the back for preparing them so well when the inevitable happened. A reporter came into Ms. Daley's office with some copy. She introduced him to the children and asked them if they had any questions. Hilda asked him a question about a story she had read recently in the paper and as he was answering her question, he turned to Ms. Daley and said, "Why don't you take them down into the morgue and show them some of the dead ones?" Roberta's head twitched with excitement; Betty fainted! The reporter quickly explained that the newspaper morgue had "dead" newspapers, not dead bodies, while Mrs. Smith and I revived Betty. A striking example of the multiple meanings of common words!

We then did go into the morgue, however, and spent a long time there. Ms. Daley showed us the newspapers that recorded such historic events as the end of the Civil War, the Lincoln and Kennedy assassinations, and the state's celebration of its 100th birthday. She pointed out the difference between history books that are written long after the actual events have occurred and newspaper accounts that are written immediately. She also pointed out how newspapers are one very important source of historical data. The children were particularly impressed when she showed them a copy of a biography of a famous general and explained that the writer of that book had spent many days in this very morgue doing research about our town where this general had grown up.

Upon our return from the newspaper, we looked at our collected data, computed the mileages and times, decided that the shortest route in distance was not the quickest route, and discussed reasons why this was so. We also looked to see which of our questions had been answered and decided that six had been answered quite thoroughly, three partially, and two not at all. Finally, each child **Focused** composed a short note to Ms. Daley thanking her for her time and telling her **Writing** what he or she had found most interesting about the visit. Here is Roberta's letter:

Dear Ms. Daley,
Thank you for letting us come down to visit your newspaper. There was lots to see and I can only apologize for Betty's fainting in your office. She is always doing things like that and I can't understand why. The dead newspapers were interesting but I would have liked to have seen some dead bodies since I never have. Being a newspaper lady I bet you have seen hundreds of them.

Sincerely,
Roberta Smith

Our other field trip this month was to the county seat. This was an all-day **Direct** field trip, and we packed a picnic lunch. Thank goodness it didn't rain! We **Experience** prepared for this one as we had for the newspaper office, by having discussions and coming up with a list of questions we wanted answered. This time, Hilda wrote down the list to make sure that we came back with at least a partial answer to all our questions.

In the morning we visited the county courthouse. When we got to the county clerk's office, a young couple was waiting to get a marriage license. All the boys plus Pat and Roberta thought that was hysterical. The children were most fascinated by the sheriff. They wanted to know what happened when a person got arrested and what a sheriff and his deputies did. The sheriff showed them the county map, which was very detailed, and helped them to locate our school and some of their homes.

When we went into the court, the judge was hearing a traffic case. He revoked the license of a person arrested for driving recklessly and speeding. This impressed the children greatly. When we got to the tax assessor's office, Hilda was busily checking her list to see what we might have forgotten to ask. When her question was finally asked, it came out as "We want to know how you decide how much taxes everyone should pay, and my Dad says you must be a friend of our next door neighbor's because his house is twice as big as ours and he pays less taxes!"

That afternoon we toured the county historical museum. The children were especially intrigued by the original state flag and the lists of names of all the men who had died in the major wars we have fought. The restored log cabin behind the museum added much realism to our study of how people used to live in our state and, of course, the children were fascinated by the Indian artifacts.

Focused Writing　Upon our return, we made a list of all the people we had visited or seen in the courthouse and what their functions were. We also referred to our question chart and, with Hilda's help, did indeed have at least a partial answer to all the questions we had raised. I then helped the children form five groups. Each group composed a letter thanking one of the people who helped us on our visit.

November

What a great month this has been! Normally, we don't go to the state capital. It is almost a two-hour trip, and the legislature is usually not in session during the fall when we are studying our state. Three weeks ago, however, the legislature was called into special session in order to consider a new water pollution bill. Everyone in the state has been debating this issue for some time now, but it took a tragedy to get the legislators moving. Four weeks ago, five people died in a small downstate industrial town. The cause of death was determined to be the high level of industrial chemical wastes in the water—way above the standard already set but never enforced. The antipollution forces were able to rally support around this emotional issue, and the governor called the legislature into special session to consider a more stringent water pollution bill with provisions for enforcement and severe penalties for lack of compliance.

Attitudes　The children came back to school on the Monday after the five people had died and they were all upset. Many of them brought the various newspaper stories and related the discussions they had had about this issue at home. The children, unlike the adult population, were almost unanimous in their insistence that the water pollution standards be much stricter. Not being burdened with financial responsibilities, they could see the need for clean water much more clearly than they could understand the financial strain the new controls would put on industry and, if industry is to be believed, the entire state population.

Of course, we put our chairs in a circle immediately and discussed the problem. I tried to raise questions and interject information that would allow them to consider the issue in its broadest terms. Many of the children were unclear about words like *chemicals* and *bacteria,* and I began to make mental notes on which words we might want to explore more fully and add to our wall vocabulary. Later, I decided that the subject was such an important one and the children were so naturally motivated that a unit on ecology and pollution would be first on our agenda after Christmas.

Meaning Vocabulary

It was Mrs. Penn who suggested that we take the children to the state capital. She came in after school that very afternoon and told me that she would be going over to meet with a citizen's action group later in the week and that she would be glad to make all the arrangements at the capital and to be one of our drivers. She added that she had seen Mrs. Smith that morning and had mentioned the possibility to her and that Mrs. Smith had agreed it would be a great experience for the children to see the legislature in session and that she, too, would be willing to drive. I told Mrs. Penn that I would talk it over with the children but that I was all for it!

Direct Experience

The children, of course, were most excited. In addition to the general excitement of going on a trip that long and being "at the capital" was the excitement generated by the knowledge that Ms. Maverick had never taken any of her other classes to the state capital. They were not just doing the same trips all the other fourth grades did—they were doing something very special and very grown-up. As I watched their delight in this specialness, I vowed to try to think of something special for each class of children I taught.

The preparations for the trip took most of the month, and many of the activities that I had planned for this middle part of the unit went by the boards. The transportation problem was solved by Mrs. Penn, who, in addition to commandeering Mandy's father as our fourth driver, also arranged for our tour through the capitol and our visit to the gallery while the legislators were debating. And she got our local representative to agree to come up to the gallery when the session broke for lunch and talk with us and answer our questions. Our list of questions for Mr. Stans took three sheets of chart paper, and Hilda thought she would never get them all copied in her notebook.

Lunch was a problem. We were going to leave at 7:30 A.M. so that we could get there, park, and go on a 10 A.M. tour through the capitol building and be in the gallery from 11 A.M. to noon. A picnic lunch was a little risky at this time of year, and I thought it would be good for all the children to have the experience of eating in a real restaurant. They had all eaten at fast-food drive-ins, but many of them had not been to a restaurant, ordered from a menu, or paid their own bill plus tax and tip! The problem with taking them to a restaurant, of course, was that many of them could not come up with the money and that many families who would come up with the money really couldn't afford it.

As I was thinking about the lunch problem, I was also gathering up the week's supply of newspapers to take them to the recycling drop point. I then remembered that some organizations had collected money for various causes by having paper and aluminum drives. It occurred to me that if our class could collect paper and aluminum for recycling as well as deposit bottles for return to the grocery stores, we might make enough money for everyone to have lunch. We might also become more personally "pollution conscious."

In three weeks, we collected hundreds of pounds of paper and aluminum and returned $56.85 worth of bottles to the grocery stores. Several parents made voluntary donations to our lunch fund and we ended up with another $80. The children thought this was a fortune until we divided by 25 and realized that each person's share of the fortune was only $5.47.

Mrs. Penn had found an inexpenive restaurant close to the capitol that was equipped for people in wheelchairs like Danielle and had arranged for the 29 of us to eat there. She had also gotten several sample menus and from these each child figured out the various combinations of food he or she could buy with $4.56 (which is what each child actually had to spend after paying the 5 percent sales tax and 15 percent tip).

Comprehension Strategy Lesson

In order to prepare them for their visit to the capitol and the legislature, I showed a film entitled *Your State Government*, which is put out by the State Chamber of Commerce and the State Department of Education. Just as when I am going to have the class read something I do a reading comprehension lesson with them, I do a viewing comprehension lesson with a film. After previewing the film, I determine which unfamiliar concepts I want to teach and whether I will help them to build these concepts before, during, or after the film. Often the film provides visual experience for words that I cannot provide direct experience for. I stop the film at the appropriate frame and discuss the picture that makes real the unfamiliar word or concept.

I then determine my purposes for having them view the film and decide how much of the film I will show at a time. Unless it is strictly for entertainment, I never show a film all the way through. Rather, I set the purpose for viewing a particular segment, stop the film and discuss the fulfillment of that purpose, set another purpose, and begin the film again. If the film is one that the children seem to especially enjoy, I will often show it again the following day in its entirety. I then try to think of an appropriate follow-up activity to the film. My purpose in this follow-up activity is to help the children organize and evaluate the new information gained from the film.

Parent Involvement

Mr. Perkins came this month before we went to the capital. He brought his routing slips and maps and talked to the children about all the reading he has to do in his job as a truck driver. The children were quite impressed! He also showed us the best route to take to the capital and told us some interesting things to watch for on the way.

The actual trip was exhausting but very exciting. We left promptly at 7:30 A.M. I provided some apples and crackers for each car so that the children could have a little snack when we first got there. The woman who escorted us on our tour through the capitol was very sweet and very smart, so Betty and Daphne have decided to be tour guides when they grow up! Of course, while we were in the gallery, one of the "anti–the-more-stringent-bill" legislators was talking and the children were quite upset. I think they did begin to get some notion, however, that there are always two legitimate, defensible points of view. Mr. Stans was great! He spent almost 30 minutes talking with us. He commended the children on their paper/aluminum/bottle collection and told them that another way they could make a difference was by getting in the habit of writing to their legislator and letting him or her know how they felt.

Lunch was fun! The children were well prepared and most knew exactly what they wanted. The only person who overspent was Daisy. I didn't realize it at the time but Mandy's father had to bail her out with 34 cents. I told him he should have left her to wash dishes! We got back to the school at 4:30 P.M.

December

This month marked not only the end of the year, but also the end of our state unit. No small feat, I can assure you! For culminating activities on this unit, I decided to have small groups work on several different activities: a time line, a relief map, a mural, a historical drama, and a book about our state. I described the projects to the entire class, letting them know what they would be doing on each. I then had the children write down their first and second choices for the project on which they wanted to work.

Unit Teaching

Steve, Mitch, Butch, Hilda, Alexander, and Jeff worked on the relief map. Actually I probably should add Ms. Maverick to that roster since I had to help this group more than any of the others. The children had already had many experiences with all kinds of maps throughout this unit, but constructing this relief map was still a big job. (When they had finished—finally!—the map was amazingly accurate.) I then sat down with the group and had them tell me the materials needed and steps to follow in making a relief map. This served as a good language and directions-writing activity for the group, and the chart we made will help us in making relief maps in the future.

Cooperative Learning

Making a Relief Map*

Materials Needed:

opaque projector	oil paint
contour map of area	varnish
sheet of paper	paintbrush
plyboard four feet long and cut	screen
as wide as needed	sawdust
nails	wallpaper paste powder
hammer	two-gallon pail

Steps:

1. Put the contour map in the opaque projector.
2. Put the plyboard in the chalktray.

* Adapted from Preston (1968).

3. Project the contour map onto the plyboard.

4. Trace the outline and all the markings onto the board.

5. Cover the board with a sheet of paper.

6. Trace the contour map on the paper as you did the board.

7. Decide what the highest point would be on your map and that will be three inches high.

8. Divide to figure out the scale.

9. Using the scale and the sheet of paper on which you traced the contour map, decide how high in inches each area should be built. Write these heights in the right place on the paper.

10. Hammer nails into the board along the contour lines.

11. Paint rivers and lakes on the board with blue oil paint.

12. Let blue paint dry. Then varnish.

13. Screen the sawdust.

14. Mix four quarts of sawdust with one quart of wallpaper paste powder.

15. Add just enough water so it can be shaped.

16. Build the map one layer at a time using the nails as a guide.

17. When it is all built and dry, varnish the whole map.

18. Paint the rivers and lakes blue again.

19. Paint the other areas.

Paul, Manuel, Chip, Anthony, and Carl worked on constructing a time line for our state. The completion of this project was, indeed, much facilitated by the experience of making the life lines that they had done in September. They began by listing important events in our state's history and verifying the dates on which they occurred. Miss Page, our librarian, helped them to find some of the references they needed for this part of the project. They then decided to use a 20-foot piece of string and to let each foot represent 10 years. While Paul was not much help on the researching end, he did work diligently to copy the dates and events onto the markers that would go along the line.

Rita, Mandy, Danielle, Larry, and Horace made a lovely bound book entitled *Facts You Should Know about Our State*. They took much of the information we had gained from our discussions, reading, films, and field trips and wrote several topical pieces. They also included maps, pictures of the state flower and bird, and representations of the several flags our state has had. They used the computers to type these and made a title page and a table of contents. They then bound it with a lovely cloth cover, as they had learned to do from Mrs. Wise, and took it to the library to show to Miss Page. You can imagine their delight when she told them it looked good enough to be a library book. The children asked if it could really *be* a library book, so Miss Page pasted a pocket in the back, typed up a card, gave it an appropriate number, made a card for the card file, and shelved it with the other books about our state. Needless to say it doesn't stay on that shelf long. Every child in our room wants to check it out to read, and now they are all asking to make their own bound books to put in the library. Perhaps after the first of the year, we will begin keeping writing notebooks in preparation for such a large project!

Mort, Tanana, Betty, and Daphne did the mural that covers the side of the room. This mural depicts the changes in the way people lived, traveled, and dressed in our state over the past 200 years. Again, Miss Page's help was invaluable in steering this group to reference works that contained many pictures. She also arranged for this group to view several filmstrips, including one film that helped them be accurate in their representations.

The drama group, Roberta, Alex, Pat, Daisy, and Joyce, presented several short skits representing significant events in our state's history. The funniest one was their skit of the legislators debating the new water pollution bill. Pat was the "anti" senator and Roberta, Alex, Daisy, and Joyce sat and booed and hissed as she spoke.

While these culminating activities occupied much of our time and energies this month, we did do some other things. We are now up to 18 minutes of SQUIRT time each day, and many of the children are choosing to read from the state books, magazines, pamphlets, brochures, and maps displayed on the back table. We have had lots of fun devising math word problems for each other to solve. The ground rules were that (1) each word problem had to involve our state in some way and (2) the person who made up the problem had to be able to solve it. The children worked out the problems at odd times during the day, and then, just before lunch, five children would come and write their problems on the board. The rest of us would then work at solving the problems. The children learned that writing clearly stated mathematical word problems that contain all the information needed to solve them is a difficult task.

Self-Selected Reading

We had a whole-school party on the day before school let out for the holidays. Mr. Sweep, the custodian, was retiring after being here since the day the school opened 27 years ago. While we were all sad to see him leave, that sadness, for me, was lightened by the knowledge that Mr. Moppet, Chip's father, needed the job so badly. He has been out of work for months, and he and his family are too proud to accept "charity." I have, however, been seeing to it that Chip has some breakfast when he gets here in the morning and, now that his father is the school custodian, I know they will be all right.

Oh, I almost forgot! I am going to have a student teacher. I don't know quite what to expect, however. Dr. Link was here at the beginning of the month and told me about a young man named Donald Ditto. It seems that Donald started his student teaching in the fall but just couldn't get along with the teacher with whom they placed him. He dropped out of the program and was going to drop out of school entirely with only student teaching left to complete! Dr. Link assures me that the young man really has potential and that he had just been poorly matched with a very rigid teacher. At any rate, Dr. Link thinks he will be able to work with my program and that he will make a contribution. I hope she's right—for his sake as well as for mine. I guess we will just have to wait and see what this new year brings!

January

Mr. Ditto has been with us all month now and he is terrific! I am just so glad Dr. Link convinced him to give teaching another try and brought him out here. He has a very quiet, easy-going manner with the kids and will never be a disciplinarian, but the children respect and cooperate with him. He never talks about his other student teaching experience, but I'll just bet that in addition to the inherent problems created by matching him with an authoritarian teacher, he also experienced difficulties because of the expectations of what a male teacher is supposed to be like. I imagine that both the students and the other teachers expected him to behave like a drill sergeant. Mr. Ditto has no top sergeant qualities about him. I like him.

Unit Teaching   Our unit for most of this month has been on ecology. It has been a lot of fun, and I found many ways to help the children become involved in the community. We discussed interviewing techniques and constructed a little questionnaire to find out what people are doing about energy conservation and pollution. The children interviewed neighbors, relatives, and business owners, and we prepared a report, sort of a miniature Harris poll, which we distributed to all the people interviewed. Newspapers, magazines, and television broadcasts provided much of the input for this unit because this information needs to be the most current available.

During one of our initial sessions, the children and I decided on some categories under the general heading of ecology and began a bulletin board for each of these subtopics. The children brought newspaper and magazine articles and pictures, shared them with the class, and put them on the appropriate board. I made videotapes of the nightly national and local newscasts and played back for the children those parts that applied to our study. I also arranged for many members of the community who are involved in specific ecological concerns to come in and talk with us about their particular involvement. As a culmination to this unit, the children and I drafted a list of recommendations for conserving energy and preventing pollution, which we sent to Ms. Daley. The letter was published with all the children's names under it. The children were pleased, but their parents were ecstatic! Copies of that paper with its 15 suggestions for conserving energy and preventing pollution have gone to doting aunts and grandparents all around the country.

The children are very careful not to waste anything anymore and are quick to point out wasteful habits in others. Sometimes these others are not so pleased to have their faults aired in public. One day in the cafeteria, Mrs. Flame took her tray up to deposit it. She hadn't even touched her roll or her cake. Butch informed her that if she didn't want to eat something, she shouldn't take it in the first place!

I have used many appealing informational books with the children in connection with our pollution unit. Two books put out by The Earthworks Group, *Kid Heroes of the Environment* and *50 Simple Things Kids Can Do to Save the Earth*, are both chock-full of tips and projects that real kids really can do. We have gotten many excellent ideas from these two sources. *Greening the City Streets: The Story of Community Gardens* by Barbara Huff was another practical resource. We also enjoyed many of Dorothy Hinshaw Patent's photo essays, including *Where the Bald Eagles Gather, The Way of the Grizzly,* and *Where the Wild Horses Roam.* I also found a marvelous new fiction book with an ecological theme, *Trouble at Marsh Harbor* by Susan Sharpe, which the children all enjoyed and which many of them chose to read to themselves later.

The children have all been keeping content journals this month as we have studied about pollution. Each morning as we are finishing our unit time, I give them 10 to 15 minutes and I ask them to write down what they have learned and their reactions to it. This is an emotional issue for my children who have very strong feelings about "their earth" and what is being done to it, and their journal entries are filled with concerns, fears, and anger. I am trying to let them express these emotions but also to steer them toward thinking about solutions and what they individually, we as a school community, and our governmental bodies can do about it.

Content Area Writing

My "book board" is off to a successful start. I selected 50 titles from our classroom library that are at a variety of reading levels and that are generally popular with my fourth graders. I then wrote these titles on sheets of white paper and covered the back bulletin board with them. I had Chip, Mort, and Paul measure and cut red, blue, and yellow construction paper into 10 cm × 5 cm rectangles. These rectangles were put into pockets I made along the bottom of the bulletin board. Now that all was ready, I gathered my children together and announced a new contest. In this contest, books, not people, were going to be the winners. Together, we read the titles of the 50 books. Among these were books a few of my children had already read and they commented briefly on them. I then explained that whenever they read one of these 50 books, they were to decide what color best describes the book. If it was "super—a book everyone should read," they would put their name on a red rectangle and attach this rectangle to the appropriate white sheet. If the book was "awful—boring—a waste of time," they would put their name on a yellow rectangle and attach this rectangle. Of course, if the book was "OK—enjoyable or informative but nothing super special," that book would get a blue rectangle with their name on it. "From time to time," I explained, "we will have discussions during which you can tell us why you think a certain book rated a red or a yellow."

Literature Response Activity

The board has been there only four weeks and already there are many red, yellow, and blue autographed rectangles attached to several of the books. The children love to see their names and ratings attached to the books. When they see a book with several red rectangles, they all try to get it and read it. One book has three yellow rectangles. Now everyone is reading it to see if it is "really that bad"! Pat has rounded up extra copies of several books from the public library and Danielle's dad bought her several paperback titles at the bookstore.

The book board is a new idea I tried this year and so far I am delighted with the results. The children are motivated to read and attach their ratings to the books. I have seen classrooms in which the number of books read by each child was kept up with and in some cases rewarded with T-shirts or rewards. While I think it does encourage some children to read, I also have noticed that some children start reading only very short books or very easy books. The goal seems to become the number of books read rather than the enjoyment and appreciation of the books. Because the book board keeps up with how many children have read and how they rated each book rather than how many books each child has read, children are motivated to read many books but not to just accumulate titles. We have had two book discussions so far. Both were lively interchanges in which some children tried to convince others that the book was really a "red" or really a "yellow." I was reminded of the deadly dull oral book reports I had my students do during my first year of teaching. How could I have done that???

Assessment

Our afternoon individual and group work time is progressing quite smoothly. This started out being a time when I worked individually or in small groups with children who needed help with specific skills or strategies in any area of reading, language arts, or math. I have a notebook in which I have pages for important reading, language arts, and math skills and strategies. When I observe, based on their written work or their oral responses, that individuals are having difficulty with something, I write their name on the page that has that skill or strategy. When I have several names and enough time, I pull the children together for a focused lesson.

I also have a page in my notebook for each child. On this page, I write down any observations that don't fit on the specified skills/strategies pages. When I notice something an individual child is having trouble with, I write that down on that child's page and I call the children individually and work with them for a few minutes each. Afterward, I write on that page the date, how well the instruction went, and whether or not I need to work some more on it.

Individual Differences

This week I worked with Paul, Daisy, Chip, Butch, and Tanana on reading short informational passages and then organizing the information into a web. I worked with Butch, Chip, Tanana, Manuel, Joyce, and Mort on paragraph writing. I spent a few minutes individually with Horace, showing him the correct way to write quotations, with Daphne on dividing two-digit numbers, and with Tanana on making predictions as you read.

Children with Special Needs

Each day, I spend 10 to 15 minutes reading and writing with Paul. Although not a good reader for fourth grade, he can read and write better than I initially thought. When he is having a good day, he can independently read material at a beginning second-grade level. I have been letting him choose what he wants us to read together. He has a special notebook and each day after we read, he writes (with my help) a couple of sentences about the book we have read. He is now able to compose and correctly write simple sentences, and I am going to expand the writing to include more complex sentences and paragraphs. Recently, he has gotten into the *Curious George* books and he is reading every one I can find. He also enjoys rereading them during SQUIRT time and listening to the tapes that come with some of the books. He and Daphne are fast friends and sometimes he reads *Curious George* books with her and I also see her reading other books he chooses to him. Paul is one of those children you never stop worrying about. He is sad and withdrawn much of the time but has times when he appears involved and happier. I am just grateful that he is here at Merritt where just about every teacher accepts the fact that, even with the best instruction, not all children will function at grade level and that all children—especially the less able ones—need TLC.

The children who are not working with me do a variety of things while I am working with others. Sometimes they work alone but, usually, they work in pairs or in cooperative groups. I have centers on the periphery of the room and children can always be found in these centers. In addition to the computer center, the writing center, the library center, the listening center, the math center, and the art center, which are always options, I now have a pollution center in which the children are working on some science experiments related to pollution. Most of the time the children are working on activities of their own choosing, but sometimes I do assign them specific things to do during this time—often as follow-up practice after I have worked with them. This is also the time when projects begun during our morning unit time are carried out and when further research is done. Miss Page has an open door policy in the library and most days some of my children are in the library researching some part of our unit topic.

Last week I had visitors during this afternoon time, and they had difficulty understanding who was doing what. I explained that I use this time to make sure that I am meeting the needs of all of the children I teach. I showed them my notebook and explained how I form groups. I also explained that if the children are not working with me, I have them working on something they need to work on—or something they choose to work on. It is a little hard to figure out if you just come in and watch what is happening. But the students and I know what we are doing—most of the time!

I tried a different content comprehension lesson plan this month—the guided reading procedure (Manzo, 1975). To begin with, I chose a short selection from a magazine article on one city's successful attempt to clean up its waterways. I had this passage typed and duplicated and gave it to the entire class with the instructions to "read to remember everything." After approximately 10 minutes when I observed that most of the children had finished the selection, I told them that if they had finished, they should turn the selection facedown on their desks and that if they had not yet finished they should continue reading until they were finished. I then asked them what they remembered from their reading and recorded everything they told me on the chalkboard, numbering each response. Every once in a while, when their responses seemed to stop, I would say, "Listen as I read what we already have on the board and see if you can remember anything else." Eventually they had exhausted their memories. I asked them to listen again as I reread what was on the board and told them that when I had finished reading I would allow them one minute to reread portions of the article to correct any inconsistencies or misinformation recorded on the board.

There was, of course, some misinformation on the board, and the children couldn't wait to get back to the text to prove it. When Hilda said, "Number twenty-seven is not right. It should be . . . ," I responded, "Can you read me the part of the text that lets you know that?" Hilda then read that part aloud to verify her statement and the class agreed that number 27 was indeed incorrect.

Centers

Comprehension
Strategy Lesson

We then corrected it. In addition to correcting misinformation, the children added other bits of information they had missed or forgotten during the first reading.

Next, I asked them to listen again as I read the information on the board, but this time they were to listen and try to decide which ideas seemed to be the main idea, the most important ideas, the ideas they would like to remember or tell someone else if that someone asked them what the story had been all about. I phrased "main idea" in this way so that the children began to conceptualize that very elusive concept of main idea. After I read the items one final time, several children suggested what seemed to be the main ideas, and I circled them. Different children had different notions about which were really the main ideas, but I circled all they suggested and then reminded them that we could all agree that each item on the board was written in the text. Choosing the main ideas was, to some extent, I explained, a matter of personal judgment: "What is most important to one person may not be most important to someone else." If the children had asked me to circle an inordinately large number of items, I would have done so, and as we finished, I would have said something like "Now, as you know, not everyone would agree on which ideas are the most important. If I had to select the main ideas here, I believe I would select numbers four, six, and twenty-seven." I would then read those three items and explain that these three seemed to me to tell what the selection was primarily about and that the other items explain these three. In this way, I would try to model for them the complex process of selecting main ideas.

Finally, I asked them to take out a sheet of paper and number it from 1 to 5. While they were doing this, I erased the board. I then read them five true-false items I had constructed prior to the lesson. The children responded by putting a *T* or *F* on their papers. When we had finished the five-item quiz, I reread the items and we decided whether each was true or false. Each child checked his or her own paper.

The children then recorded the number they got correct by coloring in the appropriate area on a graph. One week later, I gave them a delayed-retention test on the information contained in the selection. I used five different true-false items but I tried to make the two tests equally difficult. Needless to say, the children did not do nearly as well on the second test. This is exactly what I wanted them to observe. To us, as adults, it is obvious that unless we make an effort and review information, we forget. Children, however, are quite unaware of this natural phenomenon. Last week, in fact, when I gave them the delayed test and they did not do nearly as well as on the first test, they accused me of making harder items for the second test. No explaining of mine could convince them otherwise. Mr. Ditto settled the controversy by suggesting that next time I should make up all 10 items ahead of time and put them in a hat. One child would then reach in and select 5 items that would be used for the immediate retention test and the others would be put away for the test one week later. I thought that was a brilliant suggestion, and I already have the 10 questions made up for the guided reading procedure I plan to do tomorrow.

February

What a strange month this has been! January, February, and March are supposed to be the calm, uninterrupted "teaching months" but so far they, like the rest of the year, have been extraordinary! I guess it all started when the legislature held the special session and we made our unexpected trip to the capital. The new water pollution bill was passed, by the way, and the time line committee added this momentous occasion as another event on their state time line. Mr. Stans did come to visit our class as he had promised and expressed astonishment at the children's political sophistication.

Then, Mr. Ditto came when I wasn't expecting to get a student teacher this year, and, as a result of his being here, I have been asked to leave my class in March and go to the university! It seems that one of the professors over there has been in the hospital for months and they are very shorthanded. She had been scheduled to teach a special seminar on the integrated curriculum during the spring quarter and there is no one else who can teach it. Dr. Link's plan is that Mr. Ditto should take over my class for the rest of the year and I should go to the university. She had already discussed this with Mr. Topps and the university administration before she let me in on her plans, so I guess the decision is mine. My first instinct was to say no immediately. How could I leave my children in the middle of the year? But, upon reflection, I had to admit that, with the exception of Daisy, the children would thrive under Mr. Ditto's continued tutelage. Next, I thought, "But I can't teach a university seminar. What could I tell them? How would I teach it?" But then I remembered some of the terrible graduate classes I sat through when I was working on my master's degree and I remembered wondering if the professors who taught our college classes could survive, let alone thrive, in a class of real children. At least I could bring some realism to that seminar. I am tempted . . . and I have one week in which to decide!

We have now completed four guided reading procedures and the children do, indeed, seem to be increasing their long-term memory of what they read. This month, I tried some "translation writing" experiences with Paul, Daisy, Butch, Jeff, Chip, Joyce, and Tanana. I got the notion for translation writing when I was reading through an old book that I stumbled across (Burton, 1952). Being curious about what educational methods were being expounded in the forties, I perused the book. One chapter was on the unit approach to teaching, which, while different in several ways, bears some striking similarities to what I call my "integrated approach." In one chapter, a fifth-grade teacher describes some of the activities she did with the children as part of her "colonial life unit." One of these activities she called "cooperative stories." To do a cooperative story, she sat down with the children who were not very able readers, read a portion of a book to them, and then had them tell her what they heard. She then recorded what they told her on the board and had them copy that "cooperative story" into their notebooks. In this way, the less able readers constructed a textbook at their own reading level.

Shared Writing

As I was reading this, I thought of Paul, Daisy, Butch, Jeff, and Chip, whose reading skills are still not sophisticated enough to read the complex materials that we often need to read to gain information for our units. I vowed to try what I termed "translation writing" with them. I worried, however, that if I took these particular five children to work with me while the rest of the class worked with Mr. Ditto, the five I was working with might feel segregated because they don't read as well. I then hit upon the idea of including Joyce and Tanana in the group. While Joyce is a very good reader, her oral expression skills are not nearly as sophisticated. Tanana, while also a good reader, is hesitant to speak out in front of the group. I knew that with Joyce and Tanana added to the original five, no one would even think to label my translation writing group as a "slow group."

The lessons were fun. I, unlike the teacher in the forties, did not have the children copy the story into their notebooks. Rather, I wrote it as they all sat around the table, then I typed it and had seven copies made. Thank goodness for some aspects of modern technology! The other children were intrigued and the members of my group read their stories to everyone. Now, of course, everyone wants to do it. Hilda remarked that this was "just like we used to do in first grade." Roberta informed her that the topics we were discussing were, as Mr. Stans had said, "sophisticated"!

February was also parent conference month. I made it a point to include Mr. Ditto in all the conferences, both because he needs to build confidence in dealing with parents, and because, if I leave, I want the parents to have met him. Daisy's mother will be furious if I leave. She just bragged and bragged about how well Daisy has done this year and how much more ladylike she has become. She is convinced that Daisy's only problem has been that she hasn't had a good teacher before!

Assessment I have added a whole-class polysyllabic decoding lesson to my afternoon skills time. I realized that many of the children have real difficulty figuring out big words. To find out which particular children needed instruction in decoding polysyllabic words, I constructed a list of 10 words of three or more syllables that I doubted most children know as sight words (*absorbent, deduction, admission, transformation, magnificent, concentration, apologetic, personality, uncontrollable, representative*). I then had each child read the list to me. Paul could not read any and in fact could not even make a good guess. Butch and Alex each got one right. The other children could read from two to seven, except for Larry who read them all!

Decoding Based on these results, I decided to include the whole class in the instruction. Daisy, Paul, Butch, and Alex aren't really ready for polysyllabic words, so I include some two-syllable words and provide the decoding instruction they need. Larry does not like to be separated from the others and is helpful in explaining how you figure out words.

We take the first 10 minutes of the skills time for this whole-class decoding lesson. I do several things during this time. One thing I always do is to model for them how to figure out a big word and then let them try to figure out a big word and explain how they did it. I always put the word in a sentence context so that we can make sure the word we figured out makes sense in the sentence. I try to construct the sentences so that sometimes the sentence context helps you figure out the word whereas other times the context is not very helpful. I usually try to make the sentences relate to some topic of interest to my students. Here are the sentences I used related to the topic of weddings, which all of the girls (except Roberta and Hilda!) find interesting but which was not a big hit with most of the boys.

Some people want a big <u>wedding</u>.
Others invite only close friends and <u>relatives</u>.
Some couples <u>elope</u>!
Some couples keep their <u>engagement</u> a secret.
Other couples have a party and <u>announce</u> their engagement!

In this example, I modeled how to figure out the word *wedding*. I read the whole sentence, saying ''blank'' when I got to the underlined word and then said something like this:

This one is simple. It is *wed* with the *d* doubled and *ing* at the end. *Wedding* makes sense in the sentence because some people do have big weddings.

I then had the class read the rest of the sentences, saying ''blank'' for the underlined word, and let different children figure out the word, tell how they figured it out, and explain how it made sense. Betty explained that ''relatives had to go in the next sentence because friends and relatives were all you invited to weddings.'' Roberta argued that you could invite other people and that besides, relatives are called relations—so the word would be *relations*. I agreed that *relations* would fit the context and had a lot of the same letters as *relatives* and then asked what letters let you know the word was *relatives* rather than *relations*. I then wrote *relations* next to *relatives* and pointed out the difference in the last chunks of the two words. Some children still seemed confused, so I tried to think of words they might know and came up with *active* and *action*. I wrote these words and showed them that *active* had the same last chunk as *relative*, and *action* had the same last chunk as *relation*. This seemed to help and was additional modeling for them of how you can use words you know to figure out words you don't know.

Elope was difficult for them. I don't think it is a word most of them have in their meaning vocabularies. I wrote *equal* and *electric* to help them with the *e* and *hope* and *rope* to help with the *lope*. Horace then explained in graphic detail how his aunt had eloped!

Hilda explained that *engagement* was just *engage* with *ment* on the end. Steve used the context and letters to figure out *announce*. Both *engagement* and *announce* turned out to be words many students did not have meanings for, so we had to explain them! I think I will stick with a less romantic topic next time!

Interestingly, when I decided to do this whole-group decoding instruction, I had not realized how much concept development was going to go on during this time. The problem many students have with big words is that they can't decode them and even after they do decode them, they can't tell if they are right because they have never heard the word before and don't know if it makes sense in the sentence. I try to choose words I think most of them have meanings for, but often I find that I assumed more knowledge than they had. I will continue to try to choose words they do have meanings for, and when I am wrong, I will just see it as one more opportunity for concept development.

Multicultural Awareness

We have done many activities this month in celebration of Black History Month. I read them several excellent biographies of famous African Americans, including *Jesse Jackson* by Patricia McKissack, *Frederick Douglass Fights for Freedom* by Margaret Davidson, *Freedom Train: The Story of Harriet Tubman* by Dorothy Sterling, and *I Have a Dream: The Story of Martin Luther King* by Margaret Davidson. I also read them some fiction that had strong African-American main characters, including *A Girl Called Boy* by Belinda Hurmence and *Phoebe the Spy* by Judith Berry Griffin. We talked a lot about biographies and my children once again amazed me by informing me that autobiographies were when you wrote about yourself! When they say how surprised I was that they knew this, they explained about the "When I Was Your Age" tales that Mrs. Wright used to write and that they convinced Miss Nouveau to write. I was amazed at how interested the children were in biographies and autobiographies, so we have launched a research/publishing project. All the children have chosen some currently living famous person and we are going to publish a book of biographies. Their chosen people run the gamut from sports heroes to rock stars to politicians to actors and actresses. They are researching their chosen people now, using resources including *TV Guide* and *Sports Illustrated.* We have posted a list in the room of who is researching whom and almost every day children bring in things for each other that they have found in newspapers, magazines, and other sources. This project is an exciting one and my children have already asked Miss Page about having it be "a real book in the library."

March (Mr. Ditto's Journal)

I have always heard the expression "Two heads are better than one." Now I know it was referring to two teachers' heads! I really didn't realize how much I would miss Ms. Maverick, I was so excited about being able to stay with this class. But I do miss her. She comes in every Thursday afternoon and we plan activities together, but that is not the same as having her here every day. Just having another adult around sometimes is important, but I guess most teachers have to do it all, all day, every day, by themselves. Maybe I'll team-teach with someone next year! I guess the success of that would depend on who that "someone" is!

This month has gone well. Ms. Maverick seems pleased with what we've done here while she's been working at the university. Fortunately, she left all her materials here for me to use. I can see that if I try to do this type of program next year, I will have to spend quite a lot of time over the summer gathering materials on the topics around which I plan to build units. (Each week Ms. Maverick comes to our planning session and gathers up something to take with her and share with her students. She brings it back the next week, however, and so far I have not had to spend a great deal of time hunting material.)

So far the children have adapted exceedingly well to the change. They miss Ms. Maverick, however, and, for the first week, they were more unruly than usual. Ms. Maverick had warned me, however, that they would test me after she left, so I was prepared. I made a special effort to be fair and firm, and to continue the usual routines. In spite of my resolve, there were occasional laments of "Ms. Maverick never did it that way!"

Daisy is the only one who seems damaged by Ms. Maverick's leaving. Ms. Maverick is very worried about her, and even invited Daisy to her house after school to try to minimize the trauma. Daisy's mother refused to let Daisy go, however, and even wrote a very angry note to the school board concerning Ms. Maverick's unprofessional behavior in leaving her class. I try to be nice to Daisy and not to push her too much, but she simply does not respond positively. Her dislike of me is quite apparent. I just don't know what to do. I hope that if I am gentle and patient, she will eventually come around.

Chip, on the other hand, is a delight! I can almost see him growing each day—physically as well as mentally. He has grown several inches since Christmas and has put on several pounds. Most important, he is beginning to get involved with books! We are now up to 21 minutes of SQUIRT time each day. Chip loves mystery stories and folktales and takes a book home almost every night.

While I have tried to follow our routines just as we did when Ms. Maverick was here, I have experimented with a new teaching strategy. For some time now, I have been curious about why children seem to understand what they listen to so much better than what they read. Even when they can read most of the words, they often have a great deal of difficulty reading for a specific purpose. I discussed this with a friend who is still a student, and she suggested I try listening-reading transfer lessons (Cunningham, 1975). To do a listening-reading transfer lesson, the teacher uses two selections (or two sections of one long selection; I chose selections that related to our unit). One of these selections is read to the children and the other is used for them to read. From these selections, I identified several unfamiliar concepts in the selection that I was going to read to them, as well as some unknown words and unfamiliar concepts in the one they were going to read. I also decided what to do about these unfamiliar concepts and unknown words; as often as possible I try to lead the children to derive the meaning of unfamiliar concepts and the pronunciation of unfamiliar words from the context of the story, in order to encourage them to become independent readers. Usually, I write the unfamiliar concepts or unknown words on the board and ask them to see if they can figure out the meaning/pronunciation of these words. Often, after listening to or reading the selection and determining what the word seems to mean because of the way it is used and because of the other words around it, we look up the word in the dictionary, read the several definitions, and decide which one applies. We then compare our guess against the dictionary definitions and usually decide that the

Comprehension Strategy Lesson

context of the story gave us a rather good notion of at least one meaning for that word.

Next, I decide on a purpose for having the students listen to or read the selection. To facilitate the transfer from listening to reading, I set the same purpose for both the listening and the reading part of the activity.

Last week I taught a listening-reading transfer lesson designed to help the children improve their sequencing abilities. I began by putting the word *rectify* on the board and asking the children to listen for this word as I read the selection and to try to figure out its meaning by the way it was used and by the other words in the story. I then taped to the chalkboard several sentence strips on which I had written the major events of the story. I read these events to the children and set the purpose for listening. "Listen as I read so you can help me put these events, which are now jumbled, into the order in which they occur in the story." After listening to the story, the children helped me rearrange the strips to put the events in their proper order and explained how they knew which should go first, second, and so on. We then discussed how *rectify* was used and several children suggested that it must mean "to fix something." We determined that the other words that let us know that *rectify* had to do with fixing were *broken*, *repair*, and *breakdown*. Hilda then looked up *rectify* in the dictionary and read us the appropriate dictionary definition. We added *rectify* to our wall vocabulary as part of our Things People Do topical word set. This ended the listening part of the listening-reading transfer lesson.

On the following day, I gave the children a selection to read and a dittoed sheet on which I had written the major events of that story. I then put the words *candid* and *sword* on the board. I pronounced *candid* for them and told them that the other words in the selection would help them figure out part of the meaning for *candid*. I told them that they all knew the meaning for the other word, but that many of them might not recognize it immediately and be able to pronounce it. I told them that as they read they would be able to figure out what the word was. Having alerted them to one unfamiliar concept and one unknown word, I then reminded them of the listening lesson we had done the day before and how we had reordered the events of the story after listening to it.

"That is exactly what I want you to do today. Only today, instead of listening to me read, you will read the story and reorder the events. First, read the list of events, then read the story. Then use your scissors to cut the events into strips and reorder them just as we did with the strips on the board yesterday."

The children immediately formed reading pairs. These pairs have been set up for months now, and each pair contains a good reader and a less able one. This works out amazingly well and allows me to occasionally give the whole class the same selection to read. After reading the events and then the selection, the children cut and pasted the events in order. We then discussed the order and the reasoning behind that order, and noted that *sword* was what a knight carried, and that to be *candid* was to be outspoken or frank. *Candid* was added to our Describing People topical word set. Finally, I helped the children to observe that what they can do after listening, they can do after reading.

I have also done a listening-reading transfer lesson in which the children

Meaning Vocabulary

Partners

selected a main idea for each paragraph, and, next week, I plan to do one in which they match certain causes with certain effects. Ms. Maverick says she always preached that a teacher must teach for transfer and that she can't imagine why she never thought about doing that.

April

Our unit this month has been on Alaska. Ms. Maverick and I have long been concerned about helping Tanana adapt to our culture, and it occurred to us last month that one way to help her feel more comfortable with us would be for us to learn more about her and her home. Tanana was a great resource during this unit and helped us empathize with native Alaskans who see their traditional ways threatened by the advance of civilization.

Unit Teaching

We have gathered and used many books about Alaska and, as a member of the American Automobile Association, I was able to get many maps and brochures from them. I read the class two informational books, *In Two Worlds: A Yup'ik Eskimo Family* by Aylette Jenness and Alice Rivers and *The Igloo* by Charlotte and David Yue. I have also read them some contemporary fiction with Aleutians as main characters, including *Julie of the Wolves* by Jean Craighead George.

The children and I are on an imaginary journey and we have a time machine that allows us to move back and forth in time as we move through the vast and diverse state of Alaska. The children are all keeping logs of our trip and each day they record the date, place, temperature, and so forth and their thoughts and feelings about all that we are seeing. At first I was afraid that the children might consider the time machine and log idea kind of "hokey," but they have wonderful imaginations and delight in using them and are clearly into our Alaska adventure.

After talking with Mrs. Wright, the first-grade teacher, I decided to try a "List, Group, and Label" lesson as a kickoff to our unit. I asked the children to tell me all the words they thought of when they heard the word *Alaska*, and listed them on the board. When the children had exhausted their Alaska vocabulary, I read the entire list to them and asked them to listen as I was reading for any that seemed to go together in some way. Mrs. Wright had suggested that the next step was to let individual children list the things they felt went together, tell why they put them together, and give a label to that group. I did this, but in order to get greater participation, I let each child write on a slip of paper the items he or she wanted to put together. Individuals then read their lists and responded to my questions on why they had put those words together and what they would call that group. When each child who desired to had read his or her group to us, had explained the reason for grouping, and had labeled the group, I suggested that each one of them make another group that was different from any they had already made. We then repeated the explaining and labeling process with these second groups.

Meaning Vocabulary

This seems to be a very effective technique to use to begin a unit. I learned what kind of prior knowledge and preconceptions the children had about Alaska, and they began thinking about Alaska and using the specialized vocabulary: *caribou, Aleuts, pipeline.* I also think it helps their classification skills and thus their thinking skills. I plan to begin many units with a "List, Group, and Label" lesson.

Discussing
One thing that I tried this month was not quite as successful, at least not at first. Ms. Maverick had always had the children in small groups to discuss various topics, so, of course, I planned for some small-group discussions too. The first ones were awful. I let them form their own groups and told them to discuss the pros and cons of Alaska's development. Absolutely nothing happened! They just sat there and looked at each other! When I told Ms. Maverick of my failure, she said, "The one direction that will ensure no discussion is to tell them 'Discuss!' If you want them to discuss, give them some concrete task to do that will require discussion for its successful resolution." She also suggested that I form groups that will remain constant over a period of several weeks so that the children in those groups will develop some group pride in what they accomplish. She further suggested that we spread the rowdy ones, the leaders, the quiet ones, and the "outcasts" among the groups. These are the five groups we formed.

Daisy	Paul	Butch	Mitch	Mort
Alex	*Betty	Carl	Chip	Daphne
*Rita	Hilda	*Joyce	*Pat	Horace
Larry	Manuel	Roberta	Tanana	*Mandy
Alexander	Anthony	Steve	Danielle	Jeff

We then planned the following structured discussion. The children were told which group they would be in and where their group would meet (the four corners and the center of the room). They then practiced getting quickly into their groups and ready to begin. Once they were in their groups, I gave them a card with their names on it and explained that the person whose name had a star next to it would be the recorder for that group for the day and would do all the writing for the group. (We picked the recorders according to their ability in spelling and writing.)

I then gave each group index cards and a felt marker and told them they had five minutes to list the resources of Alaska. They were asked to write only one resource on each index card because they would use the cards later. Since they had seen a film a few days before on Alaska's resources, and many had read about Alaska's resources in various source books, they had no difficulty thinking of resources. When the timer rang to signal the end of the five minutes, each group had a stack of cards and was still talking!

Next, I gave them two large sheets of construction paper and some tape. On the top of one sheet of construction paper, I had written "Resources that will be used up" and on the other, "Resources that will last forever." I explained the concept of renewable and nonrenewable resources to them, and gave them a few examples from our local resources. I then gave them 10 minutes to tape each of their index cards to one of the construction paper sheets. The discussion that ensued was lively and topical! Ms. Maverick had been right again. Once they had a task to do that required discussion and a strict time limit in which to complete that task, there was no dawdling or silence. (Never again will I instruct a group to "discuss" unless, of course, I want a few rare moments of silence in this otherwise noisy room.) Once the 10 minutes were up, we displayed the charts and compared the results. When two groups had put the same resource in two different categories, the groups explained their reasoning, and if we could come to any resolution, the resource was changed to the appropriate chart. In several cases, we decided we would have to do a little research to resolve a controversy—an unexpected bonus of our first successful discussion!

I have been continuing the guided reading procedures as Ms. Maverick began them but have also initiated guided listening procedures. Every other week, we do a full procedure in which the children have 10 minutes to read a selection, list what they remember, skim the selection to verify or correct inconsistencies, identify main ideas, and complete a five-item nonreading quiz. In the intervening week, we do the delayed retention quiz. The children have increased in their ability to remember information over a one-week time span and they are very pound of this growth, which is vividly displayed on their guided reading procedure charts.

I got to thinking that if the procedure was good for reading, it should also be good for listening! Last week, I tried it. I had planned to read to the class an editorial from an Alaskan newspaper. I brought a tape recorder to class and asked the children to listen to remember everything. I then read them the editorial and taped my reading. Once finished, I asked them what they remembered and listed what they told me on the board. When they had exhausted their memories, I replayed the tape, telling them to listen to make sure the information on the board was correct, and to raise their hands to stop the tape if they heard anything that contradicted the information on the board. They found several pieces of incorrect information and seemed to really enjoy this new strategy. We then circled main ideas, and I gave them a quiz. They all wanted to know if I was going to give them a delayed quiz next week and if they were going to keep a chart. I hadn't planned to be this systematic about it, but they seem to want to! They certainly did listen attentively and knew what that editorial said. I think I will do guided listening procedures on the off-week for guided reading procedures. I wonder what Ms. Maverick will say when I tell her about this!

Comprehension Strategy Lesson

May

What a terrific month this has been. I started the month a little "down," realizing that this year was ending with so much left undone and that I still had to find a job for next year. I knew I would never find a school like this one. I had made up my mind, however, that I believed in the integrated approach to teaching, and that I would move elsewhere to find a school that would allow me to follow through on my beliefs.

You can imagine my surprise when, as I was relaying my concerns and convictions to Ms. Maverick, she informed me that she knew just the principal I ought to talk to—Mr. Topps! While conducting the seminar at the university, Ms. Maverick had become even more convinced of her approach to teaching and to children, and had decided that she would stay on at the university as a graduate student in administration and supervision so that she could get her principal's certificate. Although Mr. Topps was sorry to lose her, he agreed that the principal could be an effective change-agent in the schools, and admitted that this factor had weighed heavily in his decision to become a principal. I, of course, quickly applied for Ms. Maverick's job, and although the school board has not yet acted officially, Mr. Topps assured me that they will approve his recommendation. So, I have found a job in a school that will let me teach according to my beliefs! Ms. Maverick has even agreed to leave most of her materials here. While I am delighted at this turn of events, I am also somewhat apprehensive. Even with her materials, planning this program all alone and starting a whole new class of children in this approach will not be easy.

Ms. Maverick was away at a national reading meeting at the beginning of the month and since then has been busy finishing up her seminar. The annual book fair thus became totally my responsibility. And while I survived and it got done, it was not as well planned as I would have liked. We ordered the books for the fair from several publishers of paperback books. We got catalogues, and the children met in groups to decide how many copies of each title they thought we might sell. (Fortunately, the publishers take back and credit us for any books that are not sold!) Once the books were ordered, we began to plan how to organize and promote our sale. As is traditional, the books are first put on display for sale on the evening of the last parents' meeting. My children wrote flyers encouraging the parents to come to the final meeting and informing them that many good, inexpensive paperback books would be on sale that evening. Parents were encouraged to buy the books for their children to have something new and exciting to read during the long summer months.

We then made posters that were hung in the various classrooms of our school and in the local supermarket and drugstore. A group of children composed an announcement about the book fair that they sent to the newspaper, and another group composed an announcement that was read several times a day on the local radio station.

With our advertisement campaign well under way, we began to plan how we would organize ourselves for the actual sale. After much discussion, it was decided that we would divide all the books according to topic and display them on cafeteria tables set up in the halls. We then began a lengthy classification procedure during which we looked at the titles of the books we had ordered and tried to place them in appropriate categories. After several days of discussion and argument about what the categories should be, I saw that we were getting nowhere except closer to the night of the fair. Obviously I had to provide some direction or we weren't going to make it! I then sat down with the lists and established eight categories, plus a ninth category for miscellaneous books. The next day I wrote the category names on the board and had the children get into the groups they had been in for the ordering. Each group took nine sheets of paper, put the name of one category on each sheet, and decided in which category each book they had ordered belonged. While we did have several disagreements and a lot of books relegated to "miscellaneous," we finally got our lists made. The children made a first or second choice for which books they would like to sell, and I formed them into groups of two or three based on these choices.

When the books finally arrived (only one day ahead of the fair!), it was a fairly easy job to sort them and put them in piles according to category. Then, on the afternoon of the fair, each group set up their displays. Several children who lived quite far away stayed with me at school until the parents arrived at 7:00 P.M., watching over our displays, doing some last minute "advertisement," and eating the three pizzas I had ordered. (The ones who had gone home for supper were not too pleased when the ones who stayed bragged about having pizza for supper, but you just can't please everyone no matter how hard you try!)

We sold books out in the hall that evening to the parents and all the next morning to the children who came out of their classrooms at scheduled times. We then took the 100-plus remaining books back to our room, put them on the back table, and sold about 20 more to children and teachers during the remainder of that week. Finally, on Friday, we boxed up the unsold books and shipped them back to the companies from which they had come. We also totaled our money and figured which books we would order with the profits. We decided that each child could order one free bonus book, and that with the remainder of the profits we would order books for the classroom's already large paperback library. I didn't know until I was almost through with this project that I would be in charge of it again next year!

We have been having SQUIRT time for 24 minutes for the last two weeks of this month. While this is a minute short of the 25 minutes Ms. Maverick thought they could reach, I think it is quite a long time for fourth graders to sit still and read intently. I am proud of them!

Self-Selected Reading

Since Ms. Maverick was invited to the university, people in the school system have suddenly become curious about her approach to teaching. She has been asked to address the final meeting of one of the local professional organizations and has requested that I join her on the podium. At first I protested that I had nothing to say to teachers that they would be willing to listen to, but Ms. Maverick argued that I could answer some of their questions about beginning to teach with this method. When I hesitated, she asked whether I felt strange about going because I knew that my first supervising teacher and many of the other teachers in that school would be there. I had to admit that I wasn't looking forward to meeting those people who represented my failure as a teacher. She said that that was exactly the point: I was not a failure—simply misplaced—and that was precisely the reason I should be present at the meeting, even if I didn't say a word. I have had my orders and am going, and I have even begun to think I may enjoy it!

THE PROFESSIONAL MEETING

Mrs. Wright called the meeting to order, made a few business announcements, and then said, "As many of you know, I use a multimethod, multilevel approach to get my first graders off to the most successful start possible in reading and writing. While I believe in this method for beginning readers, I realize that there are many valid approaches to the teaching of reading and that each teacher's approach must be one he or she is comfortable with and one that meets the needs of the children being taught. I have for the past five years been able to observe the results of Ms. Maverick's integrated curriculum. Often she teaches in fourth grade a group of children I had in first grade, and I am always pleased to watch these children grow in independence, self-awareness, and real-world concern under Ms. Maverick's direction. I must confess that until this year when Mr. Ditto took over Ms. Maverick's class and carried on just as she always had, I thought that Ms. Maverick's teaching method was really peculiar to her own style and personality. I have seen, however, that this was not the case, and that given the desire and the will, one can learn to teach an integrated curriculum. It gives me great personal pleasure, therefore, to introduce to you this afternoon my friend and colleague, Ms. Maverick, and her protégé, Mr. Ditto."

Ms. Maverick rose, but before she began her address made a confession to Mrs. Wright: "I must admit, Mrs. Wright, that I always thought your teaching was peculiar to *your* style and personality!" As the group nodded their appreciation of this humorous but candid confession, Ms. Maverick began her presentation.

Content Area Integration

"One of the main reasons that I teach an integrated curriculum is that there are never, for me, enough hours in the teaching day. When I help my children become better readers, more precise language users, and more competent mathematicians as they learn science and social studies content, I get almost twice the mileage out of my instructional time. I believe this is a principle that can be applied to learners of any age. Today, rather than lecture you about the wisdom of this economy, I am going to demonstrate it with you.

"While I use many teaching strategies in my integrated curriculum, a new one that I have tried out this year and that I am most impressed with is the guided reading procedure. Mr. Ditto is presently passing out to you copies of a summary of my instructional program, which I wrote. I would like you to read this summary to remember *everything*. When you have completed reading this, I will demonstrate for you the steps in the guided reading procedure."

Ms. Maverick then sat down and after a few moments the teachers realized that she did indeed intend for them to read the summary and they settled down to do so. When most of the teachers had finished reading the summary, Ms. Maverick reminded them that she had asked them to read to remember everything and asked them what they remembered. At first no one responded, but Mrs. Flame finally said, "You take a four-pronged approach." Ms. Maverick smiled and wrote Mrs. Flame's response on the overhead transparency. Slowly, others began to volunteer bits and pieces of what they remembered reading. Ms. Maverick recorded their contributions, numbering each as she went along:

1. You take a four-pronged approach
2. Reading is Real
3. SQUIRT
4. Integrated units
5. Afternoon skills and strategies time

6. Each unit has three phases
7. In the beginning phase, you provide much input and try to build interest in the topic
8. You use a lot of real-world materials from newspapers and magazines
9. You read a lot of informational books connected to the unit
10. You read fiction too
11. You read all kinds of things aloud to broaden their personal reading interests
12. The children write many different kinds of things, content journals, letters, logs, biographies
13. You take field trips and bring real things into the classroom
14. At the end of each unit you do activities that help the children synthesize, organize, and evaluate what they have learned
15. You do lots of different types of comprehension lessons
16. You teach them how to chunk and decode big words

Once the teachers got going, they, just like the children, were able to fill the board with their pooled remembrances from the summary they had read. Ms. Maverick continued through the steps of the procedure with them, having them go back to the summary for one minute to correct any inconsistencies or supply missing information, identifying the main ideas, and then giving them a five-item, true-false quiz.

When she had finished the whole procedure, she explained to them the rationale for the guided reading procedure, that it was intended primarily to help children increase their long-term memory of what they read. She explained how Mr. Ditto had adapted this procedure to listening, and reported that the procedures did indeed seem to be effective in helping the children develop a mind-set to remember more of what they read and heard. She showed them Chip's GRP progress chart, which she had brought along.

"What I have just done with you is what I try to do with my children," Ms. Maverick went on to explain. "There was some content that I wanted to teach you—in this case, a summary of how my integrated curriculum works. At the same time, I wanted to help you increase your repertoire of teaching skills, so I used the guided reading procedure to teach you about my instructional program. Hopefully, you have experienced in the last forty minutes the kind of economy teaching I practice in my classroom."

The teachers seemed much warmer and more interested than they had when the meeting started, and Ms. Maverick reaffirmed her faith in the belief that a good teaching strategy is appropriate for learners of any age. Although there was not much time remaining, several questions were asked and answered. In one of the questions, an elderly teacher referred to Ms. Maverick's integrated approach as a radical approach. Ms. Maverick informed her that while her own version of it had certain unique characteristics, the notion that learning should be integrated was hardly new. She went on to cite references for this fact. She told them that Henry Morrison in 1931 had first pointed out the need for some external organization of subject matter to achieve internal learning products, and that he had condemned the fragmenting of the curriculum.

A young teacher indicated that he was very interested in trying the integrated curriculum approach, but that the intermediate grades in his school were departmentalized, allowing him only 45 minutes of reading time for each of six classes. Ms. Maverick indicated to him that one of the greatest values of the self-contained classroom, as she saw it, was that teaching of the different subject areas could be integrated, but that he certainly could include SQUIRT and some "reading is real" activities during this reading period.

The final question had to do with beginning an integrated curriculum, and, since the time had nearly elapsed, Ms. Maverick referred the questioner to Mr. Ditto and informed the audience that both she and Mr. Ditto would be glad to stay and talk with anyone individually after the meeting. Ms. Maverick was delighted to observe that Mr. Ditto was still excitedly talking with a group of young teachers after everyone else had cleared out and gone home.

ADD TO YOUR JOURNAL

 Ms. Maverick and Mr. Ditto have a unique approach to instruction. Many intermediate teachers do some integration but now many organize their day around topics, rather than around separate subjects. What do you see as the advantages of their integrated curriculum? What problems do you see in organizing your instruction as Ms. Maverick and Mr. Ditto do? Even if you cannot or do not choose to teach an integrated curriculum, there are many teaching strategies and organizational ideas you could adapt from this chapter. List the things you think you could do like Ms. Maverick and Mr. Ditto even if you are limited in the amount of integration you can do.

REFERENCES

Burton, W. H. (1952). *The guidance of learning activities.* New York: Appleton-Century-Crofts.

Cunningham, P. M. (1975). Transferring comprehension from listening to reading. *The Reading Teacher, 29,* 169–172.

Manzo, A. V. (1975). Guided reading procedure. *Journal of Reading, 18,* 287–291.

Morrison, H. C. (1931). *The practices of teaching in the secondary school.* Chicago: University of Chicago Press.

Preston, R. C. (1968). *Teaching social studies in the elementary school.* New York: Holt, Rinehart, & Winston.

Children's Books/Materials Cited

Anastasia on Her Own, by Lois Lowry, Dell, 1986.
The Borrowers, by Mary Norton, Harcourt Brace Jovanovich, 1989.
Charlotte's Web, by E. B. White, HarperCollins Children's Books, 1974.

Curious George books, by Margaret Rey & Alan Shalleck, Houghton Mifflin, various years.
Fabulous Facts about the 50 States, by Wilma Ross, Scholastic, 1989.
50 Simple Things Kids Can Do to Save the Earth, by The Earthworks Group, Scholastic, 1974.
Fourth Grade Is a Jinx, by Colleen O'Shaughnessy McKenna, Scholastic, 1989.
Frederick Douglass Fights for Freedom, by Margaret Davidson, Scholastic, 1989.
Freedom Train: The Story of Harriet Tubman, by Dorothy Sterling, Scholastic, 1987.
A Girl Called Boy, by Belinda Hurmence, Houghton Mifflin, 1990.
Greening the City Streets: The Story of Community Gardens, by Barbara Huff, Clarion, 1992.
The Igloo, by Charlotte & David Yue, Houghton Mifflin, 1992.
I Have a Dream: The Story of Martin Luther King, by Margaret Davidson, Scholastic, 1986.
In Two Worlds: A Yup'ik Eskimo Family, by Aylette Jenness & Alice Rivers, Scholastic, 1992.
Jesse Jackson, by Patricia McKissack, Scholastic, 1992.
Julie of the Wolves, by Jean Craighead George, HarperCollins, 1974.
Kid Heroes of the Environment, by The Earthworks Group, Earthworks, 1991.
Little House on the Prairie, by Laura Ingalls Wilder, HarperCollins, 1975.
Phoebe the Spy, by Judith Berry Griffin, Scholastic, 1989.
Sports Illustrated magazine.
Tales of a Fourth Grade Nothing, by Judy Blume, Dell, 1976.
Trouble at Marsh Harbor, by Susan Sharpe, Puffin Books, 1991.
TV Guide magazine.
The Way of the Grizzly, by Dorothy Hinshaw Patent, Houghton Mifflin, 1987.
Where the Bald Eagles Gather, by Dorothy Hinshaw Patent, Houghton Mifflin, 1990.
Where the Wild Horses Roam, by Dorothy Hinshaw Patent, Clarion, 1990.

C H A P T E R 15

Mr. Dunn: Fifth Grade

THE PARENT MEETING

Ed Dunn sat at his desk waiting for the parents to arrive. Five years before at this time he had been nervously rehearsing an almost-memorized speech, but this night he was much more confident. That first year of teaching had begun as a challenge, and he soon found himself floundering. Many of his students had difficulty reading their textbooks, and he had no idea what to do for them. He tried teaching phonics during reading class, but the students hated it, calling it babyish and boring. Happily, with help and guidance from Mr. Topps and other teachers, he began to meet the challenge. He planned activities that allowed all the students some measure of success. For instance, he found that having students write is a multilevel method that can play a major role in helping students learn social studies, science, health, and literature. He even discovered that student writing can play a minor, but important, role in teaching mathematics, particularly problem solving. By the end of the year, he had survived, if not thrived, and he believed that the students too had learned something.

Over the summers since then, Ed had taken several graduate courses in teaching reading and writing at the university. While there, he had asked specific questions of many professors and graduate students. He had read several books and articles beyond those assigned to him and had participated actively in his courses. In short, he had attempted to learn everything he could about teaching reading and writing to intermediate-grade students.

This year, especially, he felt he was ready to begin. He had learned many ways to provide materials and activities that take into account the many reading levels that inevitably are found in fifth grade. He had discovered that reading instruction actually can be provided while students read materials in content areas such as social studies, science, and health. And he had come to realize that students require opportunities to read independently for their own purposes. Now he was to welcome the parents of this year's class and tell them about the reading and writing program he had planned for their children.

After everyone had arrived and was seated, he began: "Good evening and welcome to your child's fifth-grade classroom. I am Ed Dunn, and I hope to get to know all of you as I teach your children this year. So far we are still getting acquainted, but they do seem to be an interesting group.

"During this meeting, I will first give you an overview of what we will be doing to improve reading, since that is the backbone of all our studies. Even in math, fifth graders need to be able to follow written directions and to deal successfully with word problems. And in the middle school next year, your children will be expected to read well enough to be independent learners.

Content Area Reading

"Mr. Ditto and I have talked at some length about the type of reading program your children had with Ms. Maverick and him last year. I was very impressed with their reading-to-learn approach. To some degree, my general approach to reading instruction can be seen as an extension of theirs. However, I intend to follow the traditional divisions among the content areas. By this I mean that we have periods of the day set aside specifically for literature, language arts, math, music, social studies, health, and science. This basically is the way your children will spend their school days in middle school, high school, and—if they go on—in college. I am introducing them to this format this year. The difference, of course, is that I teach all the subjects as we stay in our self-contained classroom.

"One of the most important reading goals that I have for your children is selective reading. Let me give you an example of what I mean by selective reading."

Mr. Dunn displayed the following short paragraph that he had written on an overhead transparency:

A man named Eric Thorvaldsson came to the island in 982 A.D. Eric had been exiled from Iceland for three years for killing another man. When he returned to Iceland, he wanted settlers to be eager to go to this land, so he made it sound attractive by calling it Greenland!

He turned to the parents. "What are some of the things you could do in order to learn this information?"

After some silence, Mrs. Penn raised her hand. "We could try to get a basic understanding of the passage, but I know there's more to it than that."

Mr. Moppet spoke out. "When I was in school, I simply memorized all of the information. I usually got As and Bs on the tests because I could produce practically anything the teacher wanted. Of course, I promptly forgot most everything I had memorized as soon as the test was over too."

The parents obviously could relate to Mr. Moppet's confession as Mr. Dunn noted many of them smiling and nodding their heads in agreement.

"That's exactly what I hope to keep your children away from in my class as I work on selective reading," Mr. Dunn said. "In the passage I've displayed on the overhead for you, there is quite a bit of information. Students could memorize facts such as the date Eric first came to Greenland, Eric's last name, the length of his exile, and so on. However, this year we will have extensive lessons on helping students independently determine what is important. This is the key to selective reading. It takes a long time for students to acquire this ability because determining what is important depends on numerous factors."

Comprehension Strategy Lesson

Ed Dunn continued: "Two other important reading goals that I have this year are to help your children learn from their content-area reading materials and to help them become more independent learners. For example, we will study a unit on matter and energy in science, and there are many concepts in this unit that your children probably have never encountered before. It's my job to help this class learn about things in this unit such as conductors, insulators, convection currents, waves, energy chains, collision systems, and many other concepts that probably are unfamiliar. The reading materials that Miss Launch and Mrs. Wright used in the primary grades generally contained information that your children had directly experienced inside or outside of class. But the emphasis now is on reading materials that contain new, unfamiliar information.

Study Strategies

"And not only do the youngsters need help understanding new ideas, they are expected to remember those ideas too. If you'll think back, after Miss Launch and Mrs. Wright had finished with a reading passage, they didn't check at a later date to see if your children had remembered the information in that passage. The information certainly was worthwhile, but in general it dealt with familiar things and the children did not need to spend time learning it. But now in fifth grade the emphasis is on learning unfamiliar information."

Ed Dunn paused for a second to see if the group was still with him. They seemed to be, so he pressed on to what he thought would be new to them.

Guided Reading

"I must confess to you that I am of two minds when it comes to helping students learn from their texts. First of all, I want to carefully guide your children through their materials so they know what information is important and how to deal with that information. I have a pretty good idea of what I think should be learned, and I want to make sure that all of it is highlighted. Because of this, I tend to be the one to tell the class what to read or listen for, and I then ask questions that call for extra thinking about that information. Often I will lecture or show a film that gets at the desired information. Unfortunately, there's a problem with this. The problem with this approach is that if I always choose the materials, always set the purposes for reading, and always follow up those purposes, then my students come to depend totally on me for guidance. They learn a good deal of information, but they become dependent learners. And one of the goals that I mentioned to you earlier is to help your children become independent learners of new, unfamiliar information.

Student Independence

"The reason I am of two minds when it comes to helping students learn from their texts is that I know I should not continually direct my class's reading. But I often worry that they will miss important information if I'm not out there telling them exactly what to look for. In other words, I want to direct your children's reading, but I also want to let them learn how to discover information by themselves. I believe I can strike the correct balance, although I must admit that sometimes that balance is hard to find."

Ed walked to a table with a computer on it at the side of the room. As the parents turned in their chairs to face him, he removed the dust cover from the machine. "Now I want to tell you about the writing-with-computers program that I have designed for your children.

Computers

"Fortunately, we have had a computer lab at Merritt Elementary since your children began coming here, and all classrooms have had a single computer in them. I'm sure, at this point, your children know more about computers than many of you do!"

Several parents nodded, chuckling and smiling.

"While we are fortunate to have a lab with enough computers in it so the largest class in our school can all be in there at the same time, Mr. Topps and I have felt it would be even better if we could have enough computers in the classroom so they could be an integral part of the entire instructional day. Because of the expense, that just has not been feasible. This year, however, I have exciting news for you. Last winter, I submitted a grant proposal that has been funded. This year, in this one classroom, we are going to have seven computers just like the one here that I have brought from home!"

He placed his hand on top of the color monitor. The parents were obviously impressed and pleased.

"Only during September, our class will be allowed to use the school's computer lab for forty-five minutes every afternoon. I will be in there with your children teaching them how to touch type on a keyboard. While all of your children have learned to hunt and peck on computers in the lower grades, they are now old enough and experienced enough with computers to become proficient in keyboarding. By the beginning of October, I will set up the seven new computers here in the room. Your children will not have mastered keyboarding by then, but they should be far enough along so they can write without keyboarding being a hindrance.

"The Angus Restaurant, my classroom's business partner again this year, has agreed to purchase seven computer tables with lockable wheels for us. With them, we will be able to rearrange the computers around the room depending on how we are using them at any particular time. As you can see if you look down at the floor, Mr. Topps has had three floor outlets installed around the room so that we can plug the computers in there as well as in the wall outlets.

"I am spending all of my PTA money from last year and this to buy two inkjet printers with special devices so that three or four computers can share the same printer. These printers will be set up in the room by the middle of October. The computers and printers will be used primarily to teach your children to be better writers and to use writing to learn their other subjects better."

At this point, a woman raised her hand and began speaking. "Mr. Dunn, I'm Daphne's grandmother. Mr. Fields and I bought a personal computer last year to help us manage our farm. Daphne has really enjoyed several programs that we bought for her at the computer store. What software will you have for these new computers?"

"Excellent question, Mrs. Fields," said Mr. Dunn. "With money from the grant, I have obtained a site license for our class to use Works with the new computers. Works is a single piece of software that contains a word processor, a database, a spreadsheet, and a drawing program that can be used separately or together. We had to pay three times what Works usually costs, but we are permitted to make seven copies of the program, one for each computer. We are also allowed to make copies to replace any we lose if a hard disk crashes. In addition to Works, the grant has also enabled us to purchase a number of educational software packages for social studies, science, health, music, mathematics, and literature, as well as reading, writing, and other aspects of the language arts. I also have purchased books such as *From Scribblers to Scribes* by Katzer and Crnkovich that have excellent suggestions and ideas for helping children become writers on the computer. As you can see, this is going to be an exciting year for your children."

Ed Dunn was relieved. He thought he had done a fairly good job summarizing the complex reading and writing program that he had spent so much time designing. He purposely had left out discussion of his plans for lessons that fit the reading levels of all his students, even though he would spend the first few months of school doing just that. He believed what he had just covered was of more interest to the parents. He waited for a response.

Mrs. Penn broke the silence for everyone. "Mr. Dunn, we are all thankful that our children are here in Merritt Elementary, and we know that the program you have planned for our children will continue to help them grow as they have in the past. Basically, I think I know what you mean about teaching reading along with content-area subjects, selective reading, learning from text, and developing more independent learners. Although we don't always understand the philosophies behind what you do for our children, we do know that they are happy and learning here."

"I'd like to second that," spoke up a woman at the back. "We left here when Mike was about to start third grade. We are very glad to be back. Mike is a handful but at least here we know everyone will work with him. Miss Nouveau worked wonders with him and I know you, Mr. Dunn, will be able to help him behave and learn."

Few questions seemed necessary after that, and the meeting came quickly to an end. Mr. Dunn left even more determined to improve the literacy of all his students.

MONTHLY LOGS

September

What a month this has been! Establishing a classroom routine and a set of expectations always takes time because the children simply don't know what to do or what "this year's teacher's" expectations are. This group of students, as usual, tested the limits of acceptable behavior in order to find out just what those limits are. I've found that as long as I maintain consistent, firm guidelines about what I expect with regard to classroom behavior, and as long as I provide reasonably stimulating lessons that allow the children to succeed, then the class runs rather successfully.

Mike, Butch, and Daisy tried to take over the class at first, but, without overreacting, I continued to remind them of what I wanted them to do. I watched for signs of trouble and tried to prevent problems. I ignored what I could, and when I made an assignment I insisted that they stay with it. **Discipline**

My schedule shows how I divided the day. I tried to stick to it, but there were those days special teachers came. We study six main subject areas: reading/ literature, writing/language arts, math, health, science, and social studies. I use textbooks as the guide for the content areas of science, health, and social studies, and whenever possible I bring into the classroom other printed materials, AV materials, concrete objects, and guest speakers. I refer to all these sources of information as *collateral sources*. This means that all are equally important. In fact, the main contribution of the textbooks seems to be that they are reference sources for the topics we cover in class. They are not the only sources. **Scheduling**

Time	Activity
8:30- 8:40	Plan the day
8:40- 9:40	Reading/Literature
9:45-10:35	Writing/Language Arts
10:40-11:25	Math
11:30-12:15	Lunch/Recess
12:20-12:35	Music
12:40- 1:15	Science
1:20- 1:55	Health
2:00- 2:35	Social Studies
2:35- 2:45	Close the day

When I passed out the textbooks in each of the six areas, I got quite a variety of responses from the children. For instance, Danielle immediately began poring over the pages of each book. Reading does seem to provide her an outlet. Hilda pulled out her eraser and began cleaning up her books before placing them carefully in her desk. Conversely, when I distributed the social studies texts, Mike and Butch pulled out their pencils and began drawing mustaches, crossed eyes, and big ears on George Washington and Abraham Lincoln, who grace the covers of our books. Although I could remember doing similar things when I was their age, I still informed them in no uncertain terms that such action was unacceptable in my room. They grumbled, but they erased their "artwork."

Content Area Reading

In social studies, health, and science I plan lessons that develop understanding of the information and that improve reading abilities at the same time. In effect, I use these materials just as if they were written for formal reading instruction. If a key word is defined clearly by the context, then I have the class figure out what the word means from the context. If a passage we are reading is organized clearly, then I have the class portray that organization through graphic organizers. In addition, I design activities that allow students to work independently. Most of these activities are completed in centers with materials written at various levels of difficulty so different children complete different sets of activities.

Our mornings are devoted to the subjects that mainly call for learning how to do things. Reading/literature, writing/language arts, and math fill up this time. I carry over skills from one of these areas to another throughout the day. For example, if we're studying capitalization in language arts, then we notice what is capitalized in the books we read and the writing we do in reading/literature, math, social studies, health, and science.

Literature Response Activity

At present, the time set aside for reading/literature is devoted mainly to making the selections we are reading in the fifth-grade literature anthology come alive. We learned how to turn a short story with lots of conversation into a readers' theater by actually doing it step-by-step with the first story we read. After several other kinds of literature response activities with subsequent selections, we ended the month by producing another readers' theater version of one of the short stories in the book. The students did so much better and enjoyed it so much more the second time. I plan to do at least a couple more before the year ends.

My language arts and math programs are based on presenting a common topic to the class and then pursuing that topic at levels that are appropriate for the children. For example, if we're doing division, then I do whole-class presentations to get everyone thinking about dividing numbers. However, the children work on their own or in small groups with problems and exercises that are appropriate for their math ability levels.

Process Writing

Even though all my students were regularly involved in writing last year in Ms. Maverick's room and in the lower grades before that, I still find it a good idea to begin the year with several weeks of basic process writing. Regardless of how much writing children have done previously, it seems that most of them are uncertain and anxious about how their writing will be dealt with by a new teacher. Even the most advanced students I have are well aware that I could readily find things wrong with their writing if I held them accountable to all the capitalization, punctuation, formating, and usage conventions one finds in an English handbook or even a traditional fifth-grade language textbook.

Every September, I have to establish the trust between teacher and students that enables an effective writing instructional program to operate. As usual, I begin by having students write about topics of their own choosing, followed by a time of sharing in which volunteers read aloud what they have just written. The only limitation is that what they write cannot be written to offend me or the other students. Students can respond to what others have shared, but only to make positive comments or ask questions in order to gain additional information. I keep my own comments brief and positive. By the end of September every year, I find that students are willing to write for me and each other because we have established this atmosphere of trust. Once that is established, we are able to systematically improve our writing, including its adherence to conventional standards.

The children seem to be able to cope all right with my separation of the subject areas. In fact, I overheard Chip and Carl talking about how neat it was that they were studying subjects just like the high school kids do. However, Roberta pointed out to me that they studied things "together" in Ms. Maverick's room. I agreed that that was a good way to do it, and then I tried to explain how I intended to tie together reading and language arts, especially, with science and social studies. The expression on her face after we talked indicated that I hadn't totally convinced her. We'll see.

Sustained Silent Reading (SSR) and teacher read-aloud fill up the rest of reading/literature time each day. SSR is what I call SQUIRT. My "young adults" resented the term *SQUIRT* although most of them do expect and even seem to enjoy the opportunity to read silently on their own for a certain time period. I'm sure this is the result of the programs these children have been through in their earlier grades here at Merritt Elementary.

Self-Selected Reading

I started teacher read-aloud the very first day of school. Each week over the summer, I always try to read one or two children's books that are new to me. This is really no chore since these books are always fast reads and I really like children's literature anyway. I usually find them better written and less cynical than most mass-market literature intended for more "mature" audiences. Anyway, last summer I made an effort to read books set in the cultures of other nations. It seems especially important to me for fifth graders to understand how their counterparts around the world live, think, and feel. Unfortunately, social studies often seems too abstract and collective in its view. Students have trouble identifying with individuals from other countries and cultures unless they can somehow walk around in their shoes for a while. A good movie or novel has the power to provide that kind of vicarious experience.

Teacher Read-Aloud

Multicultural Awareness

The first three weeks of school, I read a chapter of *Journey to Jo'burg* by Beverley Naidoo to the class every day. That book was a good one to start with because it is not very long and has 15 short chapters. I wanted to be able to maintain students' interest during the read-aloud and leave them wanting more when it ended. I thought we could build up to longer books with longer chapters. The story of *Journey to Jo'burg* is set in South Africa in the time of apartheid and provides a frighteningly vivid portrait of life for blacks under that system. The children were riveted throughout. Some of them also became quite disturbed that no one had told them about apartheid before. I assured them that they had heard about it but had not really realized what it meant. I promised them if they would watch the news or look through the newspaper for a week or two, they would find out more about current race relations in South Africa. Before finishing the book, several of them shared in class what they had heard or read about South Africa in the news media. The last week in the month, I began reading *Year of the Panda* by Miriam Schlein. It is set in rural China.

Content Area Reading

I really enjoy listening to music, although I don't play any instruments nor do I sing especially well. I think most youngsters like music, too, and can benefit from it, so I scheduled a part of each day for it. During the 15 minutes we have for music, we simply take out our songbooks and sing. I start off by choosing a student to select a song for the class to sing. After everyone sings the song, the original student chooses someone else—usually a friend—who selects another song for us. For example, I started out one music session calling on Joyce. She chose "When Johnny Comes Marching Home" for us to sing. She then called on Roberta, who had us sing "On Top of Old Smokey." When Roberta called on Larry there were some murmurs among the class because a girl actually had called on a boy. I get some useful information about friendships while this selecting goes on, the children settle down after an invigorating recess, and they are reading and interpreting lyrics as they sing the various songs. Singing lyrics also helps build reading fluency.

Assessment

One of the most important things I did this month was classroom diagnosis. Mort and Paul put forth very little effort in completing the social studies and science activities I assigned, but at least they did not disturb others who were working. I suspected that those two had difficulty reading and writing and that that difficulty caused them to appear lazy and uncaring. But I wasn't sure. That's why I spent part of the second week of school doing group diagnosis with our content-area reading materials. I wanted to determine who required adjustments to the assignments.

The group diagnosis that I use relies quite a bit on common sense. I simply have students complete an assignment that is roughly typical of the type of assignment that I would make with that text during the year. However, the difference is that I look at the students' performance as a measure of how well they can deal with the materials, not as a measure of the grade they should receive. This is an inventory, not a test.

To construct a group reading inventory, I took the basic textbook that we have for each of our six subjects, and I identified an appropriate selection from the second 50 pages. Each selection had a beginning, middle, and end; that is, each selection stood by itself. For each section I wrote questions that were the same type that would normally occur during a regular class. In fact, my questions covered the topics that would receive emphasis if I were actually teaching them. One of the other fifth-grade teachers might ask different questions that emphasize different aspects of the passage, but that is to be expected.

After the class completed one of the group inventories, I took it home for evaluation. Last year I graded each paper and then compared percentages to see who fell into the 90s, 80s, 70s, 60s, and below. However, this year I evaluated the papers holistically because all of my questions called for short-answer, essay-type responses rather than responses that called for circling letters or underlining words.

To do holistic evaluation, I first read all the papers rather quickly one time in order to gain an overall perspective. Then I went through the papers again and sorted them into four piles according to how well they satisfied the assignment. I tried not to let handwriting influence my judgments; clear handwriting does not always indicate clear thinking, and vice versa. After obtaining four piles, I read the papers a final time and rank ordered them. I now had tentative information to help me determine how well each student could meet certain outcomes with each textbook.

Based on my group reading inventory in social studies, I came up with a tentative list of students and their ability to benefit from working with our very

TENTATIVE RANKING OF ABILITIES TO BENEFIT FROM INSTRUCTION WITH SOCIAL STUDIES TEXTBOOK

Relative Ability	Student
Independent level (little guidance)	Betty
	Danielle
	Hilda
	Larry
	Mandy
	Pat
	Rita
	Roberta
Instructional level (some guidance)	Alex
	Anthony
	Carl
	Chip
	Daphne
	Horace
	Joyce
	Manuel
	Mitch
	Steve
Instructional level (much guidance)	Alexander
	Butch
	Mort
	Tanana
Frustration level (needs accommodation)	Daisy
	Jeff
	Mike
	Paul

difficult classroom social studies text. My holistic scoring of the group reading inventory for our social studies textbook indicated that I have four students who cannot be expected to learn from it. Daisy, Jeff, Mike, and Paul appear to need special lessons and materials if they are to use reading in order to develop their understanding of social studies. If I don't provide them special lessons and materials, then they are doomed to two situations: (1) frustration with an incomprehensible text, and (2) reliance on listening to class lectures and presentations, and viewing films or other media in order to obtain information.

I seem to have 14 students who can be expected to learn from our text and increase their reading abilities while doing so as long as they receive some direct guidance from me. I realize that learning from text is not an all-or-nothing affair and that students can acquire some knowledge, even from quite difficult materials. However, it seems that this group of 14 children will learn the most information and best improve their reading abilities at the same time if I provide them clear guidance before and after they read.

The remaining eight students look as though they will be able to understand the text with ease. They still will require my help to lead them to even better understanding and insight into what they read. But from what I can tell, they should have little difficulty with my typical assignments based on the text.

I will observe my students' reading abilities throughout the year, but for the present I have a tentative idea of their relative levels. Sometime in October I will look at the permanent files of those students whom I am especially concerned about, and perhaps I will talk with some of their past teachers. I like to form my own opinions first, however, before I solicit other people's opinions about my students.

Computers
The morning after the parent meeting, most of the children had obviously heard from their parents about the new computers. "Where are they?" Mike wanted to know. "Still in the boxes," I replied, and received a chorus of groans in response. "You are not completely ready to use them yet, but I will help you finish getting ready over the next few weeks," I promised. Everyone wanted to know what they had to do to get ready. "Get better at typing on a keyboard," I answered. Almost everyone declared they were already real good at that!

That afternoon, I took them as a class to the school's computer lab for the 45-minute period that Mr. Topps had reserved for me there every day this month. I subtracted 15 minutes each out of science, social studies, and health to make time for it. It is only temporary and I am sure the learning students gain will make it well worthwhile.

Even though the computers in the lab are rather different from the ones we will have in our classroom, the children can still learn to improve their keyboarding on them. The computer lab is networked and there is an excellent keyboarding tutorial available on the network. All of my students this year had worked in the lab during past years, so they knew how to turn the computers on. I showed them how to download the tutorial from the network into their individual machines and walked around the lab as they did so. I explained to them how the introductory lesson would work and how they should proceed at their own pace. After Larry explained to me that he had already completed this tutorial at home and proved it by jumping to the last lesson and typing with impressive speed and accuracy through the first part of it, I had him help me move around among the other students to help them with the tutorial.

Every afternoon for the rest of September, Larry and I supervised and assisted the class as they moved through the keyboarding tutorial. We played down competition between students as much as possible and tried to emphasize the concept of "personal best." Of course, students still compared themselves with each other, but we were able to keep it to a minimum. When the amount of supervision and assistance being sought decreased markedly after the first week, Larry also spent most of his time at a computer with the tutorial, increasing his speed and accuracy even more.

While the students vary tremendously in their speed and accuracy of keyboarding, the only ones whose typing was still inadequate by the end of the month were Jeff and Paul. The tutorial was too demanding for them except at its slowest and lowest level. They have made some progress.

October

As I get to know my students better, I always am amazed at how different they are! Larry has an exceptionally quick mind, and his knowledge of the world is actually astounding. Occasionally I wonder if he couldn't teach the class. The students ask him for help almost as often and as willingly as they ask me.

Mike either cannot or will not stay at any task or in any one place for more than a minute or two. He does not defy me, but he does require constant reminding.

Betty, Tanana, Daphne, and Joyce are fast friends, which is not unusual of course, but individually they are such diverse people. Betty is a perfectionist who almost always succeeds. Tanana's interest in nature has dominated all her other interests. Daphne has a tremendous imagination. And Joyce has proven to be quite popular. She inevitably is called on more than once during music to choose a song.

We got off to a good start this month working on different reading-writing activities in social studies, health, and science because of the care I took getting into them. I always am careful to keep my class together as a large group during the first few weeks of school. This allows the students to learn what my limits are in regard to acceptable behavior, and it allows the class routine to become established. After a time, I gradually begin allowing the students to control some of their own learning activities. This is a yearlong process, and some classes go further than others in assuming self-control. The procedure I follow was described quite well in an article I read years ago titled "The Half-Open Classroom: Controlled Options in Reading" by Earle and Morley (1974).

Balanced Literacy Programs

The way I "opened up" my science period is a good example of getting to a half-open classroom. The first week was spent exploring our class science textbook, noting its table of contents, skimming through the chapters, and becoming familiar with the special parts of the book such as its index, glossary, and footnoting system. Other available science materials were introduced, also. I then began whole-class lessons on our first unit of study, which dealt with motion.

When reading materials were used, I always prepared students for the reading, set specific purposes, and discussed the material afterward to make sure that the purposes had been met. I did a variety of lessons with different purposes so that I could help students learn to read for many purposes. Providing repetition of purposes with various materials helps them learn better too.

When reading-writing tasks were assigned, I made them one at a time and held everyone responsible for each one. As expected, some students did better than others. Larry and Pat turned in papers that could have been displayed in a showcase, Alexander had some terrific insights but they were not stated very clearly, and Tanana and Daisy appeared to jot down whatever came to their minds. As a group, my students worked on these assignments in a rather perfunctory way.

Student Independence

Later in the month, we watched a film and a filmstrip on motion and I read aloud a short article on "Our Friendly Moving Machines." Then I listed four reading-writing activities on the board:

1. Draw arrows around a diagram of an airplane wing to show the direction and relative amounts of force pushing on the wing.
2. List names of pictured machines.
3. Construct a "web" of the information that is contained in the article "Our Friendly Moving Machines." (See Mr. Dunn for a copy of the article and a taped version of it.)
4. Complete the experiment described on page 83 of our science textbook.

"But Mr. Dunn, some of those activities have nothing to do with our textbook!" Hilda patiently explained to me.

"That's right. They all are connected to our study of motion, but they include a variety of materials. Try it, you'll like it," I assured her. "But wait 'til you hear the real surprise."

I then told the class that they were all responsible for completing all four activities, but that each student could choose the order in which to complete them. Friday of that week was set as the due date for the four projects.

This choice making was handled quite well by most students. (Again, they do reflect their previous training!) The biggest exception was Mort, who told me that he chose not to do any of the assignments. However, I reminded him firmly that he could choose the *order* of doing them and not the actual doing of them. I think he got the message.

After the class became accustomed to choosing the order of my reading-writing activities during science period, I extended this procedure to the other subject areas. I had different due dates for the various projects in the different areas so that I didn't get totally snowed evaluating papers that came in all at once. I will need to see about cutting down on the paper load, though. I am sure that planning creative lessons for which the students give each other feedback is time better spent than my evaluating uncreative lessons. Somehow I need to get the youngsters in on the act.

Content Area Reading

A committee of girls who apparently had taken an hour to pose their question met me after lunch one day. Betty, Mandy, and Roberta came up and wanted to talk about our music period.

"Mr. Dunn, we like singing after lunch, but we're not too crazy about the songs you have for us. They're too old-fashioned," complained Mandy.

Well, I thought that the songs in their songbooks like "America the Beautiful" were rather nice, but I could see their point. When we brought this up with the whole class, we decided that they could bring in song lyrics on their own, and I would duplicate them for everybody. My only caution was that the song needed to be "singable" by a group. Some of the top 40 numbers are just a little too fast and complicated for unsophisticated group singing and some of the lyrics are inappropriate.

Our short time set aside specifically for music is a high point of the day. We get a nice group feeling after each session, and the afternoons do seem to go by quite pleasantly. Sometimes we discuss the lyrics of a song. I brought in some folk songs from the 1960s, played a recorded version of them, we sang them, and then we talked about them. There wasn't much to say about "Puff, the Magic Dragon," but we did talk at some length about "Blowin' in the Wind." Some were surprised to learn that we're actually studying poetry at these times.

Multicultural Awareness

During teacher read-aloud this month, I finished *Year of the Panda* and began *The Haunted Igloo* by Bonnie Turner. The main character of Turner's novel is a 10-year-old Inuit boy named Jean Paul. Tanana was overjoyed that I was reading a book to the entire class about her culture. As we went through the book, she became bolder about making comments and even disagreeing with the book at times. Other children began asking her questions about things in the story that they wanted to know more about. Sometimes she could answer the questions and sometimes she couldn't, but she seemed to love being the center of attention.

Computers

Of course, the real excitement this month was caused by the new computers. The first Monday morning of October, the students straggled into the room to find seven carts with computers on them against the back wall. Each computer was mysteriously hidden beneath an opaque dust cover. As soon as everyone had arrived, and the lunch count and roll were completed, I pulled one of the carts into the middle of the room and allowed the children to gather around me. I removed the dust cover and the room was filled with exclamations of "wow," "bad," "cool," and "awesome!"

Briefly, I first explained to them how our class computers are like those in the computer lab: They all have a hard drive, a 3.5-inch floppy drive, and a mouse. I then showed them how our computers are different from the lab's by turning this one on and demonstrating. They soon saw that each of our new computers has a color monitor, a CD-ROM drive, and an "upside-down" mouse that is actually called a track ball. Each of our computers can have several windows open at the same time and all major commands can be accessed by clicking on pull-down menus. I also showed them that the cart has lockable wheels so that it can be moved easily but has the stability of a stationary table when we are working with the computer. By this time they were all pleading to take a turn. Quickly, I announced the seven mixed groups of three or four students that I had previously selected and written on a piece of paper. One at a time, I had each group move a computer and enough chairs to a particular place in the room, lock the cart wheels, plug in the computer, and wait to begin. I explained that the members of each group would go in alphabetical order of last name. I then led them to turn on the computers and open the hypermedia tutorials that had come installed on the hard disks. One at a time, amidst much kibitzing, they proceeded individually through the tutorial, learning how to open applications, maneuver the track ball, and pull down menus. After 35 or 40 minutes, everyone had had a turn. I then directed them to return the computers to their places against the back wall as they pleaded with me to let them continue to explore them.

Except for having to switch two children to improve the discipline of one of the groups, I kept the students in the same seven computer groups for the rest of the month. Every day, the groups worked cooperatively to learn how to use these more sophisticated computers. While the students have had some access to computers in their classrooms and in the lab since kindergarten, those computers were simpler and more basic than these. Also, the students have generally had more supervision than they will have this year. I intended for them to learn to be more mature, sophisticated, and responsible with these new computers. There were several stages of this learning, each one with several phases. The first stage consisted of the following phases:

Learning to set up the computers in working condition around the room and then return them to their permanent condition against the back wall

Learning the basic operation of these more complicated computers (using the track ball, opening more than one application at a time, clicking on a pull-down menu, shutting down all applications, etc.)

Learning to follow the checklist of rules for good computer care posted on the back wall

Each day at computer time, a different group member was responsible for doing each phase, and I observed them carefully. The groups were told that they would not be able to move to the next level of computer use until every member had mastered every phase of this level. I was thrilled at how helpful they were to each other. Having only seven computers has certainly fostered cooperation and teamwork among students. The three groups of three that had either Paul, Daisy, or Jeff as a member each allowed that student a larger proportion of time at the computer without me even hinting that it might be necessary! By the end of the first week, everyone had learned to operate the computers individually at a stage-one level.

The second stage of learning how to use the new computers consisted of these phases:

Learning to open the Works word processor and begin a new document

Learning to name and save the document you are working on in *your* folder on the hard disk

Learning to back up the document you are working on before closing it by saving it to *your* floppy disk

Each of the seven computers was numbered on the side with an adhesive metallic numeral so each group could work with the same computer every day. I placed a folder for each student in the group on the hard disk of that group's computer. The folder was labeled with the given name of the child (e.g., Mandy, Horace, Joyce). I also labeled a floppy disk with each student's name and gave it to him or her to keep in the student's cubby except when needed.

By the middle of the month, every student had written, saved, and backed up at least two documents, however short, that they had written during computer time. The difficulty for most students was in avoiding the impulse to save without making sure they were saving to their folder or their floppy, rather than to the top level of the hard disk. Again, the cooperation and support being given within the groups was the crucial factor in the success students were having.

At this point, I felt that it was time to begin integrating the computers into writing/language arts time. The students had apparently become as comfortable writing and sharing for me as they had last year for Ms. Maverick and Mr. Ditto. There was no one who refused to write. Everyone had shared something they had written, at least in pairs. I announced to the class that it was time for each one to choose a piece of writing from their folders that they wanted to publish. **Publishing** They should share it with at least two other students and get suggestions for changes to their content (no comments on form were allowed during this initial sharing). When they were ready for my evaluation, they placed it in the box on my desk designated for that purpose. The next day, I met with each student for a few minutes and discussed what I would require before the paper could be published. First, we agreed on what the content must be, then we agreed on what form conventions I would require. After our discussion, I typed the requirements we agreed on and printed out a copy for the student.

From that time on, we would set up all seven computers in the morning and leave them set up all day. That way, when a student has individual time, he or she can go to a computer and work on the paper. We also usually connect each computer to one of the two printers, so students can print when they think they have a final draft to show me.

November

This class and I are moving steadily toward a balance among whole-class, small-group, and individual projects. I want to be in front of the whole class presenting **Balanced Literacy Programs** lessons, leading discussions, and providing directions or guidance about one-third of the time. I like to spend another third of my time circulating about the class, dealing with individual problems and questions that occur as students work through their various assignments. Finally, I want to spend the other one-third of my time instructing students in small groups and individually.

My small-group and individual instruction calls for me to meet with selected students and lead them through a lesson. In math, for example, I might sit with some students and help them compose word problems that fit the mathematical operation we are studying at that time. In social studies, I frequently review vocabulary with students, and I have presented to small groups several specific lessons on reading maps.

Student Independence

The key to maintaining this balanced instruction is to ease students into working responsibly on their own. And in all six subject areas, my students are choosing the order in which to complete their assigned tasks. In fact, the children had been completing their activities in whichever order they chose and turning them in by the deadline quite well, so this month I began allowing the children to choose among the tasks.

It was Larry who pointed out to me that the time had come to begin allowing more decision making. "I would like to try this experiment on page 115 of our science text, Mr. Dunn," he said, "but you have us doing this other one. Would you mind if I did the one on my own?"

Did I ever love that question!

The next day, I told the class that they could choose any three of the four activities listed on the board. They were to complete the activities in whatever order they liked. They could do all four if they wanted, but the assignment was to complete three. I purposely included activities that varied in difficulty. This way, students like Paul and Daisy could participate fully with the class on easier tasks, and students like Larry and Hilda could be challenged by more difficult tasks.

I offered choices this month in the subject areas other than science, too. The tasks were always related to the central topic we were studying, but they varied according to how difficult they were and the type of ability they required. I regularly offered the choice of reading and responding to some material other than the basic material being used. In social studies, for instance, we studied the Middle Ages. For one assignment, the class could choose to read one of three short stories that were about King Arthur and the Knights of the Round Table. The stories ranged in difficulty from about a third-grade level to seventh-grade level. After reading their story, each child could respond to it by either writing a summary, drawing a picture of their favorite scene, or describing how Camelot differed from our town. I made it very clear that this was one task for them, but that they could decide among variations within the task. I should mention, too, that we had worked on summarizing in our writing/language arts period, so everybody at least had an idea of what to do if they chose that activity.

Grading

Report cards for the first nine weeks went out the middle of this month. Mr. Topps has long contended that a teacher's grading system is one of his or her most important professional creations. My first couple of years here, I constantly complained to everyone about the difficulties of grading, about parents' attitudes toward the school, and about students' lack of motivation. Mr. Topps would usually ignore me, but sometimes he patiently explained that my main tool in overcoming these three universal problems of teaching was the system I chose to use in assigning grades to my students and their work. At first, I defended myself by arguing that I really didn't have much leeway in how I graded. After all, there were state laws and state board policies, district policies and guidelines, and even a few schoolwide policies and restrictions. Grades were objective indicators of student learning and I just passively delivered the news to children and their parents, whether good or bad! Finally, as I became a better teacher with more experience, I began to see how certain grading practices seem related to either causing or solving problems in my classroom. With the help of Mr. Topps and teachers like Mrs. Wise, I came to understand how a teacher's grading system can either complement or undermine that teacher's instructional program. For example, a friend teaches fifth grade in a school where she has to give students a number grade in every subject every nine weeks. School board policy in that district requires that a certain minimum number of grades be averaged each grading period for each subject. I don't see how I could teach if I were forced to grade my students that way. Certainly, Paul, Daisy, and Jeff would be assured of low grades regardless of their efforts, and Betty, Larry, and Roberta would be assured of high grades without really having to try.

When I first became disenchanted with the traditional grade-everything, average-the-grades, and let-the-chips-fall-where-they-may system, I tried to move to the other extreme. Through a long, laborious process, I had developed a checklist of knowledge and strategies for every subject I teach, for each grading period. When Mr. Topps saw my checklists, his face betrayed both admiration and discouragement. "Ed," he said, "this is very thorough, but let me ask you a question."

"All right."

"Why do we send report cards home to the parents of the children we teach?"

"Obviously, so they will know how well their children are doing in school," I replied.

"Yes, you're right. So, do you think most parents will know how well their children are doing if you send them these checklists filled in?"

Part of me had the impulse to declare impatiently that they would know much more than they had in the past, but his serious expression caused me to reconsider.

After a pause, he continued. "Ed, the problem with checklists and any other indicator of what students actually know is that parents have to understand the curriculum in order to determine their child's progress. Even if they were to understand the curriculum, they don't know how well their child is doing compared with the other children in the class."

"I don't understand." There was frustration in my voice. "Don't you think I should try to improve my grading system?"

"Yes, I do. You have worked very hard, but I'm afraid that what you have produced is too different from what parents want, expect, and can understand. It creates new problems while it solves some old ones. Most of our changes in education are like that. We fail to recognize the strengths in what we are doing now. Rather than try to keep the strengths while overcoming the weaknesses, we throw everything out and start again from scratch. That's one reason why the educational pendulum continues to swing."

"What do you suggest?" I asked.

"See if you can figure out a way to modify your current grading system so that you continue to give students letter grades, but student effort is rewarded more than it is now, and the emphasis is on application of knowledge and strategies rather than on minutiae."

The grading system that I have in place this year is not perfect, but it has developed over the years since that conversation with Mr. Topps to become quite workable. It is a system that I can manage with a reasonable commitment of time, parents seem to understand how well their children are doing, and I am able to motivate students across a broad range of initial achievement levels. The system is really quite simple. It consists of daily grades, tests, small-group projects, and individual projects. Daily grades and small-group projects are where everyone who makes a reasonable effort and is reasonably cooperative with me and with other students does well. (I monitor the group projects especially carefully to make sure that everyone in the group is making a contribution.) Tests and individual projects are also designed so that students who have paid attention and made an effort can obtain satisfactory grades. Every test and individual project, however, has an aspect that challenges the most capable, creative, and hardworking student in the class. I use the following chart to determine the letter grade a student receives in each subject. During a particular grading period in a particular subject one of the columns may be missing (e.g., individual projects). If so, I just use the other columns to determine my grades.

Grade	Daily Grades	Group Projects	Tests	Individual Projects
A	S+	S+	A	A
B	S or S+	S or S+	A-B	A-B
C	S−, S, or S+	S−, S, or S+	A-F	A-F
D	S−	S−	D-F	D-F
F	S−	S−	F	F

The procedure I use is this. First, students are considered for an A or an F. Students who do not receive an A or an F are then considered for a B or a D. Students who do not receive an A, a B, a D, or an F receive a C.

Because tests are an important component of my grading system, I use test formation when I want to be absolutely sure that the children's products come only from each child. Tanana told me about test formation, saying that it was the way they took tests at her old school. I first tried it when I administered the group inventory in social studies last month, and I intend to use it more and more often. In test formation, the children spread throughout the room, and each child sits at an isolated position. I moved a few children at first just to make sure that they could not easily see another's paper. I explained to them that I occasionally needed an uncontaminated measure of their performance so that I would know exactly how they were doing. We discussed the differences between an inventory (when I want to find out what they know for the purpose of planning lessons) and a test (when I want to find out what they know for the purpose of assigning a grade). I then explained that I would not even trust my own mother in the seating arrangement we normally used because even she would not be able to resist sneaking a quick peek at another's paper. Thus, I said flatly, "When I need to take inventory or administer a test, the class needs to get into test formation." They seem to have accepted this procedure.

Interests

This month closed with a visit from Daphne's grandmother. Mrs. Fields was concerned that Daphne was developing some very bad habits. "Mr. Dunn, maybe you can help us decide what to do. This fall my husband and I have noticed that Daphne is hard to wake up in the morning. Every year before, she's always jumped right out of bed. The other night I went to her room after midnight and there she was under the cover with a flashlight reading a Nancy Drew book!

"I asked the public librarian and she said that Daphne has checked out over 15 of them in the past two months. We want her to read better books than that. What do you think we ought to do?"

I tried to reassure her. "Daphne has been reading Nancy Drew books in SSR every day since school started. Frankly, I think you should encourage her to read even more."

Mrs. Fields frowned slightly. "You mean you allow them to read those series? Aren't all the books alike, anyway?"

"Series books have some positive attributes," I explained. "They interest many children in reading. Once the reading habit is formed, books of greater literary quality can be introduced. These books also provide lots of easy reading, which is the way many children practice the skills they have learned in reading instructional time at school. Don't worry, every good reader I've known read both comic books and one or more juvenile series at Daphne's age. If these books didn't cause them to be good readers, they at least didn't prevent them from becoming good readers.

"I would suggest that you give Daphne time to read before she goes to bed so that she won't miss her sleep. I agree with you that she needs proper rest, but please don't be alarmed about these mysteries."

I haven't heard any more about it, but Daphne has continued to read Nancy Drew during SSR. Whether that 15 minutes a day is all the Nancy Drew she gets is another question!

Many of the other students have locked onto a favorite author or two and are reading them exclusively. Betty, Tanana, Daphne, and Joyce have discovered Judy Blume's books; Horace, Mitch, and Alex are going through the old Tarzan of the Apes series by Edgar Rice Burroughs; and Mandy and Pat are trading stories by Richard Peck.

Publishing

This month the students have continued to improve in their individual writing on the computers. To provide some variety and a sense of audience, we produced two class newsletters, published two weeks apart. Each of the students had to choose to write an editorial, a feature article about another student in the class, or a sports article. We had peer response groups on the first drafts, peer editing groups on the second drafts, and my response to the third drafts. The fourth drafts were all published in one or the other of the two newsletters. I used my desktop publishing program on my home computer to compile the newsletter. Every student was given a copy of each newsletter to take home. The excitement and sense of accomplishment was tremendous.

December

Balanced Literacy Programs

My attempts in the six subject areas to achieve a balance among whole-class, group, and individual instruction has been moving steadily this month. I still move gradually because I've seen some quite chaotic classes where the teacher one day simply opened everything up to learning centers or cooperative learning without preparing the class. If anything, I may prepare the class for independence too slowly.

But whatever the case, most of my students have been working quite well choosing their own assignments and finishing them in the order they choose. Consequently, I have become better and better able to work with small groups and individuals. I'm sure that much of the reason for this group cooperation is the fact that my materials and assignments have been adjusted to allow practically every student a good deal of success. By easing this class into making choices with materials and assignments that they can handle, I am able to work more effectively with small groups and individuals. Furthermore, students require materials that are written at appropriate levels if they are to learn the information and also improve their abilities to learn. Easing students into a half-open classroom situation allows them the opportunity to deal with such materials.

Meaning Vocabulary

In fact, I've been able to spend extra time emphasizing meaning vocabulary in the subject areas now that the class is working so smoothly. This month I used capsule vocabulary (Crist, 1975) to develop understanding of geometry terms during math period. For the first part of the lesson, we sat as a group and discussed the topic of geometry. I had selected the following 10 words that the group needed to know:

Geometry Terms for Capsule Vocabulary

point	plane
polygon	perpendicular
line segment	ray
angle	triangle
parallel	line

As we discussed geometry, I made a conscious effort to introduce the 10 terms in meaningful context even though I had to occasionally force the conversation in order to allow the word to fit. "The wall in front of me can be considered a *plane*," I said at one point. "The wall behind me is a *parallel plane*, then, and the walls on either side are *perpendicular planes*." The students copied these words into their math notebooks, and we continued using them in discussion until everyone felt that they understood their meanings.

In the second part of the lesson, the students paired off for one-to-one talk sessions. The requirement was that each student use each one of the new words in a meaningful context at least once while talking to the other. For instance, I overheard this part of the conversation between Manuel and Steve:

MANUEL: Yesterday, when we played softball during recess the ball came off my bat at a funny *angle*. It didn't go *parallel* to the ground; it went straight up.

STEVE: Yeah, it almost went *perpendicular* to the ground. As for me, I hit a ball that broke the *plane* between second base and third base. I actually got a hit into left field!

MANUEL: Uh huh. Well, I played second base, and I was looking at the base paths. Did you realize that some form a *ray?* Well they do! The one going from second to first, and the one going from second to third form *rays*. What do you think about that?

I always set a timer when we do one-to-one conversations like this because they tend to get a little loony if I allow them to just go on and on. But when the children know that they have only a little time, they usually work in a much more concentrated manner. Indeed, Larry and Danielle really got going, and I'm sure that they used each term at least four times in entirely different contexts.

After applying the new terms in conversation, each student then wrote a short paper using all the new words in a meaningful context. Sometimes I collect the papers and check them for proper inclusion of the specific words, and sometimes I have the original one-to-one pairs look over each other's papers for proper use of the words. With this lesson, I include reading, writing, speaking, and listening development along with the math content that I am responsible to teach.

In order to review the 10 geometry terms a few days after our capsule vocabulary lesson, I had the students web them. We still are at this level of graphically organizing information, although after Christmas I intend to jack up the pace of instruction in organization. I had the students form their pair groupings again and web the 10 words. Since we've been webbing terms in all the subjects since September, this was a fairly easy task for most children. Anthony and Steve, my whizzes in math and science who are so-so in the other areas, produced a logical web. Both boys were able to explain why they grouped the words that way.

Good news! I think a breakthrough is being made with Mike! That boy certainly has his good and bad days, but lately his good days are beginning to outnumber his bad ones. Just last week he made it through an entire day without picking on Rita even once! I'm sure that there are a number of reasons for this change in his behavior, but I believe his tutoring the second grader is part of it.

Discipline

I had looked into his permanent file for some additional information and saw that he was not here at Merritt for third and fourth grade. As a result, we don't know what type of instruction he was getting at his new school. The file did confirm the fact that he could be a bit of a behavioral problem. With this information about Mike, I decided to see about having him tutor a younger child. I figured this way Mike could work with easier reading materials and still save

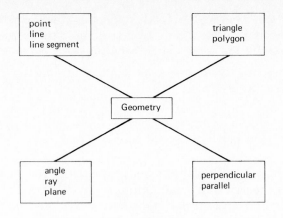

Geometry Web

face. I also thought that the responsibility of caring for a younger child might help him mature a bit. However, when I contacted Norma Flame about my proposal, she was dubious, to say the least.

"Ed," she exclaimed, "you don't realize the nights I spent in tears because of the mean things Mike did in my classroom!"

She eventually agreed that we could set up Mike with a second grader who had some reading abilities but who could benefit from some extra individual attention with word identification. (I do believe that Norma has come a long way since her first year of teaching as Miss Nouveau!) We established a three-day-a-week schedule for Mike and Jimmy, the boy to be tutored. Norma provides lessons for the boys for two days; the third day is devoted to Mike reading books aloud that Jimmy wants to hear. All I can say is that having special responsibility for another person and being able to work comfortably with easy materials without losing self-esteem seems to have given Mike a boost that he sorely needed.

Individual Differences   My other youngsters with "major difficulties" in reading are involved in their special programs during our 8:45 to 9:30 reading/literature period too, but changes with them are not so obvious as with Mike. Jeff is reading and comparing animal stories at present. Since his word identification is rather well developed, we decided that he would read about a certain topic and that we would get together once a week in order to compare the information he is learning. Miss Page, the librarian, was able to help Jeff find a good number of books and magazines about animals, since that was the topic he chose. He reads and we discuss animal books such as *The Wounded Wolf* (George, 1978), *Little Rascal* (North, 1990), *Tyrannosaurus Rex* (Selsam, 1978), and *Snails* (Zim & Kranz, 1975) along with informative magazines like *Ranger Rick* and *National Geographic World* that contain features on animals.

Daisy and Paul were started in a rather structured program largely because they seem to need clear goals and tangible evidence of progress. Daisy, especially, won't budge unless she knows exactly what she is to do. She then will do the activity at a minimal level of acceptability. On the other hand, Paul is willing to extend himself, but he seems to get lost once he does so. He will read a passage all the way through, but then he has great difficulty manipulating the ideas in a thoughtful or creative way.

The program I've devised for them is based largely on materials from high-interest, low-vocabulary book series and on collections of high-low short stories and informational passages. The high-low book series consists of hardcover books made up of about eight chapters each, with word identification and comprehension activities that correspond to each chapter. I have a chart for Daisy and Paul to keep in their personal folders. They fill in a section of the chart each time that they complete a chapter of the book and its corresponding activities. After finishing an entire book, they choose and complete at least one written composition and one artistic response.

In addition, Paul and Daisy regularly choose at least one short story or informational passage from a high-low collection to read on their own and discuss with me. I meet with these two at least once a week for about 20 minutes in order to discuss what they have chosen and to provide specific word identification and comprehension instruction with those materials. The "dynamic duo" typically take something away from our sessions to complete as follow-up and practice to my instruction.

During SSR I have noticed that Mike, Jeff, Daisy, and Paul have had some difficulty locating materials to read. We have a stack of comic books, but few students choose them anymore. In fact, Butch and Mort are about the only students who still read them. My students with "major difficulties" seem content to flip through magazines and the newspaper. I've suggested that they try some of the high-low paperback novels that are available, but none of the four has yet taken me up on them.

Since it is December, the new book I chose for teacher read-aloud this month was *Latkes and Applesauce* by Fran Manushkin. The book centers around a Jewish family's difficulties celebrating Hanukkah because of a blizzard. It's a simple story but one that fifth graders still enjoy.

Other than Works, simulation programs are the kind of computer software my students seem to enjoy most. The Oregon Trail and the various Carmen Sandiego programs are certainly among the best known of this type of software, but there are a number of others. A simulation program is almost always developed around a topic or an aspect of a content subject. Social studies, science, and health are the three content subjects I teach. Simulation programs have been developed for topics or aspects of all three of these curricular areas. In December, a simulation program helped me teach science in an interesting way that actively involved the students in their learning.

Since Thanksgiving, we have been learning about the solar system. The simulation program I purchased to use during this unit allows the students to travel by spaceship throughout the solar system. The graphics are quite detailed and accurate in their representation of each of the planets, each of the moons, the asteroid belt, the sun, and several meteor showers and comets. The challenging aspect of the simulation is trying to explore as much of the solar system as

Self-Selected Reading

Computers

possible within the shortest period of time. Without getting bogged down in the details, suffice it to say that a number of decisions have to be made, and incorrect decisions can result in a very long voyage. Moreover, there are a number of dangers that have to be anticipated or dealt with and it is possible that the ship will even be destroyed or marooned in space. Because the positions of the planets relative to each other are constantly changing, the simulation is somewhat different each time it is played.

Content Area Writing

My way of using the program was as the inquiry step of an extended content writing lesson that took place over several days of class. In a content writing lesson, the teacher has two ways to build background knowledge for students before they begin a first draft: in a teacher-directed and succinct manner before they receive the writing prompt, or in a student-directed and inquiry-based manner after they receive the writing prompt, but before they begin writing their first draft. Most content writing lessons utilize some teacher-directed background building before the prompt is presented, whether or not the lesson also has an inquiry step.

In this case, I began the lesson by reviewing the names and order of the planets in distance from the sun. I also used questions to make sure the class understood the difference between planets, moons, asteroids, meteors, and comets. From previewing the simulation program, I had determined that it would be quite frustrating for anyone who lacked this basic knowledge of the solar system. Even though we had studied all this information previously in the unit, it usually helps students to provide them with a quick review before asking them to use what they have learned.

In addition to reviewing the fundamentals of the solar system, I also taught them the meaning of two terms that would be used in the prompt, *admiral* and *cadet*. After this teacher-directed background step, I wrote the prompt on the chalkboard.

Pretend you are the captain of a space ship. Your ship has recently made a voyage through the solar system. Now that you are back on earth, an admiral has asked you to write a speech for cadets at the space academy. In your speech, explain to your audience of future space ship captains how to travel safely and quickly through the solar system.

After reading the prompt aloud, I explained to the students that, before beginning to write their speeches, they would have an opportunity to learn more about how to equip, supply, and pilot a spaceship. The way they would acquire that information would be through playing a computer game called There and Back. I then directed them to read the prompt carefully to themselves. When they finished, I answered any question a student raised to clarify the prompt except one that would have required me to tell them what to write. After answering their questions, I had them copy down the prompt.

Before long, they were in their computer groups booting up and investigating the simulation. As usual, they were very excited about learning a new computer program. They are quite sophisticated at working together, helping each other, and discovering the ins and outs of a new piece of software without needing to rely too much on the manual. When I asked them to begin their shutting down routines, there were groans and pleadings from all over the room.

The second day, each group completed a simulated voyage through the solar system, or had their voyage end with the destruction of their ship or the marooning of their crew in space. I then permitted a whole-class discussion that amounted to a sharing of tips and insights about There and Back. Mike was amazingly insightful and successful with this program. Before long, students were asking him specific questions and he was giving specific answers. This discussion really seemed to help the groups that were unable to complete their voyage safely.

The third day, I began science class by having students take out their copy of the writing prompt and reread it. I explained to them that today was the day they were to learn all they could about traveling safely and quickly through the solar system. Tomorrow, during science, they were going to write their speeches. As I walked around the room, I was asked a number of substantive questions about the solar system and about the nature of space travel. I was extremely pleased at the level of involvement with science concepts that the simulation program and the writing prompt together elicited from almost all the students.

Focused Writing

On the fourth day, they wrote to the prompt at their seats. After telling them that the papers would not be graded for mechanics or usage, I refused to answer any questions or allow any interaction during this time. Part of fading to independence is eventually requiring students to work alone on a project. They had been engaging in process writing all fall, including producing two class newsletters, and it had taken me three days of science instructional time to prepare them for this particular individual effort. Now I wanted to see what they could accomplish. Their diligence and concentration during the writing demonstrated that all the time and activity spent in preparing them to do it were well worth it.

Student Independence

The last day of this extended content writing lesson was spent having students share their papers by reading them aloud in small groups. I used a different arrangement of students so that the four students in each sharing group came from four different computer groups. I did not want the students evaluating how well a piece of writing conformed to the actual simulated voyage through the solar system. This sharing time naturally led into a whole-class discussion on the solar system and the possibility of one day being able to explore it with manned spacecraft. More than any of the other students, Hilda yearns to be a spaceship captain and pilot her ship to other planets. She really enjoyed this five-day adventure. I expect to hear one day that she has fulfilled her dream!

January

January often seemed like September; at times it felt as though we were starting anew. The first few days after the holidays were a bit hectic as we reestablished the routine that was so carefully nurtured the first four months of school. After a while, though, everyone got back into the swing of things, and I was able to regain my balance among large-group, small-group, and individual instruction.

Student Independence
January typically is a time to begin teaching new things or begin approaching instruction differently. In my case, this month signaled the beginning of my attempts to develop my students' abilities to learn independently. Up to this time, in the subject areas I had been deciding what materials the students should read and the purposes they should have for reading them. Even though I had allowed my students to choose many of their materials and activities, I was the one who dictated what the possible materials and activities would be.

Content Area Reading
In order to help develop more independent learners, I focused first on teaching students to select important information on their own. My plan for doing this began in the second week of January. One day during reading/literature period I kept the class together and showed them a picture of an aircraft carrier that I had cut out of a magazine. "If I had a book about aircraft carriers, what could I learn?" I asked.

Finally, Larry spoke up, "I think we could learn how something that big and heavy can float on top of the water."

Pat thought she would learn the name of the carrier and how many sailors it held.

Mitch was tentative, but he finally blurted out, "We could learn whether the ship can get close enough to shore so the guns and airplanes can blow up a town!"

When the time was up for suggesting what we might learn about aircraft carriers, I explained how each student could become a better reader by following this same procedure with material that he or she was reading.

After putting the picture away, I presented a short, expository passage that was about the U.S. Navy's battleships. We surveyed the passage as we normally did before reading any informative materials, and then I asked the class, "What do you think you can learn from this passage?" I listed their responses on the chalkboard. Because this activity was so similar to what we had just done with the picture, the responses came much more easily.

"I think we can learn how many ships the navy has," ventured Alex.

Larry was sure that we would learn something about the U.S. Navy's submarines because he noted the picture of one along the side of one page and he saw the subheading titled "Submarine Warfare." When I probed for a specific aspect to learn, he decided that we probably could learn the advantages and disadvantages of submarines versus surface craft.

Roberta suggested that we could learn when women first were allowed to join the navy, even though she could not point out any evidence in the passage that indicated coverage of that topic.

After the children listed what they thought could be learned from the passage, I read it to them. This way, everybody was able to receive the information, and they finished receiving it at the identical time. We then followed up the list on the board by noting which items actually were covered in the passage.

The next few days during reading/literature period, I conducted this same activity using another passage with groups of randomly assigned students. They seemed to become rather good at determining what they thought they could learn from the passages.

As a follow-up, I had the class get into test formation, and I put an overhead transparency that was made from a page in the social studies textbook. My question to the class was "What do you think you can learn from this passage?" I collected the papers and took them home in order to see who needed further work with anticipating meaning from a passage.

Although I've been emphasizing anticipating meaning throughout the subject areas, I continue to place a large emphasis upon meaning vocabulary. We do capsule vocabulary lessons frequently, and I always have students first determine the meaning of new, unfamiliar terms by noting the information that is contained in the passage about those terms. We spend time relating past experiences and previously encountered concepts to the new concepts encountered in passages. Word origins are discussed (Betty informed us just recently that *boycott* comes from a British army officer, C. C. Boycott, who was the first victim of this tactic), and the special meanings of technical terms are pointed out. For example, while studying "Coal Mining and Steel Manufacturing" in social studies, we encountered that troublesome term *coke*. I brought in a piece of charcoal as a rough example of this substance. I explained that coke is distilled from coal and that it can produce the terrific heat necessary to separate iron ore from waste rock. After this rather thorough explanation and demonstration, Jeff volunteered the opinion that he would never drink another Coke now that he knew where it came from. I'm still not sure if he was kidding or not!

Meaning Vocabulary

One vocabulary activity that we regularly pursue during subject matter instruction is to note words that contain frequently occurring morphemes. Rather than use the terms *morpheme, prefix, root, suffix, contraction,* and *compound,* we use the phrase *meaningful word part.* Whenever I am introducing or reviewing subject area vocabulary that contains meaningful word parts, I point them out. Sometimes I simply underline the meaningful parts if the words are written on the chalkboard, and sometimes I ask a group of students to identify the parts in words that have them. I always point out how that part contributes to the formation of the word. For example, one of the geometry terms that we studied last December contained a meaningful word part that occurred in other parts frequently enough to warrant attention, so I pointed out that part to the class. I underlined the *tri* in *triangle* and pointed out how it contributed to the meaning of the word. Next, I listed *tricycle* and *triplane* underneath *triangle* in order to reinforce the way *tri* functioned. We constructed sentences with the words to keep this exercise meaningful. Then, as one of the choice activities for this unit, the students were to list

Prefix/Suffix Instruction

at least five words that contained *tri* as a meaningful part and make up sentences that included their words.

Alexander and Steve got together and produced the following list:

"Tri" Words

trilogy	triplet
trio	triannual
triple	trilingual

Later I put these words on the board, and we noted how the pronunciation of the part could change drastically but that the meaning stayed the same. Hilda was quick to point out that the *tri* in *trilogy, triple,* and *triplet* was pronounced one way, that it was pronounced another way in *trio,* and still another way in *tricycle, triannual,* and *trilingual.*

Daisy got a little angry with me because she had recorded *trial, tribe,* and *trigger* among her *tri* words. When I explained to her that *tri* did not refer to "three" in those words, she became sullen. What a shame! I have shown this class that *father* is not made up of *fat* and *her* and that looking for meaningful word parts doesn't always work. I've tried to demonstrate how this word-analysis technique is useful when it is used while attending to the context of a passage. Looking for meaningful word parts doesn't always help students figure out words, but pronouncing words, recognizing them at sight, and attending to the way they are used in a passage don't always work in isolation either. However, word analysis techniques are worthwhile when readers learn to let them interact with each other. Besides, meaningful word parts frequently occur in technical, content-area vocabulary, and noting them helps students get a handle on the new terms.

I was totally surprised when Larry, Horace, and Danielle took *poly* from our geometry term *polygon* and created a list of *poly* words. They came up with *polygamy, polyester, polyglot,* and *polyhedron.* They were quite proud of themselves and assured me that they understood the meanings of all their terms. They just might! I had decided not to introduce *poly* to my fifth graders for what I thought was a good reason. Even though *poly* occurs frequently as a meaningful part in many words, those words are rarely encountered by students in the fifth grade. If I were teaching ninth grade math or science, then I probably would have presented it. At present, highlighting more common, meaningful parts such as *tri* allows students to attend to that particular element, and it helps children become accustomed to noting meaningful word parts.

Erik Haugaard has always been one of my favorite children's authors. Last summer, I read his *The Boy and the Samurai* for the first time. What an exciting story! That is the book I began reading aloud the first day back after the holidays. It is a historical novel set in ancient Japan. This was a culture few of my students knew anything about. Before long, however, they were really caught up in the story.

My students are now writing more and more, and more willingly. Every student can keyboard well enough to use the computer to write fluently. When possible, most of them will budget their time so they can do their writing on a computer. When there is not enough time, or when everyone writes at the same time, they still like to type their papers into the computer if they are editing, revising, or publishing them.

By examining my students' writing from the first four months of school, and through helping them edit and revise the papers they published, I began January with an excellent sense of how well my students were writing and what writing conventions they were consistently using. The amount of writing the students have been doing since kindergarten has really paid off in terms of their enjoying writing and having different voices and types of writing they can employ.

With respect to the conventions of writing, I am very pleased that everyone begins sentences with capital letters and ends them with appropriate ending punctuation except for an occasional careless error. Most other conventions, however, are inconsistently applied or applied hardly at all by a significant proportion of my students. I am unconcerned about this inconsistency, however. Had conventions been emphasized earlier, I doubt if the students would enjoy writing as much or be as effective at expressing ideas as they are. By postponing most formal instruction in writing conventions until now, we have made it so students will not mind the work necessary to make their writing more conventional.

I have selected certain writing conventions that are probably most important for fifth graders to learn to do consistently. I worded these conventions in the form of rules I thought my students could understand.

Writing Scale

Once I decided that these eight rules were the ones my students as a whole most needed to learn to apply consistently, I decided how I would teach them. First, after school one day, I placed a chart above the chalkboard where every student in the room would be able to see it. This chart was titled "Some Writing Rules" and had rule 1 written on it. When the students came in the next morning, they immediately noticed the new addition. I explained that I was very pleased with how well they were writing and liking to write, and that it was time for them to learn a new writing rule to keep along with the others they already followed. Mike assured me that everyone who wasn't stupid already knew that old rule. I agreed that all of them had certainly heard the rule and that everyone followed it sometimes, but that what I wanted them to learn was to do it right almost every time.

Over the next few weeks, I spent a small amount of time two or three days a week making sure they understood when a new paragraph is called for. When we were reading from the same book in a subject, I often pointed out the paragraphing used by the author and we spent a few minutes discussing it. I showed them how a web they had used to plan a piece of writing could help them decide when to begin a new paragraph (i.e., they started a new paragraph when they began writing another part of the web). We also learned that in a written conversation, each time the speaker changes, a new paragraph begins.

Once they seemed to understand paragraphing as a concept, I began having them proofread their own papers or each other's for the rule on the wall. The discussion we had around particular instances helped everyone understand paragraphing better and realize that it is not a perfect science.

Some Writing Rules

1. Indent the beginning of every paragraph.
2. Do not use run-on sentences.
3. Combine short, choppy sentences together.
4. Use commas after the first word or words in a series.
5. Use I and me, we and us, he and him, she and her, and they and them correctly.
6. Do not use double negatives.
7. Both the subject and verb of a sentence should be singular or both should be plural.
8. Both a pronoun and the noun it stands for should be singular or both should be plural.

When I began to see improvements in paragraphing in students' papers, I added rule 2 to the chart on the wall. I then began making sure they could recognize a run-on sentence. We were still working on that rule when the month ended.

February

Reading Interests Paula Danziger has been discovered. Several girls had read Judy Blume's *Tales of a Fourth Grade Nothing* (1976) and loved it. *Superfudge* (1980) came next, and it too was a hit. After reading the first chapter of Paula Danziger's *It's an Aardvark Eat Turtle World* (1985), Pat, Rita, and Joyce came up and wanted to know if she had written any other books. When I told them about her other books, they wanted to go immediately to the library and check out *Remember*

Me to Harold Square (1987), *This Place Has No Atmosphere* (1986), and *There's a Bat in Bunk Five* (1980). So now there is a new craze for Paula Danziger books.

Interests

I still am amazed at how people select one author and read everything that person has written. This seems true for series as well as nonseries books that are written by the same person. For example, during SSR I've noticed that Daphne still is reading her Nancy Drew stories. Horace, Mitch, and Alex switched from Tarzan of the Apes stories and are now into Lloyd Alexander's *Chronicles of Prydain*. And Mandy and Pat have discovered J. R. R. Tolkien.

Another interesting point about these fifth graders' reading interests is their fascination with informative books. Butch has been perusing *Tell Me Why* books, and he does take the time to really study some of the entries. Anthony has his own collection of science-oriented books at home that he brings in, and Paul has taken to an easy reading collection of animal books that is well illustrated and documented. Students at this age do like to read to learn as well as to be entertained.

My plan for developing independent learners is continuing still. The directed reading and listening activities that I do with the whole class and small groups is devoted more and more to helping them articulate what information deserves attention. I want them to decide beforehand, and afterward, what they should attend to in a passage. The activities I conducted last month on anticipating meaning with the U.S. Navy passages is one way to get children to do this.

Comprehension Strategy Lesson

For each of my content comprehension lesson plans I go through the same steps. First I teach the general background that is needed to understand what will be read. In this step I highlight key vocabulary either by teaching them the words they'll need or by just telling them that I want them to read to discover the meaning of a key word. In the second step I set a purpose for students' reading. I select my purpose to be congruent with the kind of reading they are doing. I wouldn't want them to read for sequence if there were little in the passage to be organized in that way. I frequently have students produce some kind of graphic organizer as a way to help them organize the information they are reading. I always follow up the set purpose to monitor their ability to meet the purpose. I plan reading-writing activities to extend comprehension and to help them become independent strategic readers.

Student Research

One activity, The Mag Bag, that we did during writing/language arts period got the class quite involved in independent learning. This idea came from an article I had read in the *Journal of Reading* (Adams, 1980). To begin, I brought in duplicate copies of popular magazines. The class divided themselves into groups based on interests such as sports, fashion, and the environment, and each group went through the magazines and found an article they thought interesting. After locating an appropriate article, they had three tasks. First, they created a poster to advertise the article. Headlines, blurbs, and pictures were included in the posters. (I brought in duplicate copies of the magazines partly because they had to be cut up to make these posters.) Second, the students prepared a six-by-eight-inch file card that contained complete bibliographic information about the article. Of course, I gave them a model of how to cite the articles. An identical number was written on the poster and on the card so other students could match them later. Finally, on the back of the cards each group wrote a question or two that would guide a person's reading of the article. For instance, Horace and Mitch worked together on an article about the human heart. They decided that the most important information in the article was about heart attack, so they asked two questions: "What are the most common causes of heart attacks?" and "What can people do to guard against heart attacks?"

After preparing the posters and file cards, these two items and complete, original issues of the magazines were placed in the classroom library area. The file cards were placed in a box by numbers. This way, just before SSR, students could study the posters to locate an article that seemed interesting. Then they noted the number of the poster, got its corresponding file card, and used the bibliographic information on the card to locate the correct magazine. This was a good precursor to locating information in the library, and it got the class to independently figure what was important in the articles.

Another activity that got at attending to important information used index cards also. I guided the class through a science passage about invertebrates in the ocean, the students formed pairs. To begin this activity, each person wrote four questions that he or she thought dealt with the most important information in the passage. For instance, Joyce wrote the following questions:

1. What are sponges?
2. How do jellyfish get food?
3. How do sea anemones get food?
4. Why is a coral really an animal?

After writing the questions, the partners traded cards and attempted to answer each other's questions. Then, after writing down their answers, the partners decided which questions would be best for a whole-class quiz. They rank-ordered their questions and turned them in to me. As promised, I gave a short quiz the next day using the class's own questions.

That day Tanana came up to me and complimented me for allowing them to write their own questions. I asked why she liked doing it, and her reply showed a lot of insight.

"For the first time I felt like I was in charge of the book," she said. "I had to decide what we needed to know; I couldn't just wait for you to tell us what to study for."

I knew that I had my curriculum guide to help me lead this class to the important information, and I knew I had my own opinions about what was important, but Tanana's mature comment helped remind me that children need to develop this ability for themselves.

Editing   As February ends, my students are now proofreading for three writing rules on the wall. Rather than working on the fourth rule, however, we are still concentrating on separating run-ons into short sentences and then combining those short sentences. Two interesting things happened. First, I found that it was necessary to put rule 3 up before the students had gotten very good at rule 2. The students who wrote run-on sentences were often not willing to separate them into single sentences because the separated sentences were so short and choppy. Joyce said I might not like her run-on sentences, but she liked them better than sentences that sound like what second graders write! That's when I added rule 3 to the wall. Of course, that meant I had to provide them with sentence-combining practice. As they improved their ability to combine sentences, they did become more willing to stop using run-ons.

Second, I found that I needed to teach students how to turn a run-on sentence into one or two combined sentences in the same lesson. We have a computer program that provides practice combining two or three short sentences that are given. While that program helped some, a number of my students seemed to need lessons that show them how to start with a run-on sentence and end up with one or more combined sentences. Now, in pairs, students help each other find run-ons and turn them into combined sentences.

February was also the month that the writing we have been doing in math really began bearing some fruit. Back in November, I started having students work in small groups to compose word problems that fit whatever mathematical operation we were studying at that time. I worked with different groups on different days to help them improve their problems. I used writing minilessons to model for the whole class how to compose a word problem before having them work together in their groups. Later, the groups would share one or two of their problems with the whole class. It was slow at first, but by December they were able to produce weekly word problem "tests" for each other over all the mathematics we had studied since the beginning of the year. After a while, I would vary whether they composed word problems in small groups, pairs, or individually. Once this process was operating well, it served three functions. It reviewed mathematical computation from earlier this year and previous years. It also lowered the resistance to and fear of word problems on the part of almost all the students. It also helped students improve their word problem solving somewhat by understanding how a word problem is put together and how it can help or mislead the student. This month, it has become apparent to me that their attitude toward word problems and ability to solve them has definitely improved as compared with past years. I credit our writing in mathematics with this improvement.

Content Area Writing

March

This was the month to emphasize locating information independently. We continued our study of the ocean during science period, and as a group we watched films and filmstrips, read passages from the text and from magazines I had saved, discussed our various experiences at the beach, and did several activities such as the guided reading procedure and webbing. In addition, I listed five activities for independent work and allowed the students to choose any three. The final thing they were to do was choose any animal that lived in the ocean, gather all the information they could about that animal, and write a report on it. This last assignment was the culmination of much preparation. To prepare the class for their individual reports, I listed categories of information about

Student Research

animals so that the class would know what to look for and so their reports would be well organized. The following list of categories was put on the board:

Information About Ocean Animals

Type of animal (fish, mammal, mollusk?)

Appearance (How big is it? What does it look like?)

Location (Where is it found? Describe its habitat.)

Eating habits (What does it eat? How does it eat?)

Relation to humans (How does it help or harm humans?)

After describing these categories of information, I passed out copies of an ocean animal report that was completed last year in my class. This provided a model for this year's class. Everyone seemed to be getting a fairly good idea of what to look for. Since we had worked on selecting important information in passages throughout the past few months, I figured most students would be able to identify what should be included in each category from what they were reading. I asked students to write a paragraph for each of the five categories of information. The missing component of this project was the ability to locate materials that contained appropriate information about particular animals. With this in mind, I told them all to remember which animal they had chosen to study, but that we had some preliminary things to learn. Then I turned to Miss Page, our librarian, for help.

Miss Page said we could have a 45-minute period each afternoon in the library for two weeks to work on our projects. But first, she said, she would show the class how to locate information. On our first day in the library, she taught the class for me and reviewed the concept of subject indexes. First, everyone was given a photocopy of the index of a book on animals. To see if everyone could use an index, she dictated 10 topics for each student to find. She gave topics such as "skeleton," "teeth," and "veins" and the students wrote down the page numbers where information on each topic could be found. Everyone then traded papers, and she read out the correct page numbers. No one missed any, of course, since this task required only the ability to locate a word and the ability to copy its corresponding page number.

Next, she showed them the *Reader's Guide to Periodical Literature*. As they grouped around her, she took a topic suggested by a student and looked it up for them as they watched. This task, too, seemed simple enough. She gave another list of topics, and the class spent the rest of the period writing down bibliographic information from the articles that were found under Miss Page's topics.

At the beginning of the next day in the library, Miss Page checked the students' references for the topics she had provided. Eventually, everyone had listed the correct materials that the *Reader's Guide* listed under the topics. Then she showed how to obtain the various magazines and journals from the library's collection.

"Hey, Mr. Dunn," Mitch called, "this system works almost like our 'Mag Bag' system."

"You're catching on," I thought to myself.

Finally, Miss Page demonstrated the use of the card catalogue. This time students suggested topics for which she searched and showed them what she found. If a subject was not listed, she asked for another one and searched for it. Most of the class was used to going to the card catalogue to locate a book by its title or author, but using the card catalogue by subject was a new task for most students.

At the end of the lesson, everyone was asked to write the answers to two questions:

1. How are the index of a book, the *Reader's Guide to Periodical Literature,* and the card catalogue alike?

2. How is each one different from the other two?

When all the students were finished writing, we discussed the answers to the two questions.

Following this lesson, Miss Page and I figured that this group of students had the prerequisites for locating information in a library. They knew what subject indexes were and the principle on which they work. And they knew how to use the *Reader's Guide* and the card catalogue.

For the next few days, either Miss Page or I helped the students locate a book given as a source by the card catalogue, or a periodical given to them by consulting the *Reader's Guide.* We were into our ocean animals research full blast now. Most of the students could already find books by their Dewey Decimal System or Library of Congress number, which reflected their experience with this and other libraries.

The class seemed to enjoy this time in the library. They had used the library many times for obtaining books for pleasure reading, but now they seemed to feel rather grown up using it more for obtaining information. Even Mike paid close attention to Miss Page's directions about how to locate information. He likes to know how things work, and learning how the library worked was no exception. This group had located information within materials such as encyclopedias, atlases, other textbooks, and newspapers before, but learning how to obtain those reference books in the first place was new to them.

A problem did arise, however, with selecting topic words. Chip wanted to investigate conches because his grandfather had brought him a conch shell from the Indian Ocean. He had that shell on top of his dresser in his bedroom, so he knew that there was such a thing. However, he couldn't find *conch* listed in either the *Reader's Guide* or the card catalogue.

"Now what am I supposed to do?" he moaned. "I'm stuck."

I helped Chip locate information about conches by going through the key words *shellfish* and *mollusk,* and then I raised Chip's predicament with Miss Page. She agreed that predicting key words to locate information was a problem and suggested that I prepare a lesson to develop that ability. I mentioned that I thought that she might have a "predicting key words" lesson handy, but she assured me in her good-natured way that she didn't.

"Mr. Dunn," she said, "I'd love to help you, but I'm afraid you'll have to do this one on your own. I am totally inundated trying to keep up with my cataloguing. But be a dear, do let me know what you come up with. I'm sure it will be very useful to me in the future."

"Boy, is she smooth! I thought. "Not only do I need to come up with an entirely new lesson, but I need to share it with her. I guess flattery *will* get you everywhere."

Like many abilities that are part of reading to learn, the ability to predict key words for locating information is a complex one. The lesson I used to develop this ability had two parts. First, the class tried to think of all the possibilities for key words, given a particular topic. Then they tried to determine which of those possibilities would most likely yield the desired information.

The sample topic we chose was last month's holiday, Valentine's Day. Using a chalkboard, they brainstormed all the possible key words that, regardless of source used, might yield information about Valentine's Day. We listed the following possible key words:

Valentine's Day Key Words

hearts	Cupid
St. Valentine	romance
Valentine's Day	February
holidays	February 14
love	red
candy	saints
greeting cards	

After compiling the list, we considered each item as a possible key word for use in researching Valentine's Day. After the discussion, everyone wrote down three topic words to consult and handed in these choices. I sorted the ballots and placed votes by the items in our list as they had been chosen by the group.

Four possible key words received the most votes by far: *St. Valentine, Valentine's Day, holidays,* and *February 14.* As a group, we then discussed why these four might be better than the others.

The follow-up activity for this lesson was to go to the library with the key words the class had selected, and to use those key words to see if information could be found about that topic. Alexander, Manuel, and Carl were selected, and they reported the next day that there was a wealth of information about Valentine's Day under *Valentine's Day* and *holidays* in the *Reader's Guide,* card catalogue, and various encyclopedias. Thank goodness!

Student Independence

This month closed with the students' written reports on ocean animals being completed. Within the limits I had set, they had selected their own topics, organized their search, located appropriate sources of information, gathered the important data, and reported it in one paper, which they had typed on the computer. Of course, the finished products varied in quality quite a bit, but even my students with the weakest reading and writing abilities had the opportunity to learn independently from printed materials.

This was the month of caterpillar jokes! What monster have I created?

Early in the month we were discussing the four stages of metamorphosis of certain insects. Butch and Mitch had brought in live caterpillars in a jar. In a moment of weakness, I asked the class, with a straight face, "What do you call a baby caterpillar?"

When no one responded, I answered, "A kitty-pillar!"

Everyone laughed loudly at the joke, and we went back to discussing insect development. Before long, Horace raised his hand, "When does a caterpillar go the fastest?" After a short pause, he said. "When it's being chased by a dogerpillar!" This, of course, brought a new round of laughter.

Ever since, during recess, lunch, and occasionally in class there has been an epidemic of caterpillar joke telling. Some of my favorites have been these:

Q: What did the caterpillar say when it climbed into its cocoon?
A: See you next moth!

Q: What do you call a caterpillar who finks on his friends?
A: A dirty ratterpillar!

Q: Where do crazy caterpillars go?
A: To the cuckoo-n.

Q: What is green and breaks into your house?
A: A caterpillar burglar.

There were many more. Why children at this age love jokes like these, I don't know. When I was in the fifth grade, we told elephant and grape jokes. (Why was the elephant hiding in the grape tree? He had welched on a bet and gotten himself into a jam.)

I thought about a way to capitalize on this interest in caterpillar jokes and decided that a graffiti bulletin board would be my best bet. I planned to wait until the middle of April to put up a sheet of white construction paper on the back wall. This would be a nice end-of-the-year type of activity. There would be the opportunity for movement and the intrigue of seeing what new inscriptions were written on the board.

The book I have been reading to the students during most of this month has been *The Middle of Somewhere* by Shelia Gordon. Like the first book I read to the class back in September, it is a wonderful book set in South Africa under the system of apartheid. The main character in *The Middle of Somewhere* is a nine-year-old black girl named Rebecca Gwala. The situation at the beginning of the novel is that the planning department of the white-only government has decided that a village for black people is to be destroyed, the people transported to a new town, and a new town for white people built on the site of the black village. Rebecca and her family live in the village. The new town to which the Gwalas and their neighbors will be transported is so far away that Rebecca's father will lose his job. This book has really raised my students' sensitivity to issues of fairness in government toward people of different races or nationalities.

Multicultural Awareness

April

What a great month! I just love April with all of nature springing back to life! We can get outside to investigate some of our science materials *au naturel*. It all starts to come together at this point.

Student Research   As a follow-up to developing abilities to predict key words for locating information, I brought in a collection of telephone books that the phone company had donated. I listed the types of phone calls I wanted to make, and the class found the page numbers in the yellow pages where I should look. For instance, the class discovered that to locate a doctor, one looked under the key word *physician;* to locate a kitchen oven, one looked under *appliances;* and to locate a store that sold baseballs, one looked under *sporting goods.* I discovered that my "predicting key words" lesson actually was a good lesson on organizing information. It's amazing how so many language arts abilities are interrelated!

Independent research projects were conducted in social studies this month according to the same general plan that we followed in science. I still was rather directive about the general topic and the report format, but there was enough room for individual decisions that allowed each final product to be unique. The general topic this time was the 50 United States, and each student chose a different one to investigate. No one was allowed to choose ours.

Again, we set out a common outline so that everybody would work toward the same general goal. However, this time I had the class decide what specific aspects of the topic deserved investigation. I knew they had studied a unit on our home state last year in Ms. Maverick's class, so I thought they would be in a good position to decide on those aspects.

Mort suggested researching amusement parks in the other states, and Daisy wanted to do restaurants.

"Very funny," I replied. "Let me give you a better perspective on why you are investigating your state. Let's say that your family is going to move out of our state, but they haven't decided where to go. They have asked you to help. Your mission, class, should you decide to accept it, is to convince your family either to move to or else avoid the state you have chosen."

Well, this livened things up a bit because this new perspective helped them focus their thinking. After all, "doing" a state is a rather global and abstract task; convincing your family of the relative desirability of moving somewhere is a much more compelling endeavor.

"We need to find out about the weather," Tanana volunteered. "My family likes the cold."

"What about deer hunting?" asked Mitch. "My dad won't go anywhere unless he will be able to take us hunting."

Larry suggested that we had better find out what the job situation was, since that was important, and Jeff wanted us to be sure to figure out how far the state was from where we lived. He gets carsick. Mike, the old pro who actually had done some moving, offered the suggestion that we should find out about the various cities so we could know exactly where to move once we had gotten to the state.

We kept this up for five minutes, and then we organized the categories of information on the chalkboard. Again, these categories, allowed each student to pursue an individual topic within a set of common guidelines. We decided that the following areas deserved special attention:

Information about the State

Location (How far away from our state is it? How long would it take to travel to by car? Where is it in relation to neighboring states?)

Weather (What are the temperature ranges in various locations? Is it warmer or colder than where we are already?)

Industry (How easily could your father and/or mother find a job?)

Major cities (Where are the major cities? Which city seems best for your family to be in or near?)

Vacation spots (Where could you go within the state for a weekend visit?)

With these categories of information in mind, we descended upon Miss Page once again. However, this time the group had a much better notion of how to locate the information that would satisfy their particular reasons for reading.

After about 10 minutes in the library, Betty and Hilda came up to me with a question that revealed a great idea. "Can we write to our states requesting information about these five areas?"

"Of course!" I said, "Why didn't I think of that?"

Talk about activity. Addresses for state and city chambers of commerce were located, letters were drafted on the computer, newspapers were consulted for weather reports, and a multitude of reference books and trade books were checked out for information about specific states. Students were even using our social studies textbook as a reference, which probably is its best use.

I did meet with Mike, Jeff, Paul, and Daisy at individual times in order to provide as much direction as possible. These four, and a few others in the class, easily get lost in such research projects. I made certain that they got off letters to their respective chambers of commerce and helped them locate understandable materials about their states. Luckily, there were such materials! I also made a deal with each of the students: If three of the five areas were investigated thoroughly, then that would be enough.

The papers this time were much more elaborate than the science research projects! When the class worked on ocean animals, they were rather intent on completing in a straightforward fashion the outline that I had presented. But this time many students completed the outline through some rather creative means. Mandy and Pat teamed up and put together a travel brochure of their state that was patterned after the ones they received in the mail. Several students produced relief maps of their states following the procedure they had learned in Ms. Maverick's class. Posters of vacation spots were in evidence everywhere. Everyone turned in a typed report dealing with the areas of investigation, but the compositions were directed toward their parents or guardians rather than me. Most students wrote their reports as personal letters to their families detailing the advantages and disadvantages of moving to their chosen state. I believe the class found this perspective more meaningful, and I do know that their writing was even better planned and more complete than usual.

To this point with the social studies research projects we had emphasized process over product, content over form, and macroform over microform. I am sure that the students learned more about both social studies and writing and that they enjoyed their learning more because they were not frustrated, distracted, or bogged down by concerns with spelling, mechanics, or usage. However, by not having emphasized the microform of a research report before, I was now in the best position I had been in all year to emphasize it! All the projects were saved on disk and most of them were quite well done as far as their content and overall organization. Here is how I made the transition to spelling, mechanics, and usage considerations.

Publishing   "Would you like your social studies reports to go home?" I asked.

Everyone was enthusiastic about that prospect. They were very proud of their hard work.

"I'm not sure it's a good idea," I continued. "What if your folks see misspelled words or some other errors in your paper? What will they think about what you've written?"

Several children declared that those things shouldn't matter. Before long, though, as the discussion proceeded, most of the students began to realize that their families probably would not be pleased if they noticed more than a few errors in a paper. They might think the children had not worked hard enough on it. As this consensus developed, I was able to convince them that another few class sessions on polishing their papers would be worth it.

Editing   First, I taught them how to use the spelling checker that is a part of Works. In their computer groups, they checked all their papers for spelling errors. This process went quickly and easily, since over a third of my students had already been using the spelling checker on their own. The only real difficulty I had with this was getting them to want to find out how to spell a word that the checker did not recognize and could not suggest a better spelling for. Still, the spelling of all the papers that had not already been checked did improve.

Second, they went through the laborious process of proofreading their papers for the writing rules on the wall. There are now five rules on the wall. The fifth rule has been particularly interesting in that most of my students never find any pronoun errors to correct, but a few students make a large number of this kind of error. To help this latter group, I have placed charts on the wall with two simple and correct sentences for each of the 10 pronouns: *I* and *me*, *we* and *us*, *he* and *him*, *she* and *her*, and *they* and *them*. Having these examples up in the room seems to have helped improve pronoun usage for the group whose spoken language violates this rule.

When the papers did go home, parents were very impressed. Time after time, the children related how their parents had responded with stories about how their first research papers were done in middle school or even later.

May

When spring comes, the sap rises, and it has certainly risen in my students! Pat and Horace are obviously in love, and Rita is constantly following Larry around and writing him notes. Daisy seems to have her eye on Mitch, but he pays absolutely no attention to her.

In reading/literature period, we completed a unit on prejudice that went over rather well. I began this unit by reading *Roll of Thunder, Hear My Cry* by Mildred Taylor (1978) to the whole class. Afterward, I set out multiple copies of various short novels and short stories for the class. For instance, William Armstrong's novel *Sounder* (1969) was made available, and Shirley Jackson's short story "After You, My Dear Alphonse" (1949) was provided.

Having students read these stories while focusing on prejudice was the perfect follow-up to the two books on apartheid in South Africa that I had read to the class earlier, *Journey to Jo'burg* and *The Middle of Somewhere*. When the racism being practiced was occurring in another country and culture, students were roundly disgusted and angered by it. By reading these books, the students had to confront the fact that racism has occurred and sometimes still occurs in our country and culture.

The students' assignment was basically the same in all cases. They were to write a short paper or else explain to me verbally the instances of prejudice that the materials protrayed. This assignment had been modeled beforehand with *Roll of Thunder, Hear My Cry* when I displayed a short composition one of last year's students had written about the prejudice Cassie encountered in that story. By providing this model, everyone had an idea of how to write the composition. This lesson was similar to the research projects we had done in science and social studies. The students knew what to read for and how to report what they read, and they were able to choose materials that were written at various levels of difficulty.

The difference between this lesson and the two others was that here I located the material to read, the project was shorter, and it was done with stories. Although no one complained about the first two differences, some students did have difficulty adjusting research and report methods to literature. I had to help about half of them figure out how to transfer the skills they already had to this kind of report. After they saw the connections, it really went well. I found that some students can write better reports based on stories than they can on facts! Not me! That was a real insight for me.

We did one final activity this month to continue developing abilities to learn independently. I called it an "open-notes" quiz. We had practiced writing notes that corresponded to outlines of passages throughout the year so the idea of note taking was familiar to the class. Indeed, the independent projects they had undertaken with ocean animals and the 50 United States had called for note taking to be applied. This particular application activity began with my telling everyone that they would have a quiz on a section of the science textbook that dealt with the formation of mountains. They were to be able to compare the effects

Literature Response Activity

Focused Writing

Study Strategies

of volcanic action, folding, and faulting on mountain formations. However, they had time to take notes on the section of the text that dealt with mountain formations, and they could use those notes during the quiz. I met in a part of the room with whoever wanted to read the section orally and decide as a group what notes to make. Most of the class found this activity worthwhile, especially after they all did so well on the quiz.

The graffiti bulletin board turned out to be a good idea for this time of the year. It gave the class an opportunity to express themselves, and they did so in a clever way. The students began writing their names beside their contributions so they would get proper credit for their creation. Some of the jokes were quite witty:

Q: What do you call a caterpillar who eats hamburgers?
A: A pattykiller. (Horace)
Q: Where does a caterpillar go to wash up?
A: A larva-tory. (Mitch)
Q: What did the caterpillar aunts say about their baby niece?
A: What a cute-rpillar. (Joyce)
Q: Why was the cocoon embarrassed?
A: Because his butterfly was open. (Butch).

When I saw Butch's contribution, I had to do a little soul searching. I didn't want to become a censor, but I didn't intend to let my students use improper language in front of me and gain my implicit approval either. I finally decided that Butch's joke was no more offensive than a lot of prime-time television jokes that parents allowed in their homes, so I let it go.

THE MEETING AT THE MIDDLE SCHOOL

Ed Dunn sat quietly by Mr. Topps as the middle school language arts teachers filed into the small meeting room at their school. The expressions on their faces indicated that they were as excited about going on vacation as he. They were smiling and kidding each other about what they would do with their upcoming vacation. For most of them, it seemed that their families and summer school at the university would take much of their time, and they were enthusiastic about the change.

Mr. Topps had known since April that he would be the new principal at Upton Hill, and he was meeting with small groups of teachers at that school ever since. He thought the meetings would help make for a smoother transition, and so far everyone agreed.

When all the teachers were present, Mr. Topps closed the door and introduced Mr. Dunn. "Ed has done an excellent job with his students this year and I wanted him to share some of his ideas with you. He has emphasized some of the areas with which you teachers are most concerned."

Ed stood to address these teachers. "When the students who will begin sixth grade this fall graduate from high school, it will be well into the twenty-first century. Whether they go on to four-year college, community college, vocational training, or a job requiring only a high school education, the reading, writing, and thinking they must do to succeed there will be quite sophisticated by the standards of just a few years ago. My goal with this year's fifth graders has been to build on what the K–4 teachers at Merritt Elementary accomplished and move the children another step closer to having the reading, writing, and thinking abilities their futures will require. This has meant that I have had to move the students beyond both what they learned in fourth grade last year and what they would have learned in fifth grade just a few years ago. In meeting that goal, I have emphasized several areas."

He paused to sip water from a paper cup. "First of all, I have stressed the gaining of knowledge. Students in middle school and above will not be able to read, write, or think well without adequate knowledge of the world in which they live. What students know already is a powerful determinant of how much they can learn that is new. You are all language arts teachers who teach literature. Think about how much most poets, playwrights, short story authors, and novelists assume their readers will know about geography, history, politics, and the particulars of food, clothes, transportation, abodes, furnishings, romance, and so on. To increase this knowledge, I have done my best to teach social studies, science, and health as effectively as possible. In all three subjects, I have placed special priority on teaching the meaning vocabulary associated with each unit, chapter, or topic we were studying. Moreover, we know that wide reading is the principal means by which most people acquire general background knowledge and word meanings, so I provided time and encouragement for self-selected reading every day. Since the K–4 teachers at my school had already been doing that, my students were able to reach thirty minutes a day of sustained independent reading by May, and I also have seen lots of evidence that the children were also reading books from the school and public libraries at home. In addition, because the knowledge students will need is of a shrinking world with many cultures, I read aloud every day from a book set in another country. As the year progressed, students discussed and wrote about the book I was reading aloud. Together, effective content instruction, meaning vocabulary building, teacher read-aloud of multicultural literature, and wide book reading build student knowledge of the world."

Again Ed paused for water. He clearly had the attention of the teachers before him. "Second, I have stressed teaching my students to read selectively and learn independently. Independent, selective reading is the foundational ability needed for most studying and library research. Even when there is only one book—the textbook—to read, a student must be able to determine what the main points of a selection are and what is most important to remember for a class discussion or a test. When one is doing a research paper, the ability to read selectively and efficiently becomes absolutely necessary. Even when reading a piece of literature to talk or write about it, one has to be able to read selectively to develop a thesis about the piece and then reread selectively to seek examples that confirm or cast doubt on the thesis.

"Fortunately, the K–4 teachers here at Merritt had students on the road to independent learning in topics they already were interested in and knew about. I have been able to move them into independent learning of new, more challenging topics. This year, I used reader response activities, some choice of assignments, content comprehension lessons, lessons in locating information, and lessons in note taking to help my students learn how to read more selectively and independently. They learned to apply these strategies to textbook reading as well as the reading of literary and informational books from the library.

"Finally, and most important, I made writing with computers the center of the fifth-grade curriculum. At the beginning of the year, all the students in my class learned to keyboard at a proficient level. After that, students worked in small groups and individually to learn how to better use the computer as a tool in writing and learning. Once students became comfortable and successful working on the computer, I emphasized helping them improve their writing abilities. They wrote several reports, each building on and extending what they had learned previously. I think you will find your new sixth graders from Merritt Elementary better able to plan, organize, and edit their papers compared with sixth graders in the past. I sincerely hope you will make use of the computer lab at Upton Hill to enable your students to use their considerable computer skills in writing or at least revising and editing the papers they will be writing for you."

Ed nodded at Mr. Topps to indicate that he had finished his prepared remarks. From his seat, Mr. Topps looked around at the middle school teachers. "Any questions or comments for Ed?"

After a few seconds, Buzz Riley responded, "I have."

Turning to face Ed, he quipped, "Seems like you would have left us something to teach them!"

Ed was expecting laughter from the others. When he didn't hear any, he laughed anyway. "That's very good, sir. Actually, I taught the students very little that is unique to the middle school language arts curriculum. You are all just too used to having to teach a lot before you can begin what is truly middle school instruction!" He smiled knowingly.

"Well, you can say that again," blurted out Norma Lee Cross.

Ed glanced at Mr. Topps. Was that a grimace on his face? Ed continued. "I believe that you will find that the students we are sending you are going to need what you have to teach them just as much as before, but that they are better able to learn it. I look forward to hearing from you next year about this very interesting group you are inheriting from us."

A tall woman with striking features raised her hand. When Ed caught her eyes, she began to speak. "I have found in recent years that the students from Merritt Elementary have been better prepared for middle school language arts than the students from any other of our feeder schools. I can tell from your presentation today, Ed, that this will be even truer in the years to come. I, for one, can't wait to try to build on what you've done."

As Ed and Mr. Topps walked out of the middle school building into the parking lot, both were silent. Mr. Topps focused on his preparation for the challenge of a new school. Ed was thinking of ways he could improve his program for next year's fifth graders and wondering who his new principal would be.

ADD TO YOUR JOURNAL

Writing has long been an integral part of learning any subject at the higher levels of schooling. Consider all the ways Mr. Dunn used writing throughout the fifth-grade curriculum. Why does writing assist learning? What kinds of learning does writing elicit that would be less likely to occur without it? How does using computers to write affect writing's potential to increase other kinds of learning?

REFERENCES

Adams, J. S. (1980). The mag bag. *Journal of Reading, 23,* 294–295.

Crist, B. I. (1975). One capsule a week—a painless remedy for vocabulary ills. *Journal of Reading, 19,* 147–149.

Earle, R. A., & Morley, R. (1974). The half-open classroom: Controlled options in reading. *Journal of Reading, 18,* 131–135.

Katzer, S., & Crnkovich, C. A. (1991). *From scribblers to scribes: Young writers use the computer.* Englewood, CO: Teacher Ideas Press.

Children's Books/Materials Cited

"After You, My Dear Alphonse," by Shirley Jackson. In *The Lottery, or The Adventures of James Harris.* Farrar, Straus, & Co., 1949.

It's an Aardvark Eat Turtle World, by Paula Danziger, Dell, 1985.

The Boy and the Samurai, by Erik Haugaard, Houghton Mifflin, 1991.

Chronicles of Prydain series, by Lloyd Alexander, Dell, various years.

The Haunted Igloo, by Bonnie Turner, Houghton Mifflin, 1991.

Journey to Jo'burg: A South African Story, by Beverly Naidoo, HarperCollins, 1988.

Latkes and Applesauce: A Hanukkah Story, by Fran Manushkin, Scholastic, 1992.

Little Rascal, by S. North, Puffin, 1990.

The Middle of Somewhere: A Story of South Africa, by Sheila Gordon, Bantam, 1992.

National Geographic World magazine.

Ranger Rick magazine.

Remember Me to Harold Square, by Paula Danziger, Dell, 1987.

Roll of Thunder, Hear My Cry, by Mildred Taylor, Bantam, 1978.

Snails, by H. Zim & L. Kranz, Morrow, 1975.

Sounder, by Willliam H. Armstrong, HarperCollins, 1969.

Superfudge, by Judy Blume, Dell, 1980.

Tales of a Fourth Grade Nothing, by Judy Blume, Dell, 1976.

Tarzan books, by Edgar Rice Burroughs, Ballantine, various years.

Tell Me Why series, by Arkady Leokum, Putnam, various years.

There's a Bat in Bunk Five, by Paula Danziger, Dell, 1980.

This Place Has No Atmosphere, by Paula Danziger, Dell, 1986.

Tyrannosaurus Rex, by M. Selsam, HarperCollins, 1978.

The Wounded Wolf, by J. George, HarperCollins, 1978.

Year of the Panda, by Miriam Schlein, HarperCollins, 1992.

Index

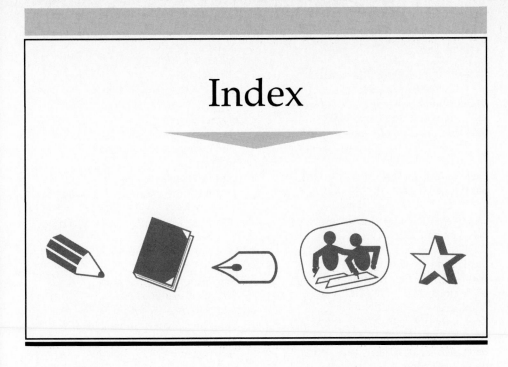